AF473996

Principles for good Layout Design

- Promotional Materials and Binding Rules
- Elements and Principles of Layout
- Output and Printing
- Layout Analysis

- Negative space
- Repetition
- Proximity
- Alignment
- Contrast

sendpoints

Principles for Good Layout Design

The third printing of the first edition, March 2024

sendpoints

EDITED & PUBLISHED BY SendPoints Publishing Co., Ltd.
ADDRESS: Unit 23, L1/F Mirror Tower, 61 Mody Road, Tsim Sha Tsui, Kowloon, Hong Kong, China
PUBLISHER: Lin Gengli
PUBLISHING DIRECTOR: Lin Shijian
ASSISTANT PUBLISHING DIRECTOR: Chen Ting
CHIEF EDITOR: Lin Shijian
LEAD EDITOR: Lin Qiumei, Waikin Ho
EXECUTIVE EDITOR: Akira Ho
DESIGN DIRECTOR: Lin Shijian
EXECUTIVE ART EDITOR: Ou Xiaoyu
PROOFREADING: Weiji Li, Carol Shields

SALES DIRECTOR: Philip Tsang
TEL: +852 6296 2246
EMAIL: sales@sppub.com
WEBSITE: www.sppub.com

ISBN 978-988-79283-7-9

Printed and bound in China.

Facebook

Instagram

X

Contents

Before Design　Promotional Materials and Binding Rules

Know Your Audience

Before you start and take any step, find out who your audience is. Analysis of the target audience helps decide what is more important for the design. To start, take a look at the subdivision of your audience including geographics, demographics, psychographics, and behaviors. Once you have formed this list, cut it down to a more targeted list by analyzing customers' recent purchases, lifestyle habits, and even magazine subscriptions. This information will provide more in-depth knowledge of what your consumers like and their purchasing habits.

Promotional Materials

Brochure

The brochure is an informative paper document with a few pages, mostly used for advertising. It is primarily used to introduce or promote a company, a product, or a service to their potential customers.

Flux Brochure
Designer: TSUBAKI KL

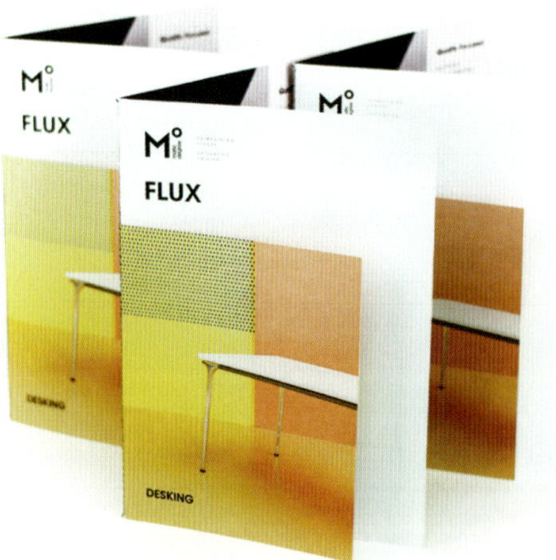

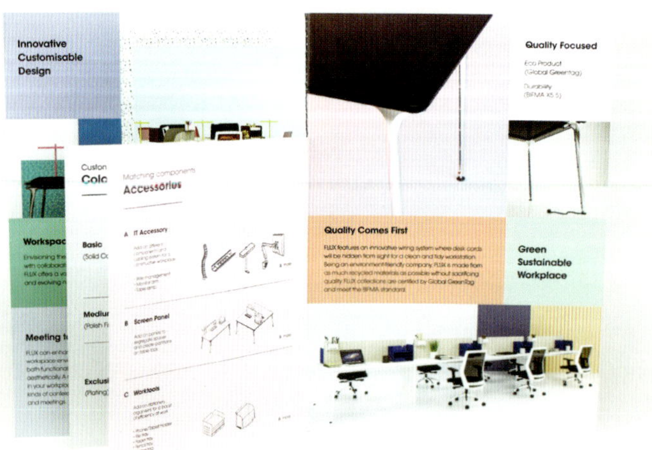

Flyer

A flyer is a form of paper advertisement intended for wide distribution and typically posted or distributed in a public place, handed out to individuals, or sent through the mail.

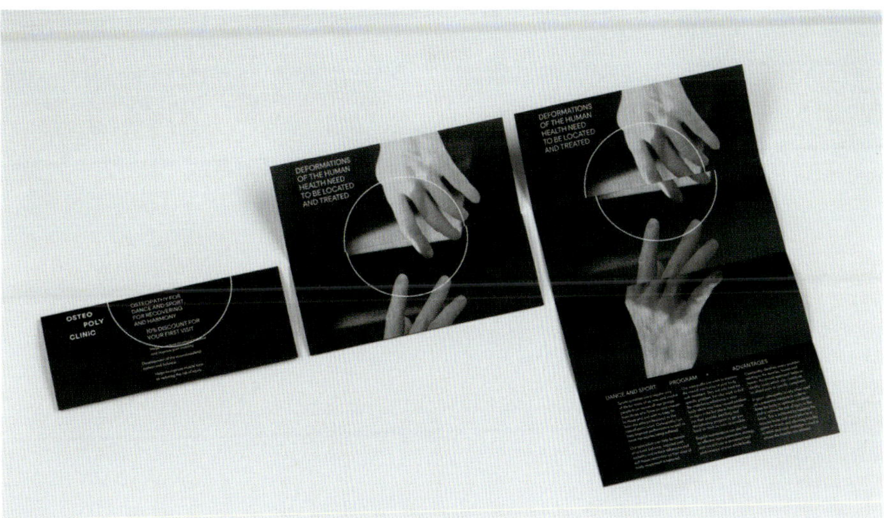

Osteo Poly Clinic Flyer
Designer: Vlad Ermolaev

Poster

Paper printed with graphic content is usually posted on a wall or on a vertical plane.

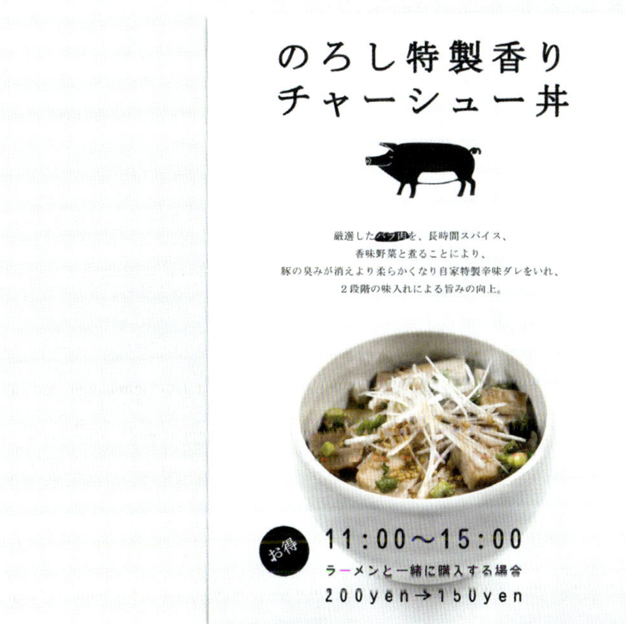

Noroshi Poster
Designer: Lee Ching Tat

Roll-up Banner

The roll-up banner, also called roller banner or pull-up banner, is a vertical display banner with a retractable banner stand, with a primary width of 80 to 120cm and height of 150 to 200cm. Its advantage is that it can be placed in any corner of the sale booth easily, and the assembled feature is convenient for storage.

Binding and Folding of Promotional Materials

Perfect Binding

In this method, glue is applied to the spine, and the pages are firmly bonded after drying. The trimming can be performed in the required size. Generally, it is divided into glue binding and perfect binding. Perfect binding with PUR (Polyurethane Reactive) hot melt adhesives is more economical and widely used. The printed products using this binding method can lie open at a flat 180 degrees.

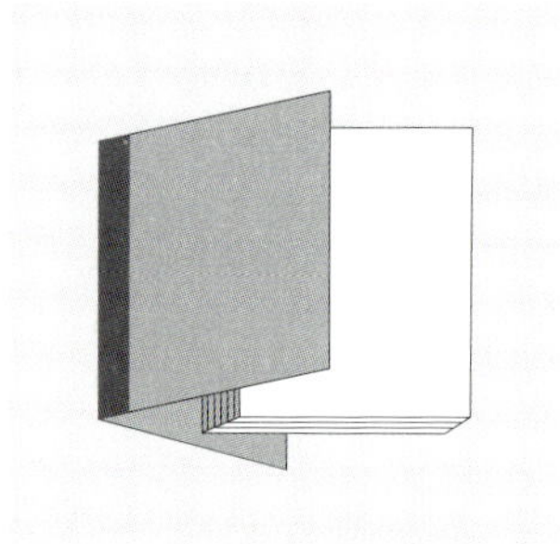

Saddle Stitching

A method in which folded sheets stacked together one on another and then stapled through the fold line with wire staples. The folded back of the paper is like a horse's back, the fold line is convenient for the staple to be accurately nailed, which just like a saddle on horseback.

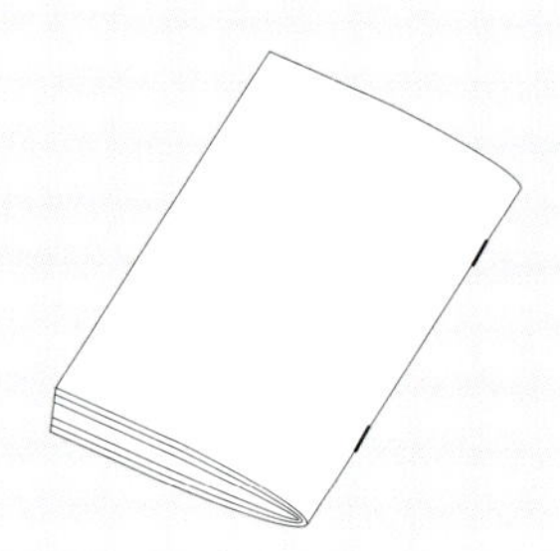

Basic Fold

Single fold is the most basic form of folding. It is so simple that it is a common folding method for invitations and leaflets.

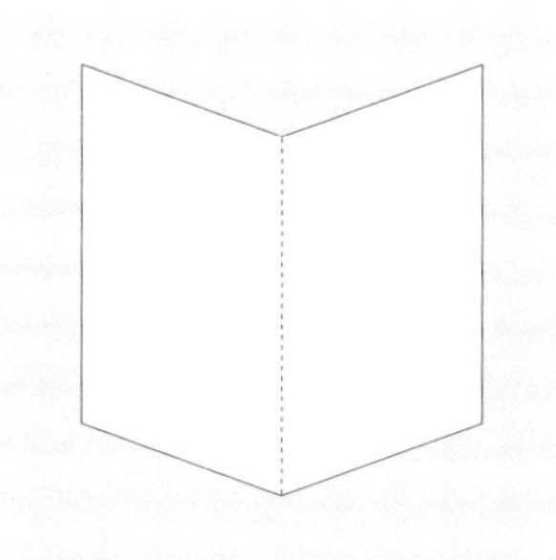

Accordion Fold

The accordion fold has almost 50 varieties. Accordions are also one of the most common folding styles used in brochure folding. It is highly identifiable for its zig-zag pattern. This style of folding offers flexibility, with the potential to add as many panels as the limitations of press and folding equipment can bear.

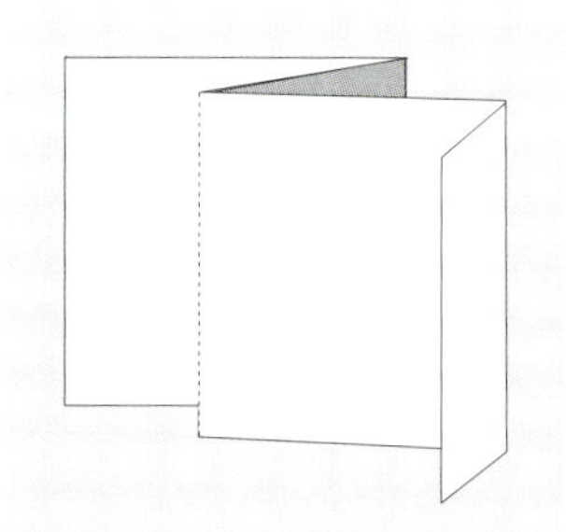

Map Fold

Map fold is constructed by making single fold, tri-fold, or quad-fold on an accordion fold. The number of foldings depends on actual need; this kind of folding requires printing materials that are relatively thin.

Gate Fold

Gate fold creates six panels by folding the outer two panels towards the central crease covering the same distance. When the central panel gets folded to create eight panels in total, it is called a double-gate fold.

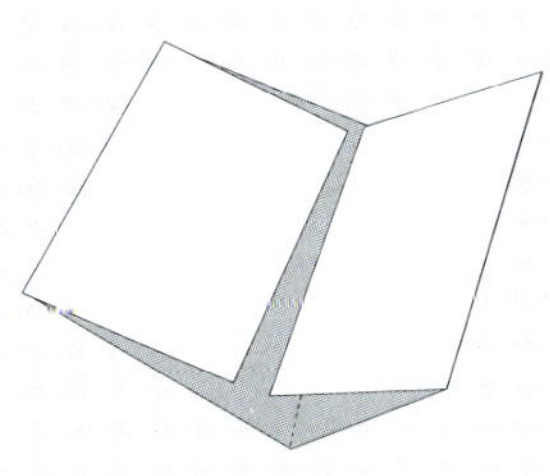

French Fold

A sheet that is a combination of one single fold and the other single fold that is perpendicular to the first one. There are eight panels after folded.

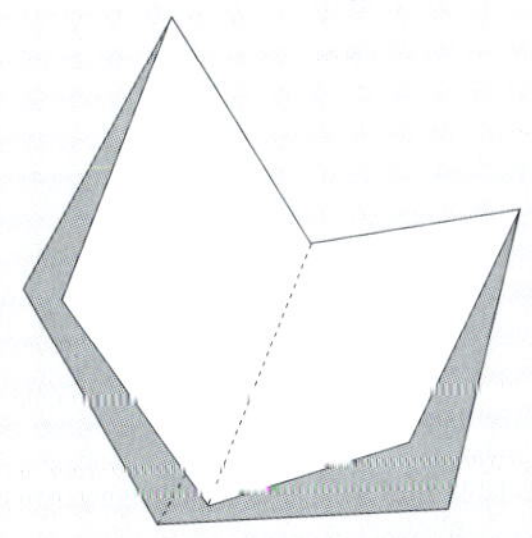

Roll Fold

Roll folds consist of panels that roll in on each other. The first two panels can have the same width, but the subsequent panels gets slightly smaller than the previous one in order to fit in each other.

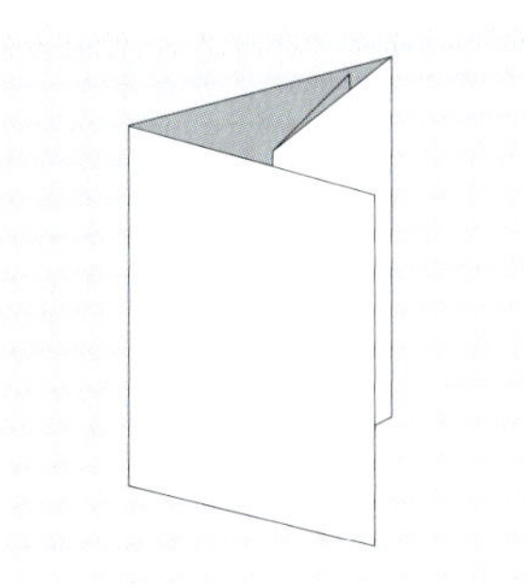

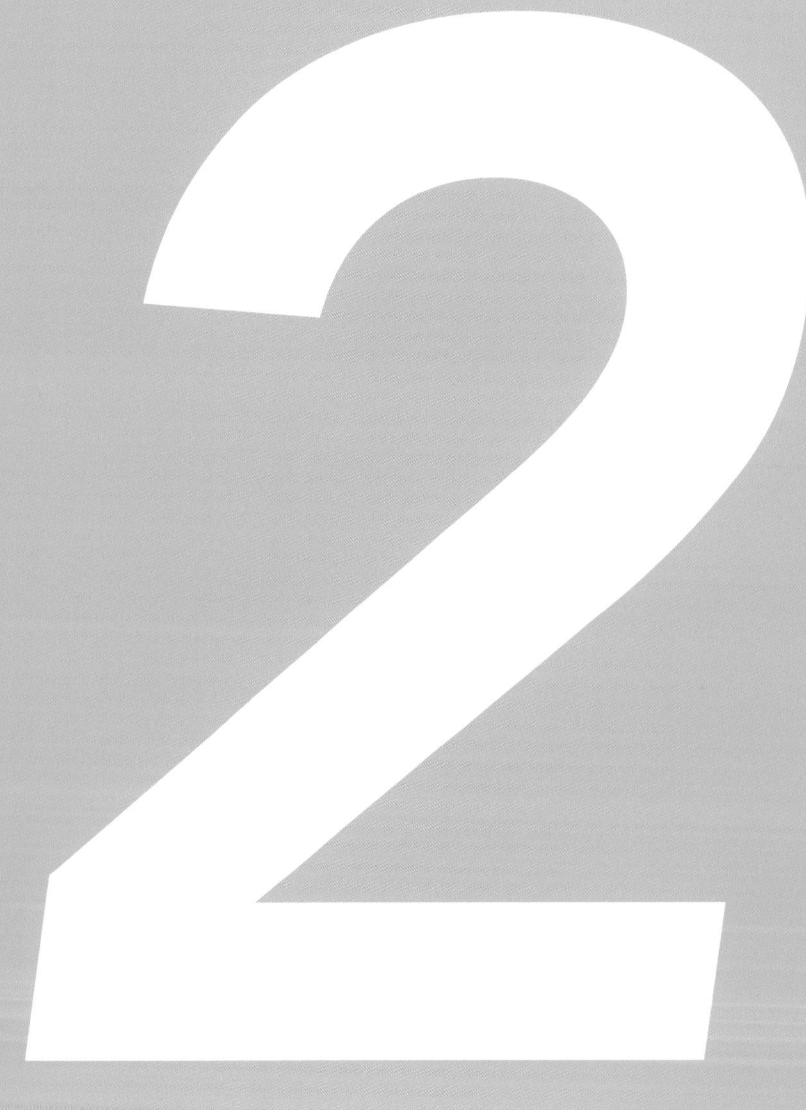

Design in Process Elements and Principles of Layout

Introduction to the Layout

Layout Elements

Layout is the process of arranging text and image elements in relation to the space that they occupy and in accordance to the overall design scheme.

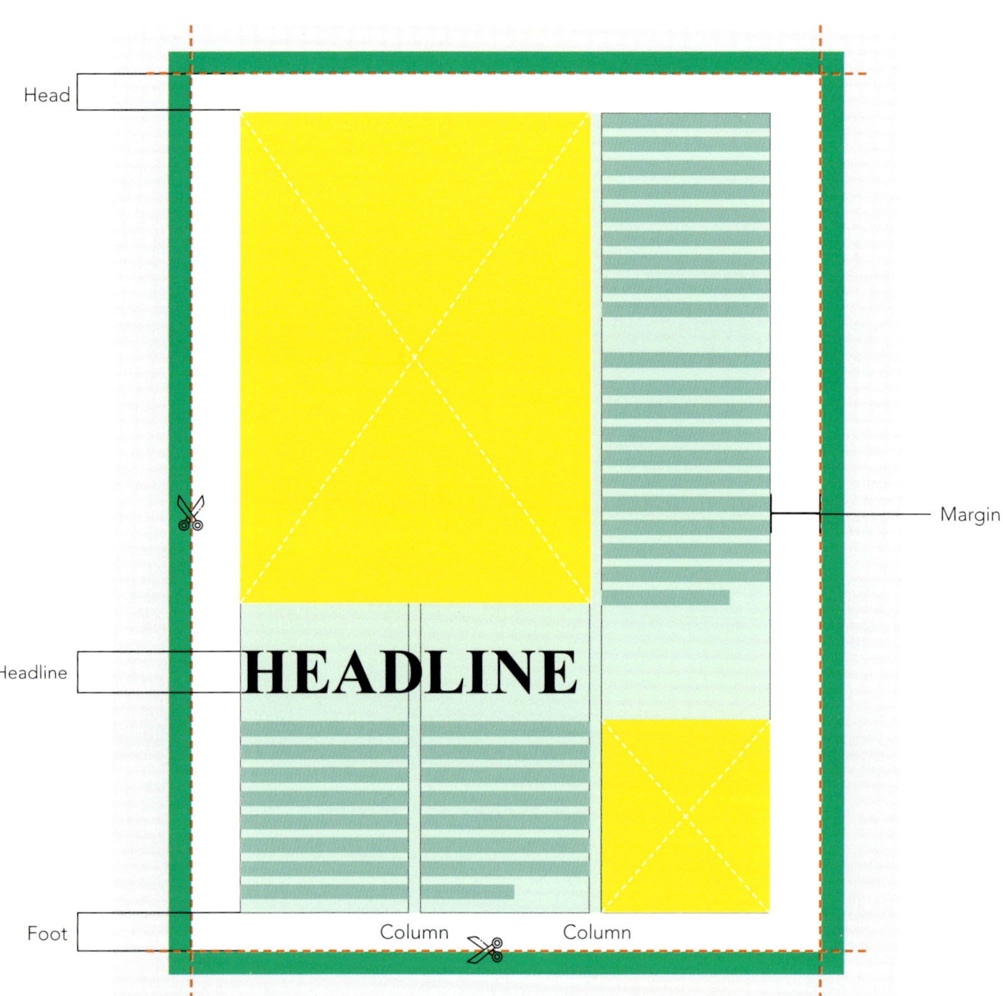

Image
Copy//Body Copy
Type Area
Bleed
Trimming Line

Head
The margin at the top of a page.

Margin
The distance from type area to the edge of the paper.

Headline
The large title for drawing viewer's attention, usually giving the main points of the copy.

Foot
The margin at the bottom of a page.

Copy/Body Copy
The main text in the type area.

Type Area
The area within the trim area where texts and images should be contained.

Bleed
To avoid cutting the type area when binding, the photos or colored area should be extended to create an area called "Bleed".

Trimming Line
The auxiliary line for cutting the paper.

The Grid System

The grid system improved in Germany and Switzerland. It is characterized by rationalization, functionalization, simplification, and geometric formalization. The grid system arranges the position of the design elements through the use of squares, thereby establishing a stable visual order. After designing a grid system, you can use it to organize a unifed layout or multi-page promotional materials.

The Column
The vertical rectangular area that carries the text is the "column". In the Microsoft Office Word software, one function is "column", which is to arrange a paragraph into several columns according to demand.

Single-Column Grid

In this case where the whole article is not divided into columns, it is called single-column grid, which is more common in brochures with more words and less content classifcation.

Multi-column Grid

If the text is divided into two columns, it is a two-column grid. If they are divided into three columns, it is a three-column grid. Both are generally applicable to most promotional materials.

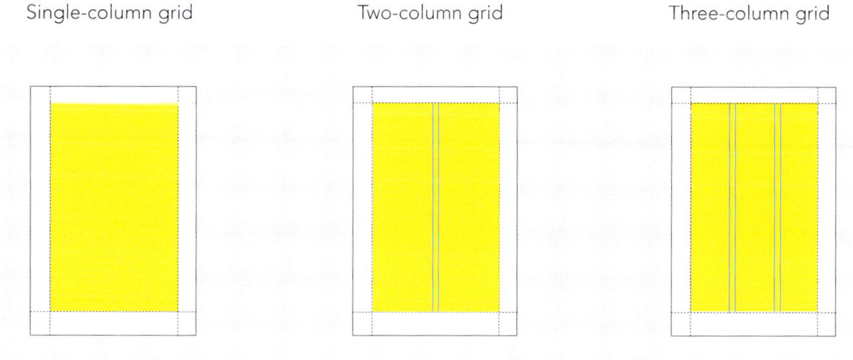

Modular Grid

A modular grid which combines many rectangle modules into the layout is the most common grid system in graphic design. This form accurately adjusts and regulates the width and height of each element.

Compound Grid

Different grid systems can be used on demand to create a compound grid. Note that the center of the layout and the column spacing has to be unified.

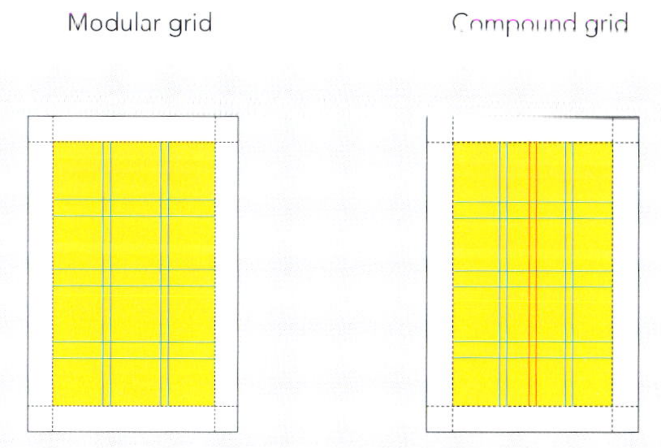

Type Area Ratio

The type area ratio is the ratio of a layout's type area to the area of the page where it is held. If the ratio is high, that means there is a full amount of information or photos in the layout. If the ratio is low, there will appear a large amount of negative space.

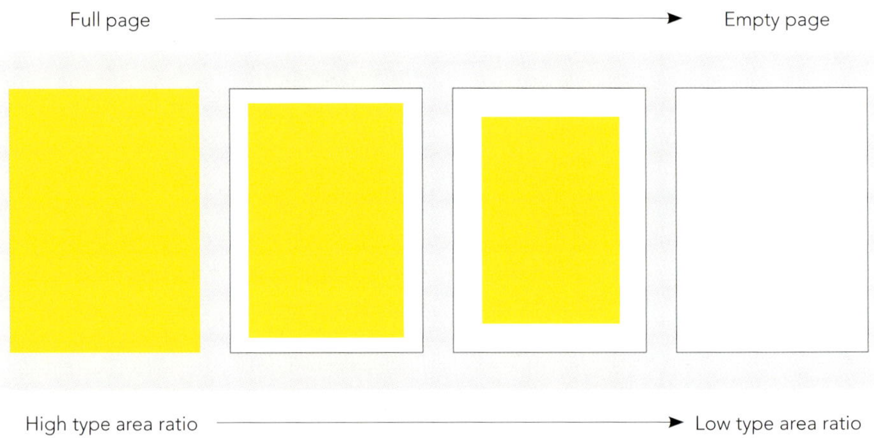

High Type Area Ratio

High type area ratio is often applied in promotional materials with a large amount of text. The designer fills in a large amount of text or large-area pictures in a limited grid system to convey a sense of information. However, if the ratio is too high, there could be an information overload and the beauty of the design will be lost.

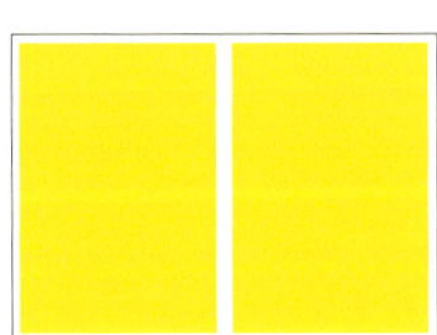

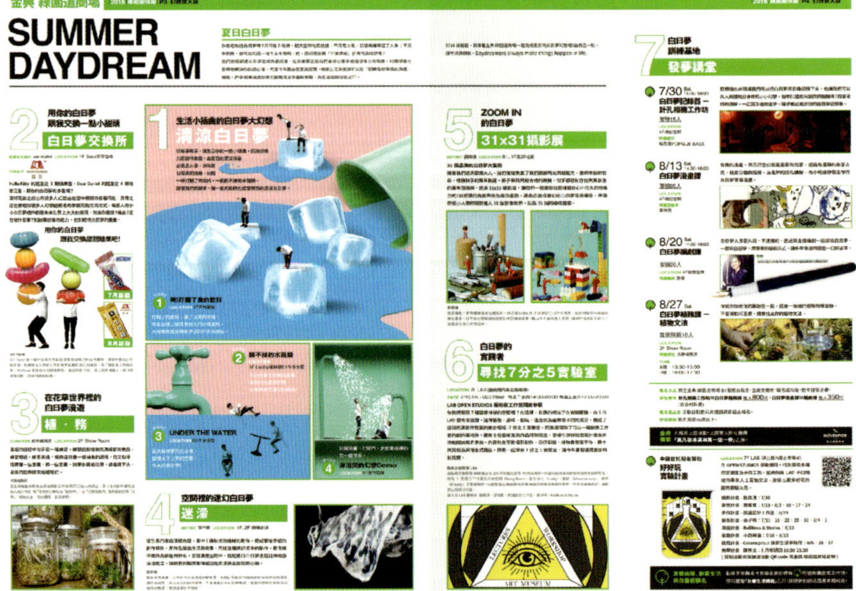

Summer Fantasy Poster
Designer: ZhongXing.H

Low Type Area Ratio

The low type area ratio can make the layout design fashionable and high-end, leaving a large area of negative space to let the design look neat and succinct. However, if the ratio is too low, the layout will lose its depth and visual impact and will make people feel mediocre.

Shimada Corporation Brochure
Designer: Masaomi Fujita

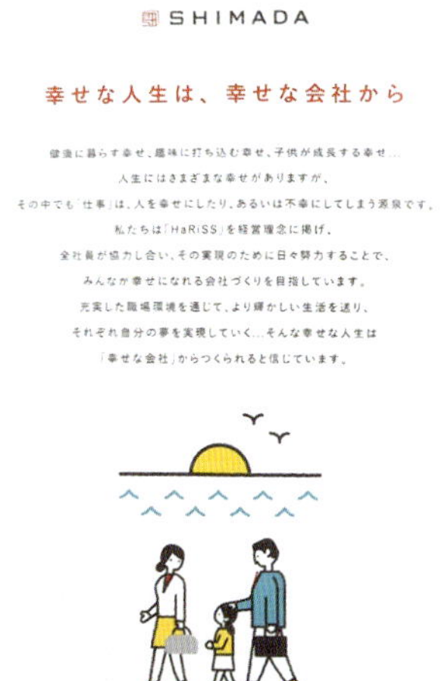

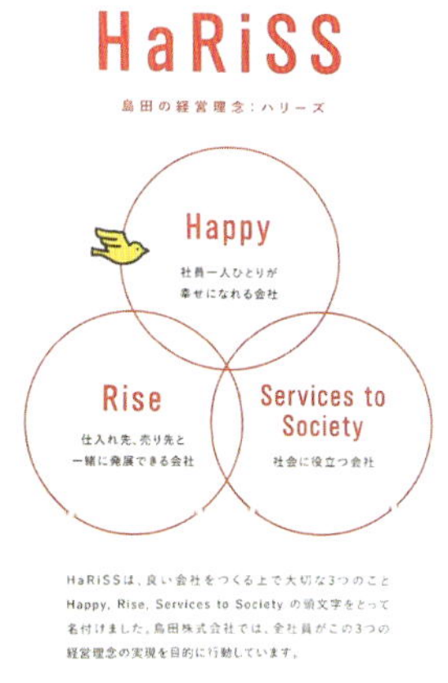

Layout Design Principles

Negative Space

Negative space can be any color, not only white, leaving it blank without any decoration. Appropriate negative space can make the layout look lighter and more spacious. It is more suitable for designs with less information and only one key visual. Reasonable use of negative space can be impressive.

How It Affects The Layout

When the negative space and main body are all in a vertical or horizontal direction, the whole layout looks stable. In this case, the customer will read the material in order from left to right, right to left, top to bottom, or bottom to top.

Fixed negative space

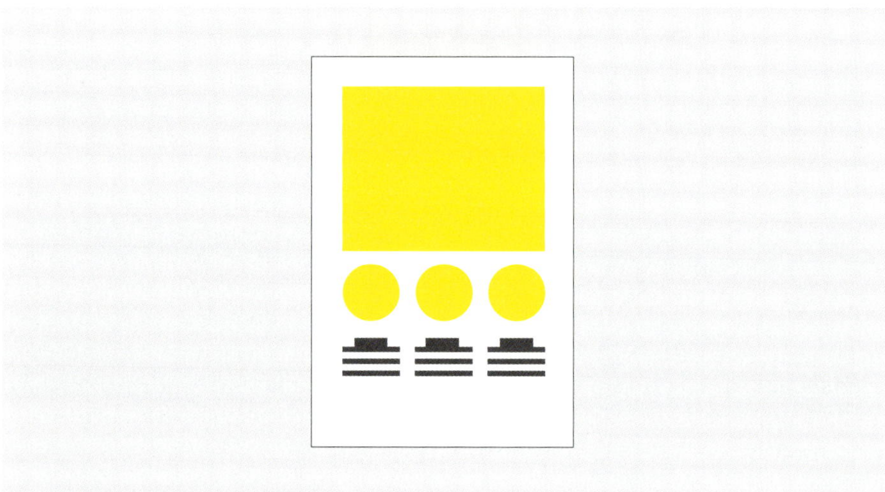

When the distribution of negative space and type area is not fixed, the whole layout gives a dynamic feeling. At this point, the consumer is no longer reading in the normal order. The most eye-catching part will be noticed first; the negative space can help shape the visual guidance route of the type area.

Dynamic negative space

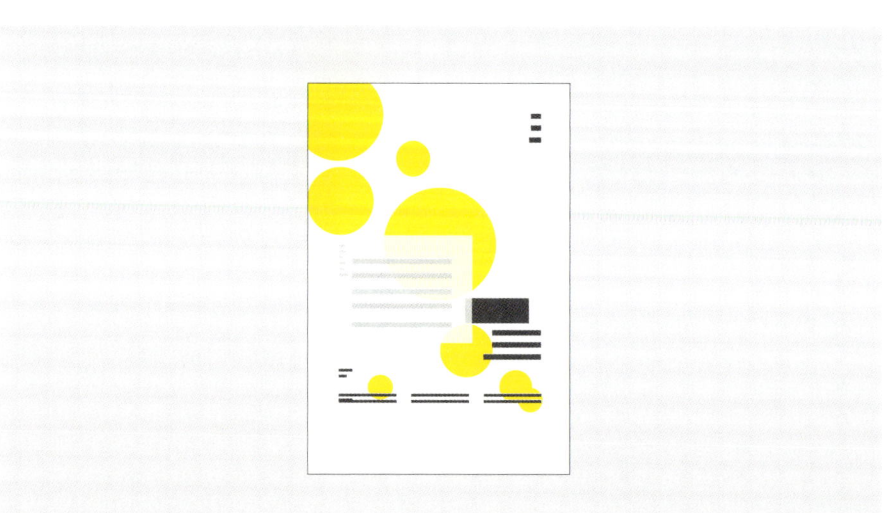

How It Affects Reading Experience

10%-20% negative space. Such intensive layouts mostly appear in newspaper and magazines, which is suitable for in-depth reading with a mass of words and does not have to meet the needs of fast access to information.

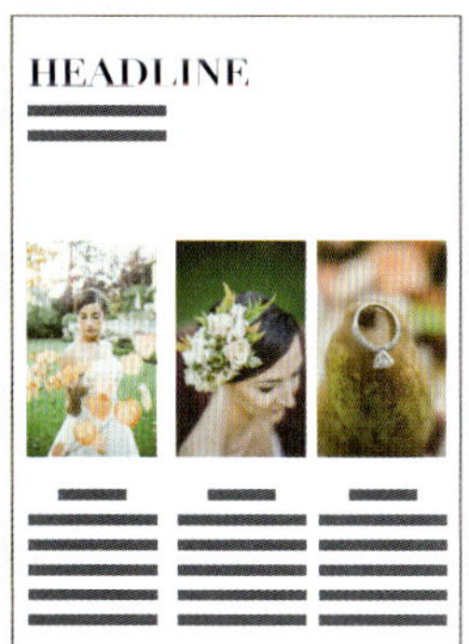

30%-50% negative space. This kind of layout has a moderate degree of negative space; its graphics arrangement is stable and comfortable to read.

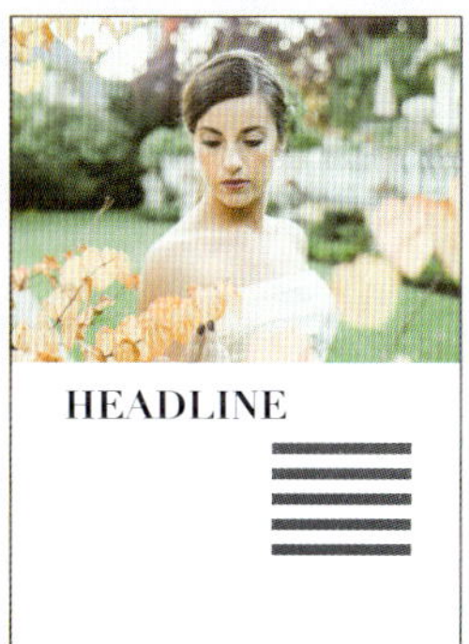

60%-80% negative space. For large scale negative space, you need to consider the design of the key elements in the layout. It would be impressive to use the "empty" space to highlight the theme.

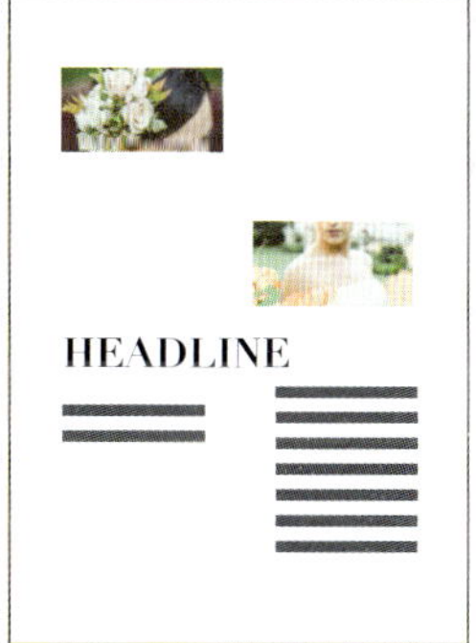

Negative Space as an Element of Layout

Spacing

Page margins, the distance between headline and body copy, the line spacing, and the word spacing all affect the negative space in the layout. When these distances are compressed, there is more negative space.

Font

Bold font makes the word spacing and line spacing look more crowded in visually, but also stands out to catch the customers' eyes.

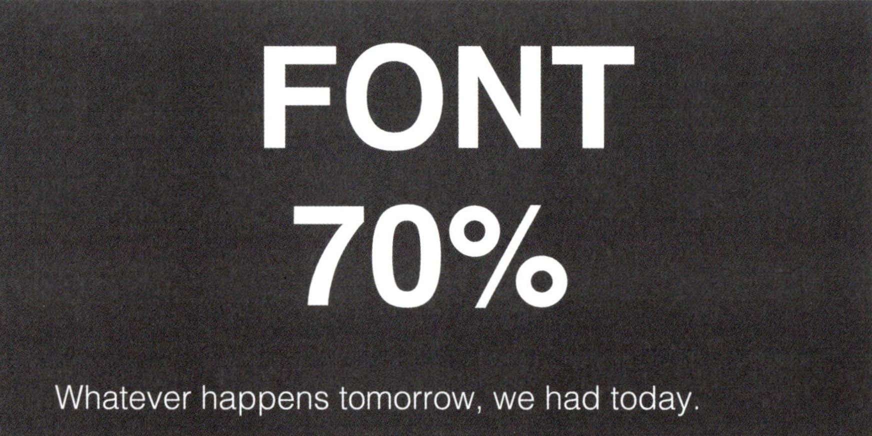

The slender fonts can let the layout looks more "breathable" and more visually refreshing.

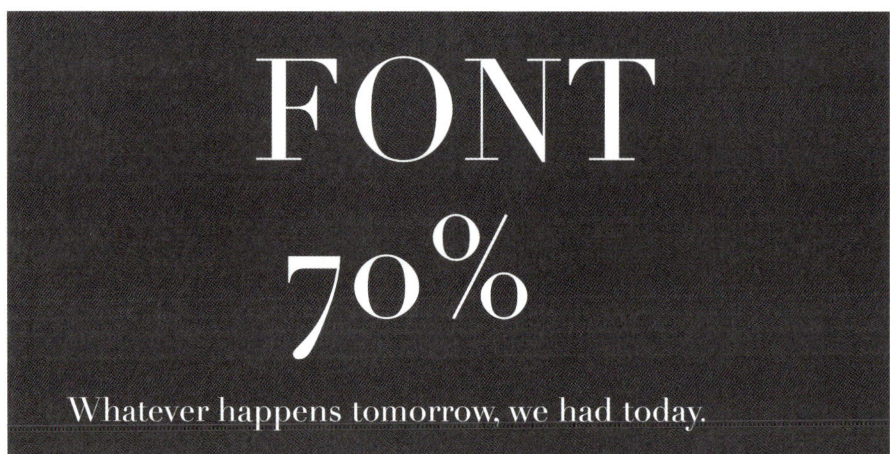

Font size

For the poster, commonly the typeface is about 17-23pt. A larger font size is more suitable to attract customers from far away. For brochures, leaflets, and other small promotional materials, you should choose 7.5-9pt that is suitable for reading.

Images

When an image stays within the type area and does not bleed to the edge, its size and its distance to the text will affect the negative space.

Man-Qi-Wu Japanese Restaurant
Poster and Brochure
Designer: Xi Jianglong

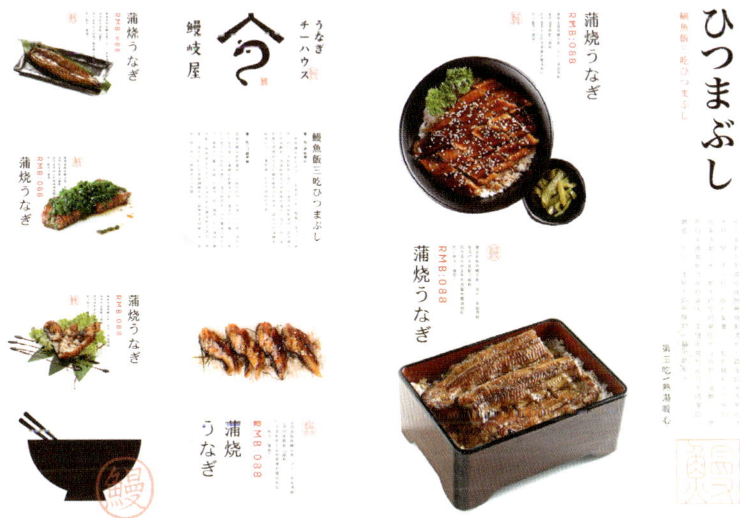

When the picture is bleeding, the size of the color block over the picture or the size of the text area will affect the negative space.

Ma-Lao-Da Sichuan Hot Pot Poster
Designer: Tsai Wei Hsin

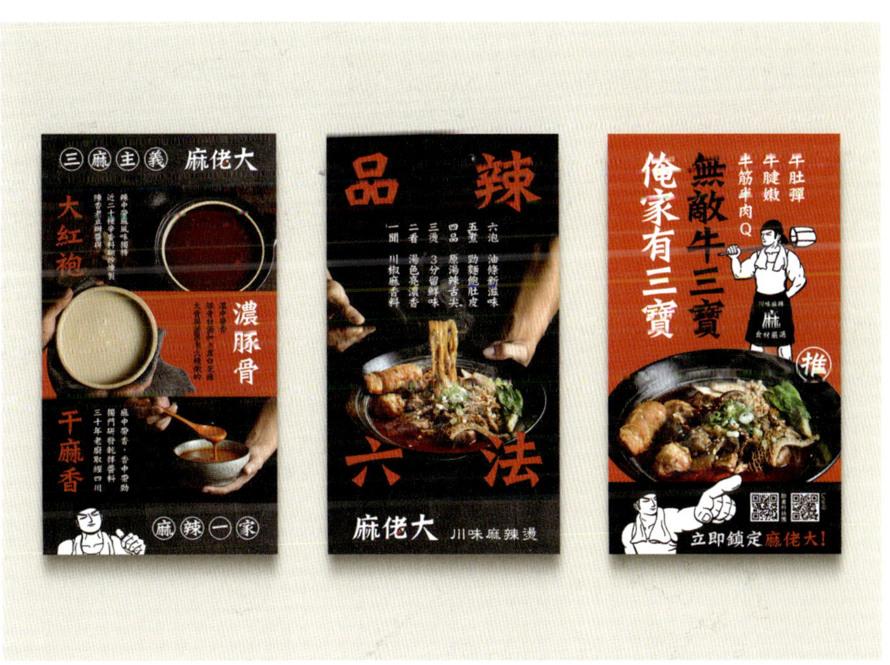

Alignment

The alignment of text and images clarifies the connection between different elements, better conveys the information, and creates beauty from regularity.

Flush Left/Flush Right

Align the text and images to the left side or right side. But one needs to ensure a good balance on the ragged side.

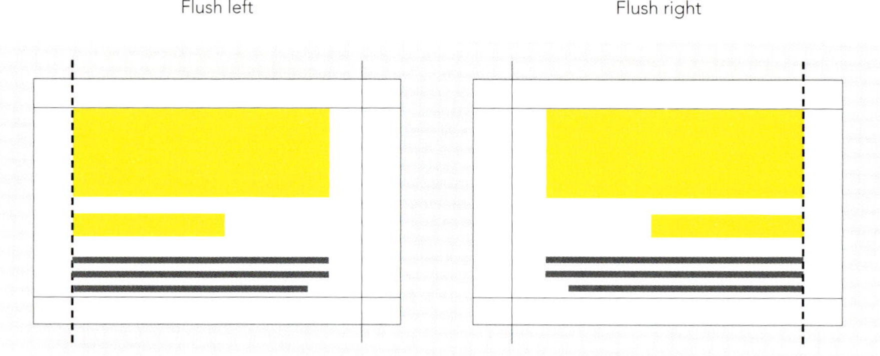

Centered

Centered text and images align with the vertical center of the type area.

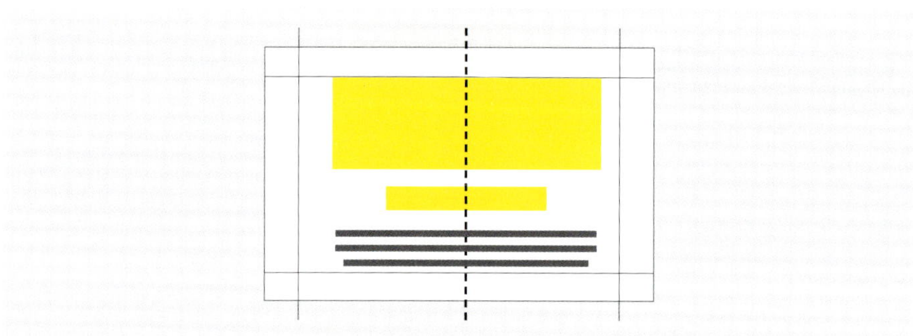

Justified

Justified text and pictures align to both right and left margins, neatly filling the column.

Case Study: Alignment

Splendid Facet Exhibition Brochure

Designer: Songah Lee

Size: 80x210mm

Applying various alignment styles in the layout will be better than only applying one type.

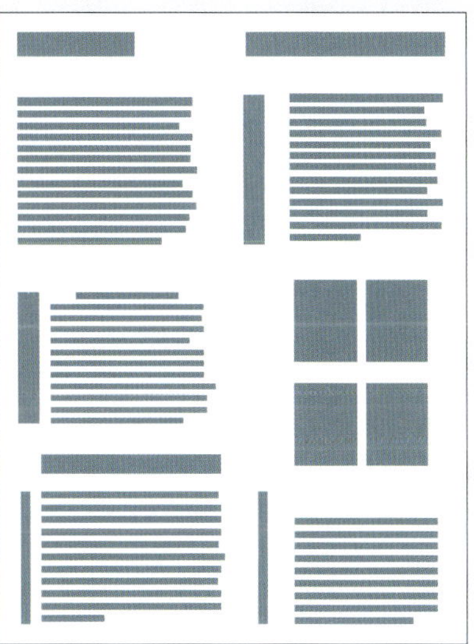

Original image

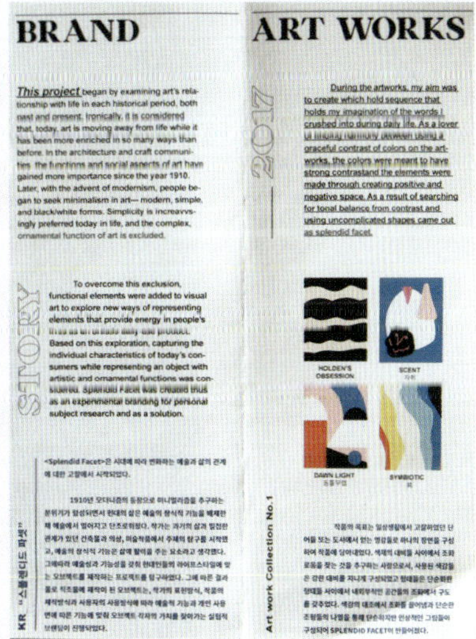

Repetition

Repetition refers to the elements that repeat in the design, such as the color, the shape, and the typeface. It is also good for enhancing the design impact. Once the reader is familiar with the image or message, they are likely to make an automatic connection when it is seen again.

Linear Repetition

Repetition of an element with the same spacing and in the same direction.

Pattern

Repetition of a group of two or more elements.

Rhythm

Rhythm is creating space and constructing a patterned grid system based on a pattern to convey a visual tempo, and make the viewer feel the rhythm. There are several types of rhythm: random, regular, alternating, space flowing, and progressive.

Linear repetition

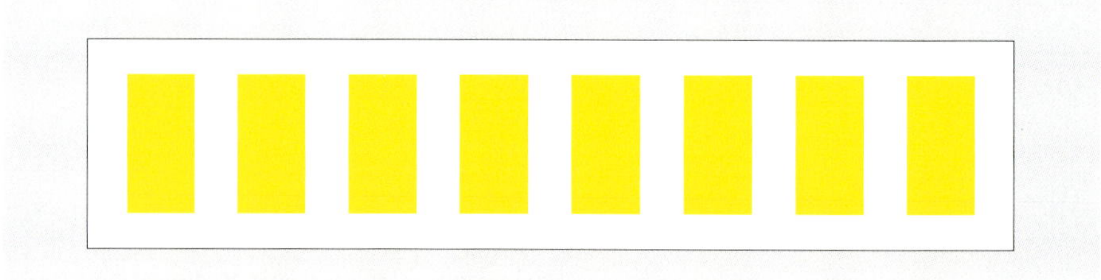

Pattern

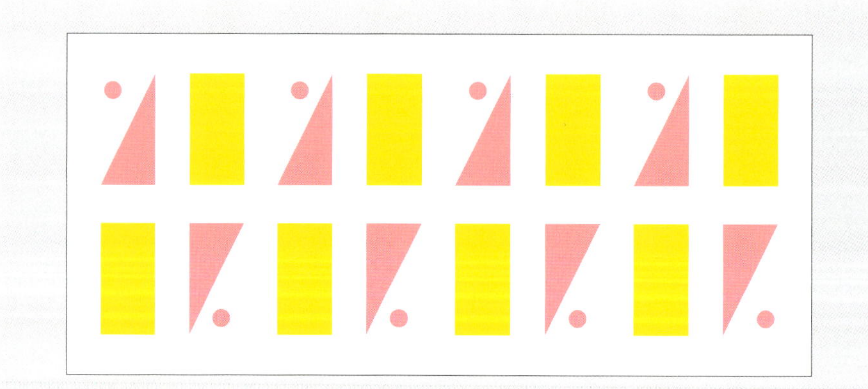

Rhythm

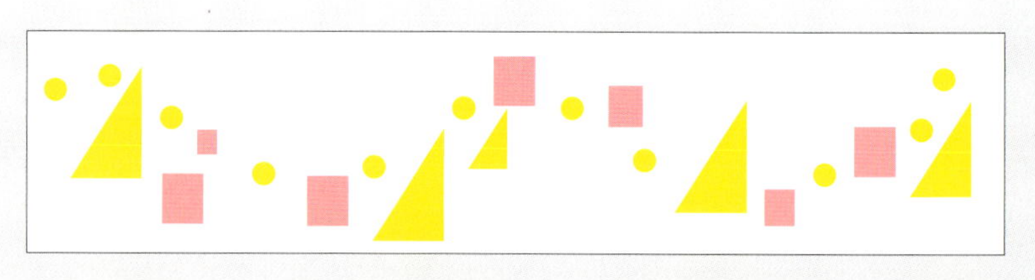

Case Studies: Repetition

Happy Birthday
Designer: ZhongXing.H
Size: 260×375mm
Advertisement type: flyer, poster, website page

Table Mountain National Park Brochure
Designer: Benthe Derks
Size: 200×200mm

Linear repetition

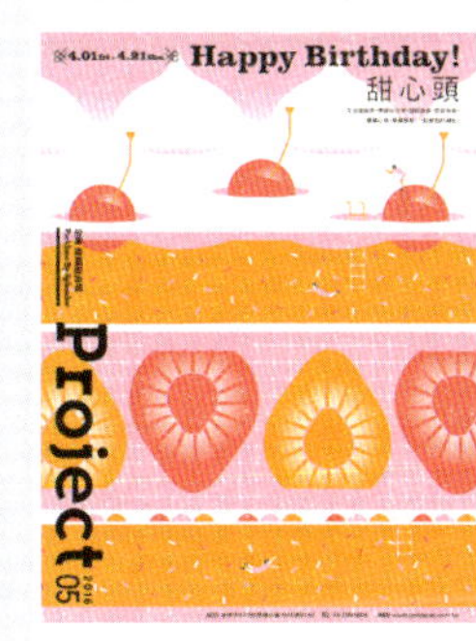

Pattern

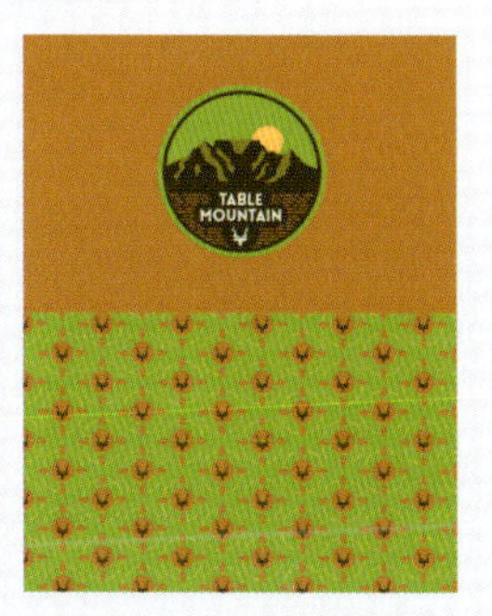

Progressive rhythm

Return Home Promotional Materials
Designer: Shao Chun Yang
Size: 270×200mm

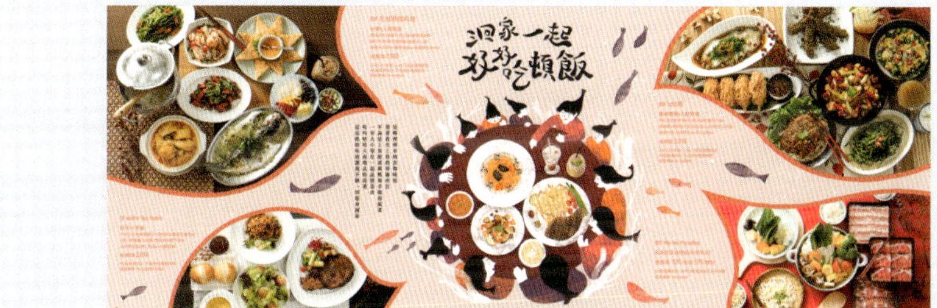

Alternating rhythm

Photo courtesy:
Rodman Browning

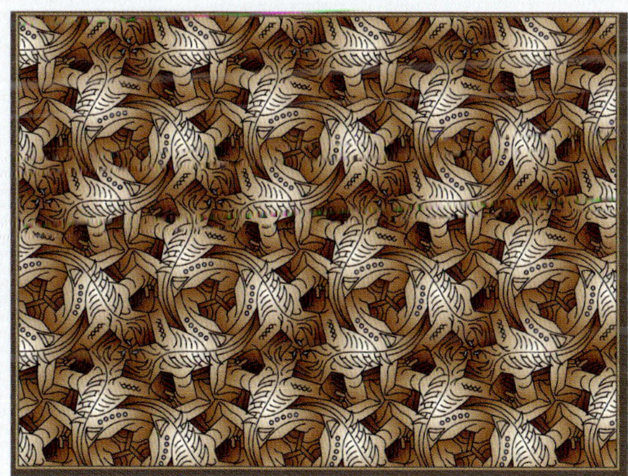

Contrast

Contrast refers to placing the different elements of a design in such a way that the contrasts between them become evident. The use of contrast on typeface, color, shape, size, or spacing, can create a dramatic effect.

Size Contrast

The contrast between different sizes and shapes. It is often used to represent the primary and secondary relationships of a layout.

Color Contrast

The contrast is created because of the difference in hue, value, and saturation of colors. It reinforces the hierarchical relationship of the information contained.

Shape Contrast

Different shapes create contrast, such as square and round.

Direction Contrast

The contrast is created by changing the direction of some elements. The contrast with direction of information blocks in the same space can create dramatic effect.

Size contrast

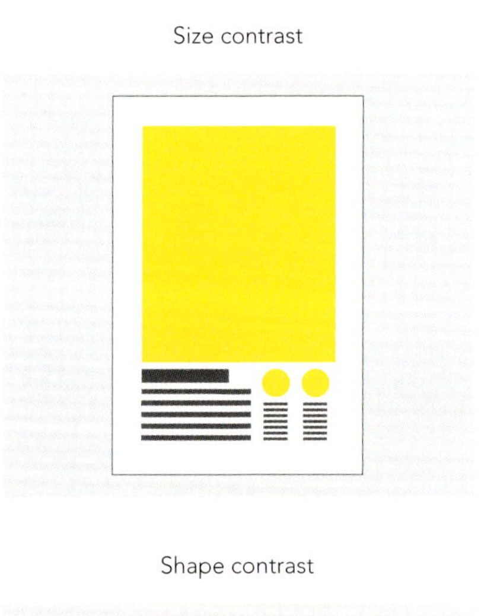

Color contrast

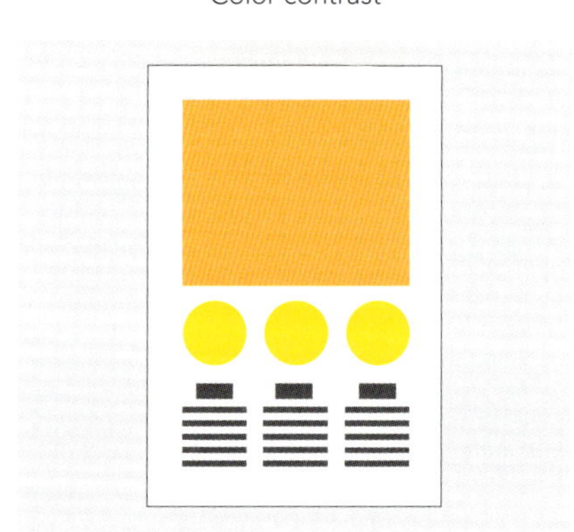

Shape contrast

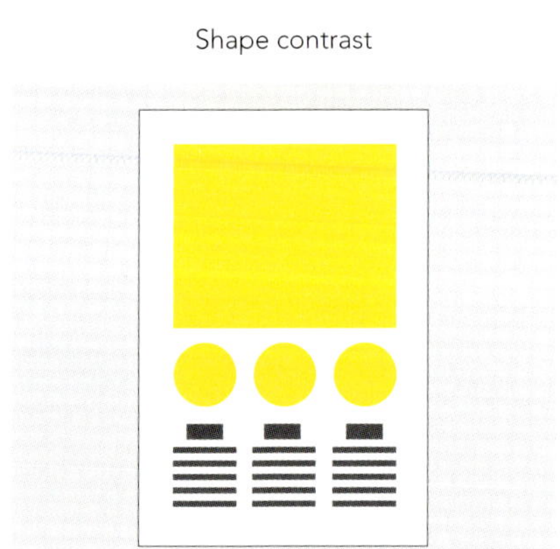

Direction contrast

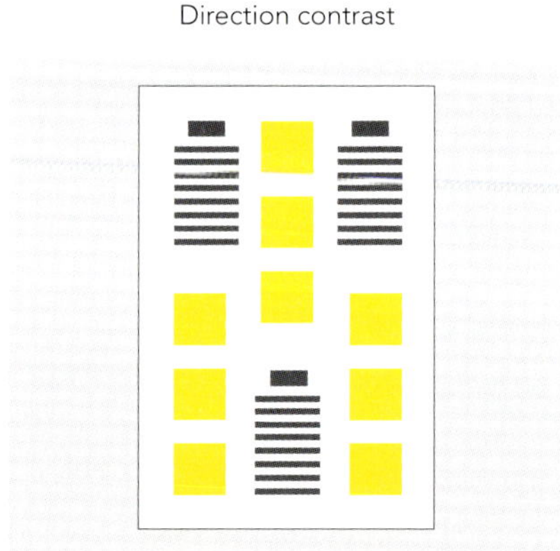

Case Study: Shape Contrast

Table Mountain National Park Brochure

Designer: Benthe Derks

Size: 200×200mm

Visual elements: a comparison of square and circle.

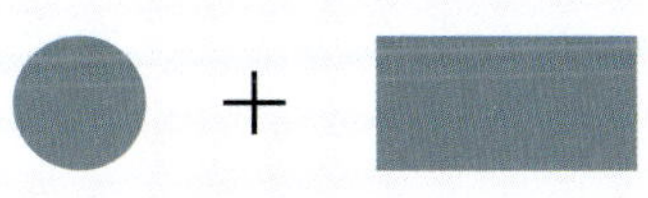

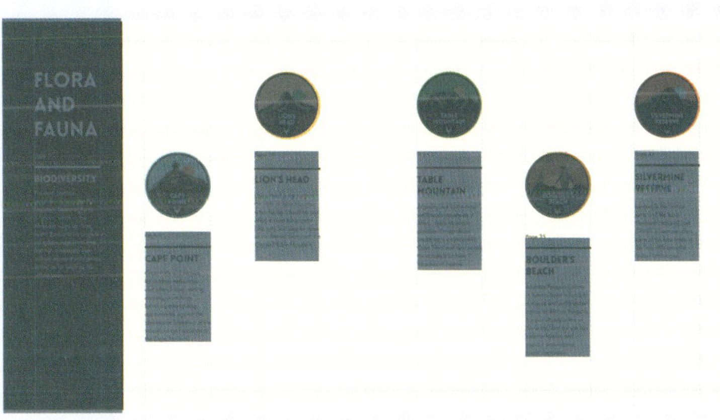

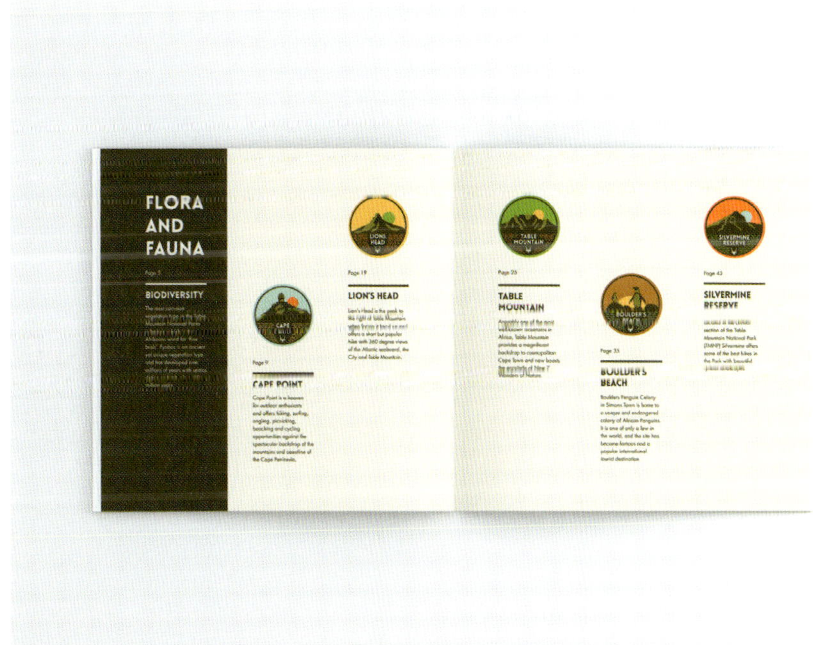

Proximity

Related information when placed together can reduce the burden of reading, and help the reader to find the information easily.

Combination of Related Elements

If the closely related elements are combined, the contents will be displayed in better order with a clearer hierarchy.

Before redesign

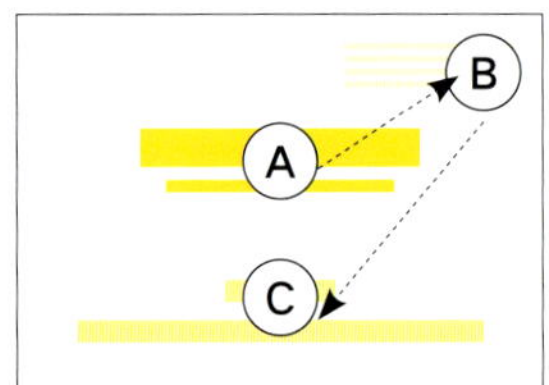

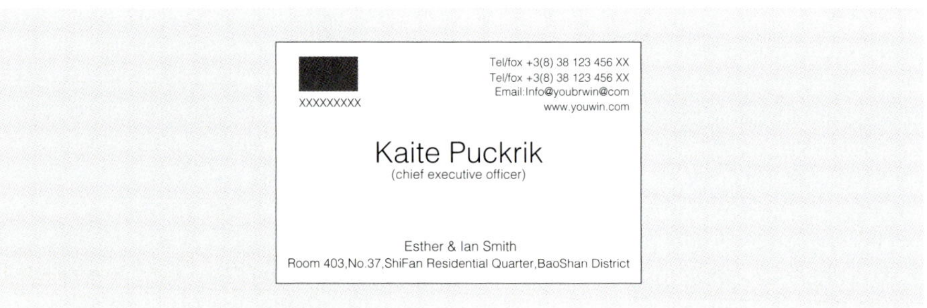

After redesign

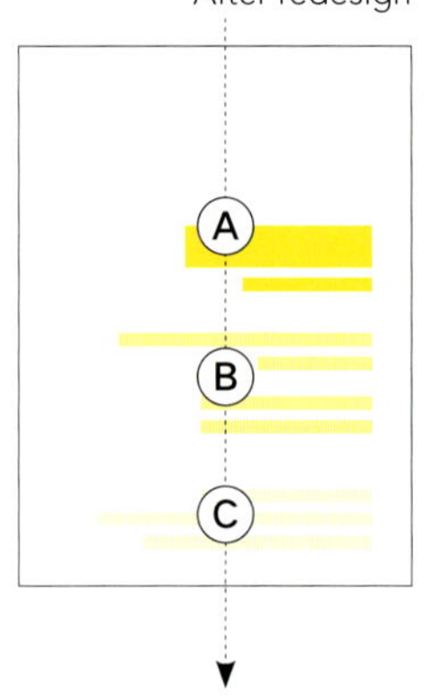

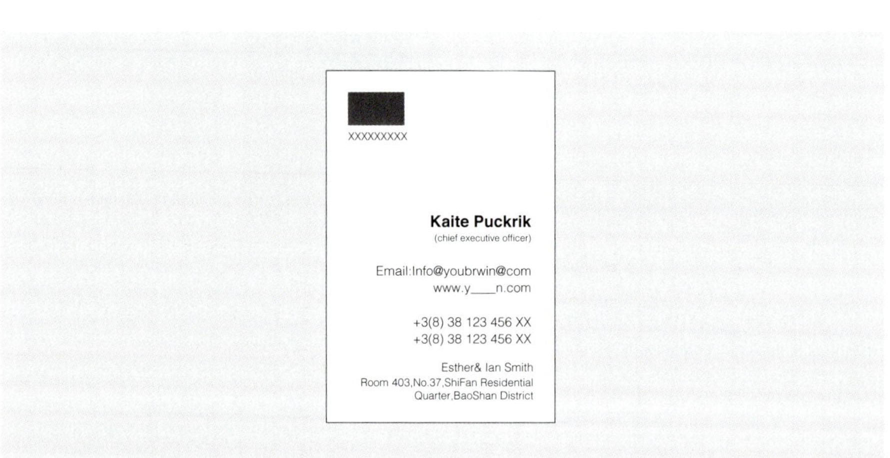

Diminishing of Difference

Fonts, shapes, or colors of different features can become a whole when they are placed closely together.

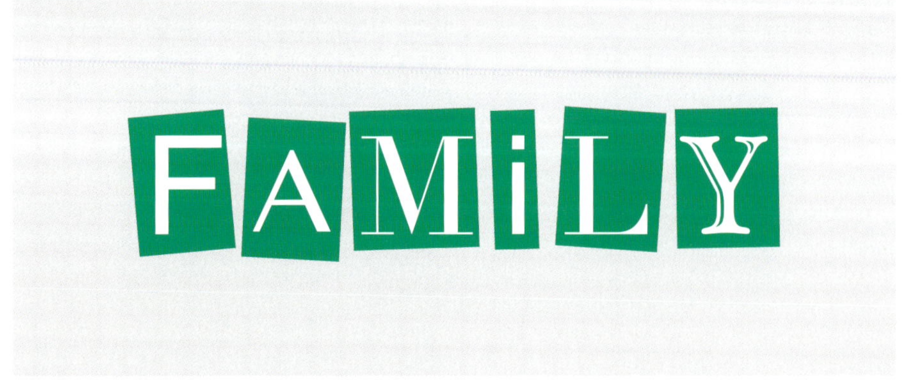

Case Study: Proximity

PARKS

Designer: Shigeki Kondo

Size: 210×297mm (A4)

Various type of plants all in the same green cube.

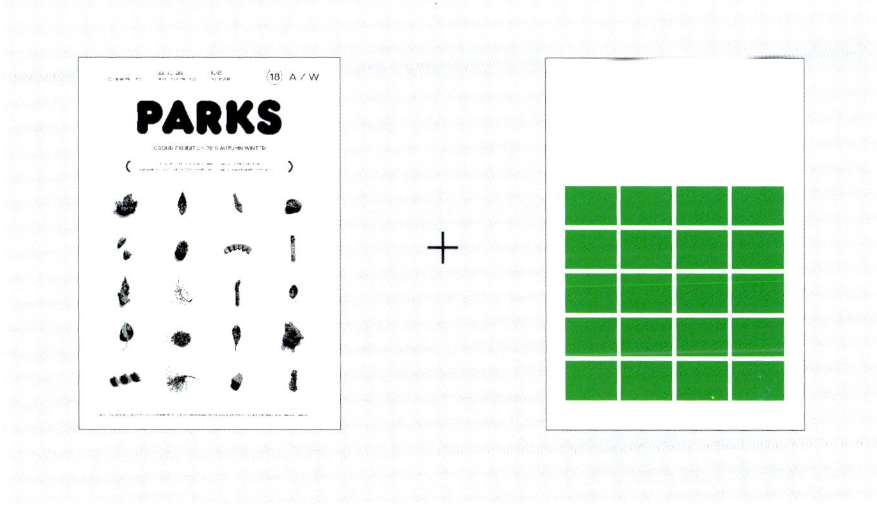

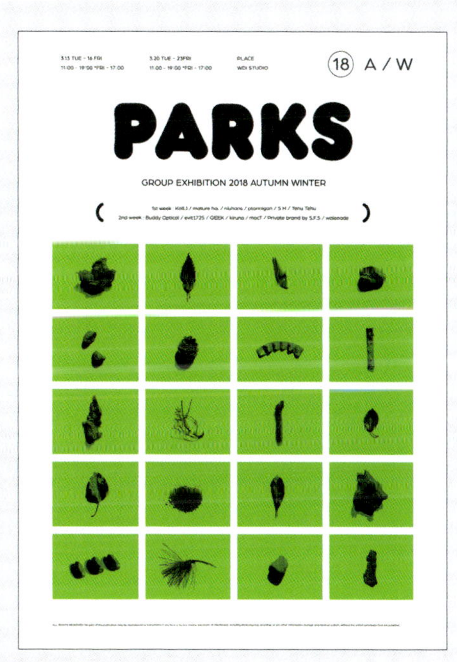

Visual Flow

Visual flow is the trajectory of our sight when tracing the layout elements. It can be understood how the layout guides the consumer to browse the contents in a certain order. After consumers get the promotional materials—which part to read first, which part will the trajectory of our sight stay in most longest—all this appeal can be achieved through layout design.

Vertical Visual Flow

The design elements in the layout are arranged in a vertical direction with a clear feeling. The reader is guided to focus on the key area first, and then browse the page from top to bottom or bottom to top. Primarily used in poster and flyer design.

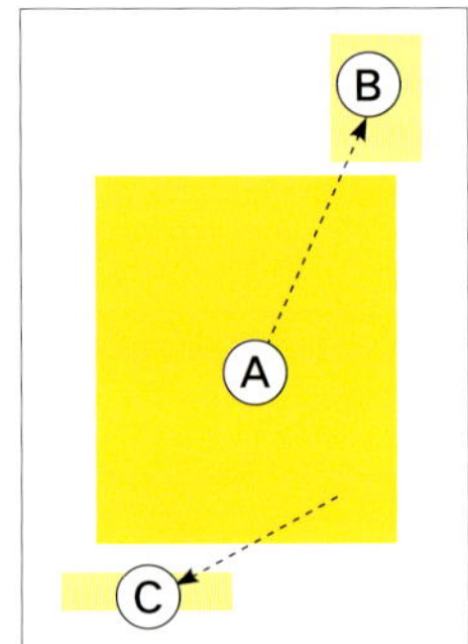

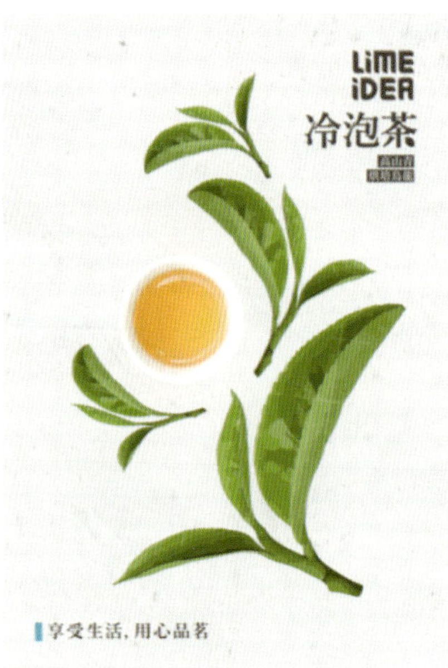

Horizontal Visual Flow

The design element is placed in a horizontal direction with a stable and harmonious feeling. The reader is guided to focus on the key area first, and then browse the page from left to right or right to left.

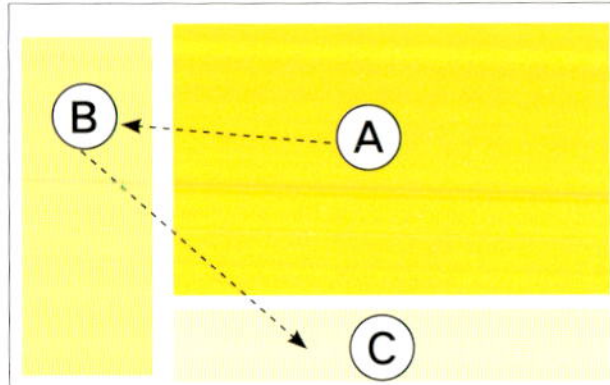

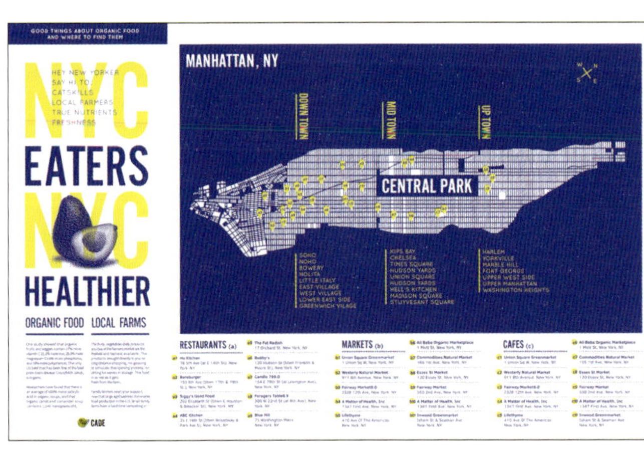

Slanted Visual Flow

The main design elements in the layout are arranged in a slanted direction. The whole visual gives people the feeling of instability, vitality, and non-conformity, which is easy to attract the customers' attention. The layout center has a main design element that attracts the customers' eyes. The text and images surrounding it work as a compliment, and the center part is the most prominent and most eye-catching. If everything was emphasized the design will lose interest, because only one focus gives the information a clear contrast for interest in the layout.

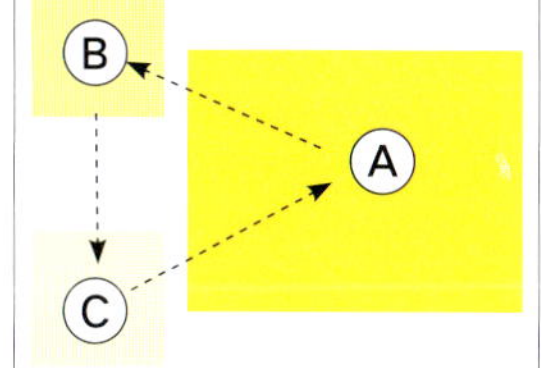

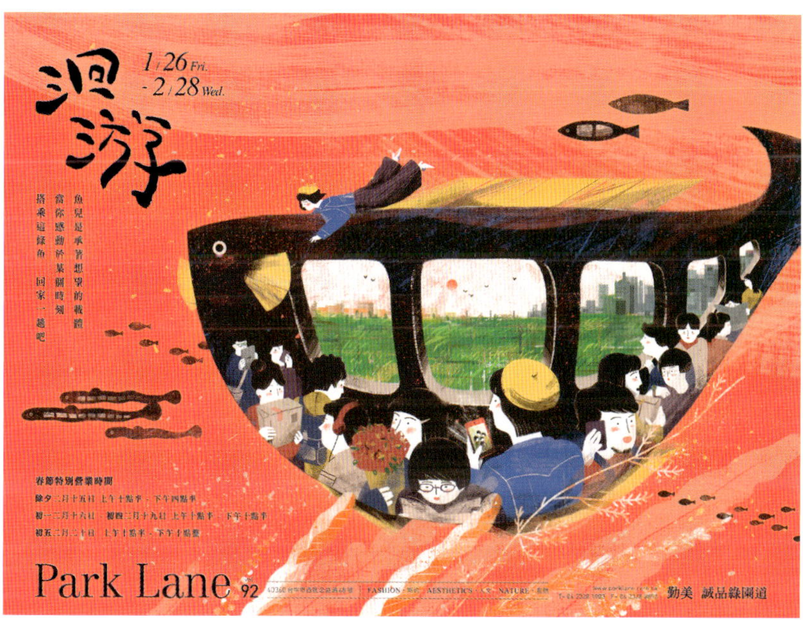

Images or Text Oriented Visual Flow

The elements in the layout are not arranged in a single direction, but instead the images and text area lead the consumer to browse the layout of the entire promotional material in a certain order.

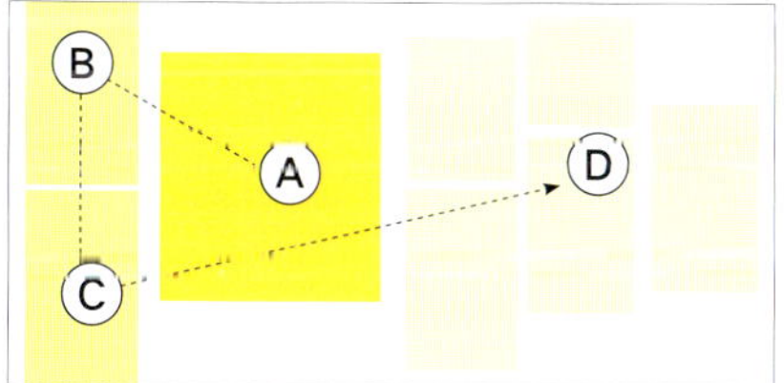

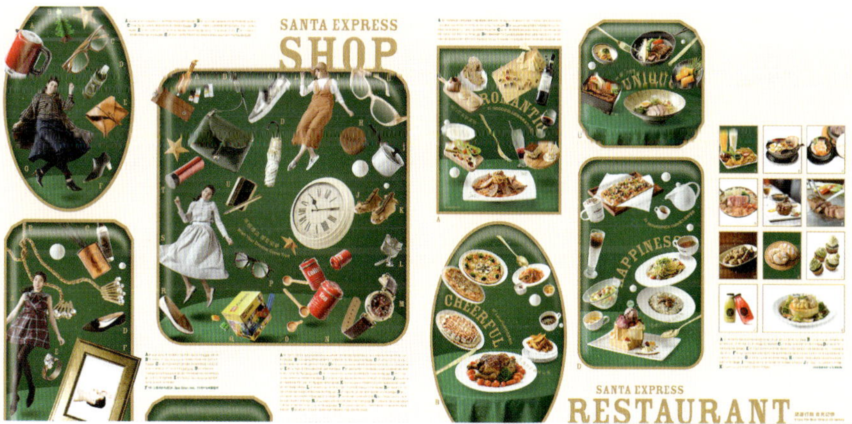

All about Color

Color Wheel

An abstract illustrative organization of color hues around a circle, which shows the relationships between different colors, including primary colors, secondary colors, and tertiary colors.

Color Temperature

Cold colors

Cold colors are often said to be the hues from blue green through blue violet.

Warm colors

Warm colors are often said to be hues from red through yellow, browns and tans included.

Neutral colors

Neutral colors include black, white, gray, and sometimes brown and beige.

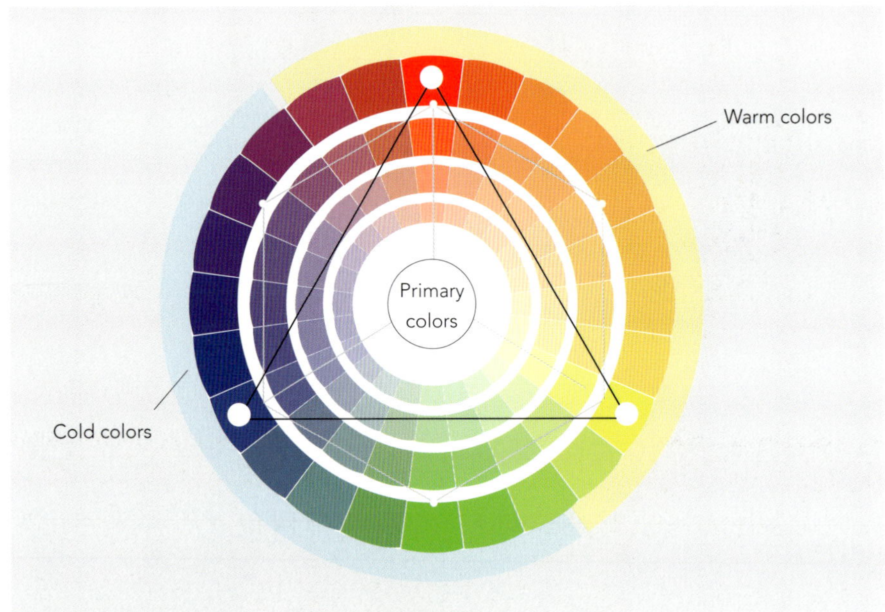

Three Properties of Color

Hue

Different wavelengths of light appear as different colors when they reflect in human eyes, such as red, yellow, blue, and so on. When adjusting the hue in design software, it is not to adjust a single color, but to adjust the overall color in the order of the color wheel.

Saturation

Saturation defines the purity or intensity of a color. High saturation will make the color of the page more gorgeous, which is suitable for colorful design. Low saturation design may look grayish and not fancy, which is more suitable for business or minimalist design.

Value

Value refers to the lightness or darkness of a color. When light is at its fullest intensity, a color will become bright. At its least intensity, a color becomes dim.

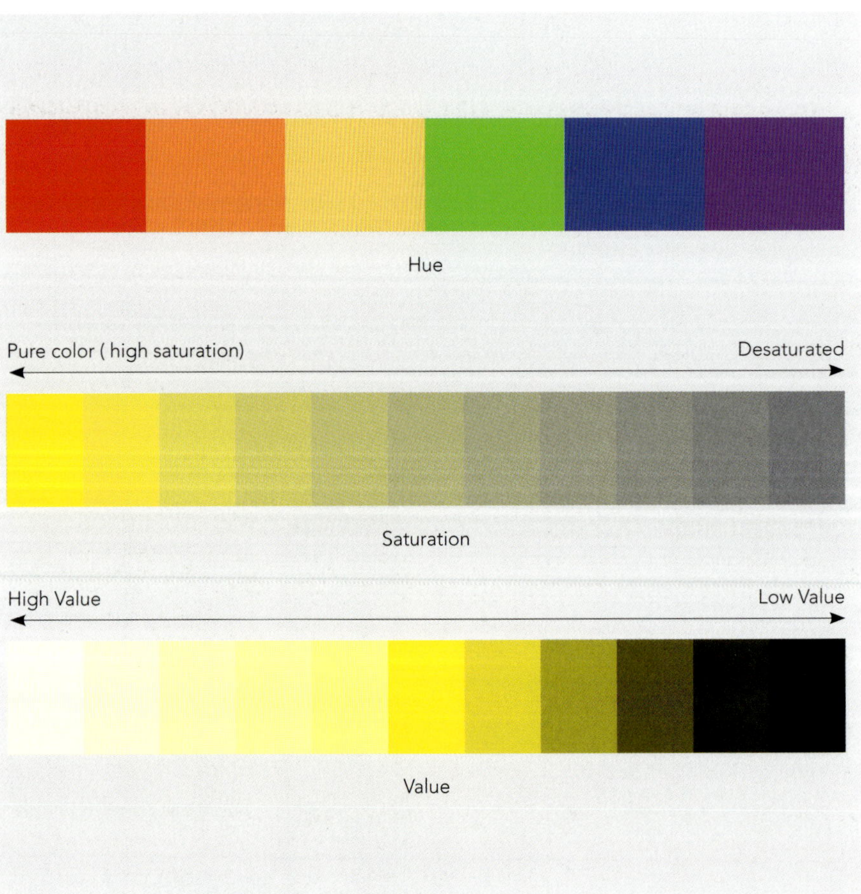

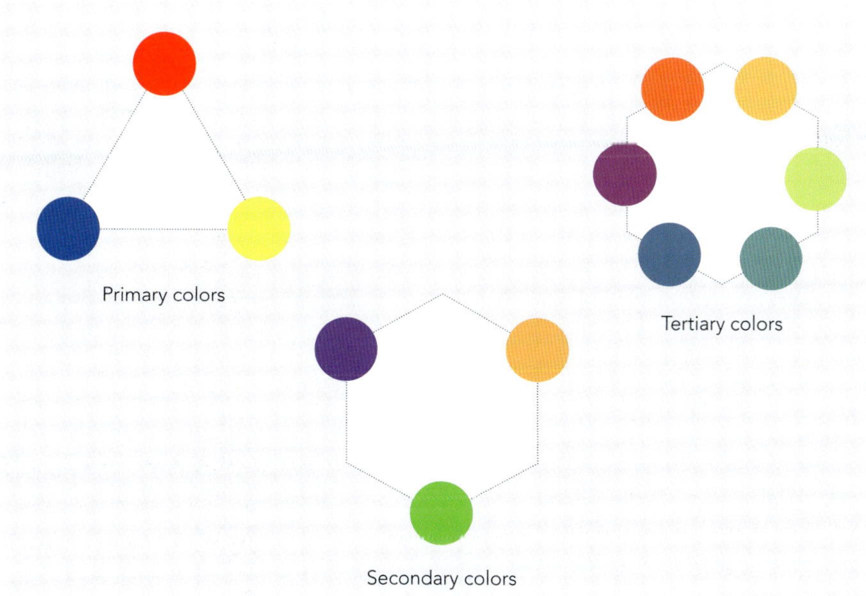

Color Combination

Primary colors

Colors at their basic essence, which cannot be made from a combination of any other colors. Red, yellow, and blue are the primary colors.

Secondary colors

Colors created from a combination of two primary colors.

Tertiary colors

Colors created from a combination of a primary color and a secondary color.

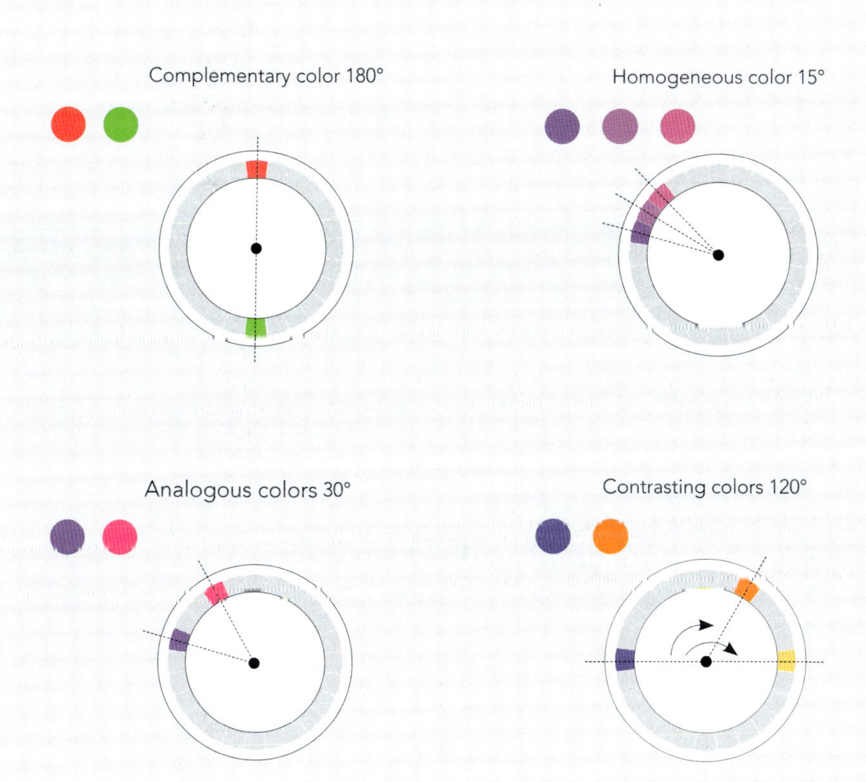

The Relationship of Color

Complementary colors

The completely opposite color on the color wheel. Most common complementary colors are red-green, orange-blue and purple-yellow.

Analogous colors

Colors lying within 30 degree angle of the color wheel which are composed of two or three adjacent colors. These colors share the same color tone, creating a harmonious combination.

Homogeneous colors

Colors lying in the 15 degree angle of the color wheel that have a similar hue, such as red, scarlet, purple, pink and orange.

Contrasting colors

Refers to two colors in the color wheel with an angle between 120 degree~180 degree. The further their location apart, the stronger the color contrast effect.

Color Psychology

People have five senses, and in design, vision is most influenced by the perception of color. If a hungry consumer happens to get a restaurant leaflet with bright red lobster and fragrant yellow lemons. It is possible to mobilize the taste and smell of the picture as if the next second the consumer could eat it.

When dealing with page layout and design elements, we have to consider how a color would affect the perception and experience of a visual. What is the color of the main body of the promotion or what color is suitable for it? We have to understand the color attributes and color psychology to better determine the color matching.

Red

Passionate, hot, dangerous, alarming

Being the longest wavelength and one of the primary colors, red is powerful as well as basic. It appears to be nearer than it physically is and is often where our eyes look first. That is the reason why red is effectively used in traffic lights and some warning signs all over the world. Hence, it is a good choice to grab attention. However, too much red may cause people's hearts to beat faster and feel a bit out of breath. It is commonly seen during holidays that are about love, happiness, and giving.

Orange

Lively, energetic, flamboyant, noisy

Orange combines red and yellow, and is a vibrant, flamboyant, and warm color. It is associated with the sun and with feelings of adventure, enthusiasm, optimism, self-confidence, and sociability that vitalizes, inspires, and creates enthusiasm. It is considered to be a fun color that can stimulate appetites and social conversation, and therefore works well in restaurants. Meanwhile, orange can be used to give the impression of approachability and affordability. The negative implications of this color, however, suggest a lack of quality.

Yellow

Energetic, uplifting, bustle, vulgar

Yellow is the color of the sun, associated with laughter, confidence, happiness, and playfulness. People surrounded by yellow feel optimistic, uplifting, and illuminated. The yellow wavelength is relatively long and stimulating. Besides emotional feelings of confidence and optimism, yellow can also stimulate mental activity. The contrast of yellow with black provides a warning and is often used in safety signs for this reason.

Green

Peaceful, youth, immaturity

Being in the center of the light spectrum, green is a calming and restful color. It suggests balance and harmony. Green is the color of nature: giving a feeling of growth, freshness, fruitfulness, contentment, vitality, healing, and hope. It also relates to the environment and is commonly used to convey a kind of sustainable, organic, natural sense. Negatively, it can indicate stagnation and, incorrectly used, will be perceived as being too bland. In the Western world, it is regarded as the color of money. Too much green may cause feelings of envy, greed, and selfishness.

Blue

Rational, cool, cold, calm

Blue is associated with the sea and the sky, which both can make people feel calm. Blue is the most universally favored color. Although cool blue is known to curb appetites, it is not as noticeable as colors like red or yellow. In its negative mode, people may be reminded of the "blues"—the implication being one of sadness, passivity, alienation, or depression.

Purple

Noble, high-class, mysterious

Purple is a secondary color which is mixed by red and blue. Bright purple indicates a healing and peaceful feeling while dark purple represents nobility and mystery, and turbid purple makes the design look unclear. So, be careful of the value and saturation of purple when using it in design.

Black

Formality, luxury, terror, mourning

Black is the strongest of the neutral colors. Positively, it communicates sophistication, luxury, power, elegance, formality, and uncompromising excellence. Negatively, it can be associated with evil, death, and mourning. Black is commonly used in design to convey a sense of sophistication or mystery.

Grey

Unobtrusive, uncertain, indifferent

Grey is the transition color between black and white. Gray is reminiscent of burnt ashes, environmentally polluted haze, or grey wild wolf. Grey is easy to integrate with the environment and match with other colors, brining a sense of the mysterious.

White

Clean, innocence, cold, disinterest

White connotes purity, simplicity, cleanliness, innocence, and perfection. It is often used in baby care and health-related industry, especially hospitals. As opposed to black, white can work well with any other color. In design, it is often use to convey a minimalist aesthetic and clean, modern quality.

Pink

Cute, girlish, Innocent

Pink is a pale red color that is named after a flower of the same name. It was first used as a color name in the late 17th century. According to European and U.S. surveys, pink is often associated with many beautiful, romantic words that make people feel good. It is commonly used in children's and women's clothing.

Case Study: Color Combination

Cool Wind Natural Mineral Water Brochure

Designer: G.H.Leong

Size: 200×270mm

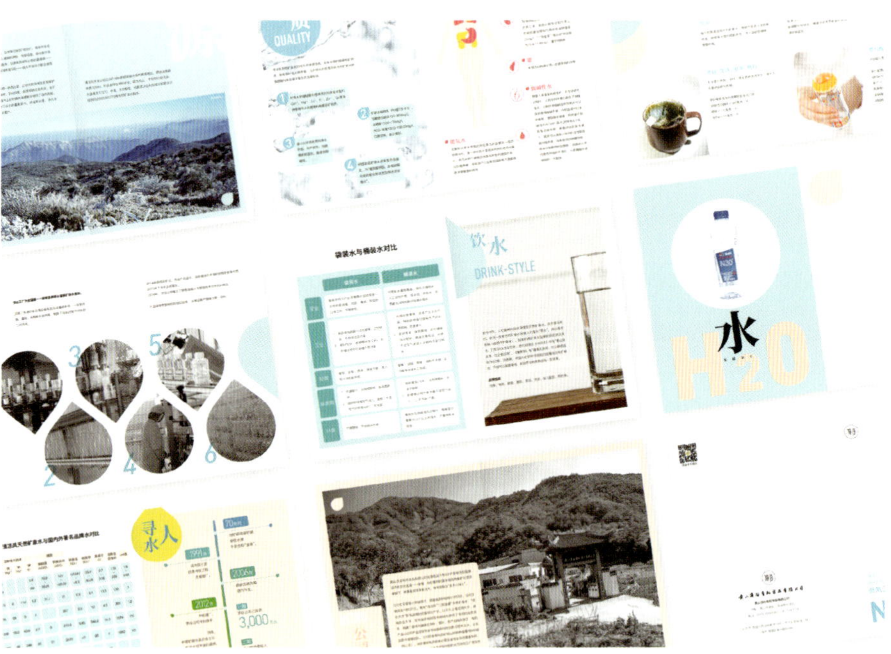

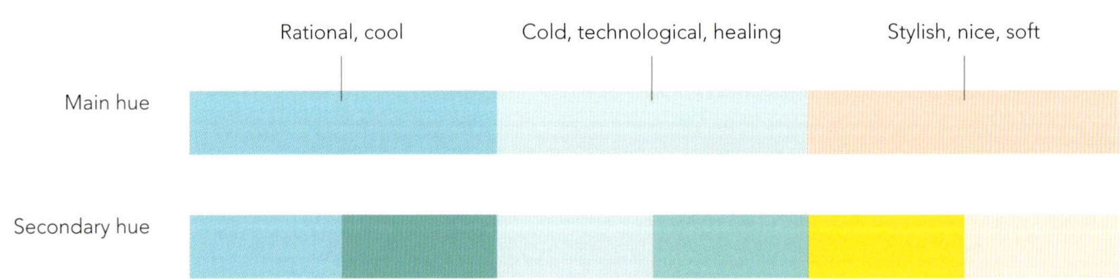

This brochure is designed for N30 mineral water brand to introduce the hit product. The glacier water is collected at 30 degrees north latitude; blue is a symbolic color of glaciers. This color also gives people a cool, cold feeling. Then add the powder orange neutralization, which can form a contrast between cold and warm, and give the color of the picture have a sense of layering. The yellow, pink, and orange colors used for highlighting are a similar color, bright but not abrupt.

Cover

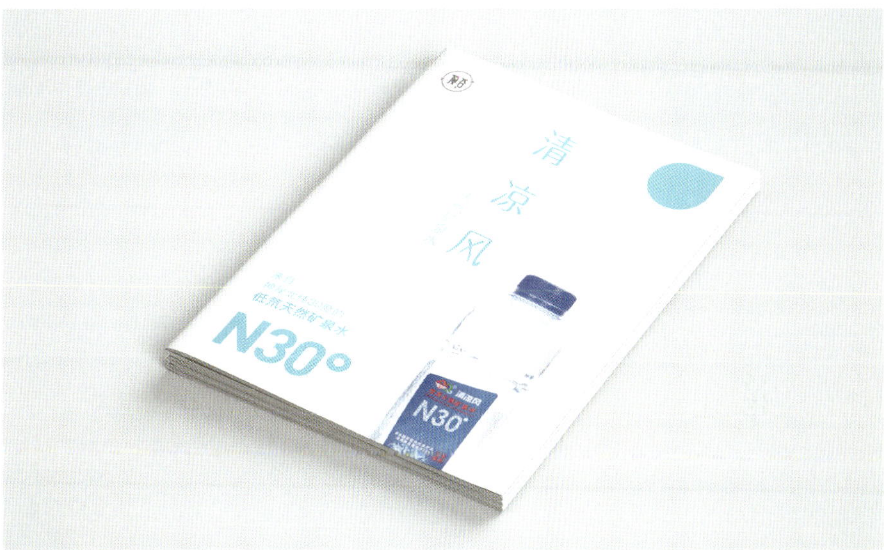

Layout of pages

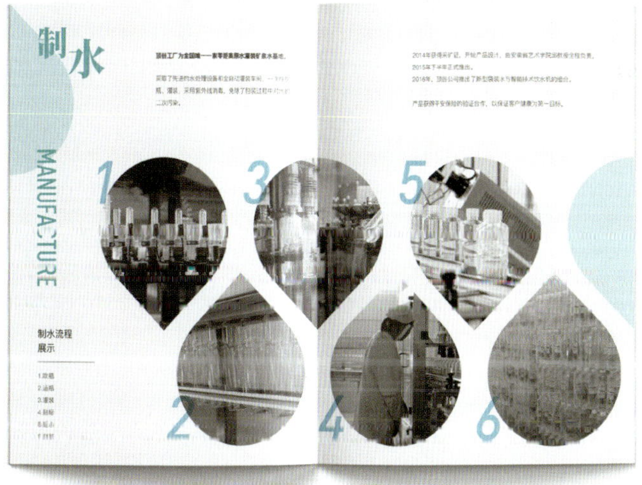

The Font and Text

Typeface

Structure of Chinese Characters

Chinese characters can be divided into two types: single-component and compound. Single-component is a single structure composed of strokes that can't be separated into multiple parts, while compound character has several assembly parts.

Strokes

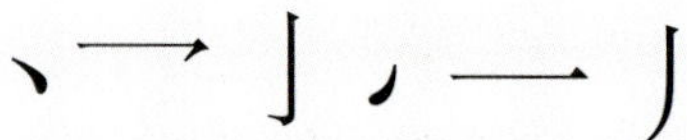

Radical

Single-character and compound-character

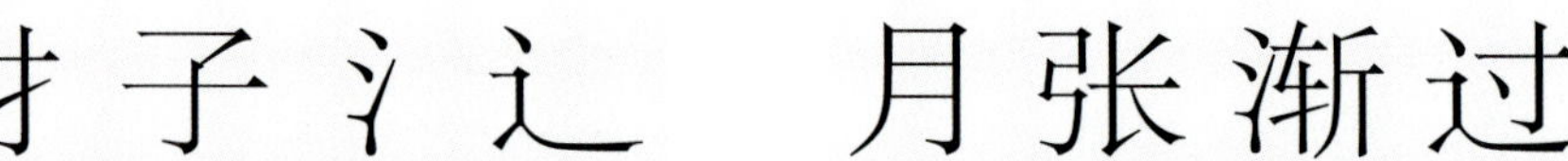

The arrangement of the Chinese character structure will influence the visual effect of them, the concept of nine-square grid originates from Chinese calligraphy that can be regarded as a reference grid system to determine the position of each stroke when writing calligraphy. The distance from strokes to Zhonggong (the central square) of the grid will influence the visual of the character.

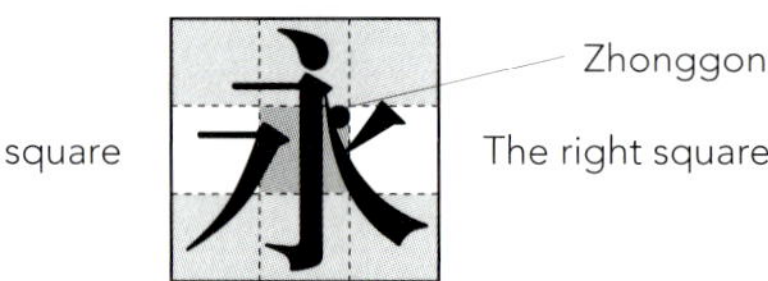

Relationship Between Radicals

According to the spatial relationship between components in Chinese characters, the compound characters can be divided into four categories: split, enclosed, flanked, and integrated. There are also variations within categories according to the structural features. The following examples are some of the most commonly seen structures.

Split structure

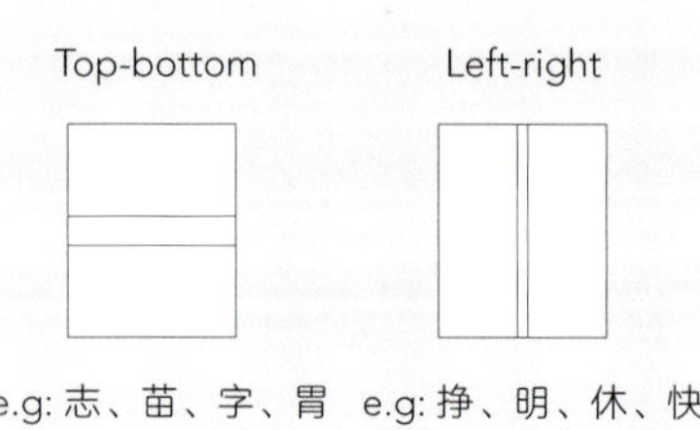

Enclosed structure

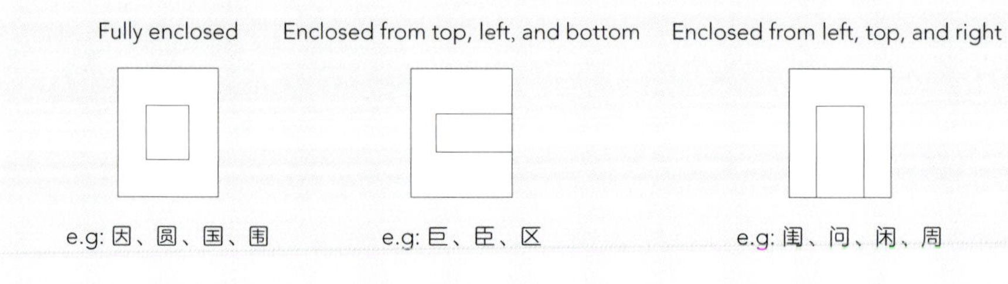

Enclosed from left, bottom, and right

e.g: 击、凶、函、画

Enclosed from top and right

e.g: 句、可、或、勾

Enclosed from left and top

e.g: 疾、反、虎

The Core of Chinese Character

The intersection point of the diagonal line is the geometric center in the grid. If the Chinese characters are placed in the grid, then the center of character is located in the vertical line. Consider both the center of the character and the Zhongong when you want to design an original typeface and apply it in the layout.

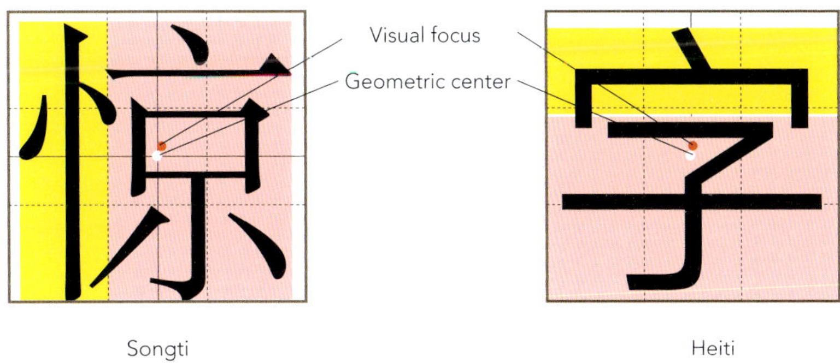

Structure of Latin Alphabet

Serif and sans serif are two main typefaces of Latin Alphabet according to the features of strokes. A typical serif font has decorative details at the end of the strokes, while non-serifs retain only the backbone of the strokes.

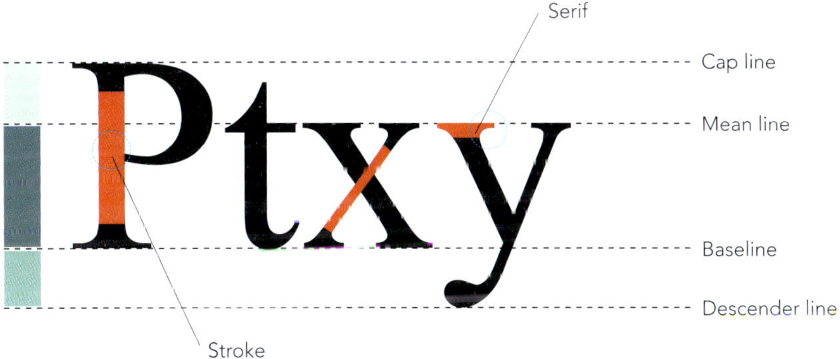

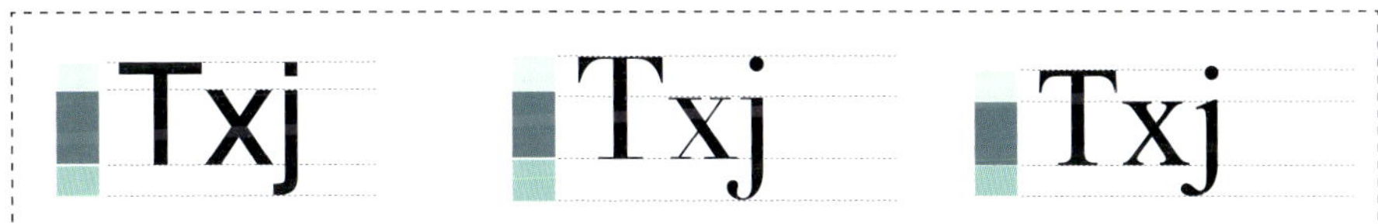

How the reference lines are set has a strong impact both on the shape and the function of the typeface.

Most typefaces can be divided into four main categories: serif, sans serif, script, and decorative.

Serif

Serif typefaces include embellishments at the ends of the letterform strokes, which originally are intended to resemble the pen strokes of embellished script. Serif typefaces are most often used for body copy in print documents.

Times New Roman

Times New Roman is a serif typeface designed for legibility in main body text. It was commissioned by the British newspaper *The Times* in 1931 and conceived by Stanley Morison, the artistic advisor to the British branch of the printing equipment company Monotype, in collaboration with Victor Lardent, a lettering artist in *The Times'* advertising department.

Songti

This is a typeface that was improved in the process of imitating the script of the Song dynasty in China. The original left low and high right strokes were gradually changed to horizontal. The strokes of the Song dynasty vary in thickness, with serifs at the ends, and strokes such as dot, left-falling stroke, right-falling stroke, and hook are pointed. By the Ming dynasty, this type of font and the script had a clear distinction, becoming a mature serif font.

Times
Designer: Stanley Morison

Times New Roman

a b c d e f g h i j k l m n o p q r s t u v w x y z

ABCDEFGHIJKLMNOPQRSTUVWXYZ

1234567890

HYZhongSong
Design: Hanyi Fonts

宋体

a b c d e f g h i j k l m n o p q r s t u v w x y z

壹贰叁肆伍陆柒捌玖拾佰仟万亿元角分零整年月日时分秒

1234567890

Sans Serif

Originating in the early 19th century, sans serif typefaces have no serifs and less line width variation than serif fonts. They are often used to convey simplicity, modernity, or minimalism, and have become the most prevalent for displaying text on computer screens.

Helvetica

Helvetica is a widely used sans serif typeface developed in 1957 by Swiss typeface designer Max Miedinger with input from Eduard Hoffmann.

Heiti

Heiti refers to an oriental font modifed according to the western sans serif font, and its striking features are suitable for headlines. Due to the lack of serif at the end, it may appear unclear when used with large amounts of text. However, with the development of font design, the font company has developed sans serif suitable for text.

Helvetica
Designer: Max Miedinger

Helvetica

a b c d e f g h i j k l m n o p q r s t u v w x y z

ABCDEFGHIJKLMNOPQRSTUVWXYZ

1234567890

HYQiHei
Design: Hanyi Fonts

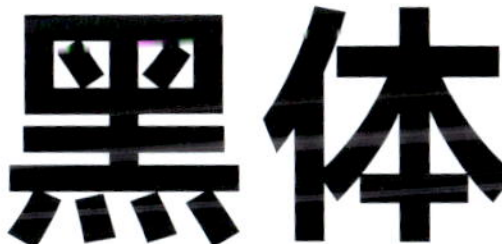

a b c d e f g h i j k l m n o p q r s t u v w x y z

壹贰叁肆伍陆柒捌玖拾佰仟万亿元角分零整年月日时分秒

1234567890

Script

Script typefaces are based on handwriting, and offer ultra-fluid letterforms. They are generally used for display or trade printing rather than for extended body text.

Brush Script

It was a popular font used in the retail industry and the advertising industry in Europe and America during 1940s~1950s. We can recognize the beginning and the ending of the strokes with the strong handwriting characteristic and the typeface that looks like writing in concatenation.

Clerical Script

Clerical script originated in the Qin dynasty and reached the pinnacle in Han dynasty. As a classic calligraphy font, its greatest features are that the end of the strokes are round, the horizontal stroke is long and the vertical stroke is short, and the shape is stable.

Brush Script
Designer: Robert E. Smith

Brush Script

a b c d e f g h i j k l m n o p q r s t u v w x y z

A B C D E F G H I J K L M N O P Q R S T U V W X Y Z

1234567890

HYZhongLi
Design: Hanyi Fonts

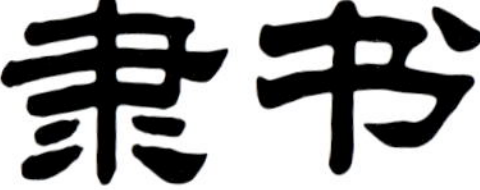

a b c d e f g h i j k l m n o p q r s t u v w x y z

壹贰叁肆伍陆柒捌玖拾佰仟万亿元角分零整年月日时分秒

1234567890

Decorative

Font design ideas emerge in endlessly, decorative typefaces from the largest to the most diverse and expressive categories. Their shapes are creative and expressive, but rarely work for lengthy blocks of text.

Burnstown Dam
The design of imitative wood blocks indicated the pastoral style.

HYYouYuan
Round-ended strokes make the font full of modern fashion, with a lovely and leisurely feeling.

Burnstown Dam
Designer: Larabie Fonts

BURNSTOWN DAM

A B C D E F G H I J K L M N O P Q R S T U V W X Y Z

A B C D E F G H I J K L M N O P Q R S T U V W X Y Z

1234567890

HYYouYuanTiW
Design: Hanyi Fonts

游园体

a b c d e f g h i j k l m n o p q r s t u v w x y z

壹贰叁肆伍陆柒捌玖拾佰仟万亿元角分零整年月日时分秒

1234567890

Text

The thickness of strokes, the font size, the leading and line length are three basic typographic elements that affect the reading experience the most.

Size and Thickness
Leading
Line spacing
8pt
The value of Leading
8pt

A readable and sharp font can reduce the tiredness of eyes and make the text visually clear, which can reduce any mis-understanding during reading.

When designing a text with a massive amount words, a highly legible font, like serif fonts, is the first choice. A readable and sharp font can reduce the tiredness of eyes and make the text visually clear, which can reduce any misunderstanding during reading.

Serif: Times New Roman
Font size 8pt, leading 14pt

When designing a text with a massive amount of words, an "easy-to-read font" will become the first choice. A readable and sharp font can reduce the tiredness of eyes and make the text visually clear, which can reduce any misunderstanding during reading.

Sans serif: Helvetica
Font size 8pt, leading 14pt

When designing a text with a massive amount of words, an "easy-to-read font" will become the first choice. A readable and sharp font can reduce the tiredness of eyes and make the text visually clear, which can reduce any misunderstanding during reading.

Sans serif: HYZhongSong
Font size 8pt, leading 14pt

印刷字数较多的文章时，首先要选择“易于阅读的字体”。如衬线体，衬线装饰让字体更便于分辨，能减轻眼睛的疲劳，易于阅读，还能减少误读。屏显设计中则多使用无衬线字体，因其笔画棱角较少，便于在电子设备的屏幕中渲染并呈现。

Sans serif: HYQiHei
Font size 8pt, leading 14pt

印刷字数较多的文章时，首先要选择“易于阅读的字体”。如衬线体，衬线装饰让字体更便于分辨，能减轻眼睛的疲劳，易于阅读，还能减少误读。屏显设计中则多使用无衬线字体，因其笔画棱角较少，便于在电子设备的屏幕中渲染并呈现。

Leading

In general, the font size is around 1.5 to 2 times wider than the leading. Too wide or too narrow will both influence the visual result.

Font size 8pt, leading 8pt

When designing a text with a massive amount of words, an "easy-to-read font" will become the first choice. A readable and sharp font can reduce the tiredness of eyes and make the text visually clear, which can reduce any misunderstanding during reading.

Font size 8pt, leading 14pt

When designing a text with a massive amount of words, an "easy-to-read font" will become the first choice. A readable and sharp font can reduce the tiredness of eyes and make the text visually clear, which can reduce any misunderstanding during reading.

Font size 8pt, leading 20pt

When designing a text with a massive amount of words, an "easy-to-read font" will become the first choice. A readable and sharp font can reduce the tiredness of eyes and make the text visually clear, which can reduce any misunderstanding during reading.

Line Length

Short line length will be best for reading narrow line width paragraphs, and the line length has to be longer when the line width is wide.Therefore, a well-balanced manipulation of line length is essential for readability.

Font size 8pt, leading 16pt

When designing a text with a massive amount of words, an "easy-to-read font" will become the first choice. A readable and sharp font can reduce the tiredness of eyes and make the text visually clear, which can reduce any misunderstanding during reading.

When designing a text with a massive amount of words, an "easy-to-read font" will become the first choice. A readable and sharp font can reduce the tiredness of eyes and make the text visually clear, which can reduce any misunderstanding during reading.

When designing a text with a massive amount of words, an "easy-to-read font" will become the first choice. A readable and sharp font can reduce the tiredness of eyes and make the text visually clear, which can reduce any misunderstanding during reading.

Indent

A reasonable indent makes the information in a layout easy to read and communicate, which lets the readers recognize the beginning and the ending of the text clearly. Indents are often used in promotional materials with massive amounts of text, but not common in posters and flyers.

Four Basic Types of Indent

Successive indent

left indent 5mm
right indent 5mm

SimHei refers to an oriental font modified according to the western sans serif font, and its striking features are suitable for the title.

First-line indent

left indent 5mm
right indent 5mm

*It's suitable to apply indents in the second paragraph of Latin text; it can bring visual harmony to the layout.

Heiti refers to an oriental font modified according to the western sans serif font, and its striking features are suitable for the title.

Due to the lack of serif at the end, it may appear unclear when used in a lot of texts.

Heiti refers to an oriental font modified according to the western sans serif font, and its striking features are suitable for the title.

Due to the lack of serif at the end, it may appear unclear when used in a lot of texts.

Hanging indent

SimHei refers to an oriental font modified according to the western sans serif font, and its striking features are suitable for the title.

Indent on point

Heiti refers to an oriental font modified according to the western sans serif font, and its striking features are suitable for the title.

Bilingual Typography

Height

The Latin characters are smaller than Oriental language characters, about 0.5pt in common. We have to adjust the height of Latin characters if apply Latin characters and Oriental language characters in one paragraph.

Weight

Refers to the thickness of strokes. English typeface is abundant in more than ten different weight versions, but Chinese typeface only has five versions: light, fine, regular, bold, bolder.

Width

Most Chinese characters look like a square because of the structure while English typeface boast three versions (Regular/Light/Bold), so the letter height should be taken into consideration before using Chinese font and English font in one paragraph.

The Latin Fonts from Chinese Typeface

Latin alphabet is included in most Chinese typefaces, but it would be advisable to carefully select it before putting it alongside the Chinese font otherwise the style and the thickness of strokes may not be uniform that influences and the accuracy of communication.

Univers,1952-1957
Design: Adrian Fruitiger

Univers LT 39 ThinUltraCn
Univers LT 49 LightUltraCn
Univers LT 59 UltraCondensed
Univers LT 47 CondensedLt
Univers LT 47 CondensedLt
Univers LT 57 Condensed
Univers LT 57 Condensed
Univers LT 45 Light
Univers LT 45 Light
Univers CE 55 Medium
Univers CE 55 Italic
Univers CE 55 Bold
Univers CE 55 Bold Italic
Univers LT 73 BlackExtended
Univers LT 73 BlackExtended
Univers LT 93 ExtraBlackEx
Univers LT 93 ExtraBlackEx

FZYouHK
Design: FounderType

悠黑 501L
悠黑 502L
悠黑 503L
悠黑 504L
悠黑 505L
悠黑 506L
悠黑 508R
悠黑 509R
悠黑 510M
悠黑 510M
悠黑 512B

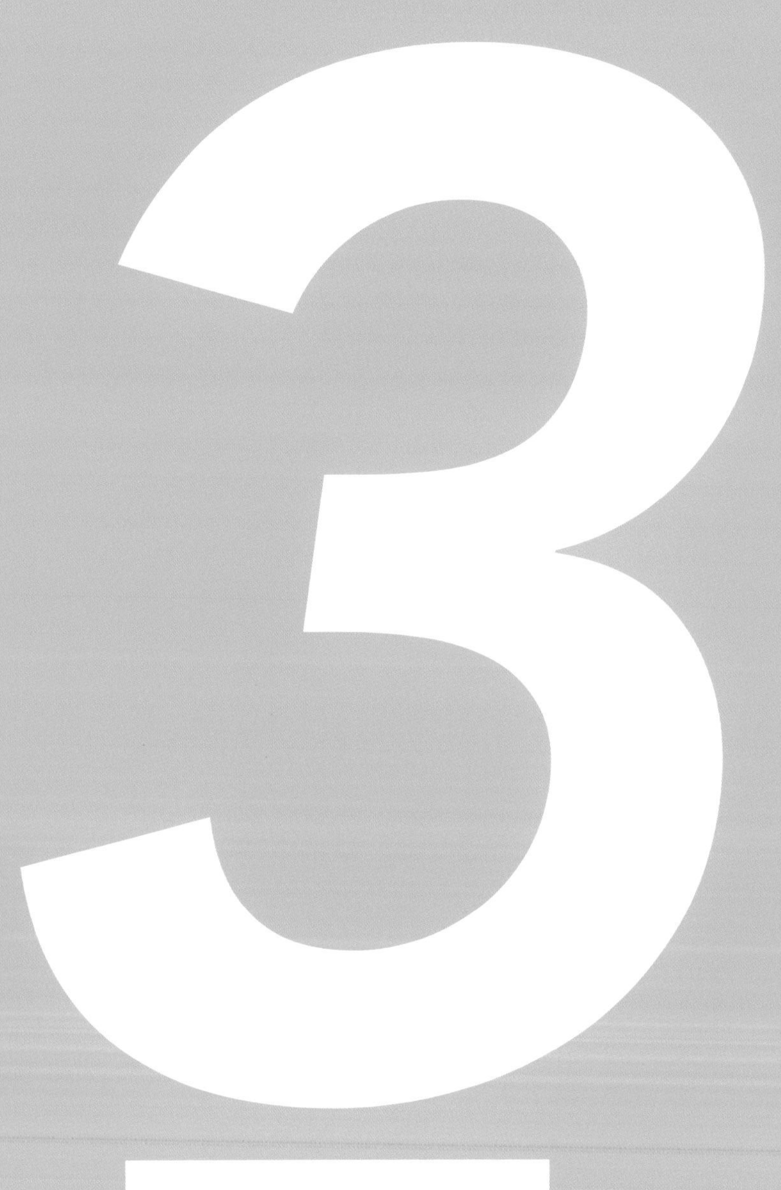

After Design Output and Printing

Output

Color Mode

Since printing uses the subtractive color mixing method, getting accurate color reproduction can only be achieved by using CMYK. When designing your artwork for print, it's recommend that to start with CMYK color mode. It is also fine to create your designs in RGB, but never forget to convert it into CMYK before printing. However, because the two color modes are so different, such conversions are never just a simple flip of the switch. It is a good idea to view a printed proof to see how the converted colors will appear in print, and if it's necessary to make some manual adjustments to get things right.

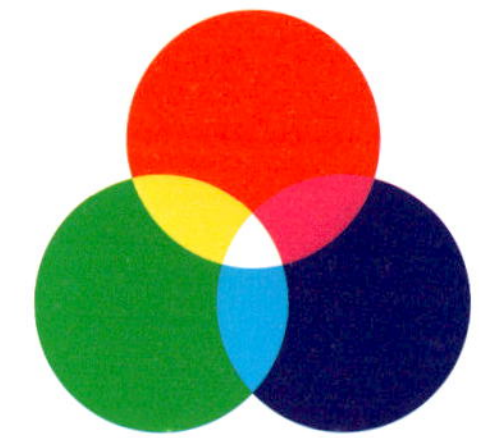

RGB

RGB stands for red, green, and blue—the primary colors of light. The RGB color model is an additive model used for displaying images on a computer monitor, televisions, or other screen device. RGB colors are composed of combinations of red, green, and blue light beams that go straight from a screen into your eyes. Each of the primary colors has a value in the range from 0 to 255.

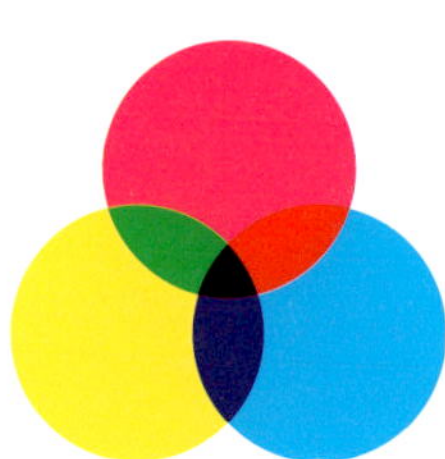

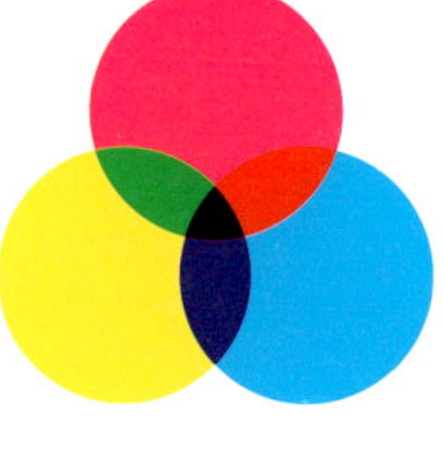

CMYK

CMYK stands for cyan, magenta, yellow, and key color (black), it is a subtractive model used specifically for printed material. CMYK colors are created by combinations of the primary cyan, magenta, yellow, and black (key color) to produce a colorfully printed result.

CMYK

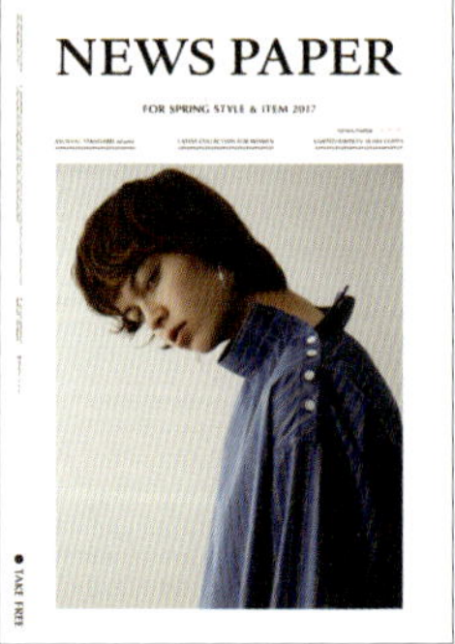

C: Cyan

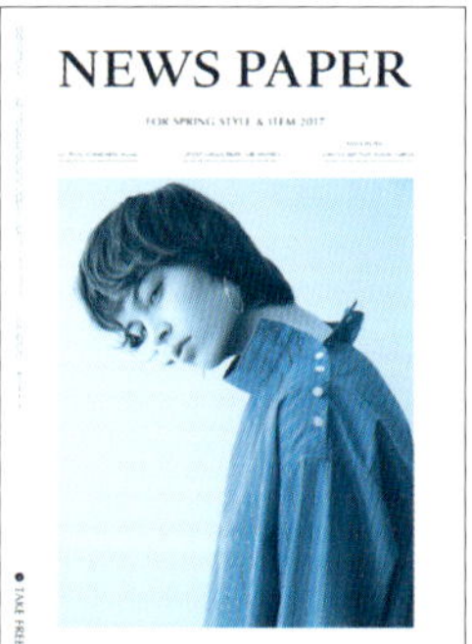

M: Magenta

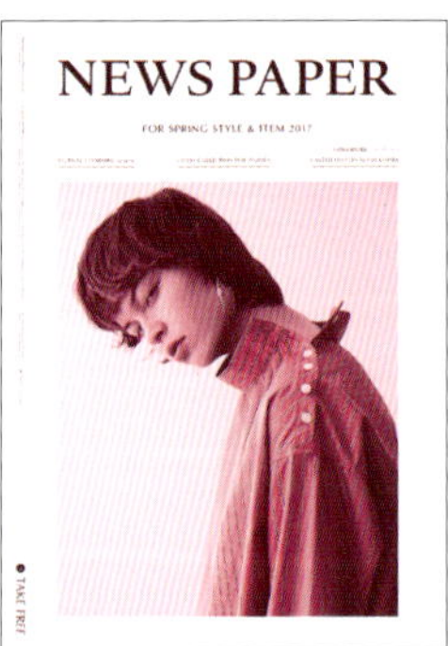

Y: Yellow

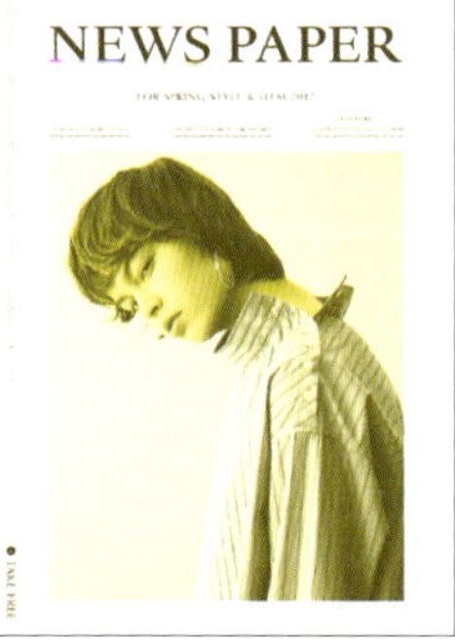

K: Key

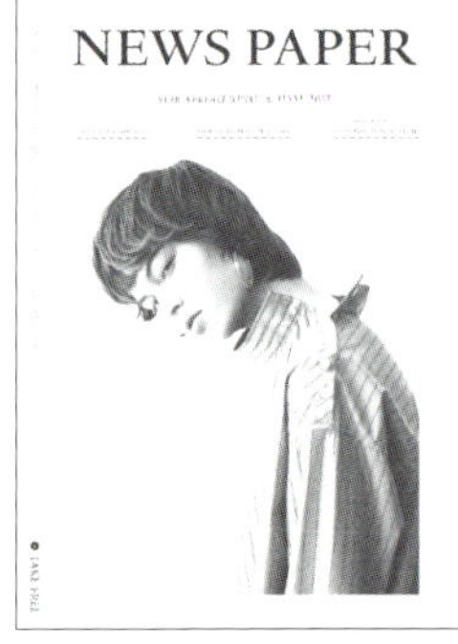

Resolution

Refers to the pixel detail in the bitmap image, measured in dots per inch (dpi). The more dots per inch, the higher the resolution. In general, the higher the resolution of the image, the better the quality of the resulting printed image. Printed promotional materials generally require a design file at least 300 dpi to ensure the high defnition of graphics.

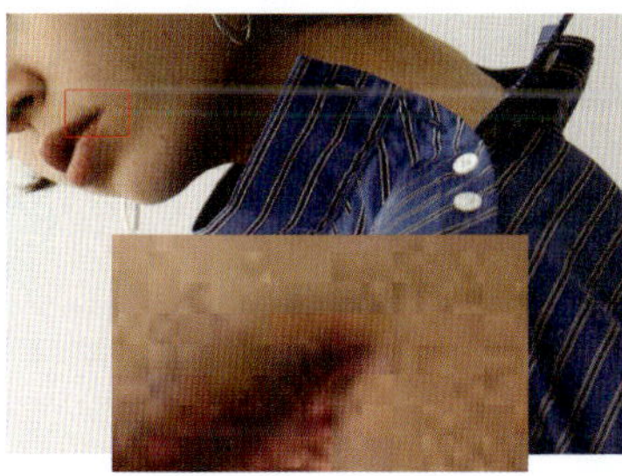

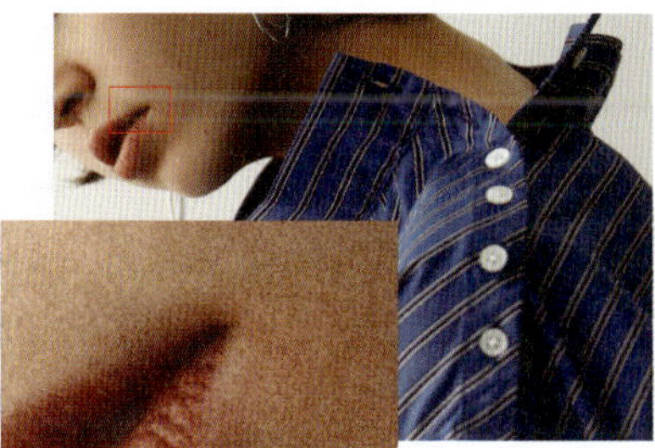

Same image at 72-dots and 300-dots, inset zoom 200%.

Sometimes the image file is large enough, but the resolution is not enough. In this case, you need to check the actual size of the image in Photoshop. If you find that the resolution is not enough for actual printing, you should replace it.

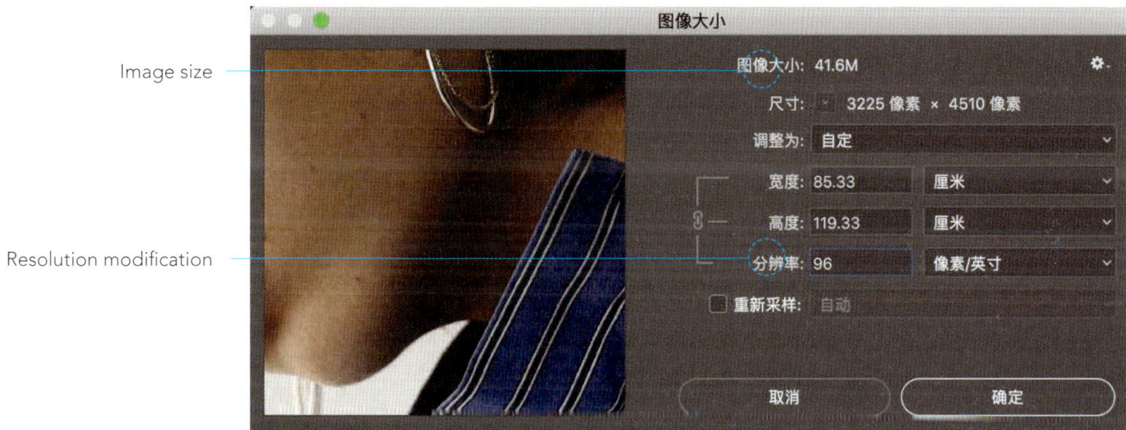

Printing

Bleed

Printing companies usually arrange the printed content on full-open paper. We often say 16mo as a page size resulted from folding a sheet of paper into 16 leaves. Therefore, when submitting printed materials to the printing house, in order to display the position of the cut, "trim marks" should be placed on the edge the printed content. In addition, when the background has color or the background is a photo, the background setting is 3mm (bleed) beyond the cutting line.The printing and binding process requires that the background or picture of the page must be at a certain position beyond the cutting line, usually 3mm, so as not to cut the contents of the page. The part outside the cutting line is called the bleed.

Paper Sizes

ISO Paper Sizes

ISO paper sizes are based on a single-aspect (width-to-height) ratio of 1:$\sqrt{2}$, or approximately 1:1.4142. We call the ratio the Lichtenberg Ratio, after the German scientist Georg Christoph Lichtenberg, who first proposed it as a basis for paper formats in 1786. This ratio is especially convenient for paper sizes that allow the halves—when cut or folded in half width-wise—to retain the same aspect ratio. Each ISO paper size is one half of the area of the next larger size. For instance, A5 is half the area of A4-size paper and A2 is half the area of A1-size paper. The system is widely used in most of the world and provides easier scaling for a consistent respect ratio.

*Both systems also define other length units equal to 12 respective points for measuring column width and depth, margins, and other larger distances. It is cicero in the Didot system and pica in the American point system.

A Series

The A series is the most commonly used page measurement standard defined by ISO 216, which is based on the German standard DIN 476, which is in turn standard for paper sizes. This series starts with the largest A0 sheet (841mm×1189mm or about 33.1in × 46.8in). Of the successive paper sizes in this series, A(n) is defined as A(n-1) halved, parallel to its shorter sides. A4 is the most frequently used paper size in this series, which measures 210mm×297mm. All measurements are rounded to the nearest millimeter. Because paper is usually specified in g/m^2, for all practical purposes, an A0 sheet is defined as an area of 1m^2. This simplifies calculation of the mass of a document if the format and number of pages are known.

B Series

The B series has been introduced to cover a wider range of paper sizes. The area of B-series sheets is the geometric mean of successive A-series sheets (Bn= $\sqrt{A(n+1)\times An}$). So, a B1 sheet is between A0 (1m^2) and A1 (0.5m^2) in size, with an area of 0.707m^2. The B series is commonly used for posters and books.

C Series

The C series is meant for envelopes that hold A-series counterparts. For example, a C5 envelope will fit an unfolded A5-size letter or an A4 sheet folded in half.

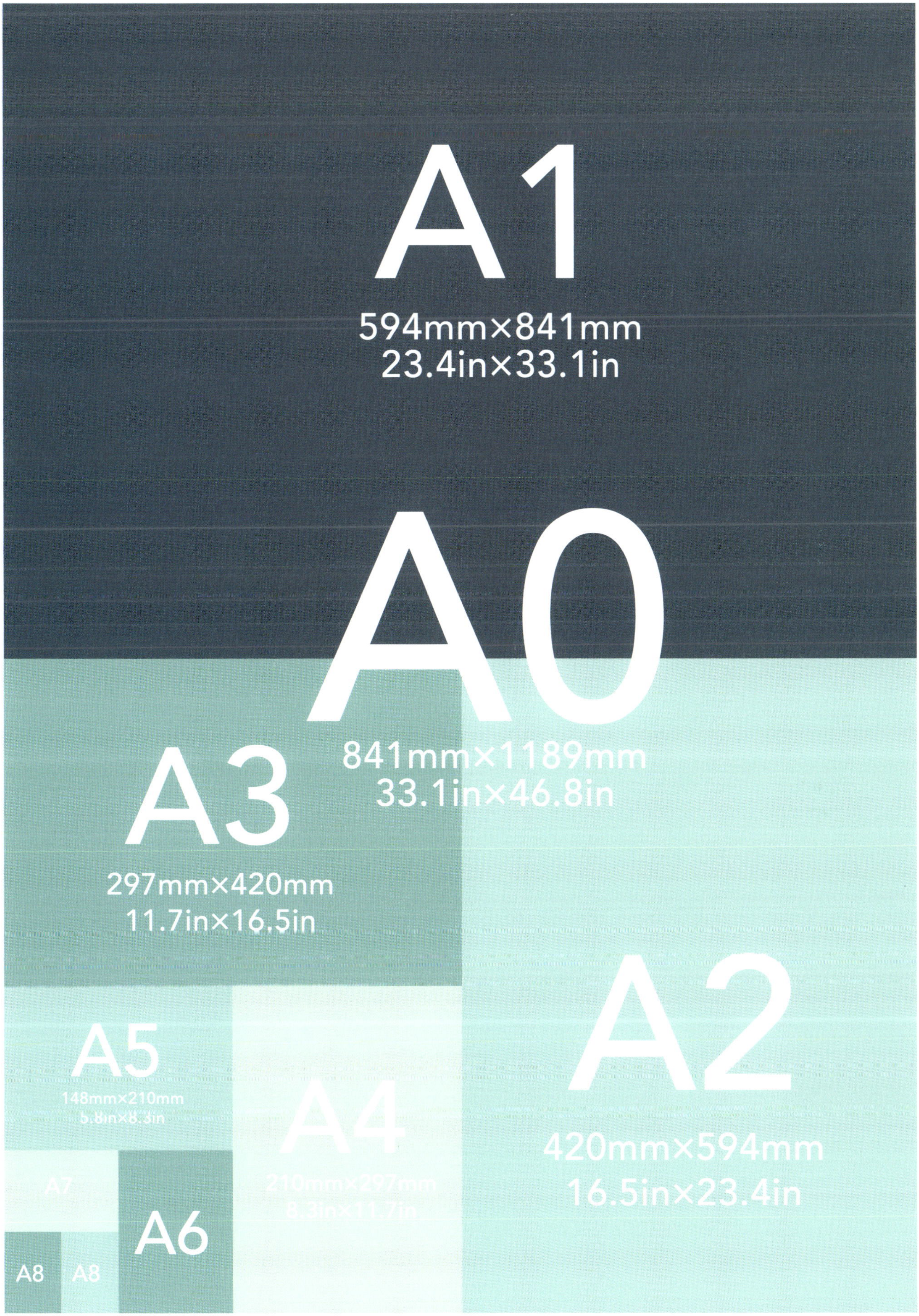

A1
594mm×841mm
23.4in×33.1in

A0
841mm×1189mm
33.1in×46.8in

A3
297mm×420mm
11.7in×16.5in

A2
420mm×594mm
16.5in×23.4in

A5
148mm×210mm
5.8in×8.3in

A4
210mm×297mm
8.3in×11.7in

A7

A6

A8

A8

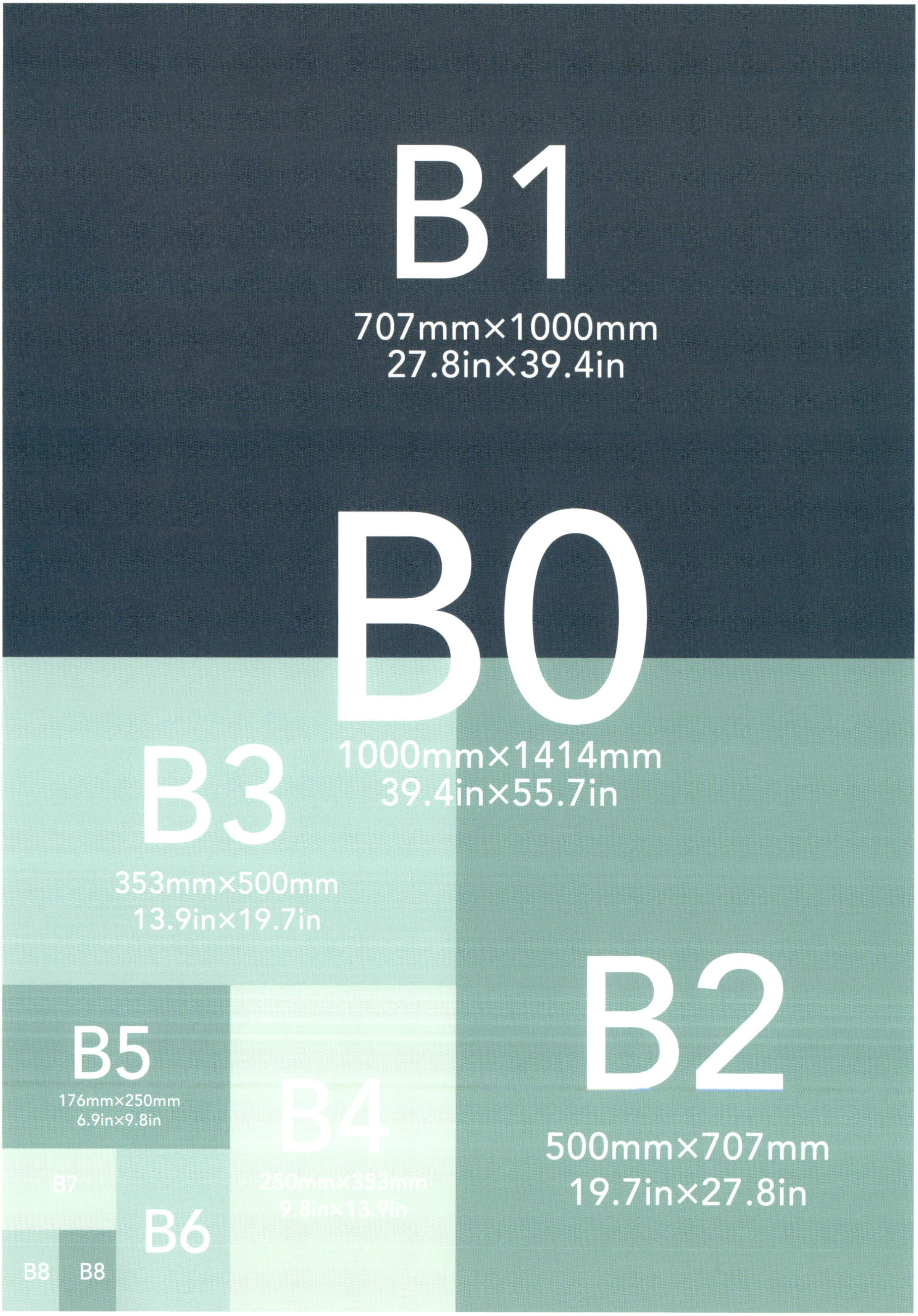

B1
707mm×1000mm
27.8in×39.4in
B0
1000mm×1414mm
39.4in×55.7in
B3
353mm×500mm
13.9in×19.7in
B2
500mm×707mm
19.7in×27.8in
B5
176mm×250mm
6.9in×9.8in
B4
250mm×353mm
9.8in×13.9in
B7
B6
B8
B8

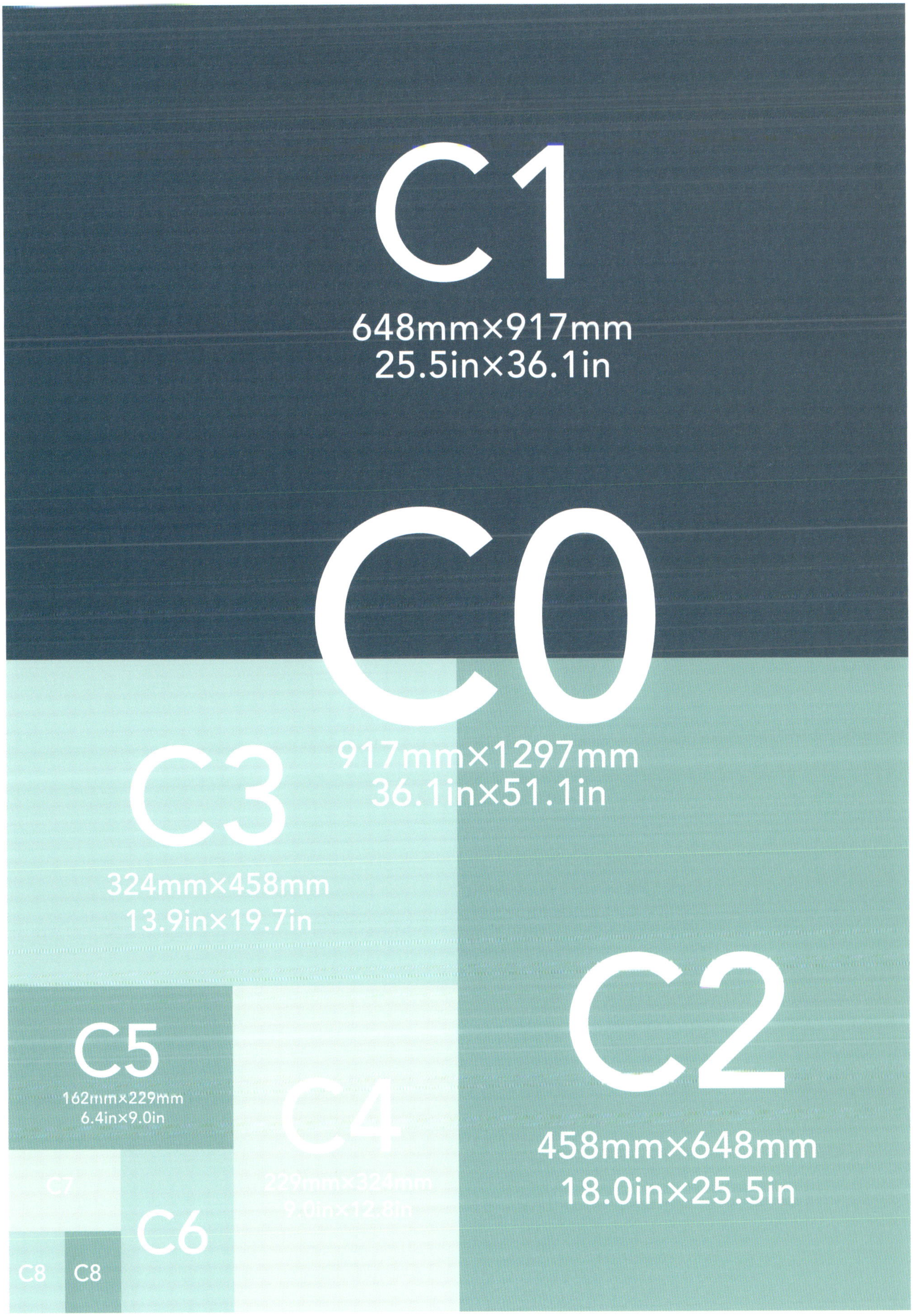

C1

648mm×917mm
25.5in×36.1in

C0

917mm×1297mm
36.1in×51.1in

C3

324mm×458mm
13.9in×19.7in

C2

458mm×648mm
18.0in×25.5in

C5

162mm×229mm
6.4in×9.0in

C4

229mm×324mm
9.0in×12.8in

C7

C6

C8 C8

Printing Methods

Offset Printing

Refers to a printing method in which lithographic printing transfers printing ink onto a paper by a blanket. The printing step is to first transfer the inked image onto the blanket and then transfer it to the surface of the printing material. The offset technique uses a rubber blanket that receives ink from ink rollers, while non-printing areas attract a water-based film which keeps the non-printing areas ink-free. This ink is then transferred to the printing material. Offset printing requires the production of plates for each of four colors.

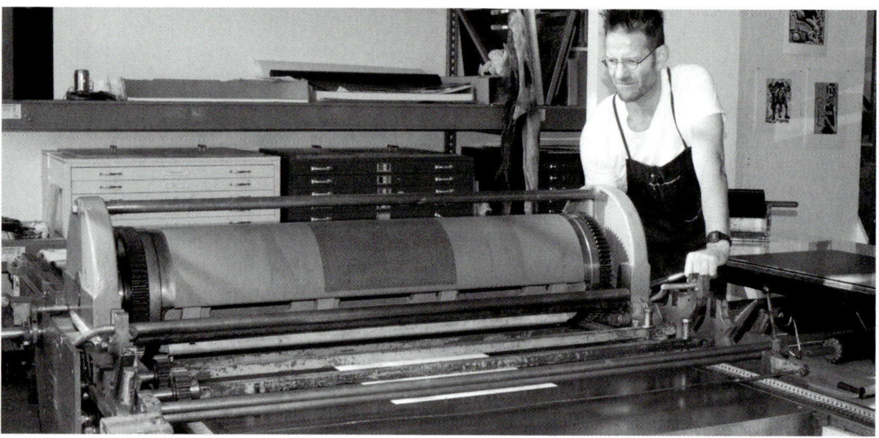

Screen Printing

Refers to a printing method in the stencil printing classification. The name is derived from the screen printing plate. In fact, screen printing used to use silk cloth. Most of them are now made of synthetic polymer, which is more durable than the silk. Screen-printed inks are thicker and have excellent color reproduction. Screen printing transfers ink through a mesh to the substrate with a certain pressure to form an image or text. The ink directly reaches the substrate for printing, leaving a thicker ink layer so screen printing is among the four printing methods most preferred for color performance.

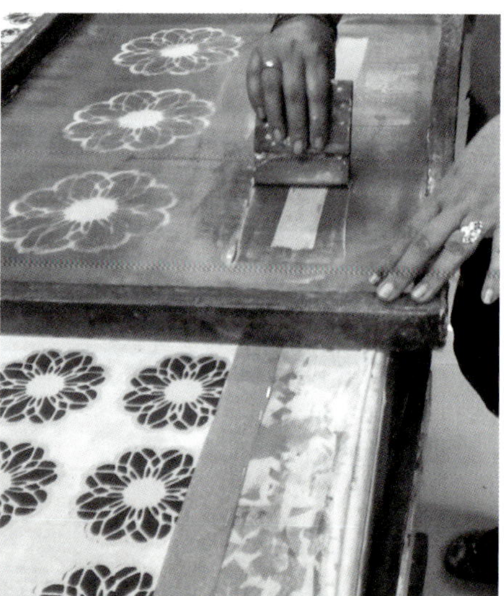

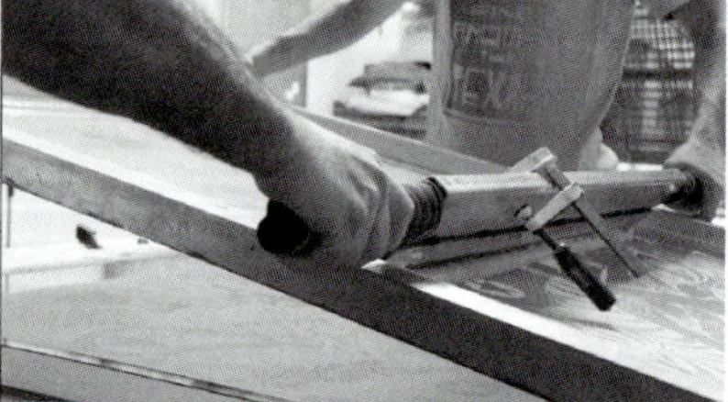

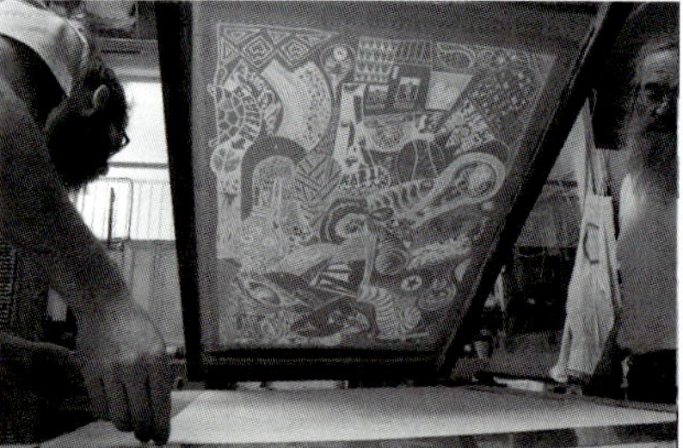

Flexographic Printing

Refers to a printing method that uses an flexible relief plate in letterpress printing, which is also called flexography. Only the text and image area are raised on the plate, primarily used in packaging printing.

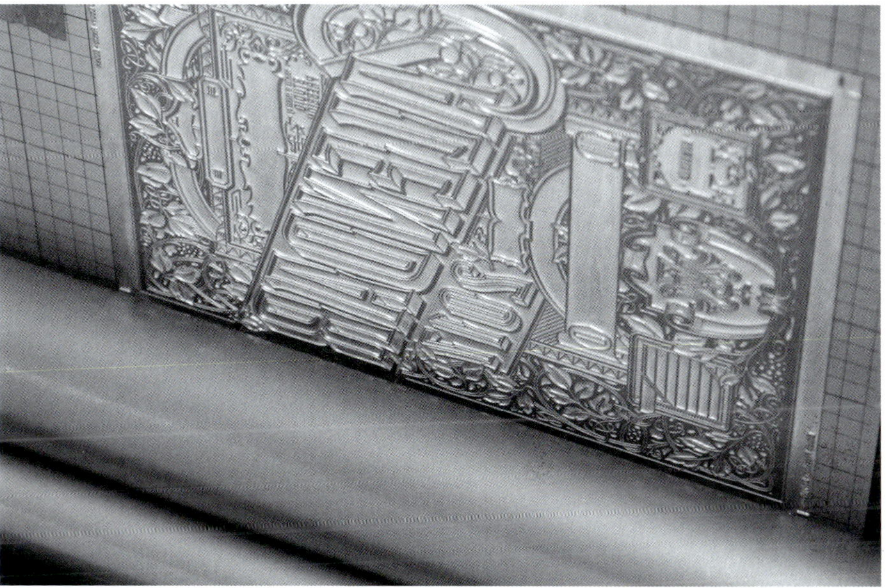

Inkjet Printing

Refers to a contactless digital printing method without the need of plate nor pressure. The information stored on the computer can be printed by inputting into an inkjet printer. Inkjet printing generally uses direct ink jets, as the name indicates, this method directly images onto the surface of the substrate.

Photo courtesy: juanjo6560

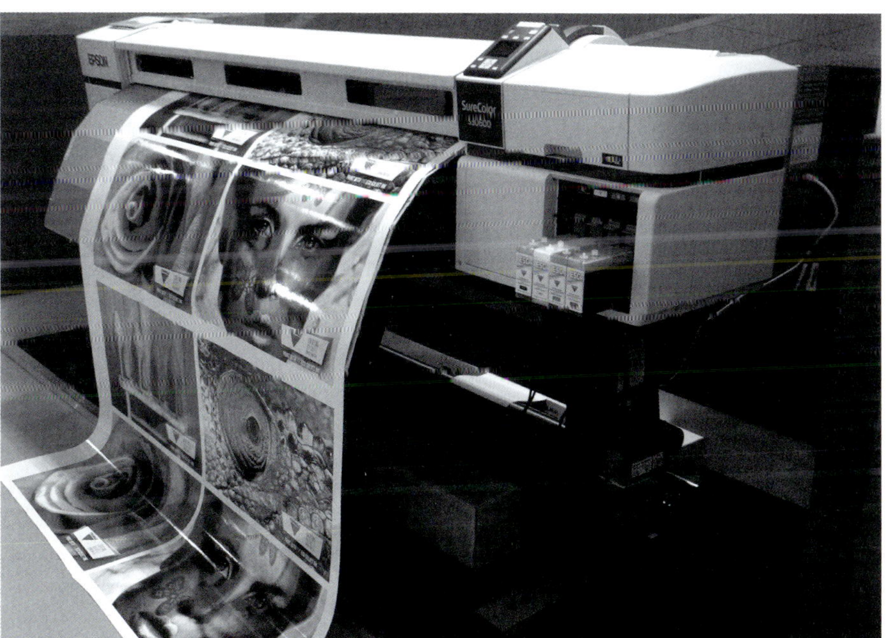

Printing Techniques

Foil Stamping

Foil stamping is a popular printing technique. It uses heat and pressure to apply metallic foil to materials such as surface, wood, and leather. The foil is positioned between the heated metal die and the surface receiving the foil. The die presses the foil onto the surface with heat and pressure, which melt down the foil to firmly stick to the material. When the pressure stops, the foil cools and solidifies quickly and permanently adheres to the substrate.

Sliver foil on stamping machine

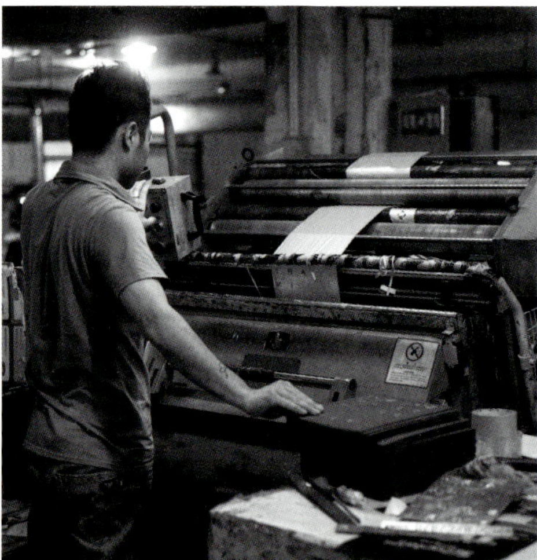

Copper plates

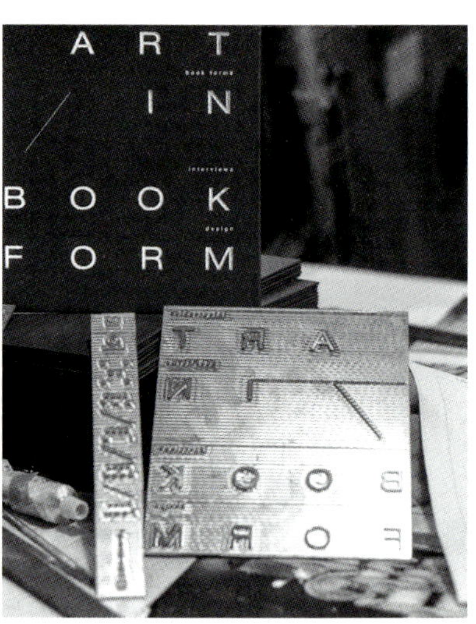

Embossing and Debossing

Embossing and debossing are two frequently used techniques for creating raised or recessed relief images and designs in paper and other materials. This results in the so-called relief effect, which enhances the product's artistic appeal. Paper is the most common substrate for an emboss or deboss, and the paper's quality will greatly affect the printing result. If paper is too thin and lacks stiffness, the printed image may be blurred. If the paper is insufficiently compliant, it cannot withstand the pressure of embossing and may become torn.

Details

Front and back

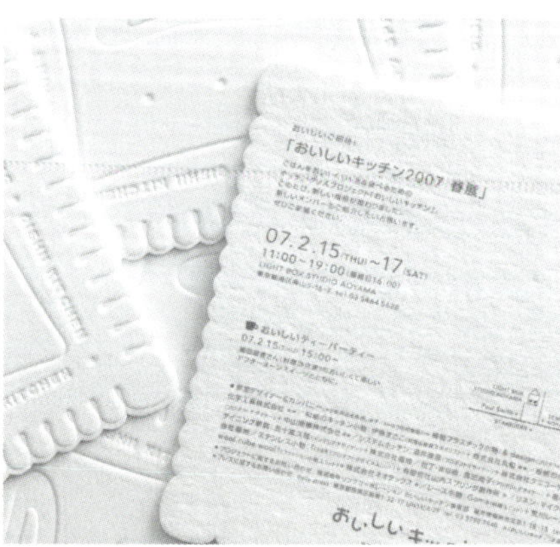

UV Printing

Ultraviolet (UV) printing is a printing technique which involves using ultraviolet light to dry the specially formulated ink. UV curable ink is widely employed in offset printing, screen printing, inkjet printing, and pad printing. UV printing is traditionally referred to as UV coating; a surface treatment, that adds a high gloss varnish to the printed material. UV coating forms a solid surface, protecting the printing effect from scratches, corrosion, and friction. The UV curable ink dries instantly under the ultraviolet light, so the paper can be piled up immediately after printing. UV printing does not pollute the environment because UV curable ink doesn't contain any volatile solvent.

Cover

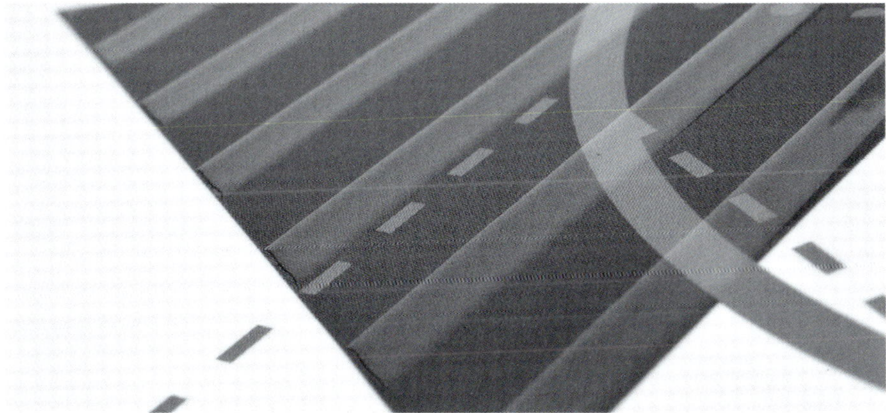

Die Cutting and Creasing

Die cutting is a process in which a desired shape can be cut out of the material based on a steel rule die, be it paper, plastic, leather, rubber, fiber or even sheet metal. During the process, the sheet material is laid on a machine where a steel rule die is mounted. There are cutting rules and creasing rules. With the right amount of pressure from the cutting die towards the paper, a desired shape would be cut out of it. While using the creasing rule, the paper can be easily folded into a certain structure or shape, thanks to the crease lines. The two rules can be fitted into one die plate so that cutting and creasing can be carried out simultaneously or separately.

Die cutting product

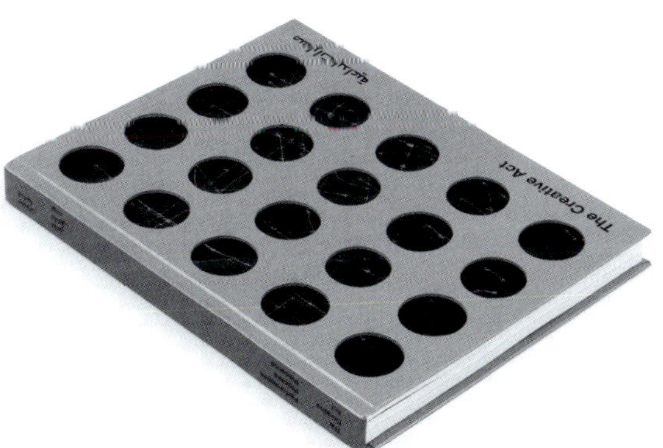

Laser Cutting and Engraving

Laser cutting uses a laser to cut materials. The focused laser beam is directed at the paper, which then either melts, burns, or vaporizes and is blown away by a jet of gas. With CNC (computer numerical control) used to direct the cutting path, a high standard of cutting can be ensured, meaning more precise than die cutting. The speed of cutting and the depth that is cut depends on the power of the beam. The high-powered beam can ensure a faster cutting speed and a higher standard of cut. And using the low-powered beam, a piece can be engraved, leaving a cavity on the surface rather than cutting through.

Laser drill

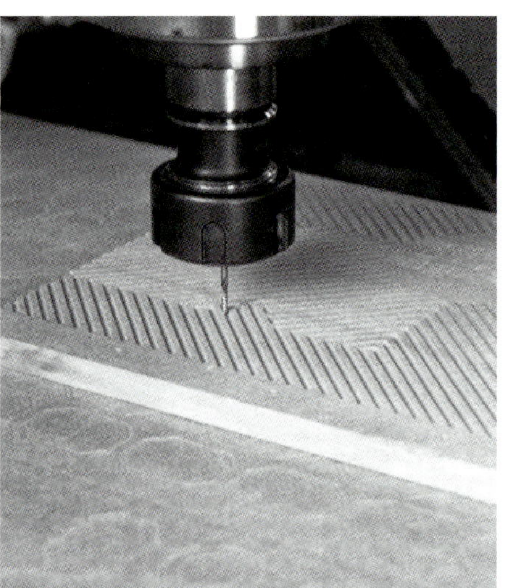

Different laser drills create different depths

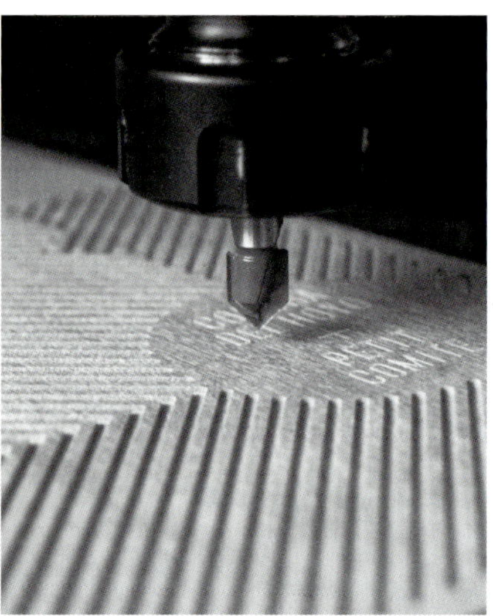

A laser cut piece

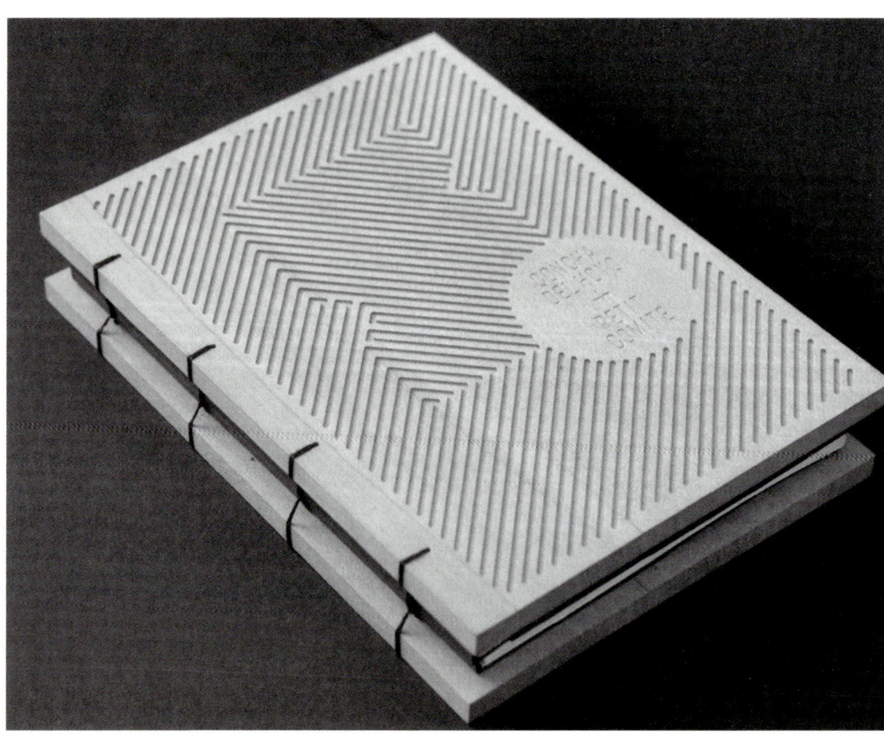

Lamination

Lamination is using a transparent plastic film that is applied to the surface of the printed materials by hot pressing; the film protects and increases the gloss. There are two types of laminate that are commonly used: gloss and matt. The gloss laminate has a shiny surface, which offers a smooth effect, whereas the matt laminate has a dull surface.

Matt laminate on the machine

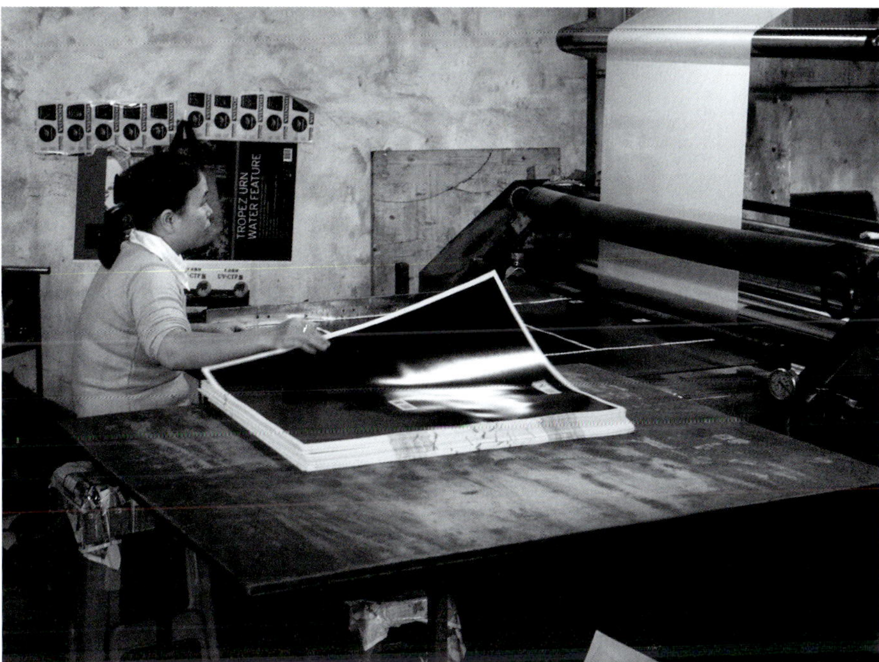

The rollers of a laminating machine

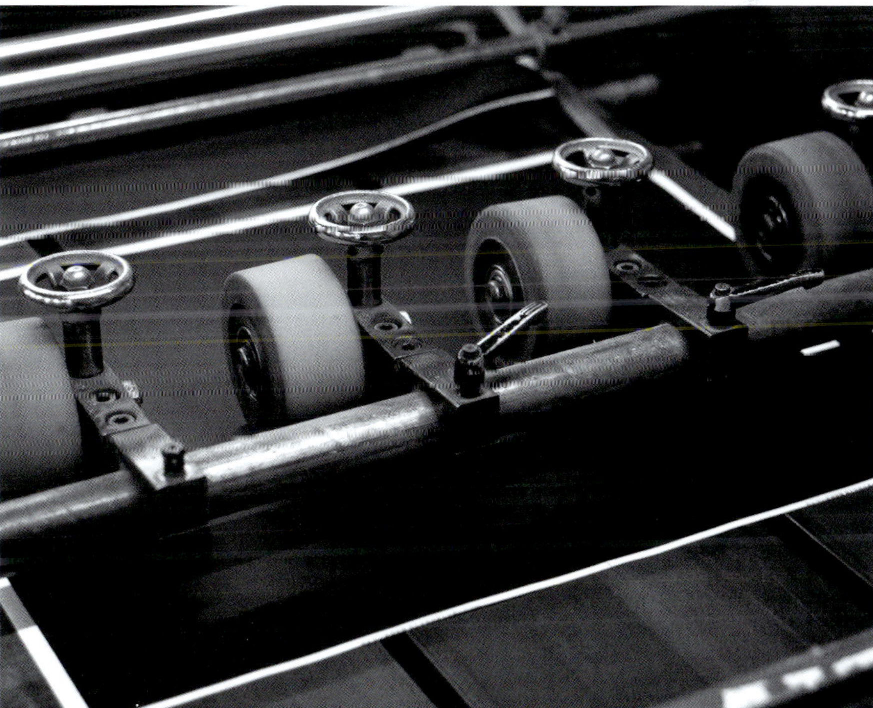

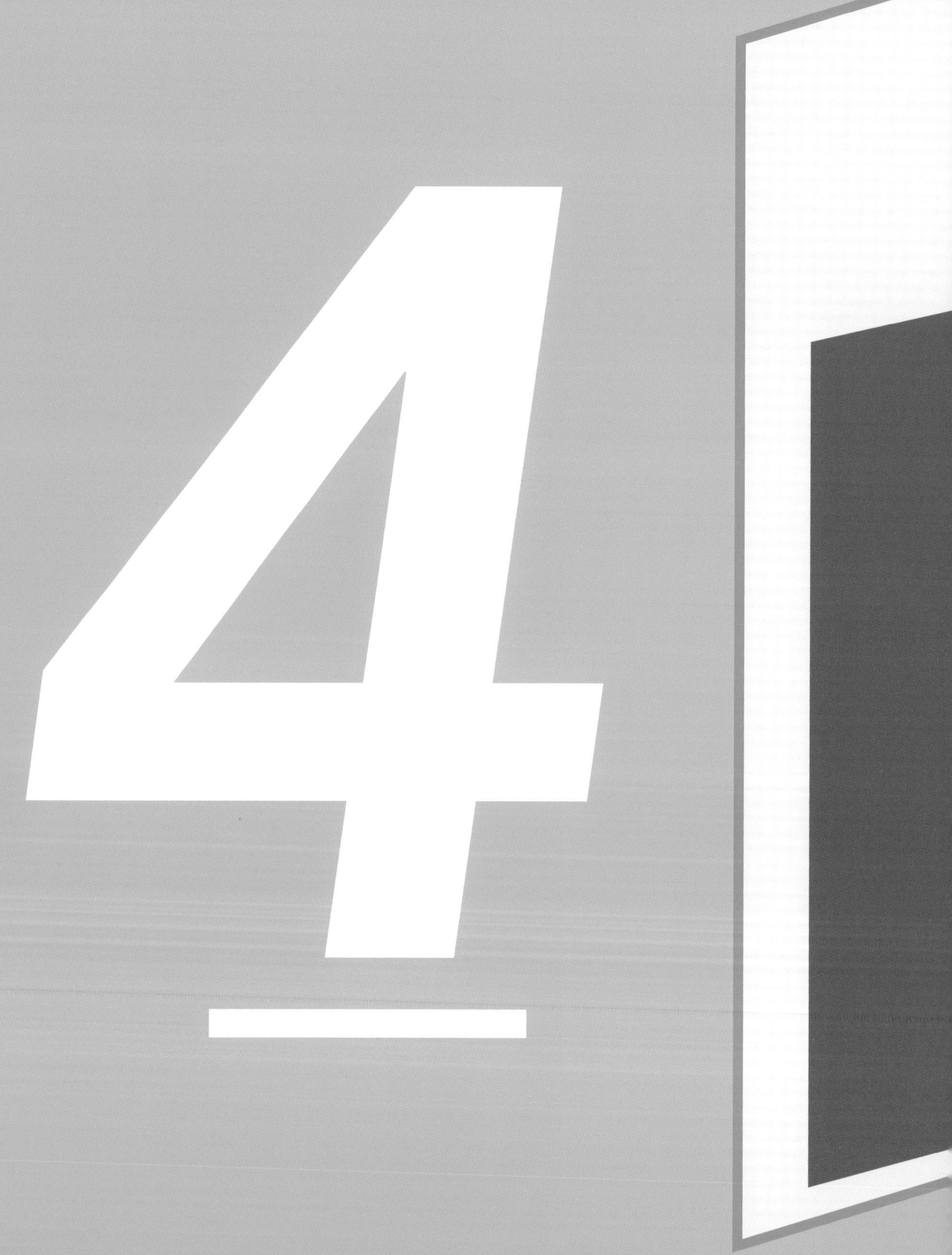
4

Case Studies Layout Analysis

Key Diagram

Typeface

Color

Layout

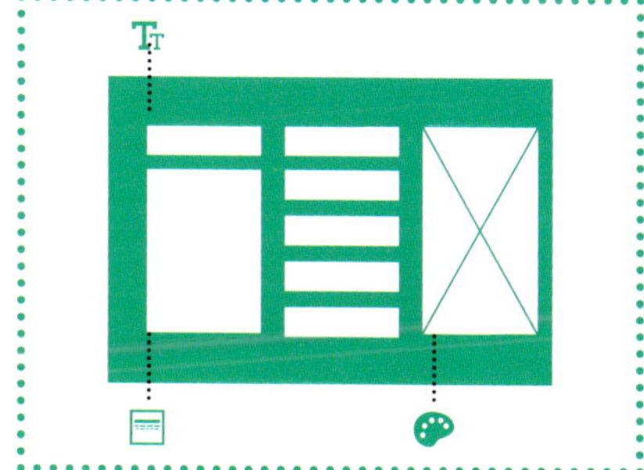

The Grid

Column

Distribution of content

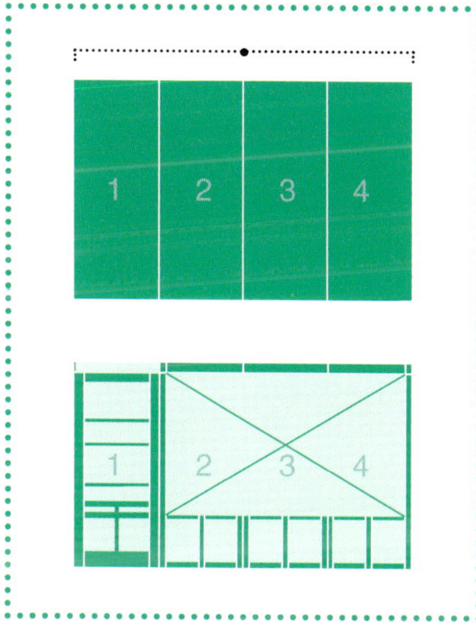

Visual Flow

The importance of each part

Distribution of content

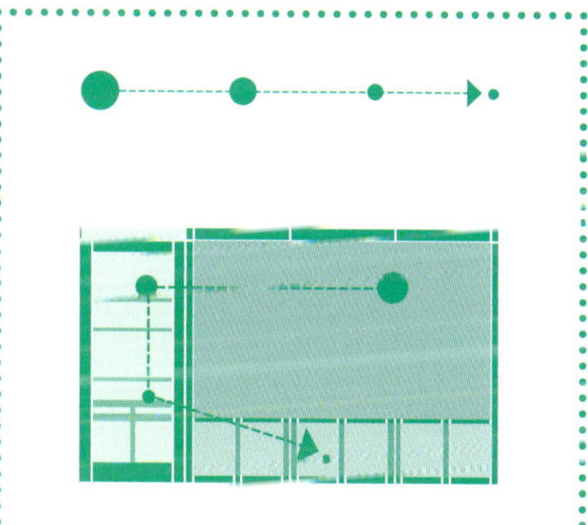

NYC x CATSKILLS: Healthy Map

Designer

Thitipol Chaimattayompol

Client

Local farms in Catskills

Key Diagram

Font	Paper	Size
Alternate Gothic	Newsprint paper	W16"×H10"

A clear and sharp feeling is created by using sans serif typeface. The sense of layers has been deepened through enhancing the contrast between different text, changing the font's size and the colors of the headline, subtitle, and main body.

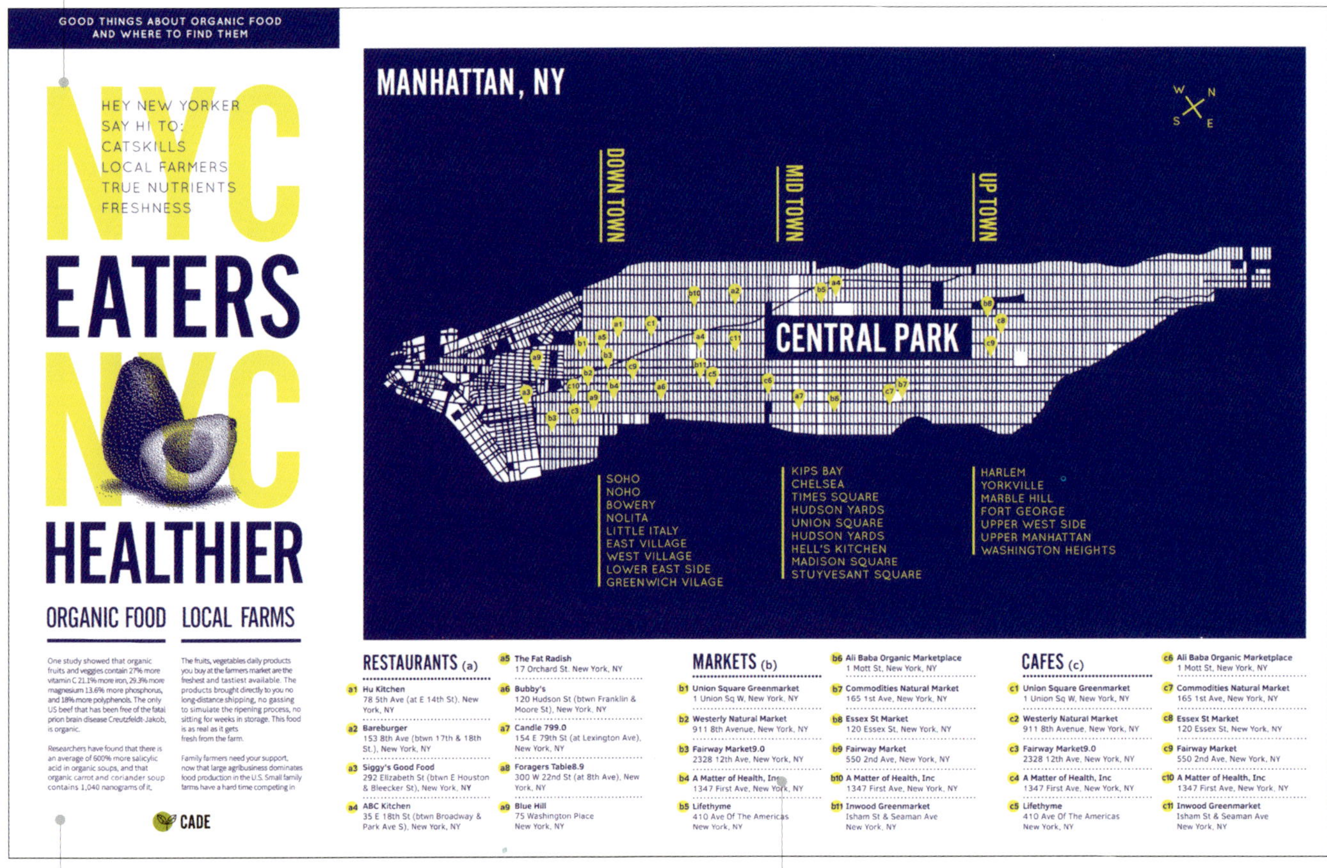

The rule of repetition has been applied to create similar sections, which contribute to the unity of layout. Whichever contents you have, it's not advisable to place the image and text too close to the edge of the page. White space is needed.

While there is a stark contrast between the large area of blue and the sparingly used yellow color, they complement each other: the blue, being calm and stable, fits to cover a large proportion of the visual, whereas the highly saturated, warm yellow lights it up.

Grid

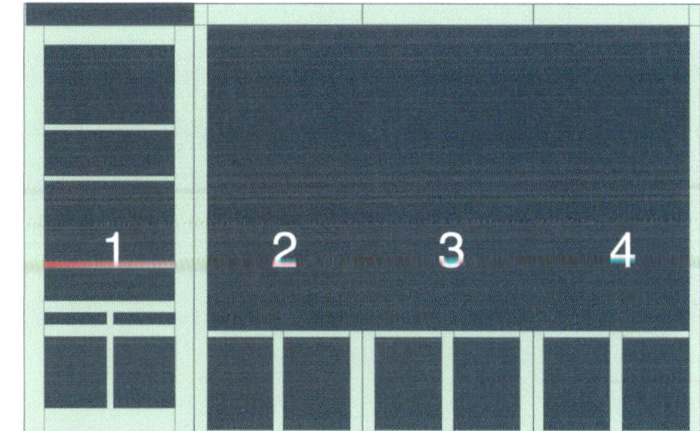

Visual Flow

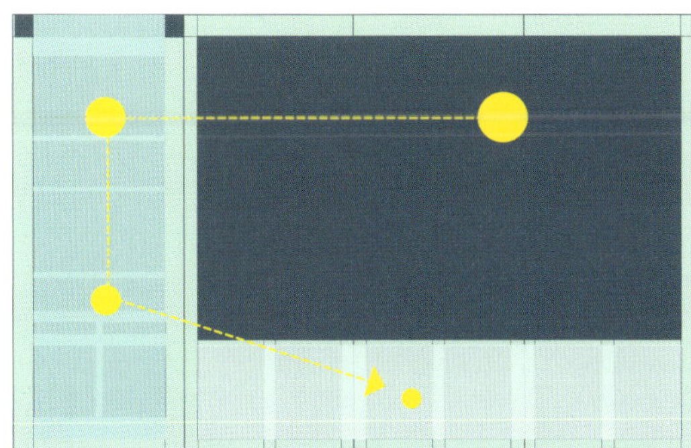

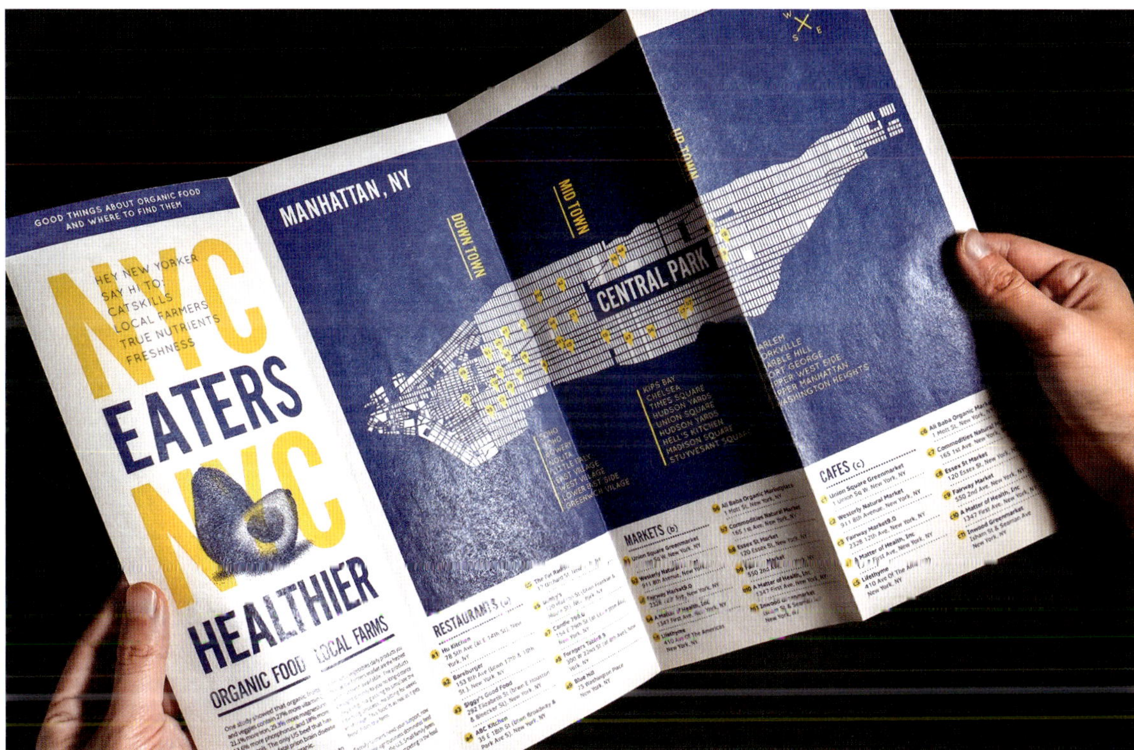

NYC x CATSKILLS is a printed material to promote local farms in the Catskills. The designer's idea was to develop a double-sided folding map that would be easily distributed to restaurants around New York City. The map exhibits the information and locations of the restaurants, café, and markets in Manhattan that use the organic ingredients from the Catskills. The other side displays a map of the Catskills that shows the locations of the farms. The designer utilized a sharp contrast between colors and condensed typeface to have an urban look.

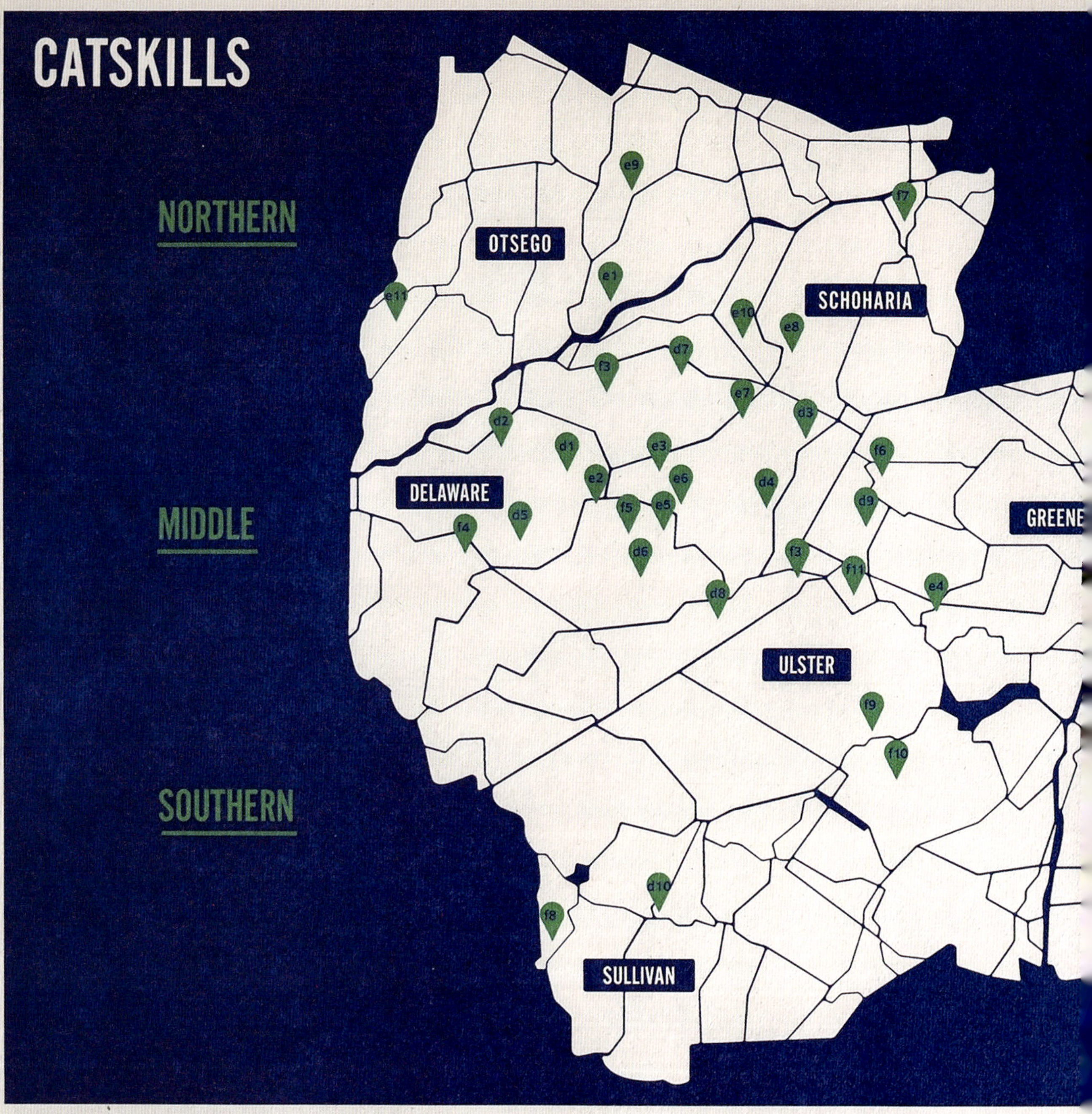

DAILY PRODUCTS (d)

- d1 **Bovina Valley Farm** (607) 746 8192
  77 Huff Rd, Delhi, NY
- d2 **Burn Ayr Farm** (607) 746 7287
  21031 NY-28, Delhi, NY
- d3 **ByeBrook Farms** (607) 538 9796
  Co Rd 18, Bloomville, NY
- d4 **Dirty Girl Farm** (845) 676 4000
  539 Perch Lake Rd, Andes, NY
- d5 **Eagle Hollow Farm** (607) 865 7215
  2004 Mac Gibbon Hollow Rd, Walton, NY
- d6 **East Brook Farm** (607) 746 8192
  2253 County Highway 22, Walton, NY
- d7 **Gelnanore Farm** (607) 832 4472
  2363 Bramley Mountain Road, Bovinia Center, NY
- d8 **Gray Goose Farm** (607) 746 3645
  83 Maggie Hoag Road Delancey, NY
- d9 **Crystal Valley Farm** (845) 254 4009
  253 County Route 3 Halcott Center, NY
- d10 **Dirai's Dairy Farm** (845) 4824301
  1345 Shandelle Road, Livingstion Manor, NY

VEGGIES & MEAT (e)

- e1 **Applegarth Farms** (607) 638 5784
  137 Axetell Road, Maryland, NY
- e2 **Eternal Flame Farm** (607) 865 7597
  61 Conclin road, Walton, NY
- e3 **Rich Farm** (607) 538 1317
  13075 County Highway 18, Hobart, NY
- e4 **Story Farms LLC** (518) 678 9761
  4640 State Route 32, Catskill, NY
- e5 **Fall Brook Farm** (607) 326 2897
  2590 West Settlement Road, Roxbury, NY
- e6 **Berry Brook Farm** (607) 267
  2369 Back River Road, Delency
- e7 **SaJoBe Farms** (607) 865
  286 Hoyt Road, Walton, NY
- e8 **Horton Hill Farm** (607) 652
  127 Harton Road, Jefferson, N
- e9 **Nectar Hills Farm** (607) 638
  393 Peeter Road, Schenevus,
- e10 **Buck Hill Farm** (607) 652
  185 Fuller Road, Jefferson, NY
- e11 **Good Fields** (607) 859
  1277 Copes Coner Road, Sou
  New Berlin, NY

GOOD THINGS ABOUT ORGANIC FOOD
AND WHERE TO FIND THEM

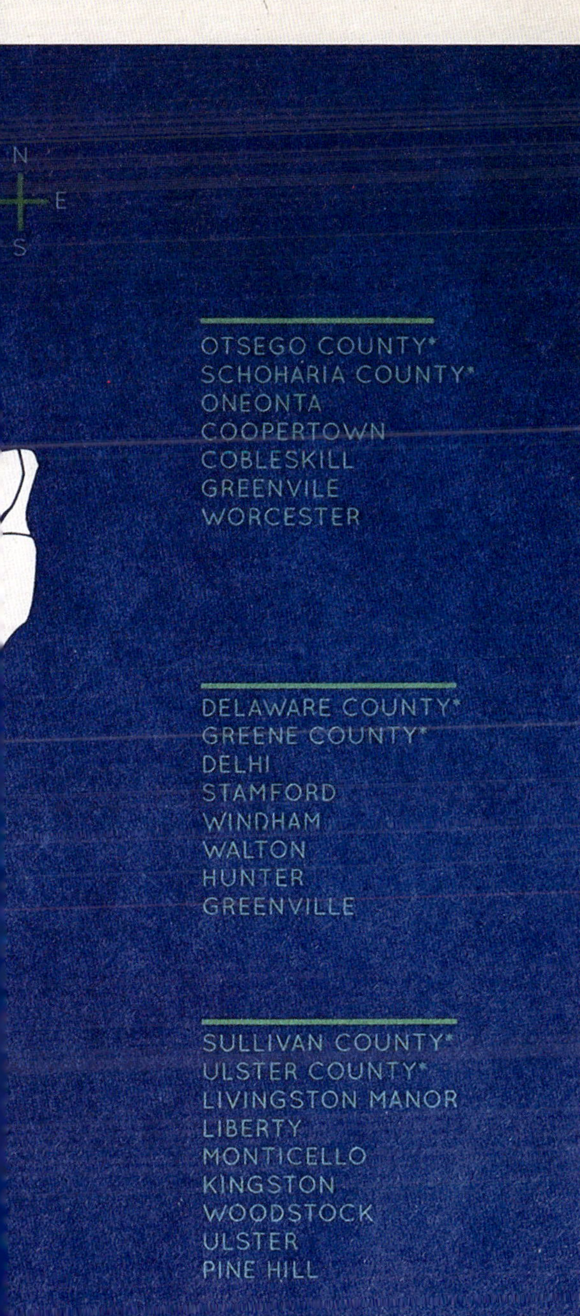

LIVE LONGER LIVE HEALTHIER

SAY GOOD BYE TO:
SYNTHETIC PESTICIDES
CHEMICAL FERTILIZERS
IRRADIATION
INDUSTRIAL SOLVENTS
CHEMICAL FOOD ADDITIVES

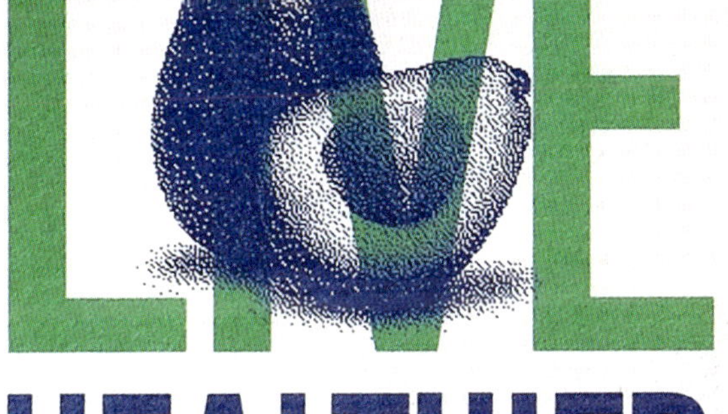

NYC LIFE

One study showed that organic fruits and veggies contain 27% more vitamin C 21.1% more iron, 29.3% more magnesium 13.6% more phosphorus, and 18% more polyphenols. The only US beef that has been free of the fatal prion brain disease Creutzfeldt-Jakob, is organic.

Researchers have found that there is an average of 600% more salicylic acid in organic soups, and that organic carrot and coriander soup contains 1,040 nanograms of it, compared with only 20 nanograms in typical nonorganic soups!

CATSKILLS

The fruits, vegetables daily products you buy at the farmers market are the freshest and tastiest available. The products brought directly to you no long-distance shipping, no gassing to simulate the ripening process, no sitting for weeks in storage. This food is as real as it gets fresh from the farm.

Family farmers need your support, now that large agribusiness dominates food production in the U.S. Small family farms have a hard time competing in the food marketplace.

HONEY & MAPLE (f)

Tree Juice (607) 267 0184
251 Rider Hollow Road Arkville, NY

Catskill Provision (607) 267 0184
244 Delawear Lake Road, Long

MT Acrec Farm (607) 434 4321
1933 MacDougall Road, Oneonta, NY

Pure Mountain Honey (607) 865 5738
Walton, NY

Catskill Provision (845) 418 6482
244 Delawear Lake Road
Long Eddy, NY

f5 **RSK Farm** (518) 299 3128
13255 State Route 23A, Prattsville, NY

f7 **Cold Spring Farm** (518) 234 4268
4953 State Route 145, Lawyersville, NY

f8 **Heirloom Acres** (845) 554 3722
23 Main St. Narrowsburg, NY

f9 **Edge Wood** (845) 245 9819
22 Lasher Road, Big India, NY

f10 **Kelder'S Farm** (845) 626 7137
5755 Route 209, Kerhonkson, NY

f11 **Griffin Conners** (313) 242 7324
189-829 Brush Ridge Road
Fleischmans, NY

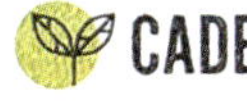

GMoMA Sculpture Park Guide Map

Designer
Kimgarden Studio (Kim Kang in, Lee Yun Ho)

Illustrator
Ha Jeong Yeong

Client
Gyeonggi Museum of Modern Art

Key Diagram

Font	Paper	Size
Sandoll GothicNeo 1, HG Gothic Ssi, LL Brown	Munken Polar Rough	105×210mm/4 fold

A clear and sharp feeling is gained by using sans serif fonts.

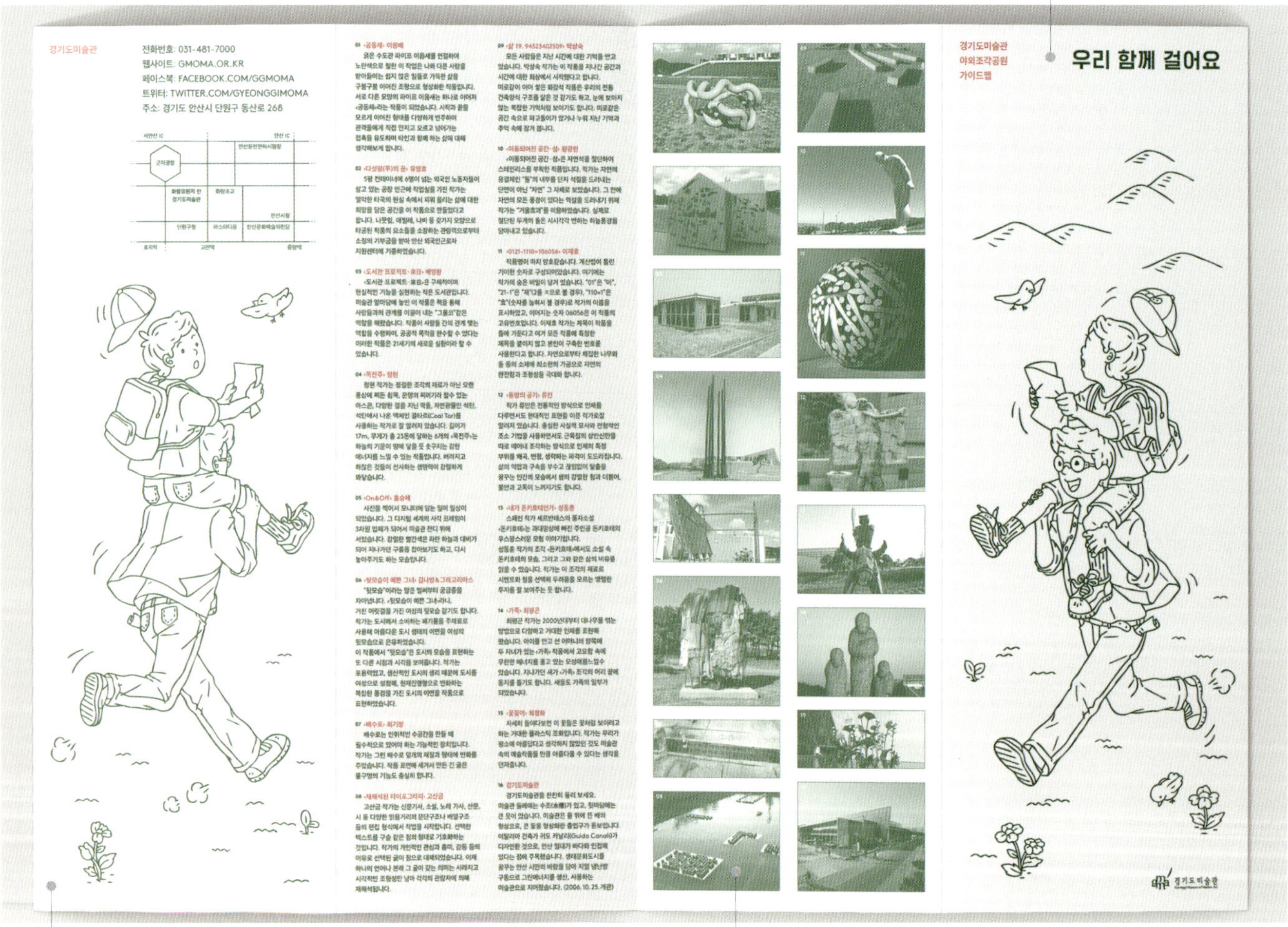

The use of alignment and proximity gives a sense of order without loosing flexibility. The illustrations are also lively and vivid and fit the theme perfectly.

The most relaxing color for our eyes is green. Most plants appear in green color, which can give us a fresh and natural feeling, and the pink dots have a decorative effect.

Grid

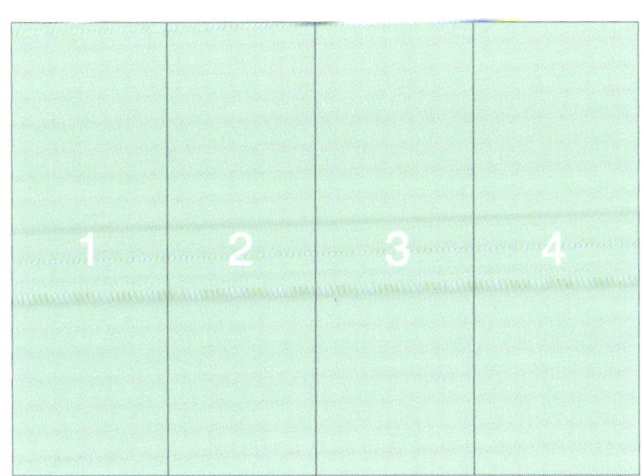

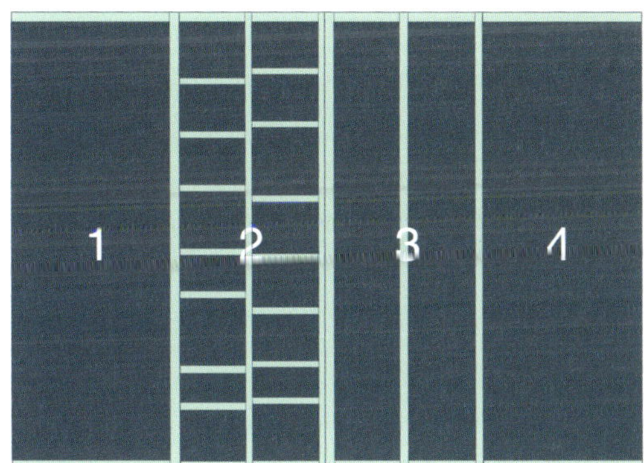

Visual Flow

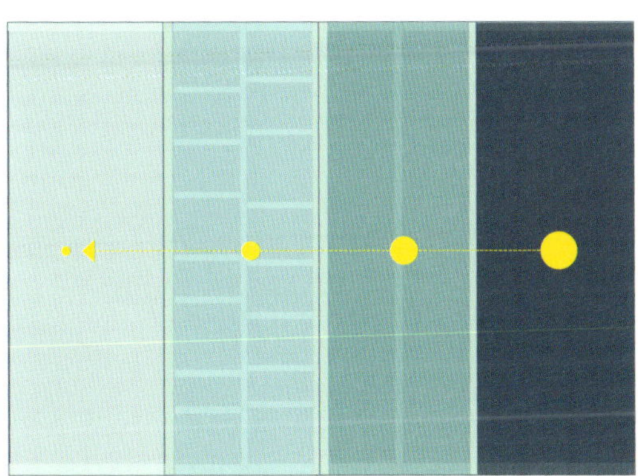

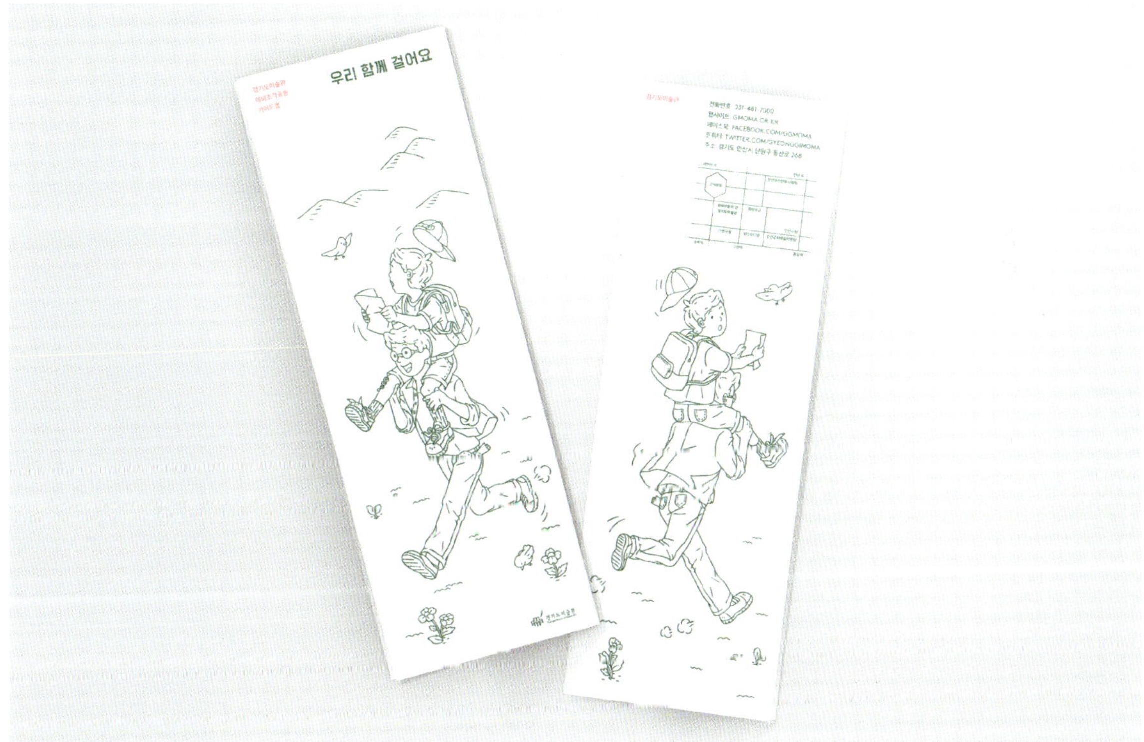

The Gyeonggi Museum of Modern Art has a large sculpture park, which has more than 30 sculptures. Visitors walk through the sculpture park before entering the museum. The sculpture park is also open separately. This is a guided map that introduces the park and sculptures. Visitors can check the location of the sculptures and read a brief description of the works.

경기도미술관 야외조각공원
전체 작품 목록 (총 32점, 2015년 11월 기준)

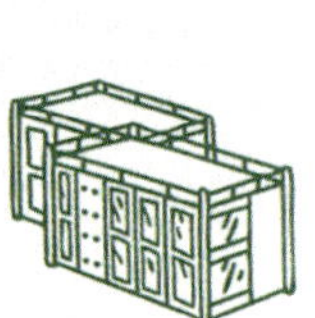

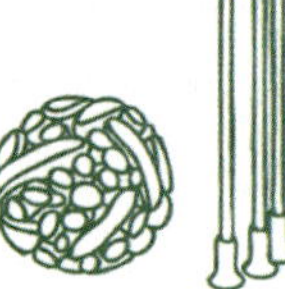

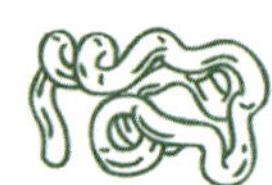

01 ‹꽃꽃이›
최정화, 2004
F.R.P, 철에 용접
500×590×590cm

02 ‹On&Off›
홍승혜, 2010
철 파이프에 폴리우레탄
460×345×345cm

03 ‹도서관 프로젝트-来日›
배영환, 2009
혼합재료
260×700×300cm,
260×350×300cm

04 ‹다섯평(平)의 꿈›
유영호, 2010
철, 우레탄도색
600×600×280cm

05 ‹공동체›
이용배, 2010
철, 우레탄도장
230×290×150cm

06 ‹바른자세›
전덕제, 2010
브론즈에 화강석
90×200×40cm

07 ‹뽀뽀›
전덕제, 2010
브론즈에 화강석
90×180×35cm

08 ‹투명함09›
정보원, 2009
레이저 컷, 조립 용접, 도장
300×474×200cm

09 ‹배수로›
최기창, 2010
코르텐 스틸
가변설치

10 ‹삶 19.945234025092009›
박상숙, 2009
화강석 쌓기
94.5×230.4×25cm

11 ‹The Giving Tree›
박안식, 2013
스테인리스 스틸
450×200×100cm

12 ‹AD4000›
박미나, 2009
접착제를 바른 비닐
580×5800cm

13 ‹목전주›
정현, 2006
나무, 철
1726×497×597cm

14 ‹뒷모습이 예쁜 그녀›
김나영&그레고리마스, 2008
철, 스폰지, 플라스틱, 페인트 등
350×250×250cm

15 ‹0121-1110=106056›
이재효, 2005
참나무, 볼트, 조립 후 연마
지름 240cm

16 ‹동방의 공기›
류인, 1992
브론즈, 철
330×150×230cm

17 ‹인간은 태어나서,
살다 죽는다 1›
배형경, 2004
브론즈
170×65×30cm

18 ‹원›
이민수, 2006
청동, 화강석
70×70×200cm

19 ‹내가 돈키호테인가›
성동훈, 1997
철, 브론즈, 특수 시멘트
190×120×230cm

20 ‹자연으로부터›
이상헌, 2004
아프리카 흑석
190×100×98cm

21 ‹기다림›
양태근, 2005
스테인리스 및 철 와셔, 알곤용접
407×407×65cm

22 ‹축제›
양태근, 2004
스테인리스 및 철 와셔, 알곤용접
340×350×130cm

23 ‹가족›
최평곤, 2007
철, 대나무, 철끈
1050×60×35cm

24 ‹애증의 덫›
이행균, 1996
대리석
47×85×129cm

25 ‹사랑으로 감싼 무한공간›
이일호, 2006
철
560×490×120cm

26 ‹재해석된 타이포그라피›
고산금, 2010
스테인리스 스틸 공
27×600×1200cm

27 ‹성 2010›
김상균, 2010
그라우트 캐스팅
270×160×160cm

28 ‹존›
홍승남, 2005
스테인리스 스틸
100×140×200cm

29 ‹하나에 관한 명상›
강신영, 2005
스테인리스 스틸
90×120×167cm

30 ‹대나무›
서정국, 2007
스테인리스 스틸
가변크기

31 ‹이동되어진 공간-섬›
왕광현, 2008
자연석, 스테인리스 스틸
가변크기

32 ‹경기도미술관에서 만나자→›
권남희, 2010
혼합재료
250×1400×50cm

지면의 제약으로 일부 작품만을 그림으로 표현하였으며, 그 외 작품들은 번호로 표기하였습니다. 본 가이드맵에 소개된 조각작품의 위치는 추후 변경될 수 있습니다.

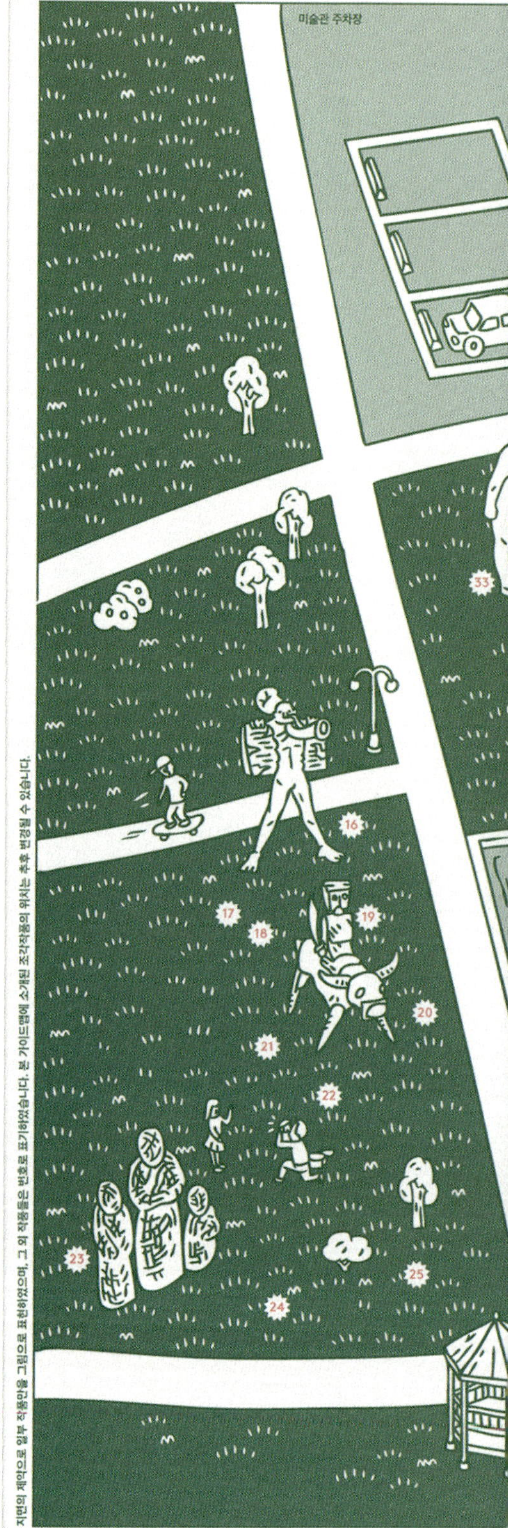

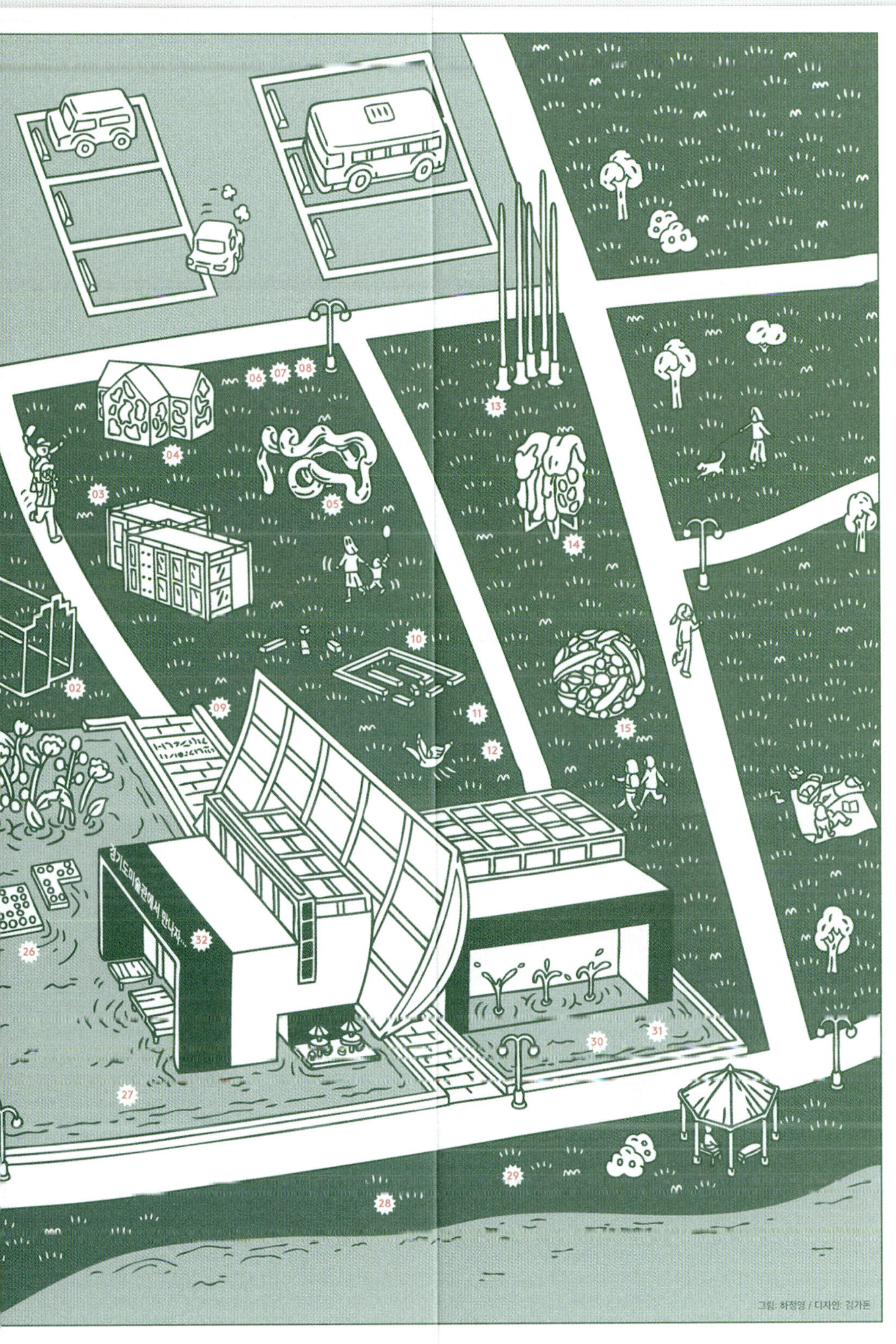
06
07
08
04
03
05
13
14
10
02
09
11
12
15
경기도미술관에서 만나자…
32
26
30
31
27
29
28
그림: 하정영 / 디자인: 김가돈

Pop Art Exhibition Catalog

Designer

Agata Jeziurska

Key Diagram

Font

Cooper Black, Open Sans, Times New Roman, Impact

Size

160mm×230mm

Four types of font clearly distinguish the hierarchical relationship of the text and add interest to the design.

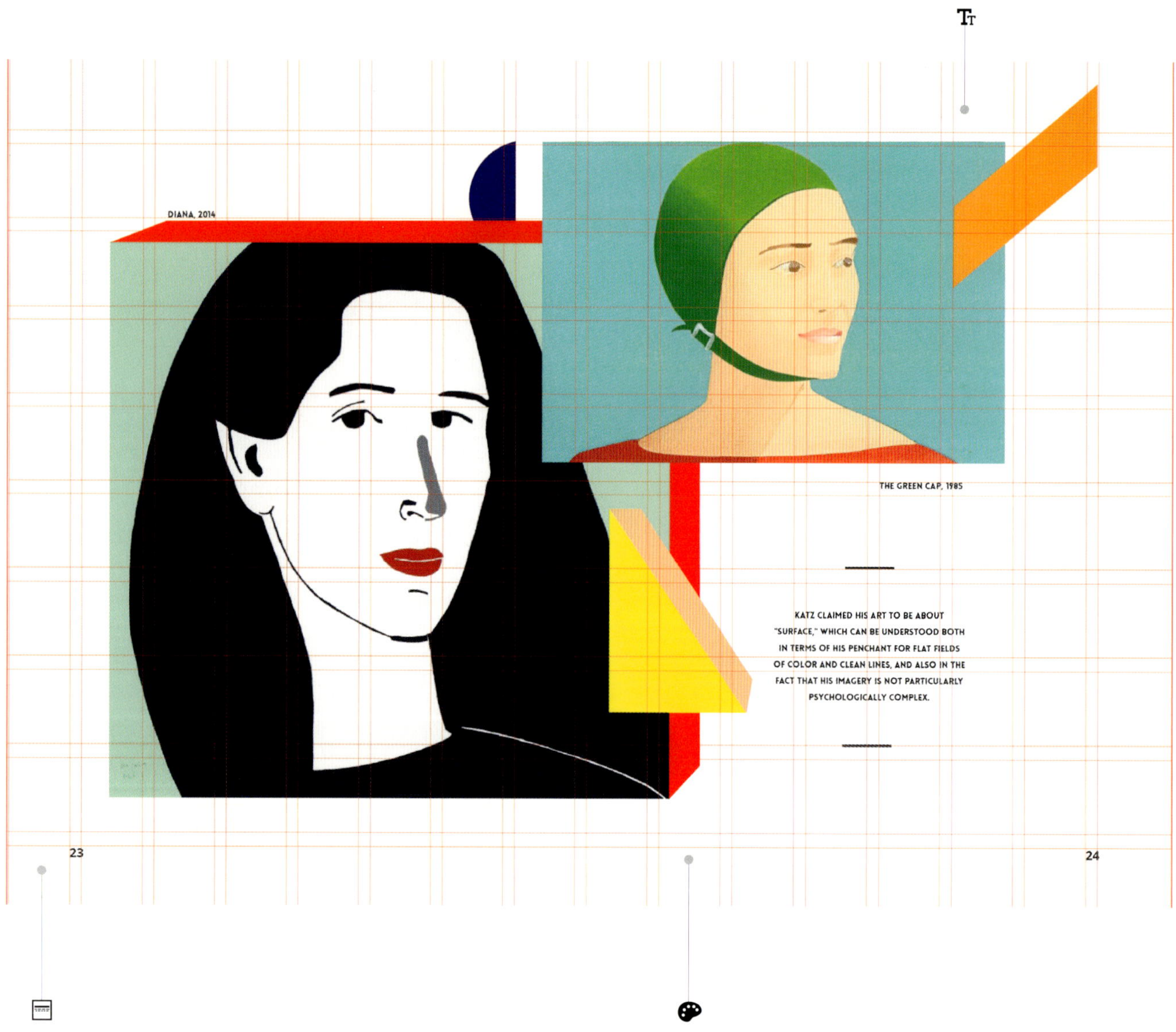

Designer aims to create a colorful, different look for each page of the catalog. However, all pages need to fit in and be connected to each other.

A large amount of high-purity colors are applied in the design, which can better highlight the characteristics of Pop Art.

Grid

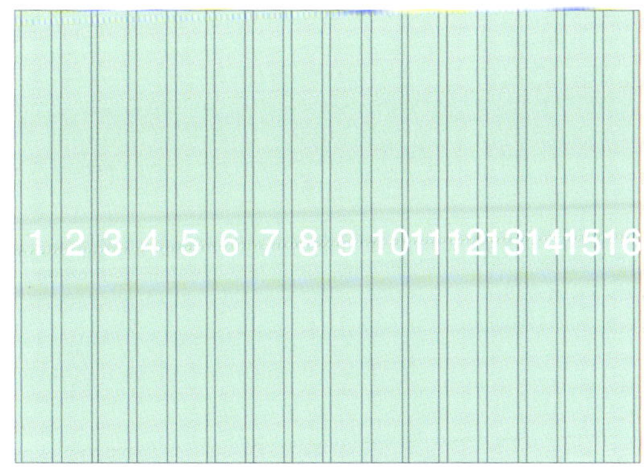

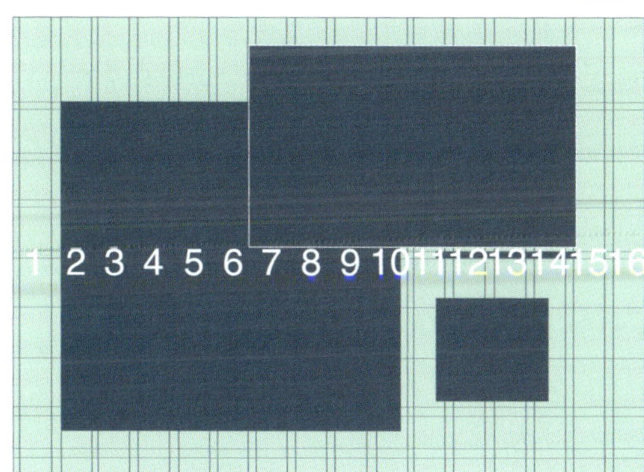

Visual Flow

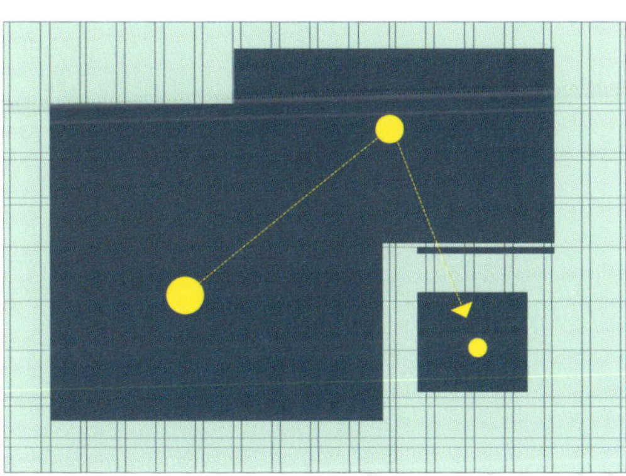

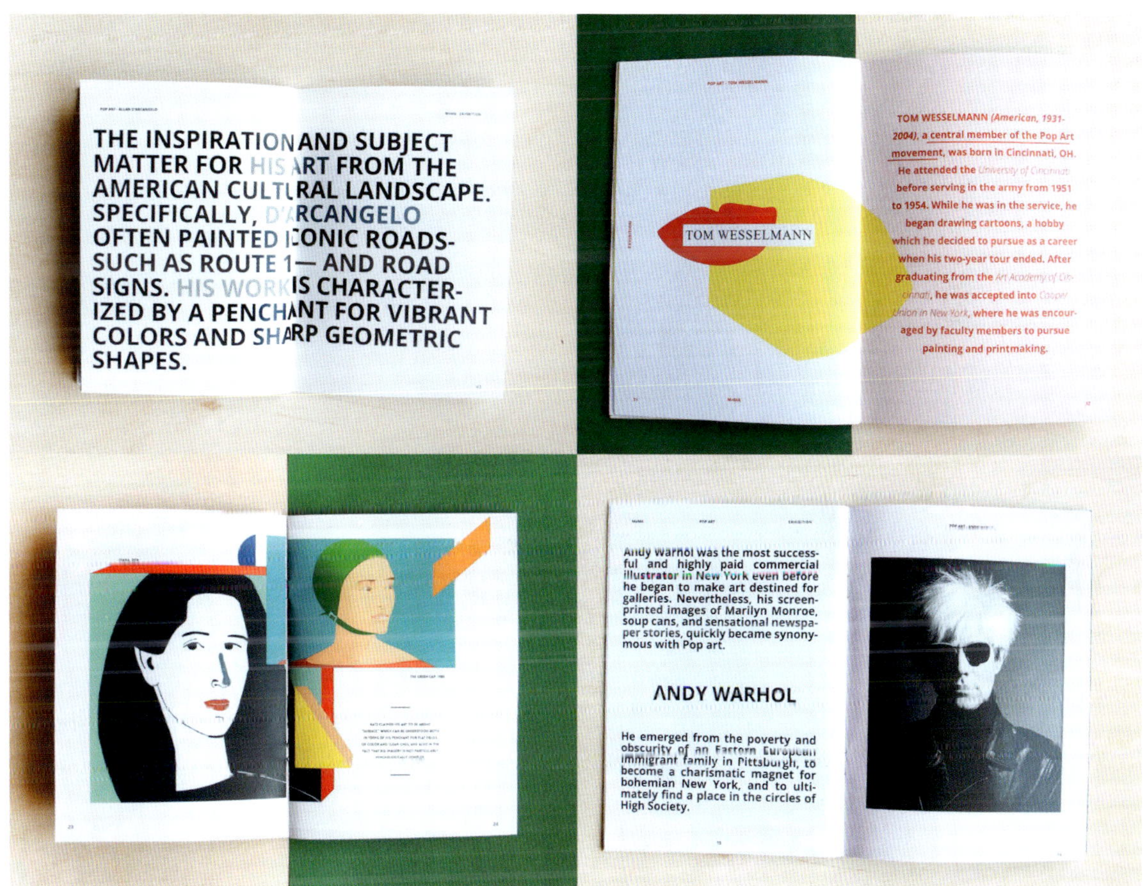

The Designer created a whole catalog promoting the Pop Art exhibition, which would take place at the Museum of Modern Art in New York.

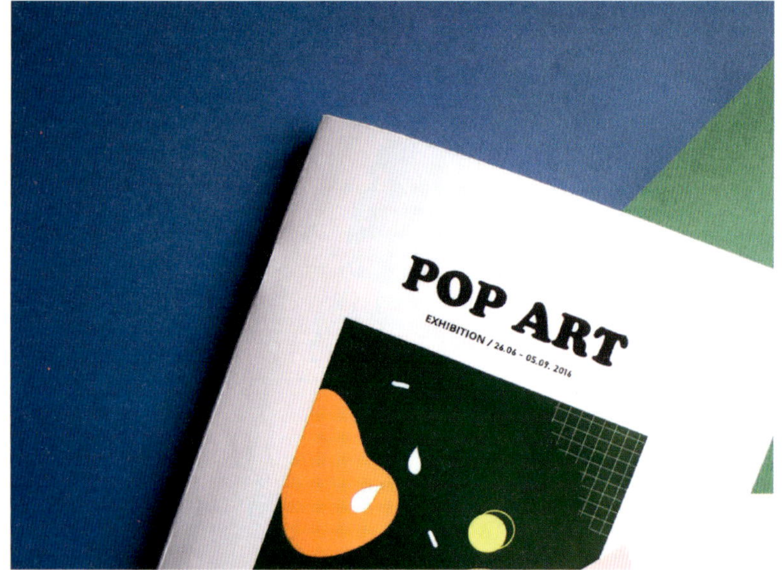
POP ART
EXHIBITION / 26.06 - 05.09. 2016

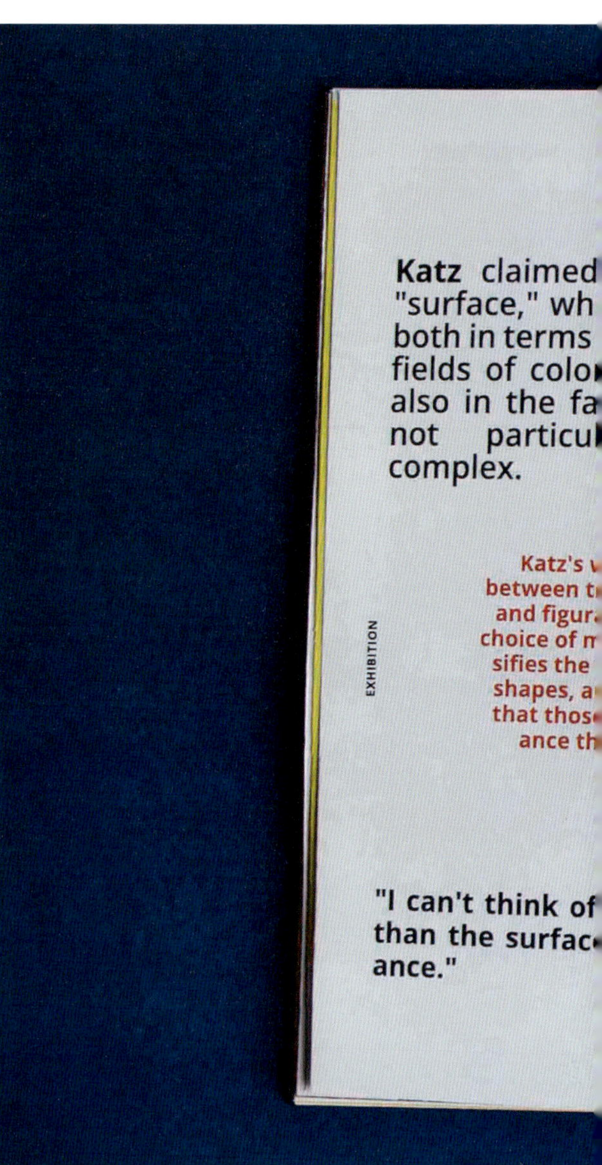
Katz claimed
"surface," wh
both in terms
fields of colo
also in the fa
not particu
complex.
Katz's
between t
and figur
choice of m
sifies the
shapes, a
that thos
ance th
EXHIBITION
"I can't think of
than the surfac
ance."

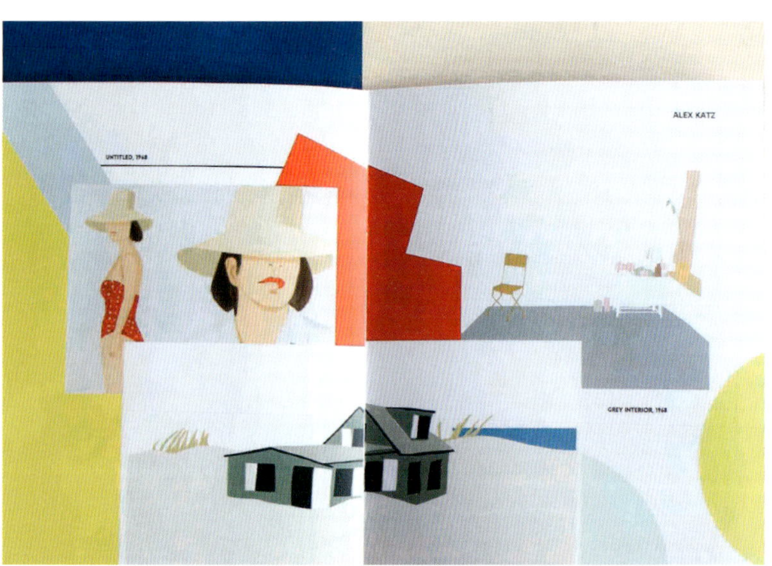
ALEX KATZ

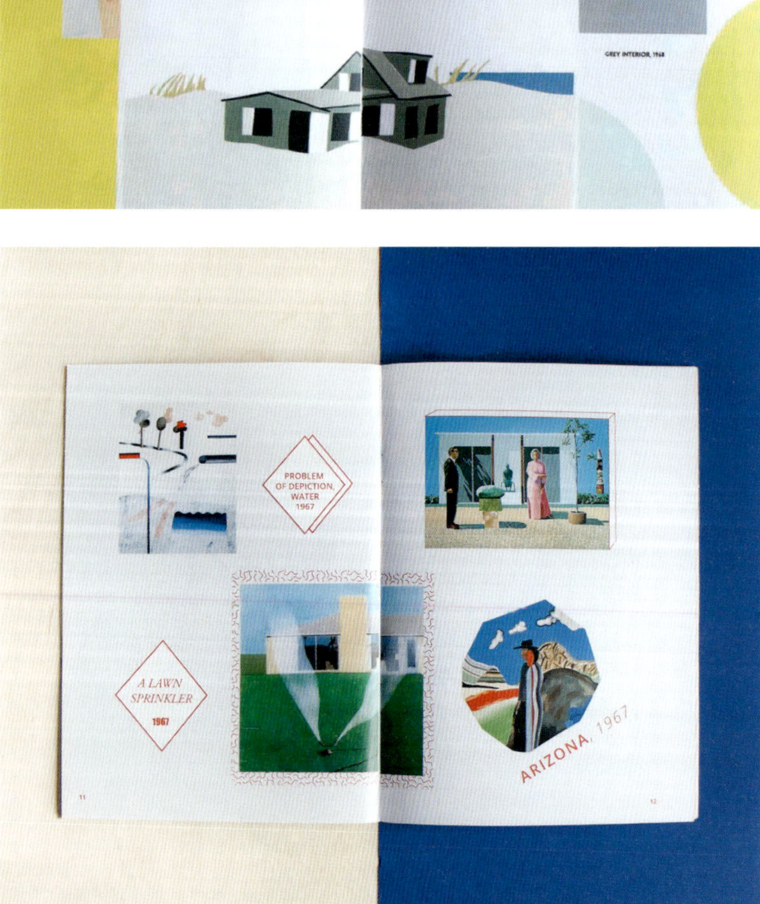
PROBLEM OF DEPICTION, WATER 1967
A LAWN SPRINKLER 1967
ARIZONA, 1967

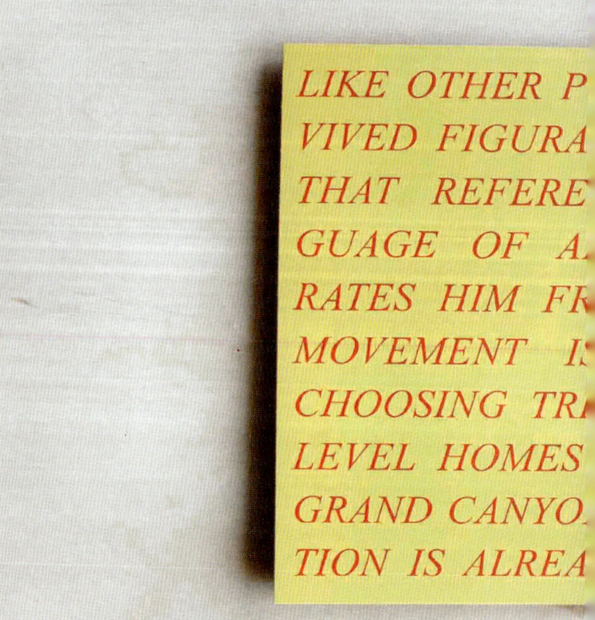
LIKE OTHER P
VIVED FIGURA
THAT REFERE
GUAGE OF A
RATES HIM FR
MOVEMENT I
CHOOSING TR
LEVEL HOMES
GRAND CANYO
TION IS ALREA

art to be about
n be understood
penchant for flat
clean lines, and
t his imagery is
psychologically

idge the gap
s of abstraction
r instance, his
ntal scale inten-
ntours, colors,
chnique, such
elements bal-
tive subject
r.

ing more exciting
ings. Just appear-

ONE OF THE MOST IMPORTANT ARTWORK

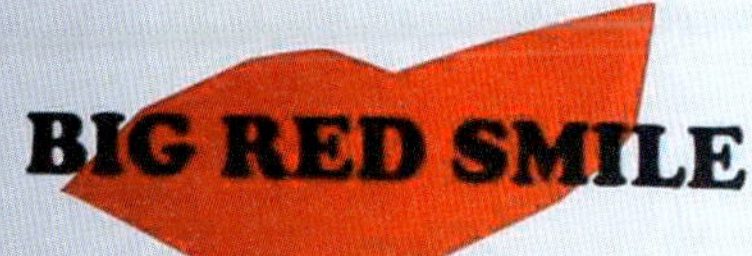

EXHIBITION

This work exemplifies Katz's highly polished, mature technique where there is little trace of the work's making. In the 1960's, Katz began to produce paintings inspired by the aesthetics of commercial advertising, film, and television, demonstrating his work's parallel with the burgeoning Pop art movement. Red Smile is nearly ten feet wide, and is one of his largest portraits to date. The composition resembles a billboard or a cinematic close-up in a widescreen view. The cropped view of Ada on the right side with her pale skin, clothing, and linear detailing of face, shirt, and hair, is balanced by the bold expanse of flat red to the left. The red ground seems to caress the contour of her face, and this feature, along with gleaming smile, expresses the warmth and contentment for which Katz's art is so often celebrated.

RTISTS, HOCKNEY RE-
PAINTING IN A STYLE
THE VISUAL LAN-
TISING. WHAT SEPA-
OTHERS IN THE POP
S OBSESSION VIEW,
SPACES, LIKE SPLIT-
ALIFORNIA AND THE
ERE DEPTH PERCEP-
CHALLENGE. HOCK-

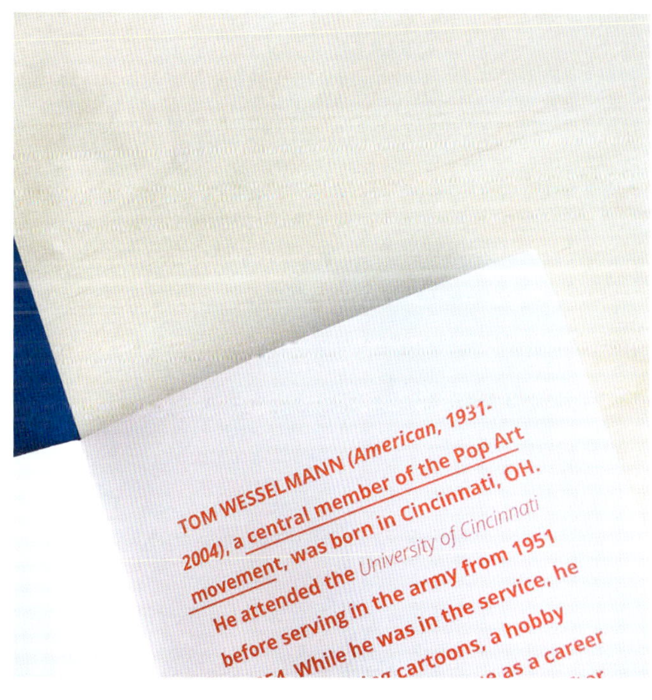

Macao Doulao Poster

Designer

Chen Guanyu, Xue Wenxin, Dawei

Client

Macao Doulao

Key Diagram

Font

custom font

Paper

Coated paper for advertising
Coated art paper
Specialty paper

Size

1189×841mm (A0)
297×420mm (A3)

A variety of fonts and buzz words, which is consistent with young people's attitudes, makes the whole visual vivid and vigorous.

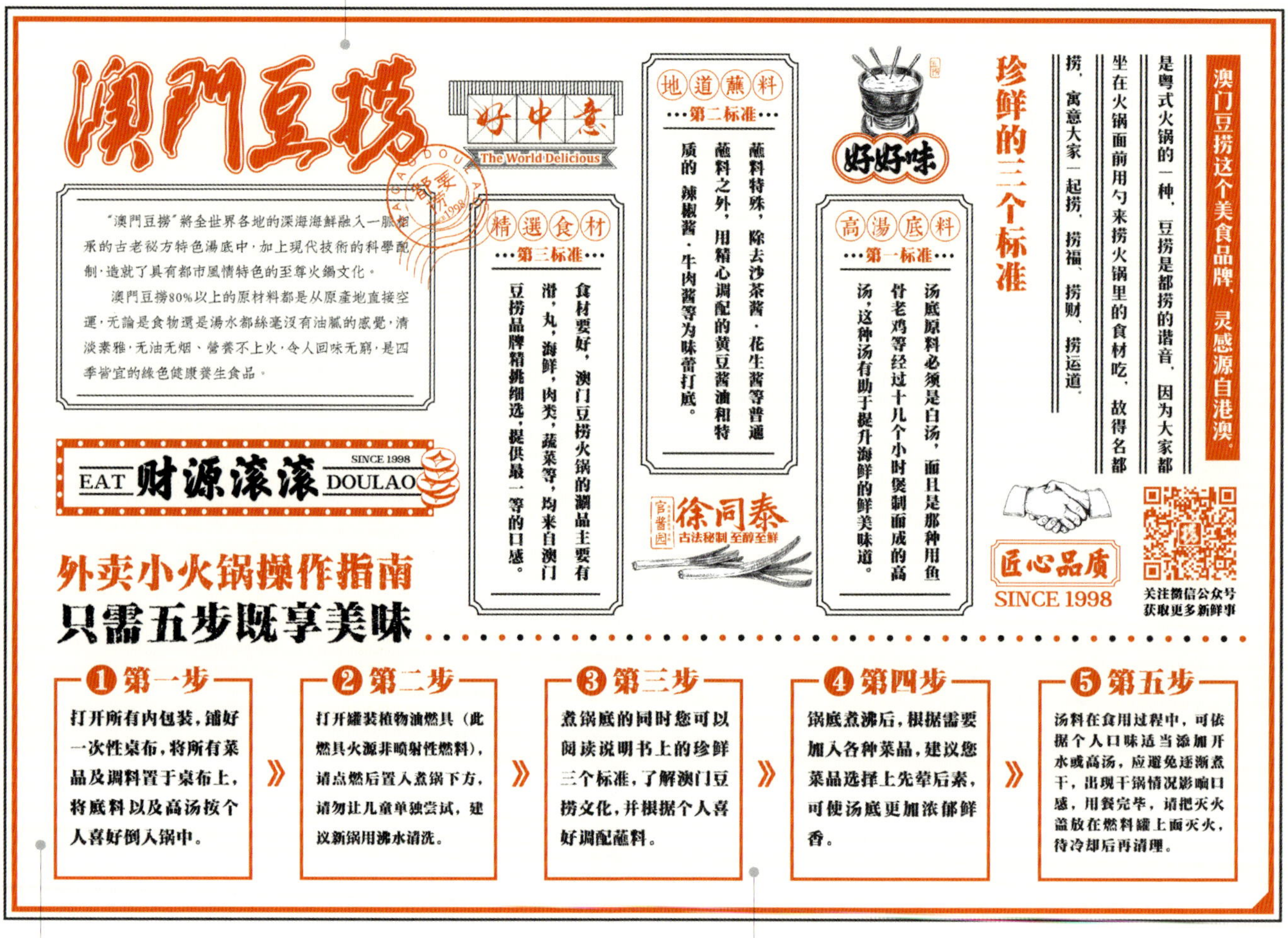

Elements and illustrations of Hong Kong and Macao culture are used in posters and different borders are added with shading added to the words. Words and illustrations are exquisitely laid out, based on certain rules which that achieves the sense of wholeness.

The main colors orange and gray generate a vintage feel belonging to a particular time. The bold use of contrasting colors deepens the brand image.

Grid

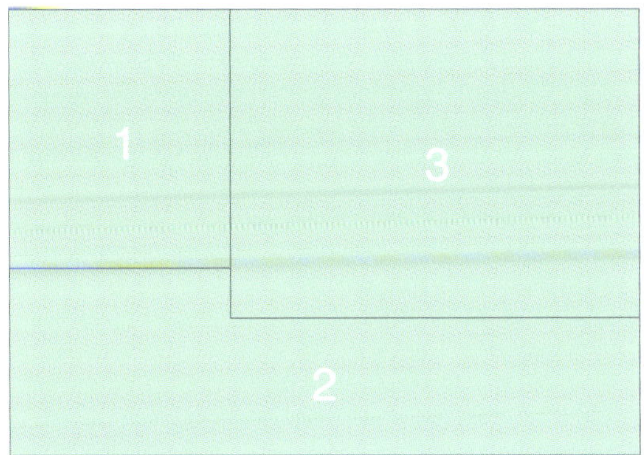

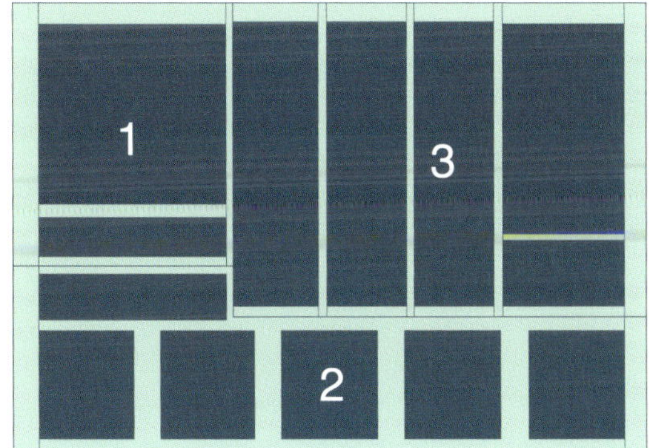

Visual Flow

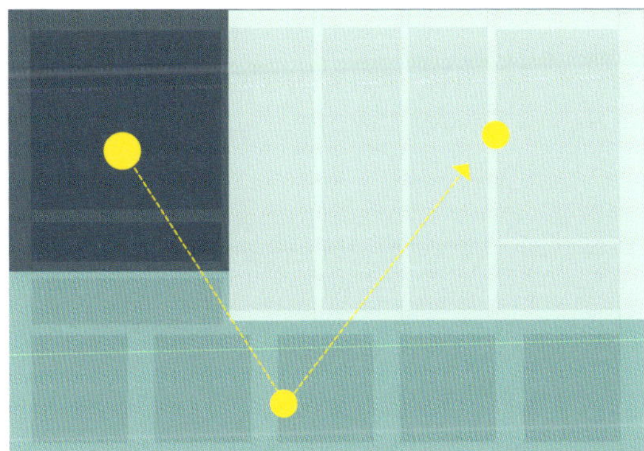

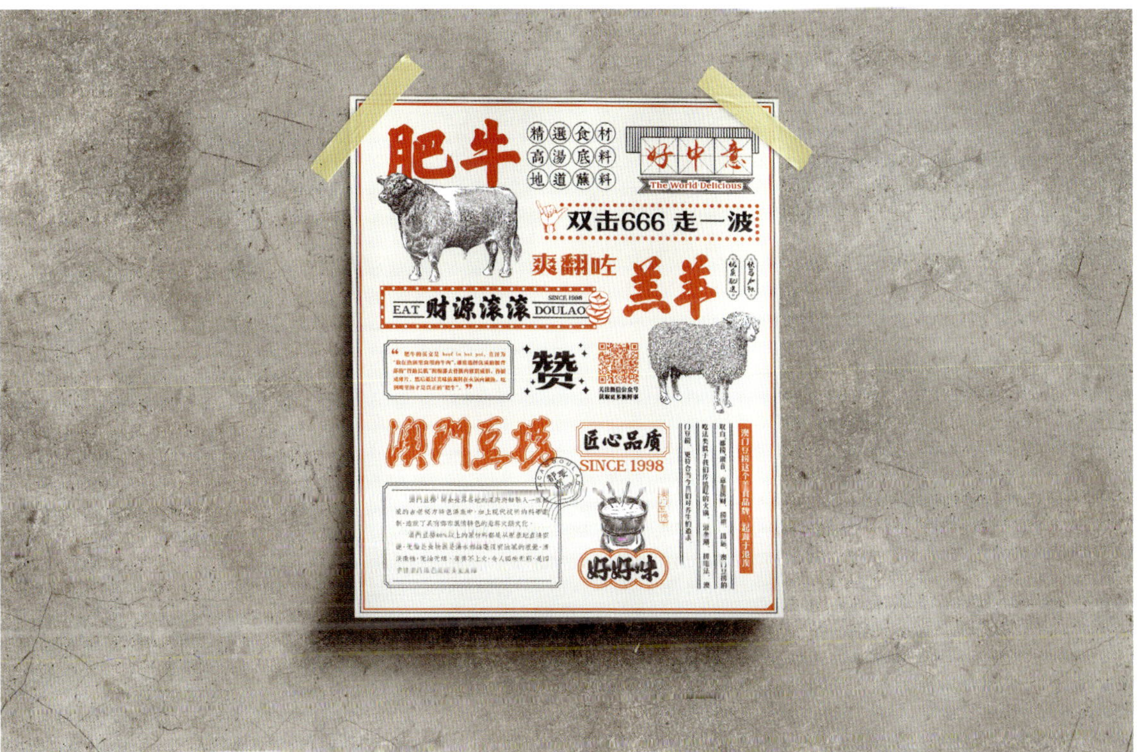

Macao Doulao is a hot pot brand with strong local characteristics. It combines an ancient secret soup recipe with a scientific food formula to create an unprecedented gourmet experience. Macao Doulao not only provides high-quality food materials from all over the world but also gives best wishes to all customers. All these have been reflected in the poster design.

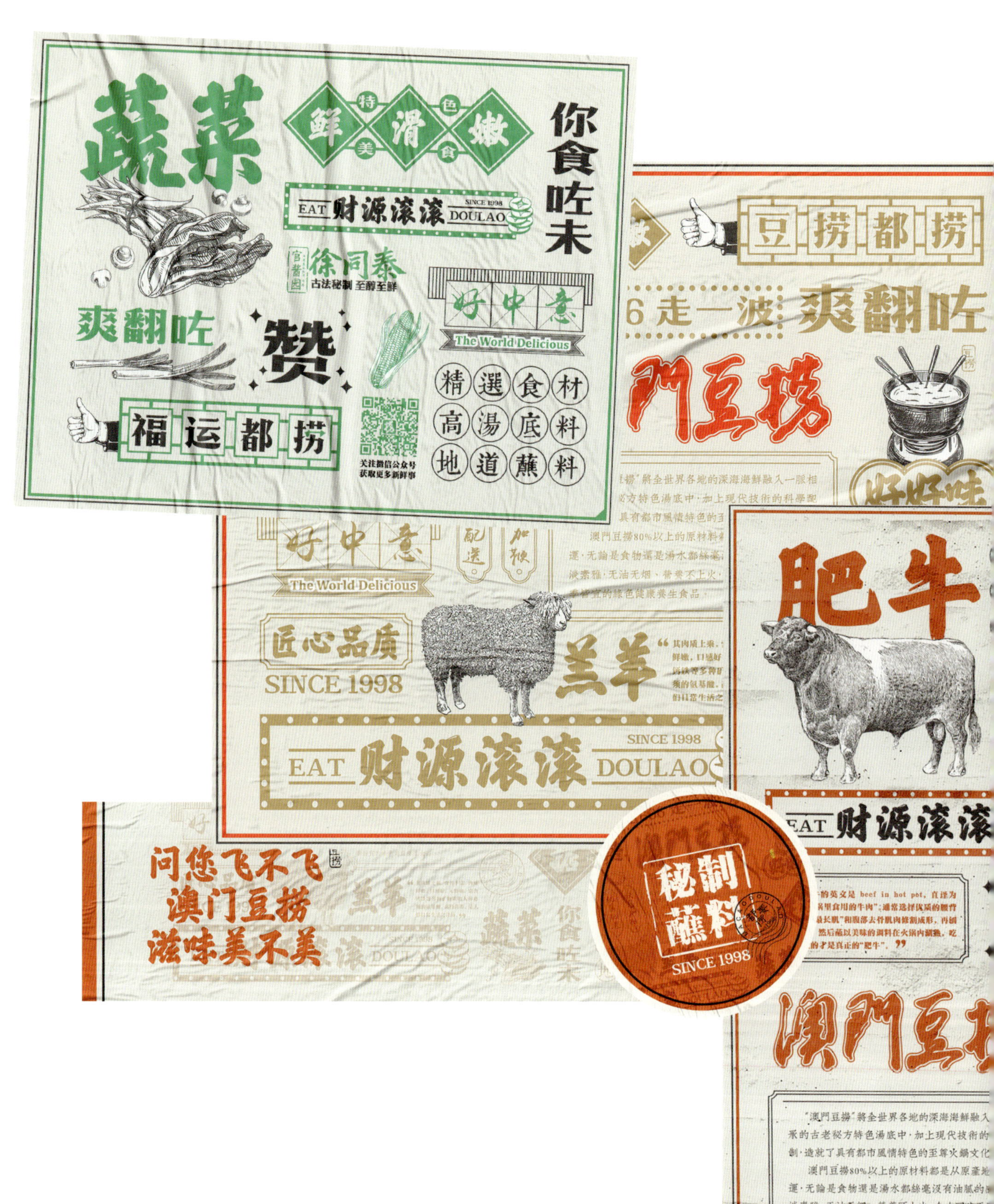

蔬菜
鲜 滑 嫩
特色美食
你食咗未
EAT 财源滚滚 SINCE 1998 DOULAO
徐同泰
古法秘制 至醇至鲜
爽翻咗
赞
好中意
The World Delicious
精選食材
高湯底料
地道蘸料
福运都捞
关注微信公众号
获取更多新鲜事
豆捞都捞
走一波 爽翻咗
門豆捞
好中意
The World Delicious
匠心品质
SINCE 1998
羔羊
EAT 财源滚滚 SINCE 1998 DOULAO
肥牛
EAT 财源滚滚
问您飞不飞
澳门豆捞
滋味美不美
秘制蘸料
SINCE 1998
澳門豆捞

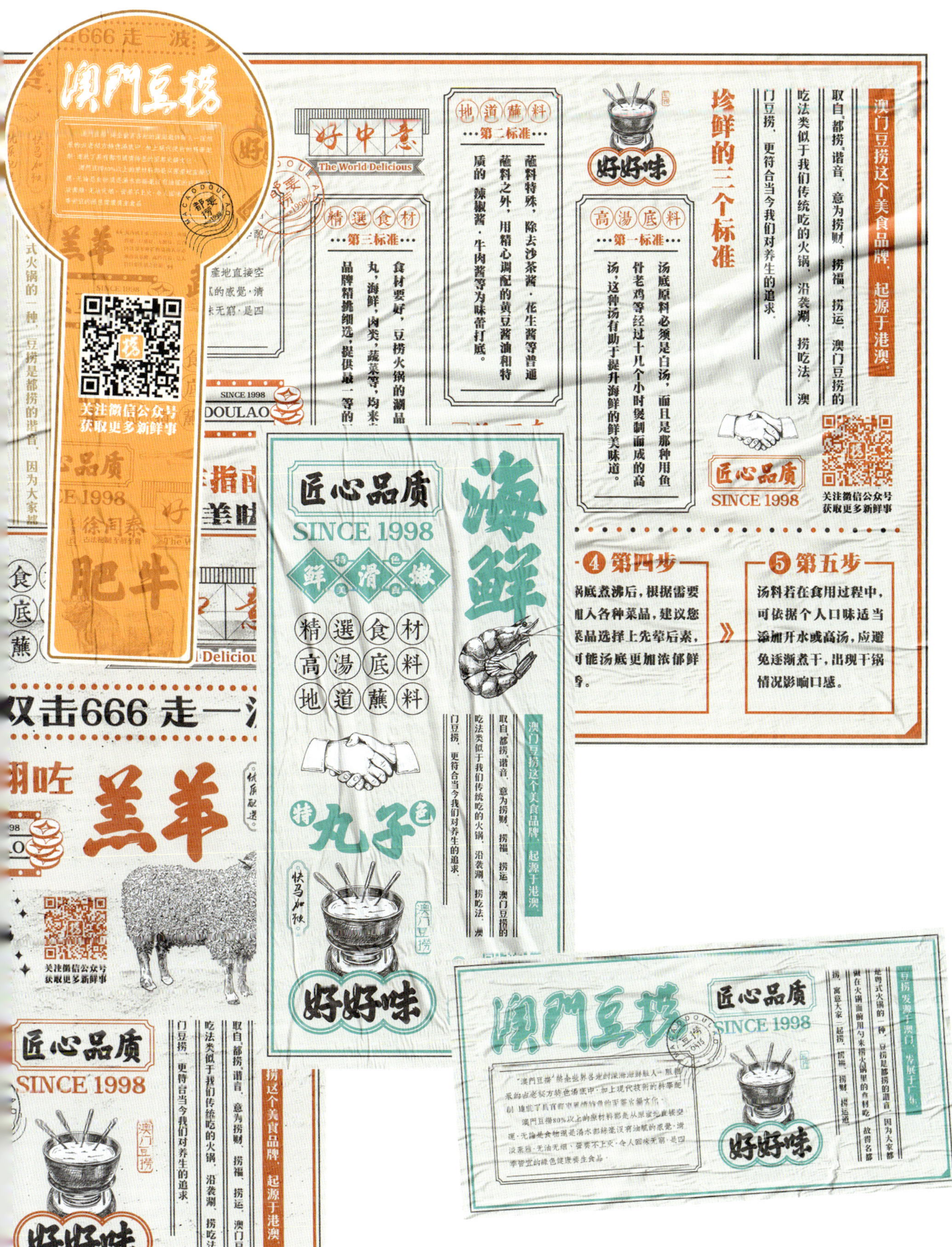

澳門豆捞
关注微信公众号
获取更多新鲜事
澳门豆捞这个美食品牌，起源于港澳
取自"都捞"谐音，意为捞财、捞福、捞运，澳门豆捞的吃法类似于我们传统吃的火锅，沿袭涮、捞吃法，澳门豆捞，更符合当今我们对养生的追求。
珍鲜的三个标准
好好味
好中意
The World Delicious
高湯底料
第一标准
汤底原料必须是白汤，而且是那种用鱼骨老鸡等经过十几个小时煲制而成的高汤，这种汤有助于提升海鲜的鲜美味道。
地道蘸料
第二标准
蘸料特殊，除去沙茶酱、花生酱等普通蘸料之外，用精心调配的黄豆酱油和特质的辣椒酱、牛肉酱等为味蕾打底。
精選食材
第三标准
匠心品质
SINCE 1998
4 第四步
5 第五步
汤料若在食用过程中，可依据个人口味适当添加开水或高汤，应避免逐渐煮干，出现干锅情况影响口感。
海鲜
鲜 滑 嫩
精選食材
高湯底料
地道蘸料
特色丸子
快马加鞭
澳门豆捞
羔羊
肥牛
双击666 走一

Ma-Lao-Da Sichuan Hot Pot Poster

Designer

Tsai Wei Hsin

Client

Wowprime Group

Key Diagram

Font	Paper	Size
DFP Long Men	Coated paper	420×594mm (A2)

Strokes are forceful and imposing which conforms to the image of the brand whose name phonetically reminds people of "boss".

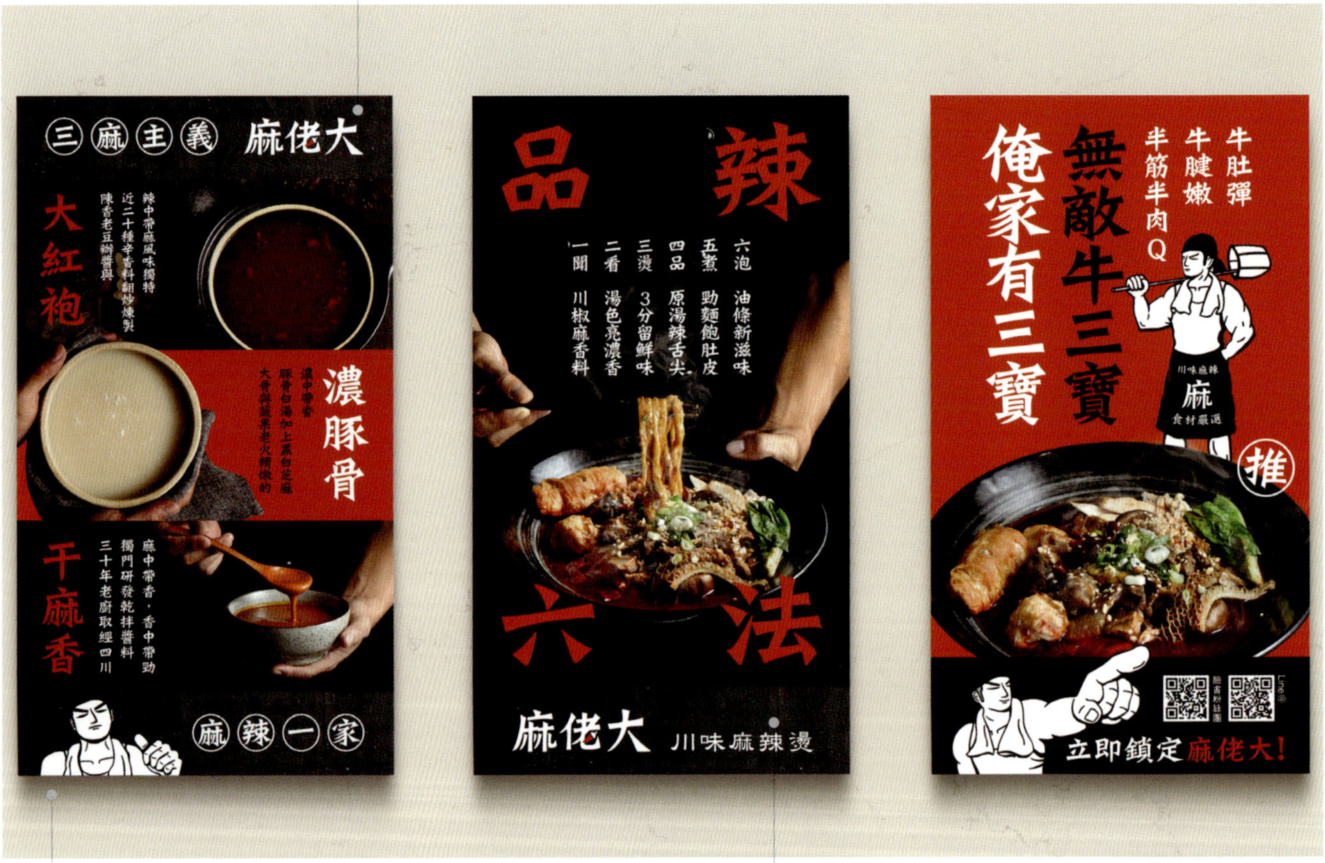

Words maximize the beauty of the pictures at their best and presents the charm of the hot pot. The selected fonts and colors echo the atmosphere of hot pot restaurants.

Black and red are the product colors. Red as a warm color reminds people of chili and provokes the appetite. The combination of red, white, and black can create a strong visual impact.

Grid

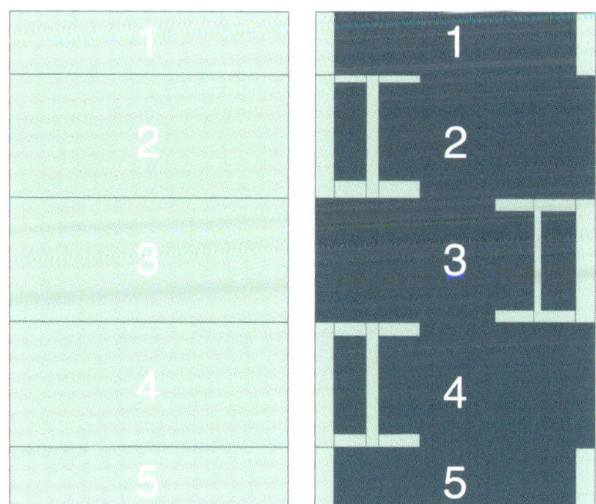

Visual Flow

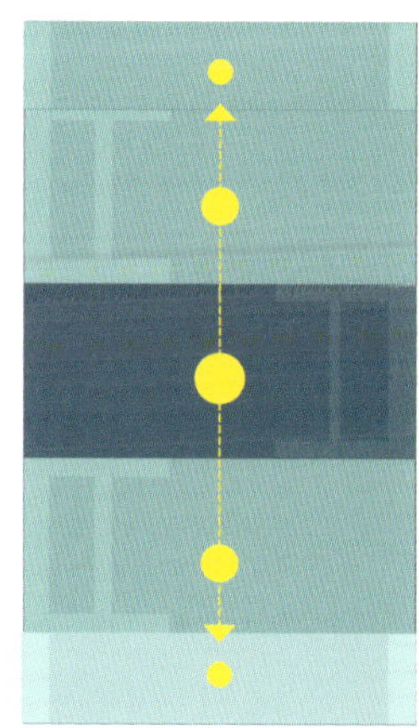

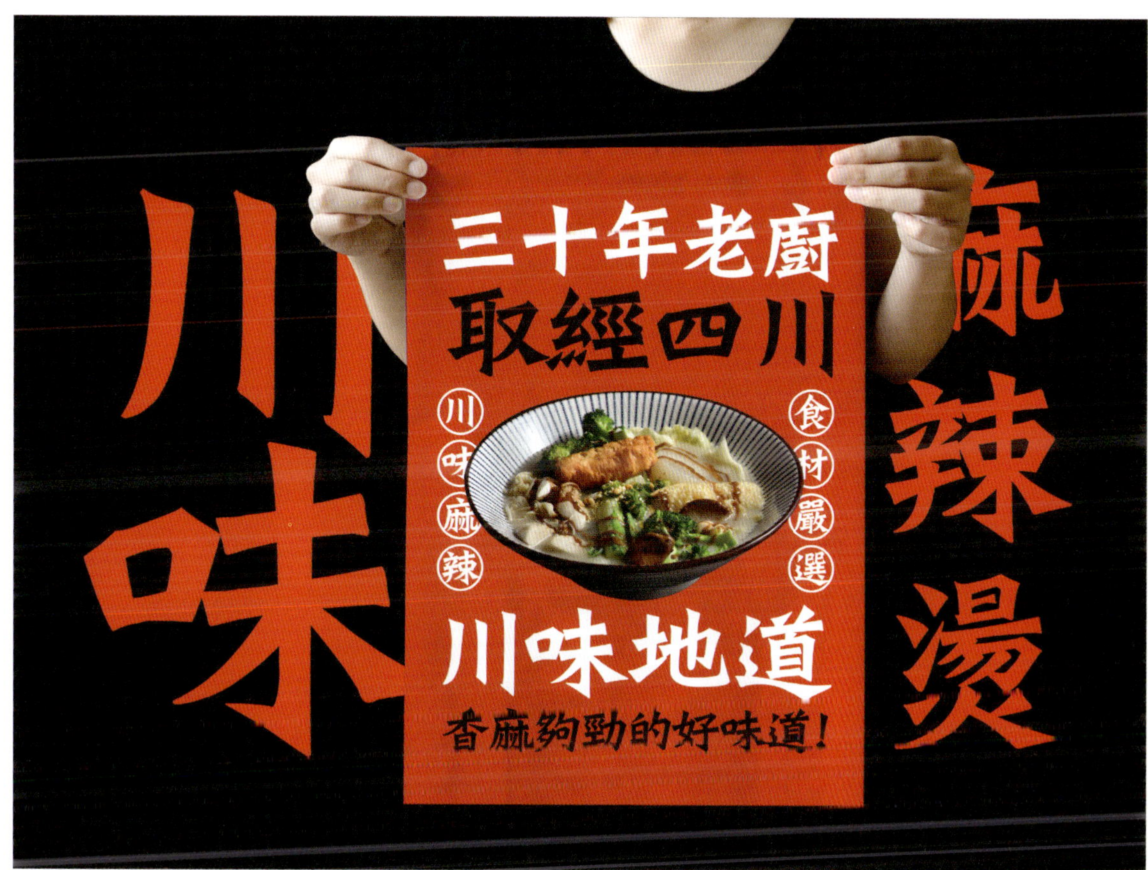

Ma-Lao-Da, part of Wowprime Group, is a new Sichuan hot pot brand. It serves fresh hot pot food and special spicy soup. The brand image of Ma-Lao-Da delivers the founders' obsession with Sichuan hot pot. The unique brand style and flavor break down the stereotype of hot pots and brings a huge surprise to his consumers. The poster continues its brand style and improves people's appetite with a special taste.

Man-Qi-Wu Japanese Restaurant Poster and Brochure

Designer

Xi Jianglong

Client

Hangzhou Ningnuo Investment Management Co., Ltd.

Key Diagram

Font	Paper	Size
HYYiSong Regular (Title)/ TypeLand KhangXi Dict, Mingliu (Text)	Off-white blanket-texture paper Matt art paper Colored dermatoglyph paper	900×600mm

HYYiSong Regular and TypeLand KhangXi Dict are antique and elegant. Mingliu appears to be soft and light, which are suitable for Japanese fresh styles.

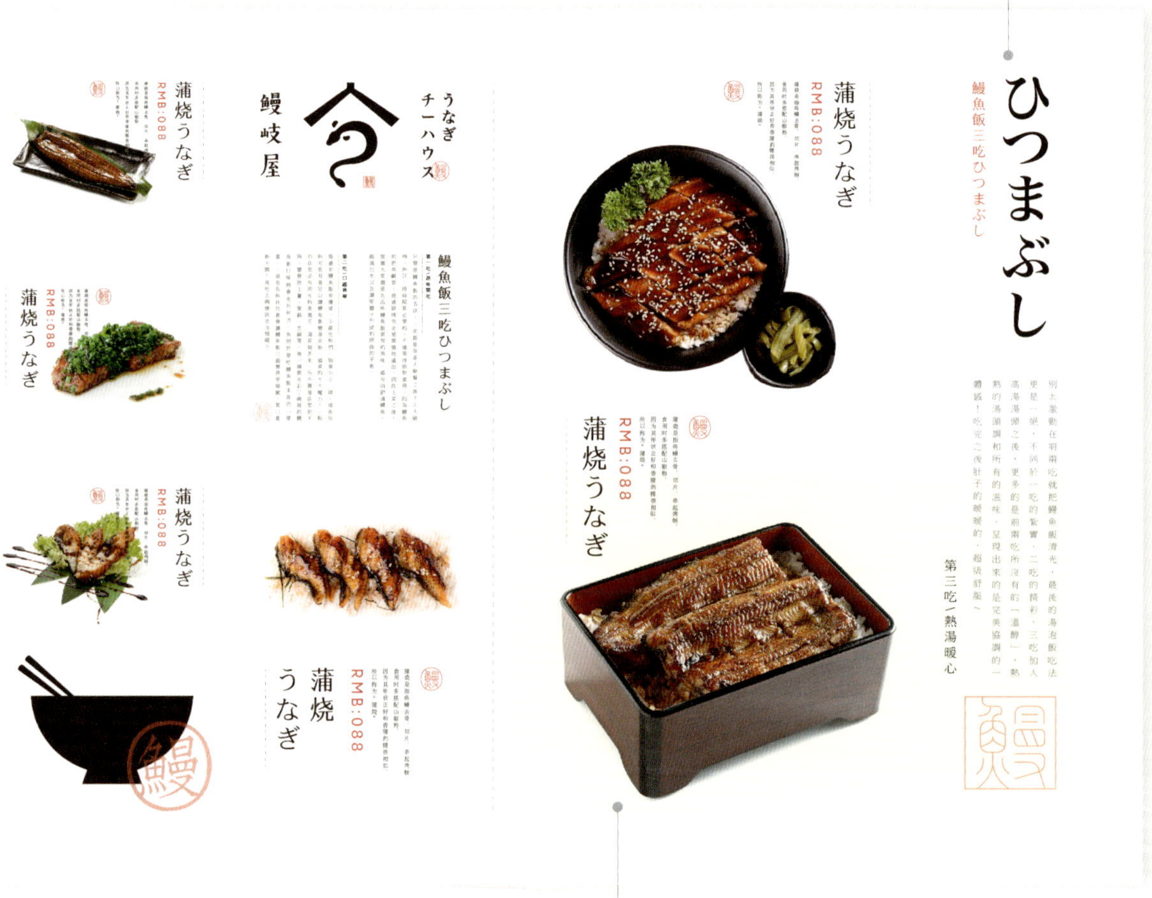

The large area of negative space has a unique quietness and gives readers a steady and calm feeling. White space surrounding words contributes to comfortable reading.

Off-white as the main color shows the characteristics of purity and calmness and creates a warm and cozy atmosphere.

Grid

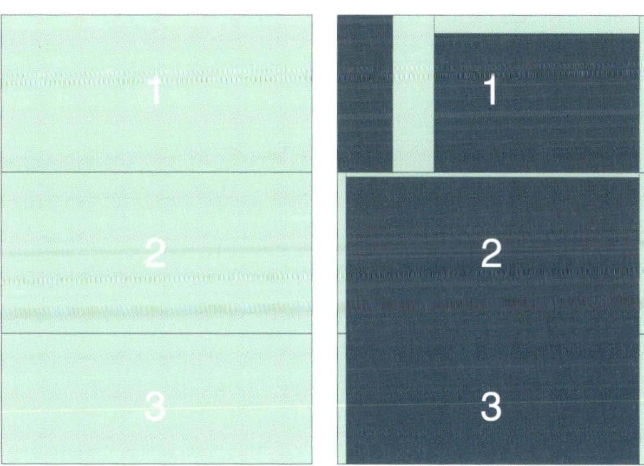

Visual Flow

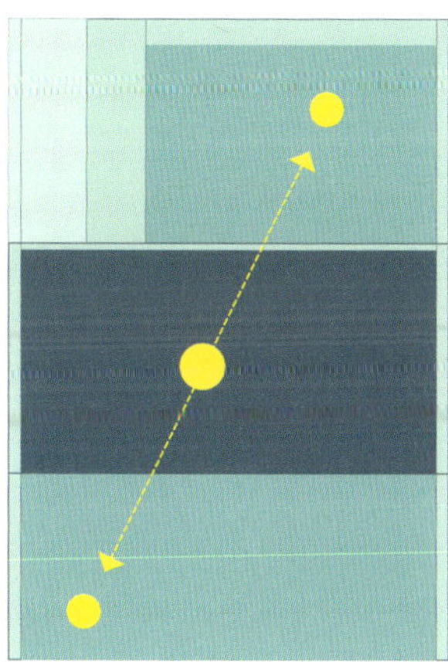

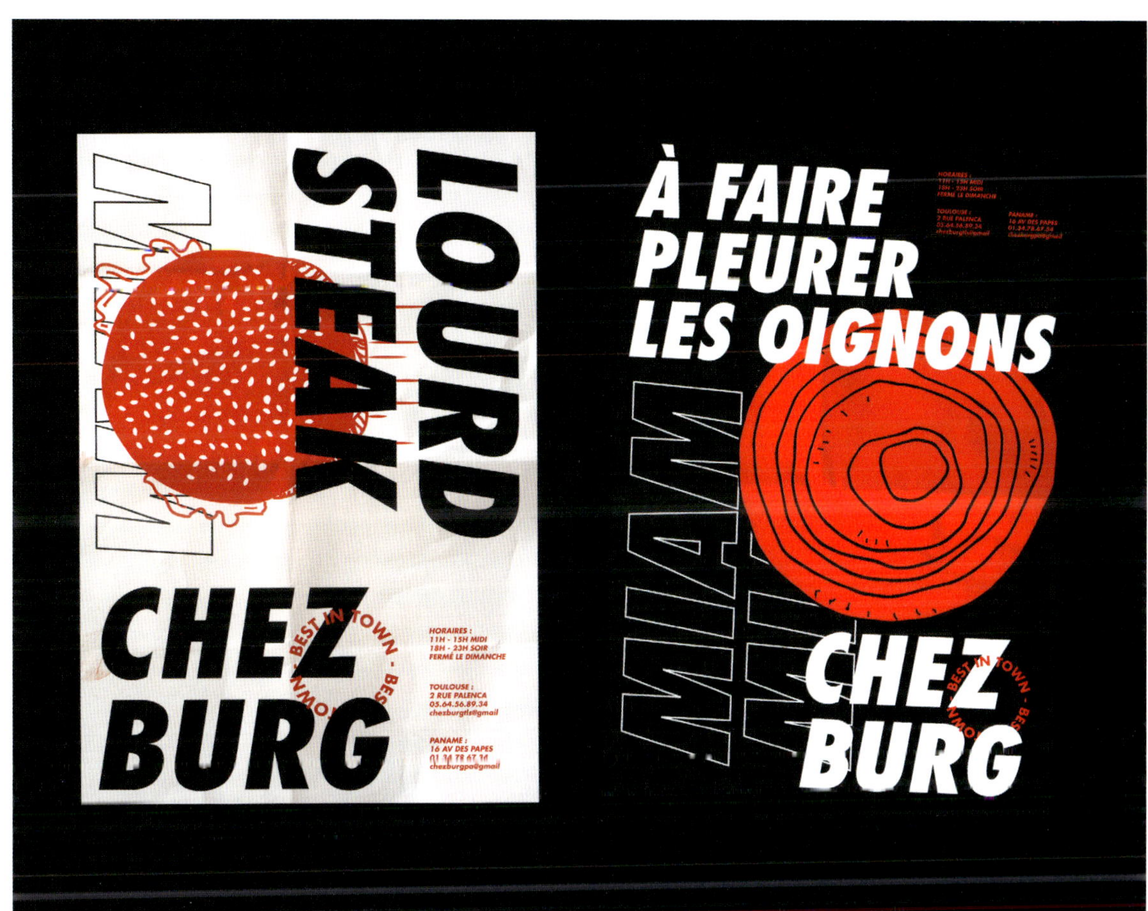

Chez Burg as a fast-food restaurant wants to attract more young clients. The strong, unique, and recognizable identity is what they need to maximize their impact on people's minds. The designer breaks the monotonous traditional layout and employs mixing popular elements in posters to achieve the double effects of art and commerce.

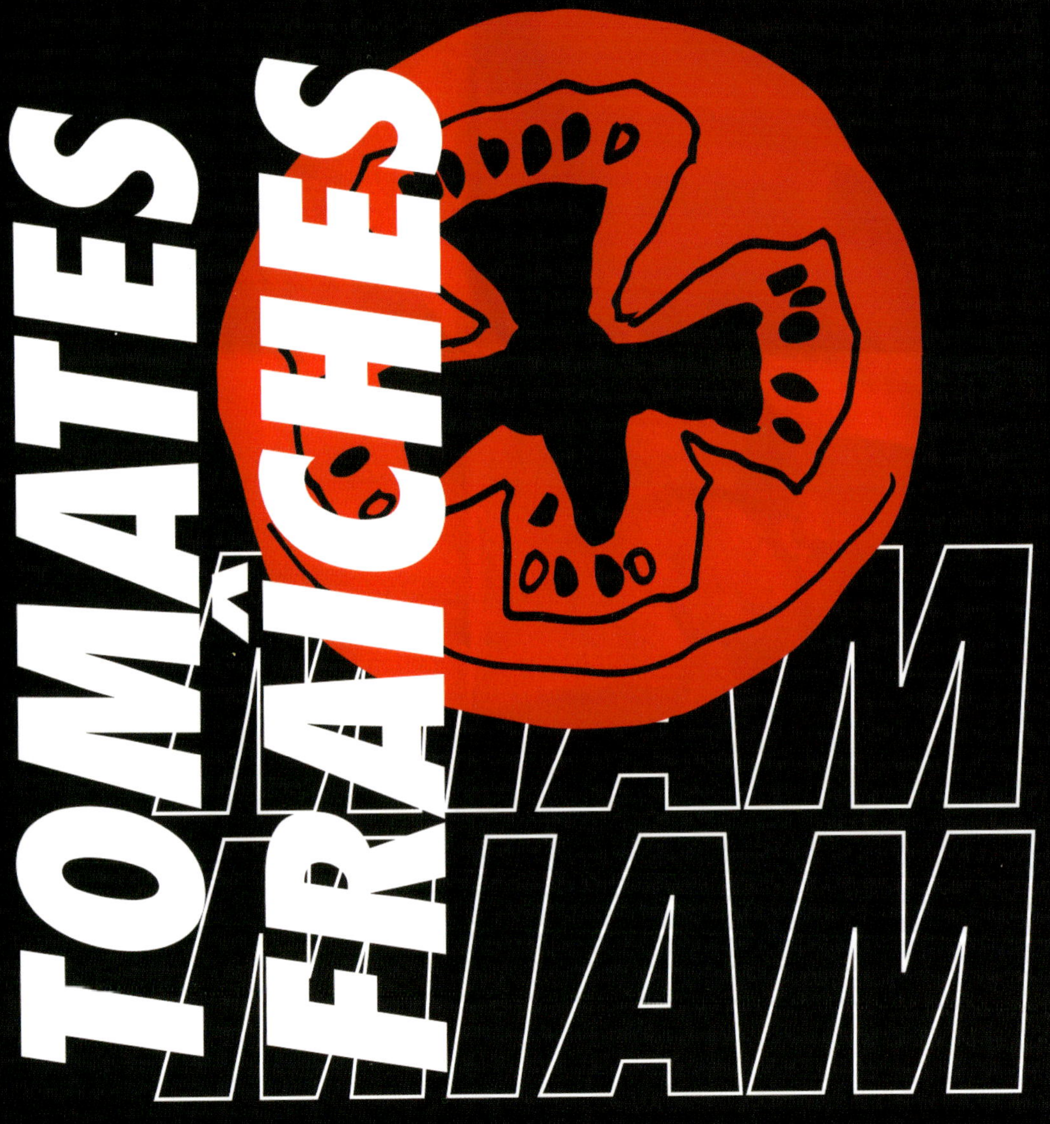
CHEZ
BURG
BEST IN TOWN - BEST IN TOWN -
HORAIRES :
11H - 15H MIDI
18H - 23H SOIR
FERMÉ LE DIMANCHE
TOULOUSE :
2 RUE PALENCA
05.64.56.89.34
chezburgtls@gmail
PANAME :
16 AV DES PAPES
01.34.78.67.34
chezburgpa@gmail
TOMATES
FRAÎCHES
MIAM
MIAM

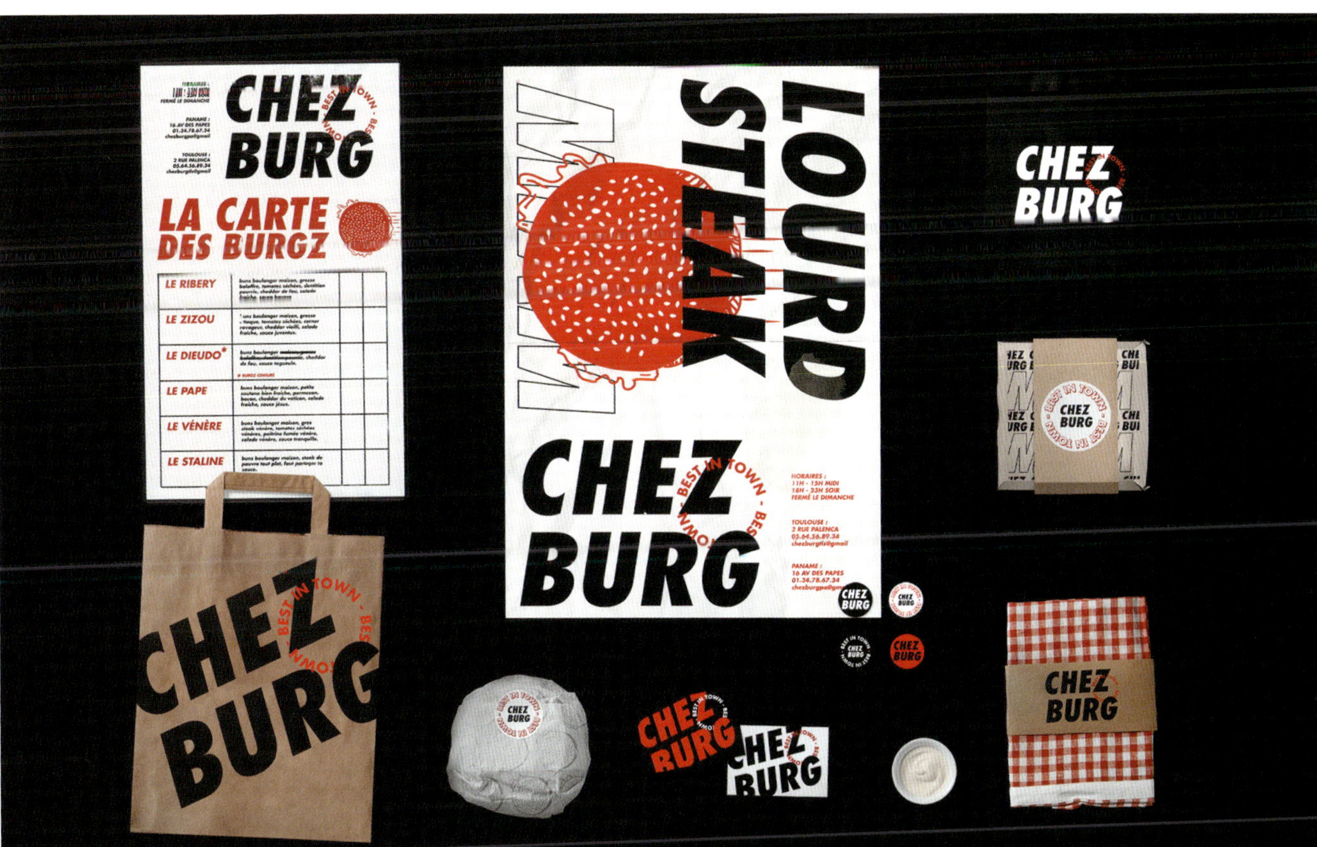

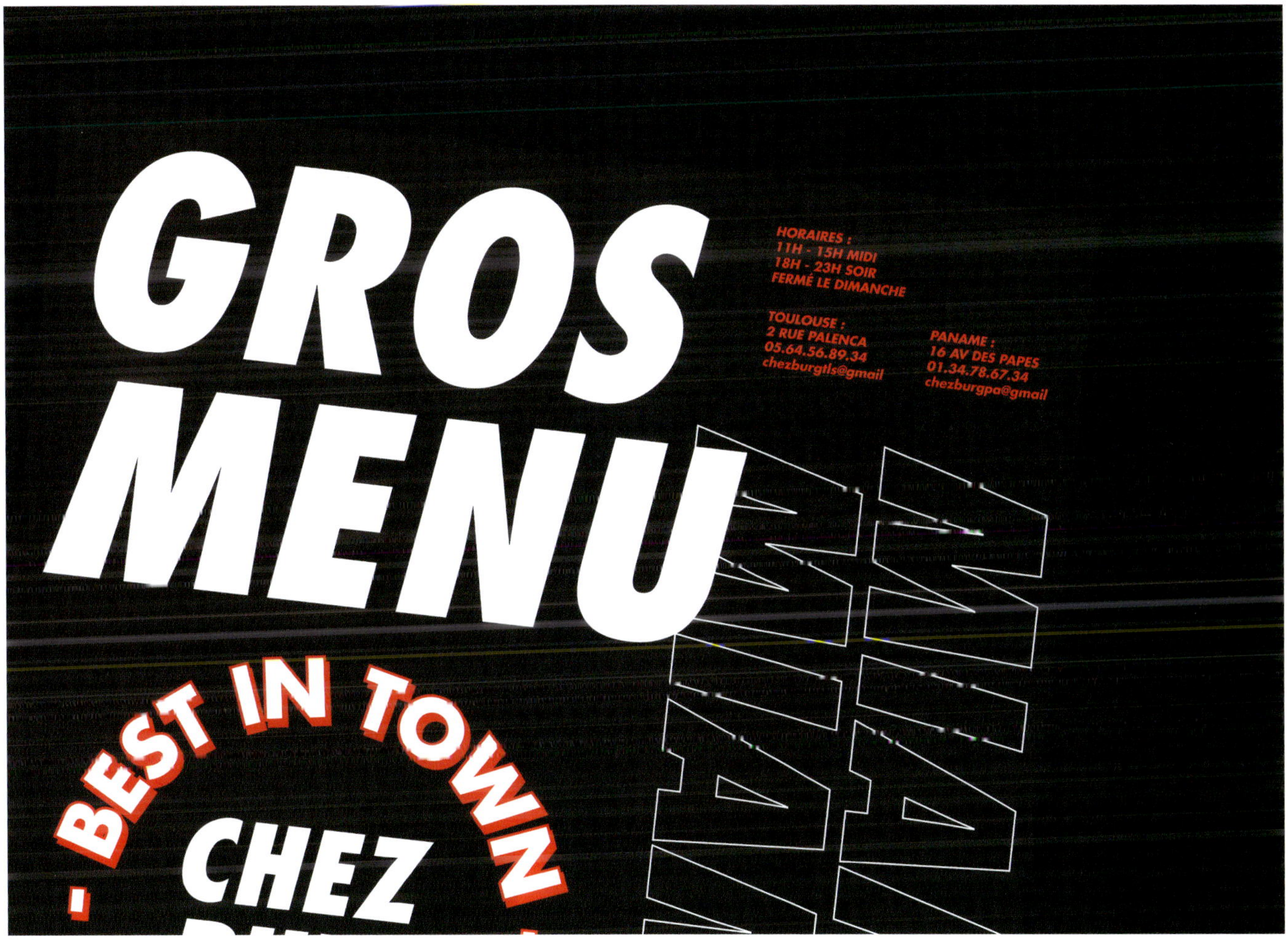

GROS
MENU

HORAIRES :
11H - 15H MIDI
18H - 23H SOIR
FERMÉ LE DIMANCHE

TOULOUSE :
2 RUE PALENCA
05.64.56.89.34
chezburgtls@gmail

PANAME :
16 AV DES PAPES
01.34.78.67.34
chezburgpa@gmail

- BEST IN TOWN -
CHEZ

Noroshi Poster

Designer

Lee Ching Tat

Client

Noroshi

Key Diagram

Font	Paper	Size
Aoyagi Soseki Font 2OTF	Poster paper	420×594mm (A2) 210×297mm (A4)

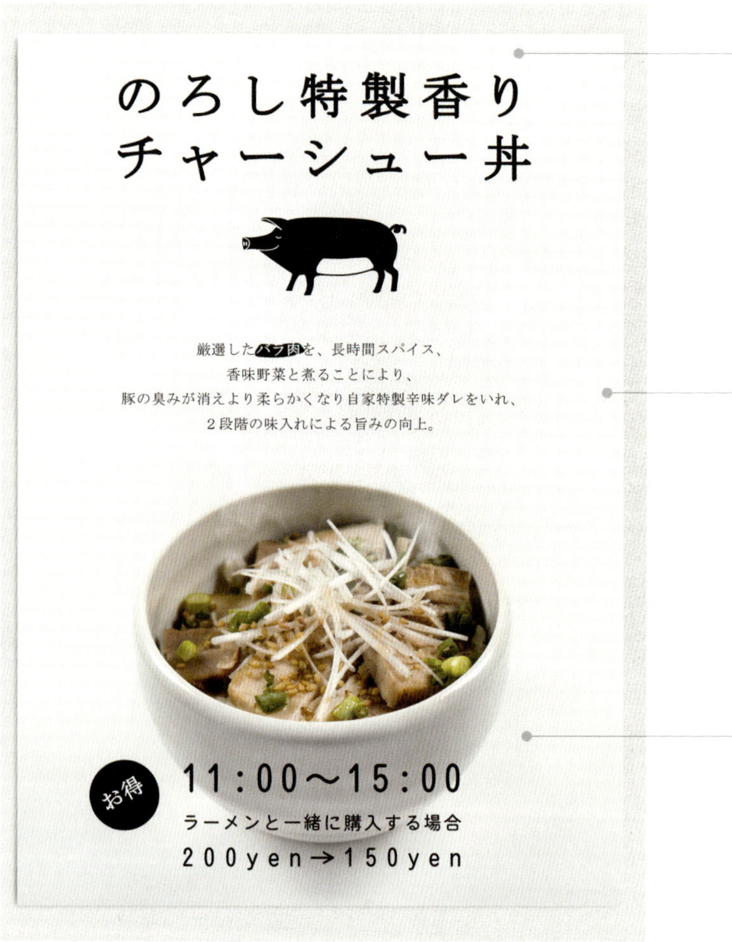

The font is distinguished by its casual but powerful quality expressed in the strokes.

The background color, pale gray, together with the black words makes the poster more elegant and graceful.

The layout is simple but vivid with the well-designed typography. All images are located on the central axis of the poster in order to keep the subtle balance. Fresh and natural food photographs make viewers sense the unique quality of the Hakodate forest.

Grid

Visual Flow

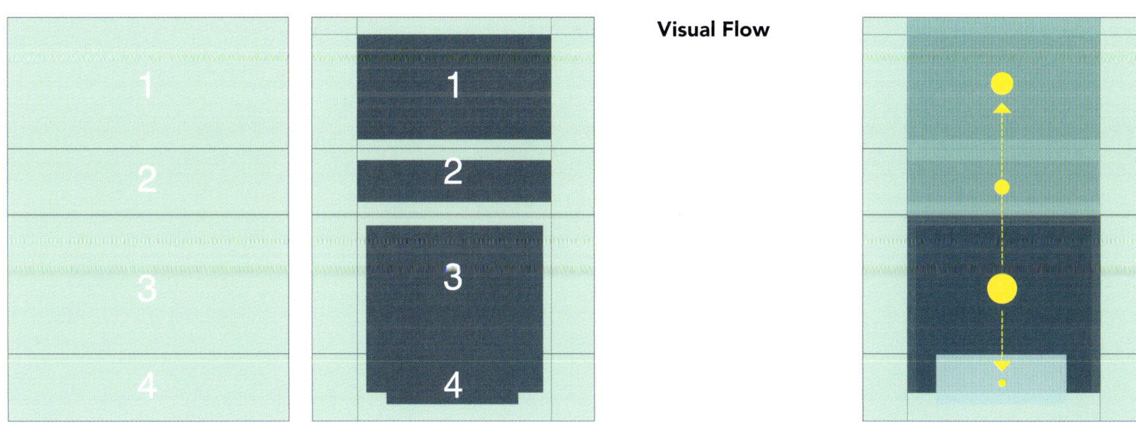

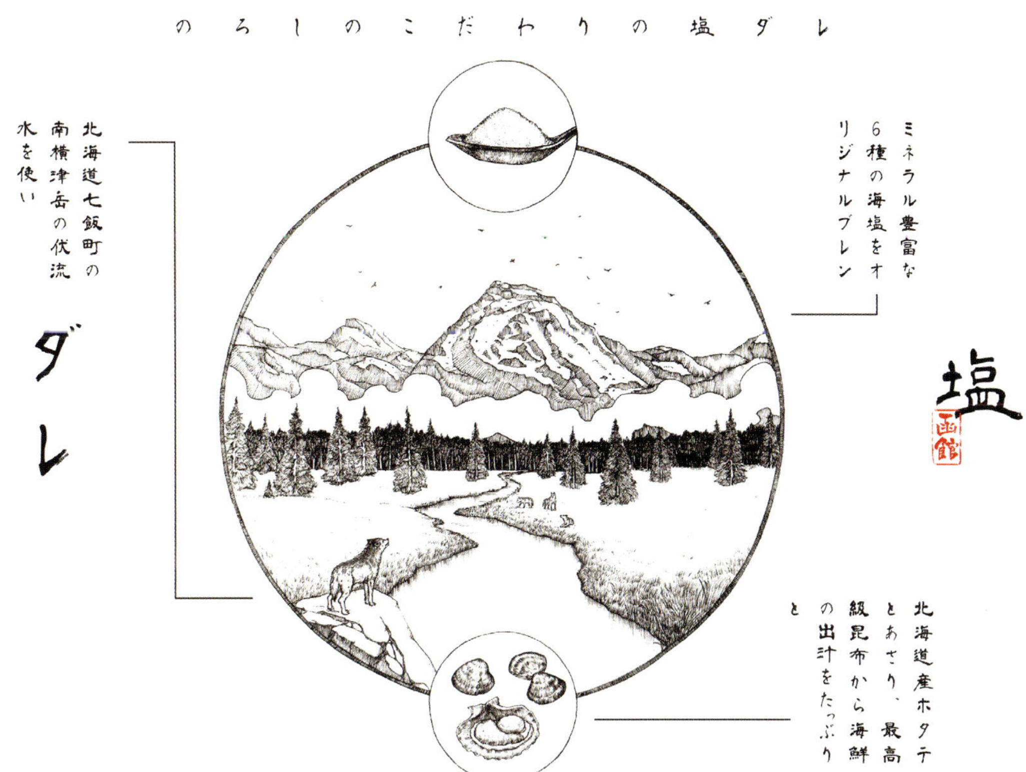

Noroshi is a regional noodle restaurant in Japan. The restaurant is characterized by its new flavor noodle of Hakodate. To attract consumers and offer a glimpse of ingredients, the posters mainly introduce the origins and property of the local products. The brand name, Noroshi, in Japanese means "smoke signals". The designer subtlety incorporated the concept into his works.

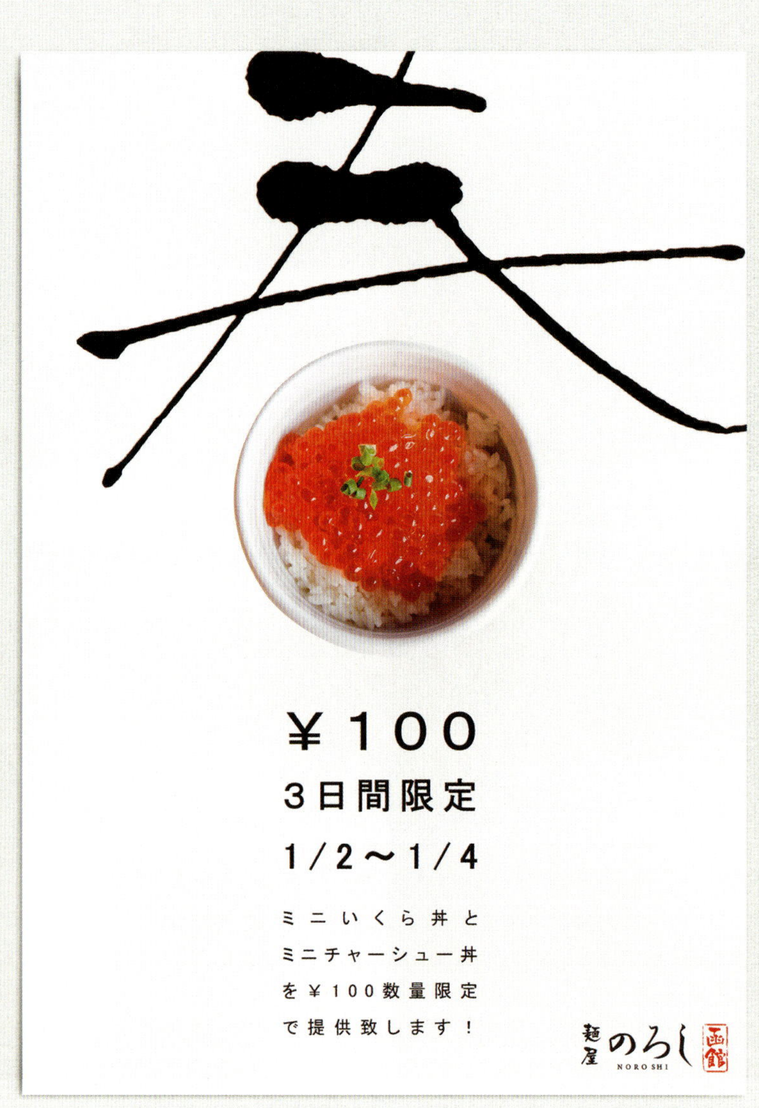
¥100
3日間限定
1/2〜1/4
ミニいくら丼と
ミニチャーシュー丼
を¥100数量限定
で提供致します！
麺屋のろし
NOROSHI
函館

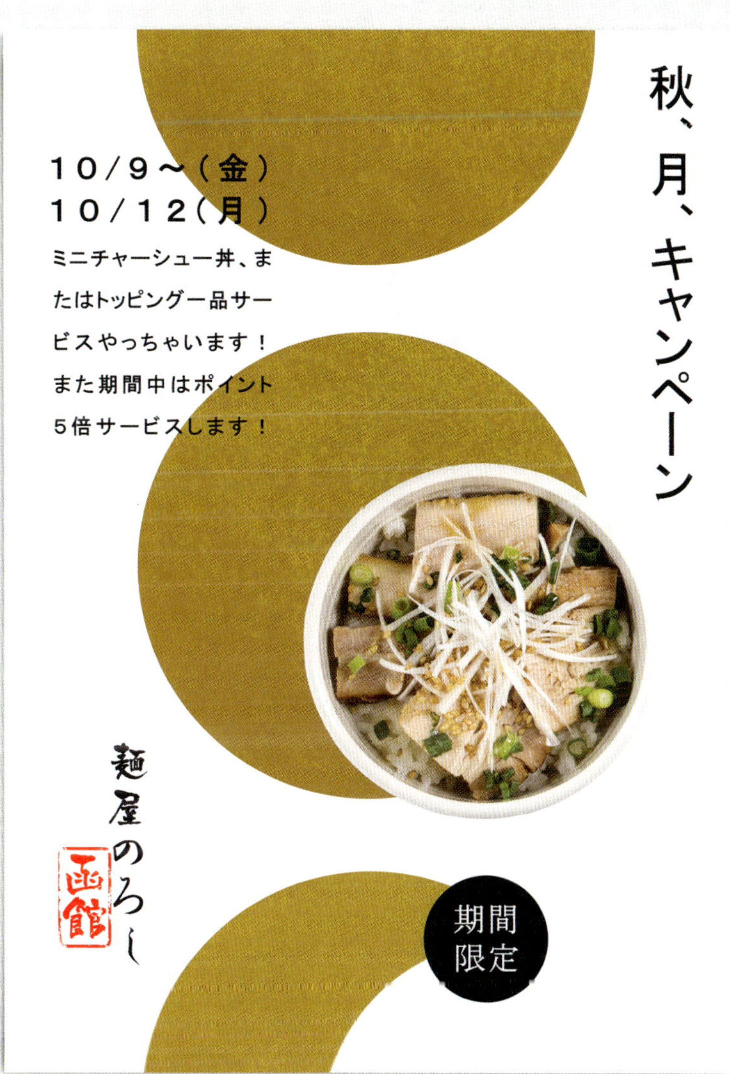
秋、月、キャンペーン
10/9～(金)
10/12(月)
ミニチャーシュー丼、またはトッピング一品サービスやっちゃいます！
また期間中はポイント5倍サービスします！
麺屋のろし
函館
期間限定

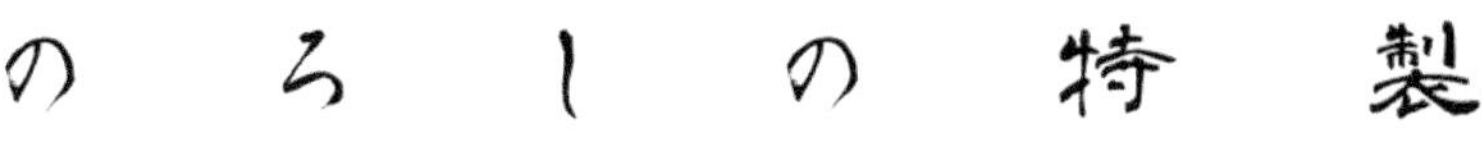

オリジナルにブレンド、一週間熟成させる

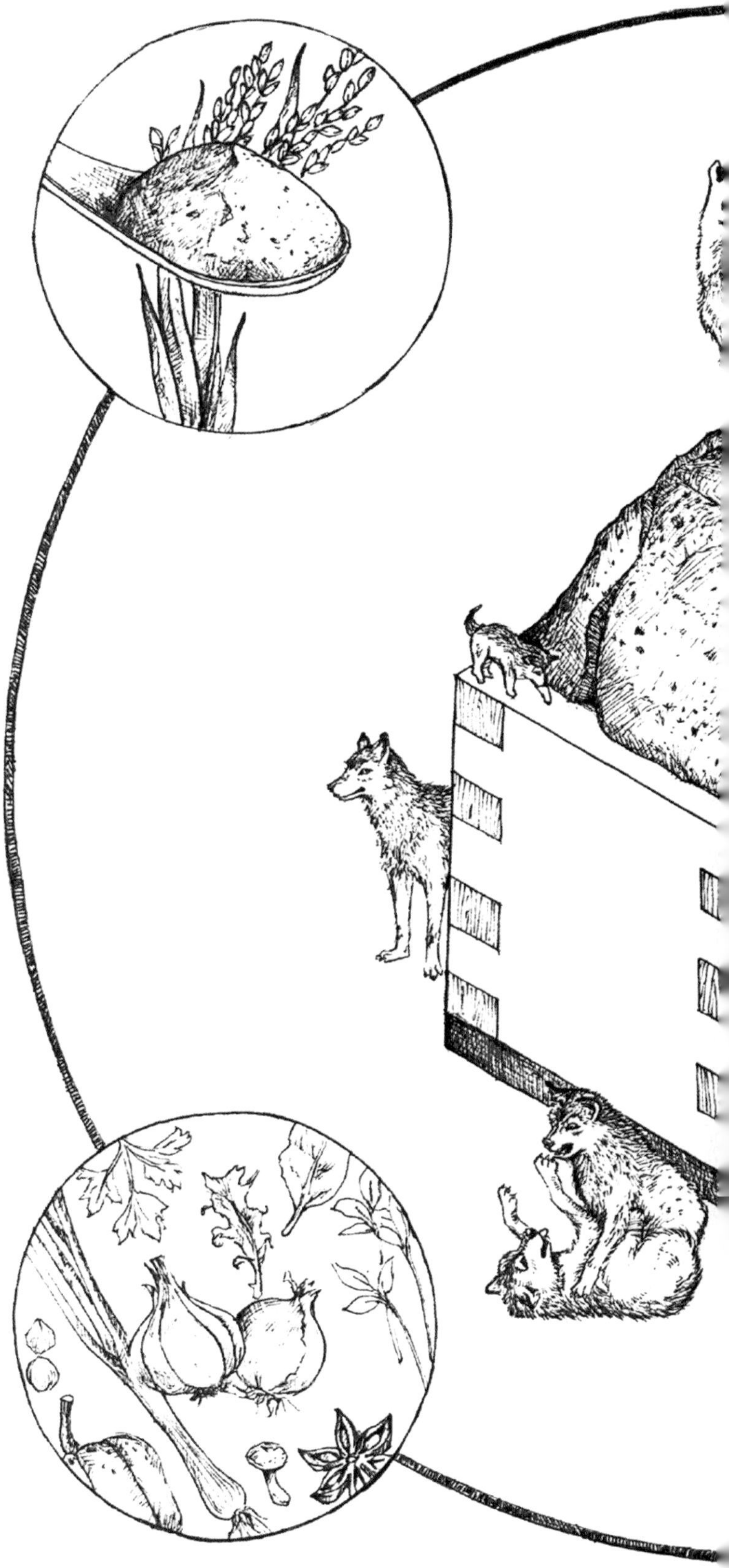

ダレ

深みのある味わいとなっています。

味噌

函館

四種類の
北海道の
赤味噌、白味噌

数種類の
特製スパイ
スと香味野
菜

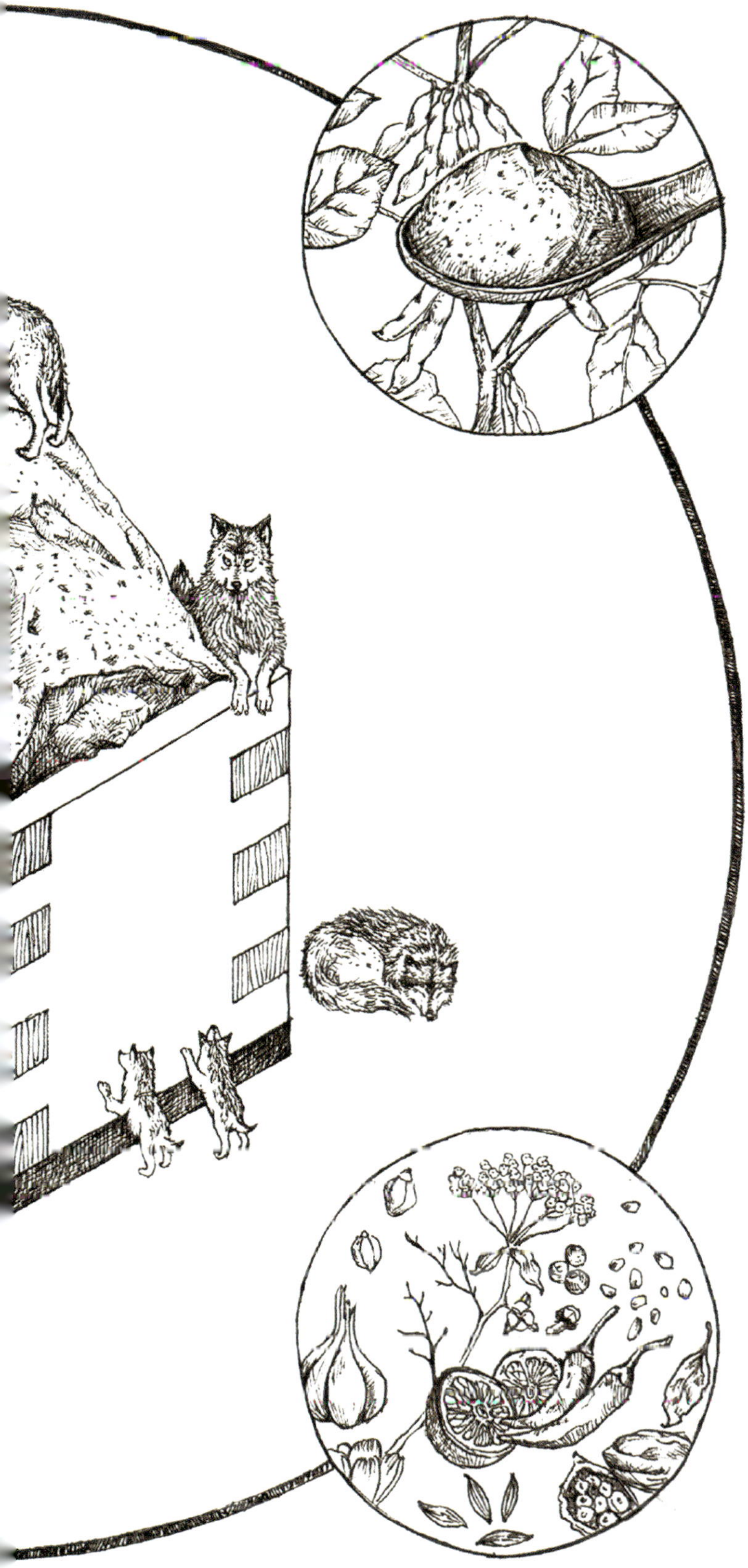

Lime Idea Flyer

Designer

Chang Xun Branding & Design

Client

Lime Idea

Key Diagram

Font	Paper	Size
Kozuka Mincho Pr6N	Wood-free paper	210×297mm (A4)

The serif font is very dignified and elegant, the price is made bigger in size to highlight key information.

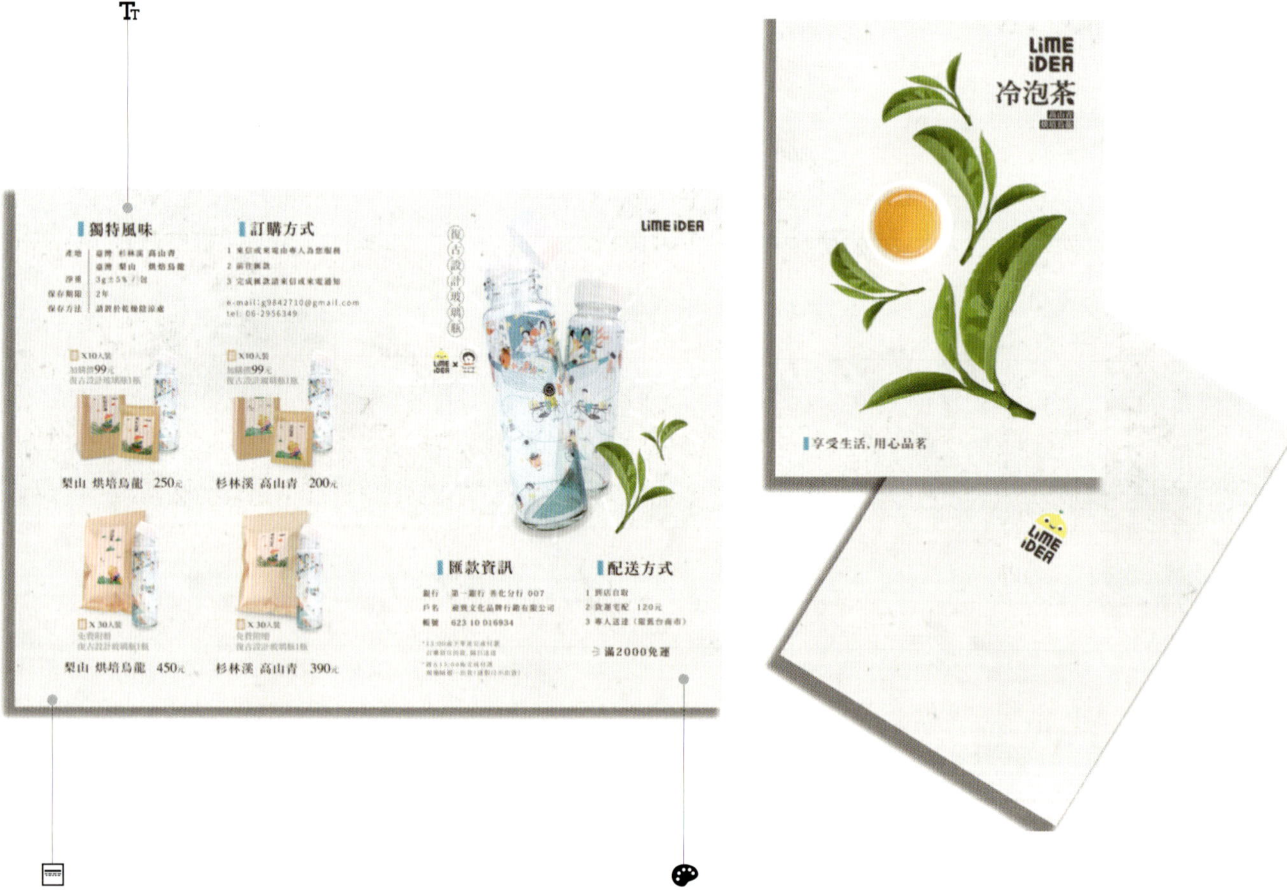

The layout reflects the principles of symmetry and proximity, and makes product images the main visual.

Simple color is used to highlight the products.

Grid

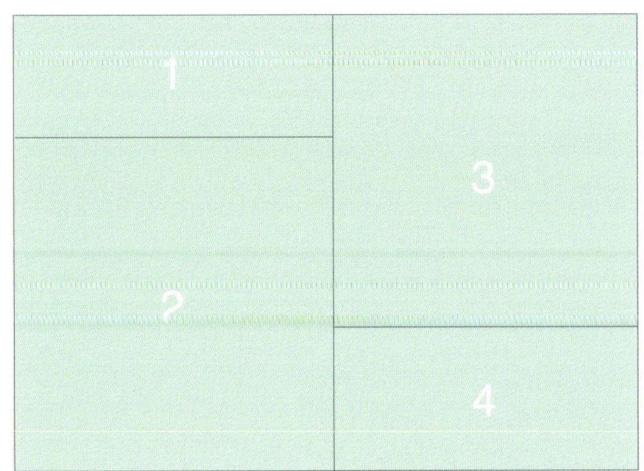

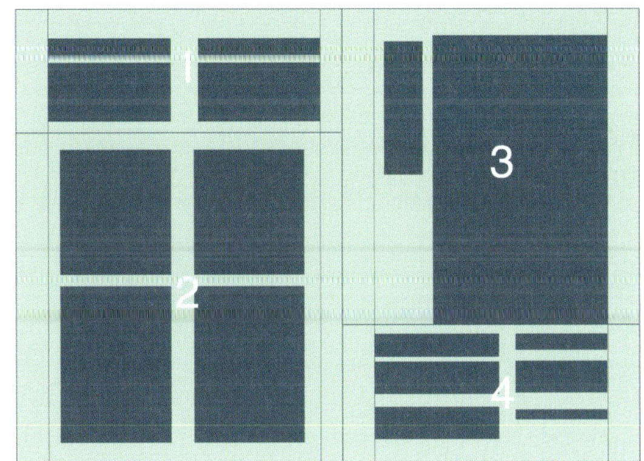

Visual Flow

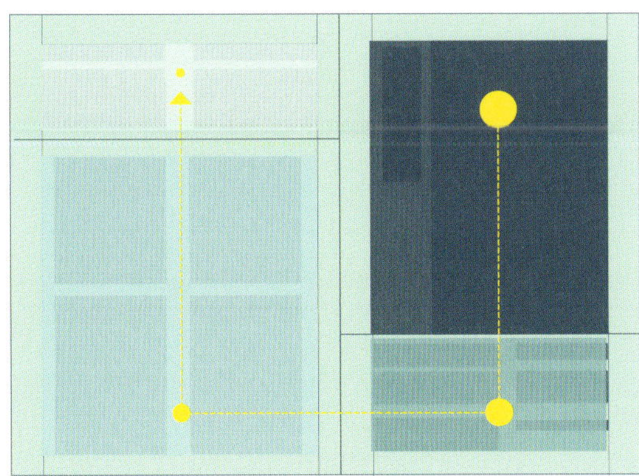

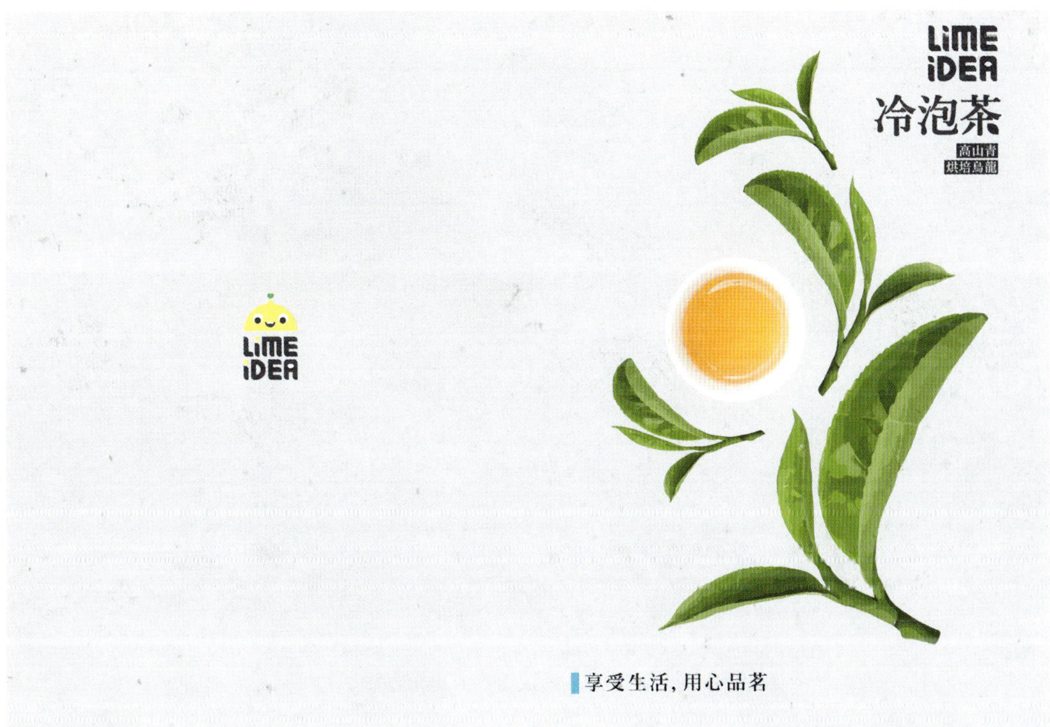

Lime Idea is a brand specializing in tea and dried fruits. Taking the promotion of Taiwanese tea as the starting point, whether it is product packaging or direct mail promotional materials, the hand-painted style is the main theme to match with the "tea" culture. The integration of product images and typography reduces an intuitive sense of resistance from customers when directly showing the price of the products. The gentleness and coziness of the hand-painted style and the simple typography, make the information easy to read.

Wuyi Ruifang Tea Brochure

Designer

ONE & ONE DESIGN

Client

Wuyi Ruifang Tea

Key Diagram

Font	Paper	Size
Source Han SerifSC	Herbage (Cover)	150×245mm
	US recycled paper (Inside Page)	135×185mm

The font in an elegant style echoes the brand's one hundred year history.

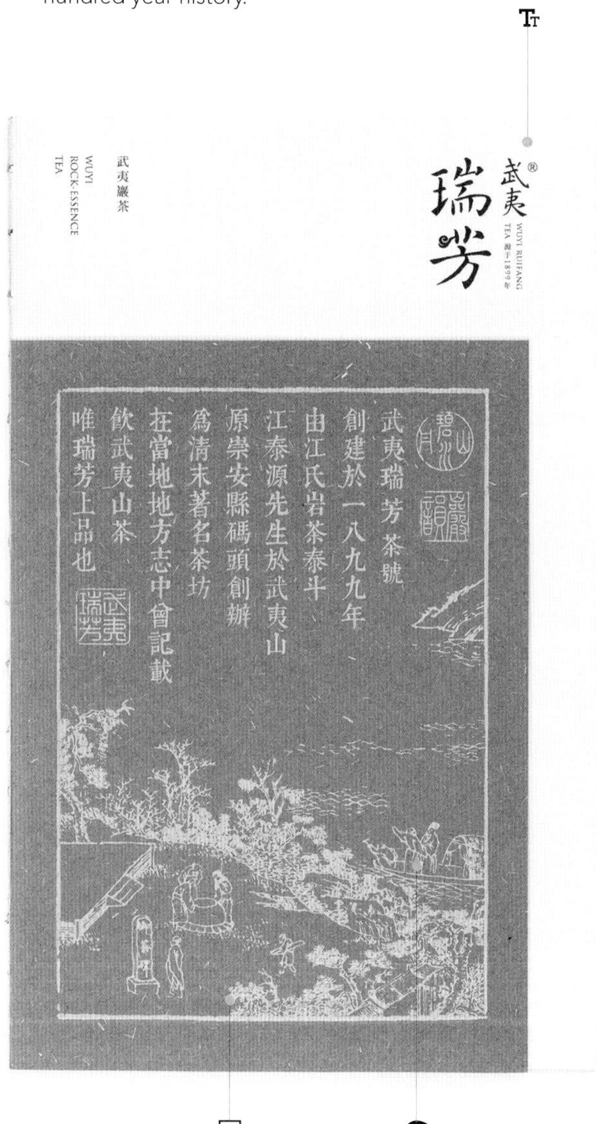

Readability is crucially important. It is affected by classification of information, fonts, font size, line spacing, type area and the structure of chapters, even the overall structure of the brochure. The core purpose of all this is to reflect and enhance the brand temperament.

The gray and beige color of the cover is contrasted, which reduces the brightness of the design and makes it looks harmonious. The engraving style is also echoed by the feeling of tranquility as with the tea brand.

Grid

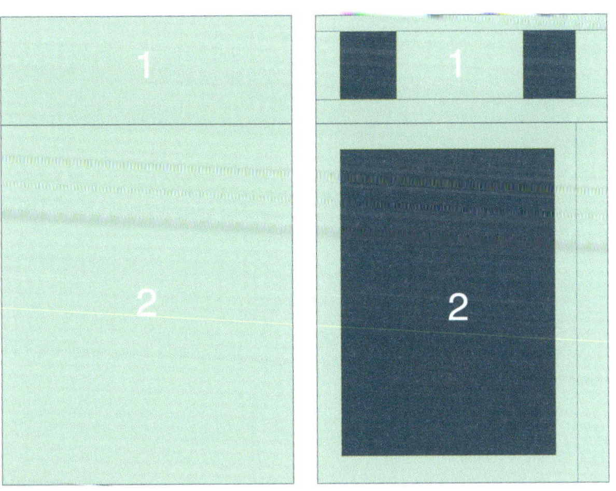

Visual Flow

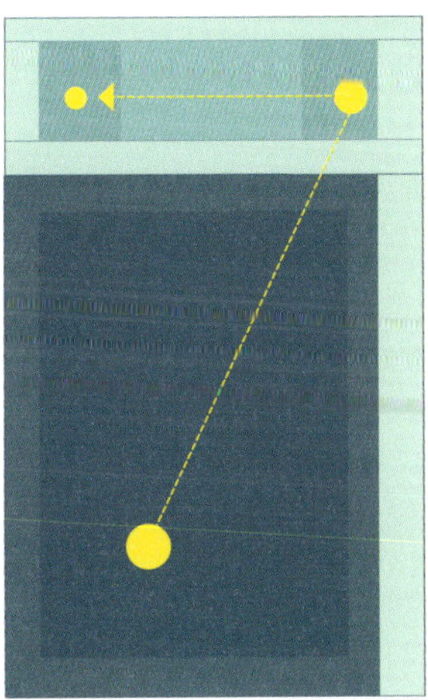

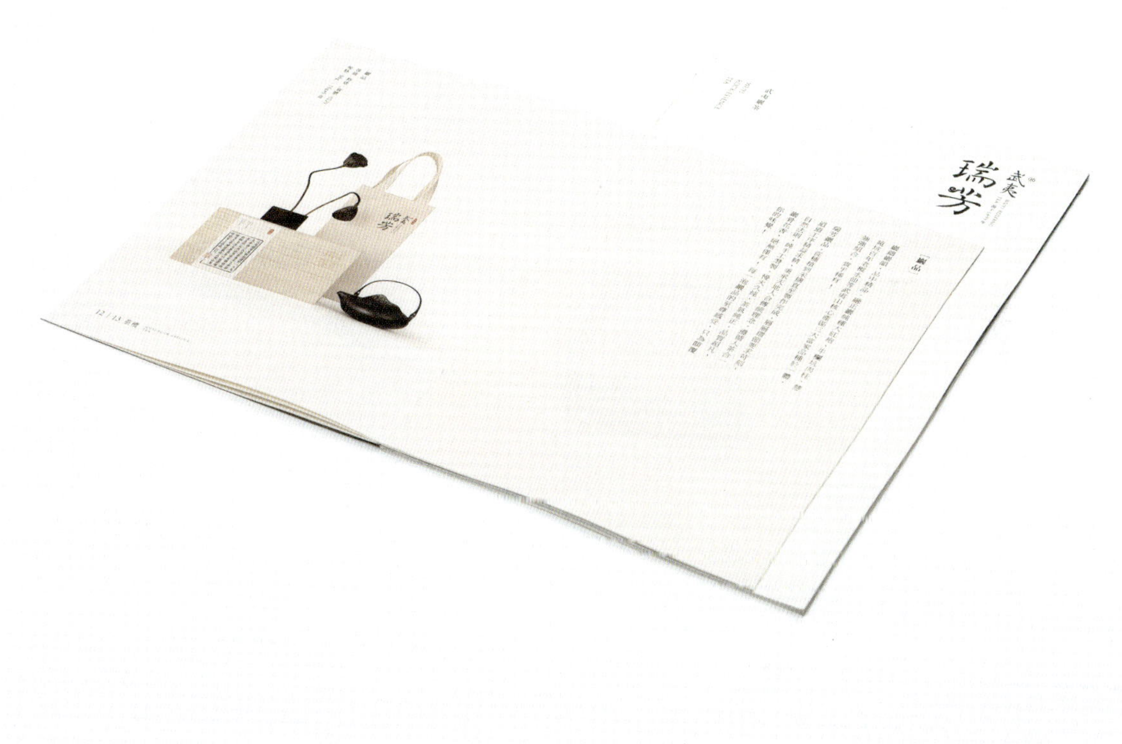

The brochure consists of two different sized parts. The small part introduces products of Wuyi Ruifang, while the bigger part tells Wuyi Ruifang's history, culture, tea hill, and the tea factory environment. The structure is derived from the ancient thread-bound format, yet combined with a modern layout design.

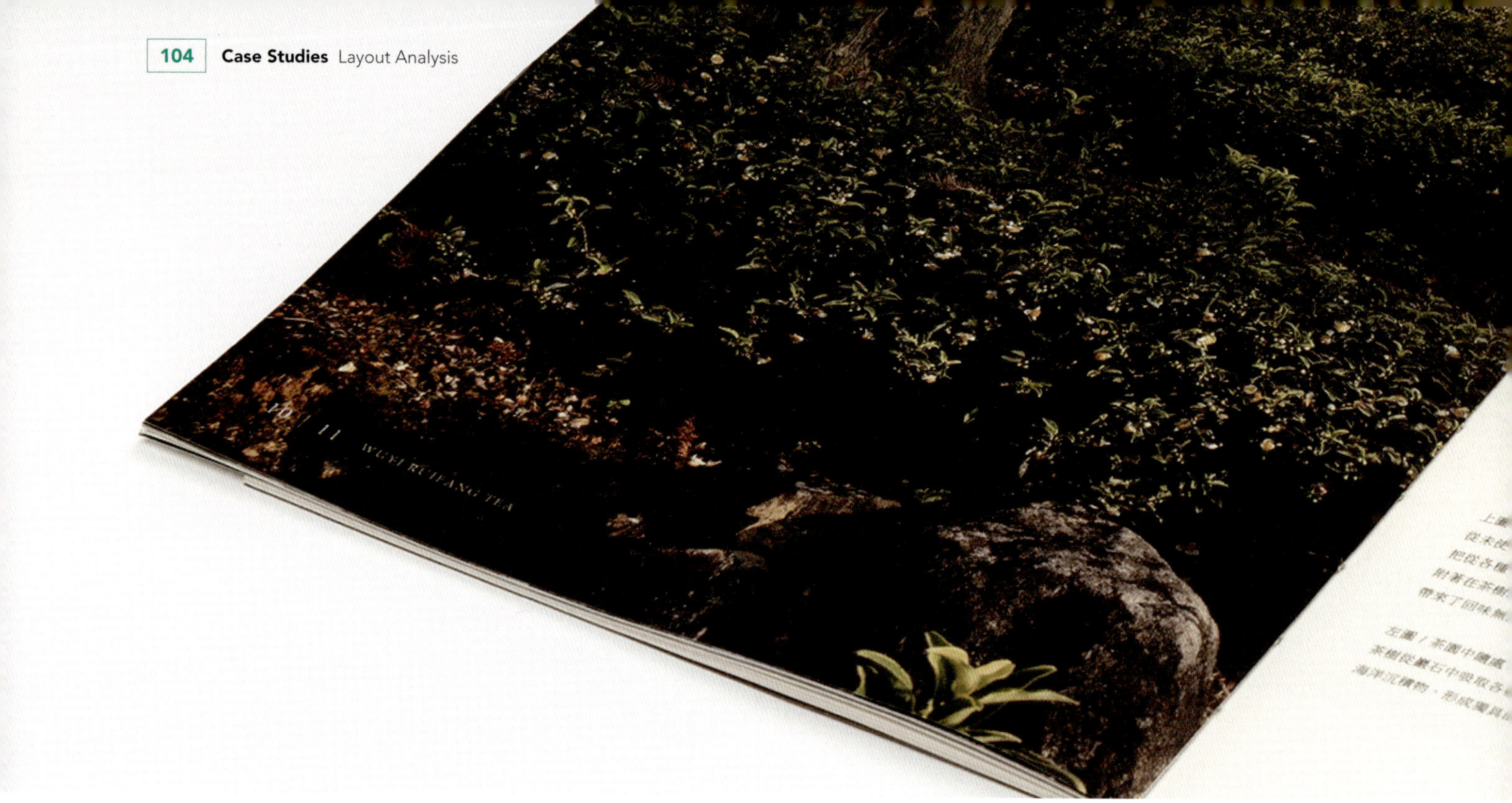

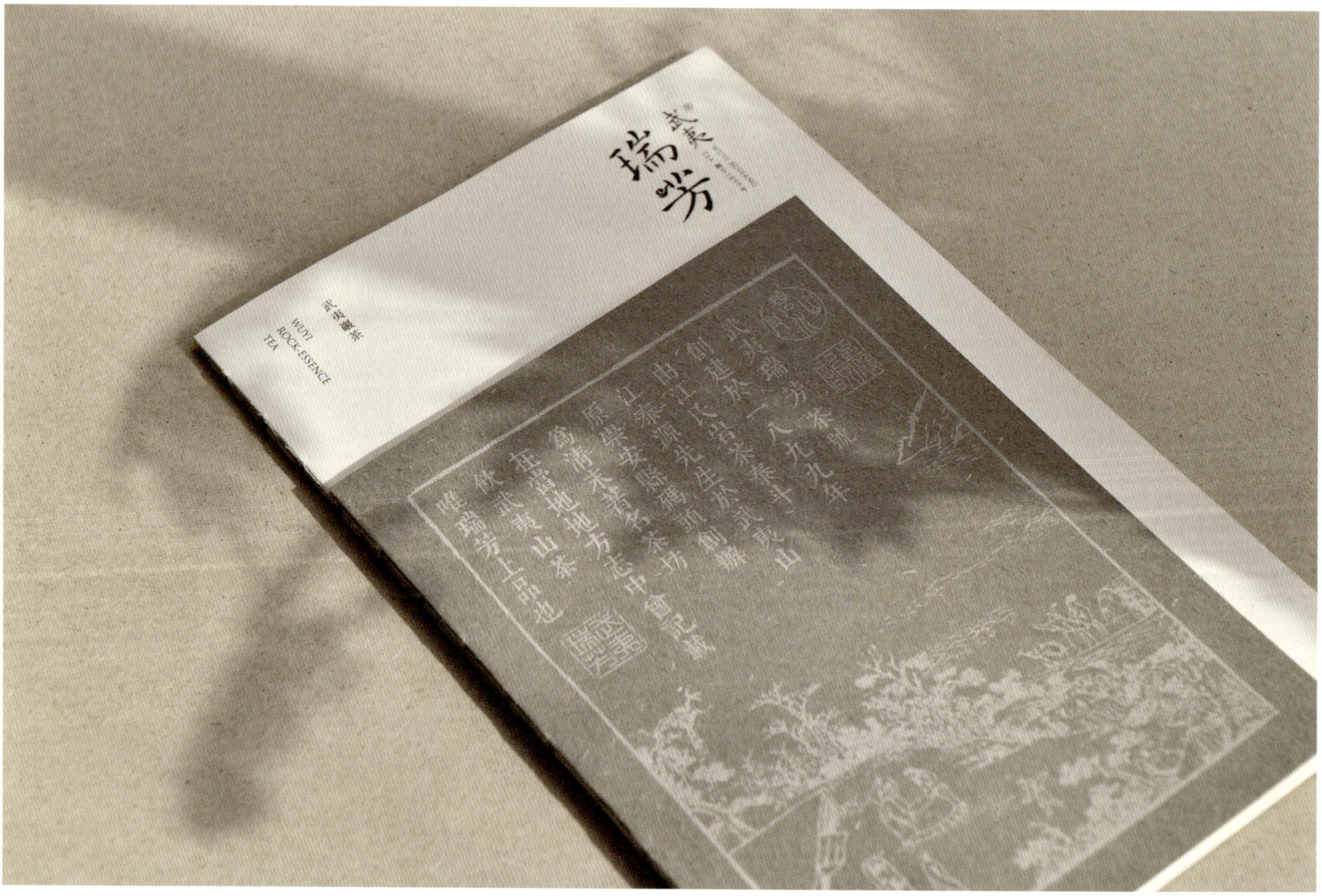

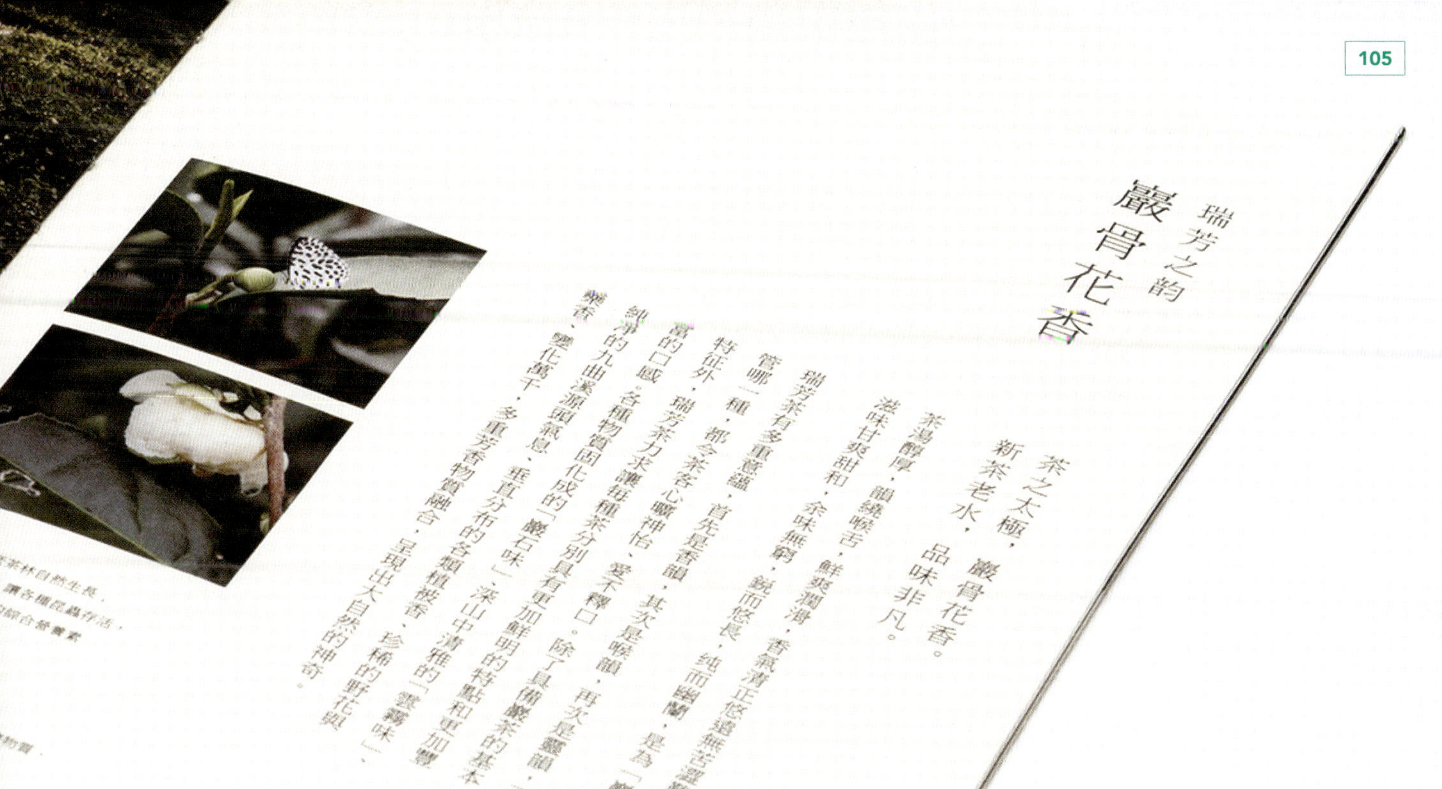
瑞芳之韵
巖骨花香
茶之太極，巖骨花香。
新茶老水，品味非凡。
茶湯醇厚，韻繞喉舌，鮮爽潤滑，香氣清正悠遠無苦澀難咽 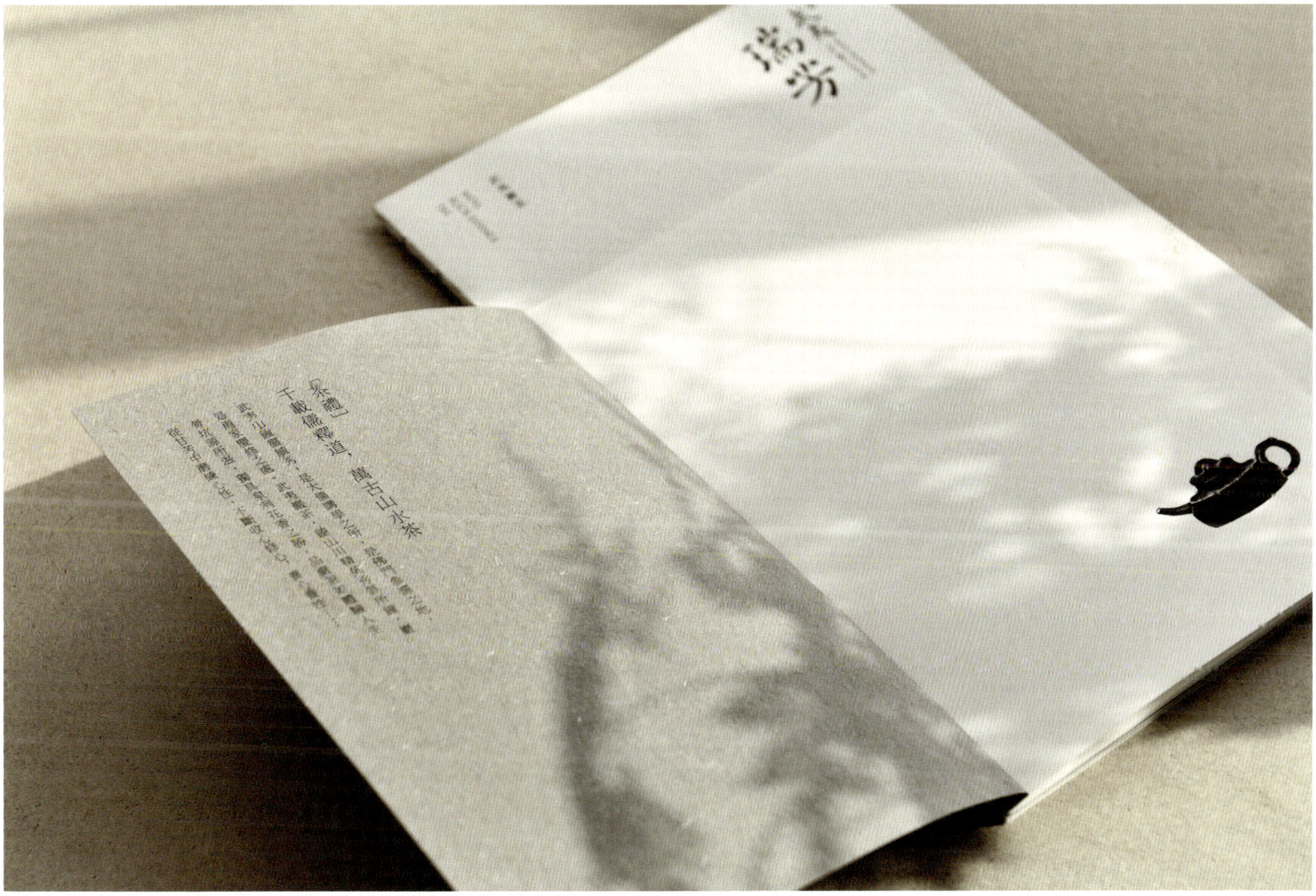
滋味甘爽甜和，余味無窮，銳而悠長，純而幽蘭，是為「巖韻
瑞芳茶有多重意蘊，首先是香韻，其次是喉韻，再次是靈韻，不
管哪一種，都令茶客心曠神怡，愛不釋口。除了具備巖茶的基本
特征外，瑞芳茶力求讓每種茶分別具有更加鮮明的特點和更加豐
富的口感。各種物質因化成的「巖石味」、深山中清雅的「雲霧味」、
純淨的九曲溪源頭氣息，垂直分布的各類植被香，珍稀的野花與
蘭香，變化萬千，多重芳香物質融合，呈現出大自然的神奇。

Healthy Noodle Brochure

Designer

Yu Shan Tsai

Client

Hua Yang Food Co., Ltd.

Key Diagram

Font	Paper	Size
Dejima Mincho	Coated paper	210×297mm (A4)

The serif font conveys a sense of serious and traditional, in line with the image of the time-honored brand.

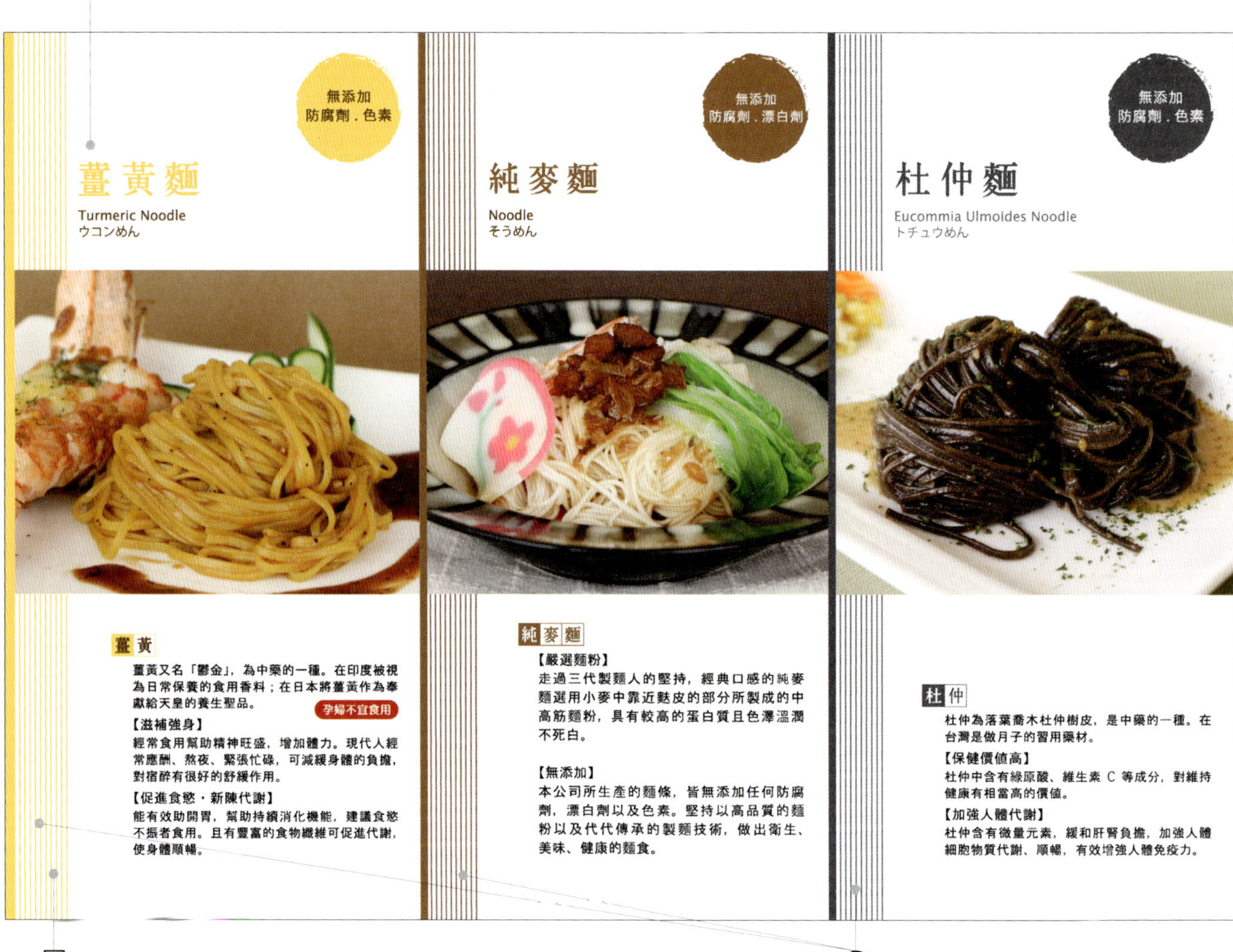

It is important to provide information clearly and correctly as in a commercial design. The layout concentrates on organizing information instead of design itself. Repetition is used to make the layouts neat and consistent with the brand image.

Four different colors represent four different flavors of noodles, and the color should be related to the product photo.

Grid

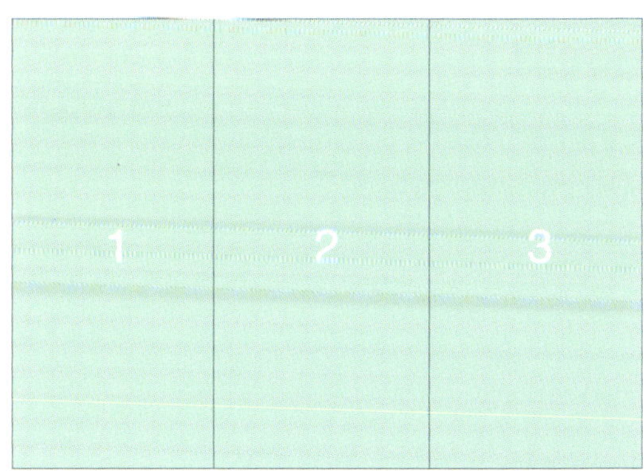

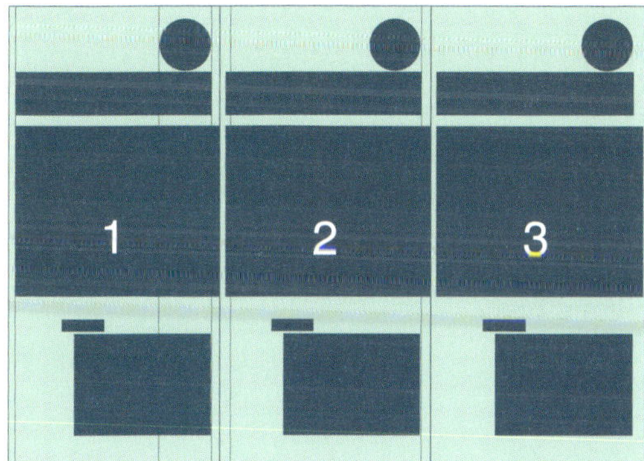

Visual Flow

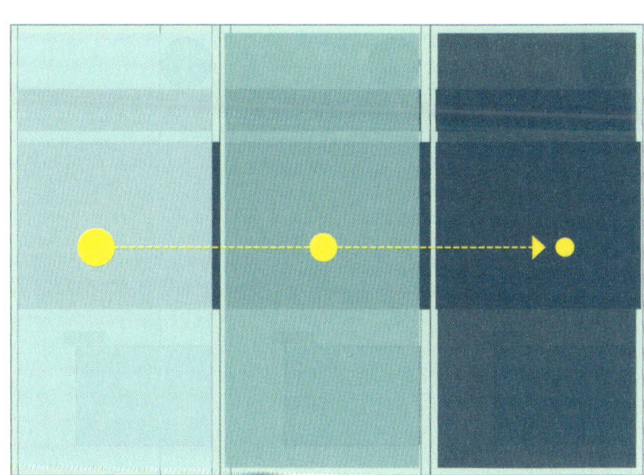

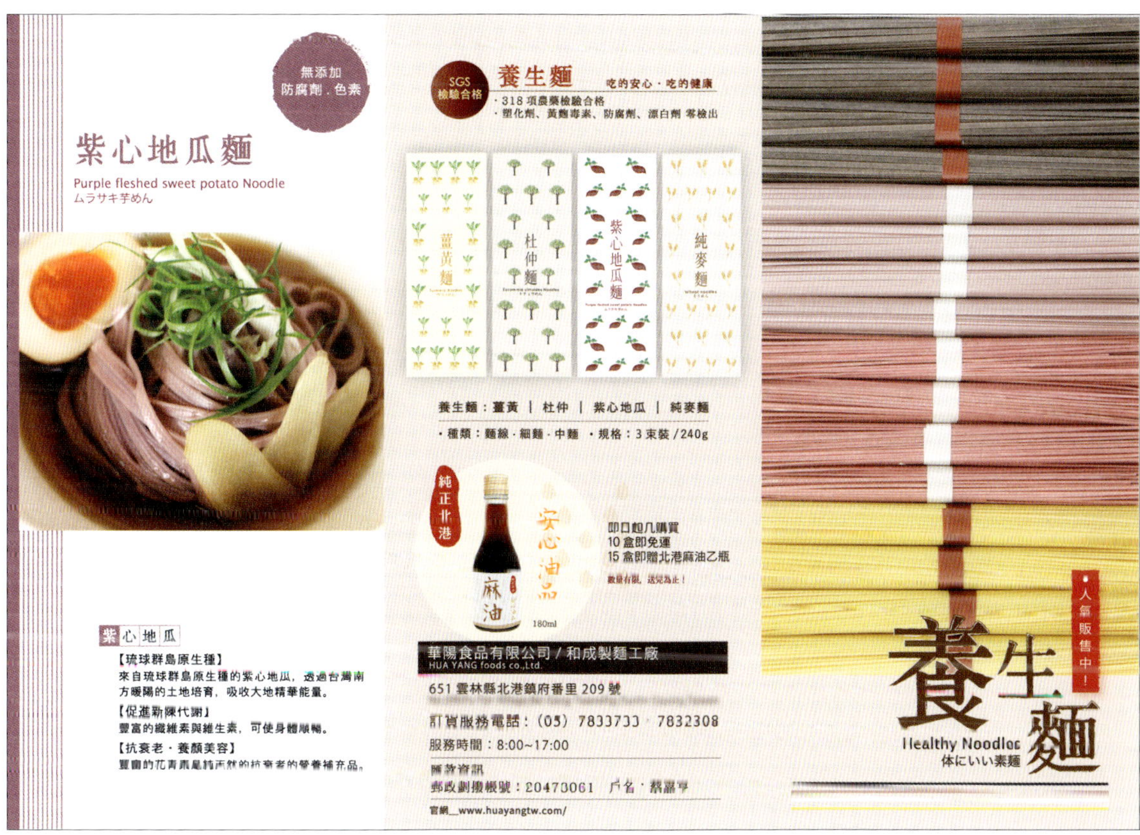

Healthy noodles are the main product of Hua Yang Food Co., Ltd., and the four flavors are distinguished by four colors. When designing the brochure, the designer used the colors of the noodles—yellow, brown, black, and purple as the main color on each page. In order to highlight the delicious taste of the noodles, the featured pictures show the four types of noodle cooked and nicely prepared.

Wormwood Powder Promotional Materials

Designer

Yu-Jhen Lai

Client

Tea Power Company Limited

Key Diagram

Font	Paper	Size
DFLiSong-Md DFLiHei-Lt	250g Ivory paperboard	148×105mm

The use of serif font highlights the elegant design and conforms to the brand image.

自然力 Nature Power 漢方艾草靜心粉 20入（加附棉袋10個）

優質艾草粉・舒心好生活

「艾葉」經過曬乾後再加以搗樁，篩去雜質呈柔軟如絨的纖維，稱為「艾絨」，點燃後散發艾草香息，可驅除蚊蟲蟑螂跳蚤等害蟲，並淨化空氣、平靜思緒、舒暢心靈，持續為您帶來一整天的舒適生活。

100%天然艾草粉　篩去雜質，質地細緻柔軟

天然驅蟲，淨化環境　清新香息，開運靜心

使用方式 ※點燃時請小心使用，遠離易燃物及置於孩童不易取得處。

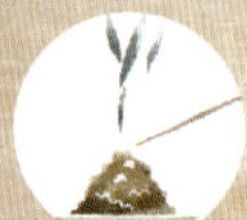

淨化環境

每日10分鐘，取適量（約半包至一包）艾絨倒入陶瓷器皿中，直接點燃淨化空氣。

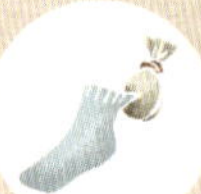

除臭驅味

1.放於襪內，可避免腳汗之異味。
2.放置於衣、鞋櫃消除異味。

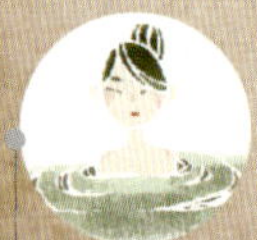

泡澡淨身

取適量裝入棉袋，放入浴缸後浸泡使用。（請勿直接倒入浴缸）

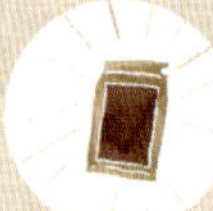

除穢開運

隨身攜帶，或誠心置放於書房、供桌、床頭、玄關。

Designers are accustomed to using "highlight the key information" as a principle for layout design to introduce the features of the product in promotional materials. Customers will not spend much time focusing on reading a massive content brochure in today's busy life; therefore, the key to make commercial design successful is to create an effective clear layout design that can deepen the image of the brand.

The main color in the layout is brown, which is reminiscent of the color of the wooden tea set and the wormwood tea powder. The rustic color scheme also echoes the brand's main feature: "use of Chinese traditional medicines".

Grid

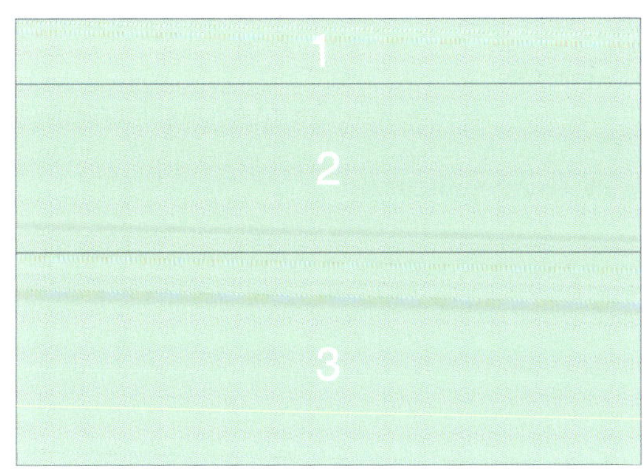

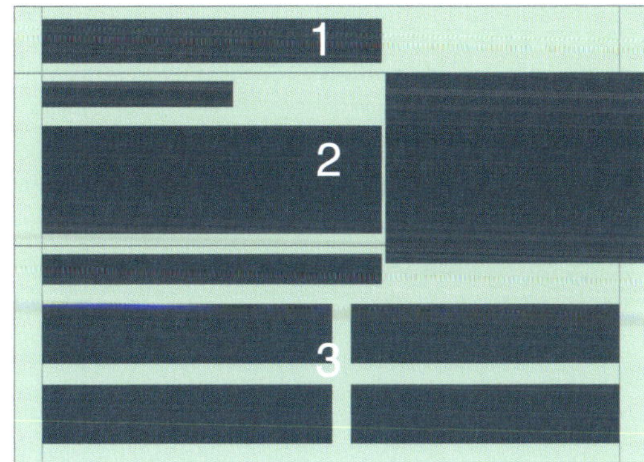

Visual Flow

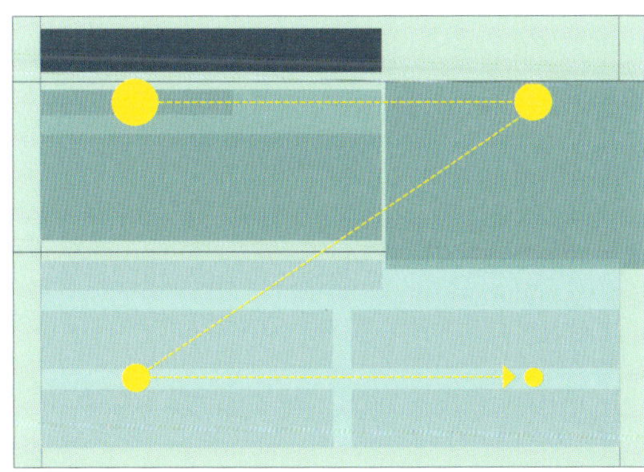

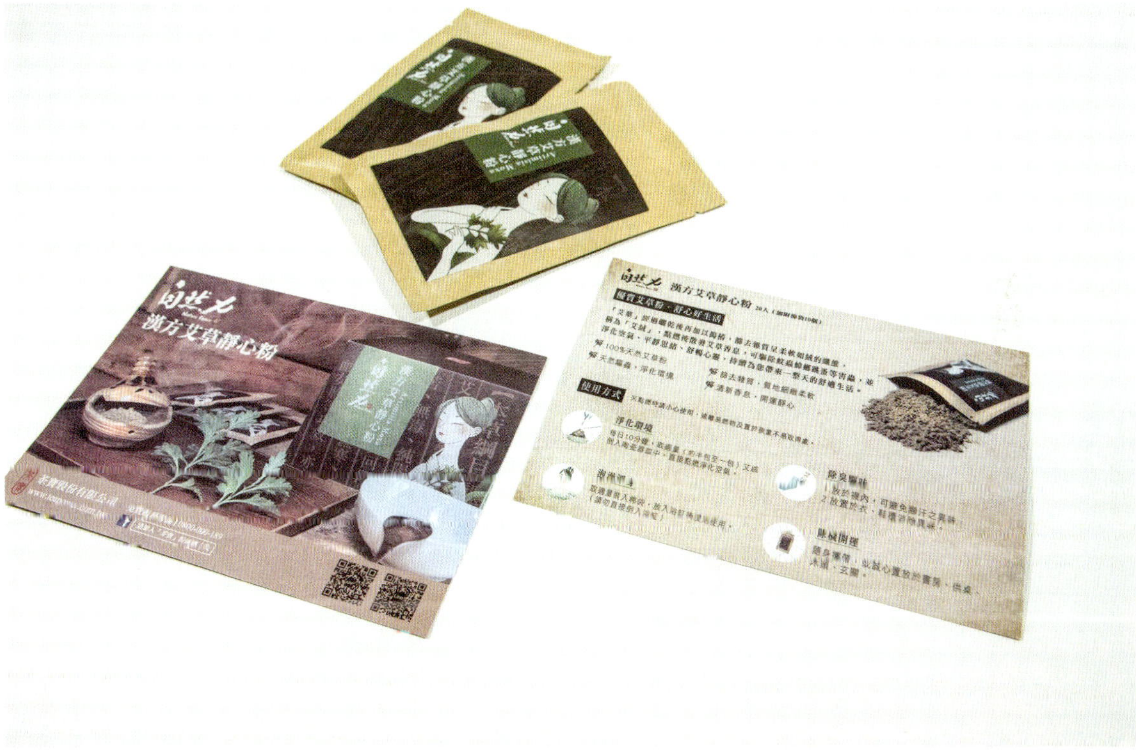

The design of this brochure uses key descriptions with some illustration to briefly introduce the use of wormwood powder and its features. The design takes advantage in using the characteristics of different typefaces to convey the visual relationship between title and text, which lets consumers read in a comfortable way.

Cool Wind Natural Mineral Water Brochure

Designer	**Client**
G.H.Leong	**Top Valley Organic Food**

Key Diagram

Font	Paper	Size
STSong, SimHei	200g Specialty paper 120g Offset paper	200×270mm

The font STSong/SimHei is upright, graceful, and dynamic.

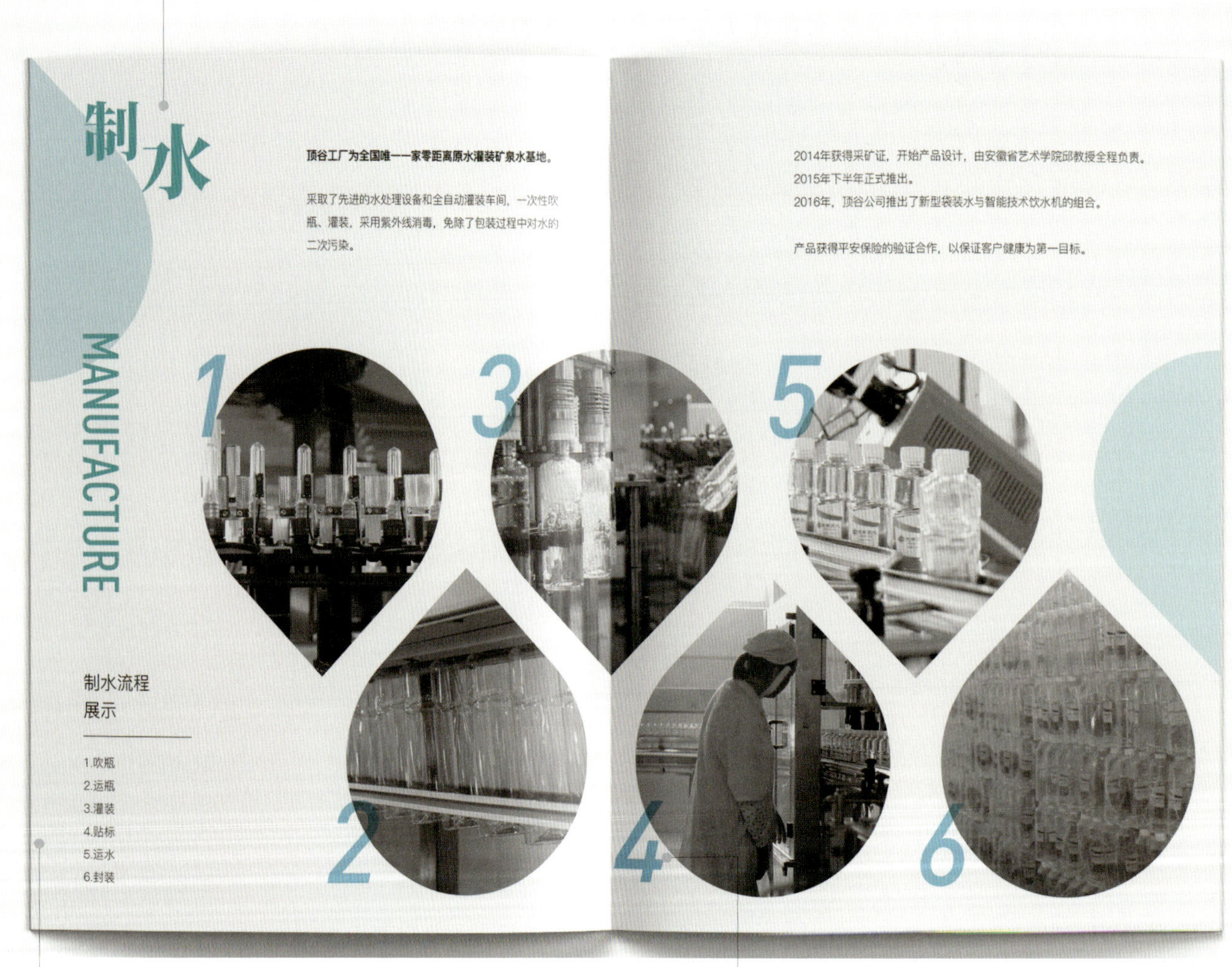

The designer reduces the number of words, but uses graphics of water drop shapes to show the production process. The special design makes reading not so boring. In addition, white space is used to create cool and refreshing feelings.

Blue and white colors highlight the purity of the products. Blue is also the product image color, so using it often can leave a deep impression on consumers.

Grid

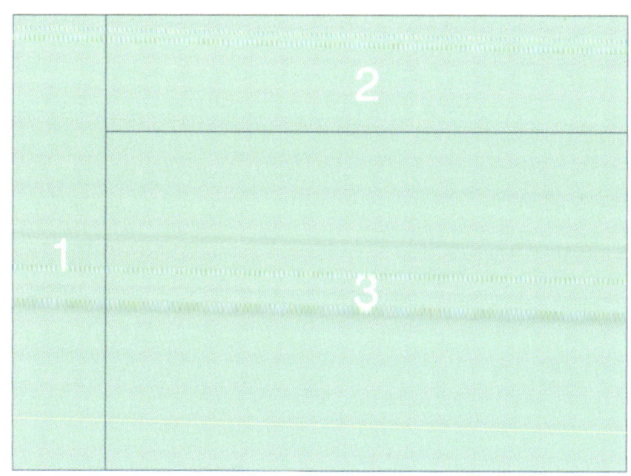

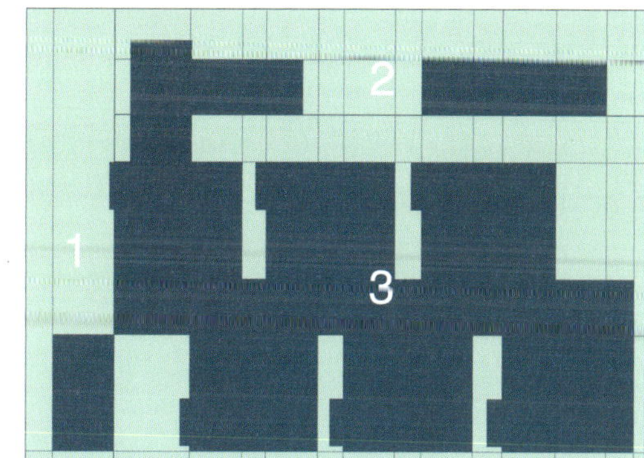

Visual Flow

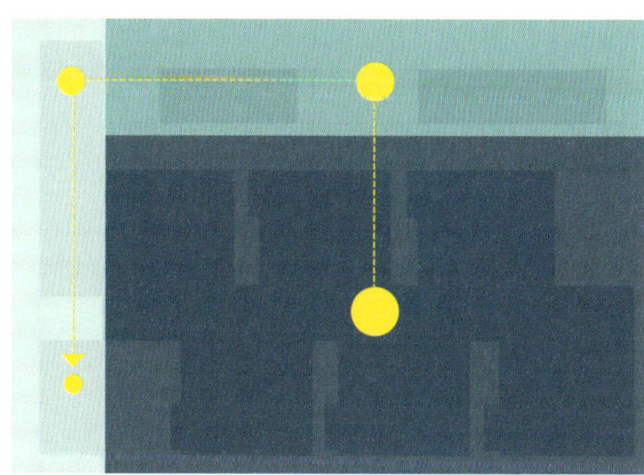

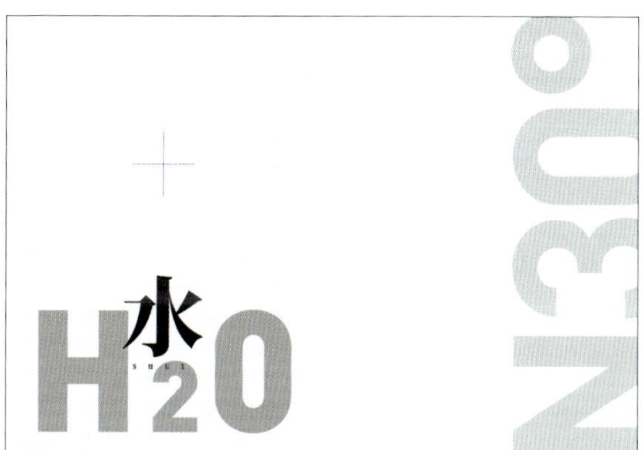

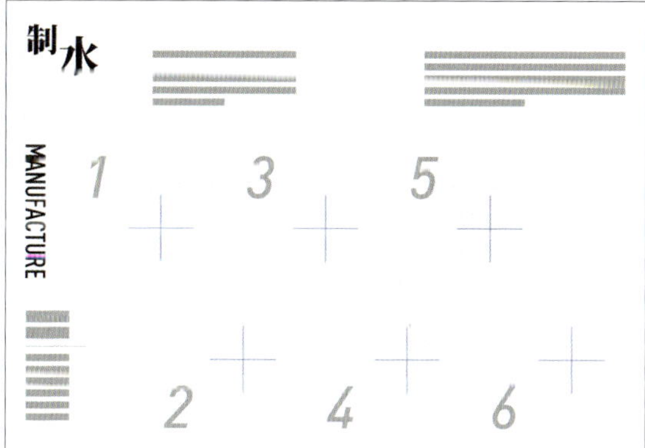

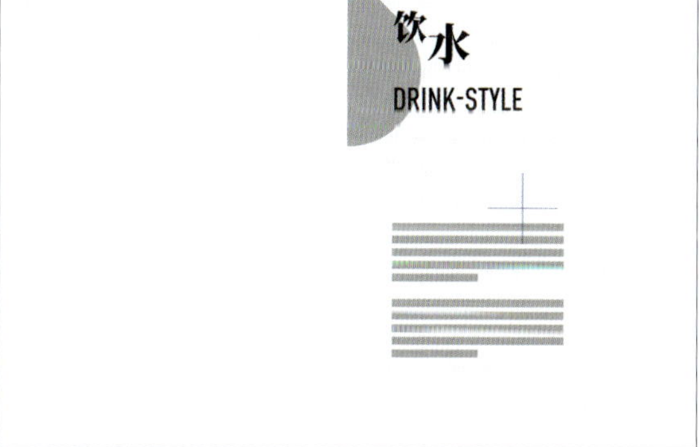

Cool Wind natural mineral water is a high quality mineral water brand whose products meet the national standard. Its natural mineral water is clean, transparent, delicious, and rich in minerals and trace elements for the human body. The brochure revolves around the core element , water, and impresses people with its pure and natural imagery.

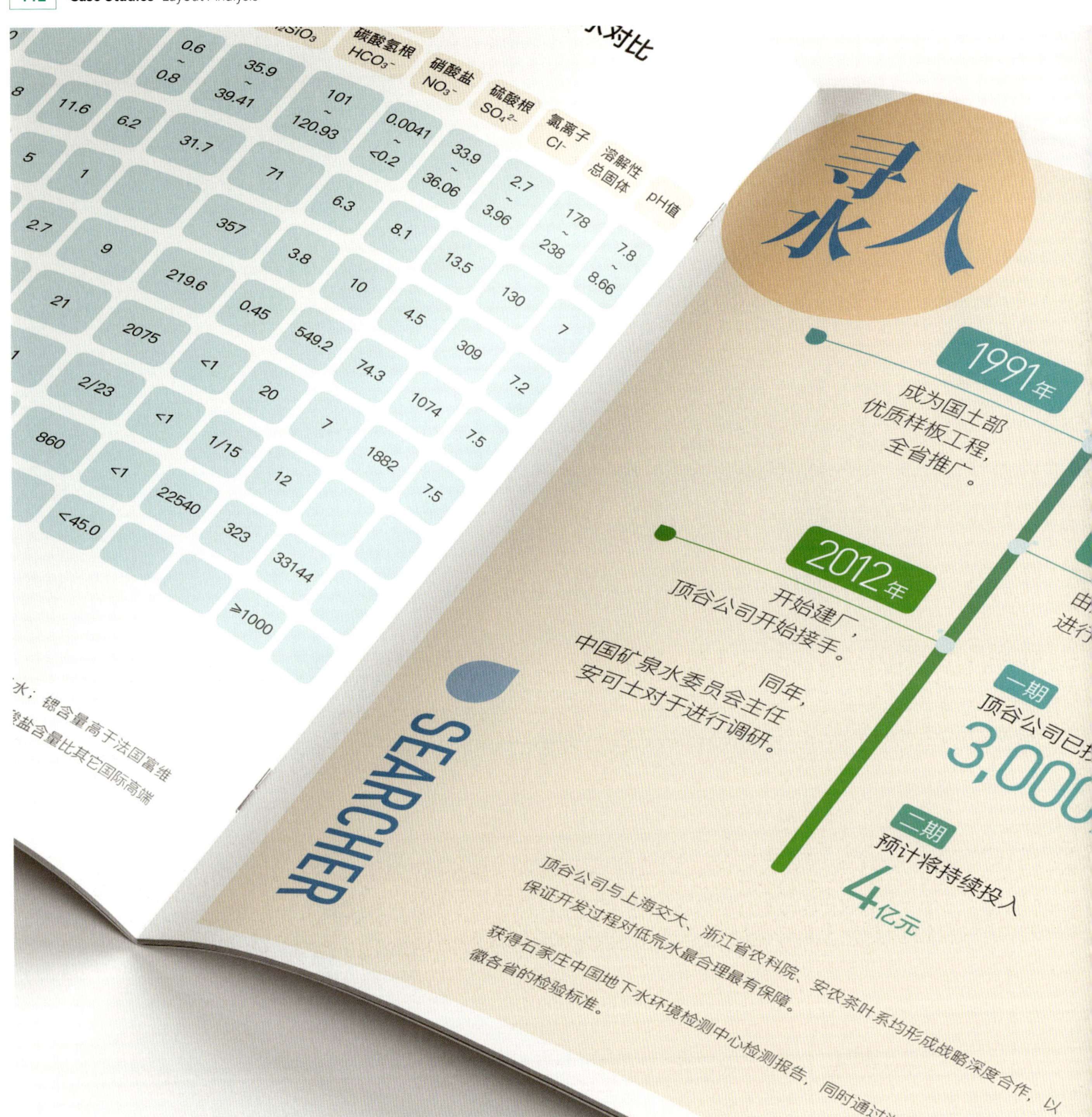
寻水人
SEARCHER
1991年
成为国土部
优质样板工程，
全省推广。
2012年
开始建厂，
顶谷公司开始接手。
同年，
中国矿泉水委员会主任
安可士对于进行调研。
一期
二期
预计将持续投入
4亿元
顶谷公司与上海交大、浙江省农科院、安农茶叶系均形成战略深度合作，以
保证开发过程对低氘水最合理最有保障。
获得石家庄中国地下水环境检测中心检测报告，同时通过浙
徽各省的检验标准。
碳酸氢根
HCO_3^-
硝酸盐
NO_3^-
硫酸根
SO_4^{2-}
氯离子
Cl^-
溶解性
总固体
pH值

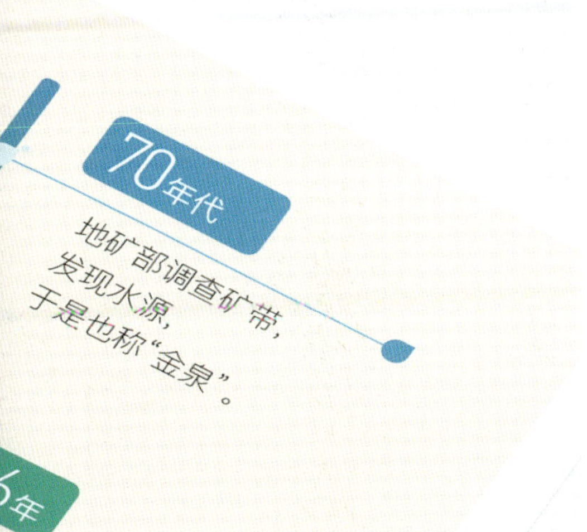
70年代
地矿部调查矿带，
发现水源，
于是也称“金泉”。

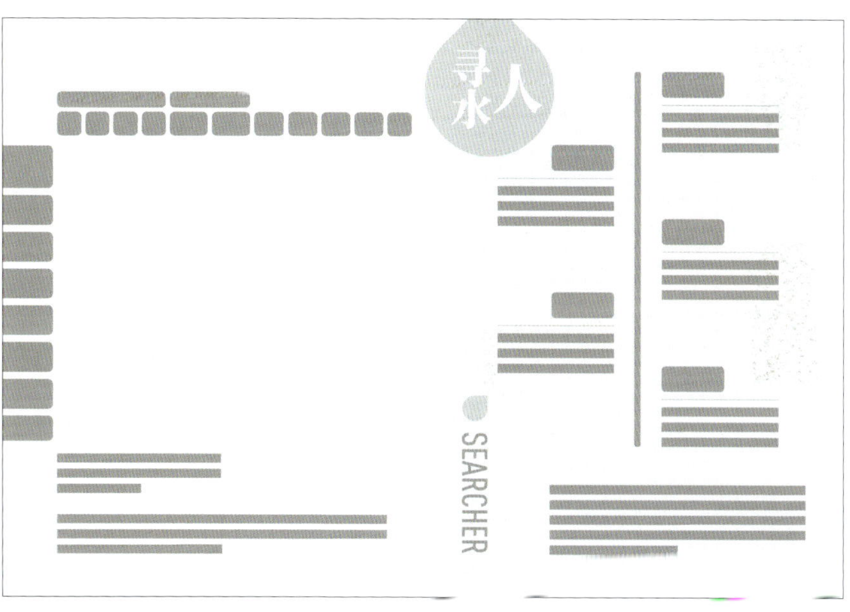
寻水人
SEARCHER

PENG PAI Marimba Concert

Designer

Studio Pros

Client

Ju Percussion Group

Key Diagram

Font

Noto DemiLight (Chinese)
DIN Medium (English)

Paper

Poster paper

Size

594x841mm (A1)

The style of the calligraphy for the headline is suitable with this emotional performance. Besides, the serif fonts for both English and Chinese represent the exquisiteness of the performance.

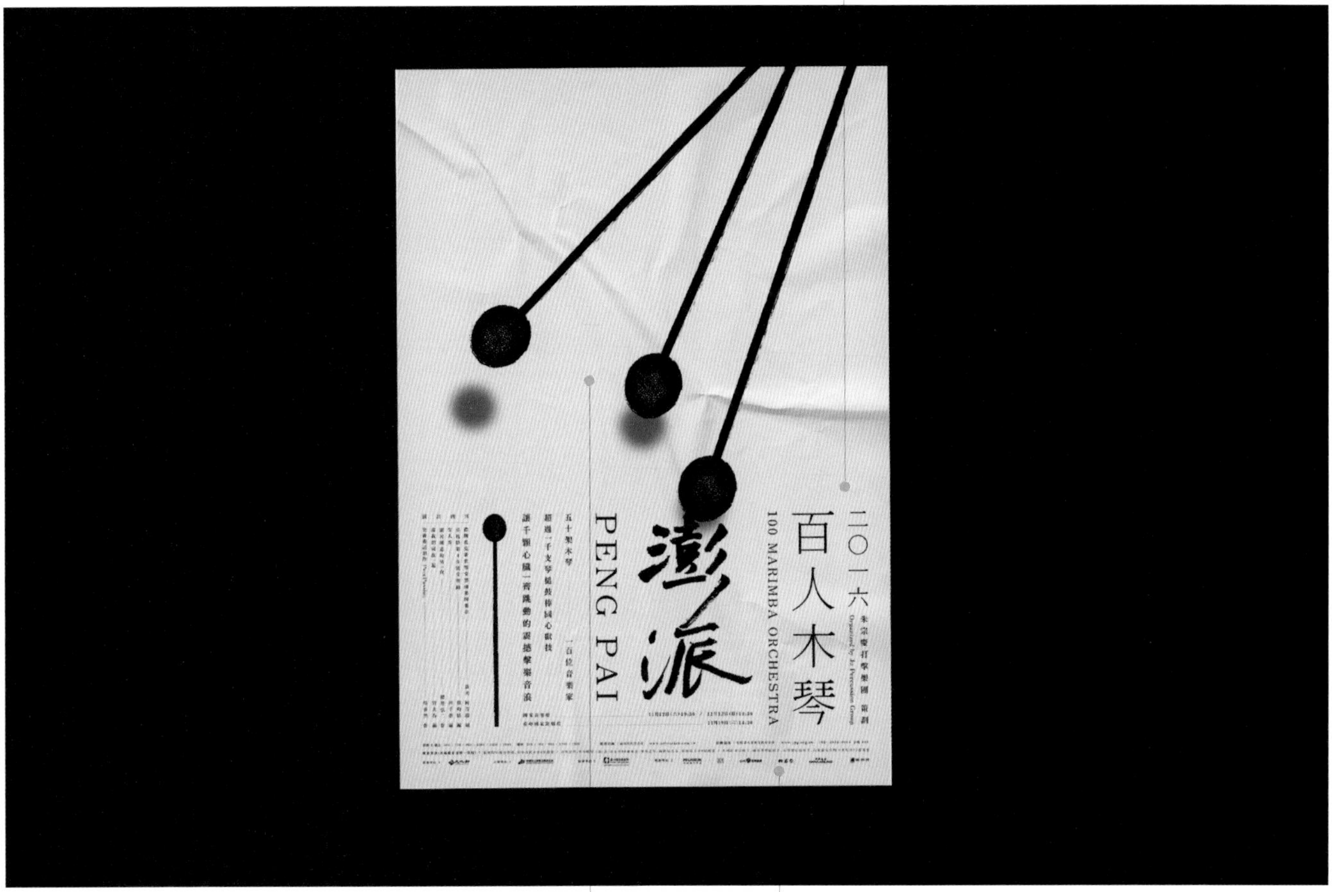

The visual flow starts from the graphic of a musical instrument, then the calligraphic title, and then to the main body text, leading the views step-by-step into the visual. In addition, a subtle contrast is made between the dynamics in the graphics and the neatly arranged typography.

White represents quiet, black contains unknown power. The designer wants to express an idea in these two different colors that the brilliant percussion performance will be peaceful instead of noisy.

Grid

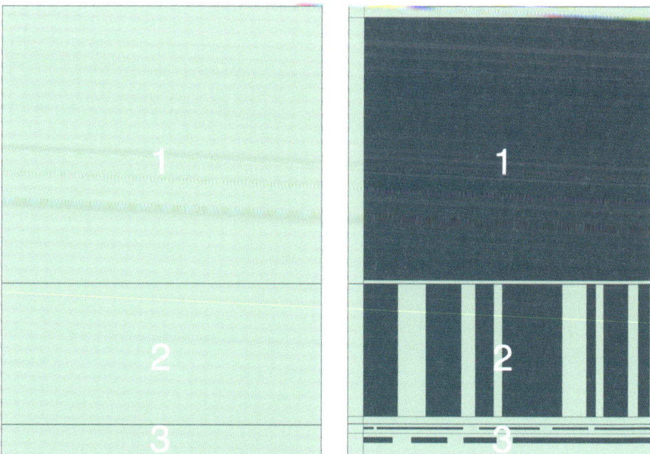

Visual Flow

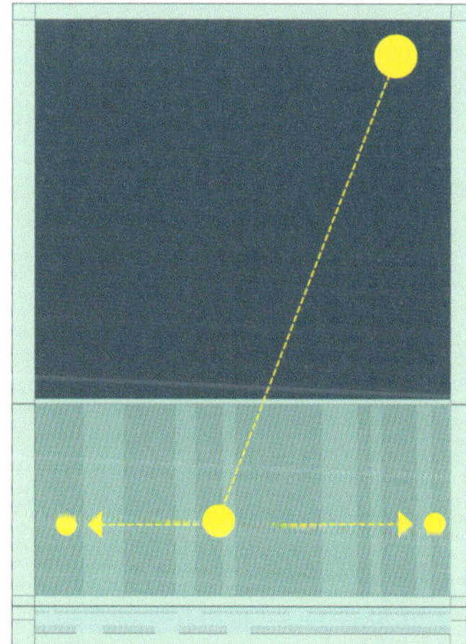

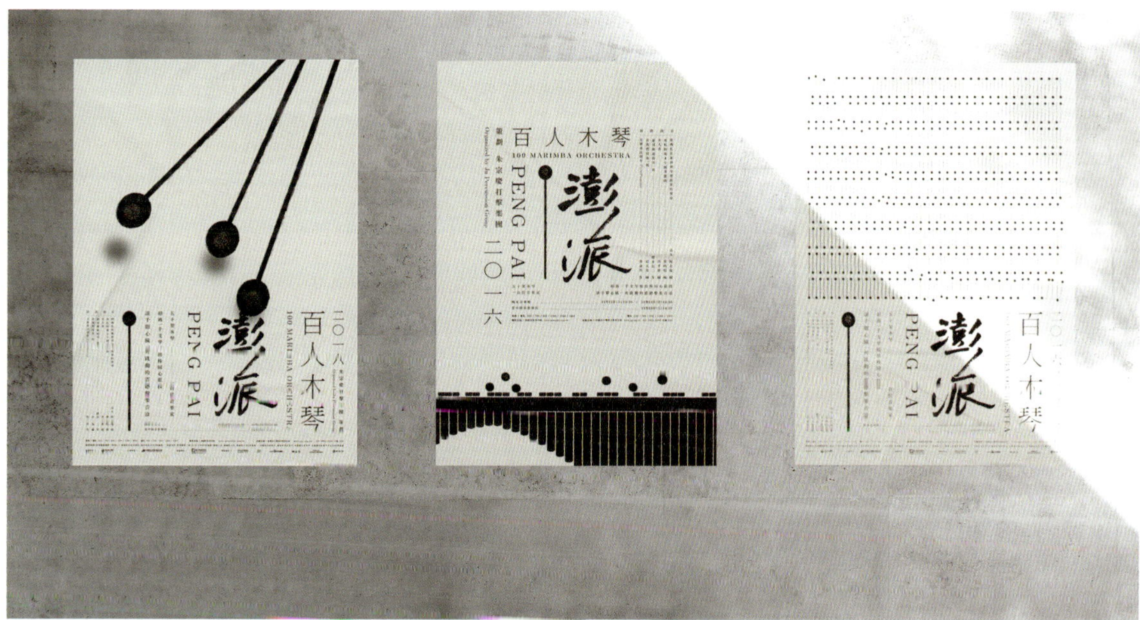

PENG PAI is a chamber concert organized by Ju Percussion Group which is combined of more than 100 marimba players. To portray the beauty of marimba, the designers emphasize the shape and structure of this graceful musical instrument for its promotional materials. Moreover, the design is based on an important concept that is "a successful percussion performance is peaceful", so the designers try to create a quiet atmosphere in the work. Although there are lots of details, people still can feel calm when they look at these posters.

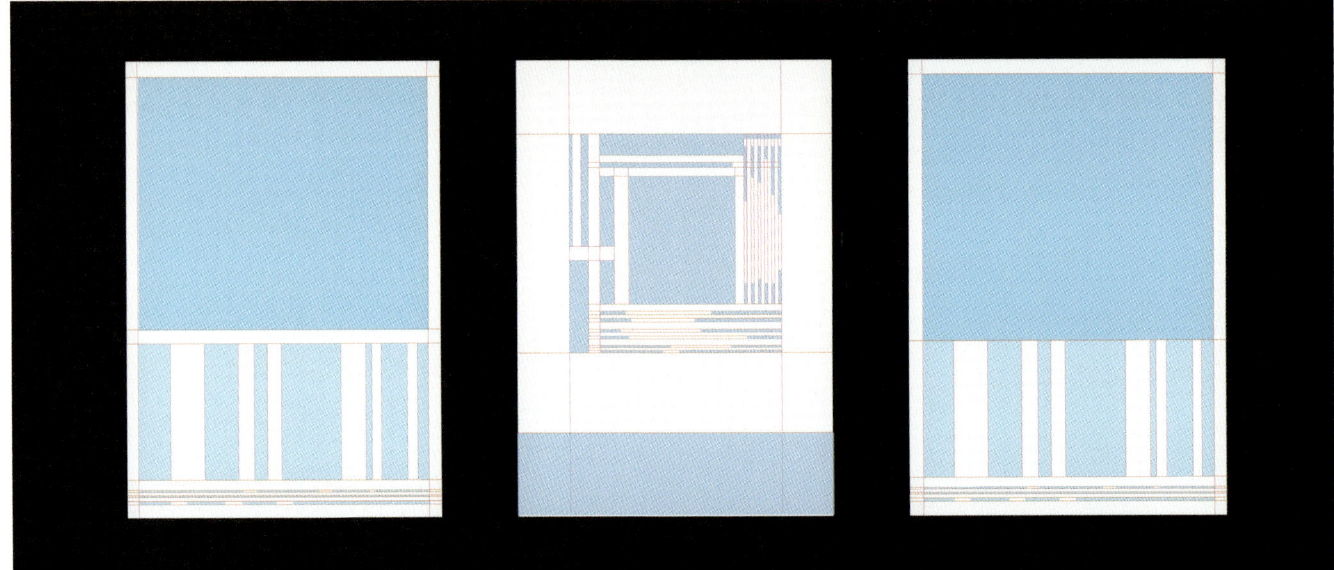

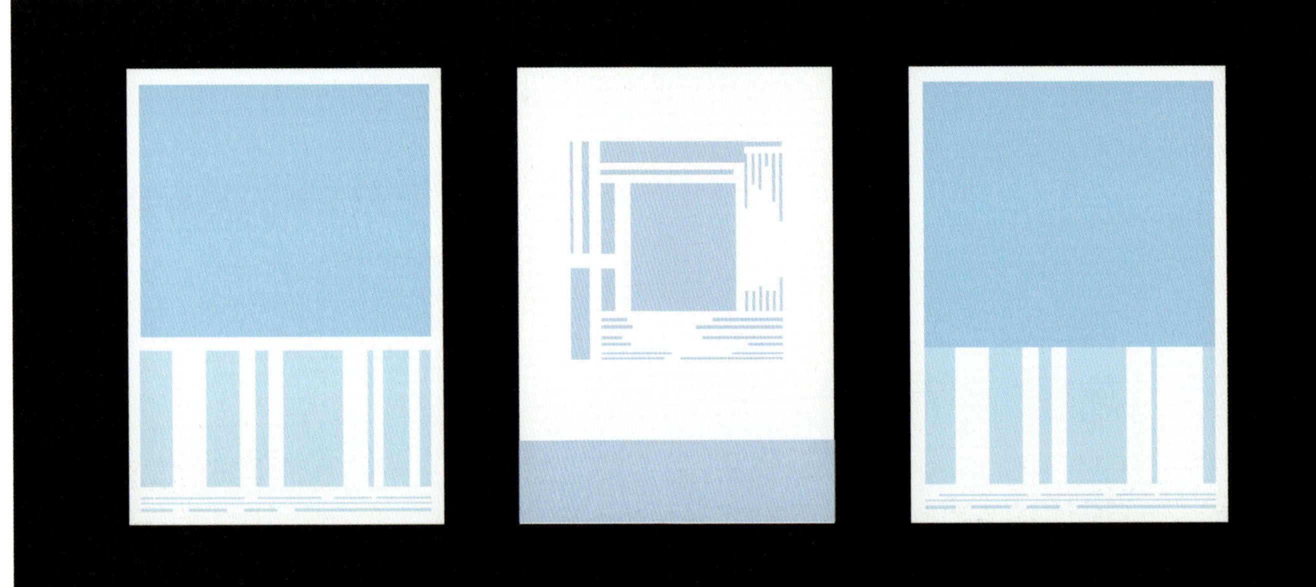

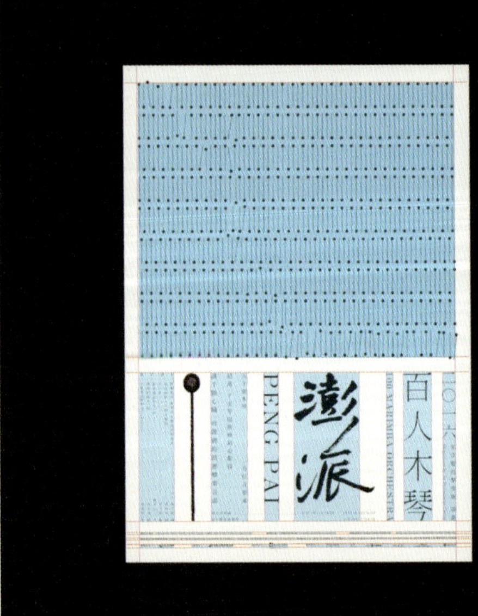
PENG PAI
澎湃
百人木琴
100 MARIMBA ORCHESTRA

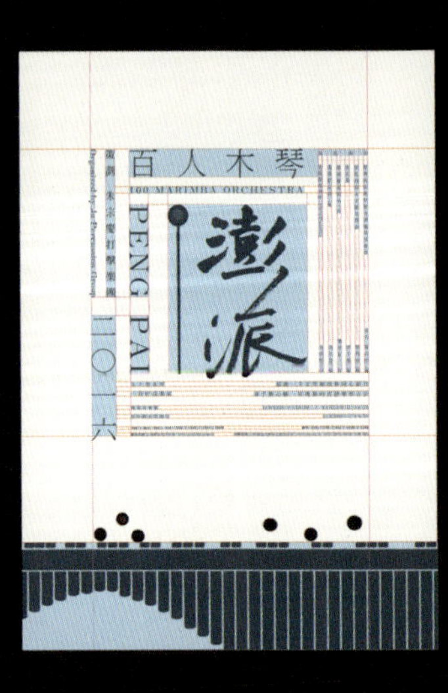
百人木琴
100 MARIMBA ORCHESTRA
PENG PAI
澎湃

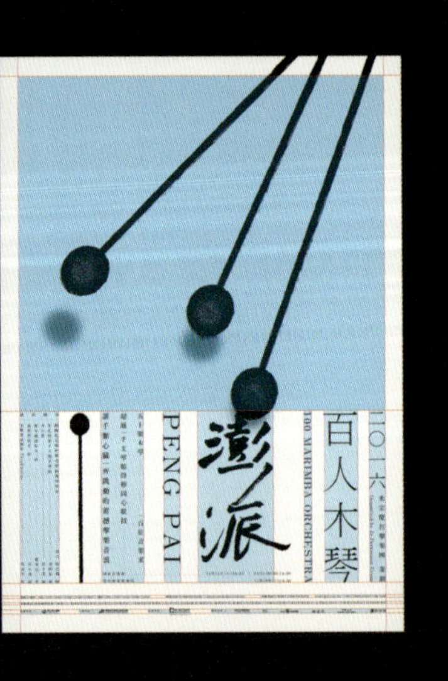
PENG PAI
澎湃
100 MARIMBA ORCHESTRA
百人木琴

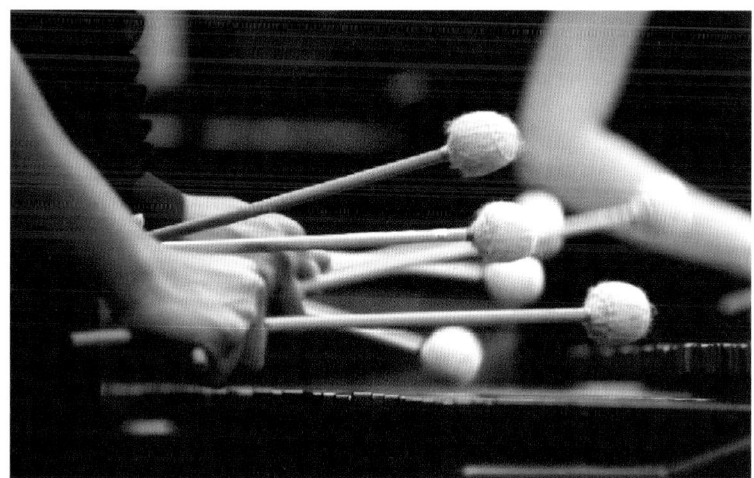

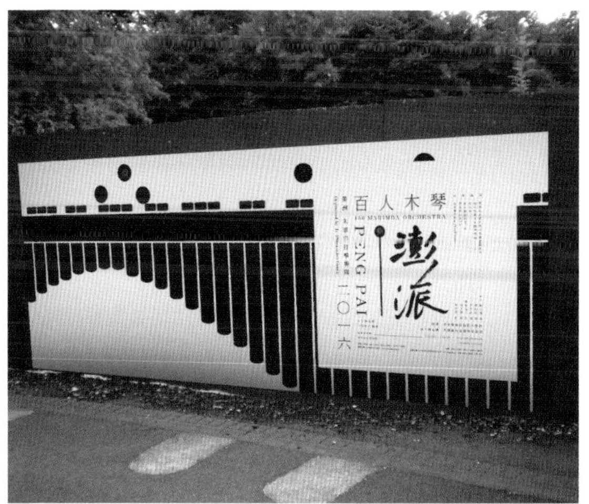

百人木琴
100 MARIMBA ORCHESTRA
PENG PAI
澎湃
二〇一六

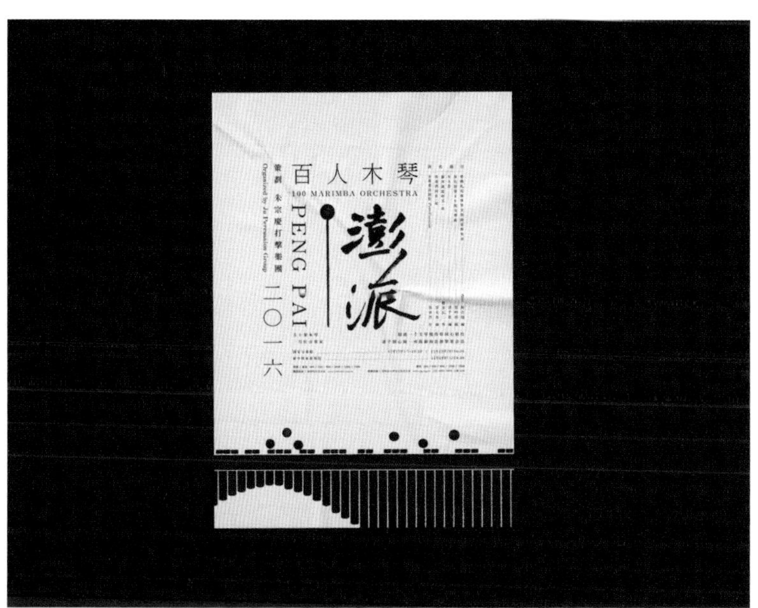

百人木琴
100 MARIMBA ORCHESTRA
策劃 朱宗慶打擊樂團
Organized by Ju Percussion Group
PENG PAI
澎湃
二〇一六

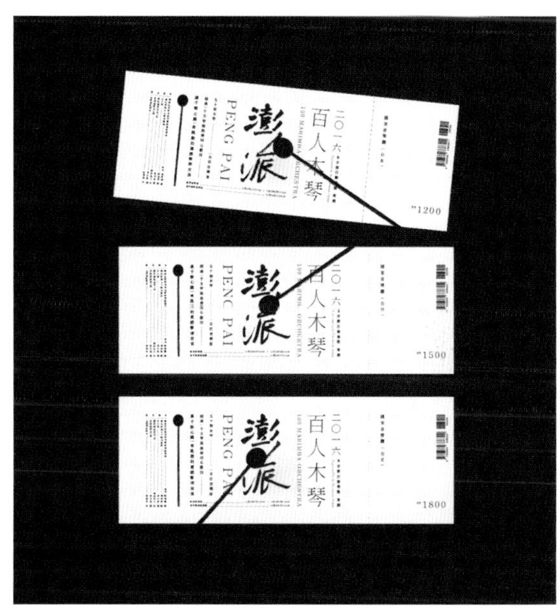

二〇一六
百人木琴
100 MARIMBA ORCHESTRA
PENG PAI
澎湃
1200
1500
1800

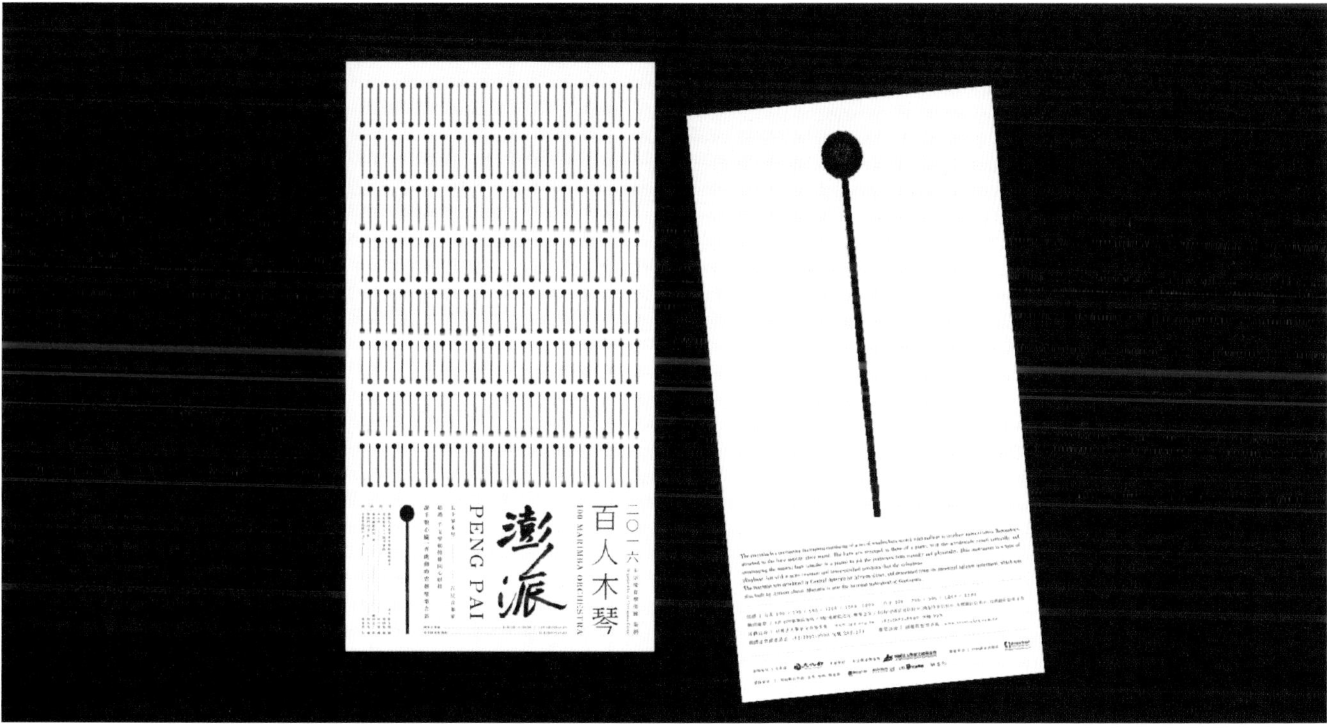

二〇一六
百人木琴
100 MARIMBA ORCHESTRA
PENG PAI
澎湃

Hunting and Nature Museum of Paris Promotion Poster

Designer

DES SIGNES

Client

Musee de la Chasse et de la Nature de Paris

Key Diagram

Font	Paper	Size
Unknown	Poster paper	210×297mm (A4)

This series of posters are all in a serif font, reflecting the feeling of calmness and technology, echoing the theme of exploring nature. Through the comparison of font sizes, it enriches the sense of layers.

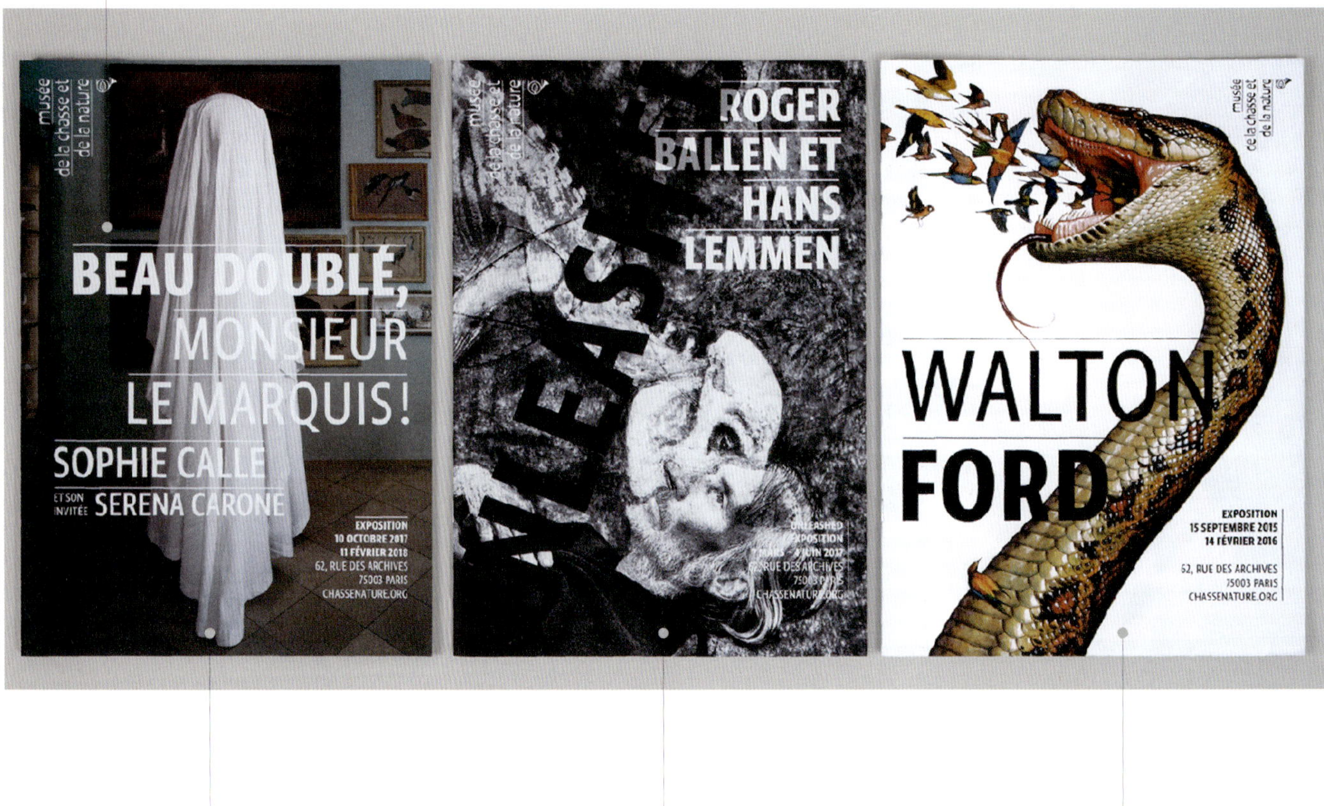

The text and layout are centered, giving people a sense of stability and balance.

The main characters of the poster are at an oblique angle, plus an oblique heading, which can attract the attention of the audience.

The large area of negative space highlights the main body of the poster. The swing of the snake, the flying of the birds, and the fixed title text produce a strong contrast between movement and static, which is impressive.

Grid

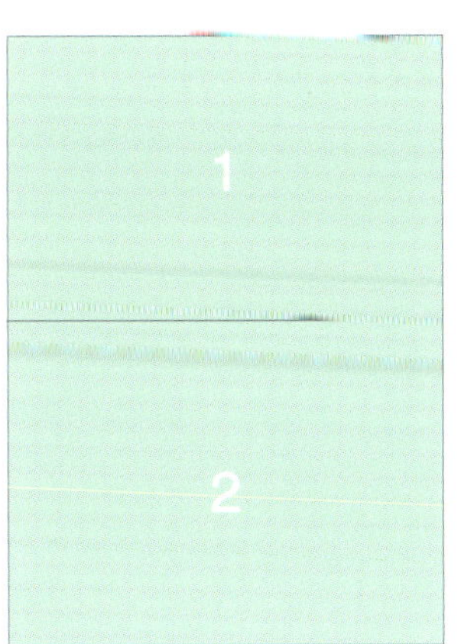

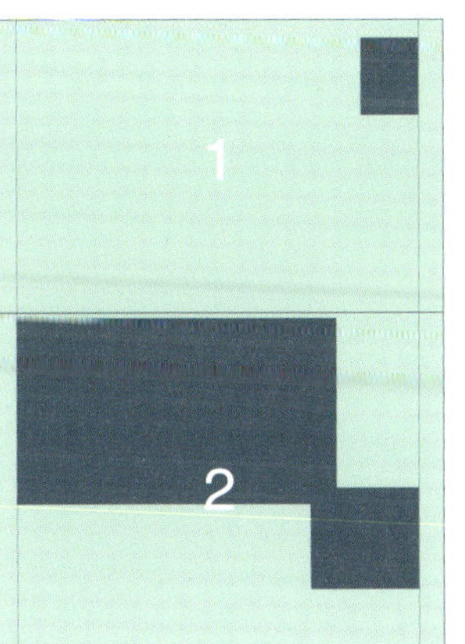

Visual Flow

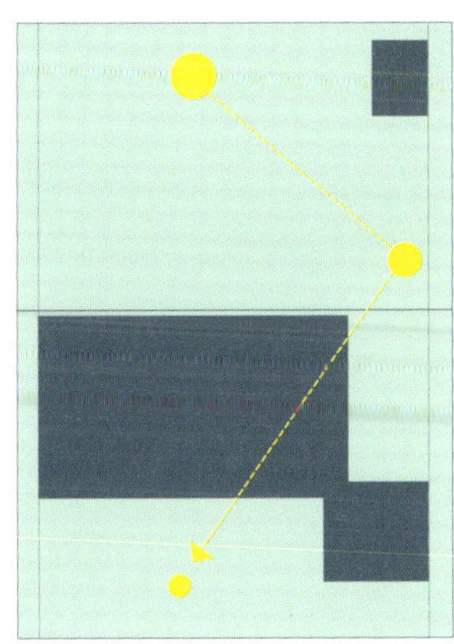

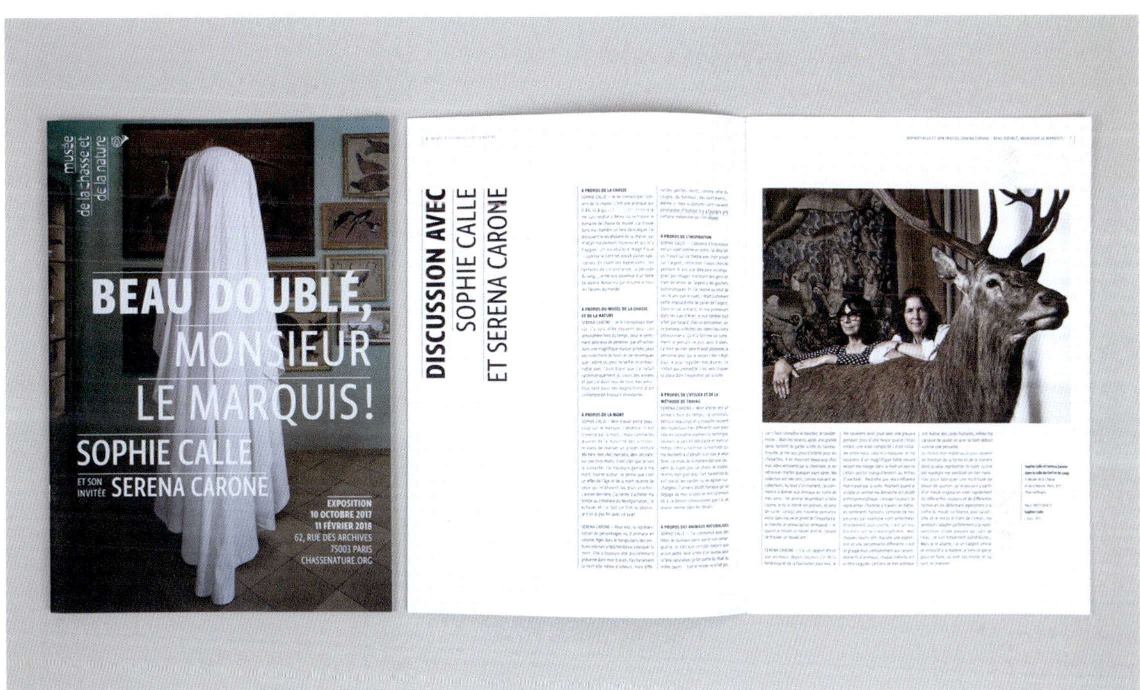

Program for the different exhibitions of the Musee de la Chasse et de la Nature de Paris (Museum of Hunting and Nature of Paris).

Kunihiro Suzuki Solo Exhibition Poster

Designer

Kunihiro Suzuki

Key Diagram

Font

Morisawa, Charcoal, Helvetica, Times

Paper

Matt coated paper
Araver paper

Size

100×148mm
210×297mm (A4)
210×148mm

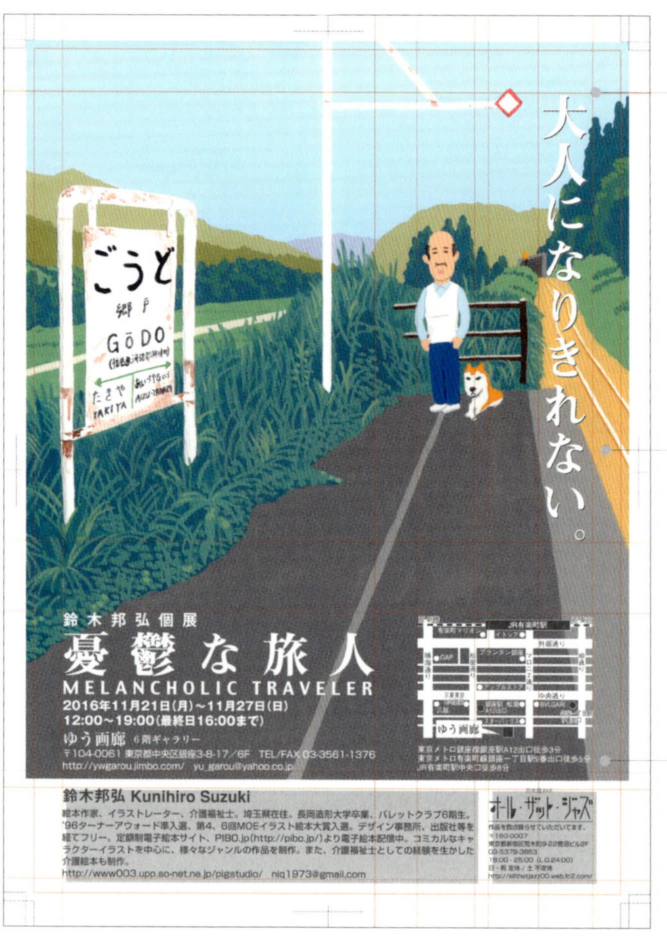

Four fonts are used to highlight different information in the layout. The time, location, and information of the exhibition are applied with sans serif to contrast with the title in serif.

In order to highlight the painting, the text is all in black and white.

The text is basically placed in the lower part of the layout, which gathers and integrates effective information so that the audience will have interest in the painting first, and then browse the exhibition information.

Grid

Visual Flow

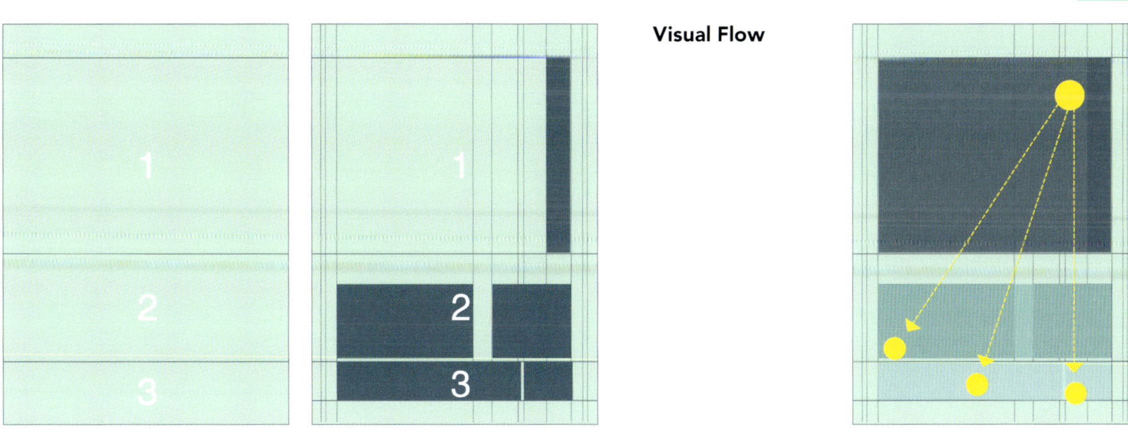

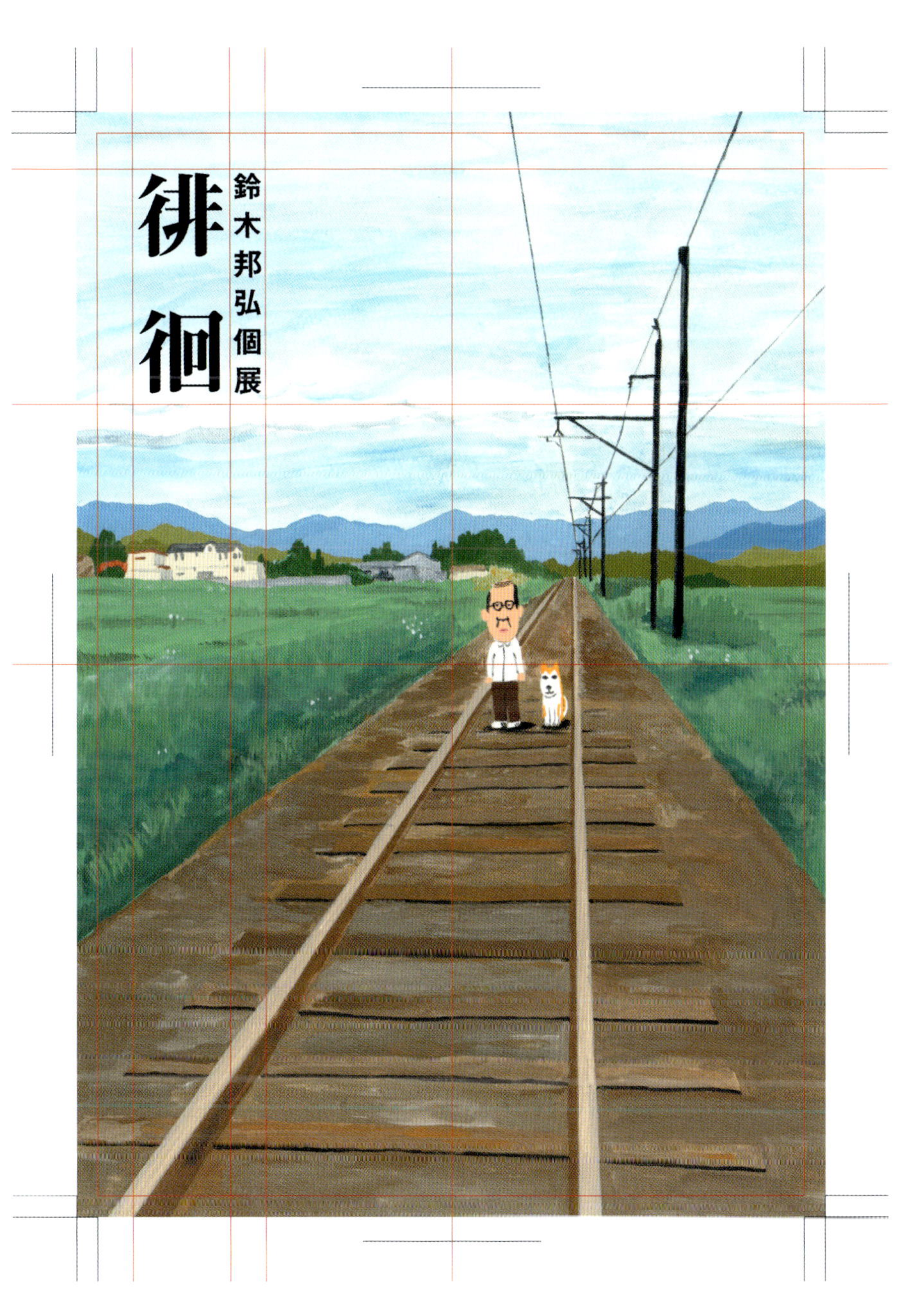

Kunihiro Suzuki designed the posters and postcard for his own exhibition, using his artwork as the main visual."Travel" and "healing" are the concepts of his artworks.The layout design concepts show an awareness of exact and neat arranging.

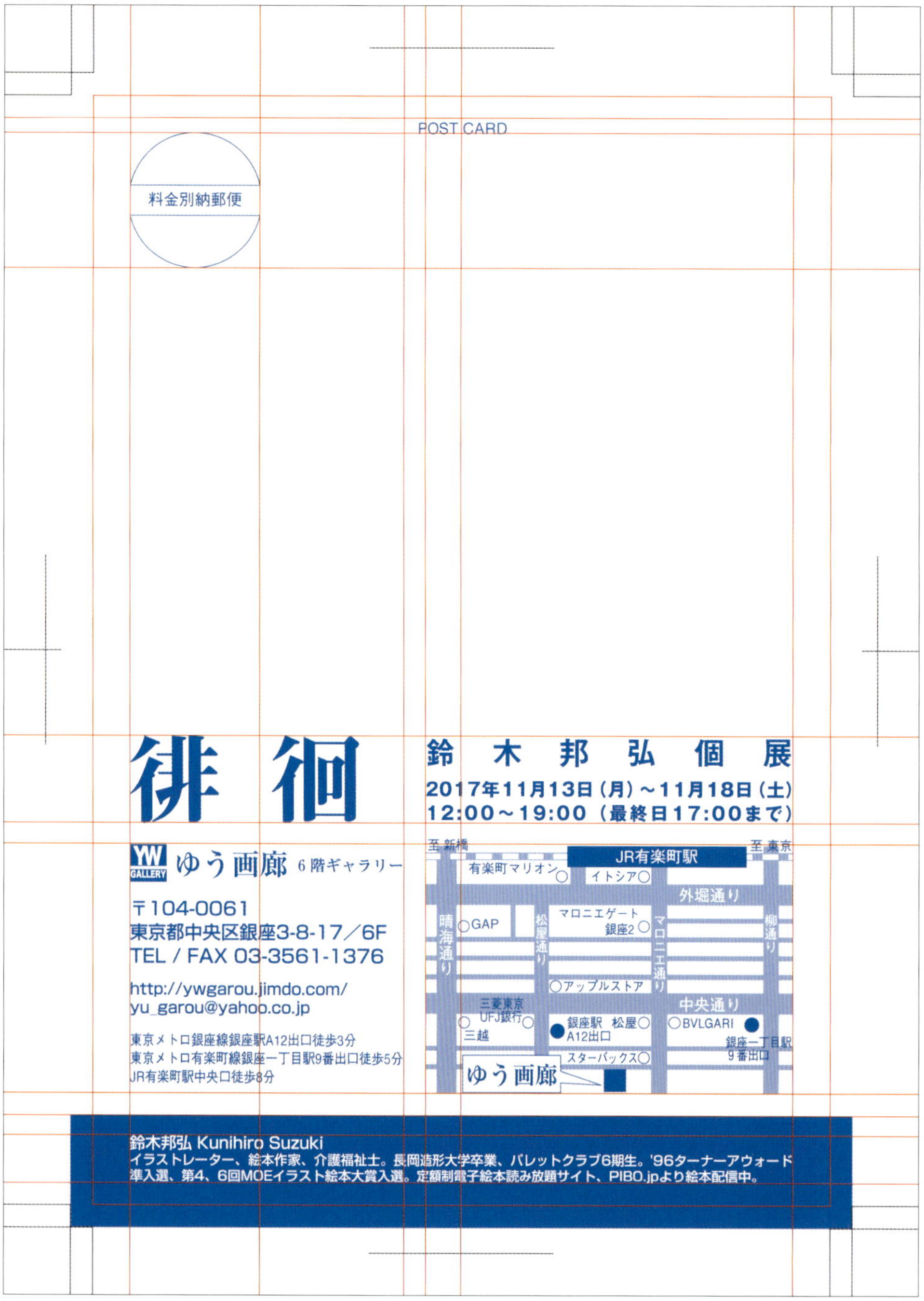

POST CARD

料金別納郵便

徘徊

鈴 木 邦 弘 個 展

2017年11月13日（月）～11月18日（土）
12:00～19:00（最終日17:00まで）

YW GALLERY ゆう画廊 6階ギャラリー

〒104-0061
東京都中央区銀座3-8-17／6F
TEL / FAX 03-3561-1376

http://ywgarou.jimdo.com/
yu_garou@yahoo.co.jp

東京メトロ銀座線銀座駅A12出口徒歩3分
東京メトロ有楽町線銀座一丁目駅9番出口徒歩5分
JR有楽町駅中央口徒歩8分

至 新橋
JR有楽町駅
至 東京
有楽町マリオン
イトシア
外堀通り
晴海通り
GAP
松屋通り
マロニエゲート 銀座2
マロニエ通り
柳通り
アップルストア
中央通り
三菱東京UFJ銀行
三越
銀座駅 A12出口
松屋
BVLGARI
銀座一丁目駅 9番出口
スターバックス
ゆう画廊

鈴木邦弘 Kunihiro Suzuki
イラストレーター、絵本作家、介護福祉士。長岡造形大学卒業、パレットクラブ6期生。'96ターナーアウォード準入選、第4、6回MOEイラスト絵本大賞入選。定額制電子絵本読み放題サイト、PIBO.jpより絵本配信中。

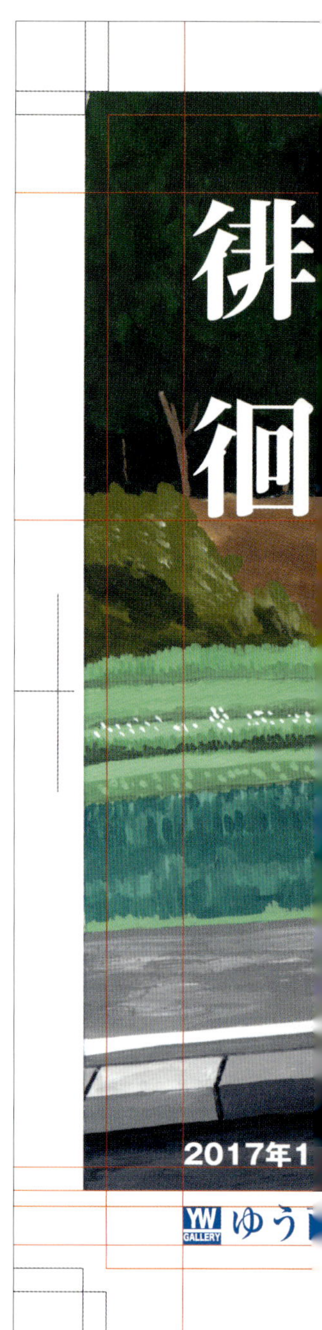

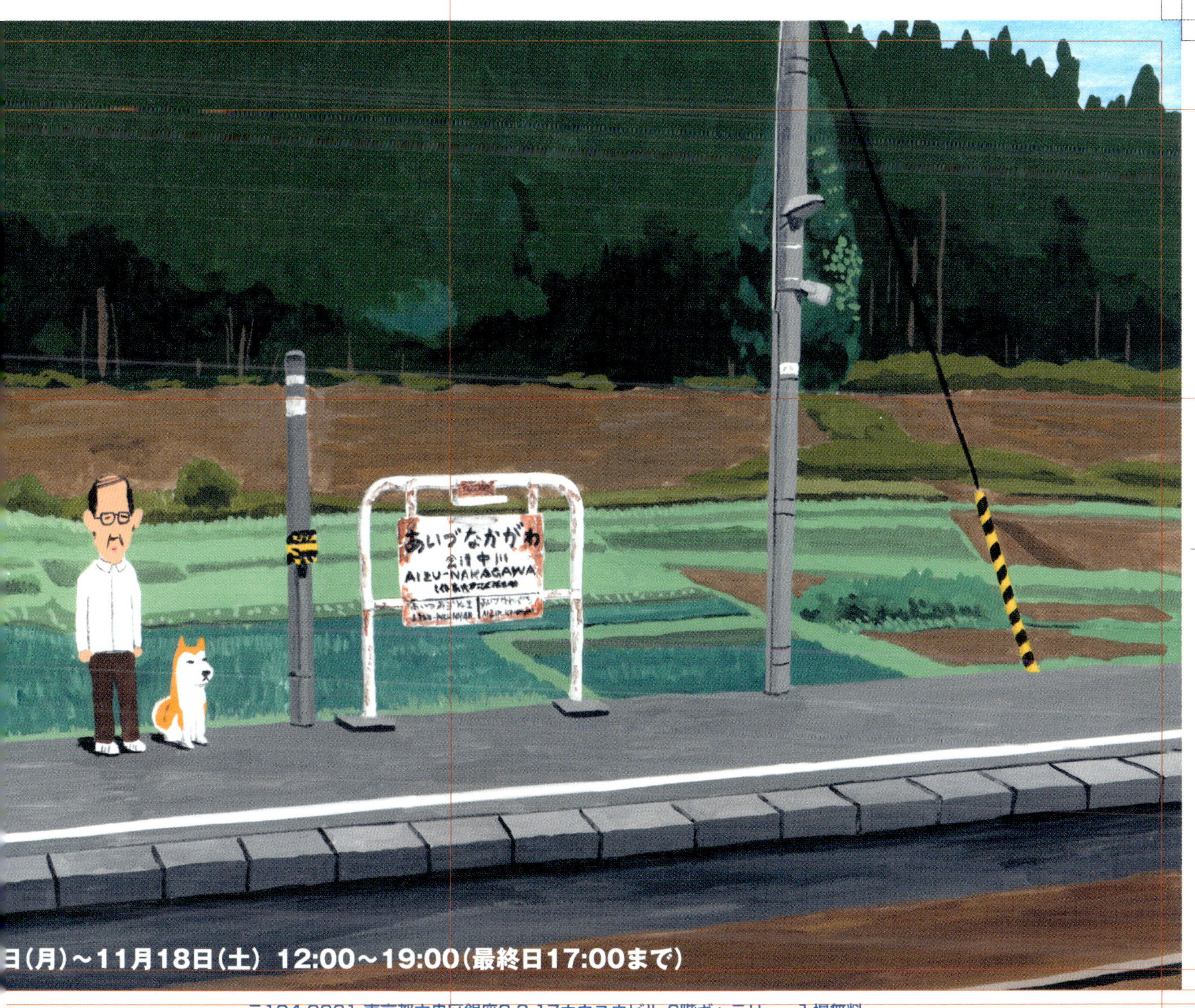

YW GALLERY 〒104-0061 東京都中央区銀座3-8-17ホウユウビル 6階ギャラリー　入場無料
TEL/FAX 03-3561-1376　http://ywgarou.jimdo.com/　yu_garou@yahoo.co.jp

Visual Playground 2017 Promotional Materials

Designer

Paula Rusu & Evelin Bundur

Key Diagram

Font	Paper	Size
Brandon Text Centima	140g Cyclus offset	Various sizes

Only by adapting the size and thickness of the fonts, without the need of more typefaces, the layout obtained a clear hierarchy.

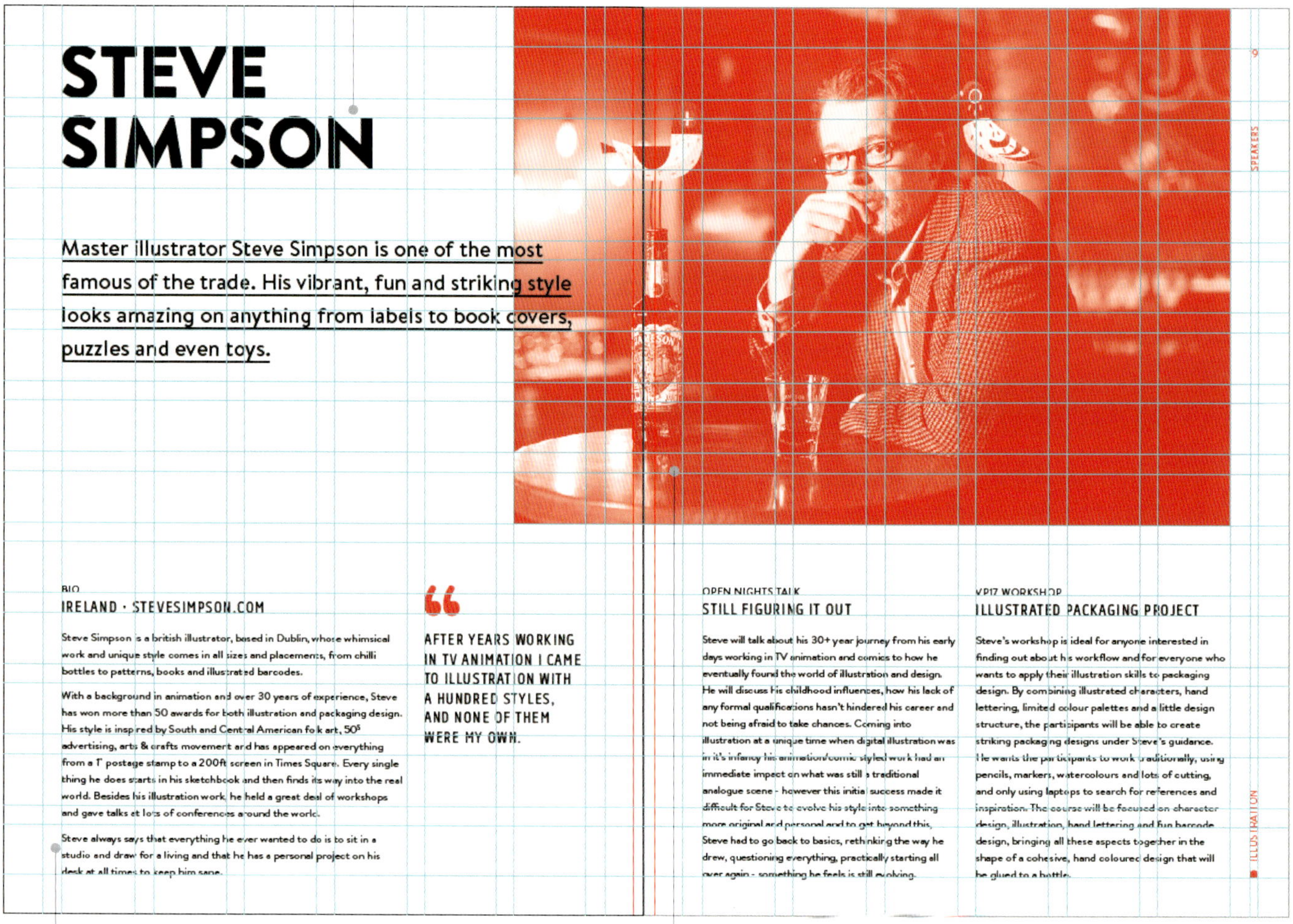

STEVE SIMPSON

Master illustrator Steve Simpson is one of the most famous of the trade. His vibrant, fun and striking style looks amazing on anything from labels to book covers, puzzles and even toys.

BIO

IRELAND · STEVESIMPSON.COM

Steve Simpson is a british illustrator, based in Dublin, whose whimsical work and unique style comes in all sizes and placements, from chilli bottles to patterns, books and illustrated barcodes.

With a background in animation and over 30 years of experience, Steve has won more than 50 awards for both illustration and packaging design. His style is inspired by South and Central American folk art, 50s advertising, arts & crafts movement and has appeared on everything from a 1" postage stamp to a 200ft screen in Times Square. Every single thing he does starts in his sketchbook and then finds its way into the real world. Besides his illustration work, he held a great deal of workshops and gave talks at lots of conferences around the world.

Steve always says that everything he ever wanted to do is to sit in a studio and draw for a living and that he has a personal project on his desk at all times to keep him sane.

"AFTER YEARS WORKING IN TV ANIMATION I CAME TO ILLUSTRATION WITH A HUNDRED STYLES, AND NONE OF THEM WERE MY OWN.

OPEN NIGHTS TALK

STILL FIGURING IT OUT

Steve will talk about his 30+ year journey from his early days working in TV animation and comics to how he eventually found the world of illustration and design. He will discuss his childhood influences, how his lack of any formal qualifications hasn't hindered his career and not being afraid to take chances. Coming into illustration at a unique time when digital illustration was in it's infancy his animation/comic styled work had an immediate impact on what was still a traditional analogue scene - however this initial success made it difficult for Steve to evolve his style into something more original and personal and to get beyond this, Steve had to go back to basics, rethinking the way he drew, questioning everything, practically starting all over again - something he feels is still evolving.

VP17 WORKSHOP

ILLUSTRATED PACKAGING PROJECT

Steve's workshop is ideal for anyone interested in finding out about his workflow and for everyone who wants to apply their illustration skills to packaging design. By combining illustrated characters, hand lettering, limited colour palettes and a little design structure, the participants will be able to create striking packaging designs under Steve's guidance. He wants the participants to work traditionally, using pencils, markers, watercolours and lots of cutting, and only using laptops to search for references and inspiration. The course will be focused on character design, illustration, hand lettering and fun barcode design, bringing all these aspects together in the shape of a cohesive, hand coloured design that will be glued to a bottle.

SPEAKERS

ILLUSTRATION

Due to the large number of themes, the designer adopted a variety of layouts. To convey a sense of freshness and impact, the designer boldly spreads the image across two pages and overlaps the text with the image, but keeps it tidy.

The colors used in each spread are different, but the main colors are always red and blue. The use of contrasting colors can stimulate the viewer's visual experience.

Grid

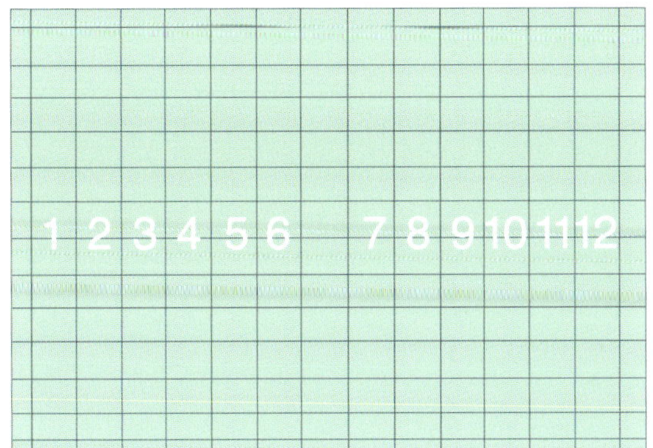

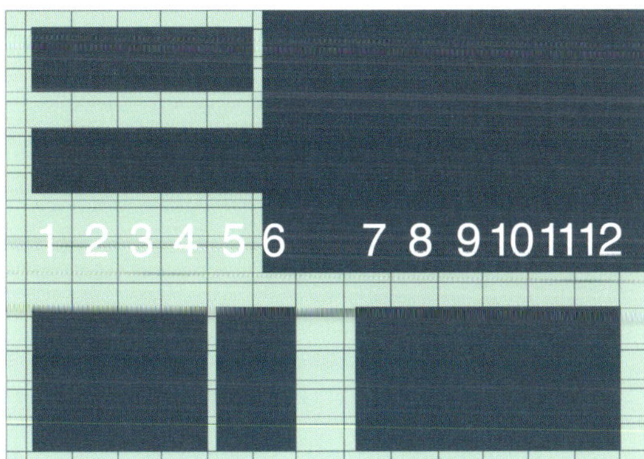

Visual Flow

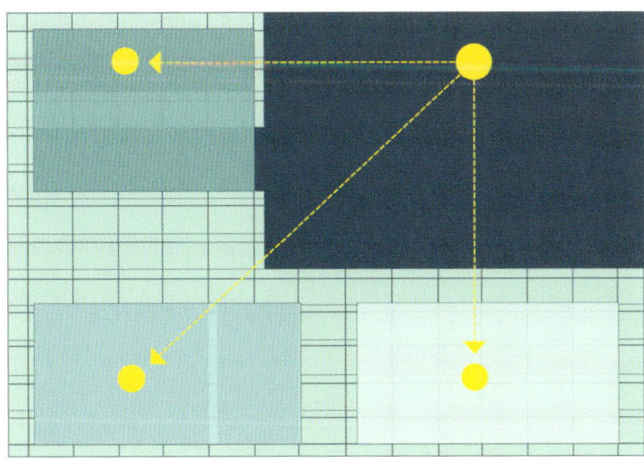

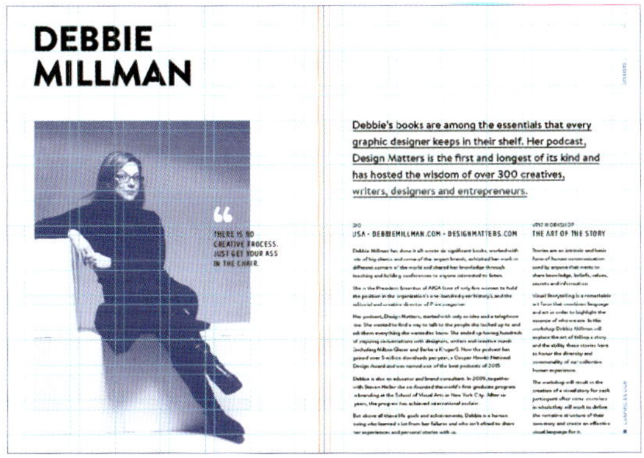

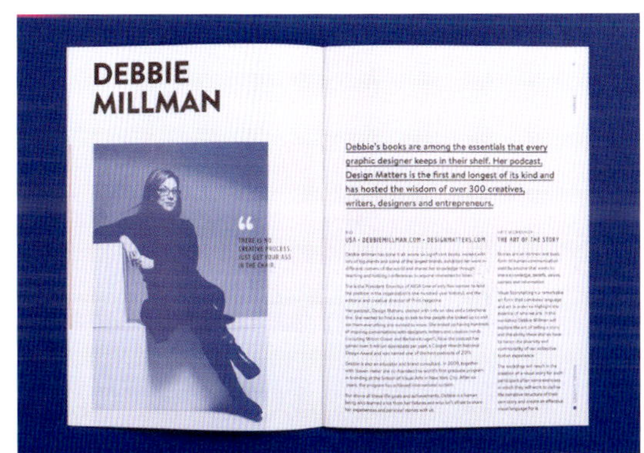

Visual Playground is a graphic design and illustration festival based in Bucharest, Romania. It involves ten days of intensive workshops, three conference nights, an exhibition of the works developed in the workshops, and a mural painting in the center of Bucharest.

Visual Playground is also a place of joyful artistic experimentation, covering all sorts of visual arts-related subjects—illustration, lettering, graphic design, animation, storytelling, printing, and many more. Therefore, the visuals for the promotional materials and stationery for the festival have to be bright, bold, and colorful, to express the playful spirit. As there is a wide range of themes for the workshops and talks, the visuals are based not just on illustration or graphic design, but a mix of all sorts. The photos, which look like 3D illustrations, work as the basic element for visual consistency.

THE NEED TO KNOWS

VISUAL PLAYGROUND is an alternative illustration and graphic design school, accessible to anyone interested in visual arts, where any design and illustration enthusiast can grow. It aims to further develop the visual arts community in Romania.

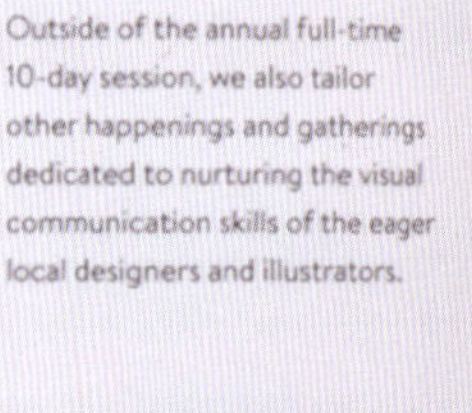

We focus on creating opportunities for creatives to both learn new skills and develop existing ones through courses and workshops held by prominent speakers, designers, illustrators and studios from Romania and abroad.

Outside of the annual full-time 10-day session, we also tailor other happenings and gatherings dedicated to nurturing the visual communication skills of the eager local designers and illustrators.

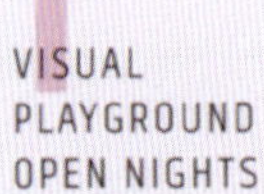

1 VISUAL PLAYGROUND OPEN NIGHTS

Inspiring conferences open to a larger audience interested in design & illustration topics, all happening after sundown.

2 VISUAL PLAYGROUND LABS

Intensive independent workshops (2-3 days), savvy and practical close-ups on various graphic design and illustration subtopics.

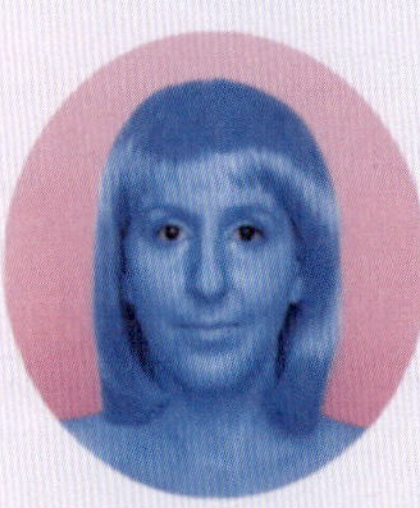

IOANA ȘOPOV

illustrator · ioanasopov.com

Illustrator and graphic designer from Bucharest, Romania. Has worked in the field for over five years, experimenting with both traditional and digital techniques. Her biggest passion is character design, especially when it comes to pirates.

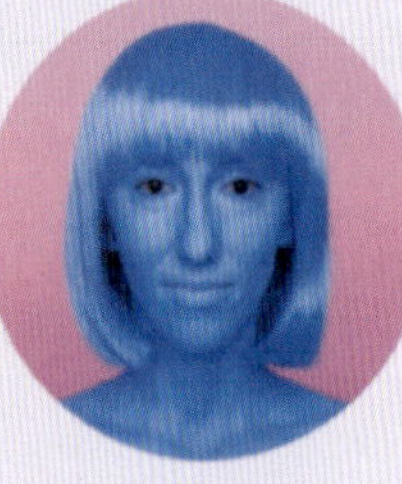

PAULA RUSU

illustrator · paularusu.com

Illustrator and graphic designer from Bucharest. Is passionate about everything related to visual arts. After five years of working in advertising she took the risk of working on her own as a freelance illustrator and now works with clients from all over the globe.

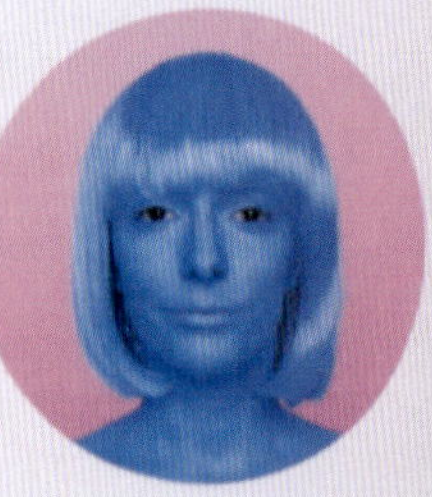

EVELIN BUNDUR

illustrator · evelinbundur.com

Freckled freelance illustrator from the East. Deeply in love with orange cats and minimalism. She likes wearing Thai boxing shorts while riding her folding bike on the crowded streets of Bucharest. Spiritual host of a true passion for kimchi.

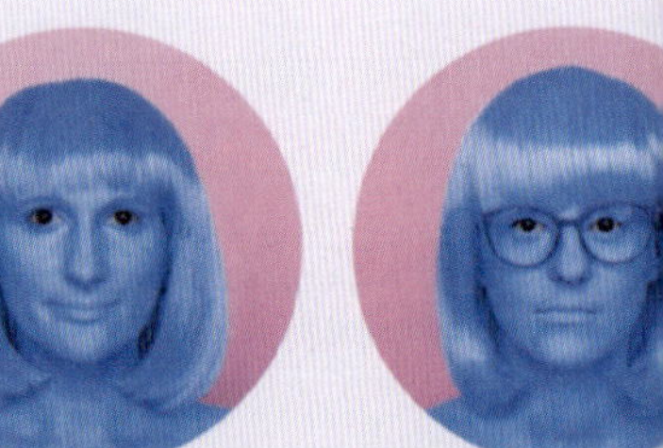

RAMONA CHIRICA

pr manager · studioreceptor.com

Ambassador and co-curator of the digital gallery Colorhood.com and illustration agent at Studio Receptor. She collects visual goodies from around the world. From 2015, Ramona has been a proud fortuneteller at VISUAL PLAYGROUND.

ROMINA BANU

photographer · dissolvedma

Freelance photographer, the run. Co-founder of D Magazine. Has too many on her laptop and would like her cats to get off the and let her work from tir Never said no to a good c tea with milk.

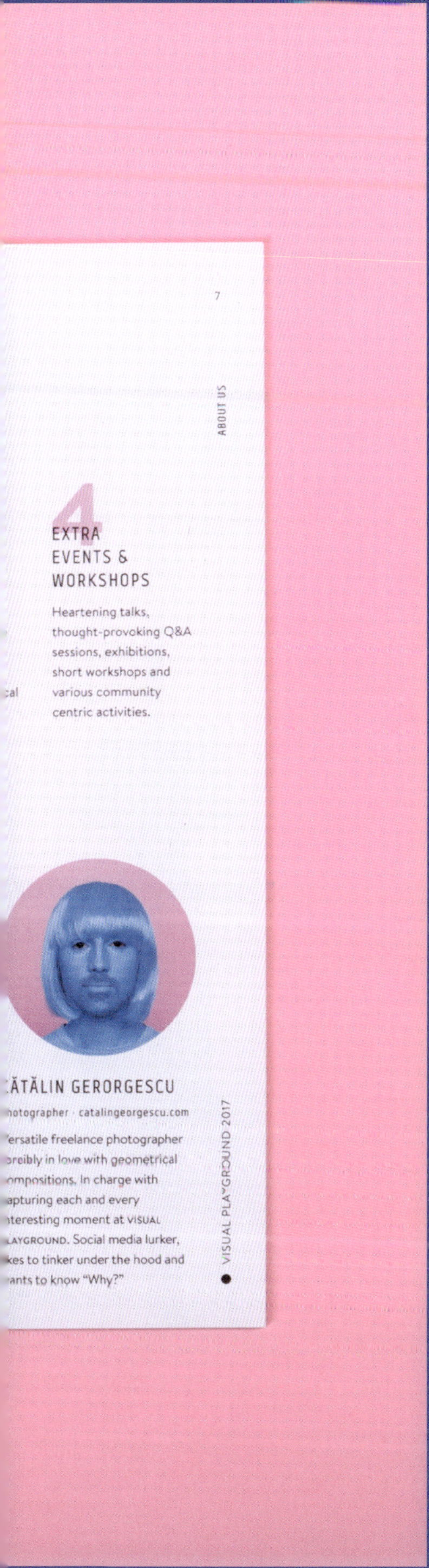

7

ABOUT US

4
EXTRA
EVENTS &
WORKSHOPS

Heartening talks, thought-provoking Q&A sessions, exhibitions, short workshops and various community centric activities.

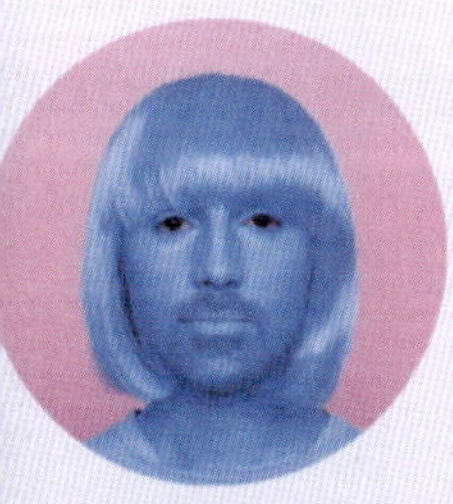

ĂTĂLIN GERORGESCU

hotographer · catalingeorgescu.com

ersatile freelance photographer oreibly in love with geometrical ompositions. In charge with apturing each and every nteresting moment at VISUAL LAYGROUND. Social media lurker, kes to tinker under the hood and ants to know "Why?"

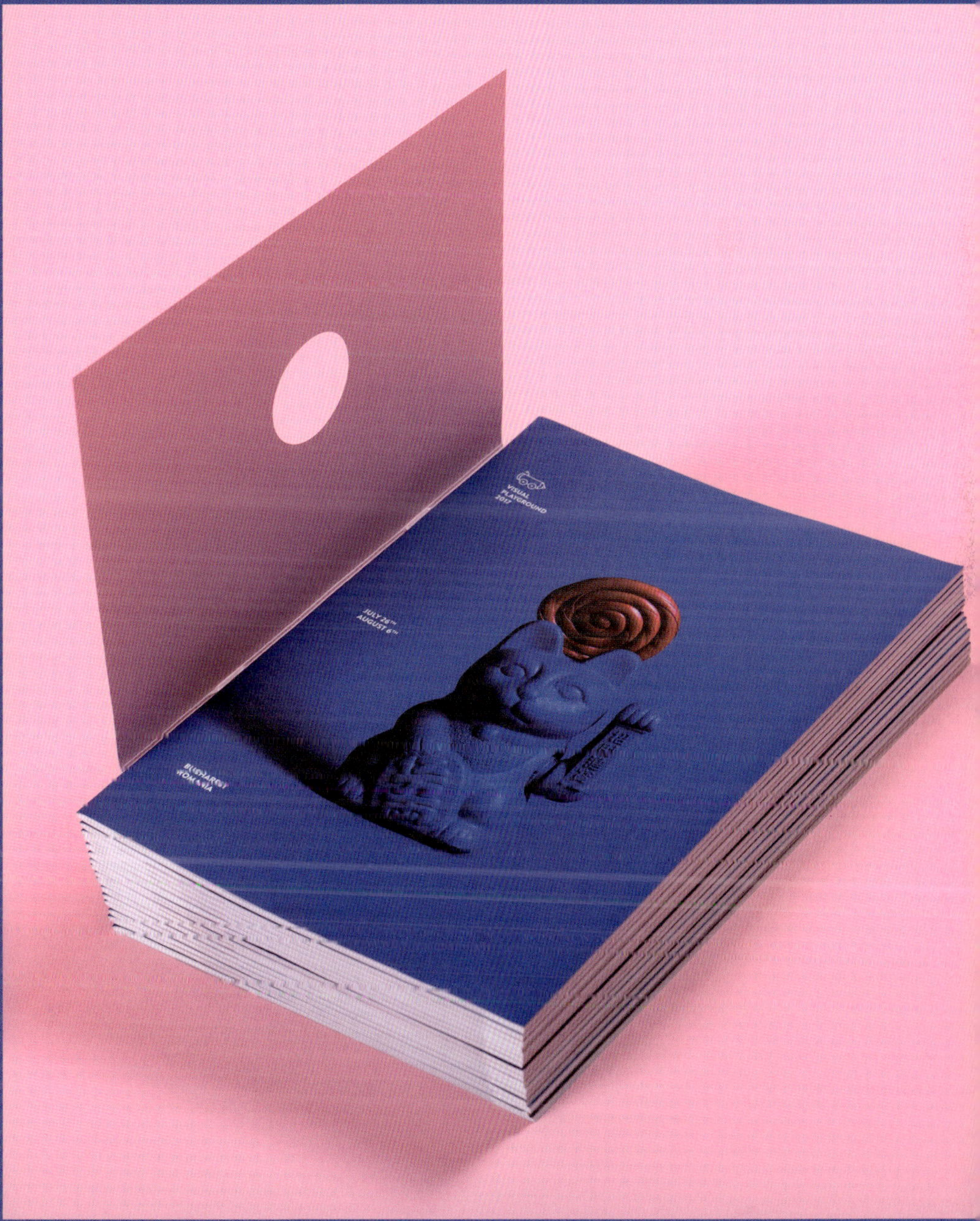

VISUAL PLAYGROUND 2017

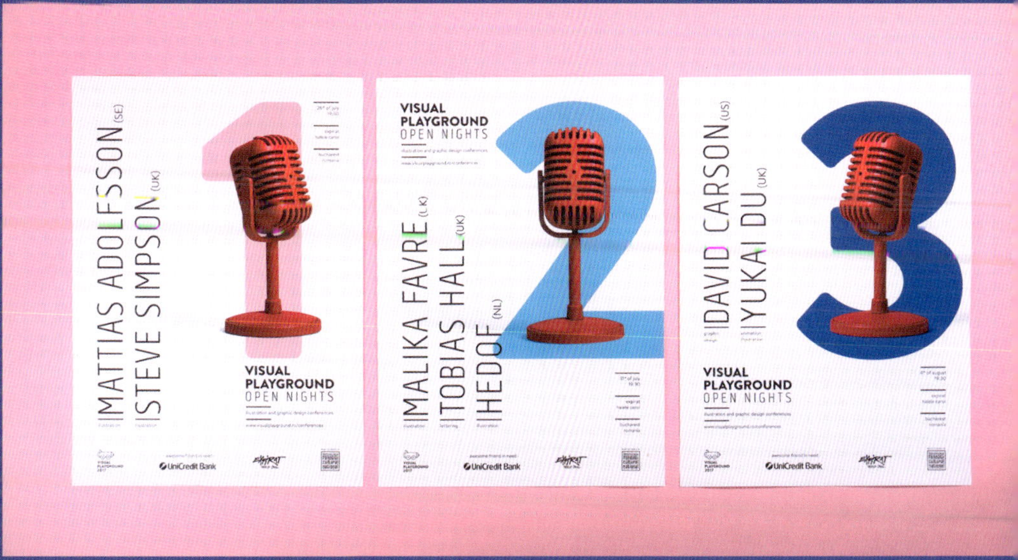

MATTIAS ADOLFSSON (SE)
STEVE SIMPSON (UK)

VISUAL PLAYGROUND
OPEN NIGHTS

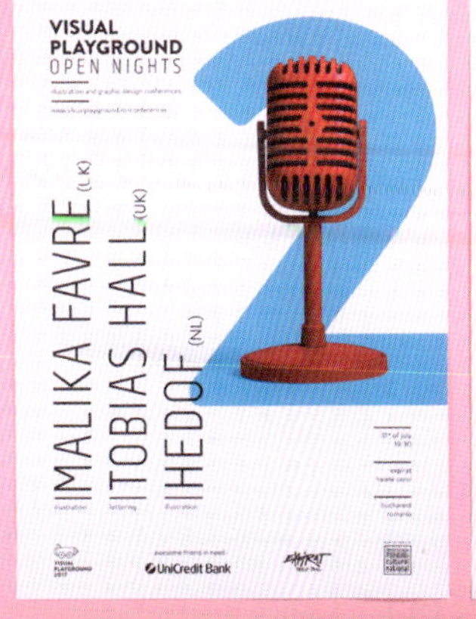

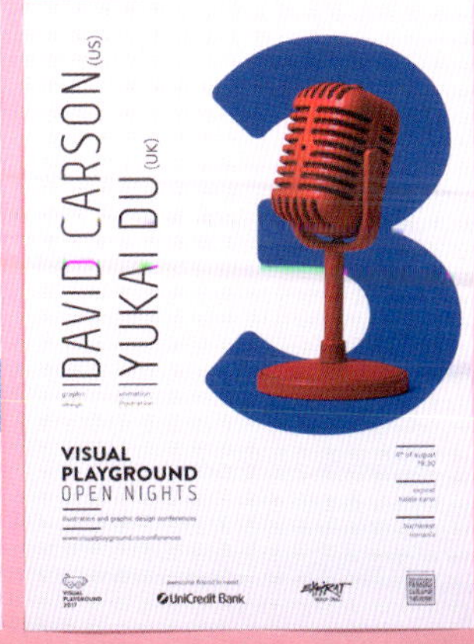

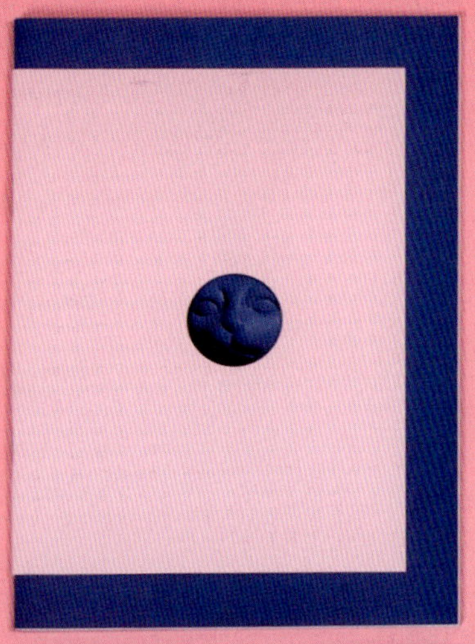

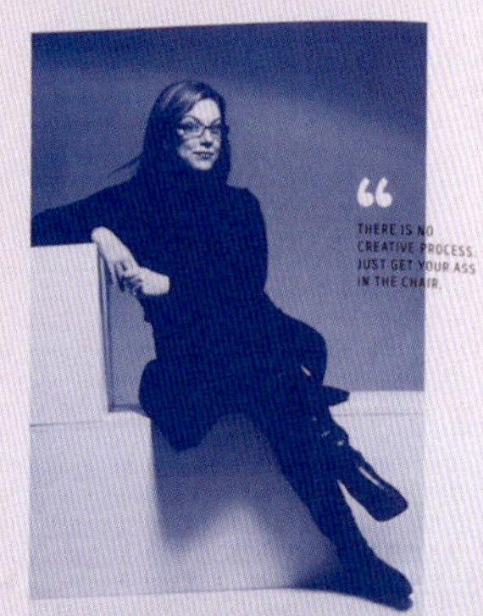
DEBBIE MILLMAN
THERE IS NO CREATIVE PROCESS. JUST GET YOUR ASS IN THE CHAIR.

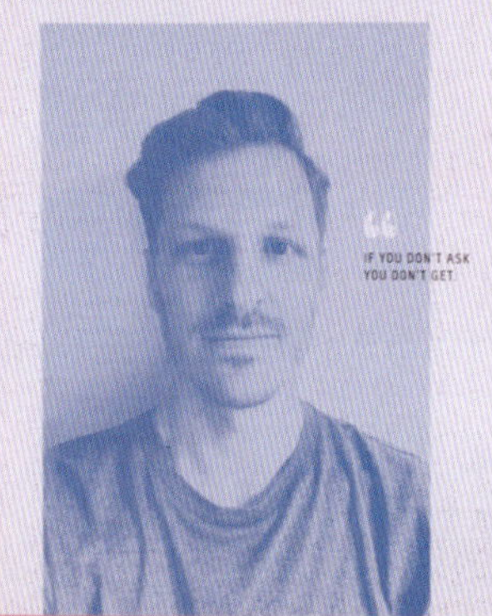
TOBIAS HALL
IF YOU DON'T ASK YOU DON'T GET
In between lettering, design and even murals, Tobias' incredibly versatile skillset is something every well rounded creative aspires to. Whether you're ogling his intricate labels, complete with his own illustrations, or drooling over his yummy hand lettering, you're sure to find something to love in his portfolio.
UK • TOBIAS-HALL.CO.UK
COPING WITH STRESS AND ANXIETY: A NEW APPROACH
HAND LETTERING: AN INTRODUCTION

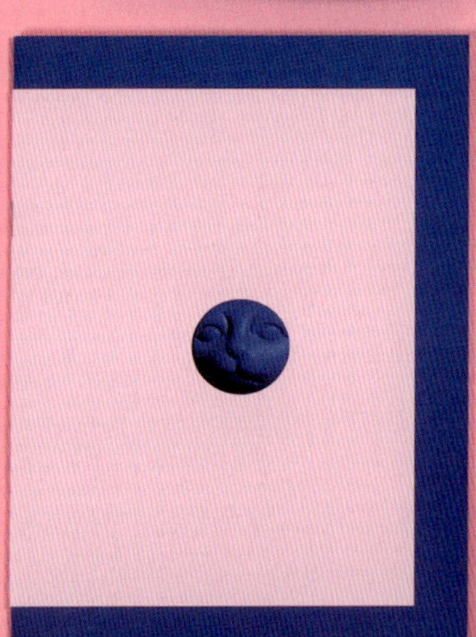

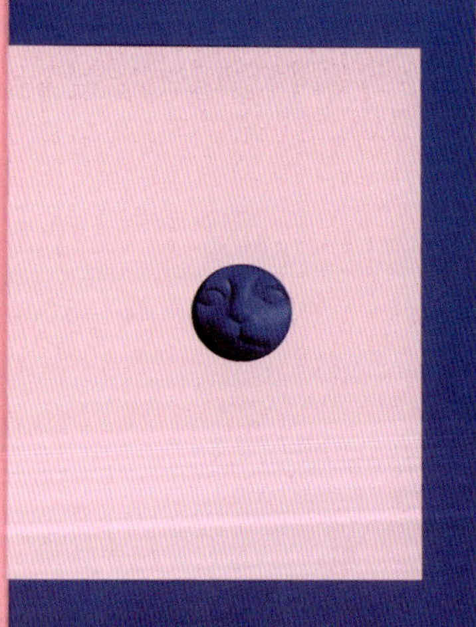

STILL & MOTION

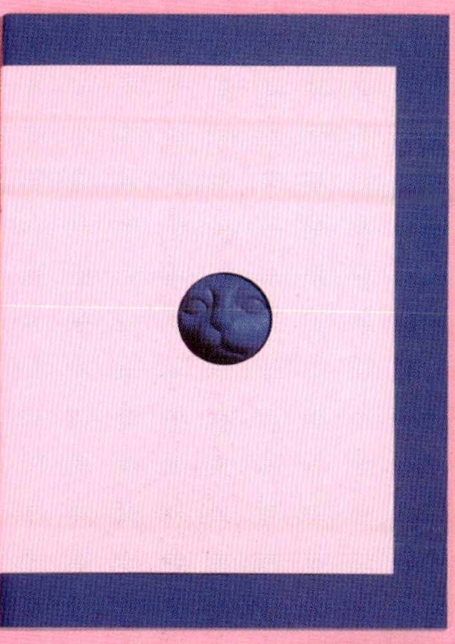
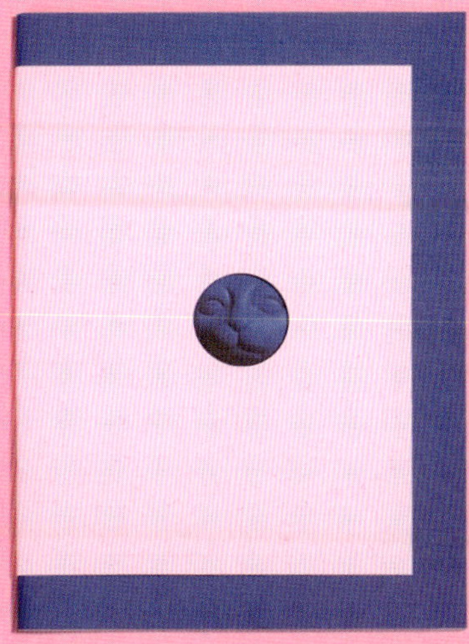
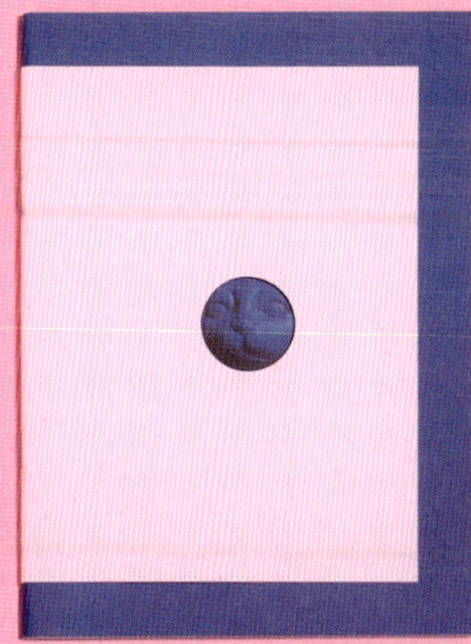
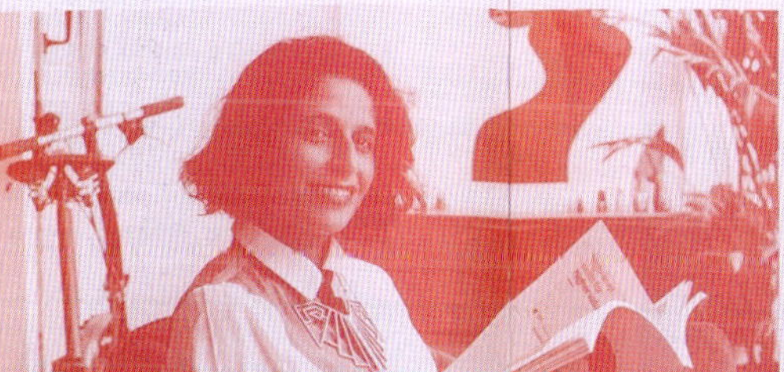

MALIKA
FAVRE
Malika's work just has that je-ne-sais-quoi that fascinates no matter what form it takes. Her iconic style is characterized by clever use of colors and spotless compositions, tackling a variety of subjects in bold images that just make your retinas tingle in the best way possible.
I BELIEVE THAT OUT OF STRUCTURE COMES FREEDOM.
UK · MALIKAFAVRE.COM
IT'S COMPLICATED
PORTFOLIO REVIEWS
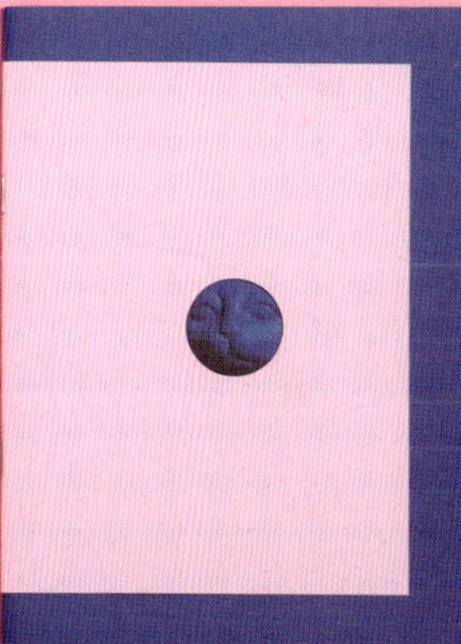
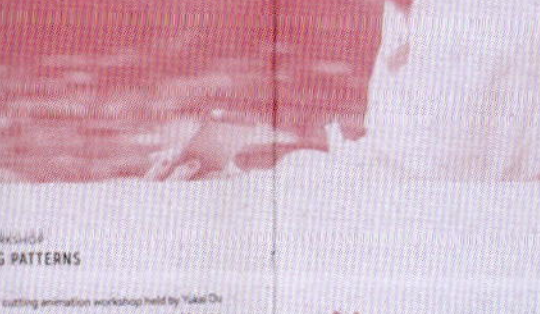
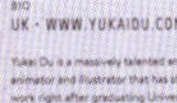
UK · WWW.YUKAIDU.COM
I OFTEN FEEL LIKE A TRANSLATOR, MY JOB IS TO TRANSLATE INFORMATION OR A STORY FROM TEXT TO VISUAL.
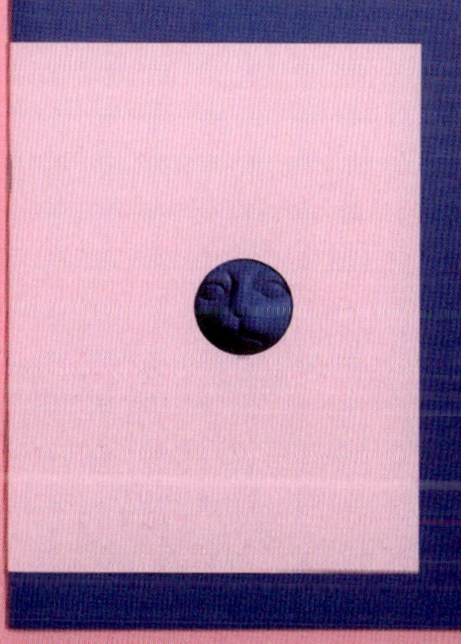
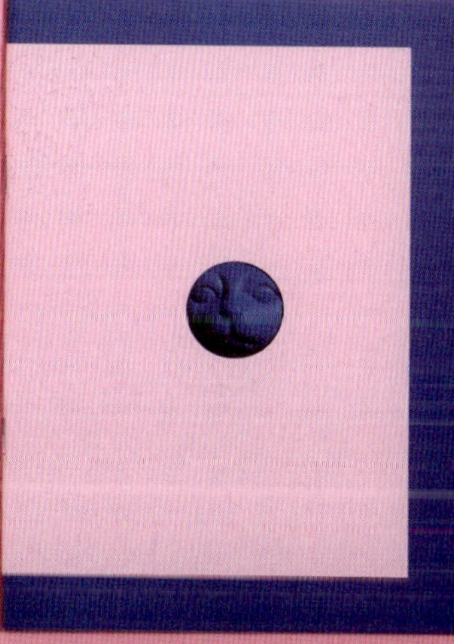

The Seoul Illustration Fair W

Designer

Hwayoung Lee

Client

The Seoul Illustration Fair

Key Diagram

Font

Proto Grotesk (English)
Sandoll Gothic Neo (Korean)

Paper

Semi-Gloss

Size

150×210mm

Two font types of similar style are applied for a perfect visual effect.

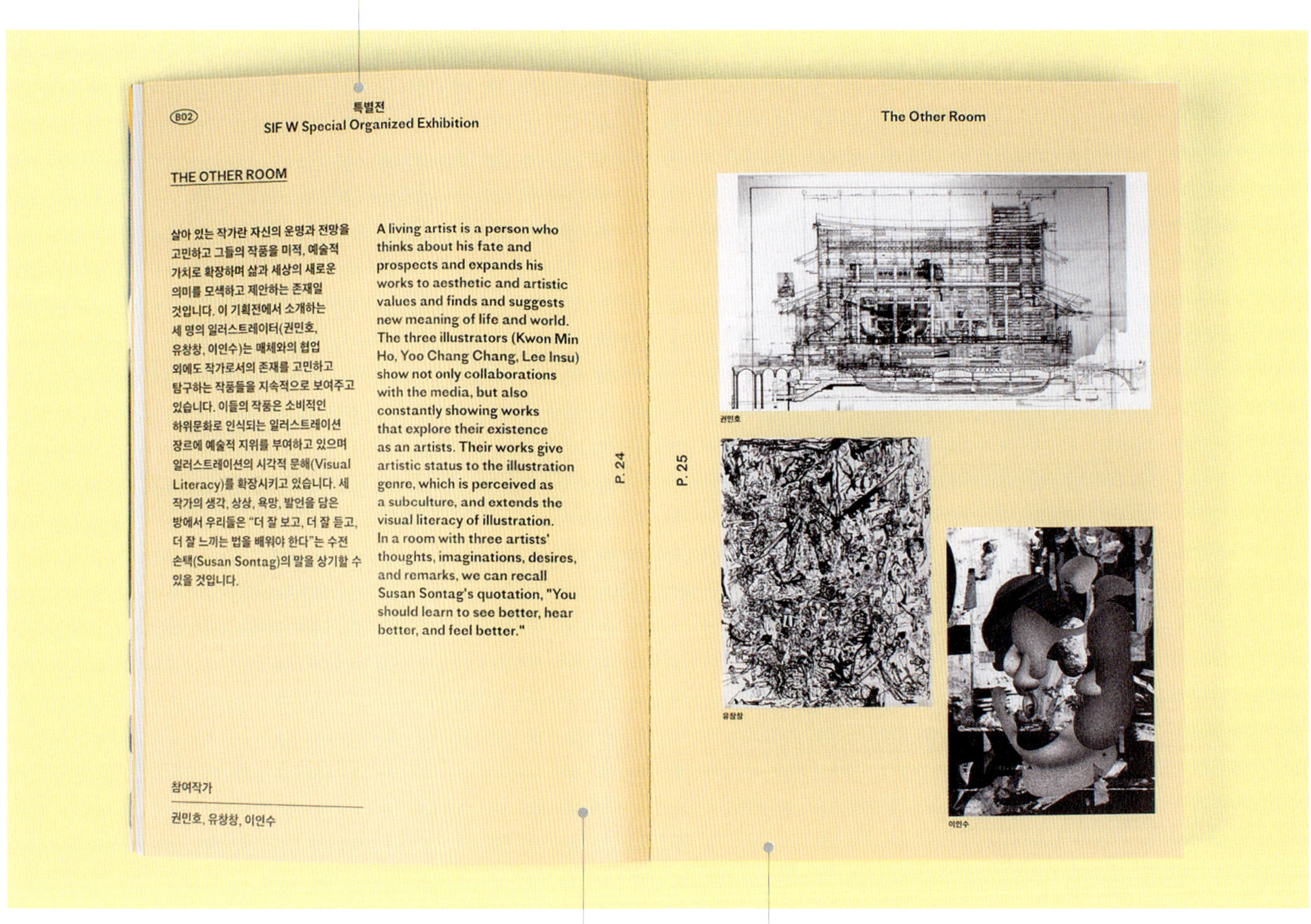

The grid system used on the cover of the booklet is applied to the inner pages as well, ensuring consistency throughout the whole design.

The color scheme varies in different contents, but the colors are always colorful and vivid and extend to the bleed of each page.

Grid

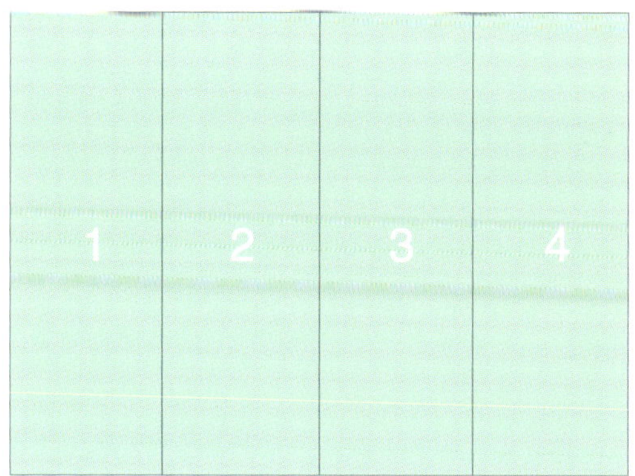

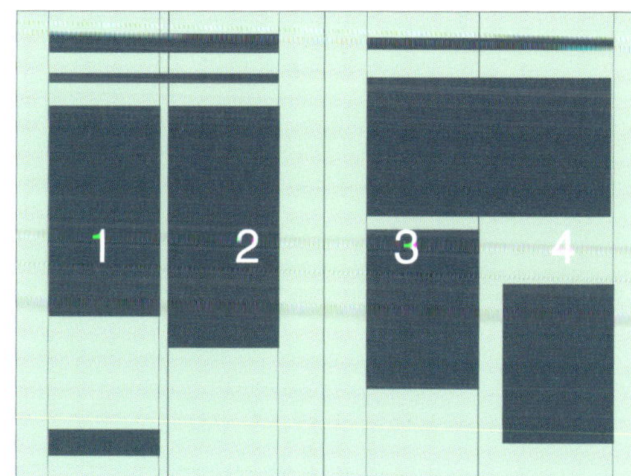

Visual Flow

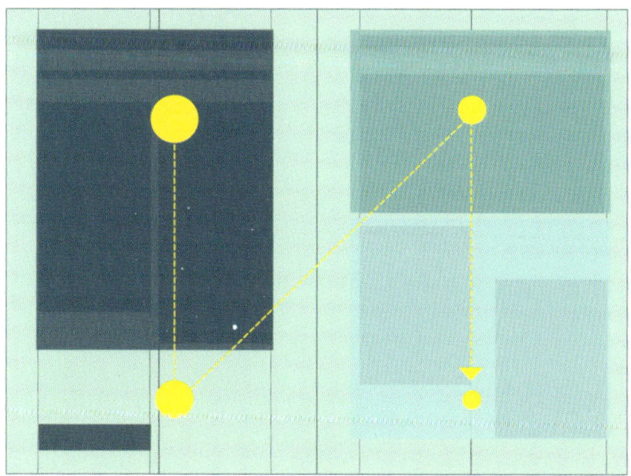

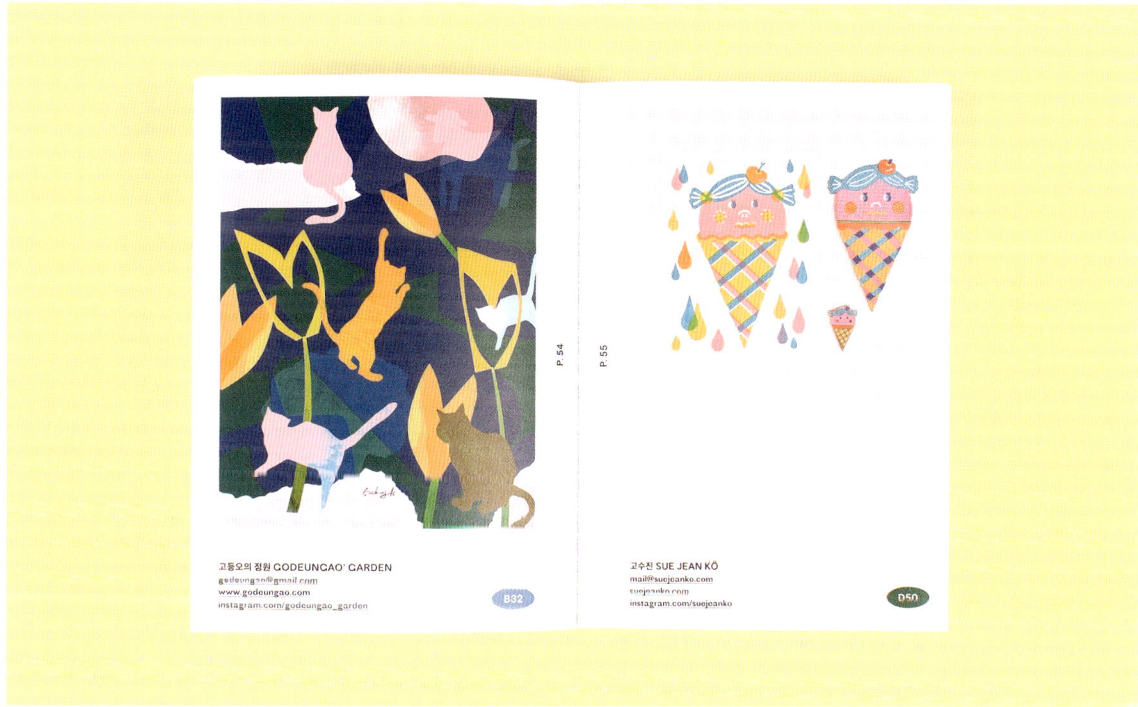

This is a booklet for The Seoul Illustration Fair, a large-scale exhibition where illustrators display their works and sell them. The event is held during Christmas season and the theme of it is Light and Winter, which is interpreted by geometric patterns.

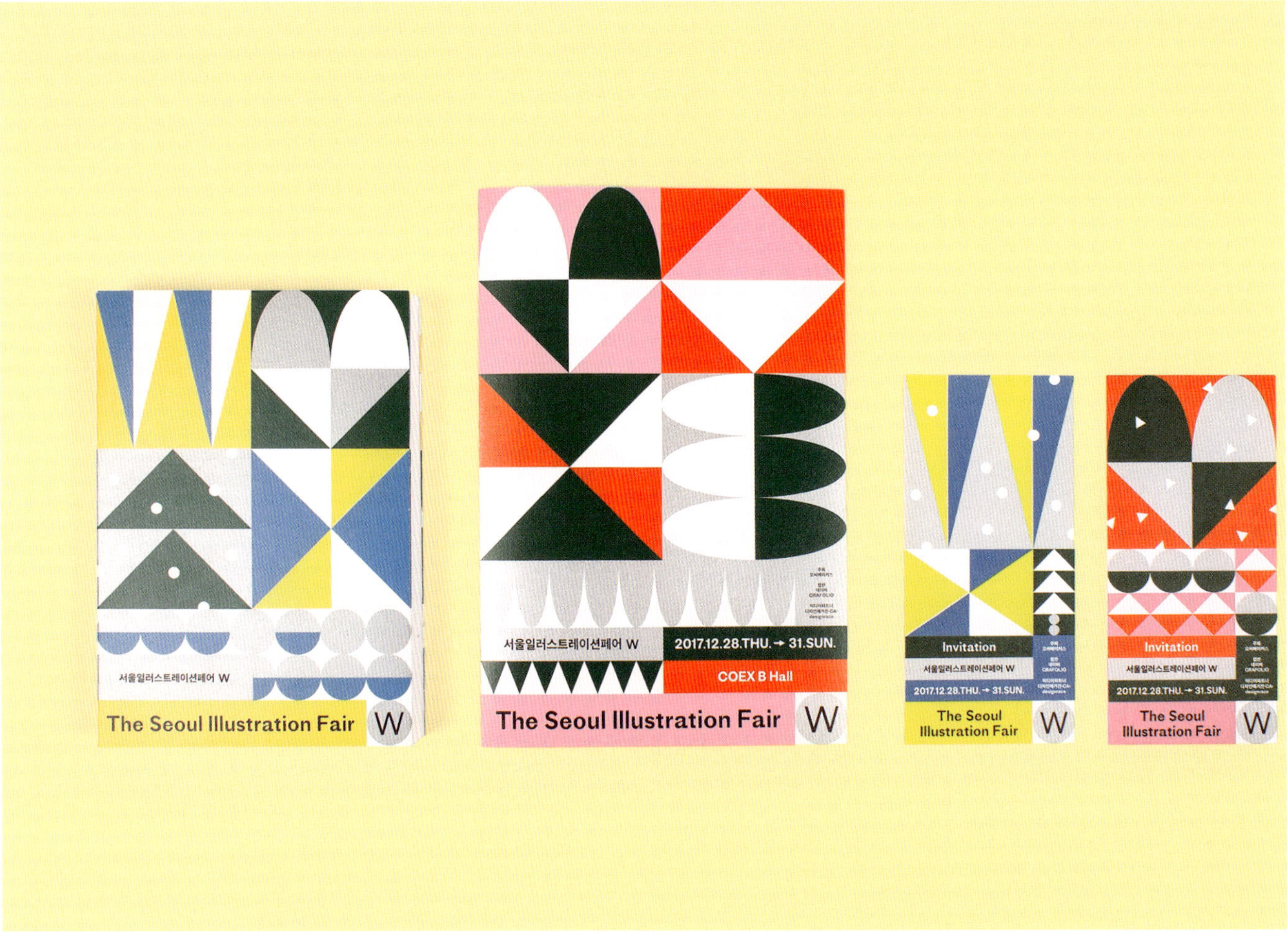

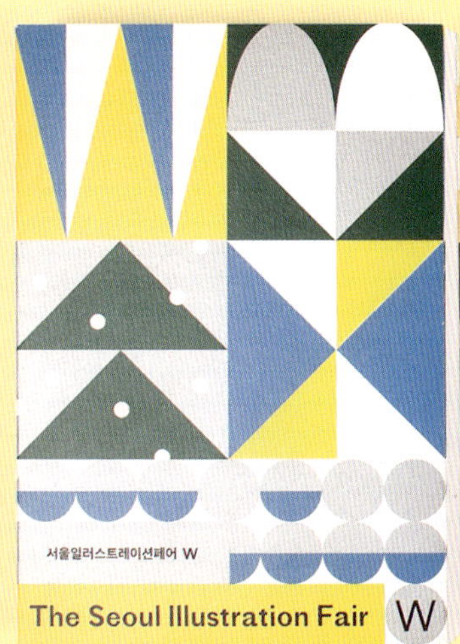

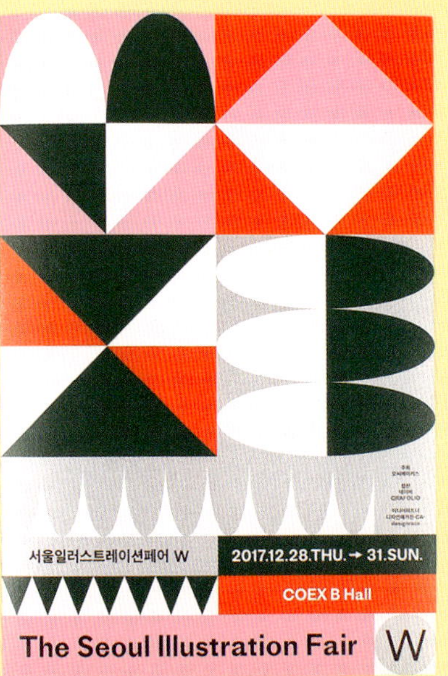

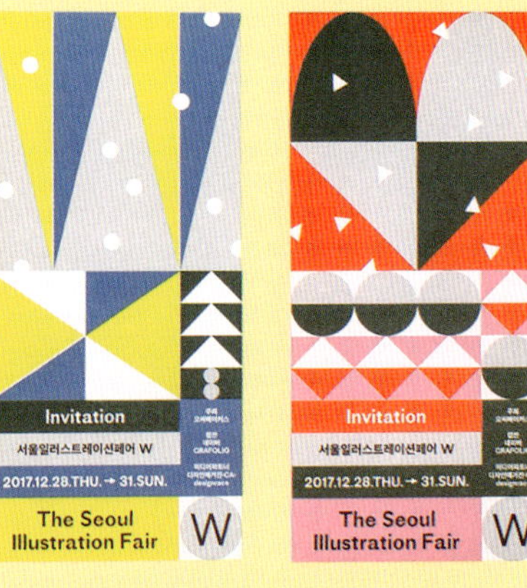

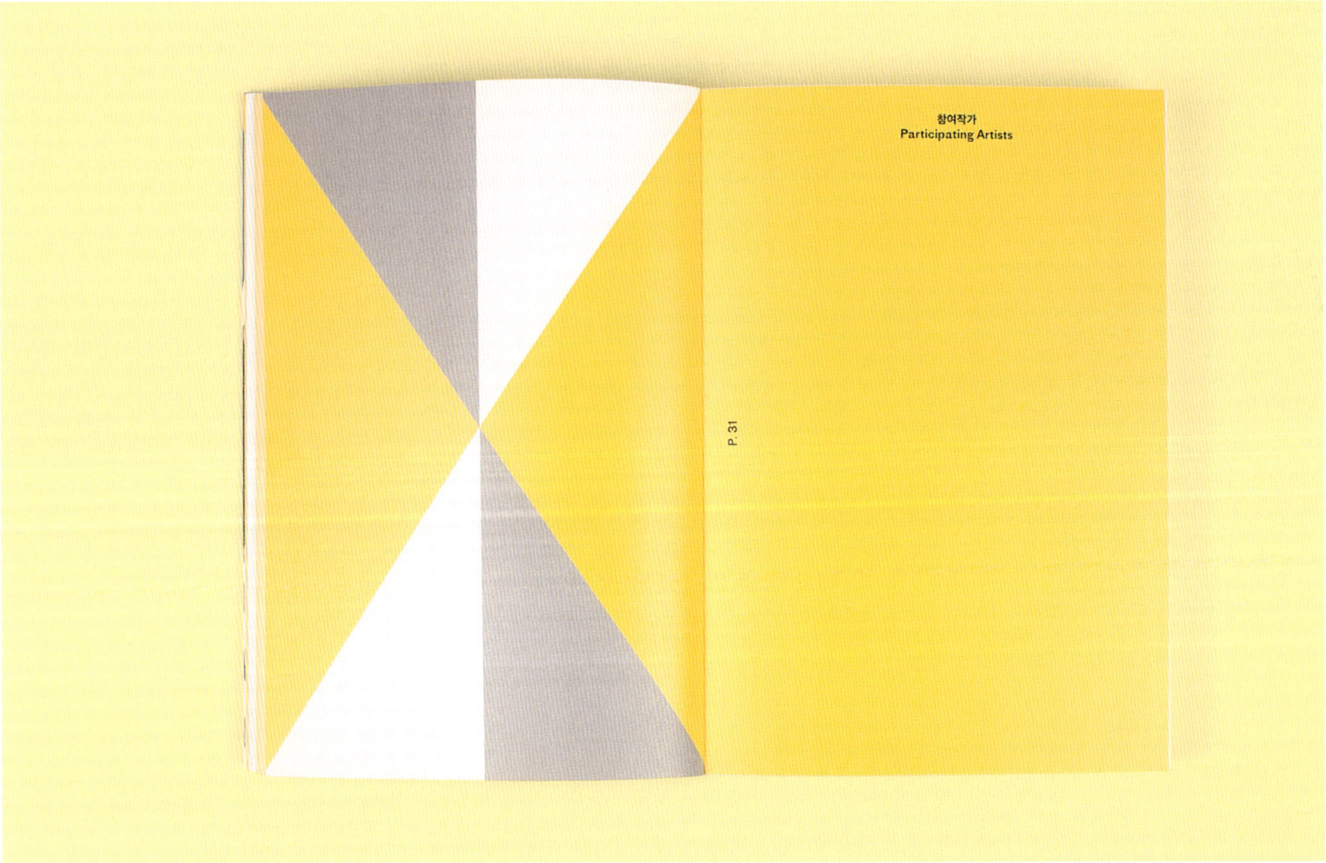

참여작가
Participating Artists

P. 31

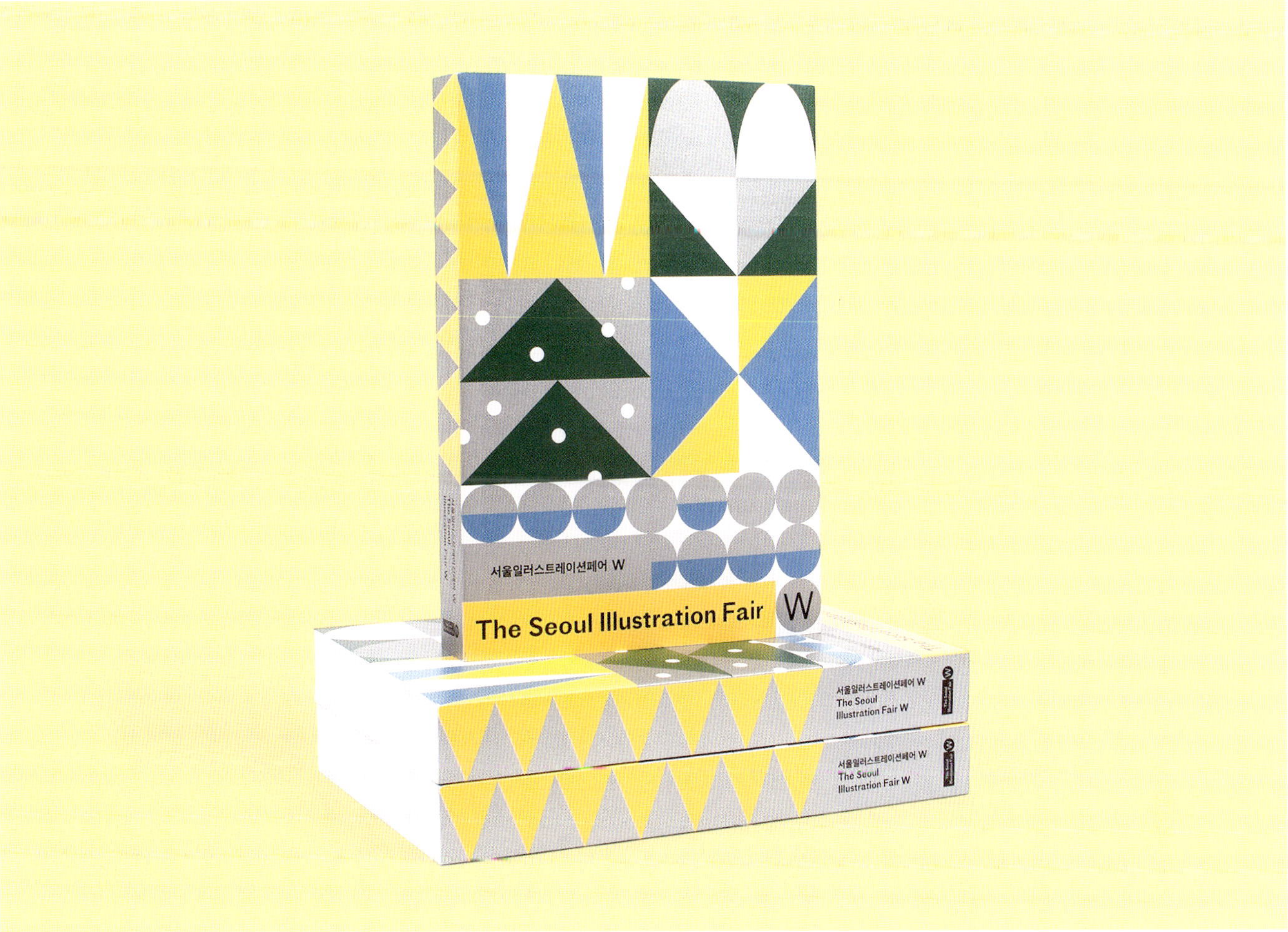

서울일러스트레이션페어 W
The Seoul Illustration Fair
W
서울일러스트레이션페어 W
The Seoul
Illustration Fair W
서울일러스트레이션페어 W
The Seoul
Illustration Fair W

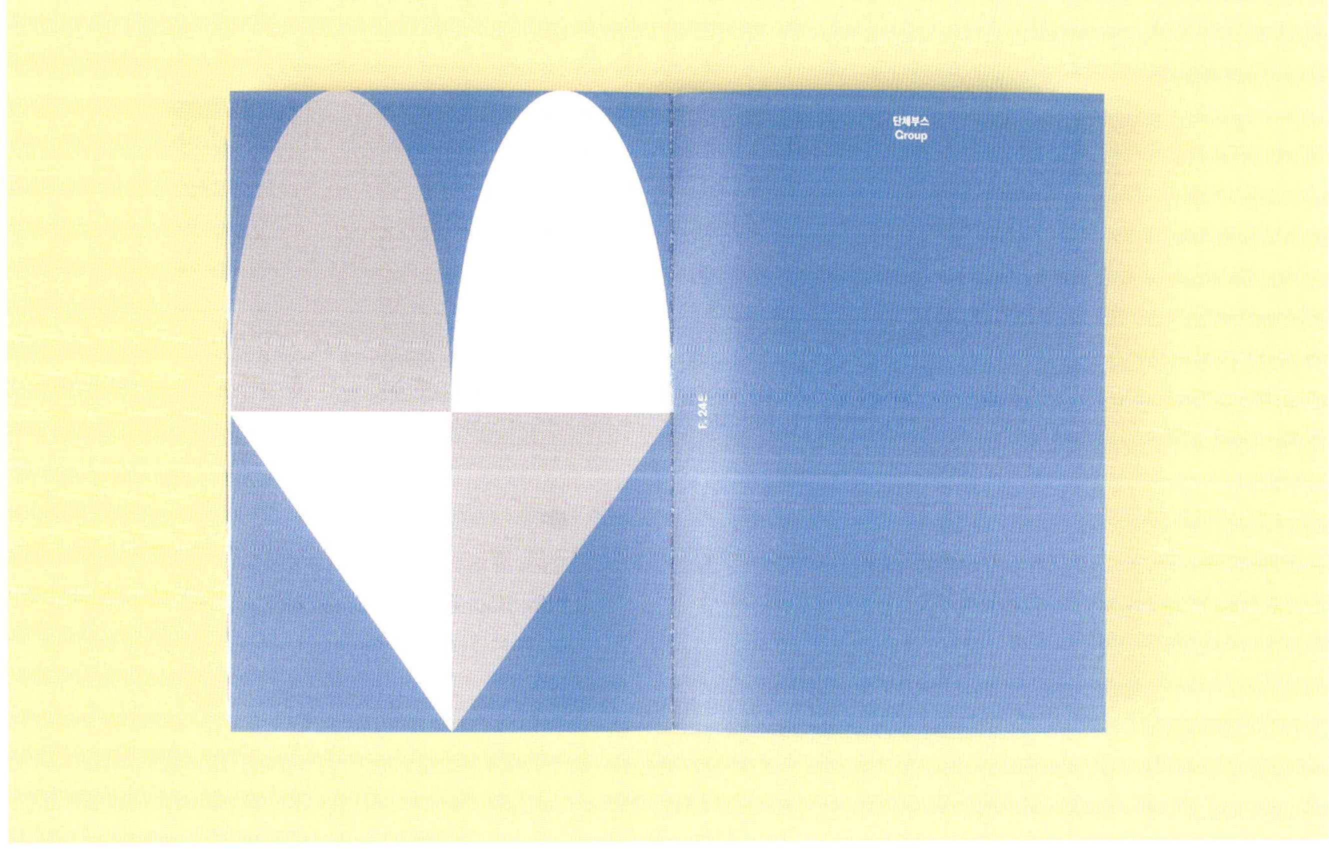
단체부스
Group
F. 24E

Fauna Primavera Posters

Designer

Sandrine Anne Sautejeau

Client

Fauna Productions

Key Diagram

Font	Paper	Size
Albus, Pier Sans Bold	Bond	770×1100 mm

Typeface is a decisive visual element here, for the artists' names occupy a large proportion of the whole visual. The most impressive might be the contrast between the lively Albus for the festival name and the calm Pier Sans Bold as the main type.

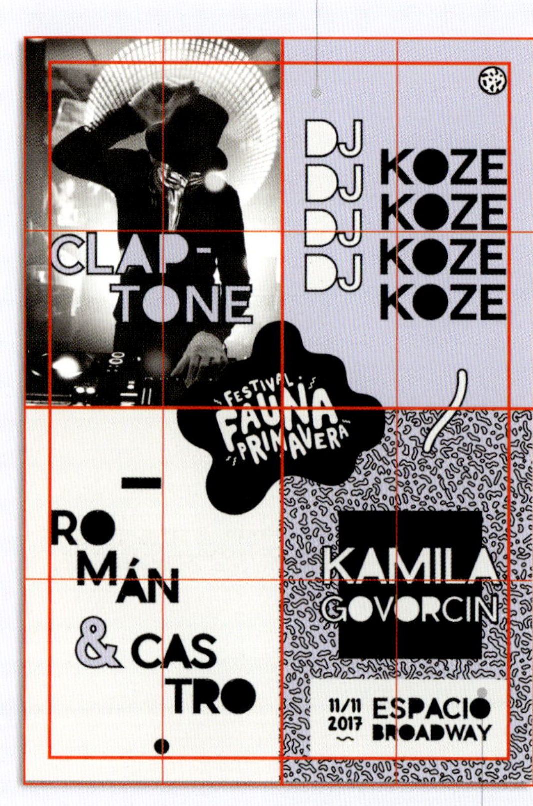

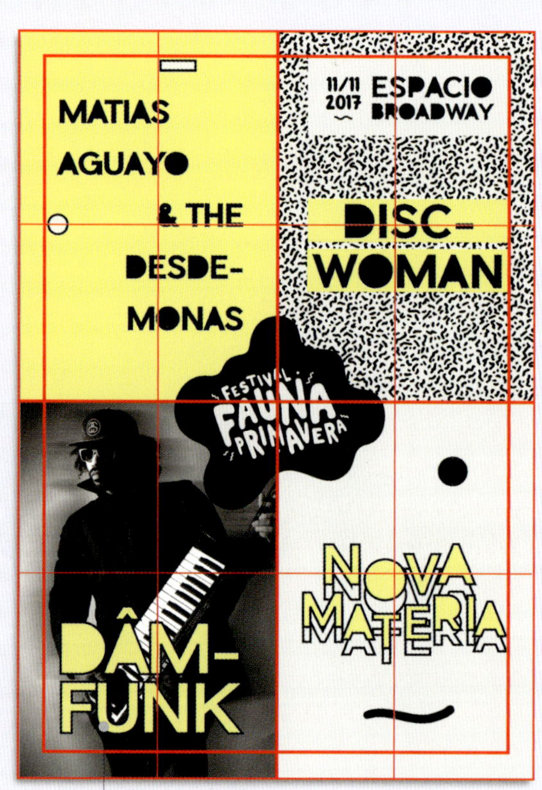

In order to present all 16 artists on four posters with no confusion, all four posters share the same grid system and each is divided into four areas to feature four artists. The principle of repetition contributes to consistency and order. Despite the many details, negative space has been adequately preserved for a harmonious visual.

Each of the four parts of the poster has a different background image: pure color, pattern, or photograph of artist. Such a difference makes an interesting contrast, too.

Grid

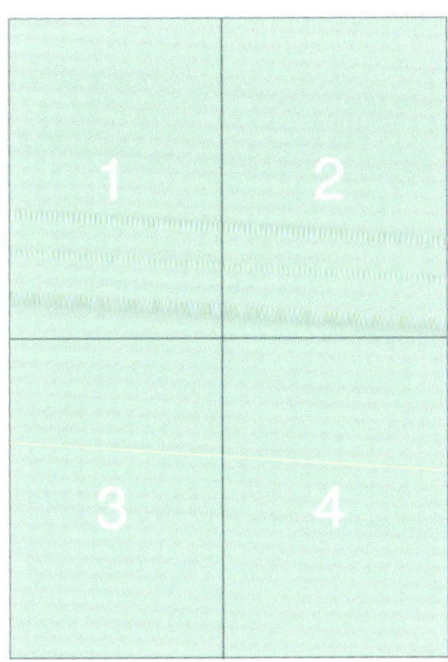

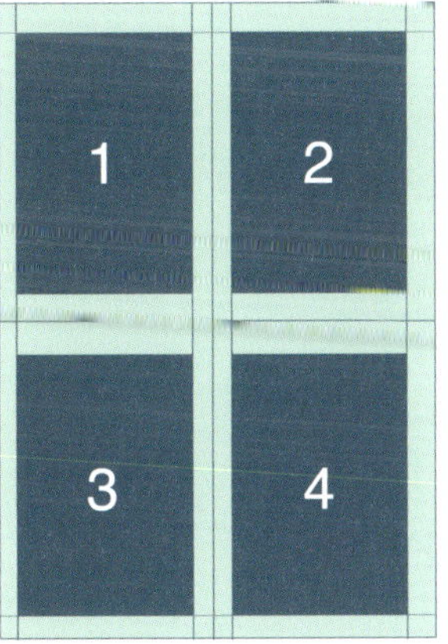

Visual Flow

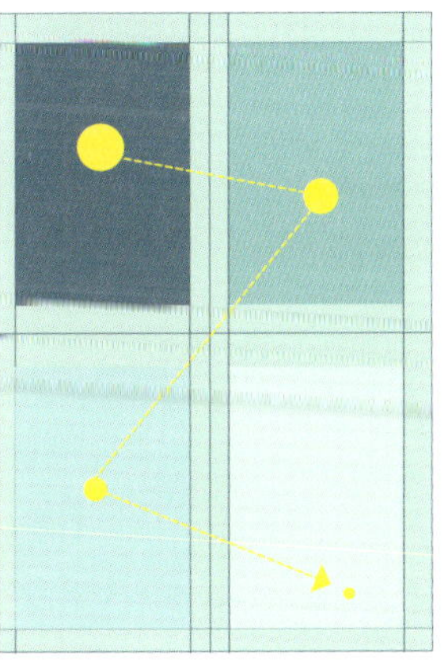

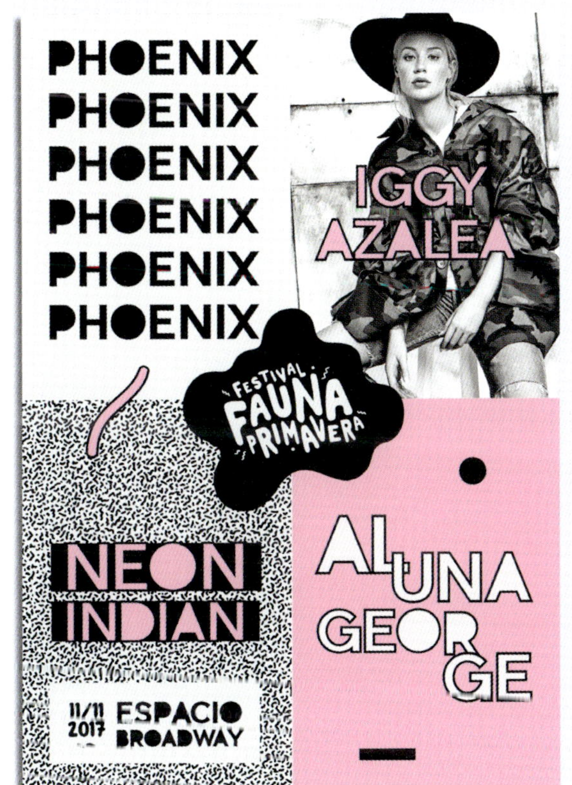

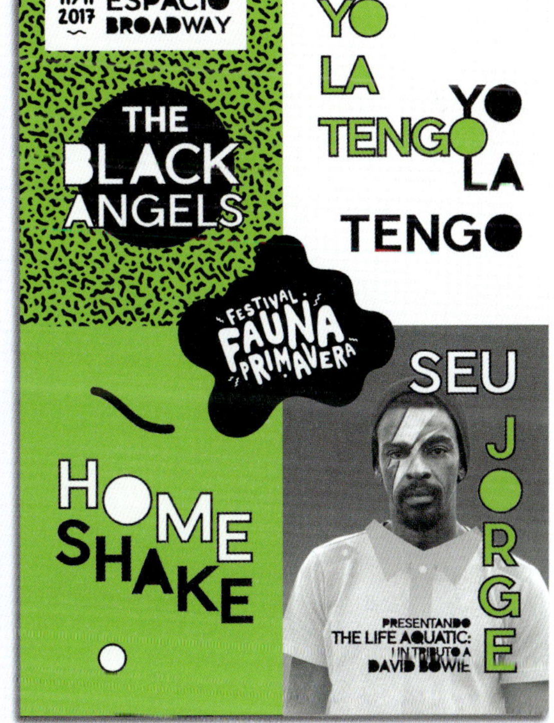

Fauna Primavera is a music festival established in 2009 at Espacio Broadway, just outside of Santiago, Chile. These posters for the festival focused on showcasing the main activities. Each poster had four different artist names designed in a playful and dynamic way to catch passerby's attention. In 2017, this series of posters were created for the festival that focused in showcasing the main acts that participated.

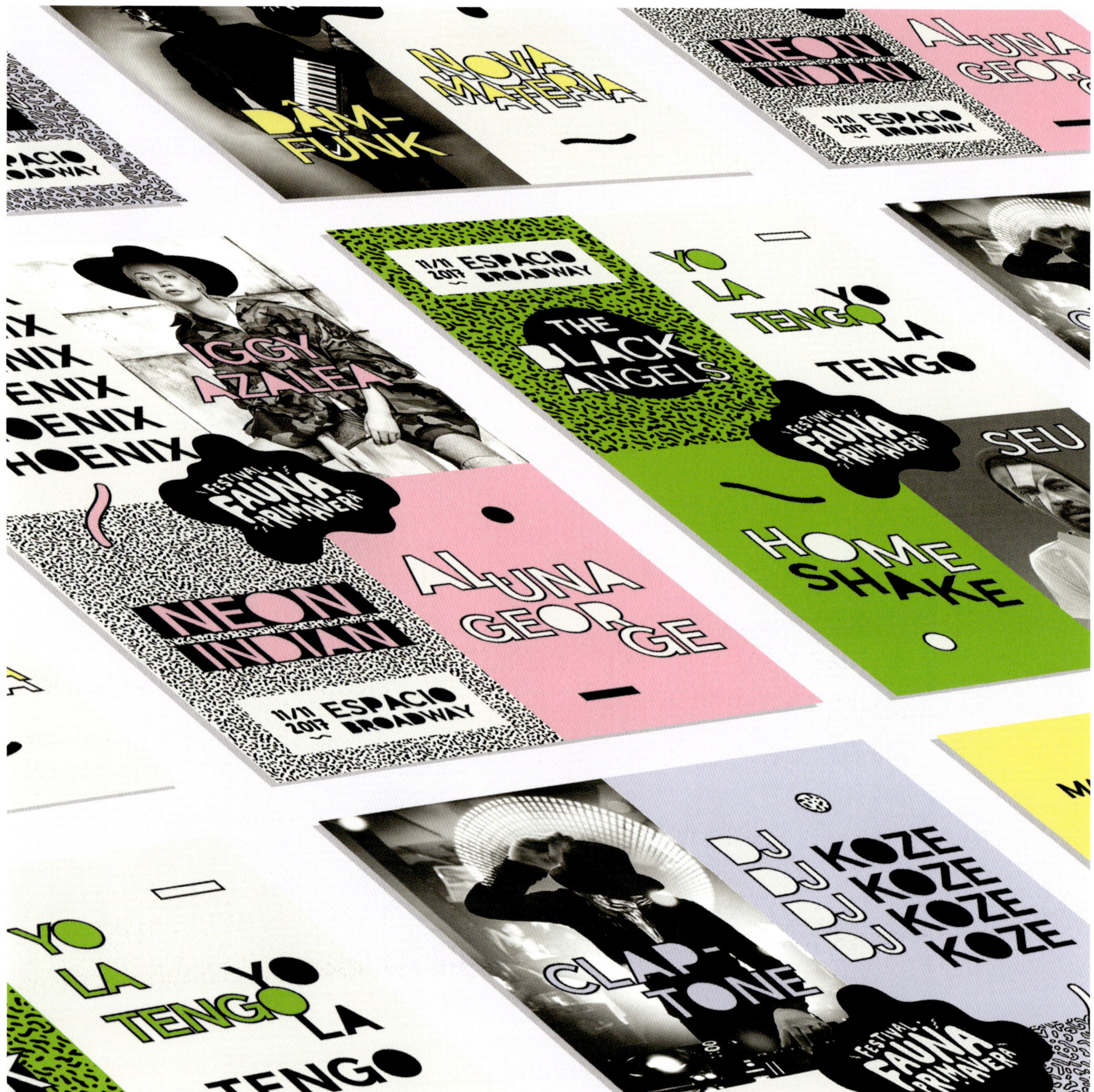
DÂM-FUNK
NOVA MATERIA
NEON INDIAN
ALUNA GEORGE
11/11 2017 ESPACIO BROADWAY
IGGY AZALEA
PHOENIX
THE BLACK ANGELS
YO LA TENGO
FESTIVAL FAUNA PRIMAVERA
SEU
HOME SHAKE
CLAP-TONE
DJ KOZE

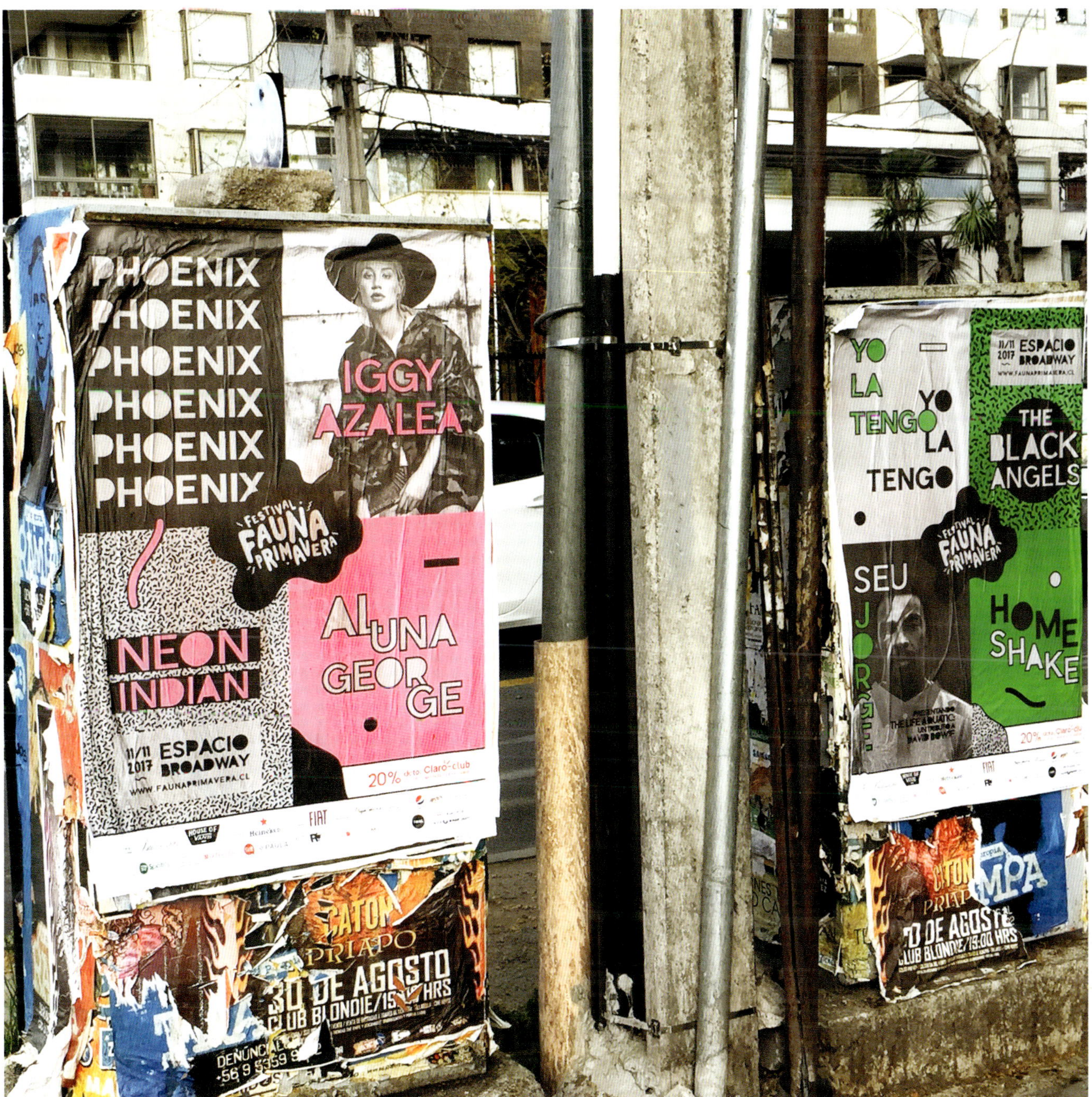
PHOENIX
PHOENIX
PHOENIX
PHOENIX
PHOENIX
PHOENIX
IGGY AZALEA
FESTIVAL FAUNA PRIMAVERA
NEON INDIAN
ALUNA GEORGE
11/11 2017 ESPACIO BROADWAY
WWW.FAUNAPRIMAVERA.CL
20% dcto Claro club
YO LA TENGO
YO LA TENGO
THE BLACK ANGELS
SEU JORGE
PRESENTANDO THE LIFE AQUATIC: UN TRIBUTO A DAVID BOWIE
HOMESHAKE
FIAT
CATON
PRIAPO
30 DE AGOSTO
CLUB BLONDIE
DENUNCIA

Architectural Odyssey

Designer	**Client**
Mane Tatoulian	**Khnko Aper Children's Library**

Key Diagram

Font	Paper	Size
Helvetica Neue	200g Matt coated paper	210×297mm (A4)

The sans serif font echoes the Soviet architectural style, and both are visually balanced and well-organized.

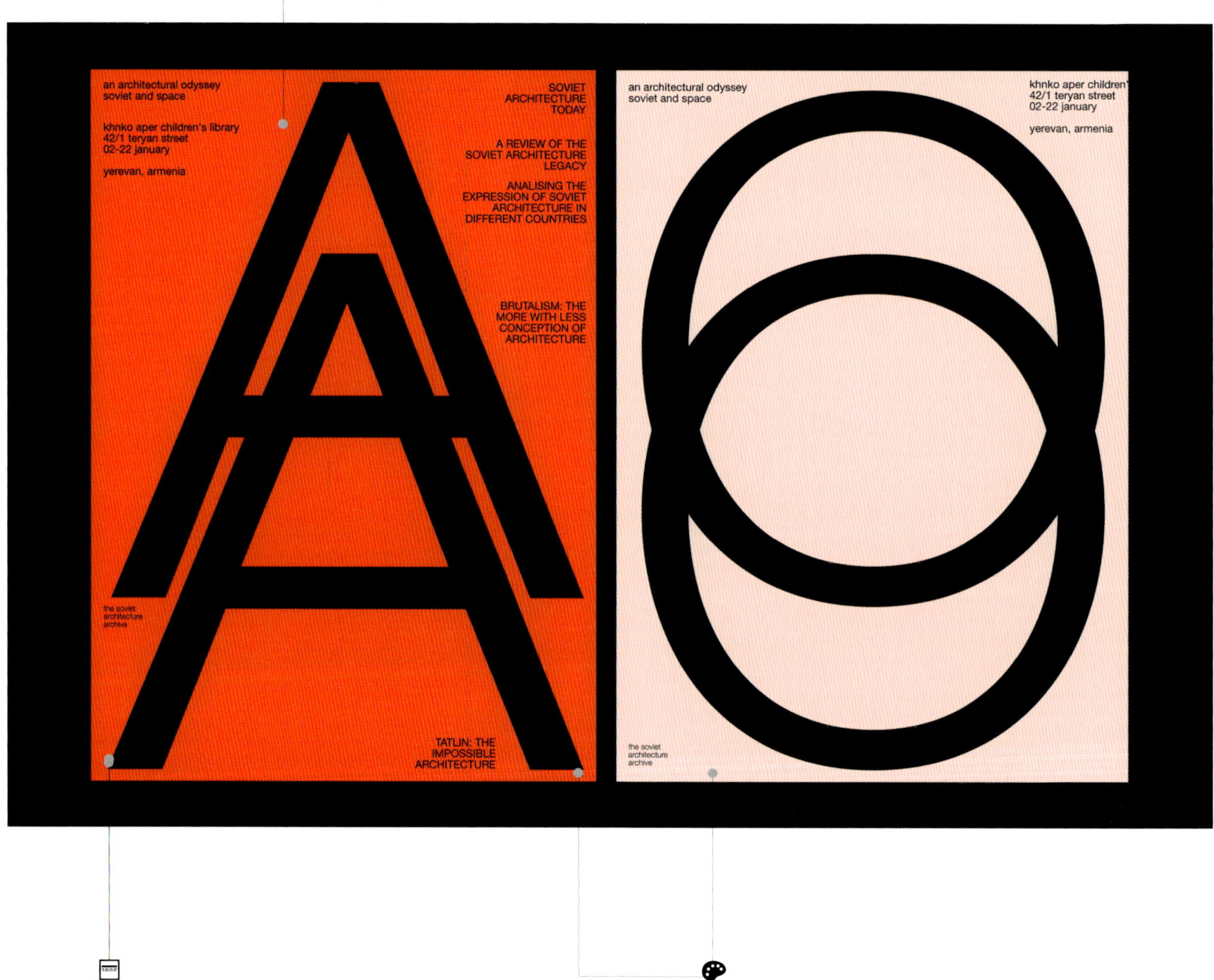

Re-interpretation of constructivism and Bauhaus visual guidelines, to empower the communication of the event and create a cohesive visual system.

Deep orange and light pink have a strong visual contrast, while reminiscent of the classic color scheme of Soviet-style graphic design.

Grid

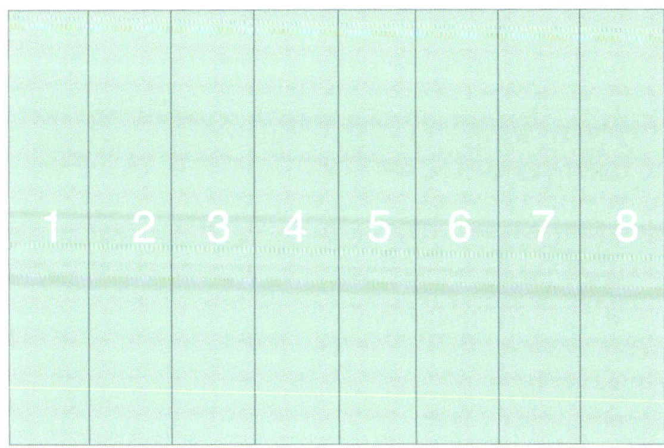

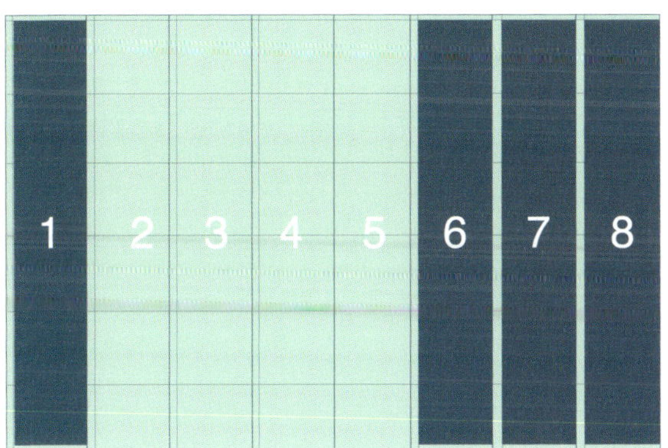

Visual Flow

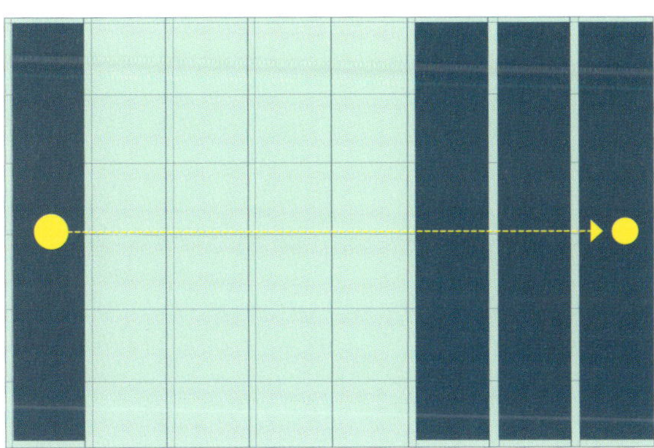

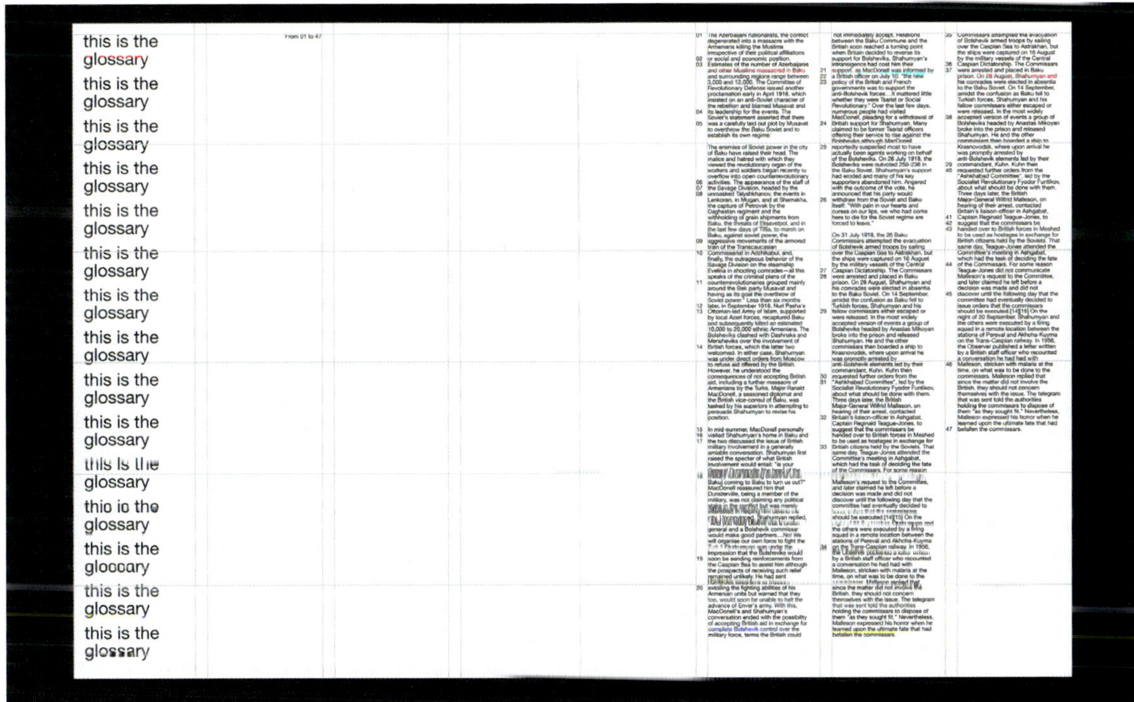

Architectural Odyssey is a Soviet architecture event held in Yerevan, Armenia, in Khnko Aper Children's Library. Soviet architecture is a symbol of the history that has gone, and the Soviet conception of construction is still alive: it is an odyssey through time. The event includes a complete experience into this "odyssey": conferences, expositions, movies and so on, so the new generation could understand better the theme of the event.

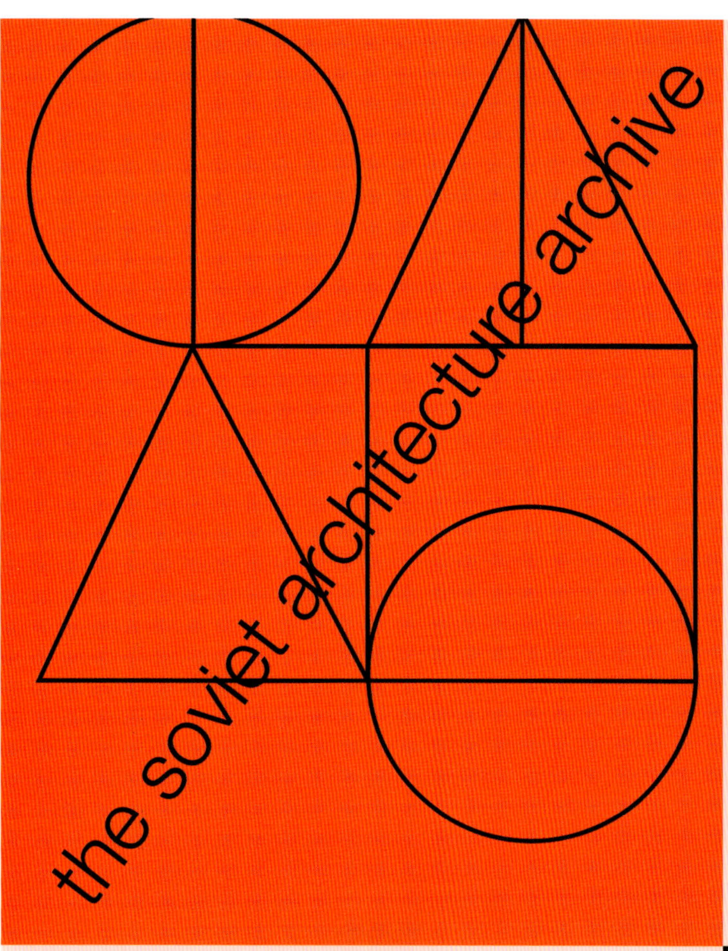

05 ARMAVIR, HOKTEMBERJAN
06 EREVAN, ARMAVIR
07 EREVAN, YEGNWARD
08 EREVAN, ARMAVIR
09 ARTASHAT, EREVAN
10 ASHTARAK-YEGNWARD
11 EREVAN, EDCHMIATZIN
12 SEVAN, EREVAN
13 SEVAN, EREVAN
14 EREVAN, GYMRI
15 SEVAN, WARDENIS

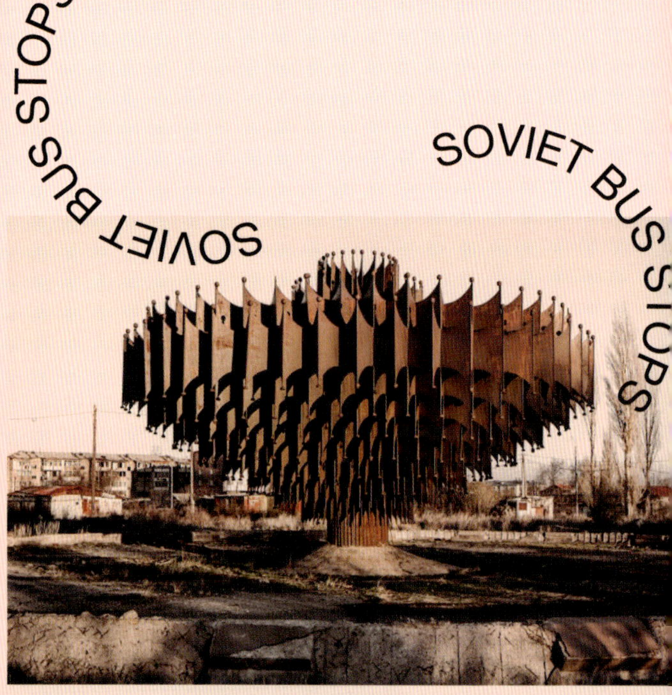

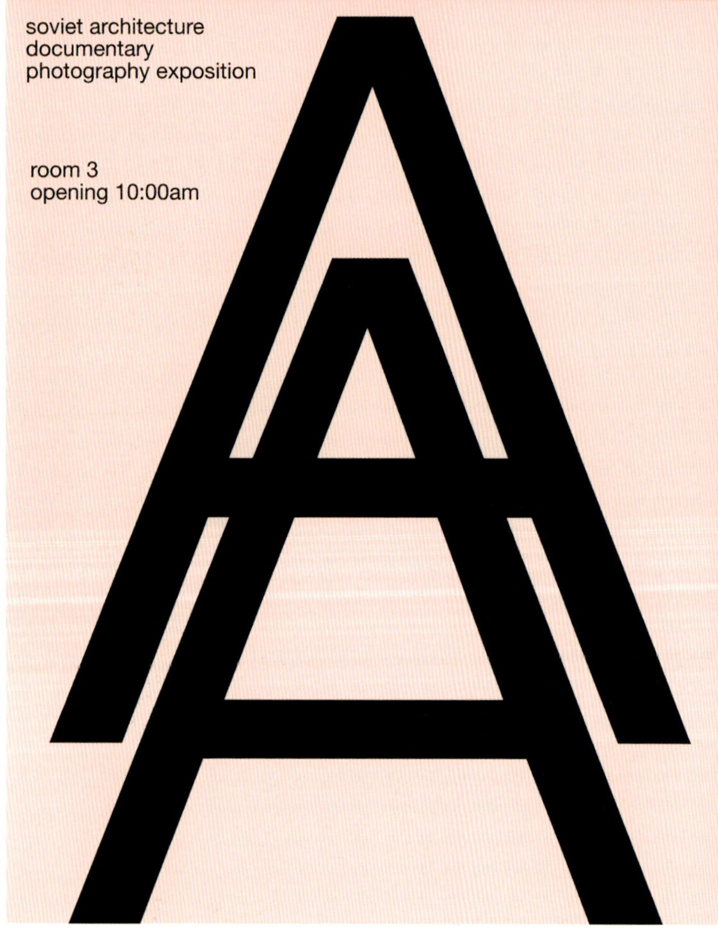

SOVIET ARCHITECTURE
TODAY

so
vie
t

02-
22
janu
ary

A REVIEW OF THE SOVIET
ARCHITECTURE LEGACY

ANALISING THE EXPRESSION OF
SOVIET ARCHITECTURE IN
DIFFERENT COUNTRIES

BRUTALISM: THE MORE
WITH LESS CONCEPTION
OF ARCHITECTURE

TATLIN: THE IMPOSSIBLE
ARCHITECTURE

he
ita

ye
re

room1

Armenia reestablished its Independence nearly 25 years ago, but the legacy of the USSR in the country lives on through leftover Soviet architecture. These buildings across the republic are as fascinating as they are monotonous; they are eerie and devoid of aesthetic. Their utilitarian purpose is incorporated into the design: colorless blocks, uniform heights. It is only with the appearance of the trappings of a modern society – like satellite dishes – that we can be sure we have not traveled back in time. Or, in some way, maybe we have. Tatevik Vardanyan leads us there with her lens.

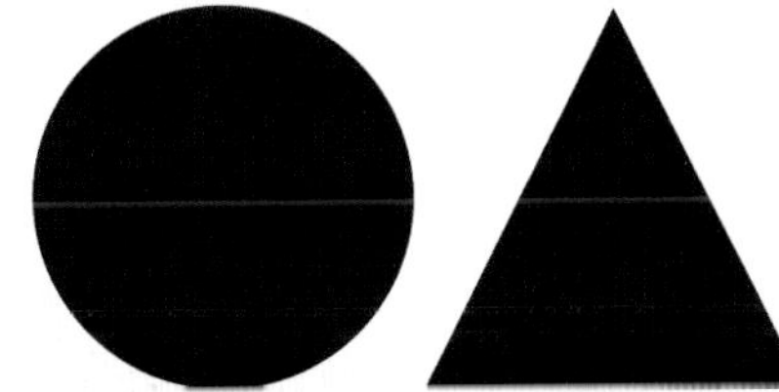

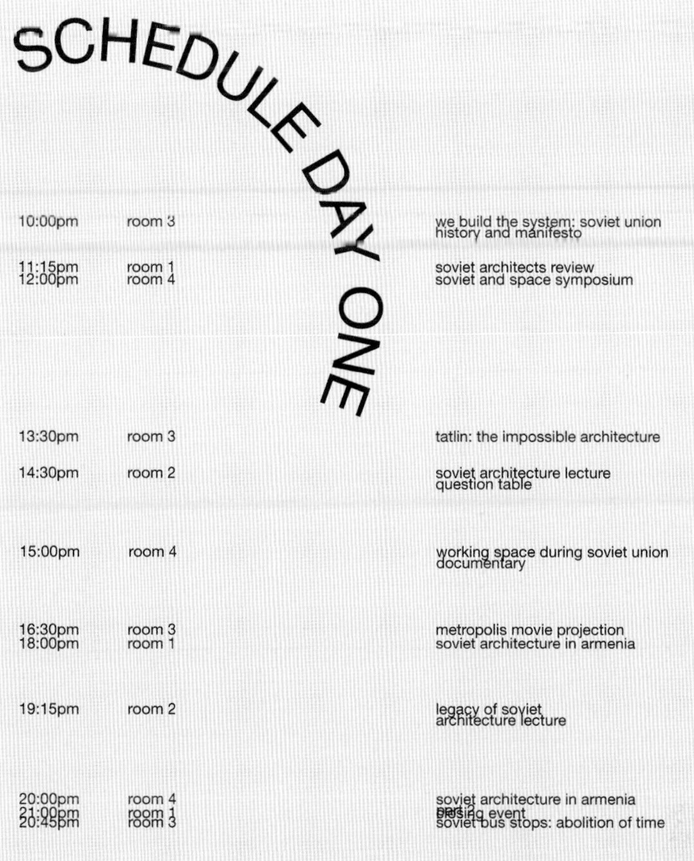

ARCHITECTURAL ODYSSEY
ARCHITECTURAL ODYSSEY
ARCHITECTURAL ODYSSEY
ARCHITECTURAL ODYSSEY
ARCHITECTURAL ODYSSEY
ARCHITECTURAL ODYSSEY
ARCHITECTURAL ODYSSEY
ARCHITECTURAL ODYSSEY
ARCHITECTURAL ODYSSEY
ARCHITECTURAL ODYSSEY
ARCHITECTURAL ODYSSEY
ARCHITECTURAL ODYSSEY
ARCHITECTURAL ODYSSEY
ARCHITECTURAL ODYSSEY
ARCHITECTURAL ODYSSEY
ARCHITECTURAL ODYSSEY

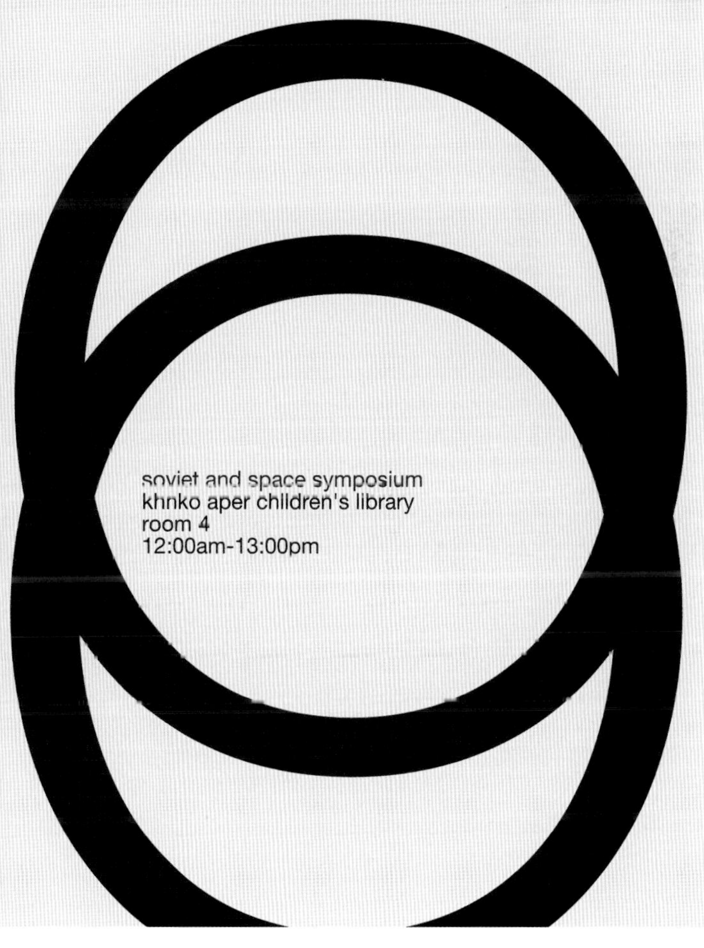

Artloop Festival Poster

Designer

Michał Mierzwa

Client

Artloop Festival

Key Diagram

Font	Paper	Size
Fabrik, Maax	Coated paper	210×297mm (A4)

The minimalist modern style fits perfectly with the sans-serif font and matches the theme of cosmic particles.

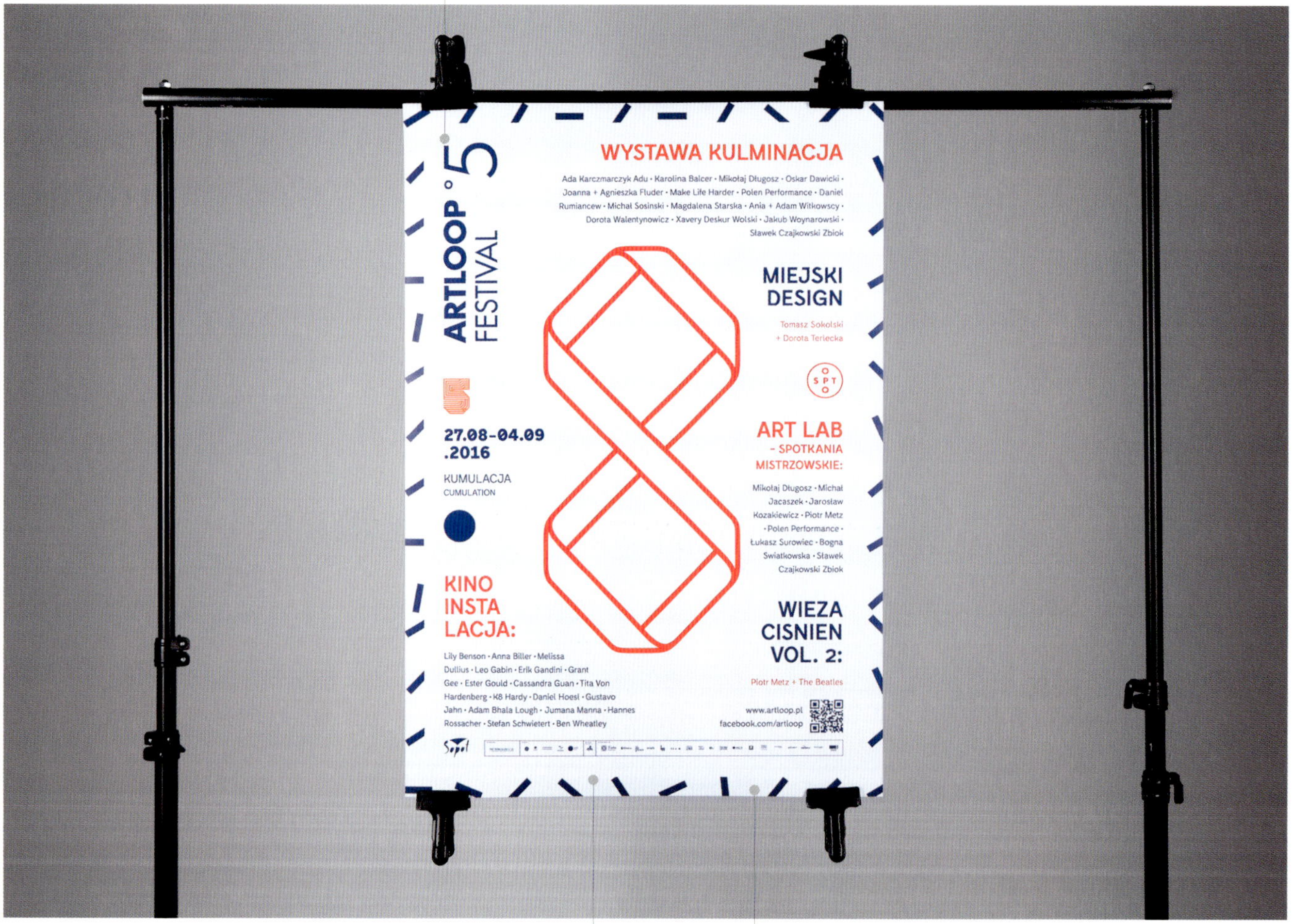

The layout is basically a 12-column grid with a lot of negative space.

Using contrast color to stimulate the visual sense also differentiates the information content that needs to be transmitted.

Grid

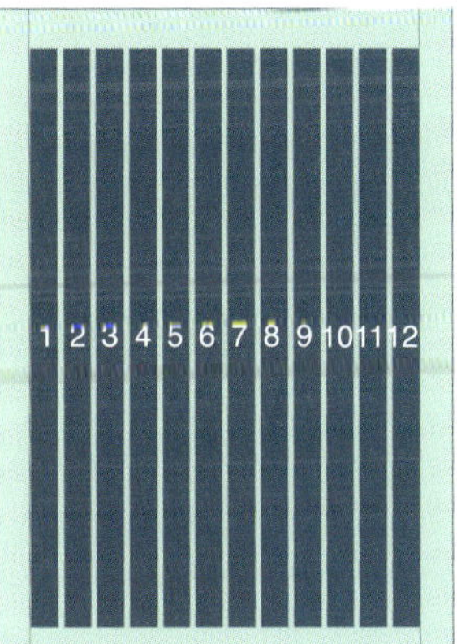

Visual Flow

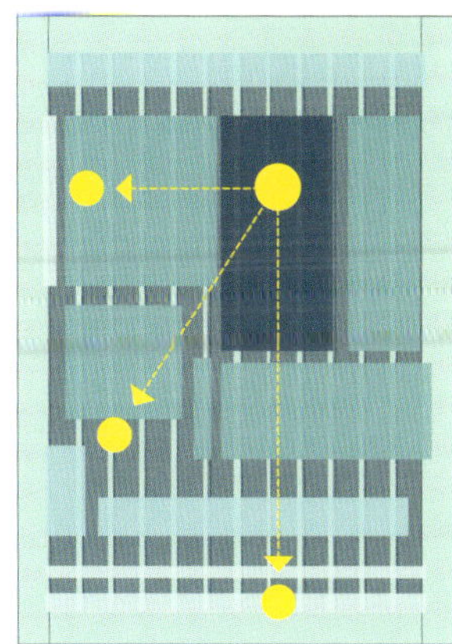

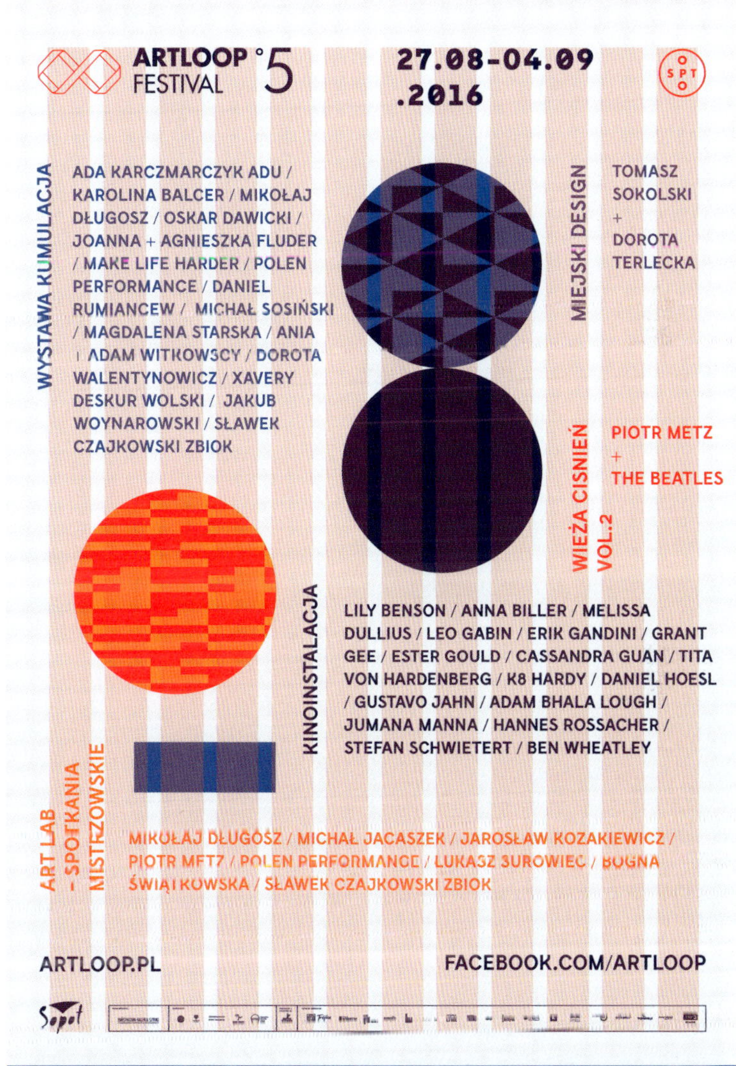

The key word of the Artloop Festival is "cumulation". The main theme refers to the concept of a cosmic black hole, which is the accumulation of particles whose visual form is a result of a particular energy bringing the particles together. Based on the theme of the festival, a number of elements were designed, such as a festival's official poster, large format printed materials, and a TV spot.

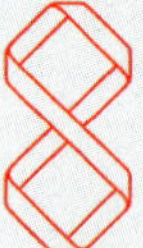

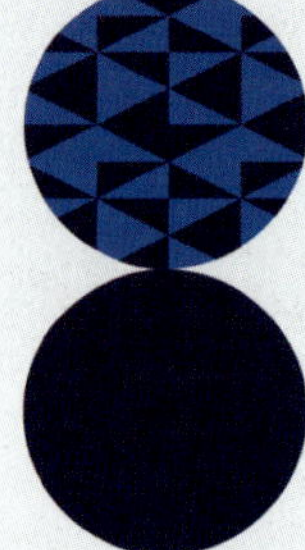

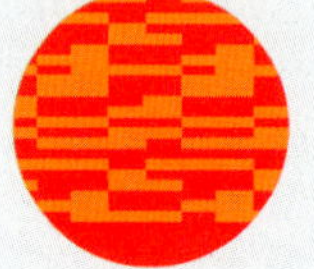

ARTLOOP °5
FESTIVAL
WYSTAWA KUMULACJA
ADA KARCZMARCZYK ADU / KAROLINA BALCER / MIKOŁAJ DŁUGOSZ / OSKAR DAWICKI / JOANNA + AGNIESZKA FLUDER / MAKE LIFE HARDER / POLEN PERFORMANCE / DANIEL RUMIANCEW / MICHAŁ SOSIŃSKI / MAGDALENA STARSKA / ANIA + ADAM WITKOWSCY / DOROTA WALENTYNOWICZ / XAVERY DESKUR WOLSKI / JAKUB WOYNAROWSKI / SŁAWEK CZAJKOWSKI ZBIOK
WIEŻA CIŚNIEŃ VOL.2
PIOTR METZ + THE BEATLES
MIEJSKI DESIGN
TOMASZ SOKOLSKI + DOROTA TERLECKA
KINOINSTALACJA
LILY BENSON / ANNA BILLER / MELISSA DULLIUS / LEO GABIN / ERIK GANDINI / GRANT GEE / ESTER GOULD / CASSANDRA GUAN / TITA VON HARDENBERG / K8 HARDY / DANIEL HOESL / GUSTAVO JAHN / ADAM BHALA LOUGH / JUMANA MANNA / HANNES ROSSACHER / STEFAN SCHWIETERT / BEN WHEATLEY
ART LAB - SPOTKANIA MISTRZOWSKIE
MIKOŁAJ DŁUGOSZ / MICHAŁ JACASZEK / JAROSŁAW KOZAKIEWICZ / PIOTR METZ / POLEN PERFORMANCE / ŁUKASZ SUROWIEC / BOGNA ŚWIĄTKOWSKA / SŁAWEK CZAJKOWSKI ZBIOK
O S P T O

ARTLOOP °5
FESTIVAL
O S P T O

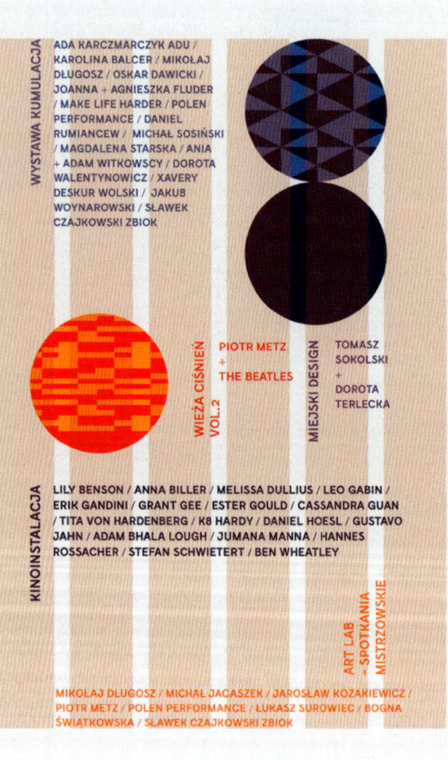

WYSTAWA KUMULACJA
ADA KARCZMARCZYK ADU / KAROLINA BALCER / MIKOŁAJ DŁUGOSZ / OSKAR DAWICKI / JOANNA + AGNIESZKA FLUDER / MAKE LIFE HARDER / POLEN PERFORMANCE / DANIEL RUMIANCEW / MICHAŁ SOSIŃSKI / MAGDALENA STARSKA / ANIA + ADAM WITKOWSCY / DOROTA WALENTYNOWICZ / XAVERY DESKUR WOLSKI / JAKUB WOYNAROWSKI / SŁAWEK CZAJKOWSKI ZBIOK
WIEŻA CIŚNIEŃ VOL.2
PIOTR METZ + THE BEATLES
MIEJSKI DESIGN
TOMASZ SOKOLSKI + DOROTA TERLECKA
KINOINSTALACJA
LILY BENSON / ANNA BILLER / MELISSA DULLIUS / LEO GABIN / ERIK GANDINI / GRANT GEE / ESTER GOULD / CASSANDRA GUAN / TITA VON HARDENBERG / K8 HARDY / DANIEL HOESL / GUSTAVO JAHN / ADAM BHALA LOUGH / JUMANA MANNA / HANNES ROSSACHER / STEFAN SCHWIETERT / BEN WHEATLEY
ART LAB - SPOTKANIA MISTRZOWSKIE
MIKOŁAJ DŁUGOSZ / MICHAŁ JACASZEK / JAROSŁAW KOZAKIEWICZ / PIOTR METZ / POLEN PERFORMANCE / ŁUKASZ SUROWIEC / BOGNA ŚWIĄTKOWSKA / SŁAWEK CZAJKOWSKI ZBIOK

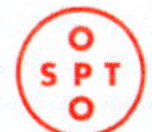

PROGRAM GODZINOWY

27.08 -04.09 .2016

Legenda

- WIEŻA CIŚNIEŃ
- ART LAB
- MIEJSKI DESIGN
- KINOINSTALACJA
- WYSTAWA

czwartek, 25 sierpnia

18:00 — 22:00	Willa na Goyki | **Inauguracja Wieży Ciśnień Piotra Metza**
19:00	Willa na Goyki | **Masterclass: Piotr Metz**

piatek, 26 sierpnia

16:00 — 22:00	Willa na Goyki | **Wieża Ciśnień Piotra Metza** | Obiekty + akcje

sobota, 27 sierpnia

11:30	Molo | **OTWARCIE 05 ARTLOOP + WYSTAWY KUMULACJA | Ania + Adam Witkowscy, „W zenicie"** | Performatywny utwór muzyczny
12:00 — 16:00	Skwer Kuracyjny | **Sławek ZBIOK Czajkowski, "Loop/pętla"** | instalacja + akcja
12:00 — 20:00	Plaża przy Molo | **Karolina Balcer, „Parawaning"** | Instalacja
	Plaża przy Molo | **Xavery Deskur Wolski, „Przybysz"** | Rzeźba
	Molo | **Magdalena Starska, „Spełnienie w Sopocie"** | Instalacja
12:00 — 21:00	Latarnia przy Molo | **Joanna + Agnieszka Fluder, „Numer Jeden"** | Projekcja
12:00 — 22:00	Plac Przyjaciół Sopotu | **Dorota Terlecka + Tomasz Sokolski, „Kumulacja marzeń"** | Obiekty
	Molo | **Mikołaj Długosz, "Głos Mola"** | Instalacja
	Plac Przyjaciół Sopotu – przy obiekcie Kumulacja Marzeń | **Ada Karczmarczyk ADU**, Biżuteria **"Amber Emperor"** + Teledysk **„Bursztynami mnie obejmij"**
14:00	Marina | **Make Life Harder + Adam Witkowski, „Sopocki Sztorm"** | Wykonanie utworu
14:00 — 15:30	PGS – Kinoinstalacja | **Dyskusja „Kumulacja / Konfrontacja"** – spotkanie z artystami biorącymi udział w wystawie – moderuje: Kolektyw Kuratorski
16:00	Marina | **Make Life Harder + Adam Witkowski, „Sopocki Sztorm"** | Wykonanie utworu
16:00 — 17:30	PGS – Kinoinstalacja | **Masterclass: Sławek ZBIOK Czajkowski**

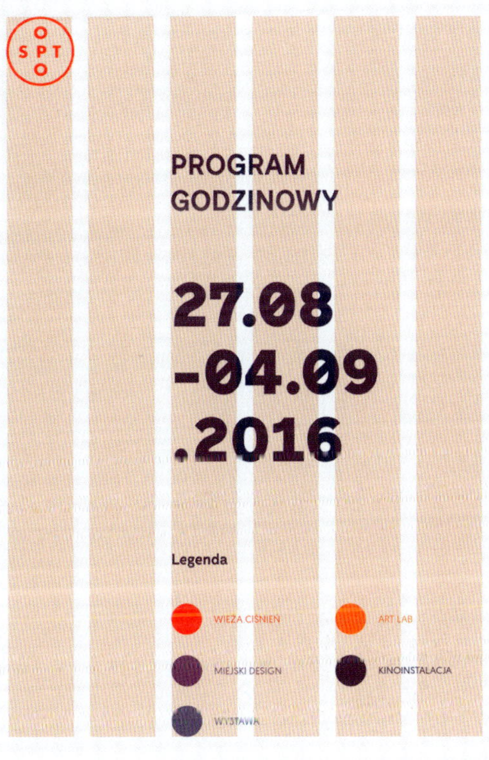

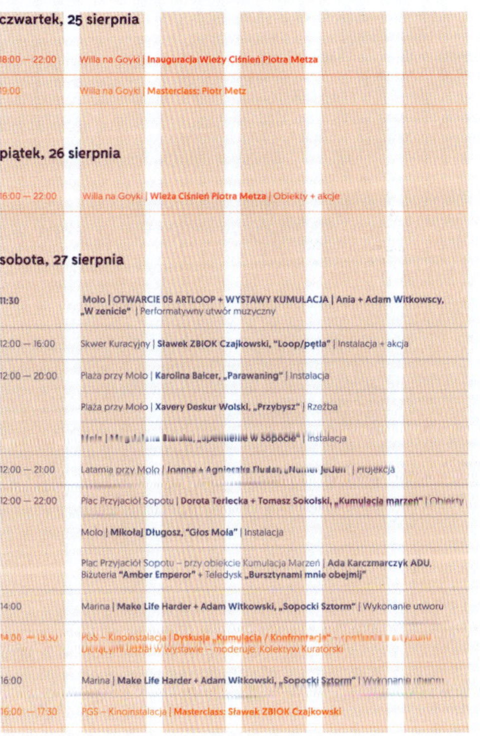

Katowice City's Anniversary Celebration Promotional Materials

Designer

Marta Gawin

Client

Katowice—City of Gardens

Key Diagram

Font	Paper	Size
GT Sectra, GT Pressura	Munken Kristall	170×240mm

The serif font is mixed with the sans serif font. In addition, the comparison of the font size also enhances the text sense of layering.

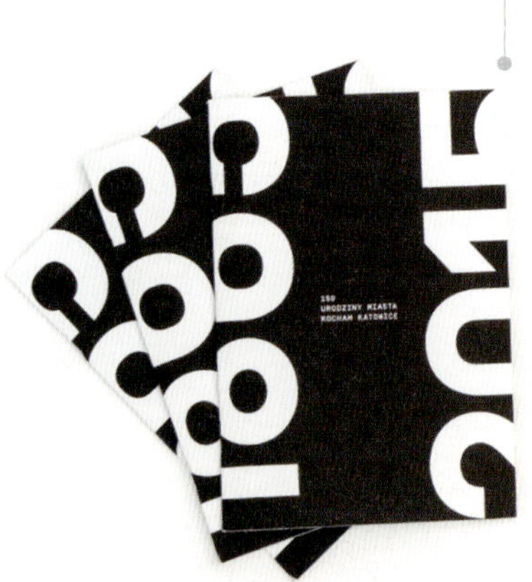

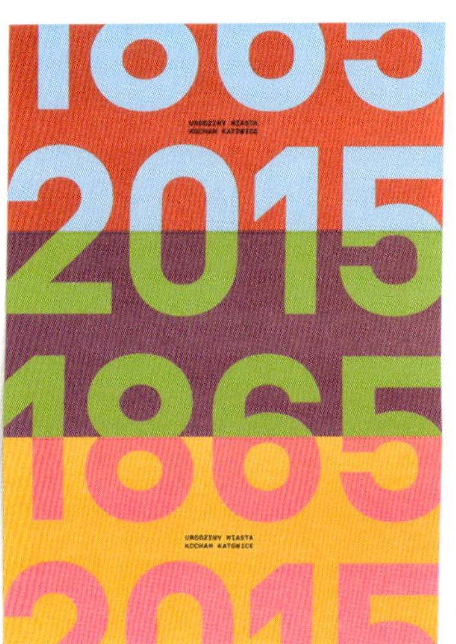

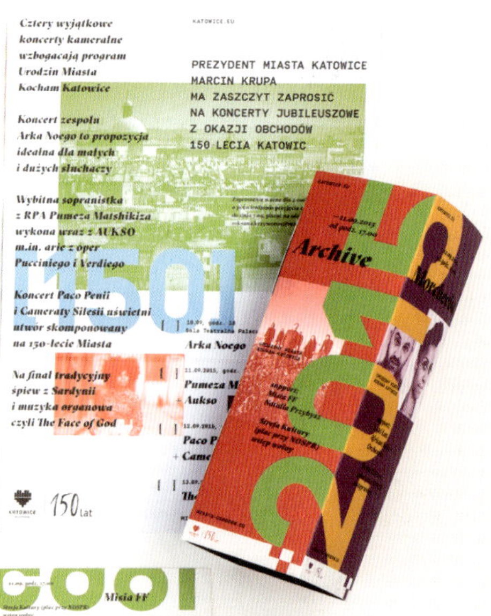

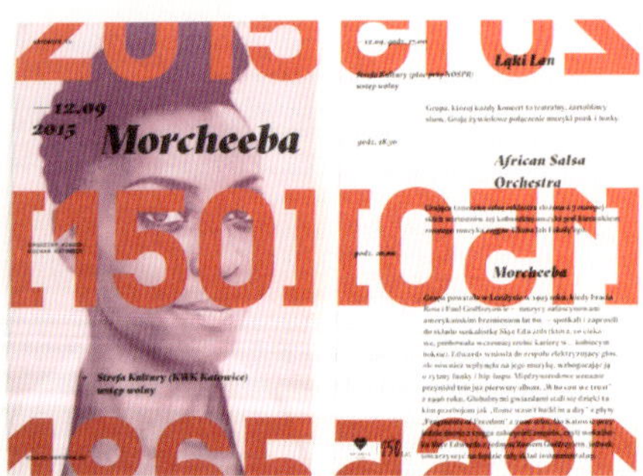

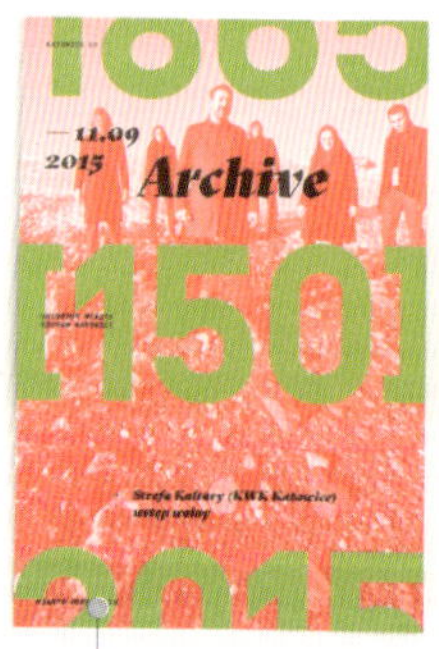

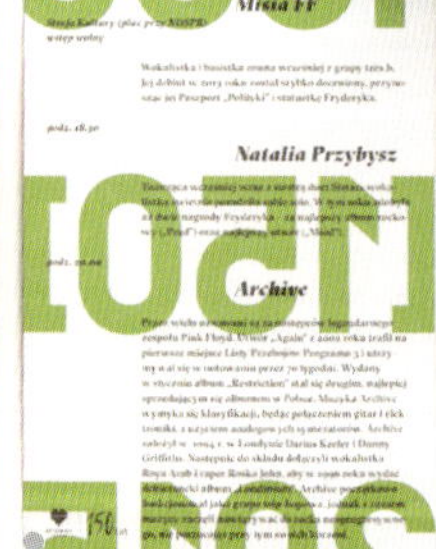

Compound grid system is used in the layout. The most visual impact is the brightly colored anniversary number and the titles.

Inspired by the vivid colors of the city's architecture, the designers applied colorful colors to design the anniversary promotional materials. With a 70% base color and 30% secondary color, the promotional materials for the three anniversaries acquire coherence and recognizability.

Grid

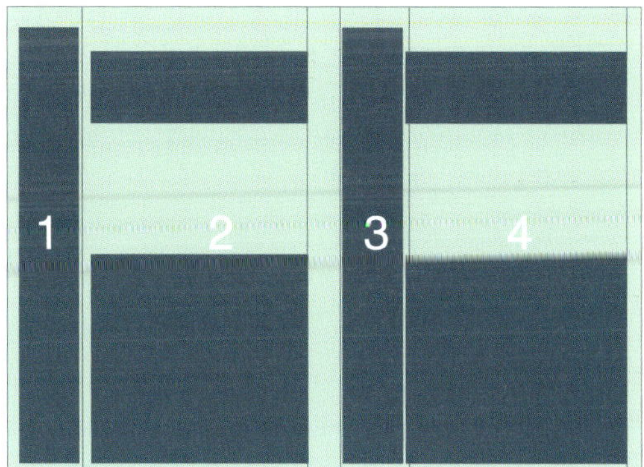

Visual Flow

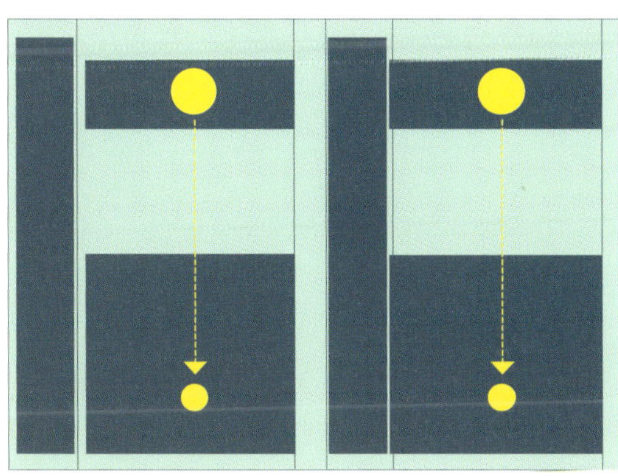

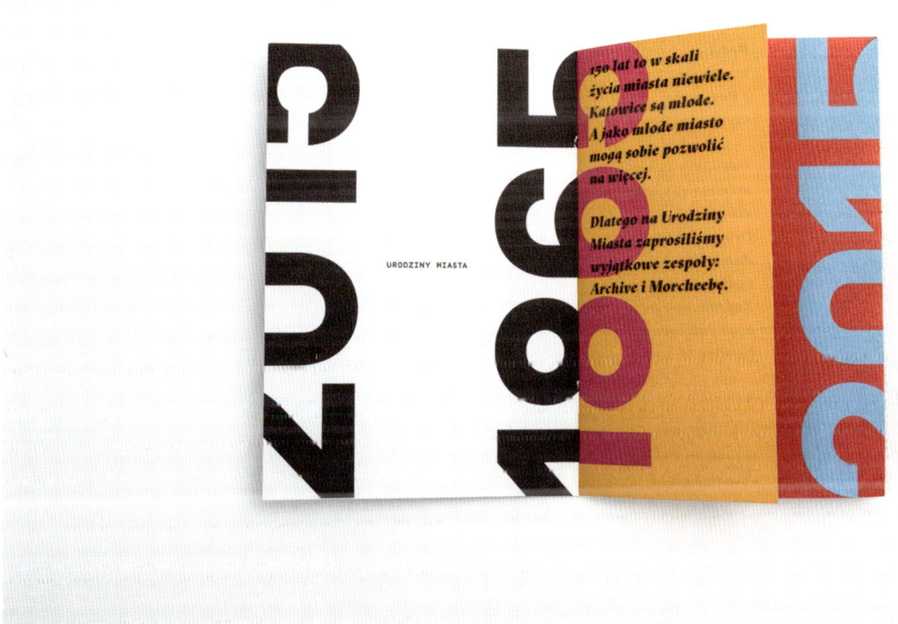

Promotional materials design for the 150th, 151st and 152nd anniversary celebrations of the city Katowice, Poland.

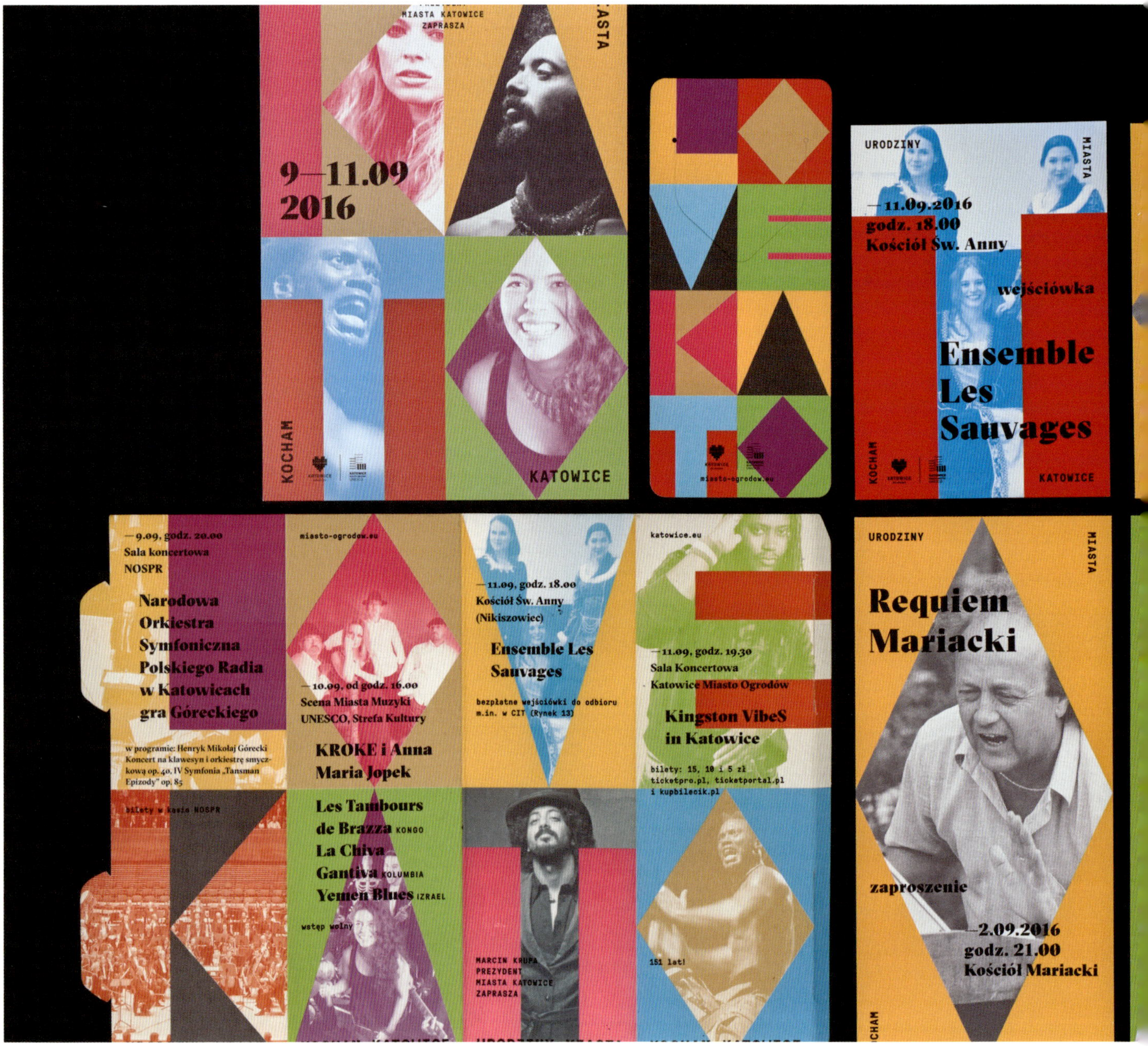

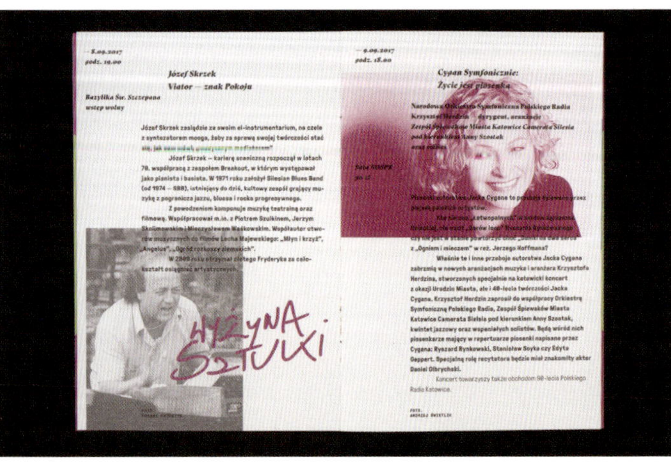
Józef Skrzek
Viator — znak Pokoju
WYŻYNA SZTUKI

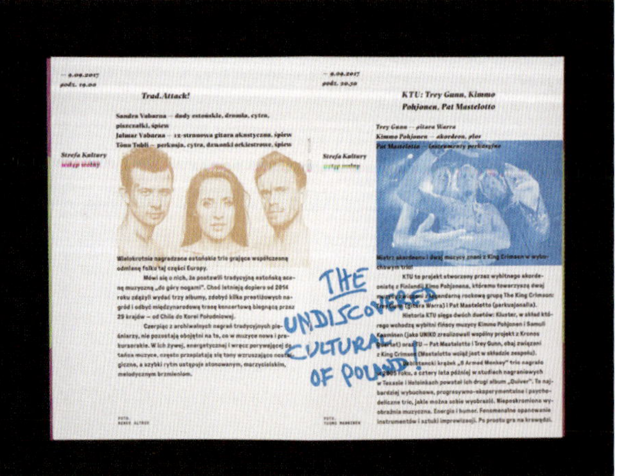
Trad.Attack!
KTU: Trey Gunn, Kimmo Pohjonen, Pat Mastelotto
THE UNDISCOVERED CULTURAL OF POLAND!

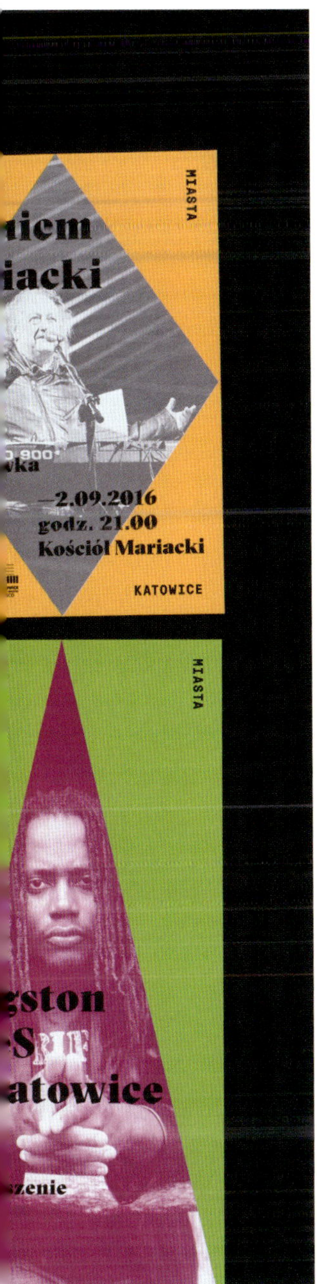

LOVE KATO

KATOWICE
KATOWICE MIASTO MUZYKI UNESCO
miasto-ogrodow.eu

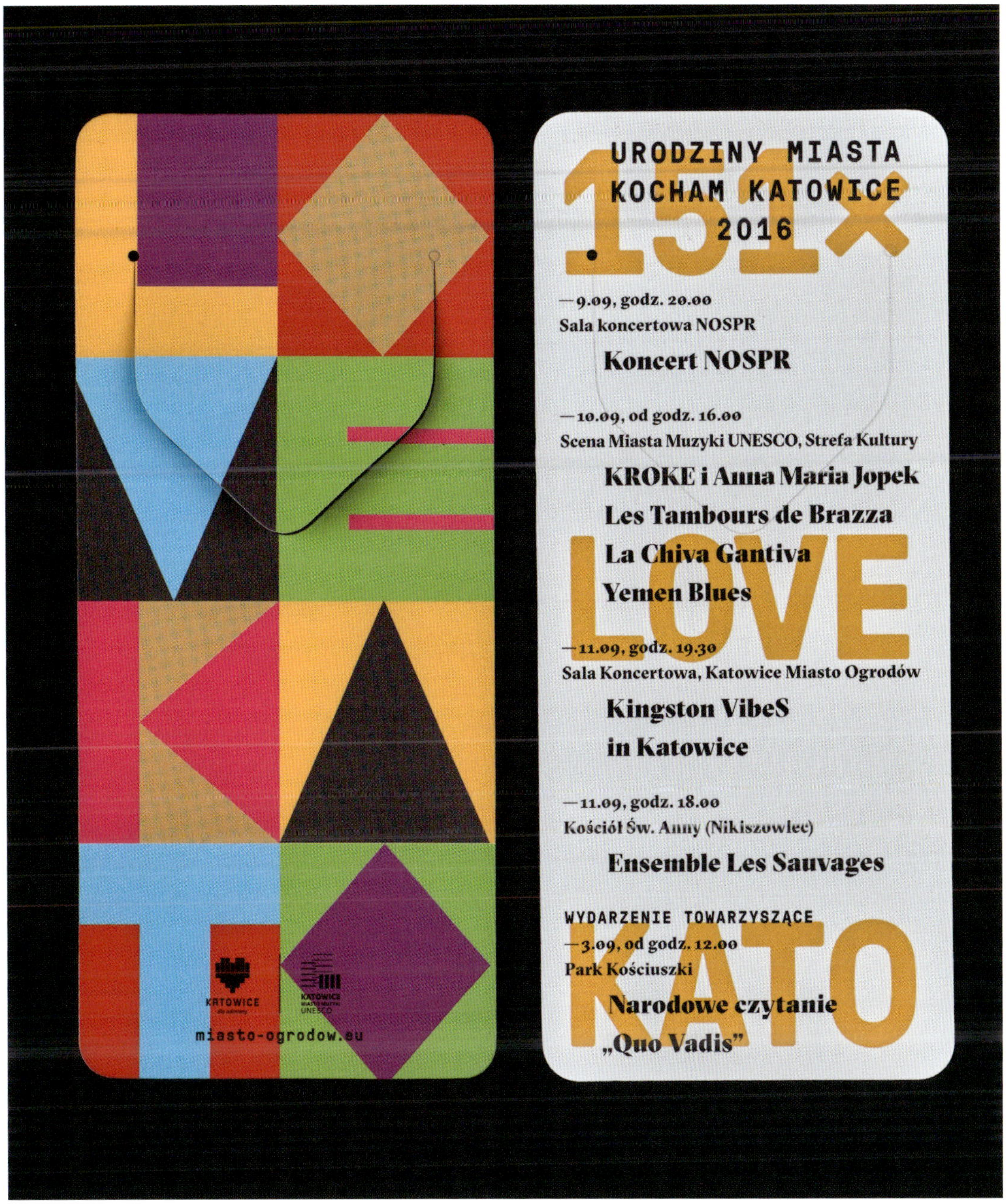

URODZINY MIASTA
KOCHAM KATOWICE
2016
151x

—9.09, godz. 20.00
Sala koncertowa NOSPR
Koncert NOSPR

—10.09, od godz. 16.00
Scena Miasta Muzyki UNESCO, Strefa Kultury
KROKE i Anna Maria Jopek
Les Tambours de Brazza
La Chiva Gantiva
Yemen Blues

LOVE

—11.09, godz. 19.30
Sala Koncertowa, Katowice Miasto Ogrodów
Kingston VibeS
in Katowice

—11.09, godz. 18.00
Kościół Św. Anny (Nikiszowiec)
Ensemble Les Sauvages

WYDARZENIE TOWARZYSZĄCE
—3.09, od godz. 12.00
Park Kościuszki
Narodowe czytanie
„Quo Vadis"

KATO

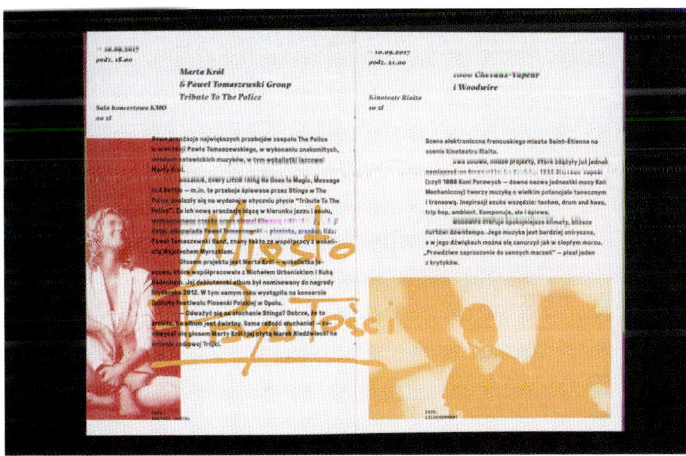

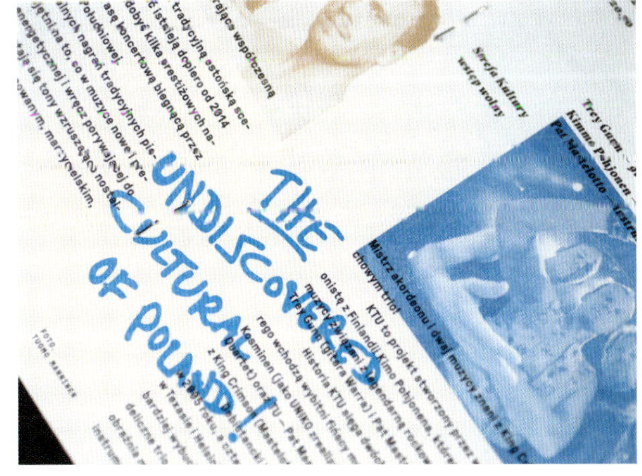

Fauna Primavera Booklet

Designer

Sandrine Anne Sautejeau

Client

Fauna Prod.

Key Diagram

Font	Paper	Size
Albus, Pier Sans Bold	106g Bond wove finish	100×200mm (Folded)

The same fonts as for posters. This makes all materials a coherent whole.

Four main colors were used across all the pages of the booklet: green, black, pink, and yellow.

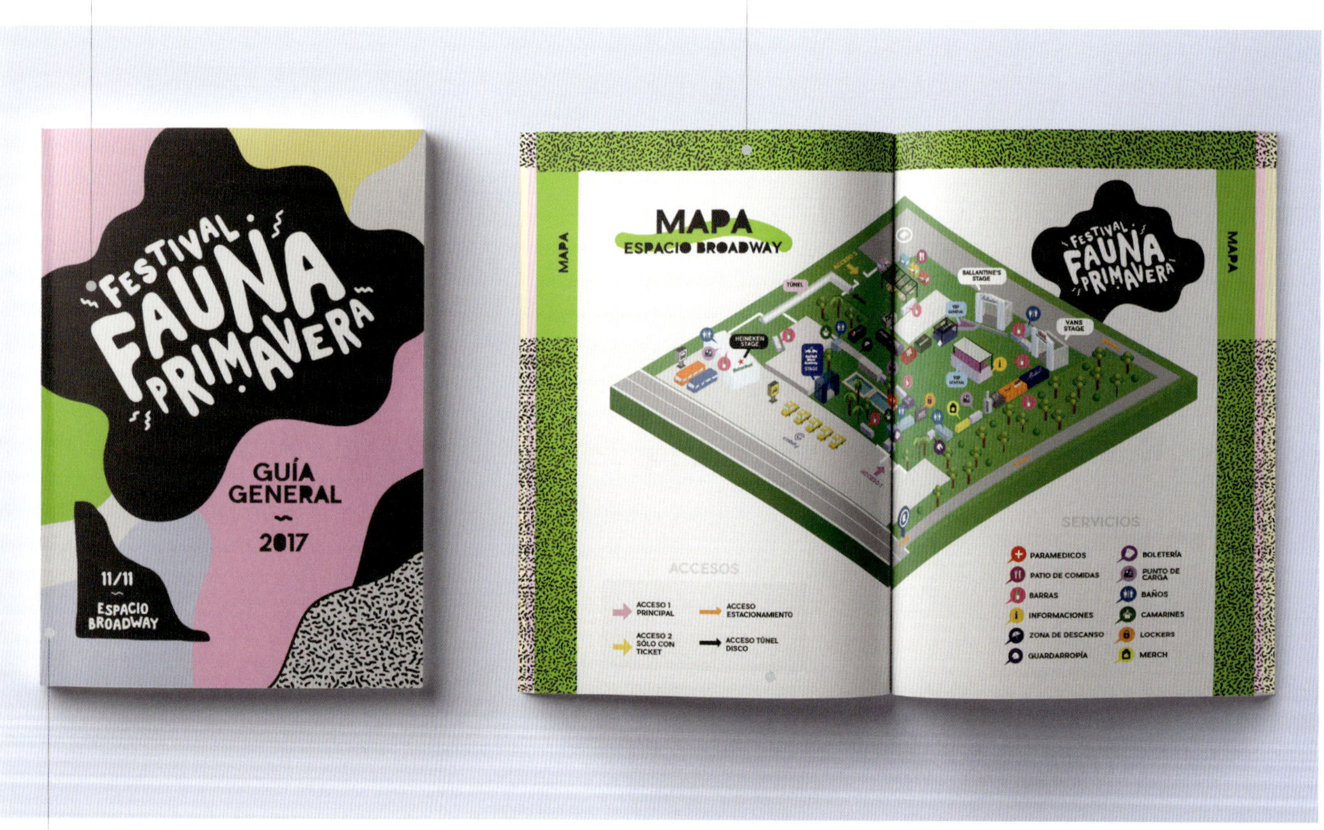

The amount of text in the booklet is much stronger than the posters and the content stays in the centered type area. By repeating the arrangement throughout the pages, the information is sorted out more clearly and neatly.

Grid

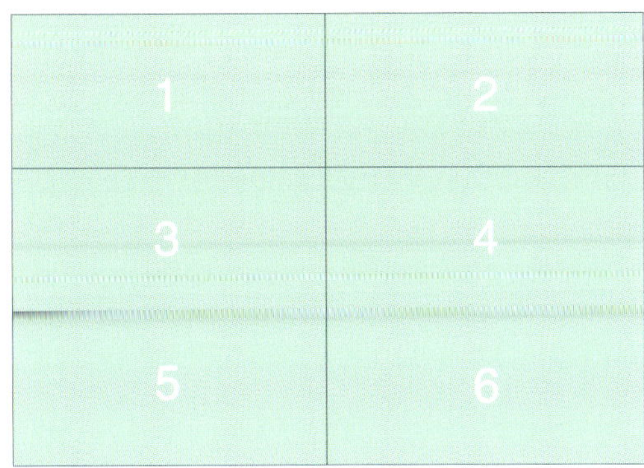

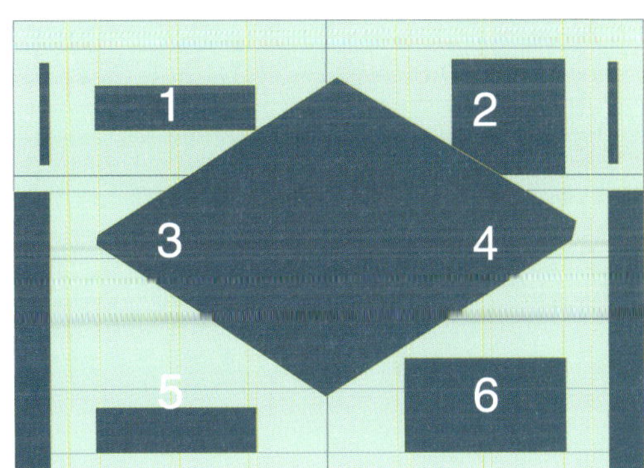

Visual Flow

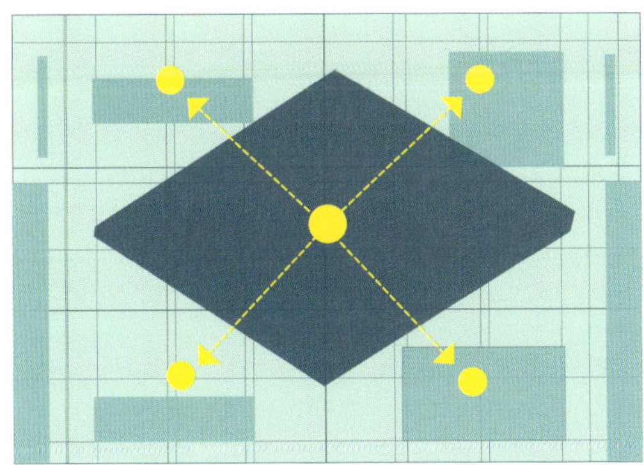

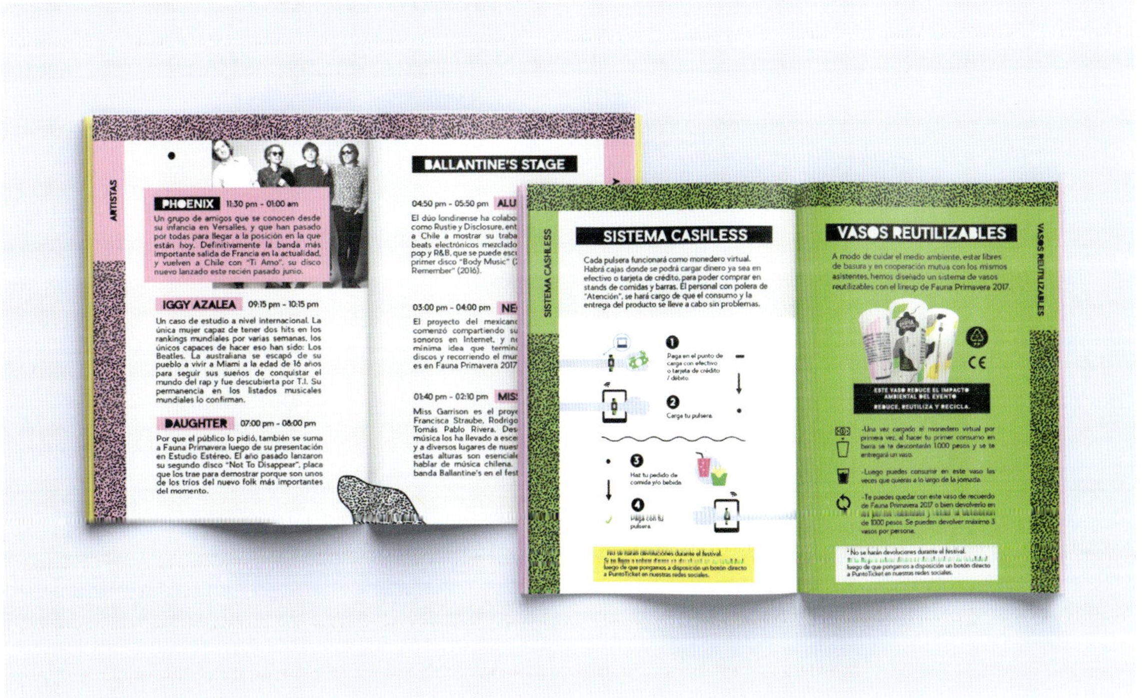

Splendid Facet Exhibition Brochure

Designer

Songah Lee

Key Diagram

Font	Paper	Size
Arial	70g Medium pulp paper	80×210mm

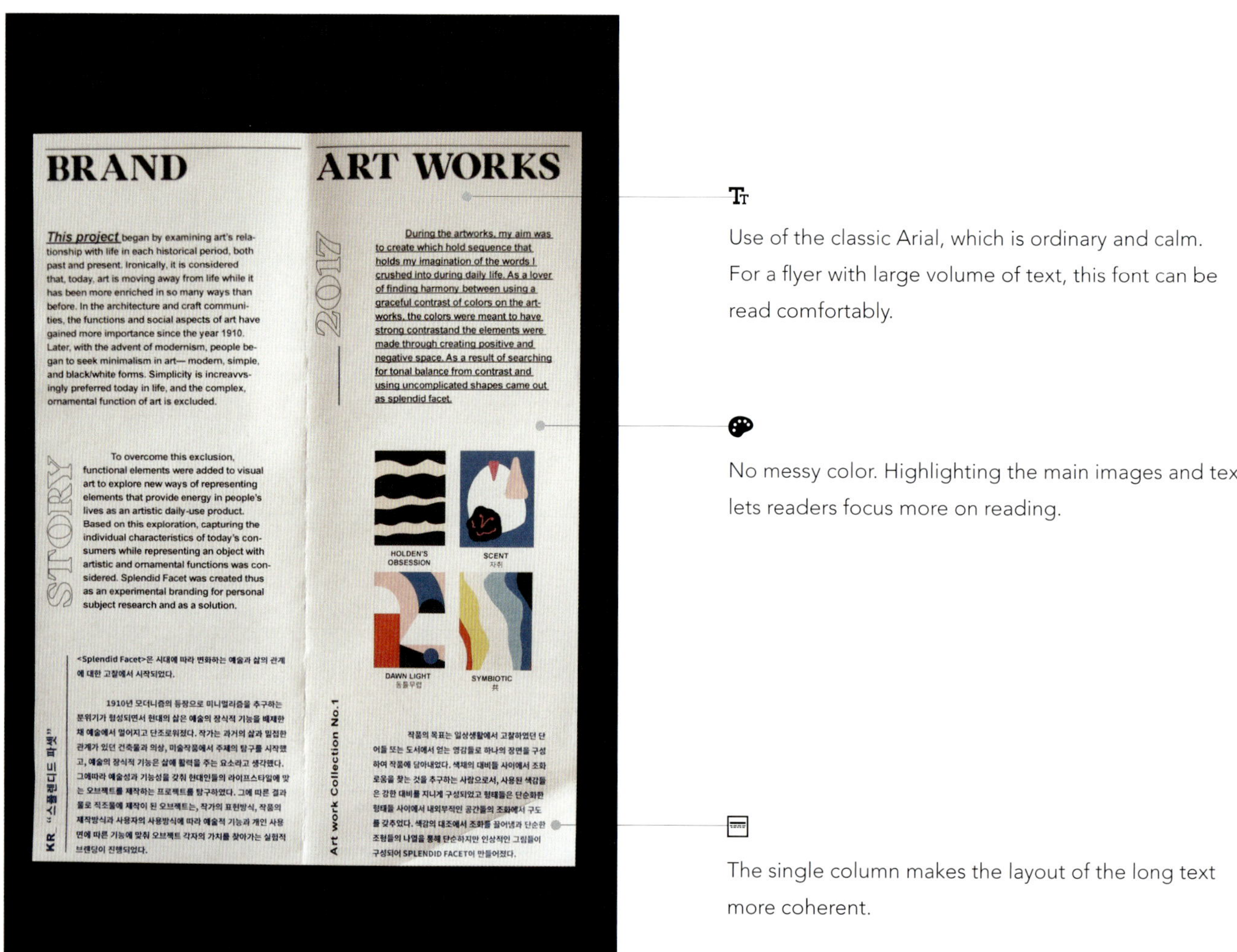

Use of the classic Arial, which is ordinary and calm. For a flyer with large volume of text, this font can be read comfortably.

No messy color. Highlighting the main images and text lets readers focus more on reading.

The single column makes the layout of the long text more coherent.

Grid

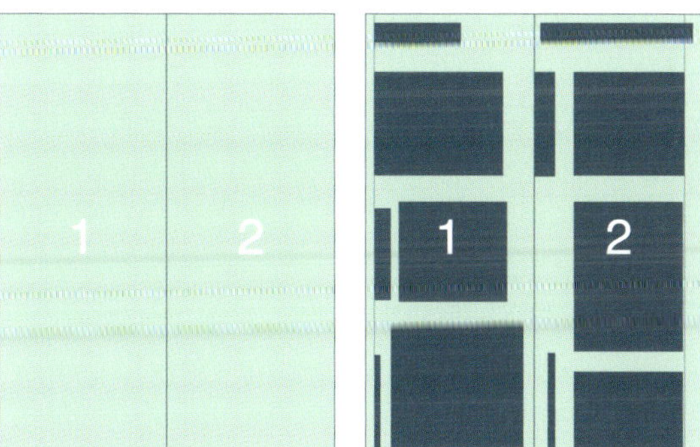

Visual Flow

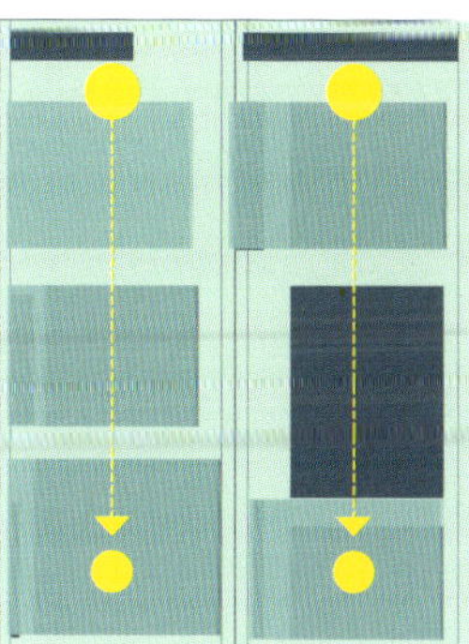

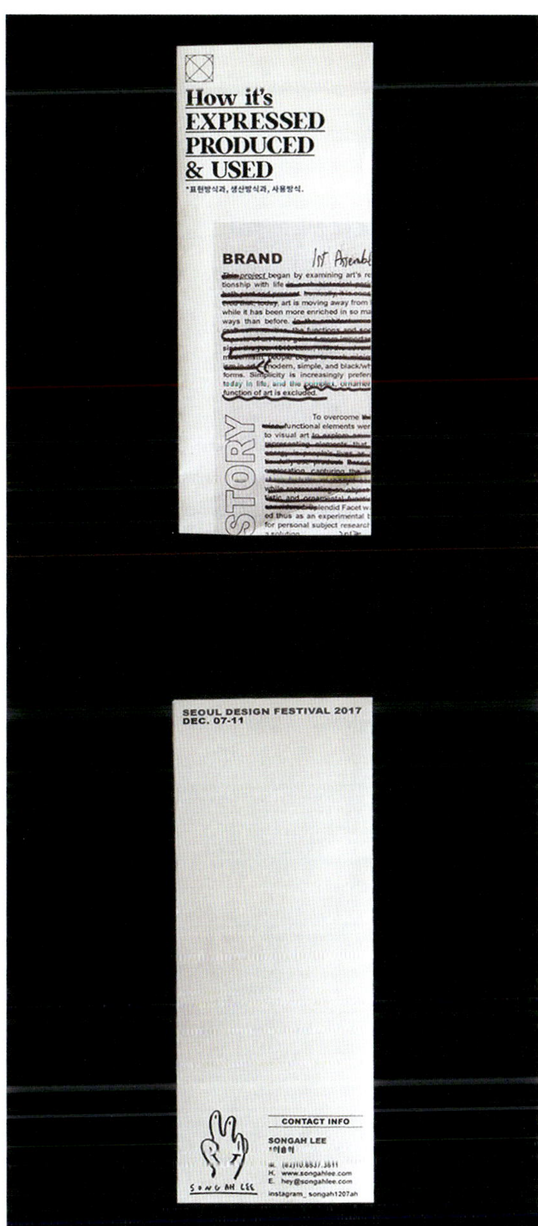

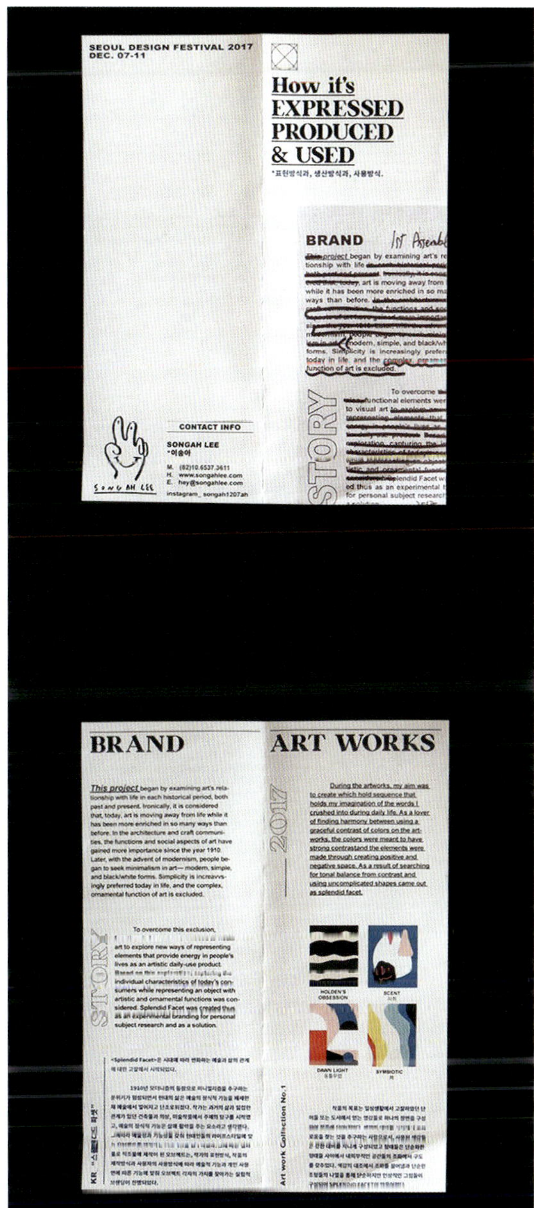

The main content of this brochure is introducing the brands that are displayed at the Seoul Design Festival. It will be used to showcase the exhibitors, the process of producing their products, and the usage of the products. The brochure aims to introduce how to build up a brand, and the background design upgrades the visual effect of the design process. The paper, a 70g medium pulp paper, was applied, in order to echo with the concept.

Breve Historia De Las Cosas Brochure

Designer

Mane Tatoulian

Key Diagram

Font	Paper	Size
Helvetica Neue Caslon	120g Fabriano matte	210×297mm (A4)

Tracking, also called letter-spacing, affects the rhythm of the text. The loose tracking of the title gives a feeling of relaxation, while the tight spacing of the main body text pulls the reader into the world of philosophy.

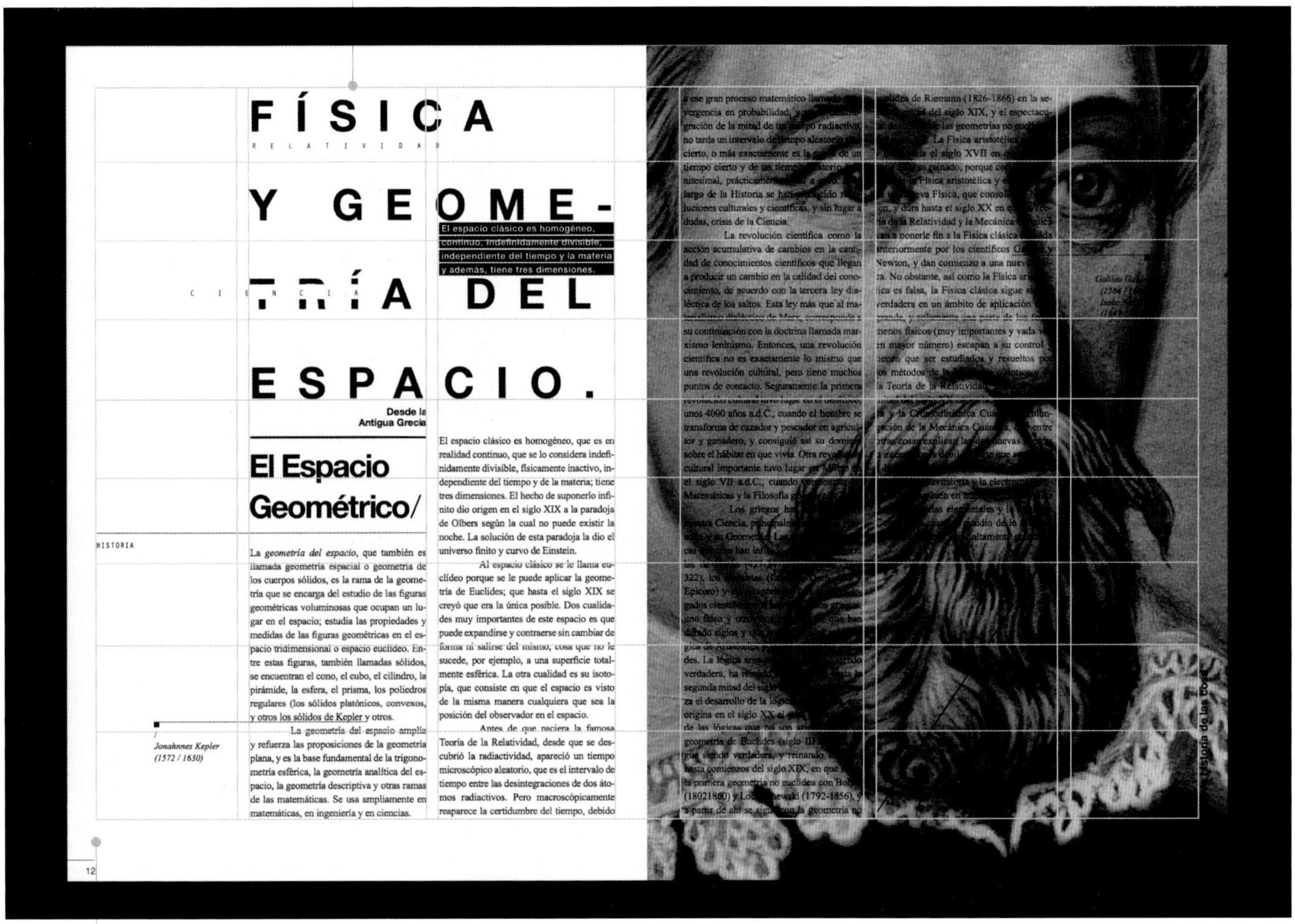

FÍSICA Y GEOMETRÍA DEL ESPACIO.

El espacio clásico es homogéneo, continuo, indefinidamente divisible, independiente del tiempo y la materia y además, tiene tres dimensiones.

Desde la Antigua Grecia

El Espacio Geométrico/

Since the text content is about philosophical thinking, the overall layout is in a stable and balanced form. The justified edge alignment makes the long text look very neat in the layout.

Grid

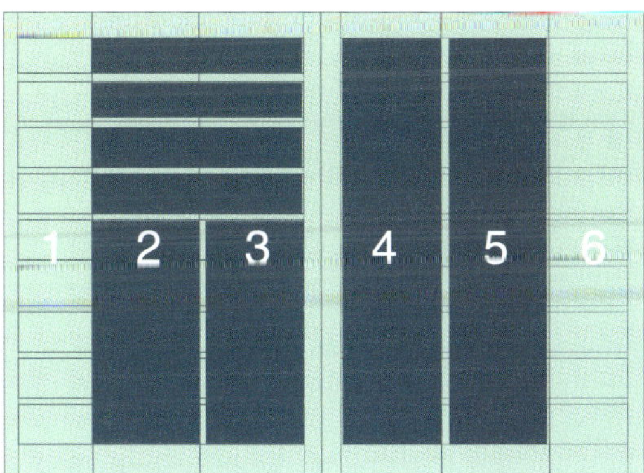

Visual Flow

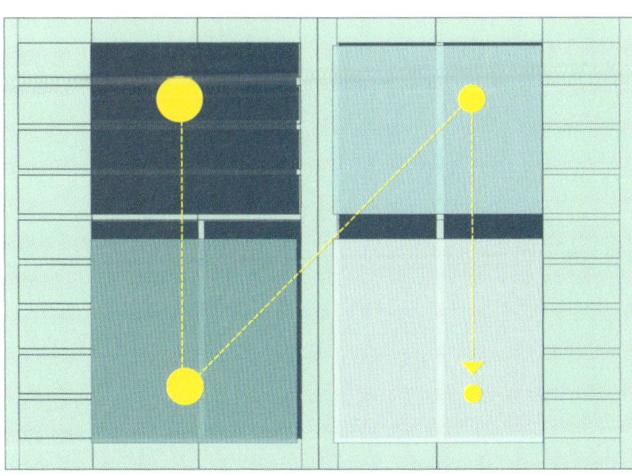

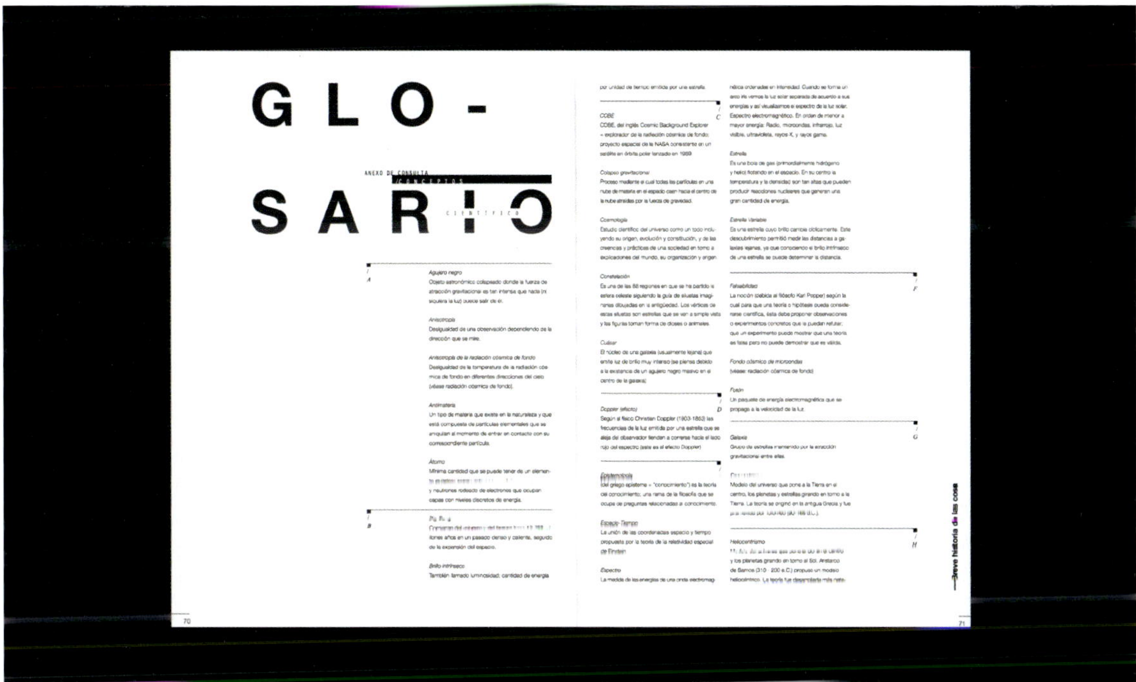

In this project, the designer explores an abstract question: How is it that man can know reality? Through coordinates of space and the implicit mathematics, we may at least know the so-called reality. The abstract nature of space and time makes them constantly in the dichotomy of truth and falsehood or existence and non-existence, which has been an eternal question for humans.

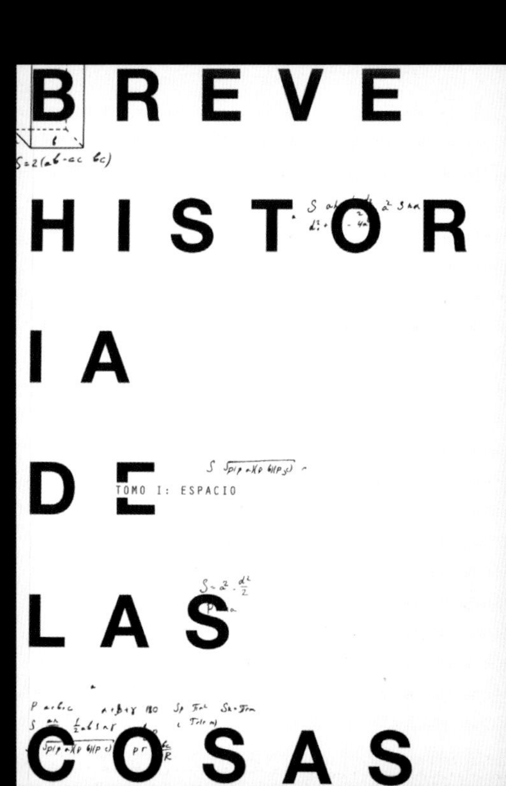

Espacio, tiempo y no tiempo, construcciones que han acompañado al hombre a lo largo de toda su existencia. ¿Cómo es que el hombre puede conocer la realidad? Esto es a través del tiempo y del espacio, de sus coordenadas y las matemáticas implícitas en la edificación de *lo real*, por lo menos, lo que nosotros llamamos realidad, lo plausible a ser conocido. Y la *naturaleza* asbtracta de dichos fenómenos, los hace permanecer constantemente en la dicotomía de la verdad/falsedad, existencia/inexistencia, en una pregunta eterna en la vida del ser humano.

Según su punto de vista, en tanto que los seres humanos y todos los cuerpos corrientes se encuentran en tres dimensiones. «Los seres espirituales», incorpóreos, «los espíritus», se sitúan en magnitudes del espacio inaccesibles a los seres comunes. De ahí deducen que «los espíritus» pueden influir en los procesos materiales y dirigirlos, permaneciendo fuera de nuestras percepciones. Pero el intento de especular con la noción de los «espacios pluridimensionales» para refutar el materialismo carece de toda base.

1

El espacio geométrico

Sección I

El espacio euclídeo

Sección I

Hilbert, Lebesgue y Sobolev

Sección I

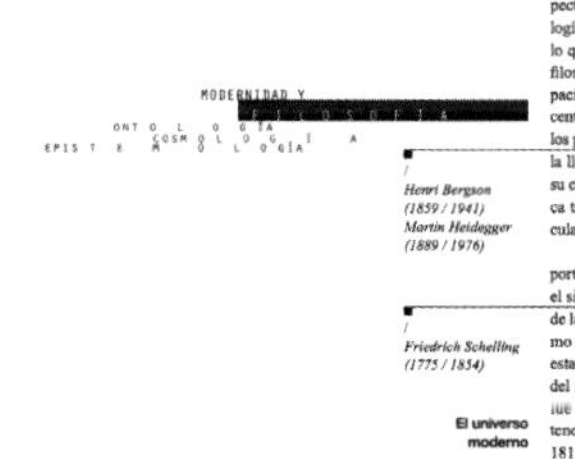

FILOSOFÍA

El universo moderno

Teorías Generales/

Ha ocurrido con muchos sistemas filosóficos clásicos que ven amenazados sus cimientos por las revolucionarias concepciones que levantan los actuales conocimientos científicos. O si no sus cimientos, algunas ideas capitales. Se torna, pues, imperiosa una autoconciencia filosófica de la crisis y una revisión, por parte de muchas doctrinas filosóficas, de sus proposiciones fundamentales. Pasos imprescindibles para salir de este estado y comenzar a remozarse son, primero, que el saber filosófico se haga cargo, en todo su impacto y consecuencia, de los resultados de las diversas ciencias (humanas y naturales); y, segundo, que los diferentes sistemas filosóficos que han levantado extensas proposiciones sobre el hombre y la naturaleza, las evalúen y examinen a la luz de tales resultados científicos Muchas supuestas verdades, muchos juicios caducos, quedarían así - para nuestro beneficio- arrumbados para siempre en los patios traseros de la historiado las ideas.

La filosofía del espacio y el tiempo es la rama de la filosofía que trata de los aspectos referidos a la ontología, la epistemología y la naturaleza del espacio y el tiempo, lo que se conoce también como cosmología filosófica. Si los problemas vinculados al espacio y al tiempo tradicionalmente han sido centrales en los sistemas filosóficos, desde los presocráticos hasta Bergson y Heidegger, la llamada filosofía analítica, en ejercicio de su crítica del método científico y la metafísica tradicionales, los ha estudiado con particular interés desde sus comienzos.

Henri Bergson
(1859 / 1941)
Martin Heidegger
(1889 / 1976)

Una de las aportaciones más importantes realizadas al estudio del tiempo en el siglo XIX es obra de F. W. Schelling, una de las figuras relevantes del llamado idealismo alemán. La obra clave para el estudio de esta cuestión en este filósofo es Las edades del mundo (Die Weltalter), un texto que no fue publicado en vida del autor y del que tenemos tres versiones muy similares (de 1811, 1813 y 1815) aunque diferentes en algunos aspectos importantes. En este trabajo Schelling pretende conocer el tiempo premundano (vorweltlichen Zeit), es decir, el tiempo anterior a la creación del mundo. Sin embargo, esto no es posible porque no tenemos fuentes directas; utiliza, por lo tanto, fuentes indirectas: estas consisten en el autoconocimiento del ser humano (método antropomorfista) y en discursos divinos revelados, básicamente en el Antiguo Testamento. Su investigación le lleva a la conclusión de que el verdadero pasado es el pasado anterior a la creación del mundo y el verdadero futuro es el postmundano.6 Defiende un concepto regional del tiempo, donde cada ser posee su propio tiempo interno y critica una concepción objetivista de la temporalidad. Su estudio del tiempo, debemos situarlo dentro de una concepción teológica, ya que identifica el pasado con el Padre, el presente con el Hijo y el futuro con el Espíritu; elabora, de esta forma, un sistema trinitario que se identifica con cada una de las manifestaciones de la divinidad defendidas por la religión cristiana.

Friedrich Schelling
(1775 / 1854)

Así, el concepto circular del tiempo, como se ha visto, en todas las épocas y regiones, tiene sus raíces, por una parte, en las ideas de eternidad e inmortalidad del Antiguo Egipto, donde, por ejemplo, el escarabajo era considerado símbolo de la renovación eterna de la vida. El paradigma de "universo cíclico" es también muy importante dentro de las doctrinas orientales hinduista y budista, a través de su noción de la rueda de la vida o samsara, que representa un ciclo sin fin de nacimiento, vida y muerte, del cual es necesario liberarse. Estas ideas fueron retomadas en Occidente por los filósofos pitagóricos y estoicos, entre otros. En el Renacimiento los alquimistas representaban el ouroboros, el símbolo por excelencia de la eterna repetición. La repetición incesante fue esgrimida por pensadores muy posteriores como Giambattista Vico, con su teoría de los cursos y recursos interminables de la historia, y Friedrich Nietzsche, con su concepto del eterno retorno de lo idéntico, en el que, a diferencia de la visión cíclica del tiempo, no se trata de ciclos ni de nuevas combinaciones en otras posibilidades, sino de que los mismos acontecimientos se vuelven a repetir en el mismo orden, tal cual ocurrieron, sin posibilidad de variación.

Científicos contemporáneos como John Richard Gott, con su teoría de los universos autogenerados, Roger Penrose, con su cosmología cíclica conforme, Peter Lynds que supone la repetición infinita del tiempo, y Henri Poincaré, con su teorema de la recurrencia, contemplan, cada cual a su manera, una visión circular e interminable acerca de la concepción del tiempo.

La dualidad realismo-idealismo es heredera de algunas de las ideas mencionadas anteriormente. Así, una postura tradicional del pensador realista en ontología es que el tiempo y el espacio tienen una existencia aparte de la mente humana. El idealista, en cambio, niega o duda de la existencia de los objetos con independencia de la mente. Algunos antirealistas que a pesar de serlo mantienen el punto de vista ontológico de que los objetos fuera de la mente existen, dudan sin embargo de la existencia independiente del tiempo y del espacio. Así, el filósofo idealista alemán Immanuel Kant, en su obra central y más conocida, Crítica de la razón pura, describió el tiempo y el espacio como formas puras a priori de la sensibilidad: se trata no de conceptos, sino, en efecto, de «formas de la sensibilidad» que suponen condiciones apriorísticas, para cualquier posible experiencia, ya que posibilitan la percepción de los sentidos. Ni el espacio ni el tiempo se conciben como sustancias, sino que más bien se trata de elementos de un armazón o estructura sistemáticos que utilizamos para organizar nuestra experiencia. De esta forma las medidas espaciales se utilizan para cuantificar hasta dónde se encuentran los objetos separados, y las medidas temporales para comparar cuantitativamente el intervalo entre los acontecimientos.

Giambattista Vico
(1668 / 1744)

John Richard Gott
(1947)
Roger Penrose
(1931)
Peter Lynds
(1973)
Henri Poincaré
(1854 / 1912)

La filosofía del espacio y el tiempo es la rama de la filosofía que trata de los aspectos referidos a la ontología, la epistemología y la naturaleza del espacio y el tiempo, lo que se conoce también como cosmología filosófica. Si los problemas vinculados al espacio y al tiempo tradicionalmente han sido centrales en los sistemas filosóficos, desde los presocráticos hasta Bergson y Heidegger, la llamada filosofía analítica, en ejercicio de su crítica del método científico y la metafísica tradicionales, los ha estudiado con particular interés desde sus comienzos.

Escenaris Especials Flyer

Designer

Miquel Amela & Ferran Rodriguez

Client

Escenaris Especials

Key Diagram

Font	Paper	Size
Futura	350g Cyclus offset	210×580mm (Open) 210×140mm (Folded)

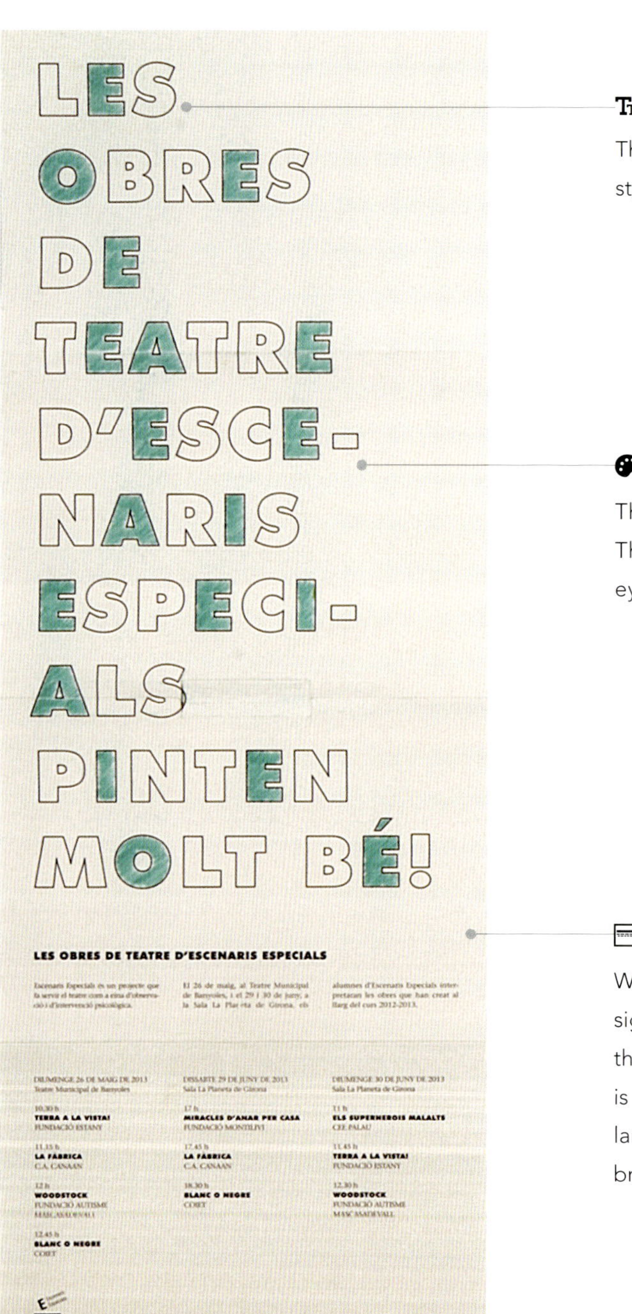

The text used is Futura font, which is in Regular shape style and its strokes are well proportioned.

The colors are chosen by the performing students. The crayons at the back of the brochure are very eye-catching and special.

When there is a lot of information to include, the designer needs to pay attention to the classification and the modular spacing. The spacing between text blocks is arranged to be neither too long nor too short, and a large area of negative space also enhances the sense of breathing in the layout.

Grid

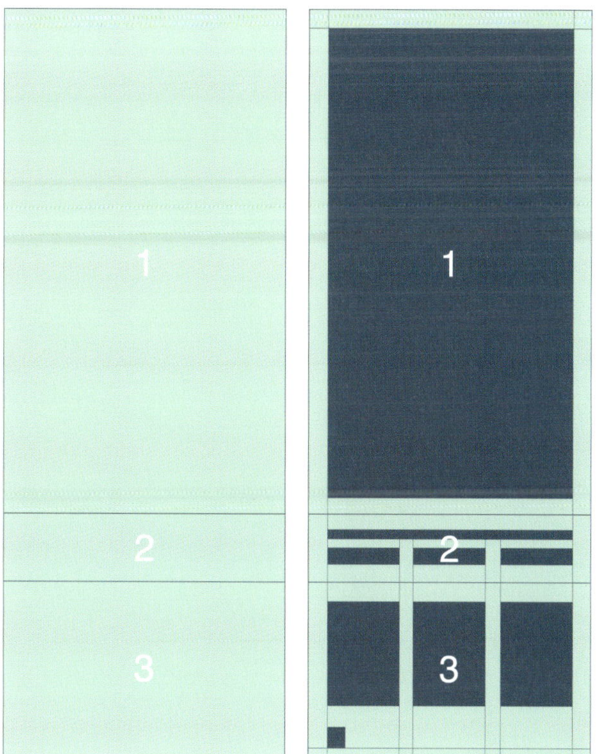

Visual Flow

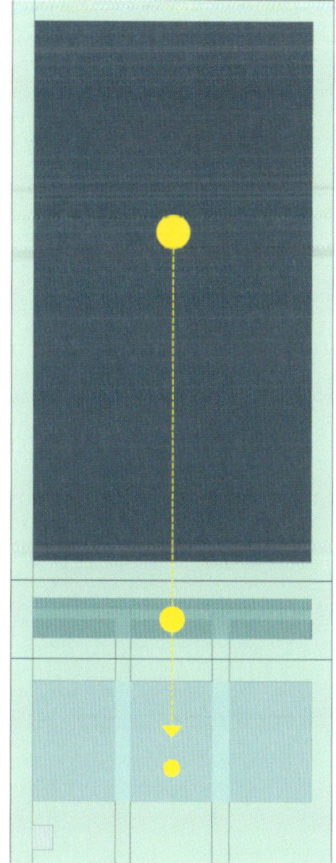

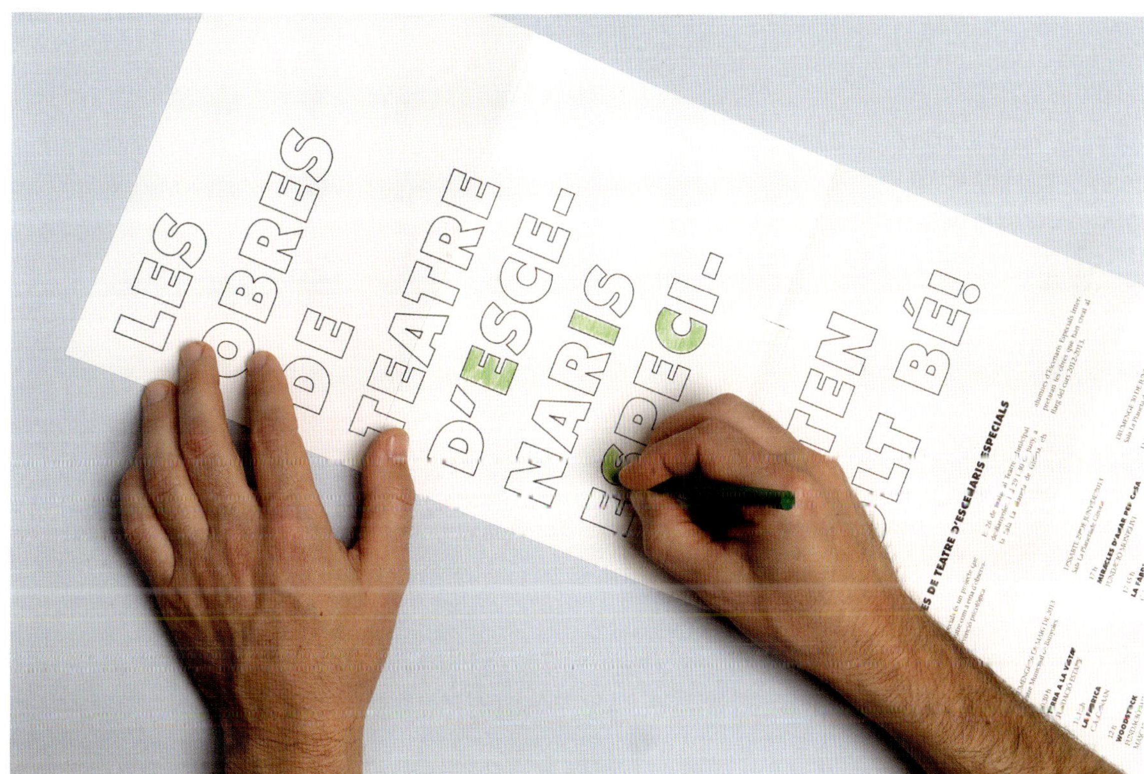

This is a brochure as well as a poster for the end of the year show, Escenaris Especials; a project that aims to reflect the social diversity on theater stage where the actors and actresses are marginal people in the society. The performing students were invited to draw on the front cover of the brochure. Their creation and the crayons they used are a part of the design.

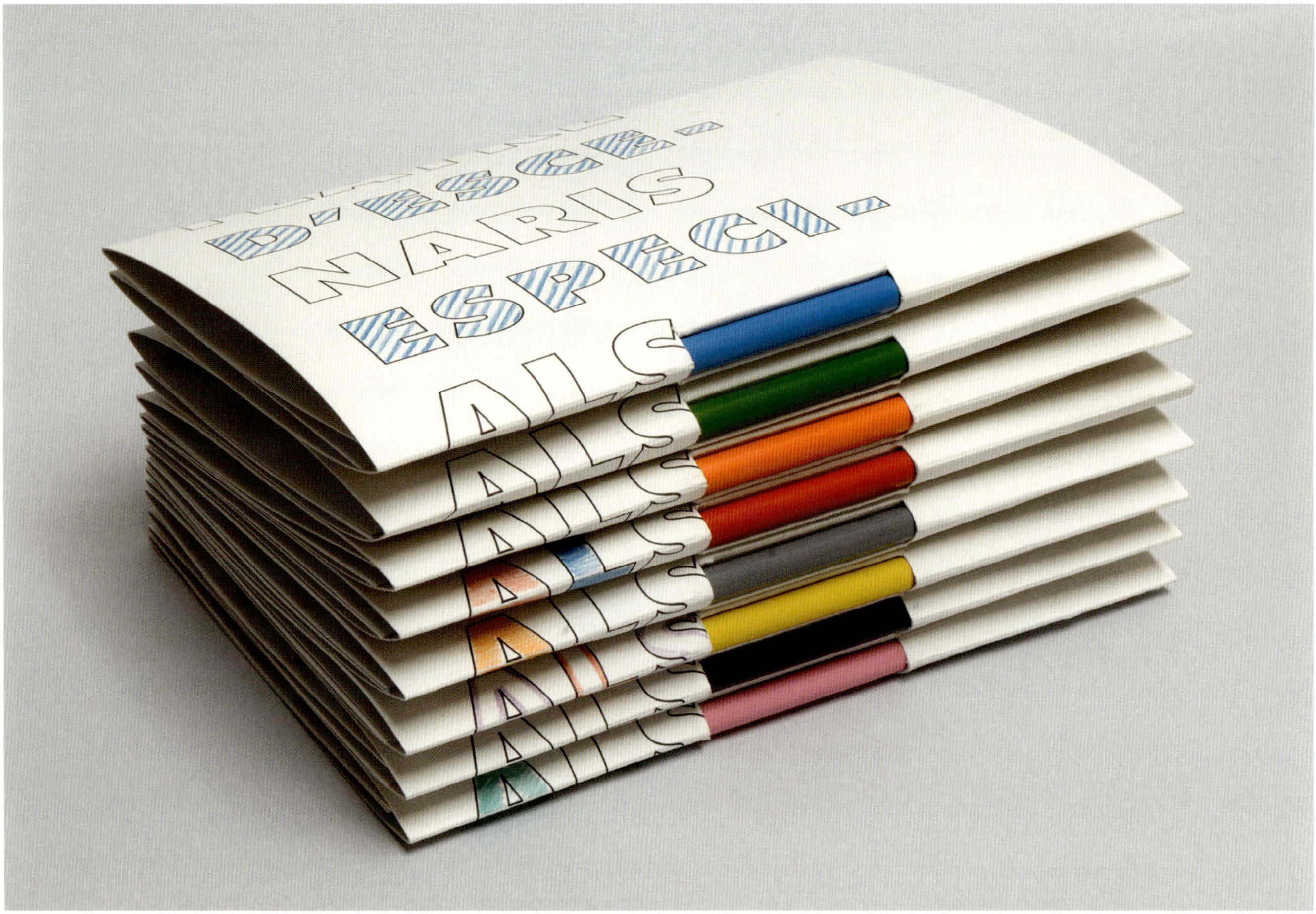

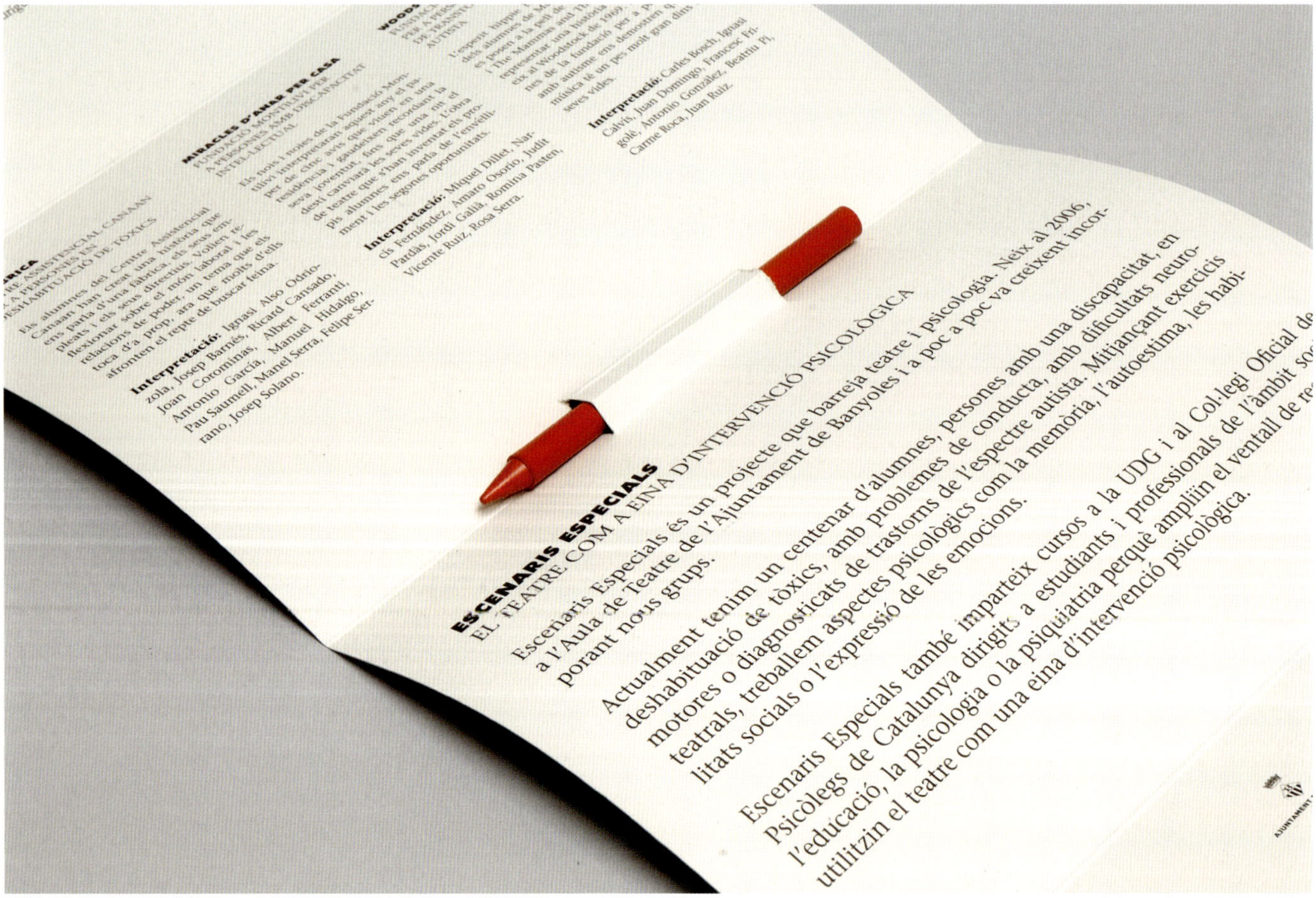
ESCENARIS ESPECIALS
EL TEATRE COM A EINA D'INTERVENCIÓ PSICOLÒGICA
Escenaris Especials és un projecte que barreja teatre i psicologia. Neix al 2006, a l'Aula de Teatre de l'Ajuntament de Banyoles i a poc a poc va creixent incorporant nous grups.
Actualment tenim un centenar d'alumnes, persones amb una discapacitat, en deshabituació de tòxics, amb problemes de conducta, amb dificultats neuromotores o diagnosticats de trastorns de l'espectre autista. Mitjançant exercicis teatrals, treballem aspectes psicològics com la memòria, l'autoestima, les habilitats socials o l'expressió de les emocions.
Escenaris Especials també imparteix cursos a la UDG i al Col·legi Oficial de Psicòlegs de Catalunya dirigits a estudiants i professionals de l'àmbit social, l'educació, la psicologia o la psiquiatria perquè ampliïn el ventall de recursos i utilitzin el teatre com una eina d'intervenció psicològica.

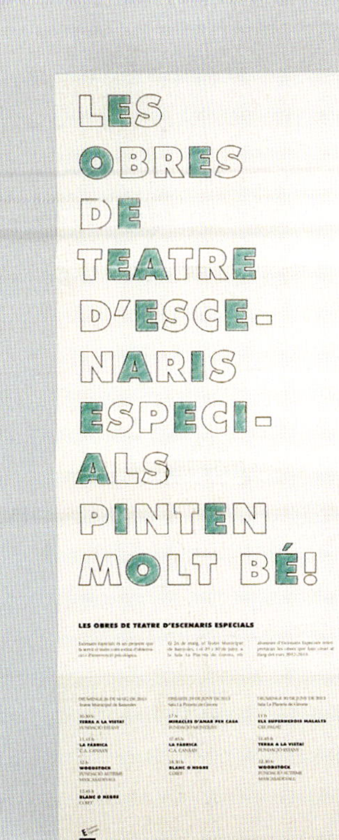
LES
OBRES
DE
TEATRE
D'ESCE-
NARIS
ESPECI-
ALS
PINTEN
MOLT BÉ!
LES OBRES DE TEATRE D'ESCENARIS ESPECIALS

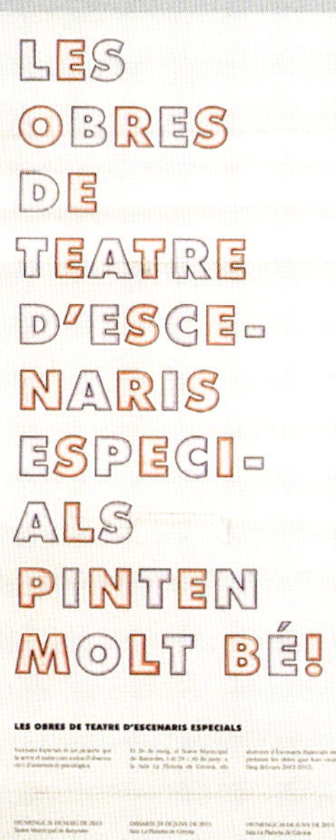
LES
OBRES
DE
TEATRE
D'ESCE-
NARIS
ESPECI-
ALS
PINTEN
MOLT BÉ!
LES OBRES DE TEATRE D'ESCENARIS ESPECIALS

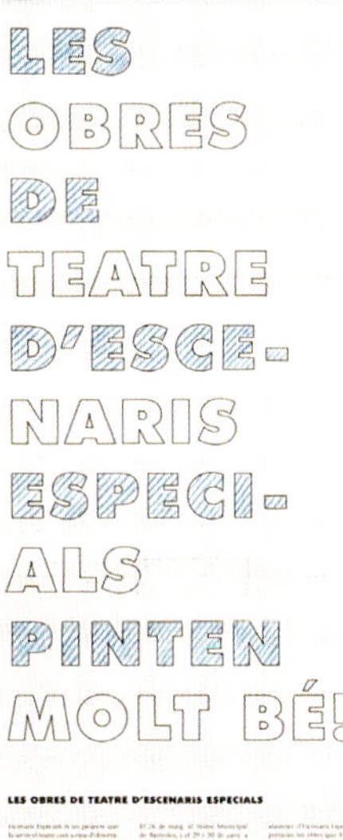
LES
OBRES
DE
TEATRE
D'ESCE-
NARIS
ESPECI-
ALS
PINTEN
MOLT BÉ!

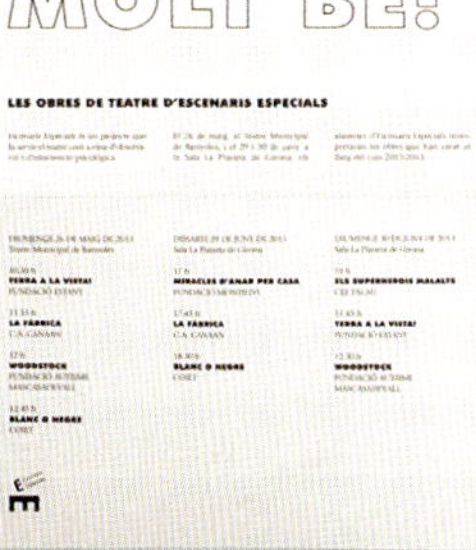
LES OBRES DE TEATRE D'ESCENARIS ESPECIALS

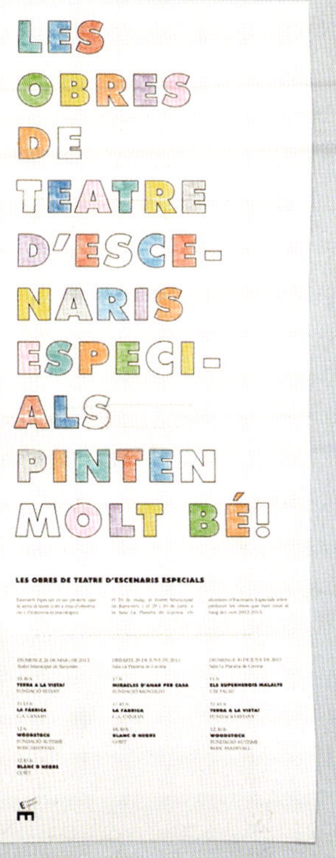
LES
OBRES
DE
TEATRE
D'ESCE-
NARIS
ESPECI-
ALS
PINTEN
MOLT BÉ!
LES OBRES DE TEATRE D'ESCENARIS ESPECIALS

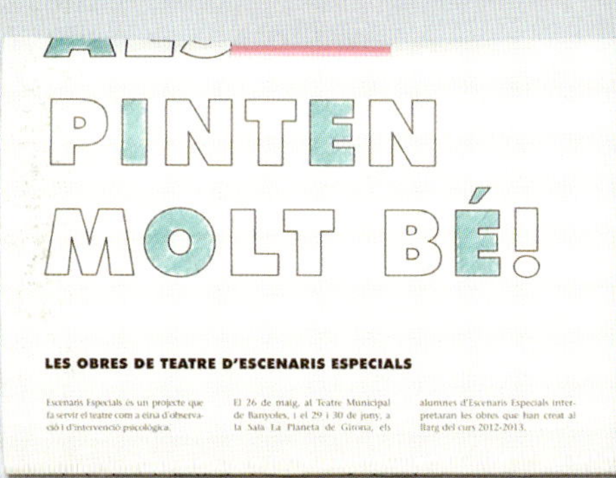
PINTEN
MOLT BÉ!
LES OBRES DE TEATRE D'ESCENARIS ESPECIALS
Escenaris Especials és un projecte que fa servir el teatre com a eina d'observació i d'intervenció psicològica.
El 26 de maig, al Teatre Municipal de Banyoles, i el 29 i 30 de juny, a la Sala La Planeta de Girona, els
alumnes d'Escenaris Especials interpretaran les obres que han creat al llarg del curs 2012-2013.

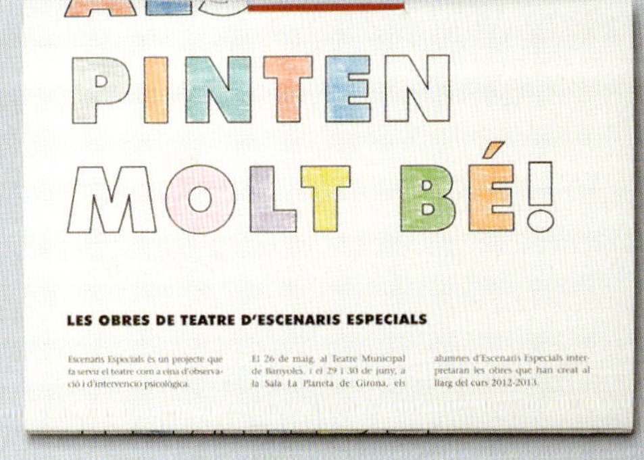
PINTEN
MOLT BÉ!
LES OBRES DE TEATRE D'ESCENARIS ESPECIALS
Escenaris Especials és un projecte que fa servir el teatre com a eina d'observació i d'intervenció psicològica.
El 26 de maig, al Teatre Municipal de Banyoles, i el 29 i 30 de juny, a la Sala La Planeta de Girona, els
alumnes d'Escenaris Especials interpretaran les obres que han creat al llarg del curs 2012-2013.

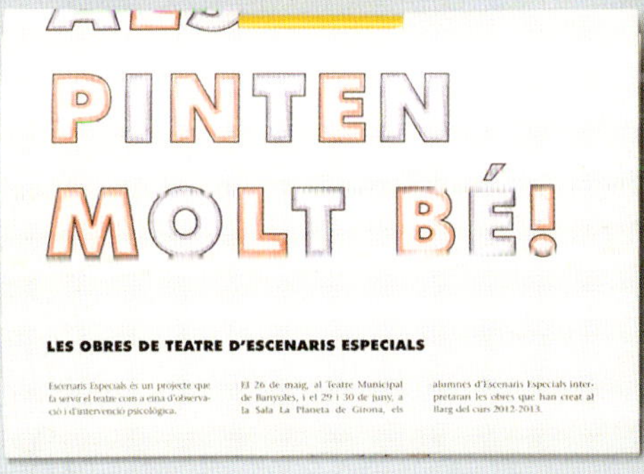
PINTEN
MOLT BÉ!
LES OBRES DE TEATRE D'ESCENARIS ESPECIALS
Escenaris Especials és un projecte que fa servir el teatre com a eina d'observació i d'intervenció psicològica.
El 26 de maig, al Teatre Municipal de Banyoles, i el 29 i 30 de juny, a la Sala La Planeta de Girona, els
alumnes d'Escenaris Especials interpretaran les obres que han creat al llarg del curs 2012-2013.

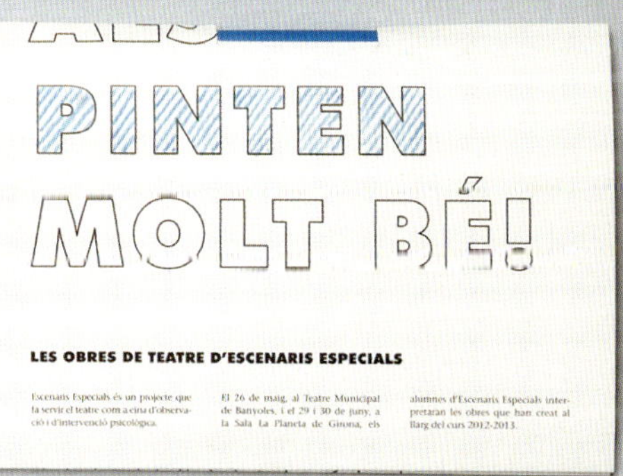
PINTEN
MOLT BÉ!
LES OBRES DE TEATRE D'ESCENARIS ESPECIALS
Escenaris Especials és un projecte que fa servir el teatre com a eina d'observació i d'intervenció psicològica.
El 26 de maig, al Teatre Municipal de Banyoles, i el 29 i 30 de juny, a la Sala La Planeta de Girona, els
alumnes d'Escenaris Especials interpretaran les obres que han creat al llarg del curs 2012-2013.

Cantonese Opera Young Talent Showcase Poster

Designer

Ray Lau Kin-her & Chu Tsz-ying

Client

The Chinese Artists Association of Hong Kong

Key Diagram

Paper

Special paper

Size

594×841mm

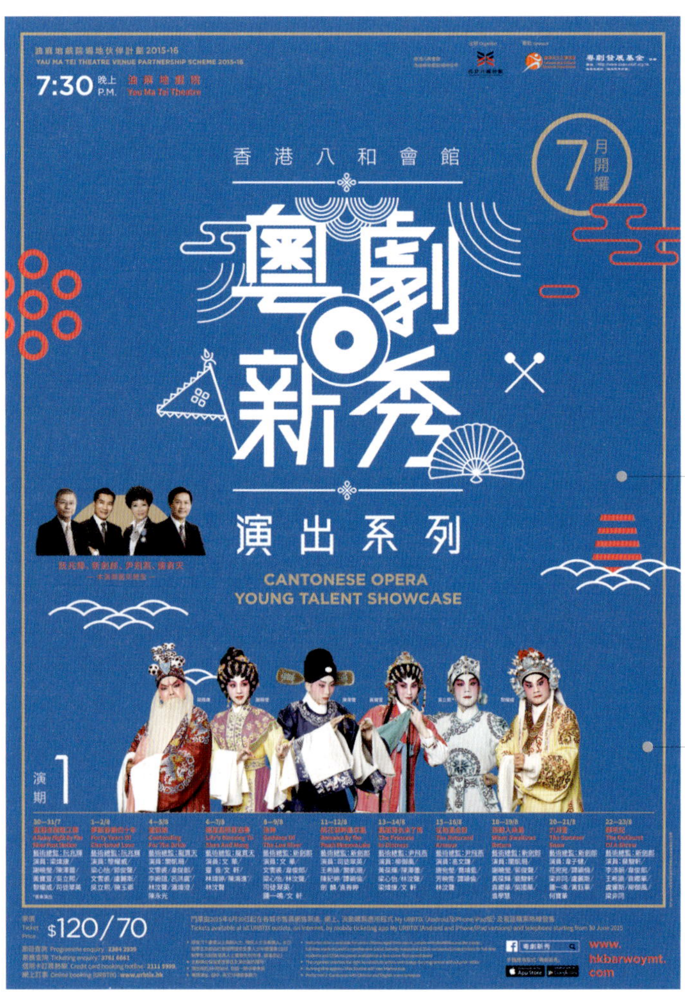

The pure color background is embellished with yellow and red decorations, and the core of the entire design is placed on the centered headline, contrasting with the background color.

The negative space guides the audience's first sight to the center of the poster, and then notices the performance information below, which is realized by the principle of proximity. In order to combine the design with the Cantonese opera culture, some decorative icons derived from the opera, such as the fan and flag, are used.

Grid

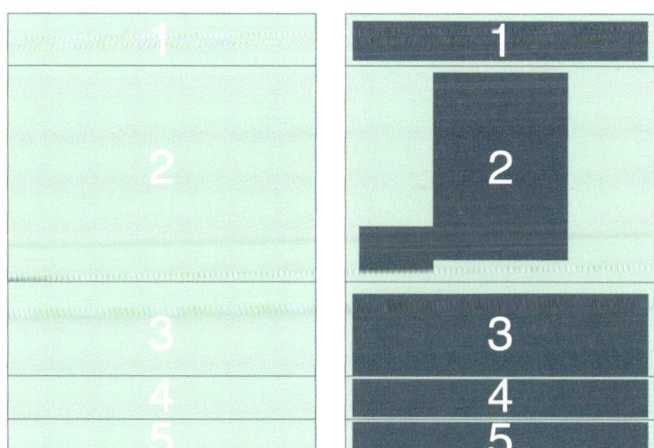

Visual Flow

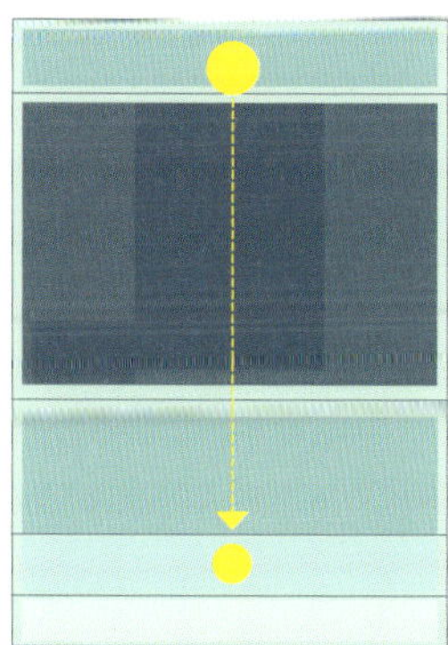

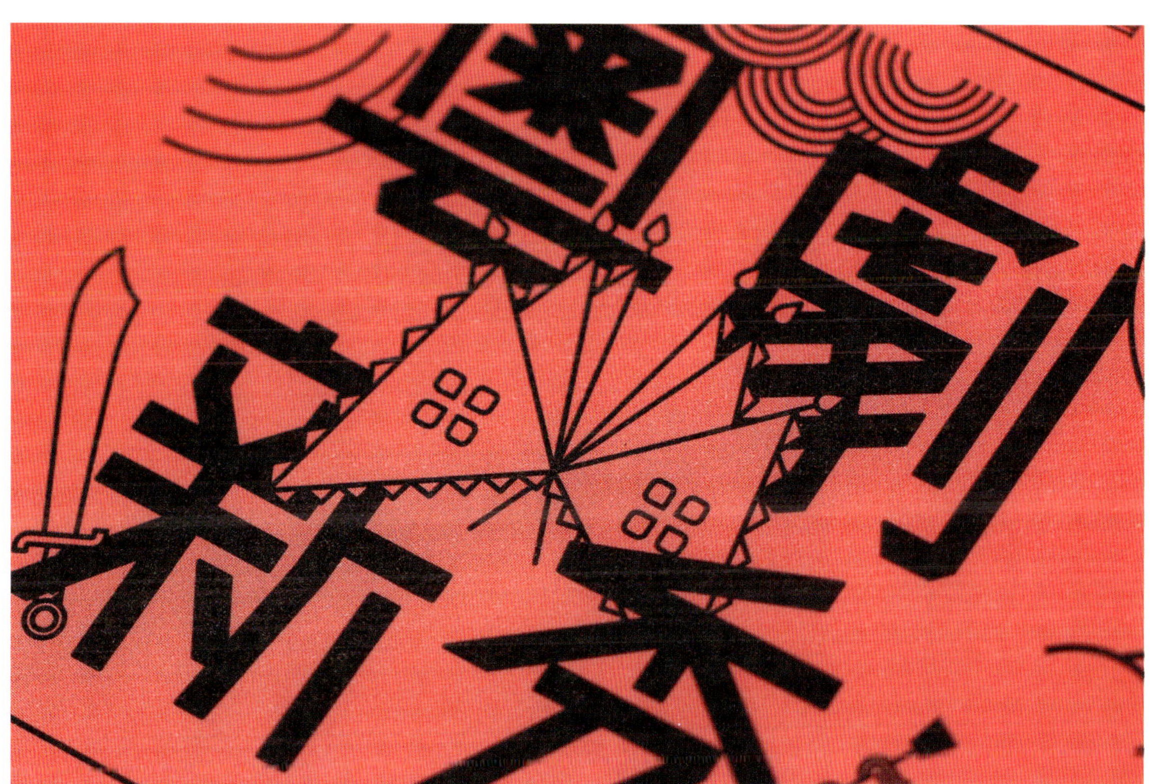

Cantonese Opera Young Talent Showcase is an important succession of work by The Chinese Artists Association of Hong Kong. The young talents will not only learn the Cantonese opera in a systematic way under the leadership of six art directors, but also, through stage performance by demonstrating their skill set. With "succession" as the design concept and to attract more young talents, the posters re-packages the traditional Cantonese opera by adding energetic and youthful elements.

油麻地戲院場地伙伴計劃 2015-16
YAU MA TEI THEATRE VENUE PARTNERSHIP SCHEME 2015-16

7:30 晚上 P.M. 油麻地戲院 Yau Ma Tei Theatre

主辦 Organiser
香港八和會館為油麻地戲院場地伙伴
香港八和會館

贊助 Sponsor
康樂及文化事務署 Leisure and Cultural Services Department

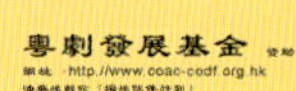

香港八和會館

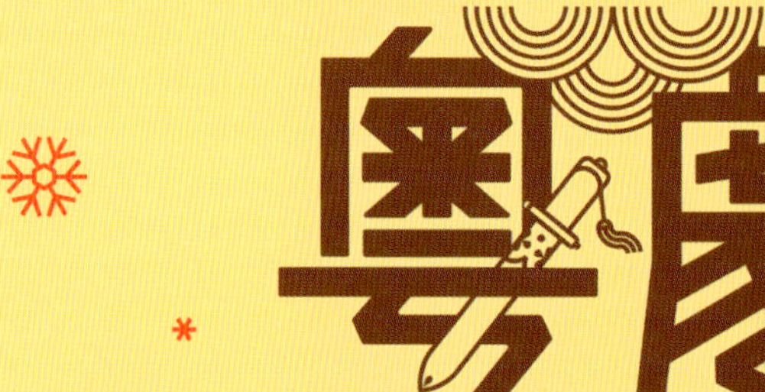

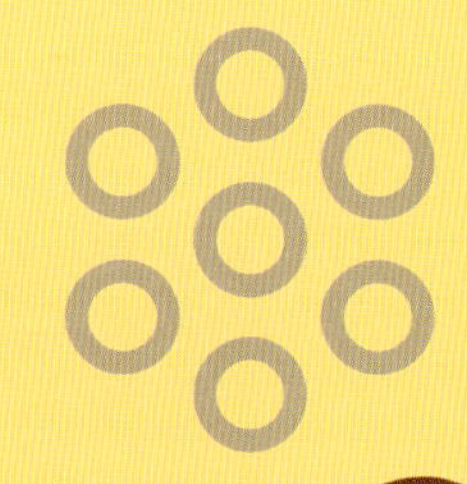

演出系列

CANTONESE OPERA YOUNG TALENT SHOWCASE

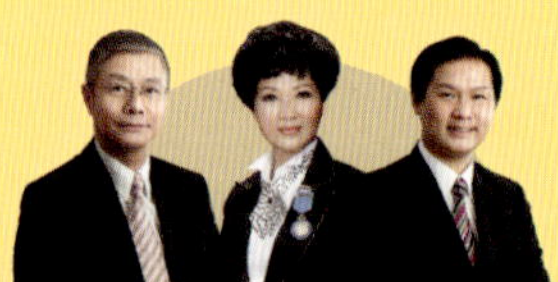

阮兆輝、尹飛燕、龍貫天
— 本演期藝術總監 —

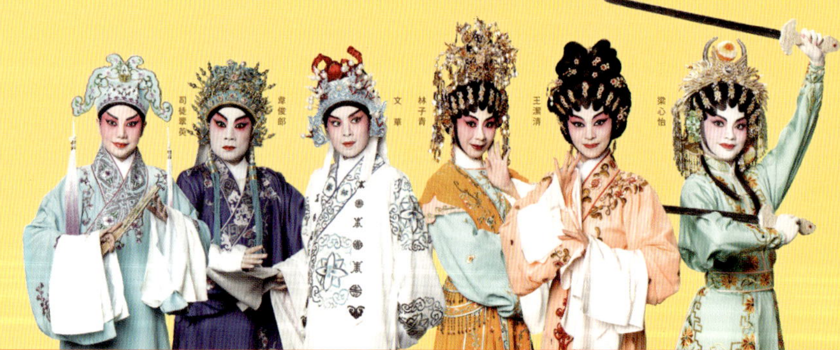

粵劇新秀・八和粵劇學院交流演出 (3・1)

演員：羅耀邦/呂智豐/李子蕊/鄺紫煌/梁芷萁/黎子樂/林貝嘉/梁非同/鄺純茵/吳思穎/葉曦甯/李懿恩/李晴茵/曹采意/蘇鈺橋/郭俊亨/謝紹岐/朱嬿瑤

演期 4

5–6/1
香羅塚
Tomb of the Fragrant Gown
藝術總監：阮兆輝
演員：宋洪波/瓊花女/陳澤蕾/陳玉卿/林子青/高文謙/梁慧珠

7–8/1
夢斷香銷四十年
Forty Years of Cherished Love
藝術總監：尹飛燕
演員：陳澤蕾/瓊花女/高文謙/李沂洛/陳玉卿/鍾一鳴/江穎紅

9–10/1
雷鳴金鼓戰笳聲
The Sounds of Battle
藝術總監：尹飛燕
演員：柳御風/林子青/楚文琦/王希頴/林汶聲/劍 麟/黃鈺華

12–13/1
古老排場折子戲
Formulaic Plays Excerpts
藝術總監：阮兆輝
《打洞結拜》
演員：黎耀威/謝曉瑩
《金蓮戲叔》
演員：宋洪波/王潔清

14–15/1
宋江怒殺閻婆惜
How Song Jiang Slew Yan Xijiao
藝術總監：阮兆輝
演員：司徒翠英/梁心怡/郭俊聲/文雪裘/譚穎倫/鍾一鳴/盧麗斯/吳國華

16–17/1
孟麗君
Meng Lijun
藝術總監：阮兆輝
演員：阮德鏘/謝曉瑩/陳澤蕾/黃寶萱/吳立熙/林汶聲/高文謙

19–20/1
紅菱巧破無頭案
Red Silk Shoes and The Murder
藝術總監：龍貫天
演員：司徒翠英/唐宛瑩/郭俊聲/林芯菱/陳鴻進*/林汶聲/袁纓華/梁慧珠

21–22/1
一曲琵琶動漢皇
The Legend of Wang Zhaojun
藝術總監：龍貫天
演員：關凱珊/王潔清/陳鴻進*/譚穎倫/袁善婷/王希頴/張宛雲/陳玉卿

23–24/1
無情寶劍有情天
Merciless Sword Under Merciful Heaven
藝術總監：龍貫天
演員：文 華/梁心怡/韋俊郎/文雪裘/譚穎倫/袁纓華/林汶聲/陳永光

*客串演出

票價 Ticket Price $120/70

節目查詢 Programme enquiry：**2384 2939**
票務查詢 Ticketing enquiry：**3761 6661**
信用卡訂票熱線 Credit card booking hotline：**2111 5999**
網上訂票 Online booking (URBTIX)：**www.urbtix.hk**

門票由2015年12月5日起在各城市售票網售票處、網上、流動購票應用程式 My URBTIX（Android及iPhone/iPad版）及電話購票熱線發售
Tickets available at all URBTIX outlets, on Internet, by mobile ticketing app My URBTIX (Android and iPhone/iPad versions) and telephone starting from 5 December2015

- 設有六十歲或以上高齡人士、殘疾人士及看護人、全日制學生及綜合社會保障援助受惠人士半價優惠（全日制學生及綜援受惠人士優惠先到先得，額滿即止）
- 主辦單位保留更改節目及演出者的權利
- 演出長約3小時30分，包括一節中場休息
- 粵語演出，設中、英文分場故事簡介

- Half price tickets available for senior citizens aged 60 or above, people with disabilities and the minder, full-time students and Comprehensive Social Security Assistance (CSSA) recipients (Limited tickets for full-time students and CSSA recipients available on a first-come-first-served basis)
- The organiser reserves the right to substitute artists and change the programme without prior notice
- Running time approx. 3 hrs 30 mins with one intermission
- Performed in Cantonese with Chinese and English scene synopses

粵劇新秀
手機應用程式「粵劇新秀」

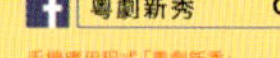

www.hkbarwoymt.com

油麻地戲院場地伙伴計劃 2015-16
YAU MA TEI THEATRE VENUE PARTNERSHIP SCHEME 2015-16

7:30 晚上 P.M. 油麻地戲院 Yau Ma Tei Theatre

主辦 Organiser 香港八和會館為油麻地戲院場地伙伴

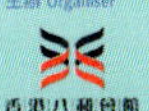

贊助 Sponsor

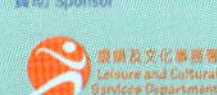

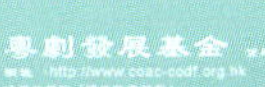

香港八和會館

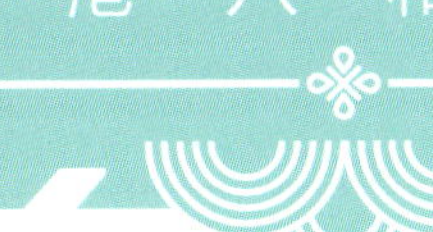

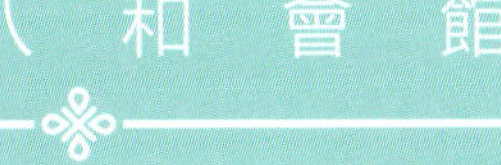

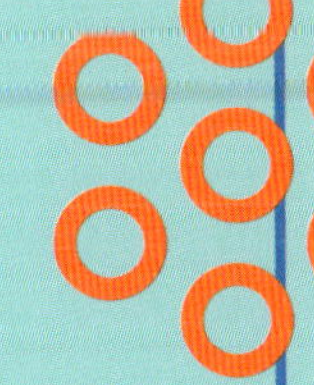

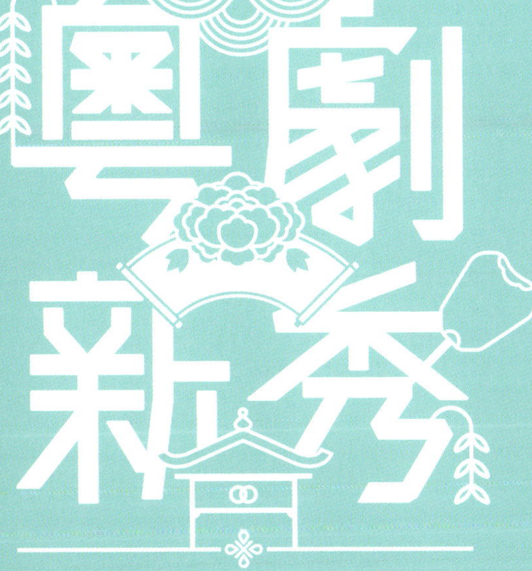

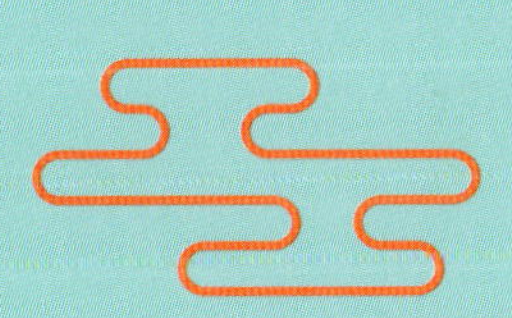

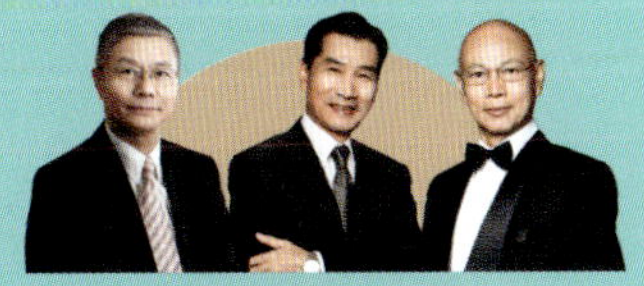

阮兆輝、新劍郎、羅家英
— 本演期藝術總監 —

演出系列

CANTONESE OPERA
YOUNG TALENT SHOWCASE

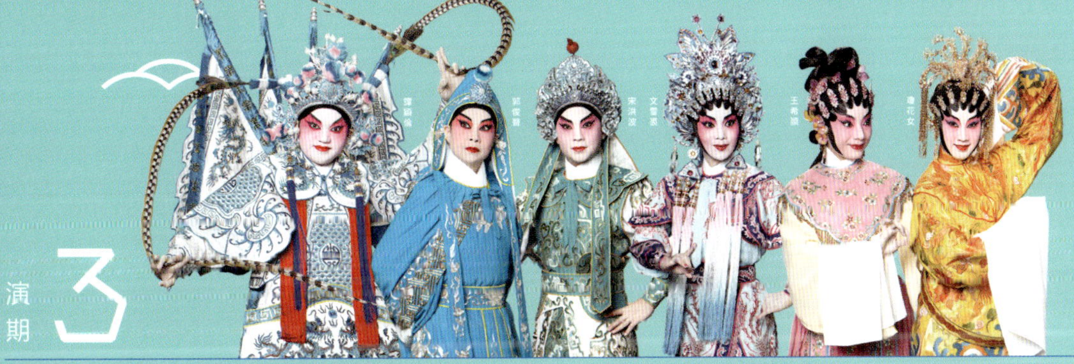

演期 3

17–18/11	19–20/11	21–22/11	24–25/11	26–27/11	28–29/11
琵琶血染漢宮花 The Mournful Melody	金釧龍鳳配 Return of True Love	十年一覺揚州夢 A Dream in Yangzhou	刁蠻元帥莽將軍 The Impetuous General	花月東牆記 Romance Across the East Wall	王寶釧 Wang Baochuan
藝術總監：羅家英	藝術總監：羅家英	藝術總監：羅家英	藝術總監：阮兆輝	藝術總監：阮兆輝	藝術總監：阮兆輝
演員：宋洪波／謝曉瑩／陳澤蕾／徐月明／裴駿軒／袁纓華／李沂洛／鄧琇娟／林汶聲	演員：關凱珊／瓊花女／柳御風／王希穎／林汶聲／韋俊郎	演員：郭俊聲／盧麗斯／蔣錦軒／張潔霞／劍麟／林汶聲／黃成彬／黃鈺華／文軒	演員：郭俊聲／徐月明／關凱珊／林瑋婷／譚穎倫／鍾一鳴／文軒	演員：關凱珊／謝曉瑩／郭俊聲／林瑋婷／鍾熙文／吳立熙	演員：郭俊聲／唐宛瑩／文軒／盧麗斯／劉惠鳴／高文謙／韋子健

1–2/12	3–4/12	5–6/12	8–9/12	10–11/12	12–13/12
十奏嚴嵩 Impeachment of Yan Song	萬世流芳張玉喬 The Immortal Zhang Yuqiao	狄青與雙陽 Di Qing and Princess Shuangyang	牡丹亭驚夢 The Peony Pavilion	販馬記 The Story of Horse Selling	百花亭贈劍 The Spy Who Loves Me
藝術總監：羅家英	藝術總監：羅家英	藝術總監：羅家英	藝術總監：新劍郎	藝術總監：新劍郎	藝術總監：新劍郎
演員：譚穎倫／瓊花女／韋子健／梁非同／劍麟／韋俊郎／林汶聲／袁纓華／司徒凱誼／蘇永江	演員：宋洪波／謝曉瑩／陳澤蕾／郭俊聲／黃葆輝／林汶聲／梁非同／盧麗斯	演員：關凱珊／黃寶萱／譚穎倫／梁煒康／黃鈺華／文雪裘／喬靖藍	演員：柳御風／瓊花女／關凱珊／文雪裘／劍麟／林汶聲／盧麗斯	演員：司徒翠英／黃寶萱／郭俊聲／梁非同／梁煒康／林汶聲／李沂洛／袁偉傑	演員：譚穎倫／文雪裘／司徒翠英／王希穎／劍麟／林汶聲／韋俊郎

票價 Ticket Price $120/70

門票由2015年10月17日起在各城市售票網售票處、網上、流動購票應用程式 My URBTIX (Android及iPhone/iPad版) 及電話購票熱線發售
Tickets available at all URBTIX outlets, on Internet, by mobile ticketing app My URBTIX (Android and iPhone/iPad versions) and telephone starting from 17 October 2015

節目查詢 Programme enquiry：2384 2939
票務查詢 Ticketing enquiry：3761 6661
信用卡訂票熱線 Credit card booking hotline：2111 5999
網上訂票 Online booking (URBTIX)：www.urbtix.hk

- 設有六十歲或以上高齡人士、殘疾人士及看護人、全日制學生及綜合社會保障援助受惠人士半價優惠（全日制學生及綜援受惠人士優惠先到先得，額滿即止）
- 主辦單位保留更改節目及演出者的權利
- 演出長約3小時30分，包括一節中場休息
- 粵語演出，設中、英文分場故事簡介

- Half price tickets available for senior citizens aged 60 or above, people with disabilities and the minder, full-time students and Comprehensive Social Security Assistance (CSSA) recipients (Limited tickets for full-time students and CSSA recipients available on a first-come-first-served basis)
- The organiser reserves the right to substitute artists and change the programme without prior notice
- Running time approx. 3 hrs 30 mins with one intermission
- Performed in Cantonese with Chinese and English scene synopses

粵劇新秀
手機應用程式「粵劇新秀」
App Store Google play

www.hkbarwoymt.com

Shopping Carnival Booklet

Designer

Shao Chun Yang

Client

Park Lane by CMP

Key Diagram

Font

Akrobat (English)
Kozuka Gothic (Chinese)

Paper

100g kouuui Geniiii

Size

270×200mm

The typography for the main visual is well proportioned and looks very dynamic.

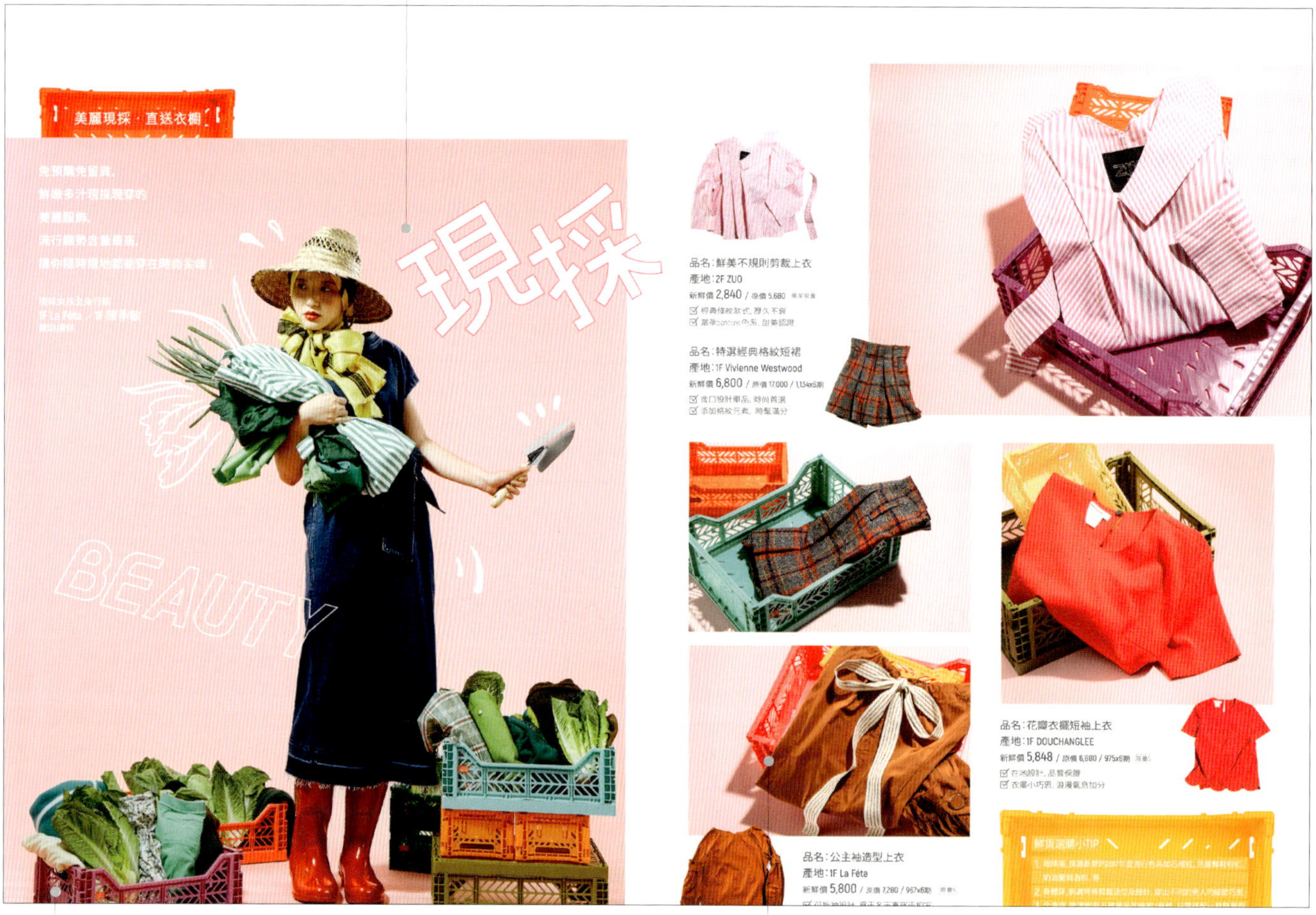

Designers are accustomed to setting a grid system on the base layer first, and then putting the sketch on the second layer, placing design elements and text into the page, and finally adjusting the overall layout. Delete the grid system in the final step, and the best positions can be fine-tuned according to our visual experience.

After removing the color, you will find that the image of the main product will be enhanced by adjusting the brightness of the background color.

Grid

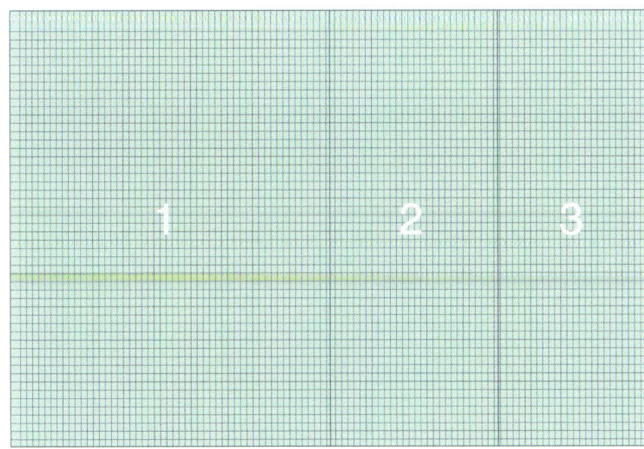

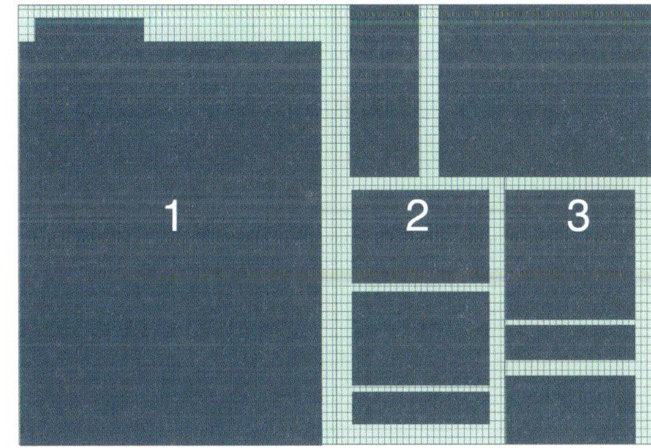

Visual Flow

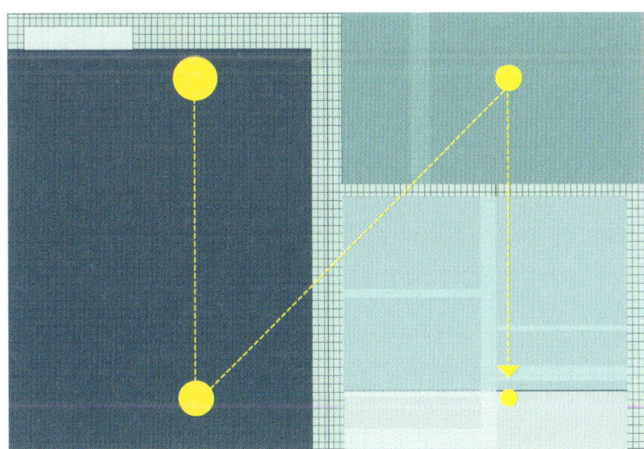

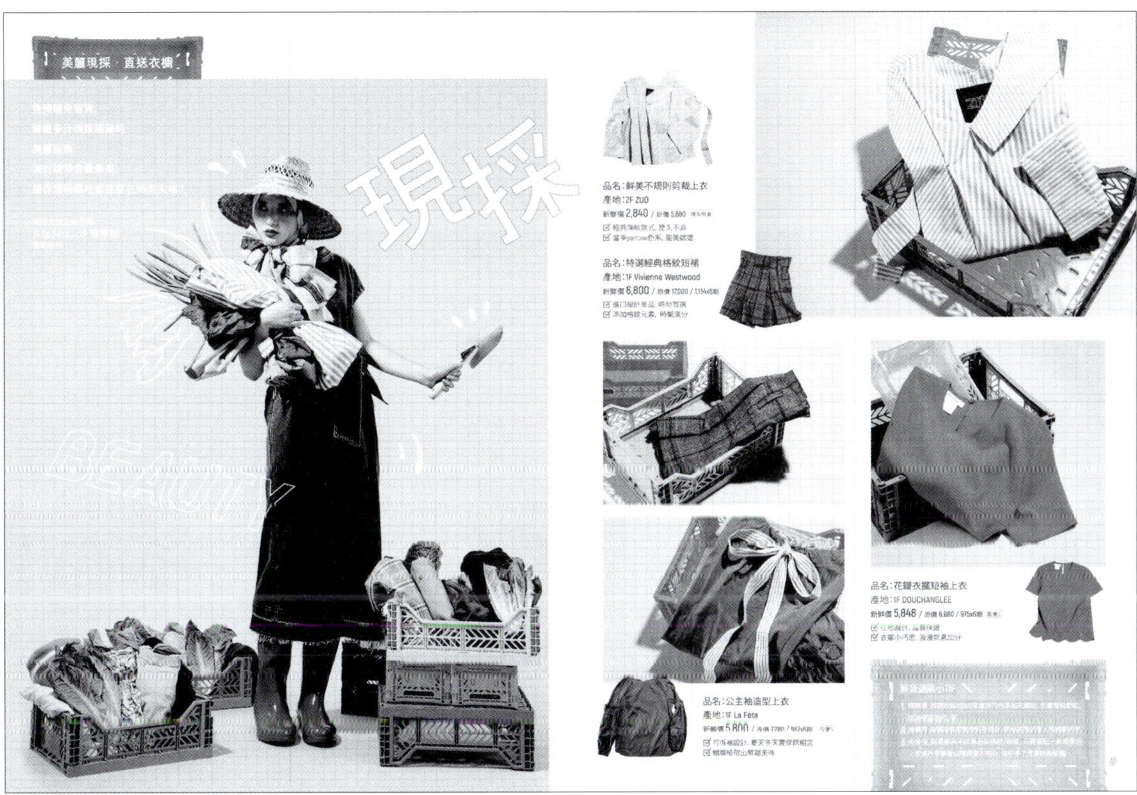

The Park Lane Shopping Mall has been known for providing valuable shopping experiences by offering interesting new products. The new campaign "Fresh Arrivals" borrowed its name from agricultural products to emphasize the "freshness" of the products in their stores. The promotional material design, including the copy writing and photography, are based on the same concept.

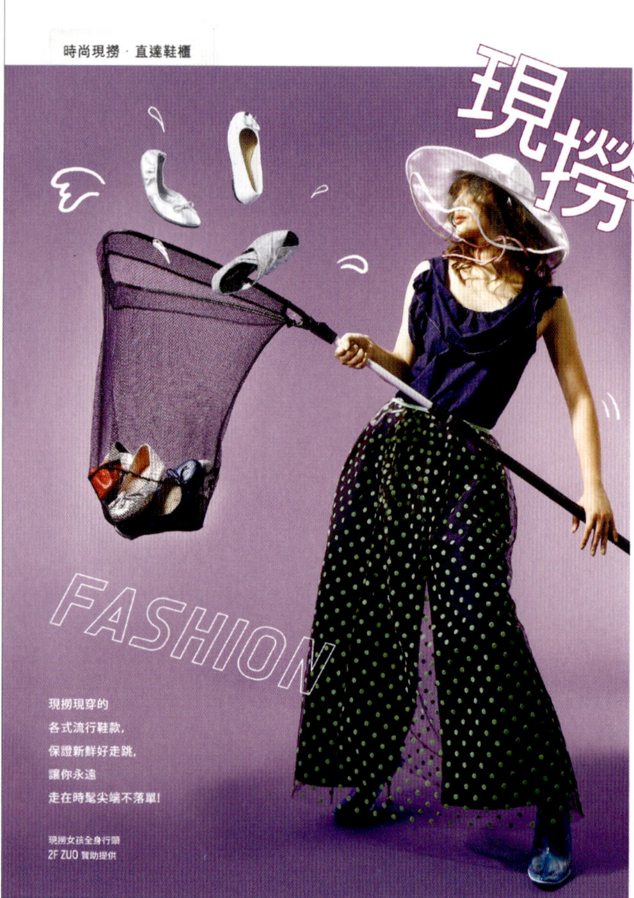

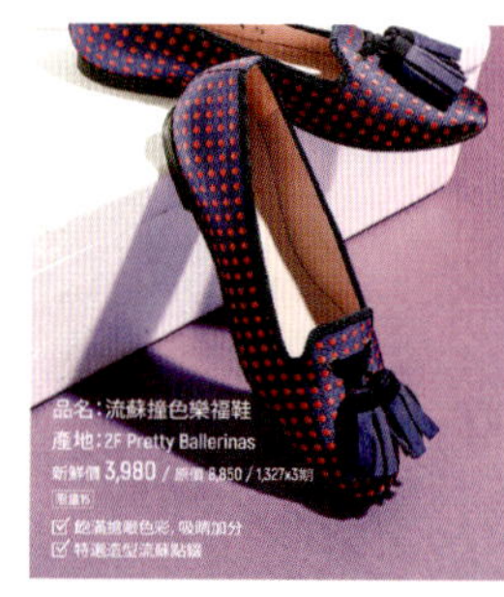

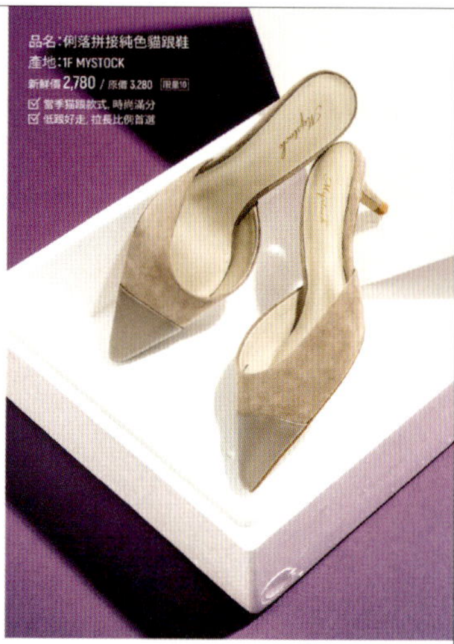

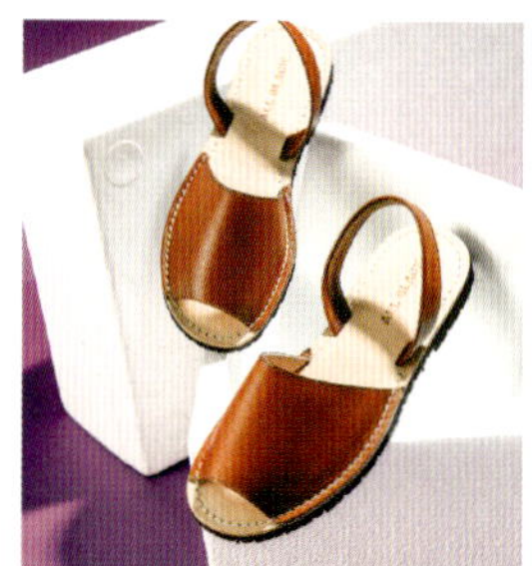

品名:平底涼鞋
產地:2F ALL BLACK
新鮮價 1,500 / 原價 2,980 限量30
☑ 舒適特潤, 好走不掐腳
☑ 在地設計, 安心使用

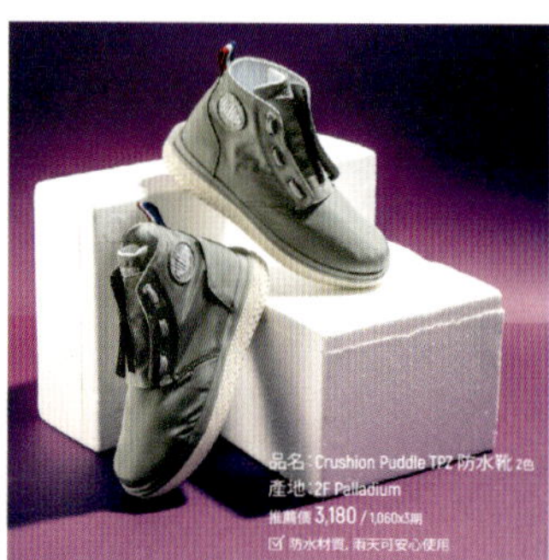

鮮貨選購小TIP

1. 跟著看, 挑選異材質拼接、撞色款式亮眼新奇鞋款
2. 雙手秤, 挑選相對輕盈鞋款, 姐妹逛街、旅行久走好上道!
3. 腳底穿, 挑選3-5cm的低跟鞋款, 舒適穩定也能修飾腳部線條, 輕鬆應對各種場合!

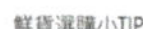

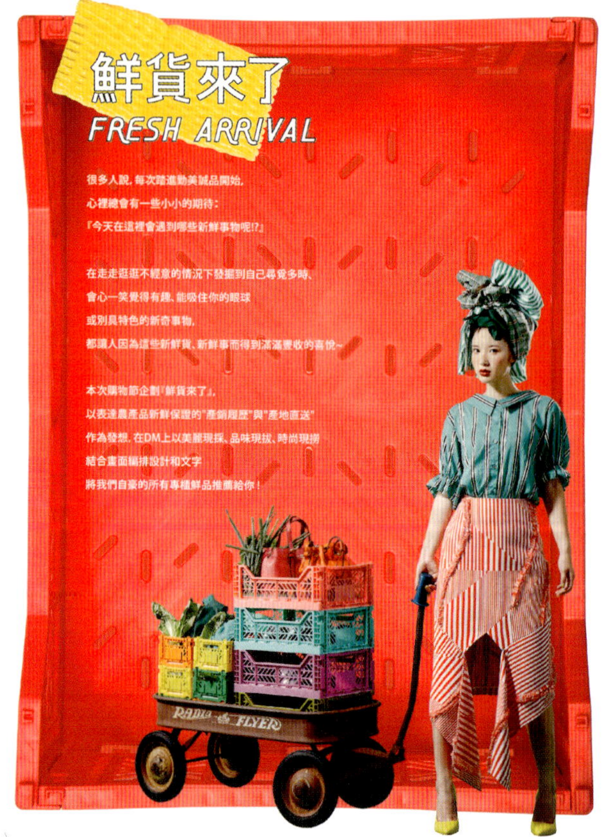

鮮櫃來了
NEW OPENING

1F M·A·C 席捲而來的黑色力量 10月上旬開幕

時尚的黑色包裝裡加入順應潮流千變萬化的色彩,
妝點每一個時髦女孩的臉龐,
有它在每一個時刻、每一種表情都如此嬌豔垂"鮮"欲滴!

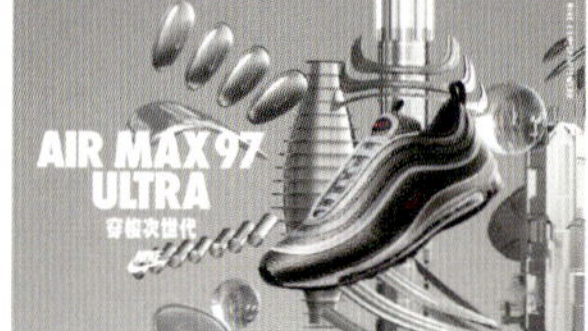

1F NIKE 腳下熱血沸騰的靈魂 9月下旬開幕

和時尚、潮流永遠連袂出席難分難捨, 不論是經典款式
或限量鞋款, 總讓你的足下嚐鮮, 邁開步伐無畏追逐夢想!

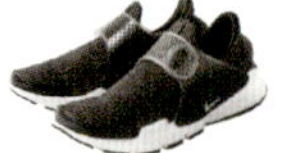
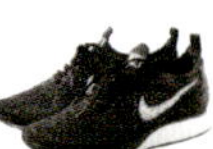

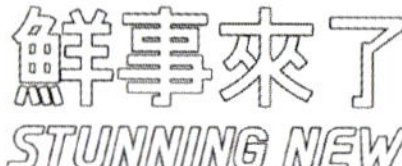

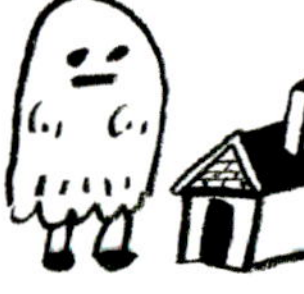

萬聖行動之鬼才來玩!鬼才遊行!

萬聖行動需要你揪出真正的鬼怪並一同參加TRICK OR TREATS搗怪大遊行!
10.28 SAT.-10.31 TUE. 10:00-20:30
變裝參與並抓出隱身人群中的鬼怪即可獲得萬聖鬼怪小物乙組
活動詳情請關注勤美 誠品綠園道FACEBOOK粉絲專頁

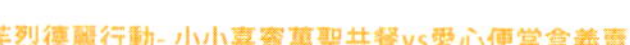

芙烈德麗行動需要你付出"食"在愛心!本季提案主題希望透過企業力量,
舉辦「小小嘉賓萬聖共餐」活動, 邀請偏鄉學校小朋友, 安排一次十月聚餐時光,
加上有趣的工作坊活動, 為孩子們留下屬於這個節日的難忘回憶

10.11 WED.-10.31 TUE. 地點:B1F會員中心

此外, 可於活動期間以250元購得獨家設計款便當盒 (限量100個),
募款目標金額25,000元, 將全數捐贈兒福聯盟「長假營養資助計畫」專案使用
透過實際行動讓有需要的孩子感受這份溫暖

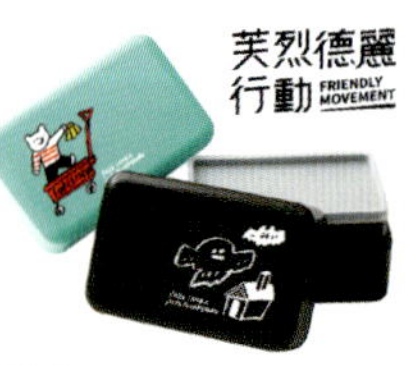

主辦單位:勤美 誠品綠園道 / 合作單位: 兒童福利聯盟文教基金會 / 合作插畫家:馨餅太郎

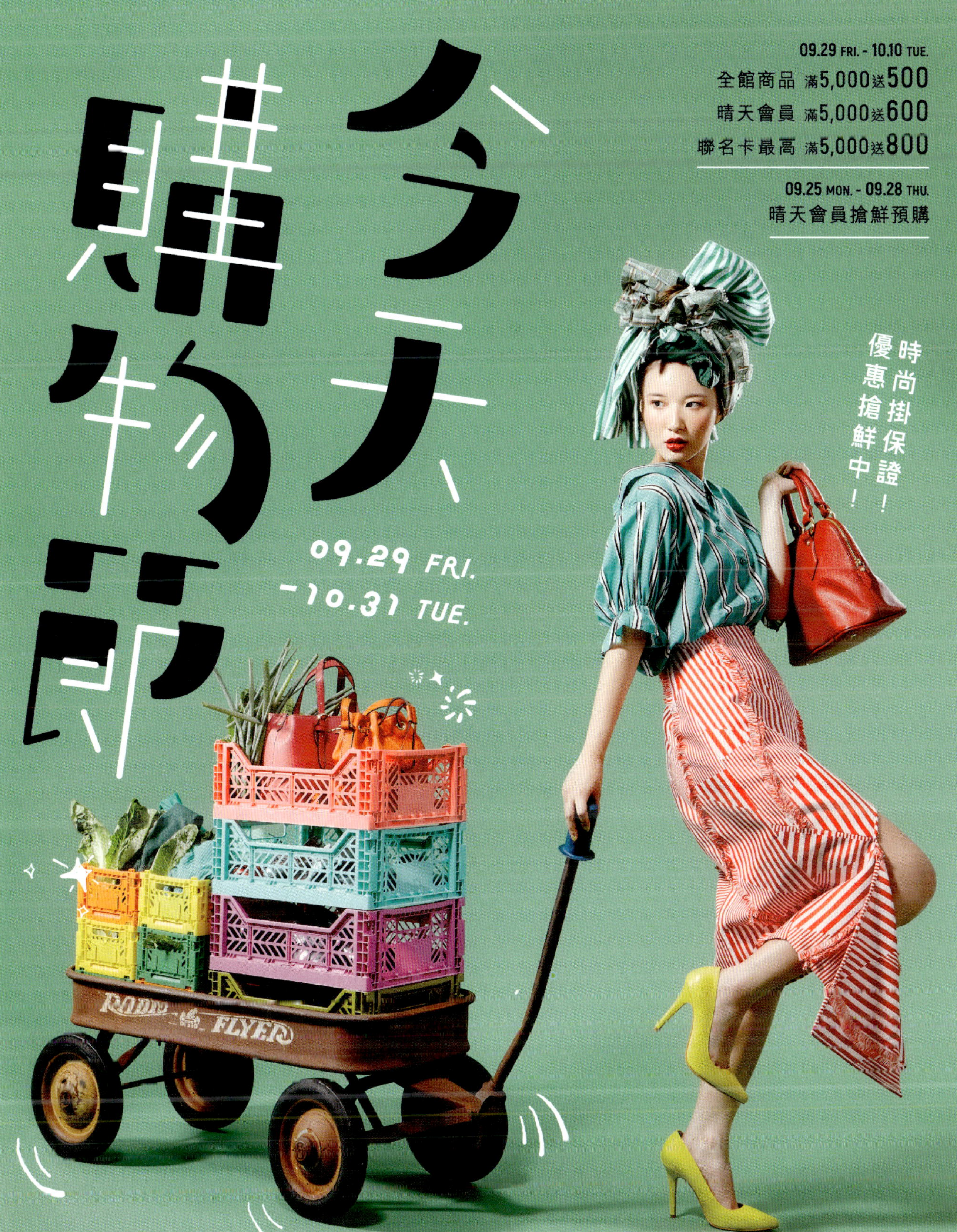

Park Lane vol. 89

www.parklane.com.tw
T+ 04 2328 1000 F+ 04 2328 8890

勤美 誠品綠園道

40360台中市西區公益路68號 | FASHION・時尚 AESTHETICS・人文 NATURE・自然

Return Home Promotional Materials

Designer

Shao Chun Yang

Client

Park Lane by CMP

Key Diagram

Font	Paper	Size
Akrobat (English) Kozuka Gothic (Chinese)	100g Dongjiu special paper	270×200mm

Compared to the upright and regular fonts, custom handwriting font for the title can match the illustration better.

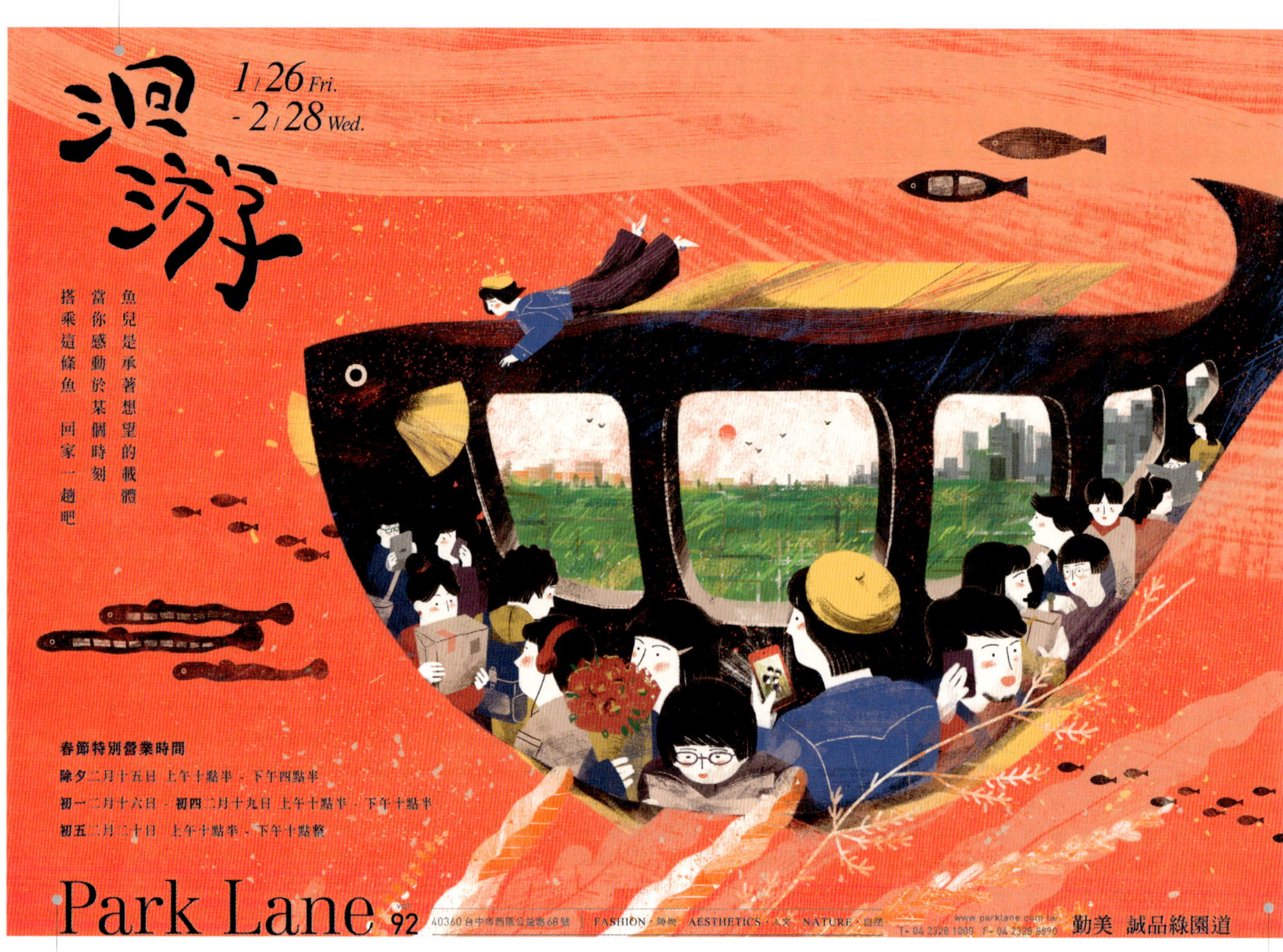

The designer uses dynamic layout to attract consumers to read all the information on the poster.

In order to express the feeling of the New Year, the large red negative space can enhance the festive atmosphere.

Grid

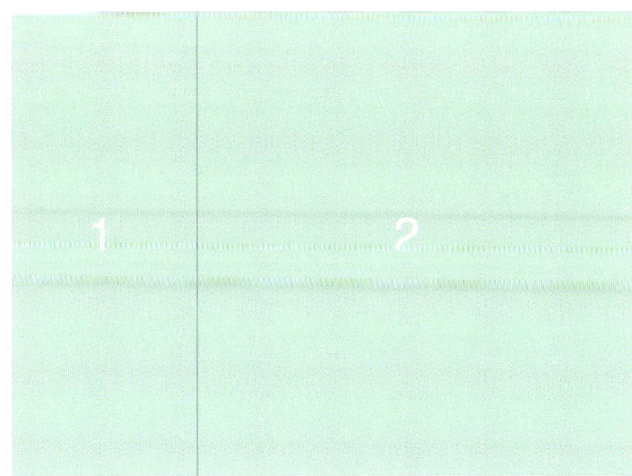

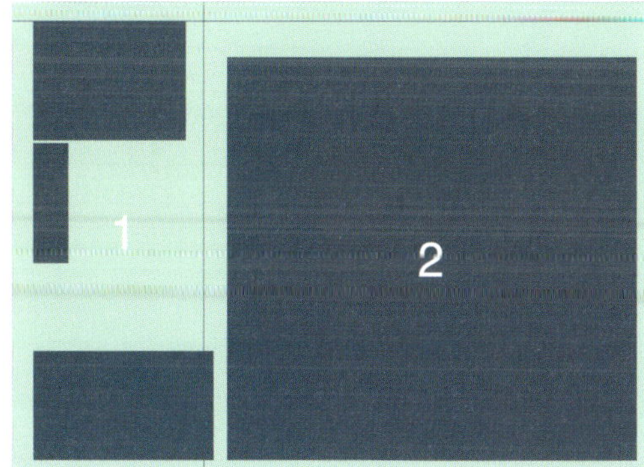

Visual Flow

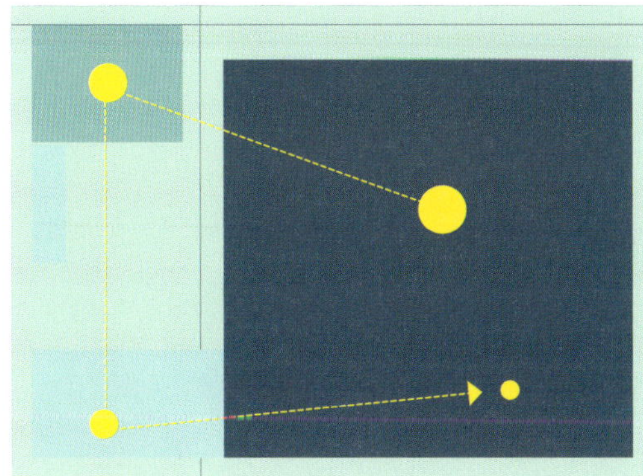

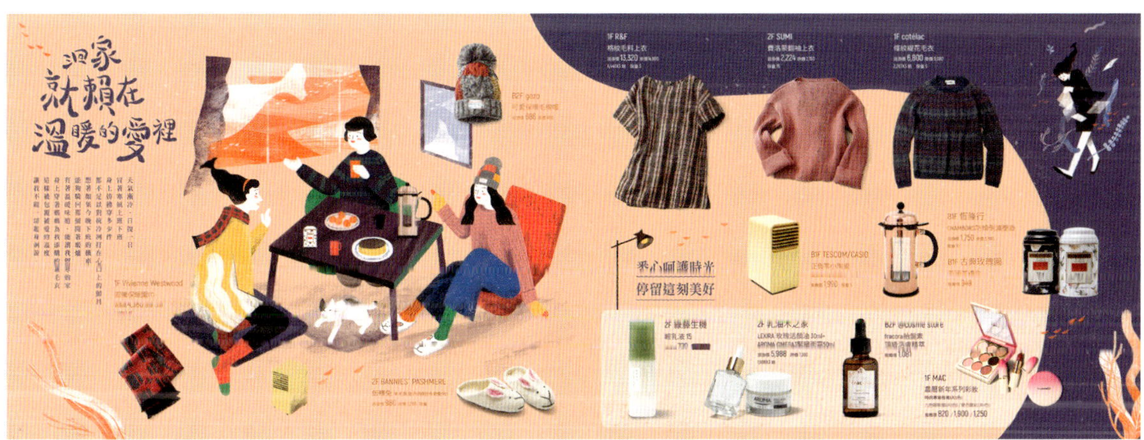

During the Spring Festival, the Park Lane Shopping Mall launched a campaign themed "Return Home", which suggests the practice of returning home for a family reunion. Following this concept, the designer worked with the illustrator to create a series of promotional materials.

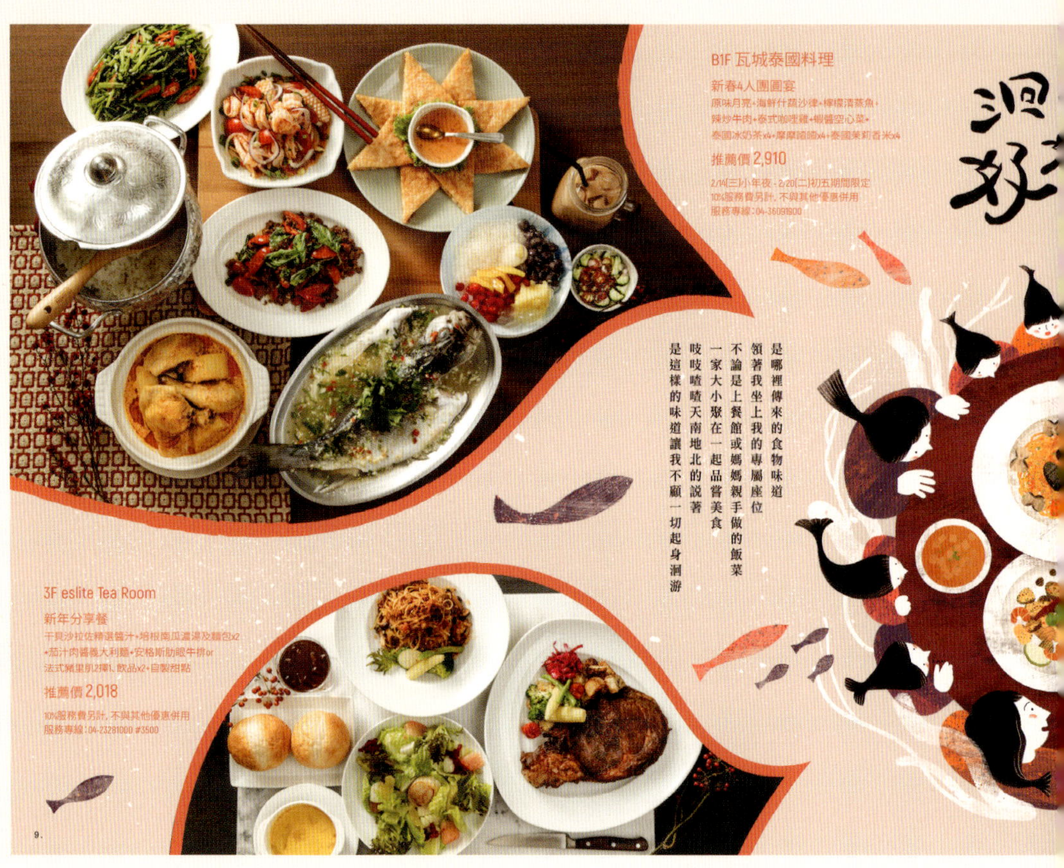
B1F 瓦城泰國料理
新春4人團圓宴
原味月亮+海鮮什蔬沙律+檸檬清蒸魚+
辣炒牛肉+泰式咖哩雞+蝦醬空心菜+
泰國冰奶茶x4+摩摩喳喳x4+泰國茉莉香米x4
推薦價 2,910
2/14(三)小年夜 - 2/20(二)初五期間限定
10%服務費另計，不與其他優惠併用
服務專線：04-36091800
是哪裡傳來的食物味道
領著我坐上我的專屬座位
不論是上餐館或媽媽親手做的飯菜
一家大小聚在一起品嘗美食
吱吱喳喳天南地北的說著
是這樣的味道讓我不顧一切起身洄游
3F eslite Tea Room
新年分享餐
推薦價 2,018
10%服務費另計，不與其他優惠併用
服務專線：04-23281000 #3500
9.

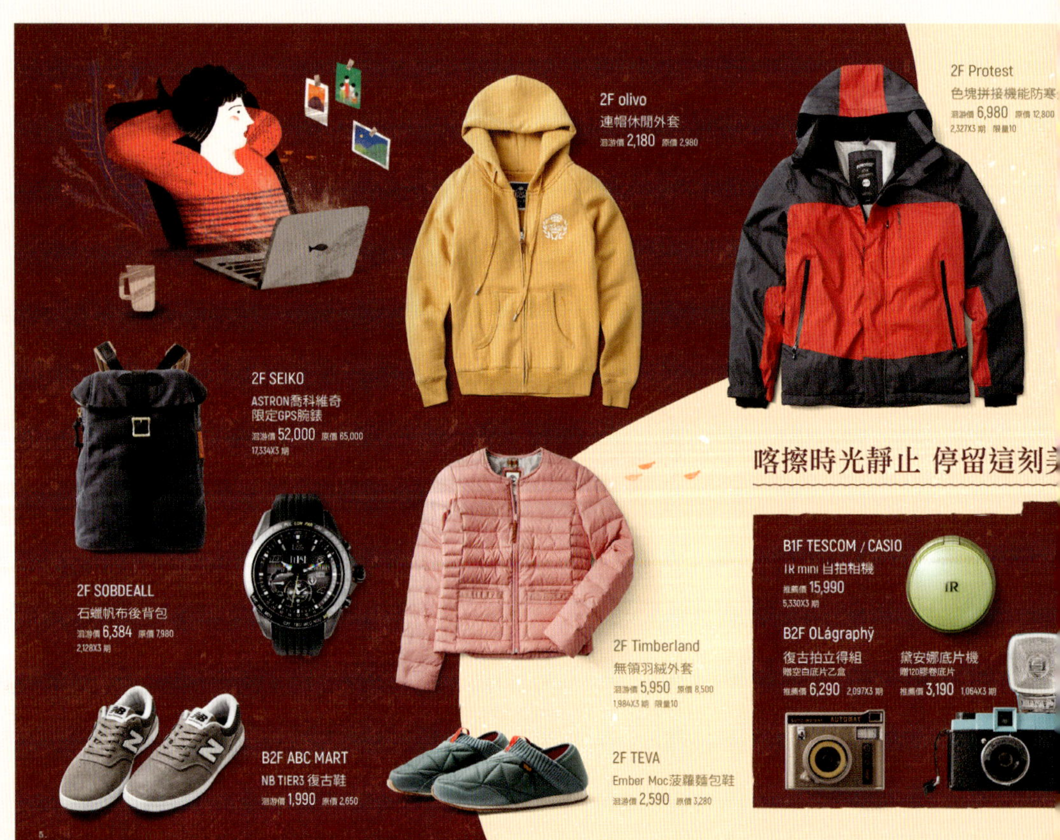
2F olivo
連帽休閒外套
洄游價 2,180 原價 2,980
2F Protest
洄游價 6,980 原價 12,800
2,327X3 期 限量10
2F SEIKO
ASTRON喬科維奇
限定GPS腕錶
洄游價 52,000 原價 65,000
17,334X3 期
喀擦時光靜止 停留這刻
2F SOBDEALL
石蠟帆布後背包
洄游價 6,384 原價 7,980
2,128X3 期
B1F TESCOM / CASIO
IR mini 自拍相機
推薦價 15,990
5,330X3 期
B2F OLágraphÿ
復古拍立得組
贈空白底片乙盒
推薦價 6,290 2,097X3 期
黛安娜底片機
贈120膠卷底片
推薦價 3,190 1,064X3 期
2F Timberland
無領羽絨外套
洄游價 5,950 原價 8,500
1,984X3 期 限量10
B2F ABC MART
NB TIER3 復古鞋
洄游價 1,990 原價 2,650
2F TEVA
Ember Moc菠蘿麵包鞋
洄游價 2,590 原價 3,280
5.

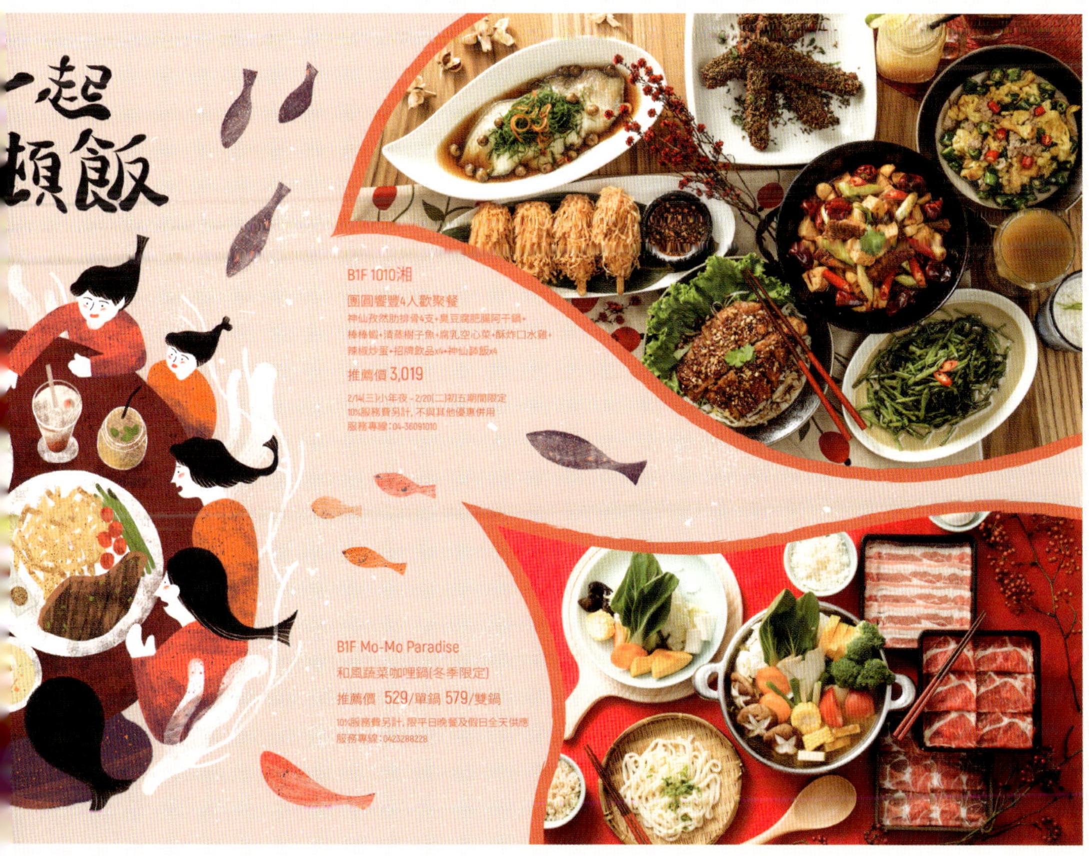
一起
頓飯
B1F 1010湘
團圓饗豐4人歡聚餐
神仙孜然肋排骨4支+臭豆腐肥腸阿干鍋+
棒棒蝦+清蒸樹子魚+腐乳空心菜+酥炸口水雞+
辣椒炒蛋+招牌飲品x4+神仙跡飯x4
推薦價 3,019
2/14(三)小年夜 - 2/20(二)初五期間限定
10%服務費另計，不與其他優惠併用
服務專線：04-36091010
B1F Mo-Mo Paradise
和風蔬菜咖哩鍋(冬季限定)
推薦價 529/單鍋 579/雙鍋
10%服務費另計，限平日晚餐及假日全天供應
服務專線：0423288228

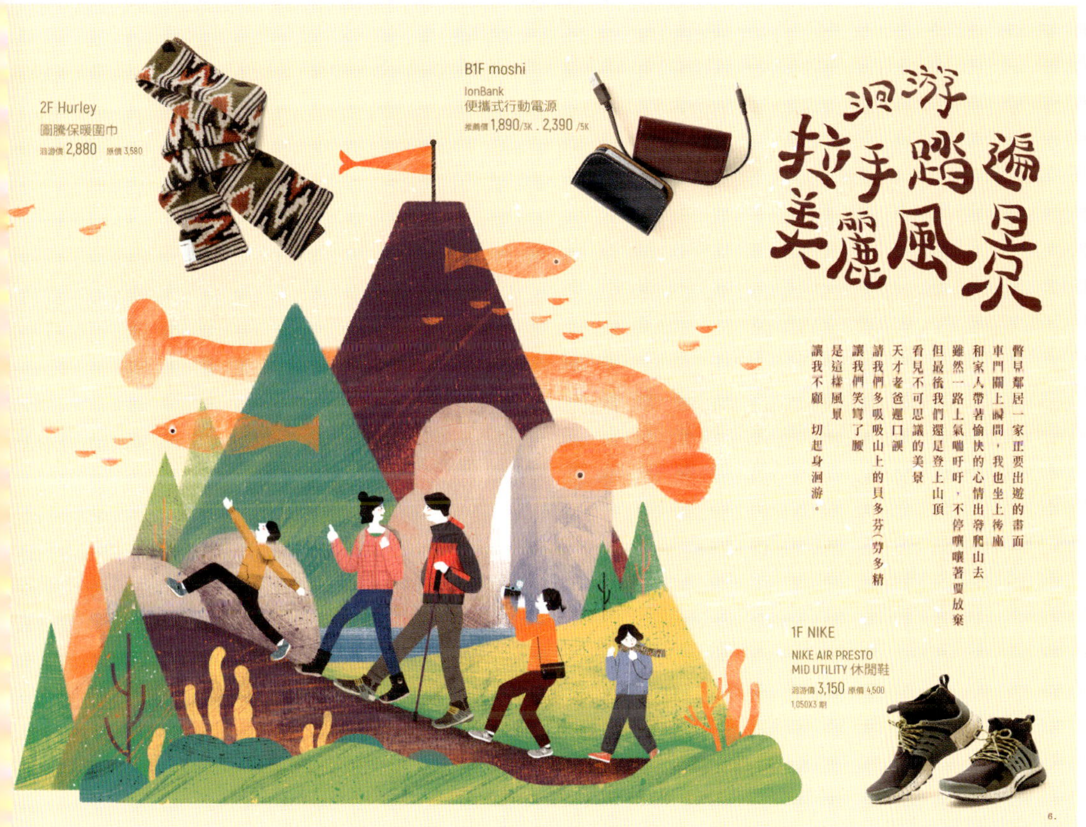
2F Hurley
圖騰保暖圍巾
洄游價 2,880 原價 3,580
B1F moshi
IonBank
便攜式行動電源
推薦價 1,890/3K . 2,390 /5K
洄游
拉手踏遍
美麗風景
瞥見鄰居一家正要出遊的畫面
車門關上瞬間，我也坐上後座
和家人帶著愉快的心情出發爬山去
雖然一路上氣喘吁吁，不停嚷嚷著要放棄
但最後我們還是登上山頂
看見不可思議的美景
天才老爸還口訣
請我們多吸吸山上的貝多芬（芬多精
讓我們笑彎了腰
是這樣風景
讓我不顧 切起身洄游。
1F NIKE
NIKE AIR PRESTO
MID UTILITY 休閒鞋
洄游價 3,150 原價 4,500
1,050X3 期
6.

You Are The One Promotional Material

Designer

Shao Chun Yang

Client

Park Lane by CMP

Key Diagram

Font

Bodoni MT (English)
Source Han Sans (Chinese)

Paper

120g Dongjiu special paper-bingli

Size

255×182mm

The serif font is very relevant to the topic of art fashion, revealing the feeling of elegance.

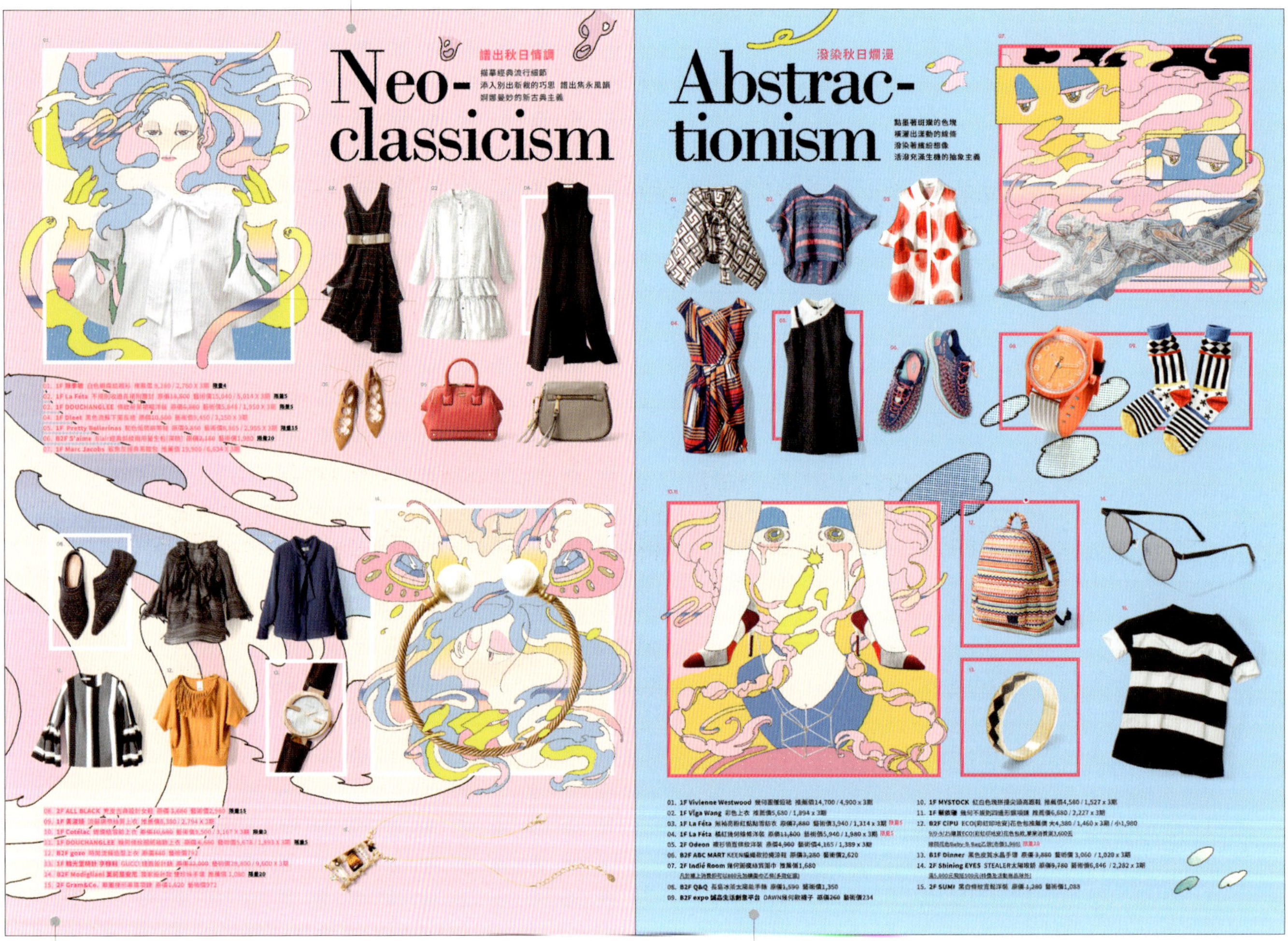

The layout is roughly divided into four parts. Product pictures and illustrations are arranged symmetrically so that all elements are placed neatly and orderly even if the size of the material is different.

The dominant color is pink, and the light color background can highlight the images of the products.

Grid

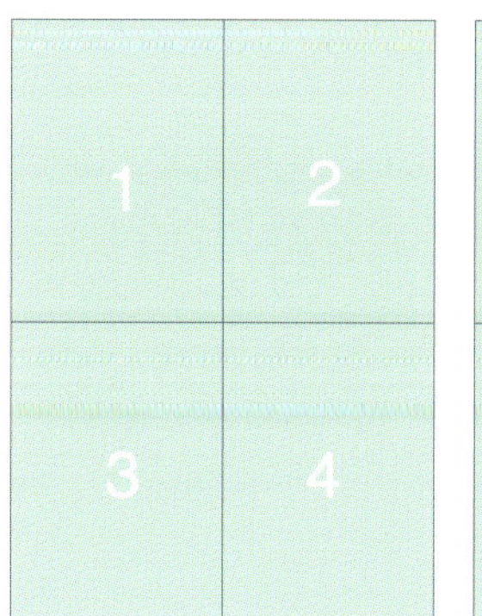

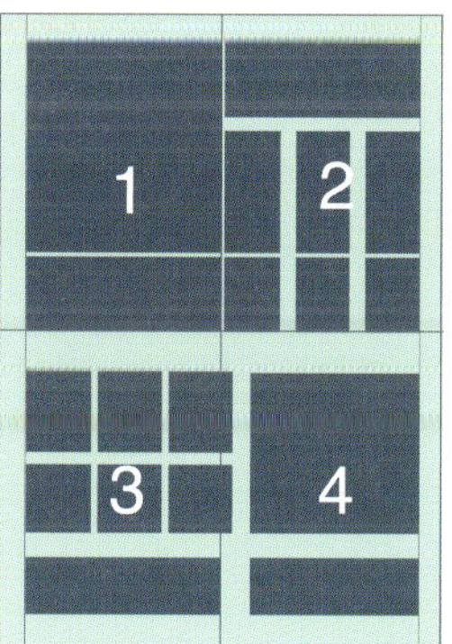

Visual Flow

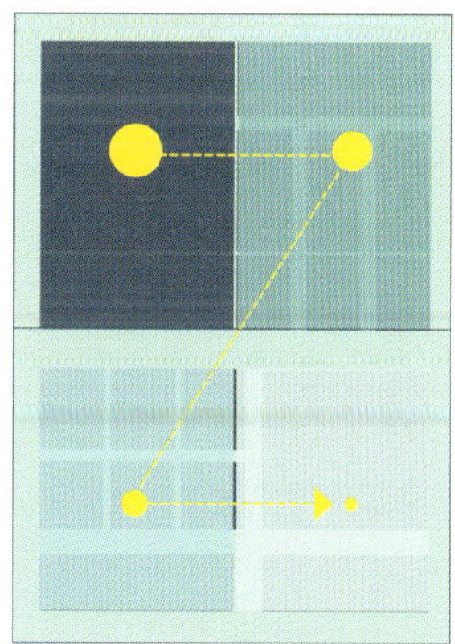

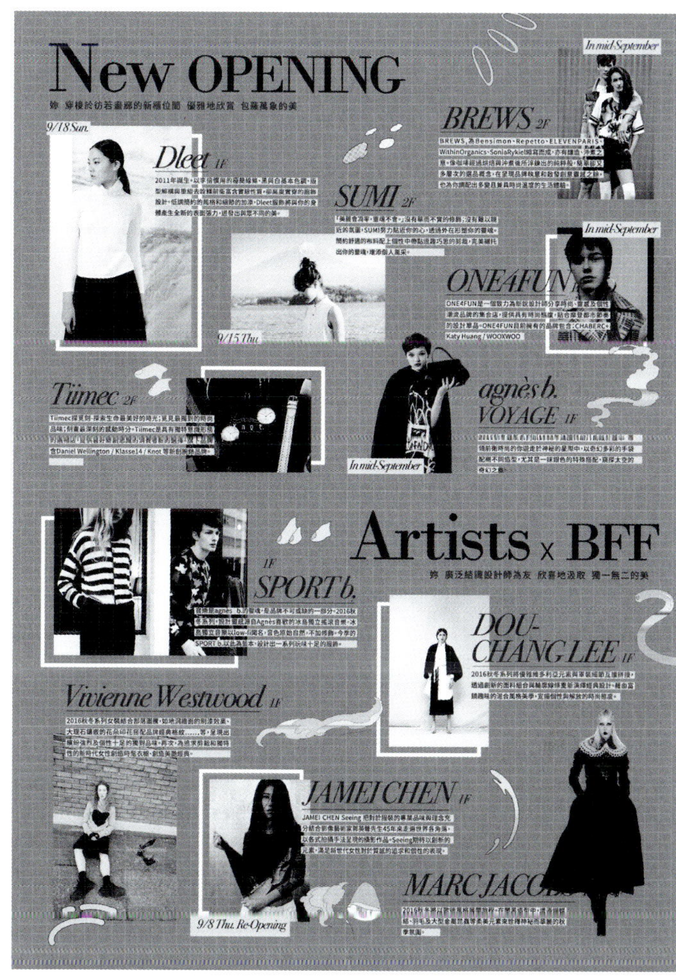

This campaign for Park Lane Shopping Mall was to promote the autumn fashion items with the viewpoint of "unique taste", conveying "whether you are liberating yourself or continuing to develop a new self-style, your beauty is defined by yourself". The new fashion photographer Fang Pin Hao, model Li Rou, and the illustrator Diji Cuowu, were invited by the designer brand Dleet to create something new. This rich multi-party co-operation led to fashionable and original visuals. The con tents of the direct mail catalog has a special classification of the autumn fashion items: neoclassicism, abstractionism, and realism.

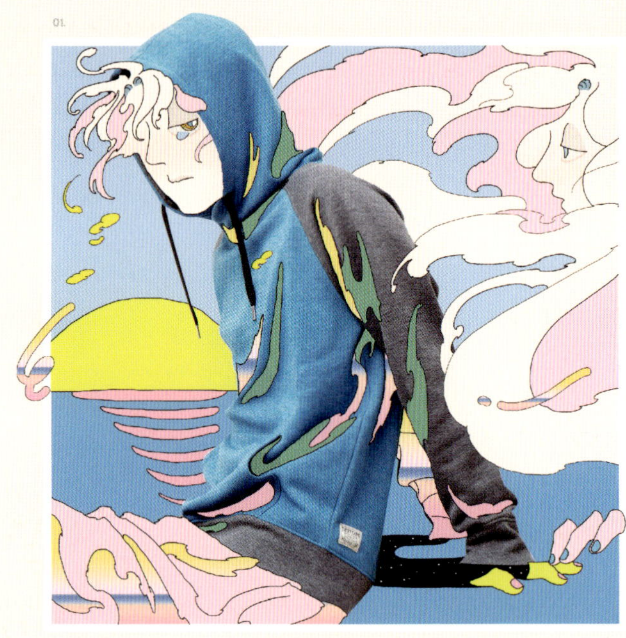

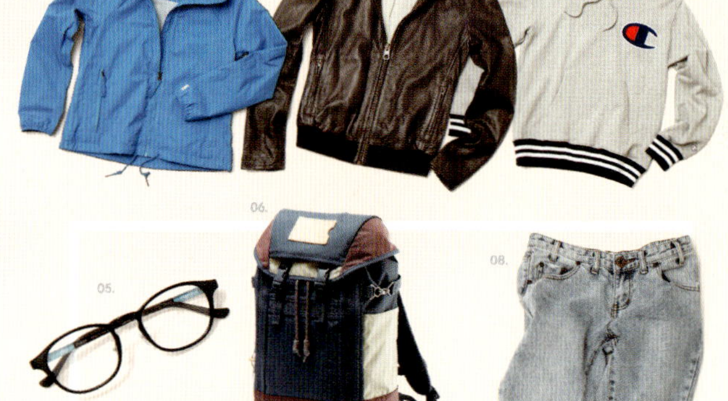

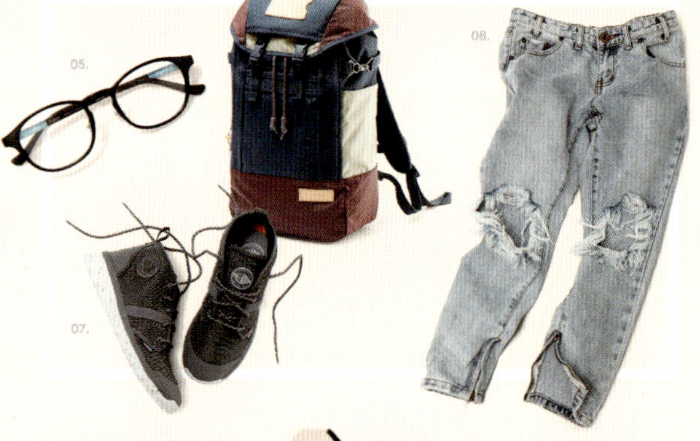

Realism"

繪上秋日底蘊

繪上基本元素 交織堆疊 相互輝映
調合出簡約大方 率性而機能十足的寫實主義

01. **2F PROTEST** 雙色帽Tee ~~原價2,980~~ 藝術價2,380 限量10
02. **2F Timberland** 風衣外套 ~~原價6,900~~ 藝術價4,140 / 1,380 x 3期
03. **2F Timberland** 真皮夾克 ~~原價27,000~~ 藝術價22,950 / 7,650 x 3期
04. **2F Champion** 灰色連帽Tee 推薦價3,680 / 1,227 x 3期
05. **B2F OWNDAYS** 簡約百搭眼鏡 推薦價2,490
06. **2F EASTPAK** 拼色後背包 ~~原價5,850~~ 藝術價4,000 / 1,334 x 3期 限量
07. **2F Palladium** 灰色高筒休閒鞋 ~~原價2,180~~ 藝術價2,071
08. **2F One Teaspoon** 淺色破損牛仔褲 推薦價5,600 / 1,867 x 3期

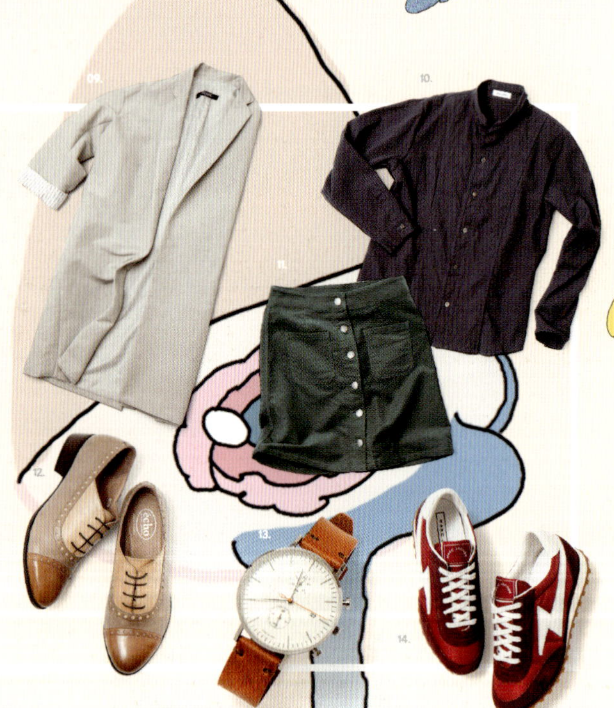

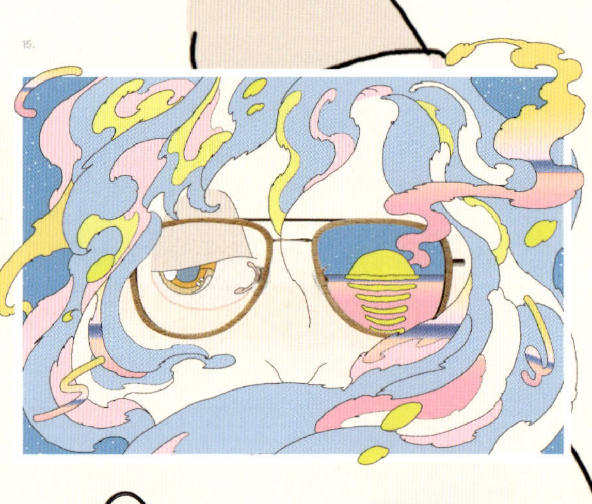

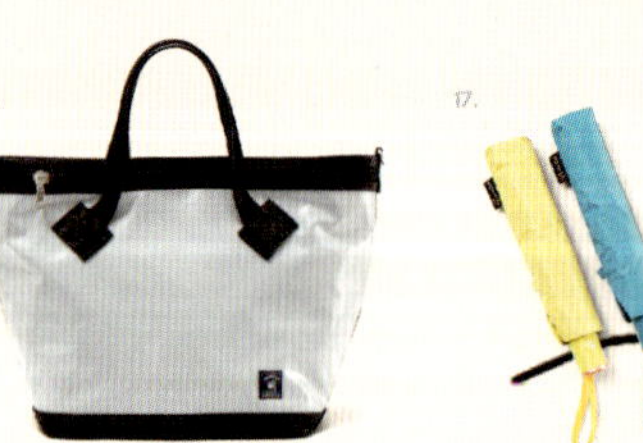

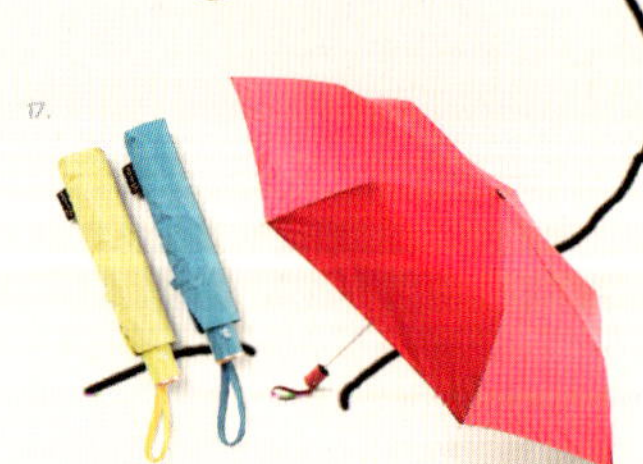

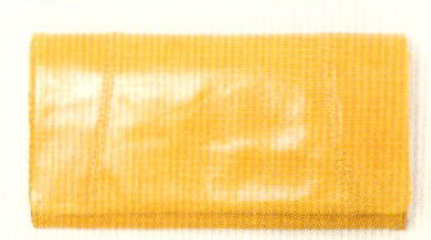

09. **2F Indié Room** 長版風衣外套 ~~原價7,580~~ 藝術價5,300 / 1,767 x 3期
VIP招募會單筆滿12,000元即贈800元購物金及限量絲巾乙條
10. **1F Plantation** 素面襯衫 ~~原價14,800~~ 藝術價10,300 / 3,434 x 3期 限量3
11. **B2F LOWRYS FARM** 單排釦氣質款短裙 ~~原價2,190~~ 藝術價1,790
12. **2F Vanger** 拼色牛津鞋 ~~原價3,380~~ 藝術價3,080 / 1,027 x 3期
13. **2F Tiimec** KNQT簡約計時碼錶 推薦價 7,350 / 2,450 x 3期
KNQT姬路手工縫線錶帶 推薦價1,900

14. **1F Marc Jacobs** MJ復古球鞋 推薦價14,900 / 4,967 x 3期
15. **1F 小雅眼鏡** 木框眼鏡 ~~原價9,000~~ 藝術價7,200 / 2,400 x 3期
送鏡片(度數800度內、散光200度內)
16. **1F PORTER** INTERNATIONAL 鯊魚灰簡約托特包 推薦價4,250 / 1,417 x 3期
17. **2F Prolla** 金屬漆色自動開收晴雨兩用傘(黃/藍/紅) ~~原價1,200~~ 藝術價900
18. **2F SOBDEALL** 芥末黃水臘牛皮長夾 ~~原價3,180~~ 藝術價2,703

New OPENING

妳 穿梭於彷若畫廊的新櫃位間 優雅地欣賞 包羅萬象的美

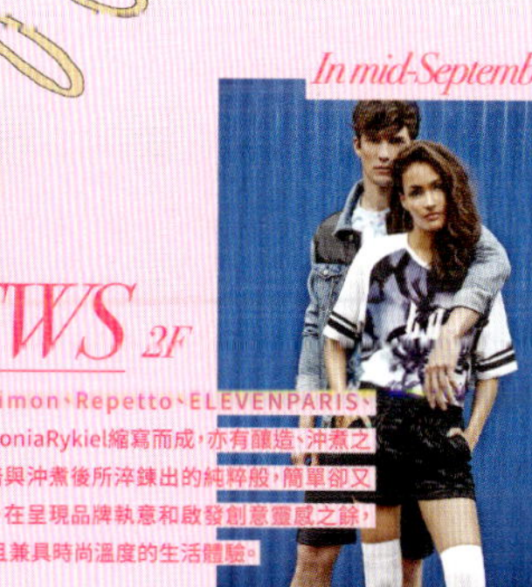

In mid-September

BREWS 2F

BREWS，為Bensimon、Repetto、ELEVENPARIS、WithinOrganics、SoniaRykiel縮寫而成，亦有釀造、沖煮之意。像咖啡經過烘焙與沖煮後所淬鍊出的純粹般，簡單卻又多層次的選品概念，在呈現品牌執意和啟發創意靈感之餘，也為你調配出多變且兼具時尚溫度的生活體驗。

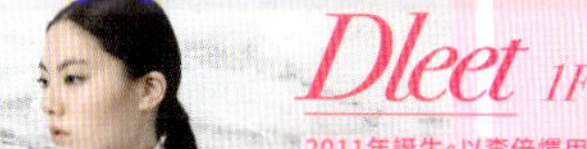

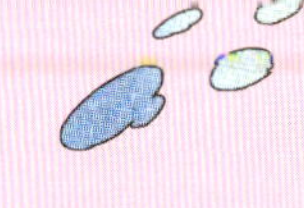

9/18 Sun.

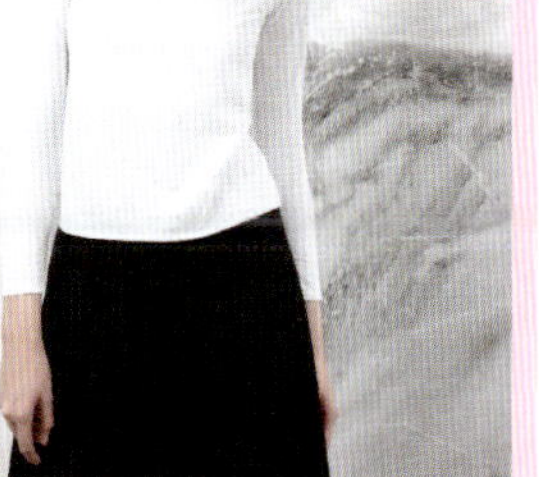

Dleet 1F

2011年誕生。以李倍慣用的極簡線條、黑與白基本色調、版型解構與重組去詮釋前衛富含實驗性質，卻高度實穿的服飾設計。低調簡約的風格和細節的加添，Dleet服飾將與你的身體產生全新的表面張力，迸發出與眾不同的美。

SUMI 2F

「美麗會凋零，靈魂不會。」沒有華而不實的修飾；沒有難以親近的氛圍，SUMI努力貼近你的心，透過外在形塑你的靈魂。簡約舒適的布料配上個性中帶點逗趣巧思的剪裁，完美襯托出你的靈魂，增添個人風采。

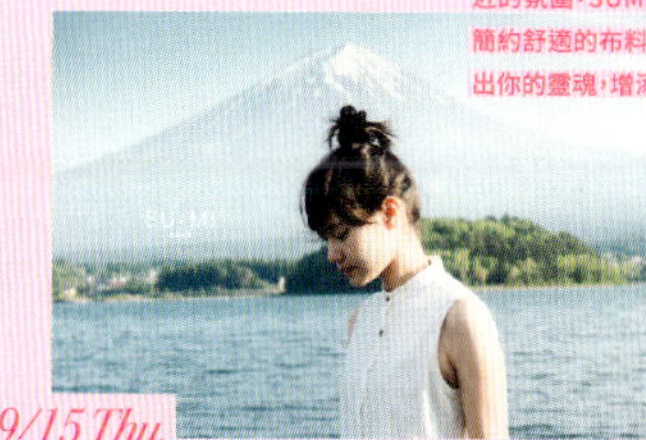

9/15 Thu.

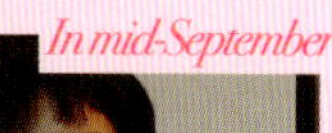

In mid-September

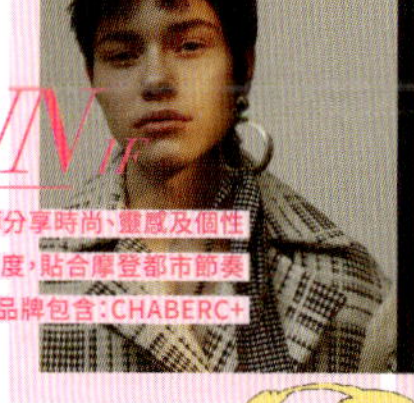

ONE4FUN 1F

ONE4FUN是一個致力為新銳設計師分享時尚、靈感及個性潮流品牌的集合店，提供具有時尚態度，貼合摩登都市節奏的設計單品。ONE4FUN目前擁有的品牌包含：CHABERC+ Katy Huang / WOOXWOO

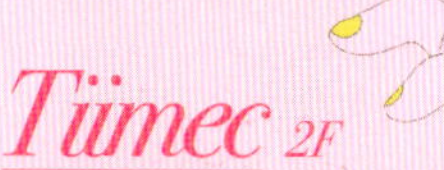

Tiimec 2F

Tiimec探覓刻-探索生命最美好的時光；覓見最獨到的時尚品味；刻畫最深刻的感動時分。Tiimec是具有獨特意識形態的選物店，提供喜好新創思維的消費者新的選擇。旗下品牌含Daniel Wellington / Klasse14 / Knot 等新創腕錶品牌。

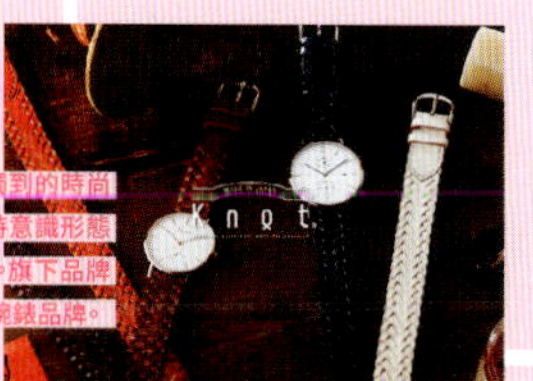

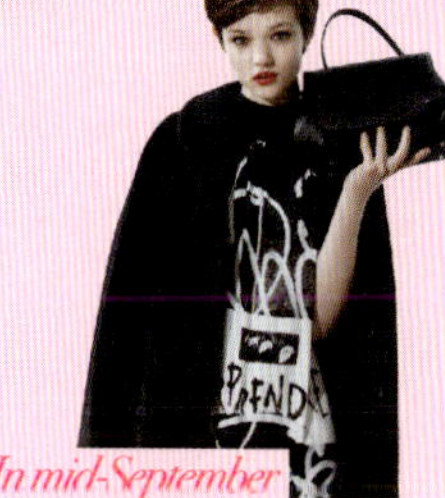

In mid-September

agnès b. VOYAGE 1F

2016秋冬最新系列以1968年法國科幻片為設計藍本，帶領前衛時尚的你遊走於神秘的星際中，以奇幻多彩的手袋配襯不同造型，尤其是一抹銀色的特殊搭配，窺探太空的奇幻之旅。

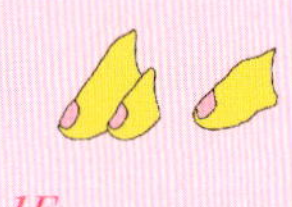

Artists x BFF

妳 廣泛結識設計師為友 欣喜地汲取 獨一無二的美

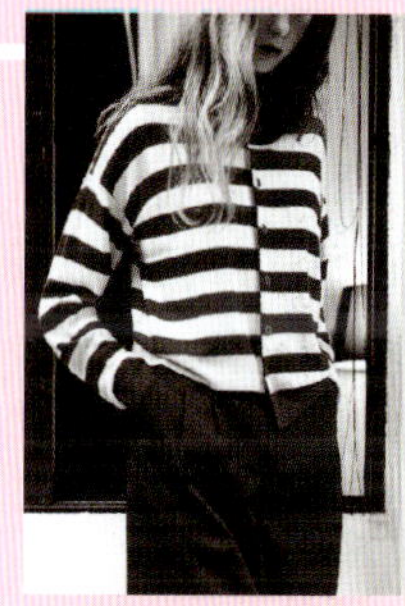

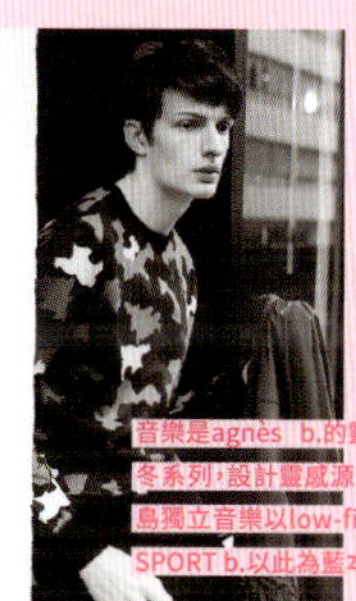

SPORT b. 1F

音樂是agnès b.的靈魂，是品牌不可或缺的一部分。2016秋冬系列，設計靈感源自Agnès喜歡的冰島獨立搖滾音樂。冰島獨立音樂以low-fi聞名，音色原始自然，不加修飾。今季的SPORT b.以此為藍本，設計出一系列玩味十足的服飾。

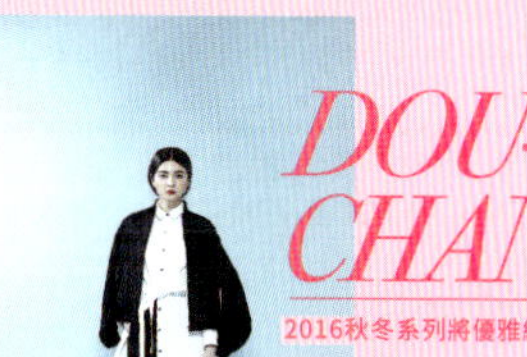

DOU-CHANG LEE 1F

2016秋冬系列將優雅維多利亞元素與軍裝細節互撞拼接，透過創新的面料組合與輪廓線條重新演繹經典設計。藉由富饒趣味的混合風格美學，宣揚個性與解放的時尚態度。

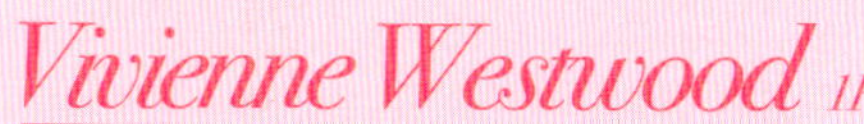

Vivienne Westwood 1F

2016秋冬系列女裝結合部落圖騰，如地洞牆面的刷漆效果、大理石鑲嵌的花朵印花搭配品牌經典格紋……等，呈現出繽紛強烈及個性十足的獨到品味。再次，為追求剪裁和獨特性的新時代女性創造時髦衣櫥、創造美艷經典。

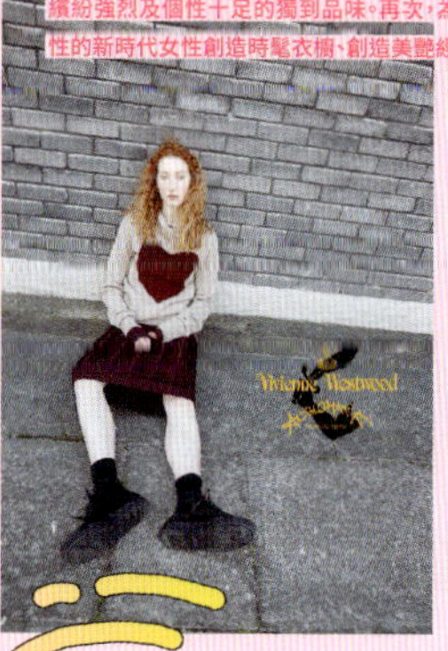

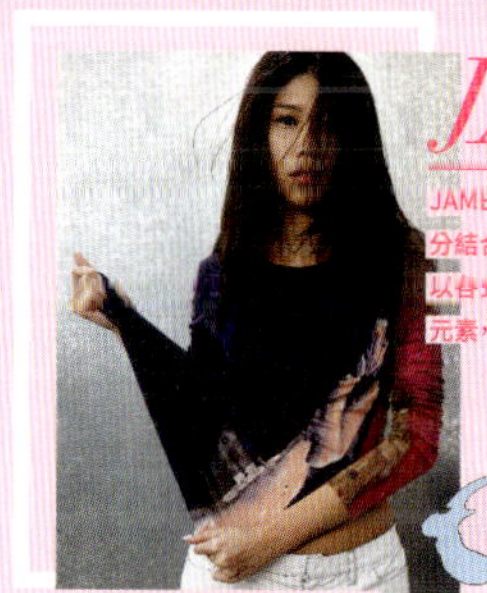

9/8 Thu. Re-Opening

JAMEI CHEN 1F

JAMEI CHEN Seeing 把對於服裝的專業品味與理念充分結合影像藝術家郭英聲先生45年來走遍世界各角落，以台式拍攝手法呈現的攝影作品。Seeing期待以創新的元素，滿足新世代女性對於質感的追求和個性的表現。

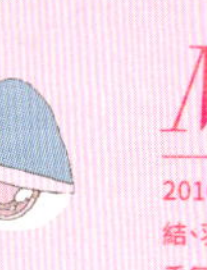

MARC JACOBS 1F

2016秋冬將以歌德風格展開旅程。在闇黑造型中，增添蝴蝶結、羽毛及大型金屬昆蟲等柔美元素來詮釋神祕而華麗的秋季氛圍。

"Something Good Something New" Poster

Designer

ZhongXing.H

Client

Park Lane by Splender

Key Diagram

Font	Paper	Size
W5-GB5	Coated paper	260×375mm

The logotype was inspired by those on the cardboard boxes seen in traditional markets. The font W5-GB5 adds a hint of vintage.

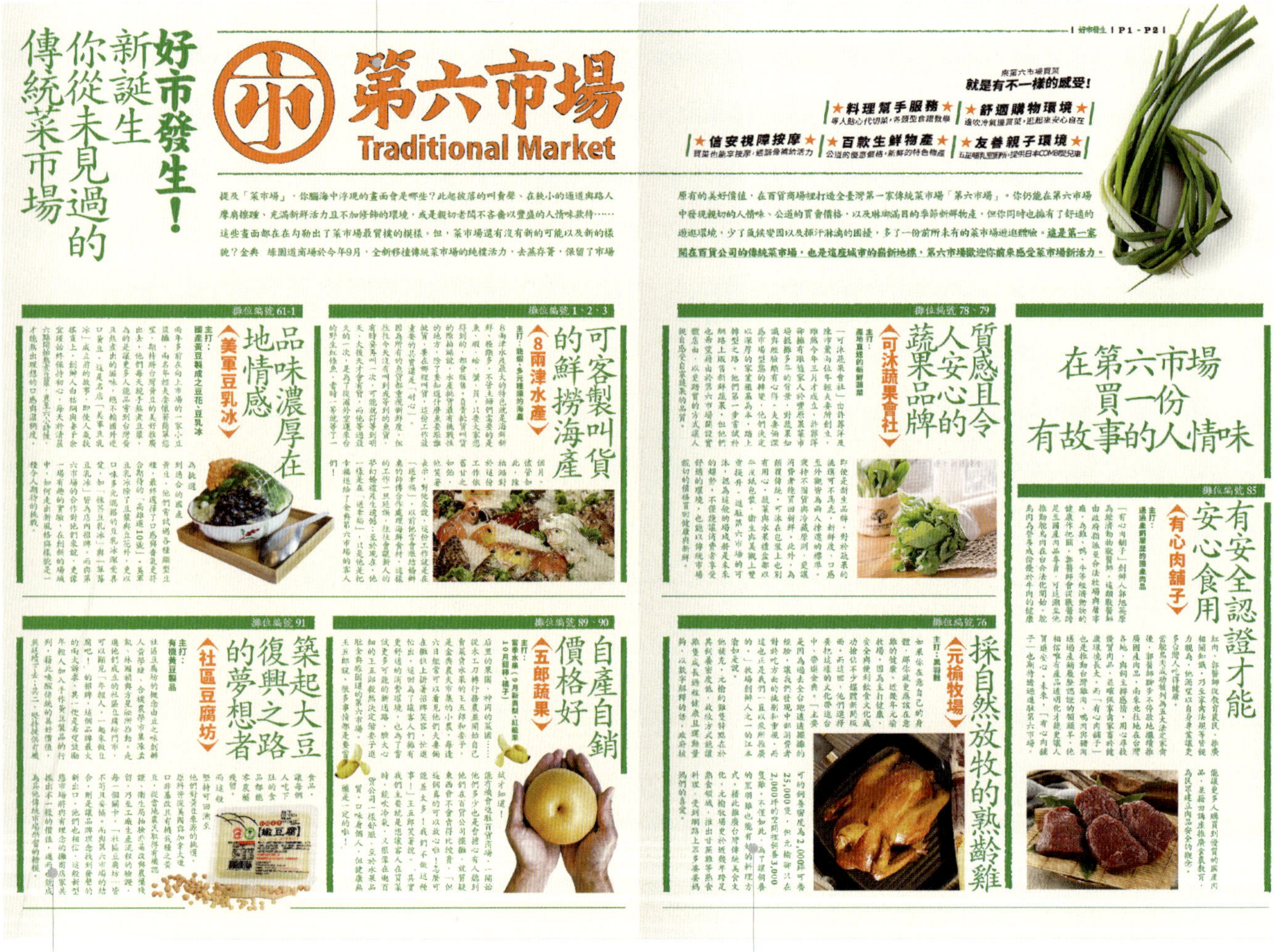

The entire page consists of neatly placed modules filled with pictures and texts, giving consumers a sense of a wide variety of products.

As the Chinese pronunciation for "good persimmon" is the same as "good things" in the slogan, the colors orange and green of persimmon are used as the main colors. Such a contrasting color scheme is also reminiscent of the vintage style on cardboard boxes of fruits and vegetables.

Grid

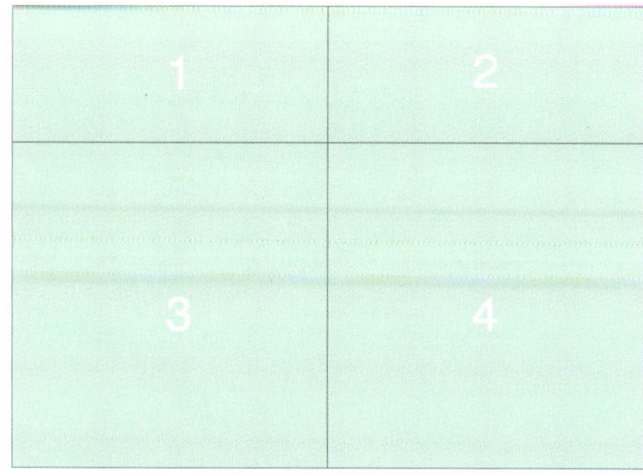

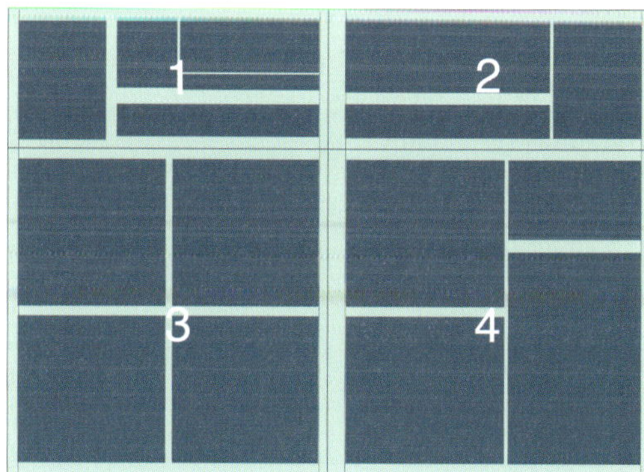

Visual Flow

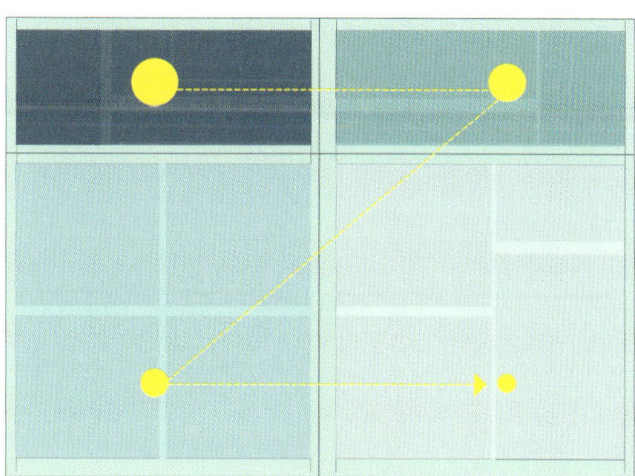

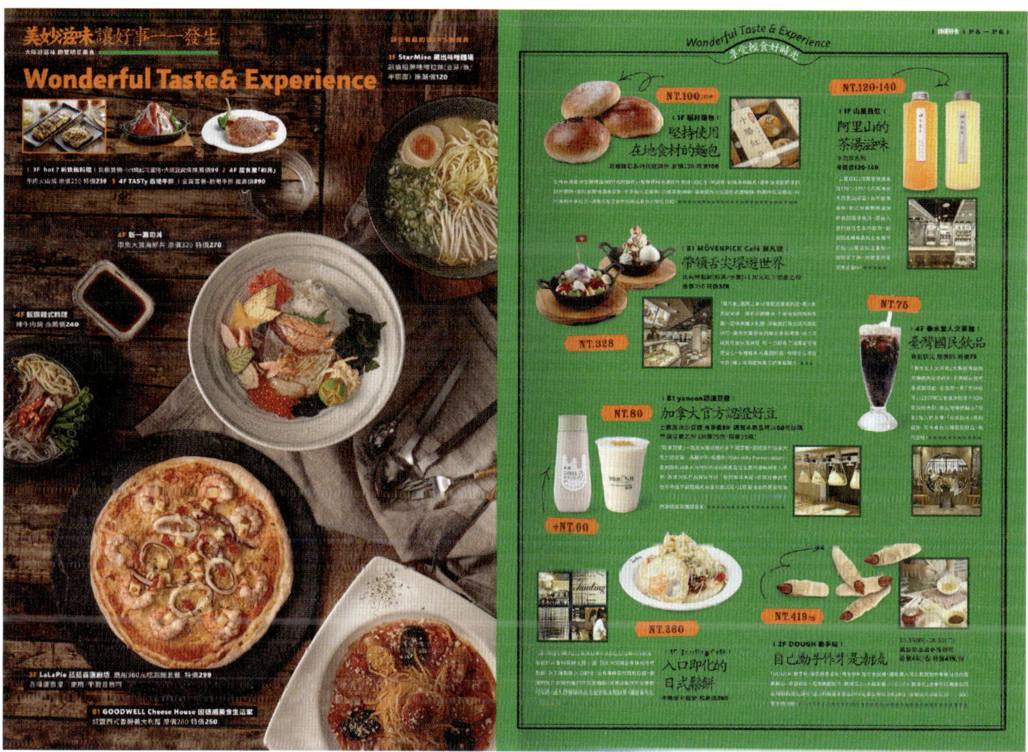

This traditional market is located in a department store, with the aim of combining the old and the new and creating a new life style. The promotional materials are designed based on the logotype style of the cardboard boxes commonly seen in traditional market. Besides, the Chinese word for "good things" (好事) in the slogan "Something good something new" sounds the same as "good market"(好市). There is another word which has the same pronunciation--"good persimmon", a fruit which serves as one of the key elements for the whole design.

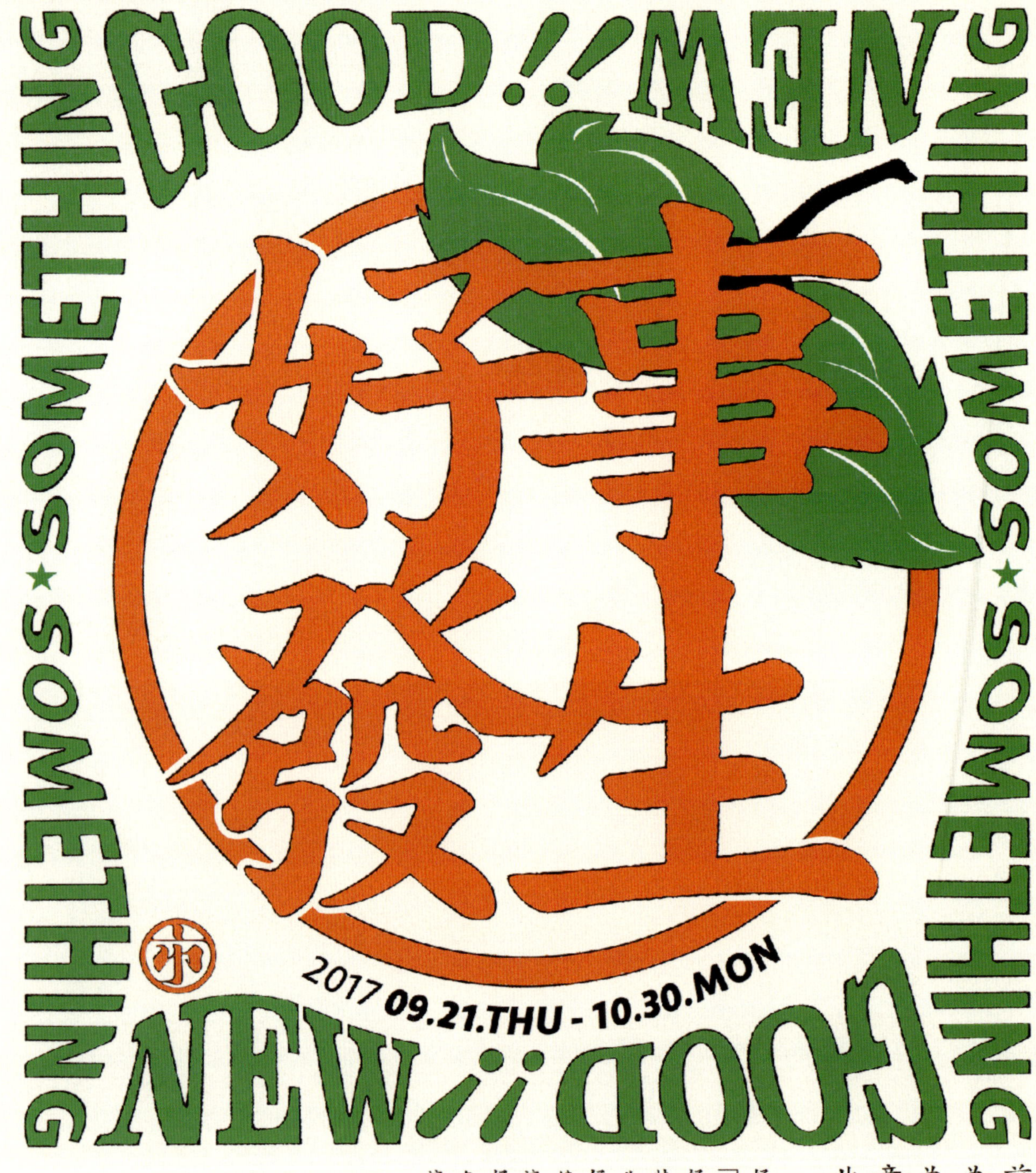
GOOD!! NEW
SOMETHING ★ SOMETHING
好事發生
2017 09.21.THU - 10.30.MON
NEW!! GOOD
SOMETHING ★ SOMETHING
前所未有的新鮮，
為日常添加新風味，
為生活調理新滋味
意想不到的各種好事，
此刻 正在發生！
好〈市〉發生
「第六市場」新鮮誕生。
好〈事〉登場
特色新櫃
為日常加值新活力。
好〈事〉精選
精選優質商品，
讓採買變得美好。
好〈事〉優惠
各種專屬好禮，
讓好事一一發生。
3F GRAND OPENING
第六市場 9/21 盛大開幕
金典 綠園道商場
台中市403西區健行路1049號B1-6F 04-2319 8000 WWW.PARKLANES.COM.TW

一起採買改變生活的美好事物

Every Good Thing Will Light UP Your Life.

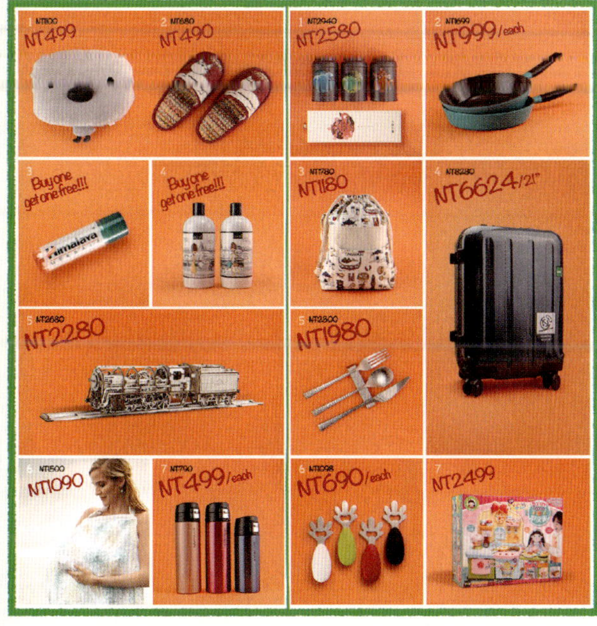

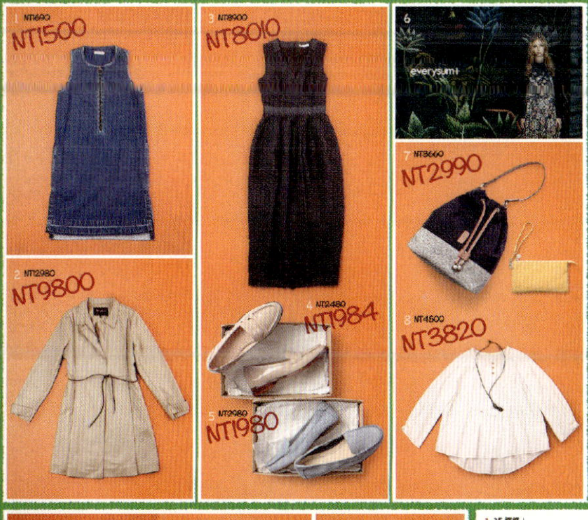

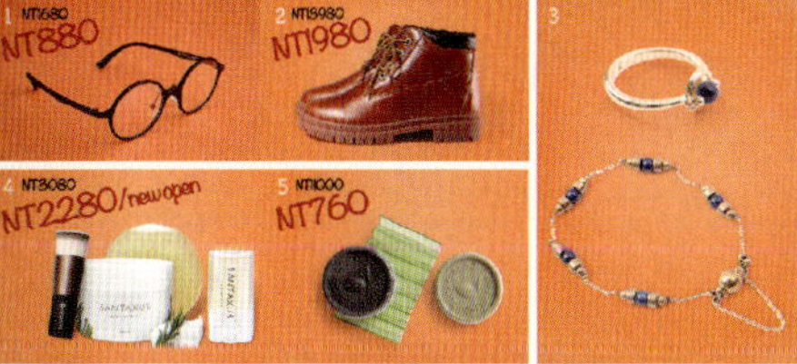

7 6F 玩具"反"斗城 | Dallimi扮家家酒-廚房組 推薦價 2,499 | 獨家販售 |

好事發生 NEW OPEN

助益身心的日常所需

LIFE 一起改造居家生活

助美化生活 PACKAGE 1

TZULAÏ

NEW OPEN

1F 居內TZULAÏ

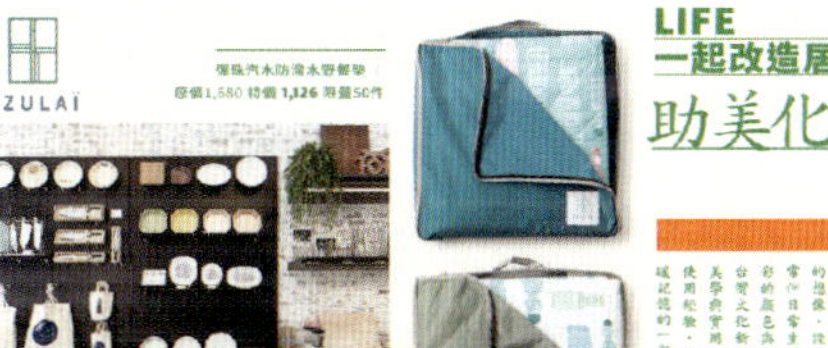

NEW OPEN

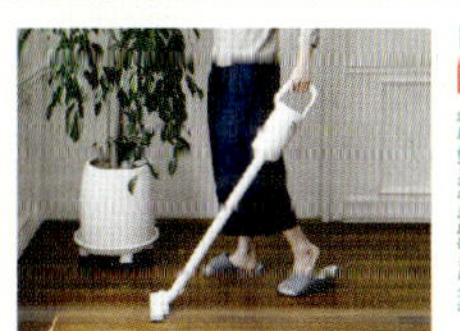

EXPERIENCE不一樣的身心體驗

助手腦並用 PACKAGE 2

2F DOUGH 動手玩

NEW OPEN

2F 達文西科技學習中心

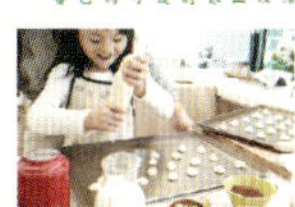

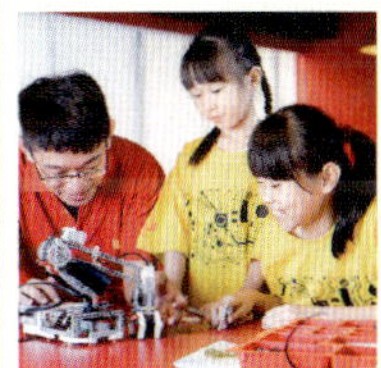

PARENT-CHILD親子樂活天地

助親子共樂 PACKAGE 3

6F 騎士堡

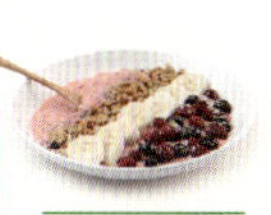

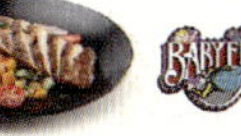

NEW OPEN

6F BABYFLY

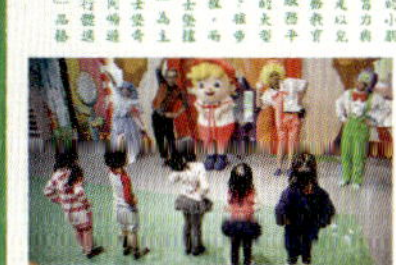

DRINK為生活乾一杯

助健康循環 PACKAGE 4

NEW OPEN

B1 iMetta

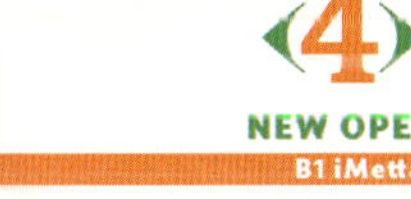

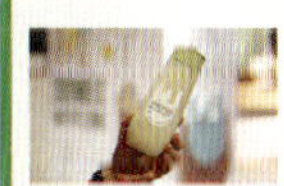

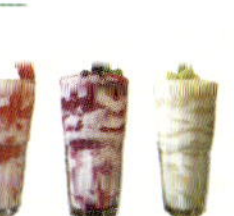

B1 yanoon耶濃豆漿

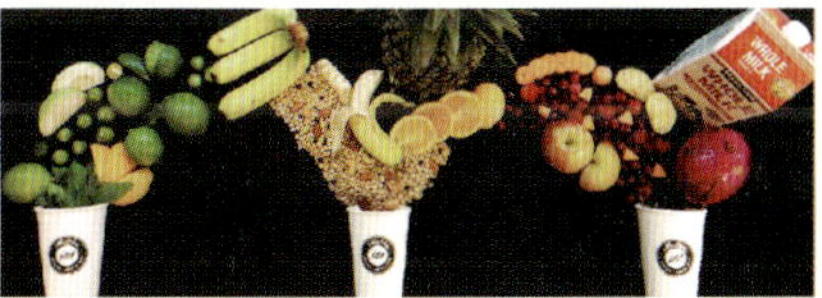

Warm House Poster

Designer

Masaomi Fujita

Client

Chiba Health and Energy Conservation Housing Promotion Association

Key Diagram

Font	Paper	Size
DIN	Coated paper	210×297mm (A4)

This sans serif font conveys minimalist aesthetics.

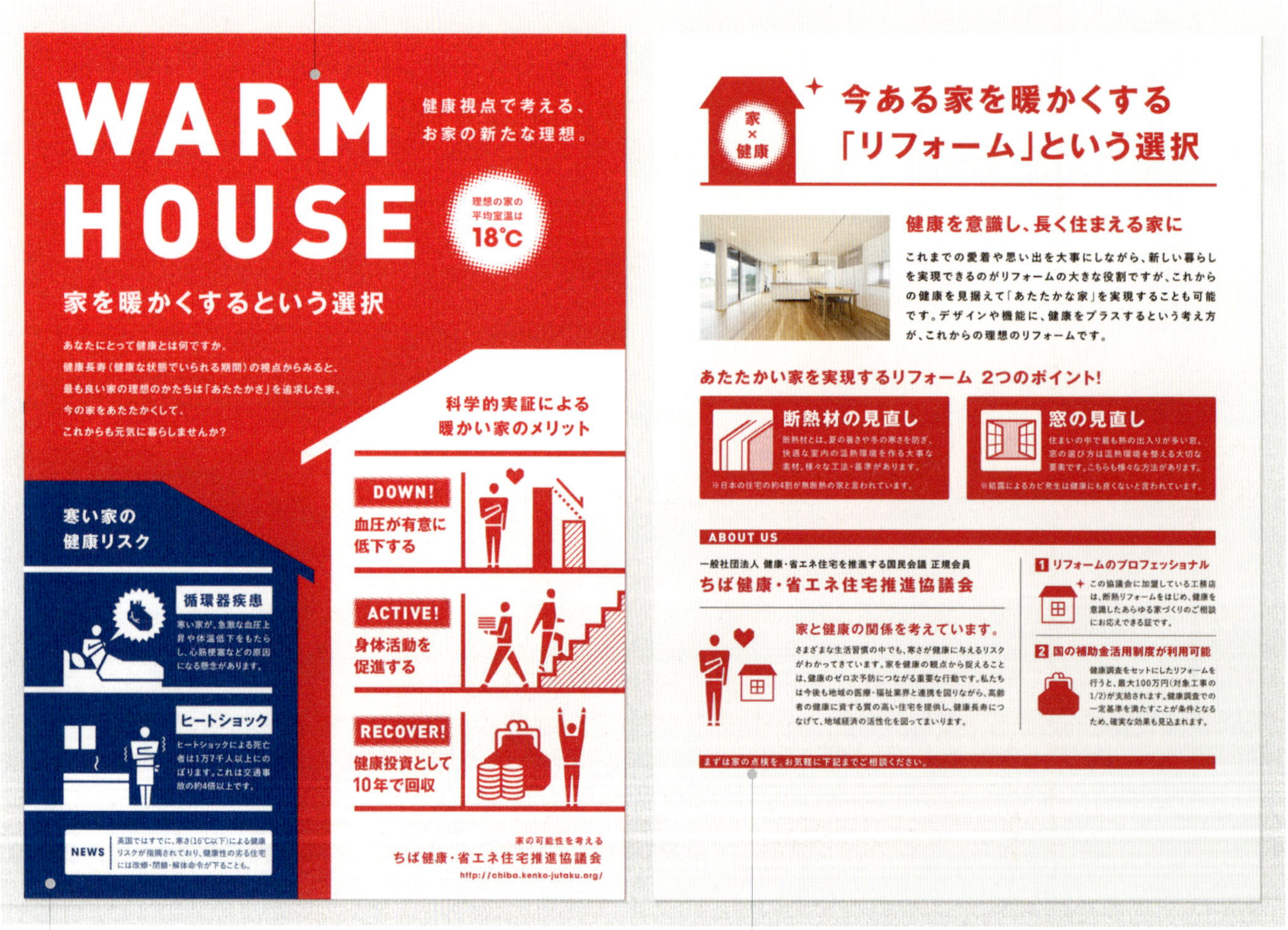

The layout principles such as alignment and proximity are applied in the design, making a relaxing sense of order. The illustrations are also lively and vivid, which fits the design goal.

The poster used red and blue as the main color, because the product is the heating system, it is very intuitive to use color to express the temperature.

Grid

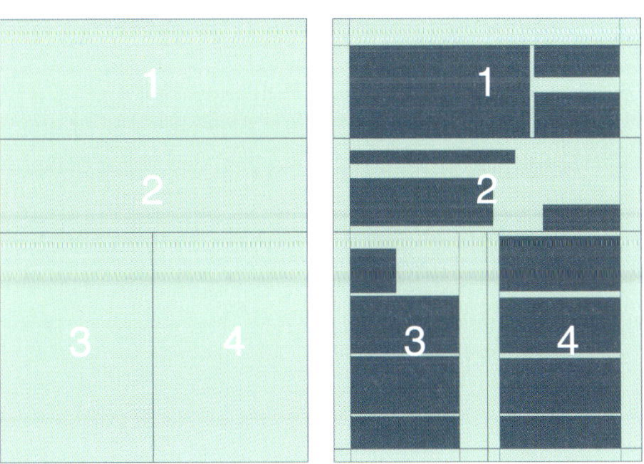

Visual Flow

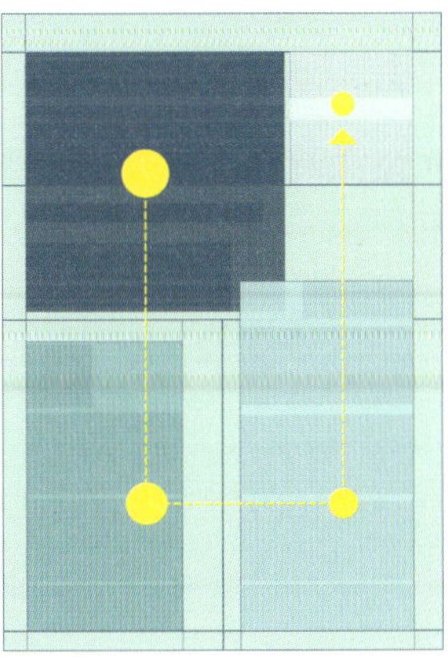

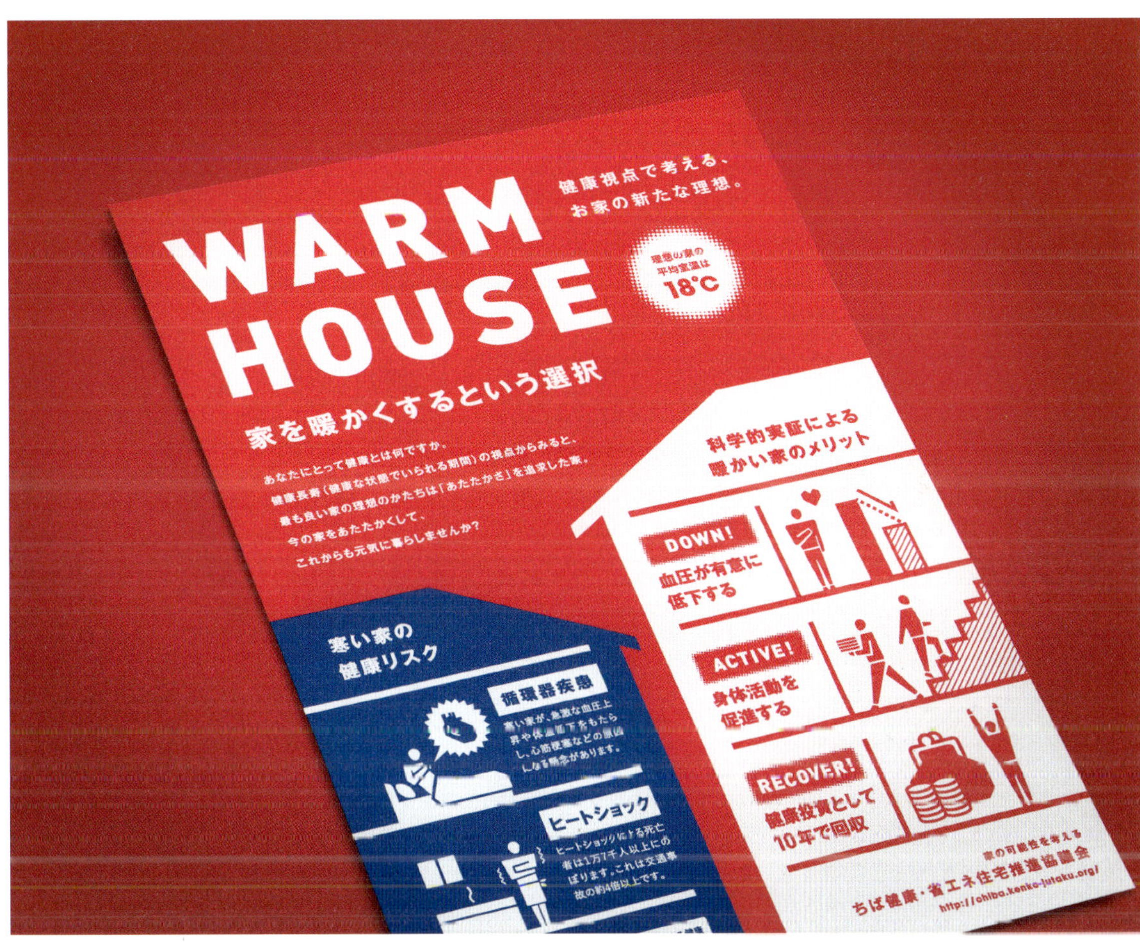

Chiba Health and Energy Conservation Housing Promotion Association is a business organization which aims for the realization of a "healthy and long-lived society", the reduction of nursing care cost, and the vitalization of local economies. Housing which has temperature-saving capabilities and a good thermal environment is said to help elders live longer. The poster and leaflet illustrate the reason such "warm houses" are effective and economical, and ways to renovate your house into a "warm house" in a simple way. The visual comparison of "cold houses" and "warm houses" using pictograms is made so that people who see it can understand the benefits and risks instinctively.

WuChun Shop Poster

Designer

ZhongXing.H

Client

Park Lane by Splender

Key Diagram

Font

W5-GB5

Paper

Coated paper

Size

260×375mm

The font in red color is related to a strong sense of traditional Chinese festivals. Mixed up fashion and traditional style is fresh and new.

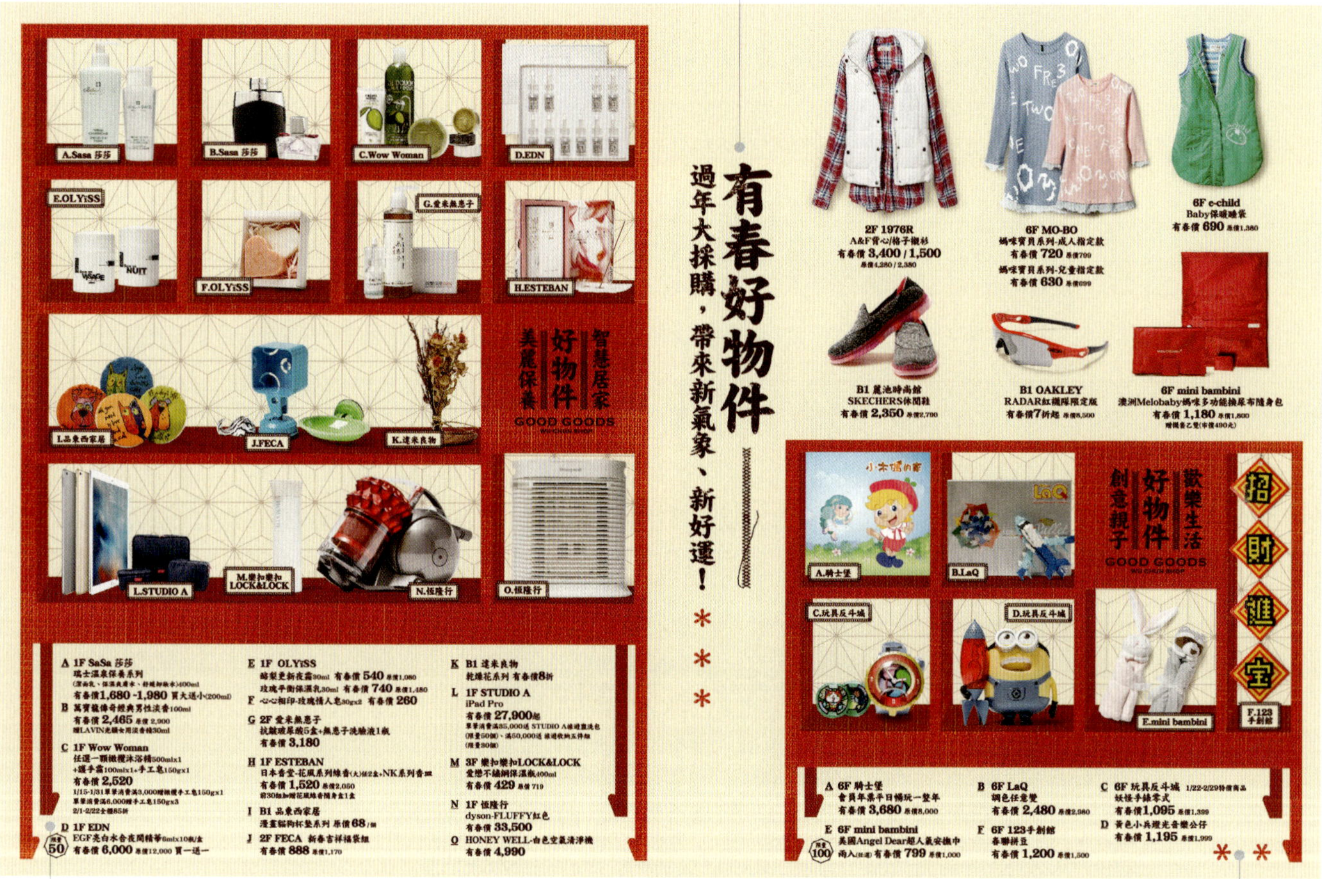

有春好物件

過年大採購，帶來新氣象、新好運！

Image classification is very important. When there are many pictures, pay attention to the order and the hierarchy. Using the principle of proximity, the products of different categories are placed in different modules, and the information is clearly classified so that consumers can get facts quickly.

Warm color gives a cozy feeling, and it is the Chinese New Year where the festive atmosphere is emphasized by the red color.

Grid

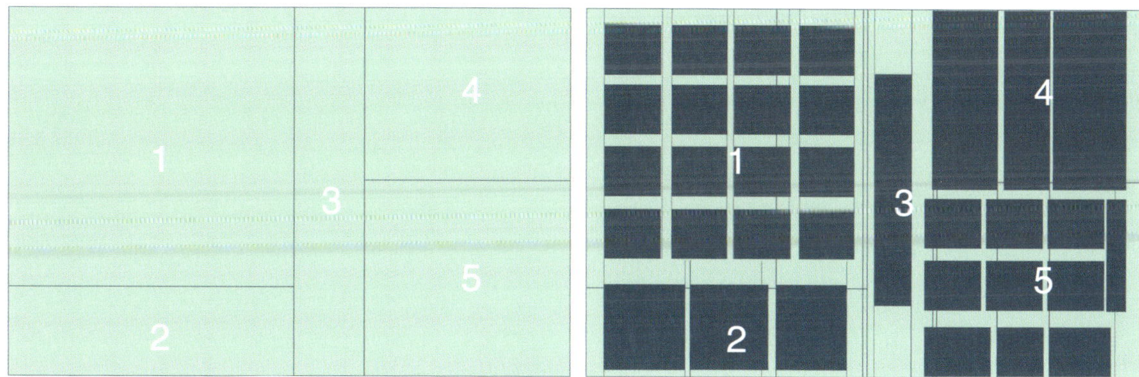

Visual Flow

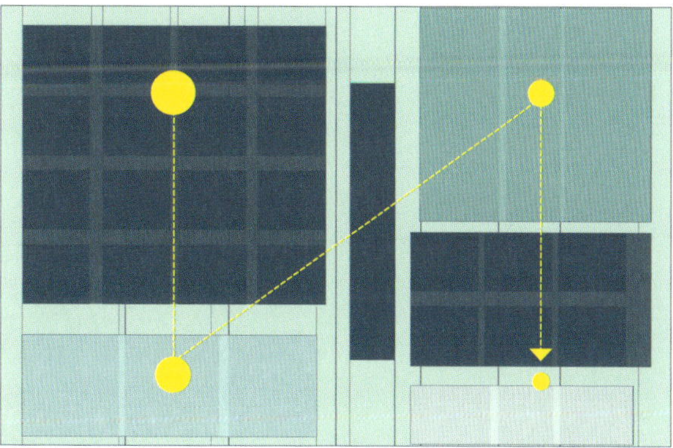

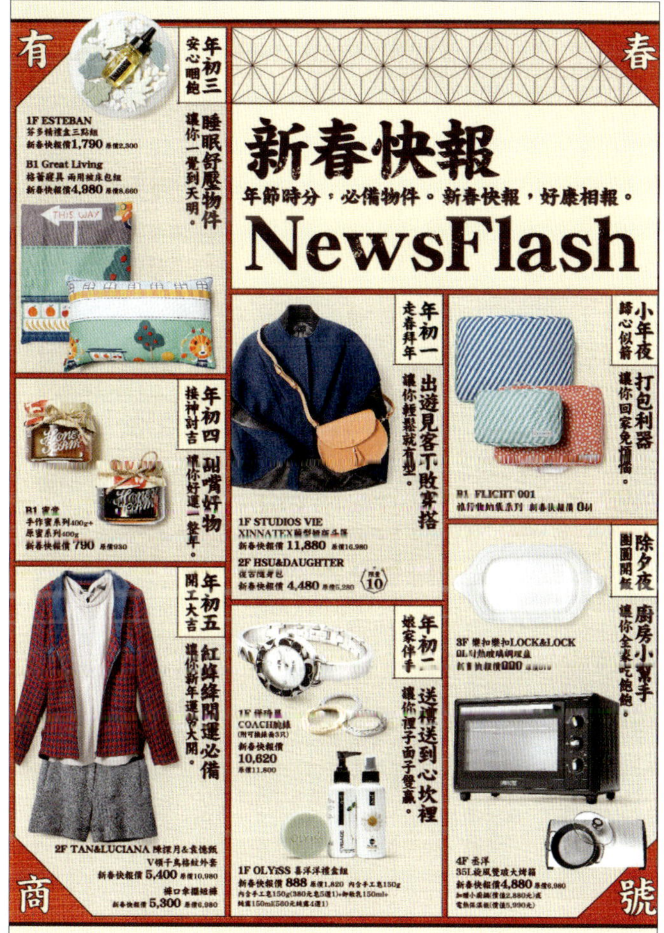

WuChun Shop is a promotional project designed for Park Lane. The design turns the mall into an old fashion shop and names it WuChun Shop. The nostalgic style brings out the atmosphere of the New Year, using vintage window displays, cabinets, tables, and chairs to present the products.

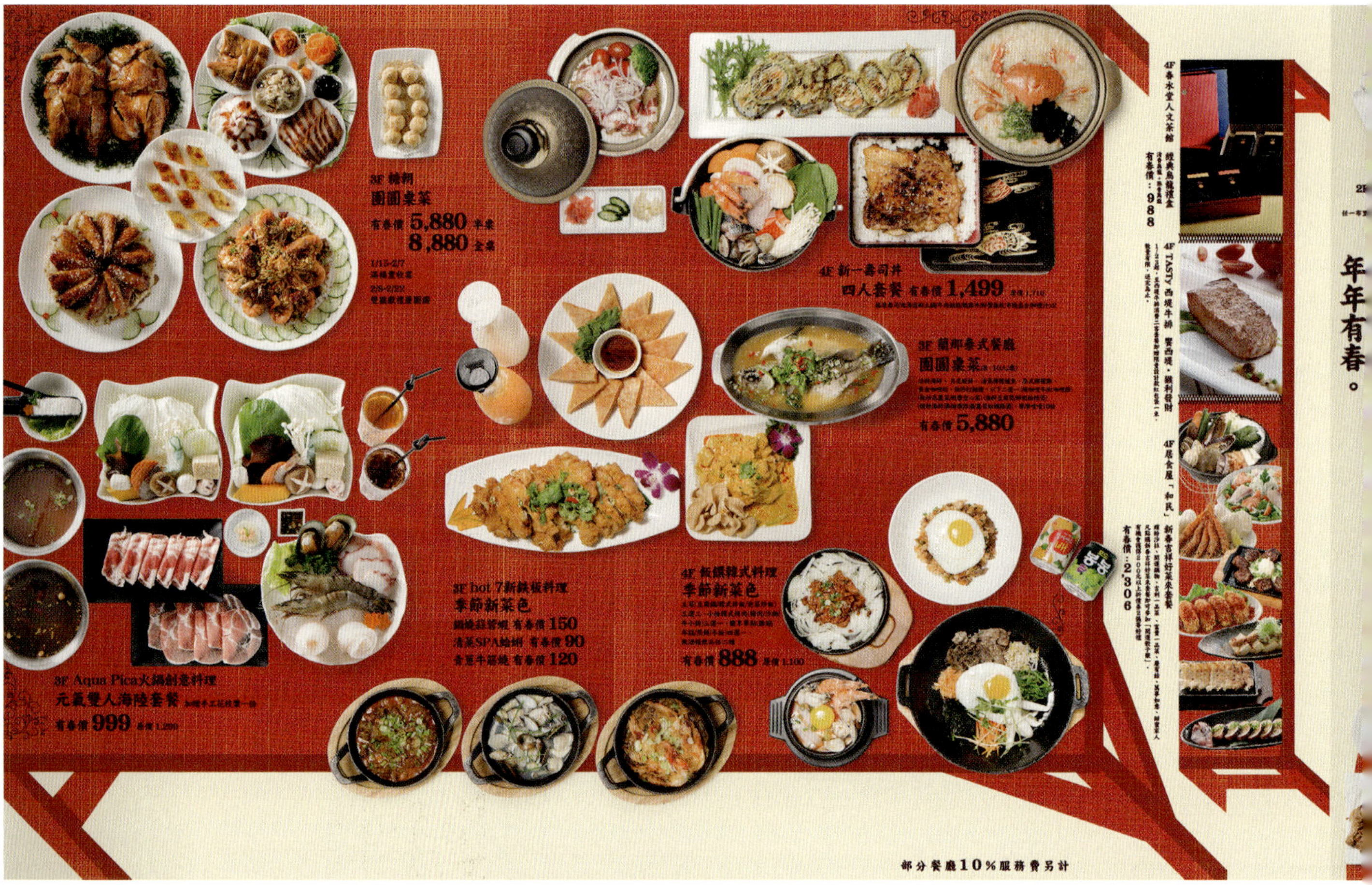

年年有春。

部分餐廳10%服務費另計

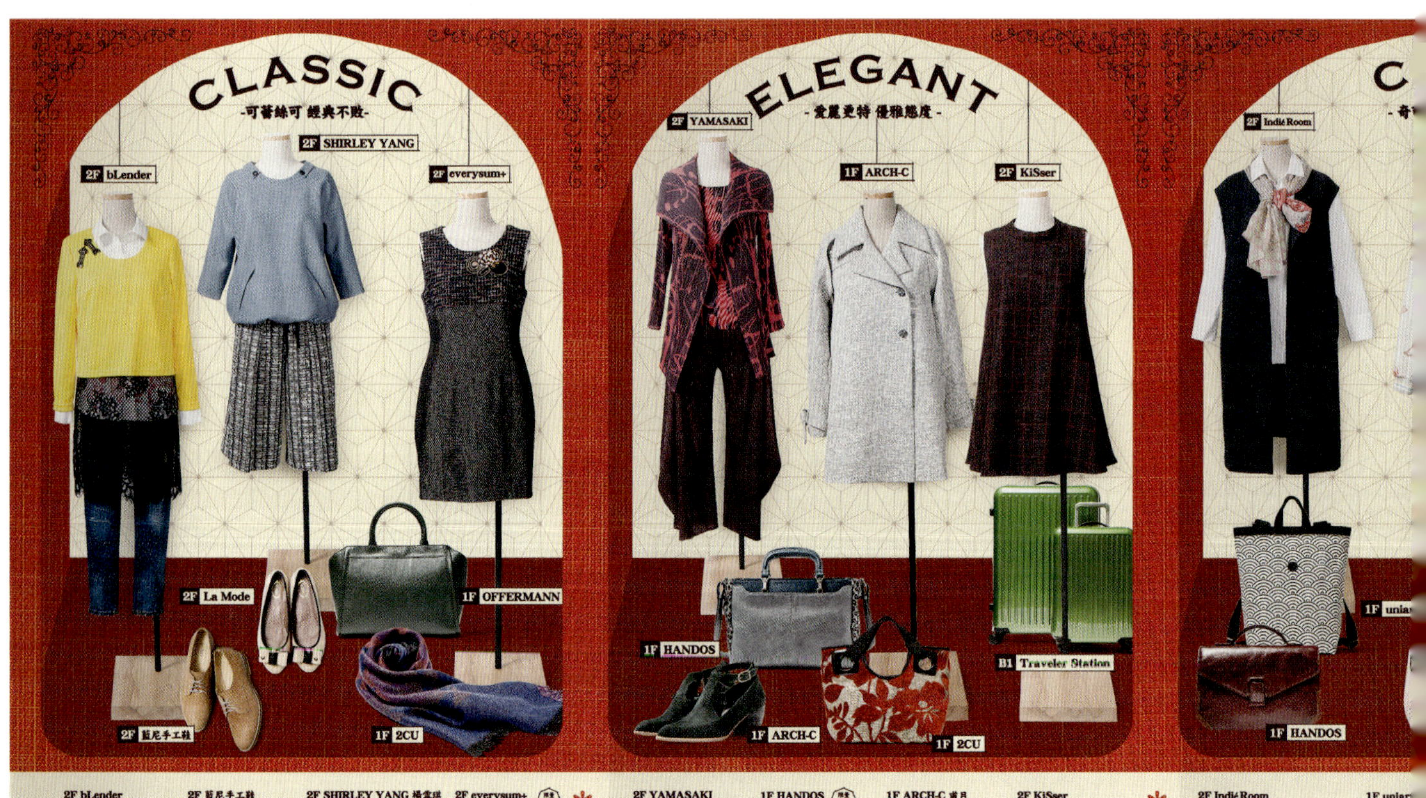

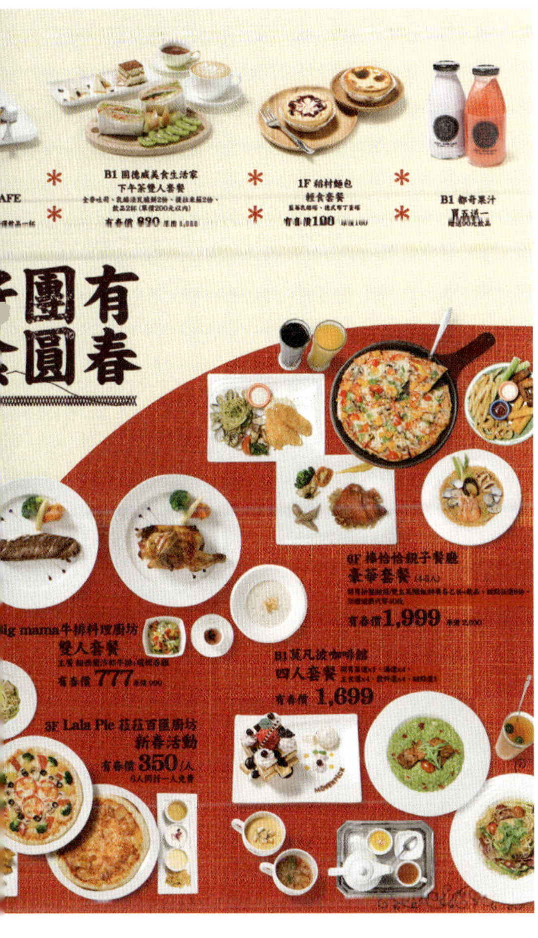
B1 國德威美食生活家
下午茶雙人套餐
有春價 890
1F 稻村麵包
輕食套餐
有春價100
B1 都奇果汁
買五送一
團圓
有春
6F 棒恰恰親子餐廳
豪華套餐
有春價1,999
雙人套餐
有春價 777
B1 莫凡彼咖啡館
四人套餐
有春價 1,699
3F Lala Pie 菈菈百匯廚坊
新春活動
有春價 350/人

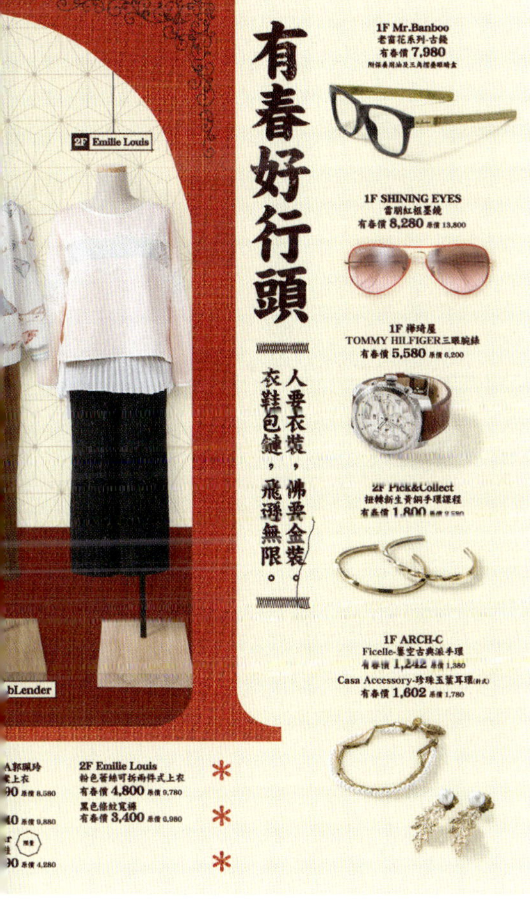
有春好行頭
人要衣裝，佛要金裝。衣鞋包鏈，飛遜無限。
2F Emilie Louis
bLender
1F Mr.Banboo
老當花系列-古銭
有春價 7,980
1F SHINING EYES
雷朋紅框墨鏡
有春價 8,280 原價 13,800
1F 樺琦屋
TOMMY HILFIGER三眼腕錶
有春價 5,580 原價 6,200
2F Pick&Collect
扭轉新生黃銅手環課程
1F ARCH-C
Ficelle-鏤空古典派手環
Casa Accessory-珍珠玉葉耳環
有春價 1,602 原價 1,780
2F Emilie Louis
粉色蕾絲可拆兩件式上衣
有春價 4,800 原價 9,780
黑色條紋寬褲
有春價 3,400 原價 6,980

Santa Express Poster

Designer

ZhongXing.H

Client

Park Lane by Splender

Key Diagram

Font	Paper	Size
Rosewood / Source Han Sans SC – Regular	Belize paper	260×375mm

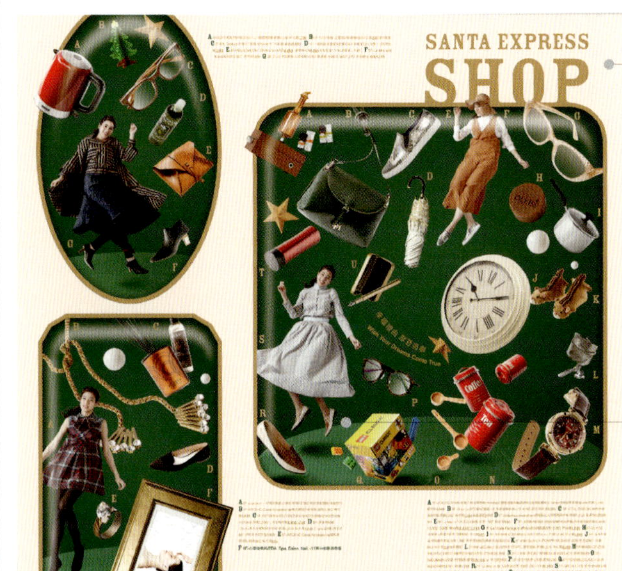

The serif fonts bring elegance to the design.

The dark green—symbolic color of a Christmas tree—matched with metallic khaki can create a festive atmosphere.

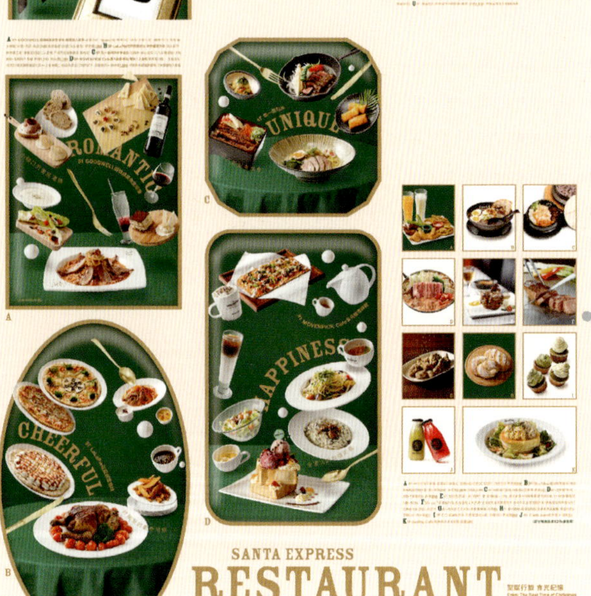

Flexibility is obtained by such a free layout. The large proportion of images work to focus consumers' attention to the merchandise.

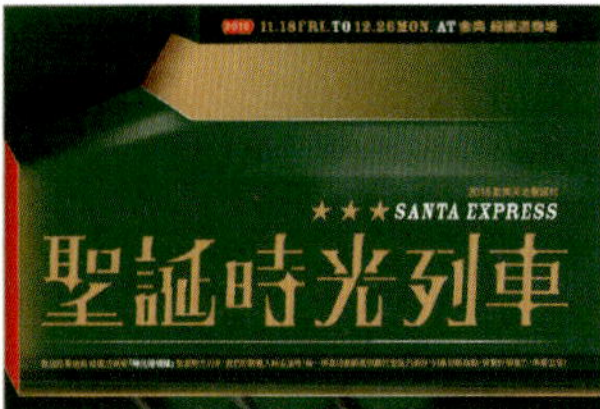

Grid

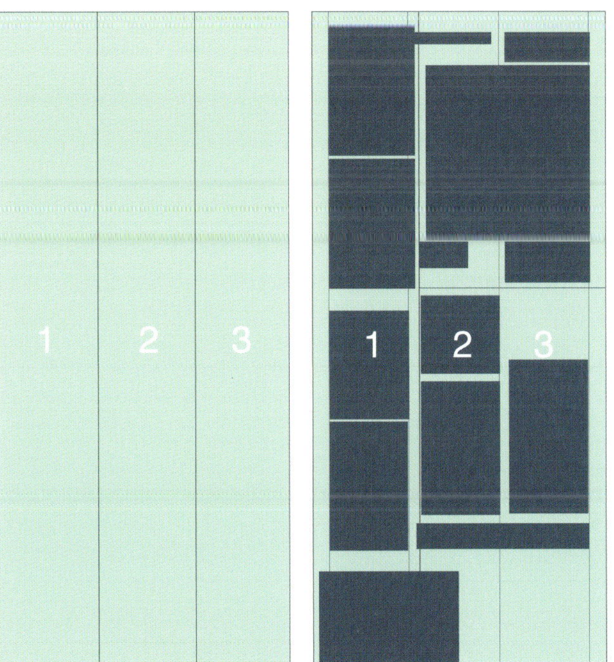

Visual Flow

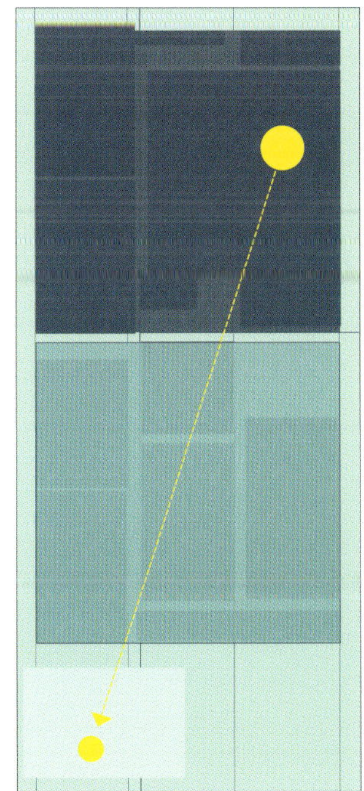

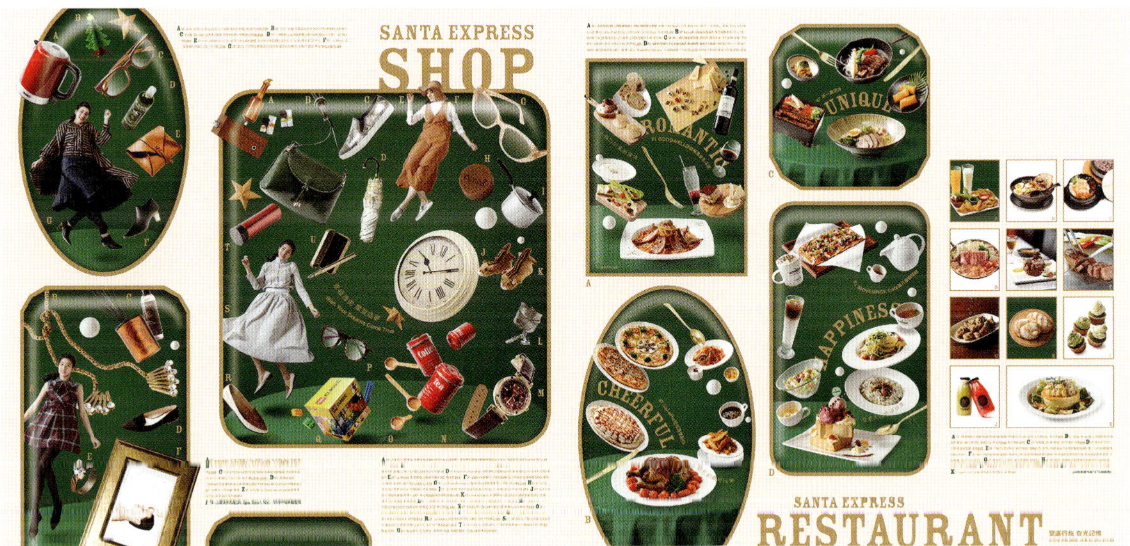

Santa Express is a promotion project designed for Park Lane's Christmas campaign in 2016, which echoed the theme of a time travel train. Customers can see the goods, and food and drinks prepared for Christmas from each window of the train.

Happy Birthday Poster

Designer

ZhongXing.H

Client

Park Lane by Splender

Key Diagram

Font

URW Clarendon
Source Han Sans

Paper

120g Dongjiu special paper

Size

260×375mm

The serif font is round and lovely, and the sans serif font is neat and fashionable, which is in line with the atmosphere of the illustration.

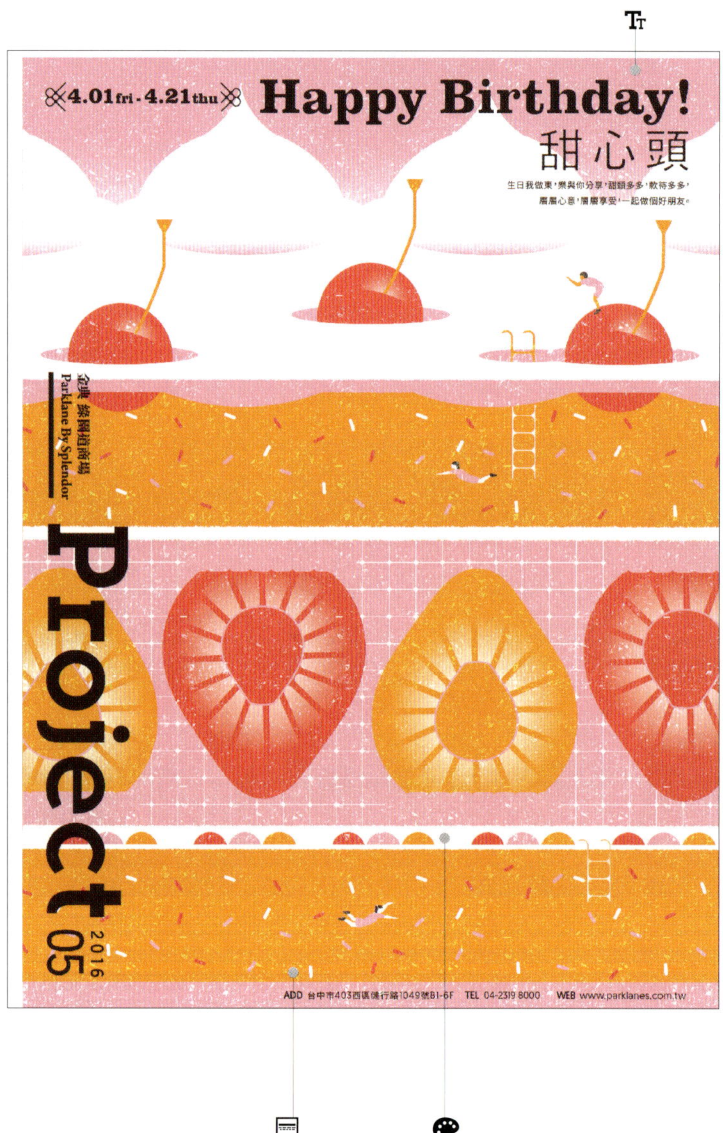

The design uses a principle of repetition to repeatedly align the key elements to guide the viewer's vision.

The warm color is filled with a festive atmosphere, which is in line with the theme of the anniversary. The use of analogous colors make the design more harmonious.

Grid

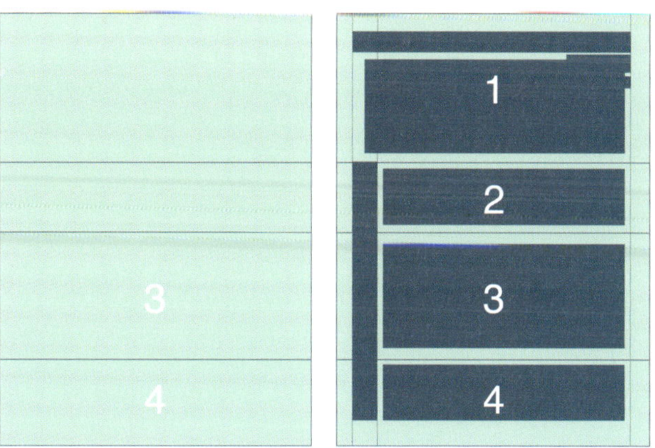

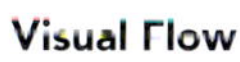

Visual Flow

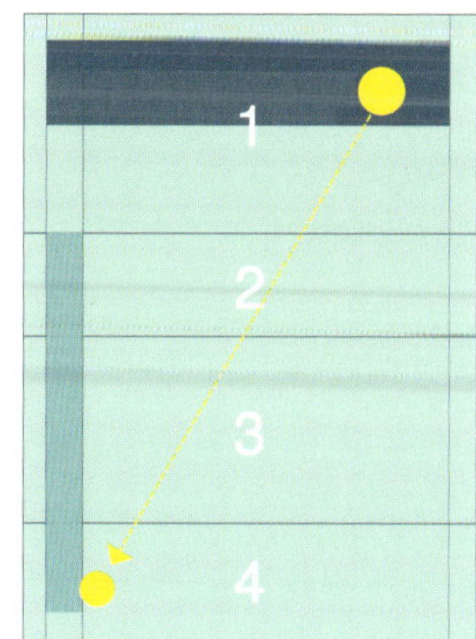

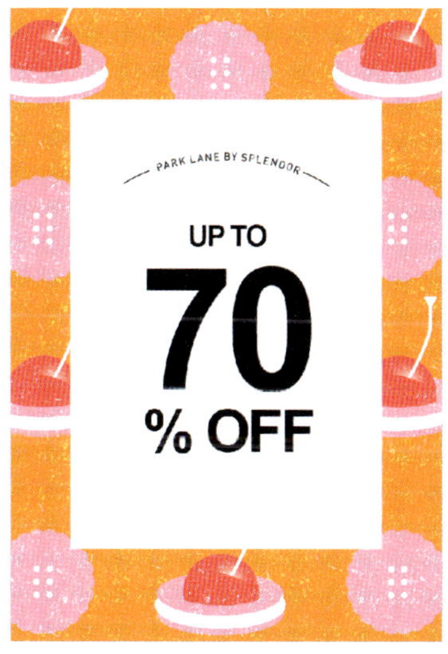

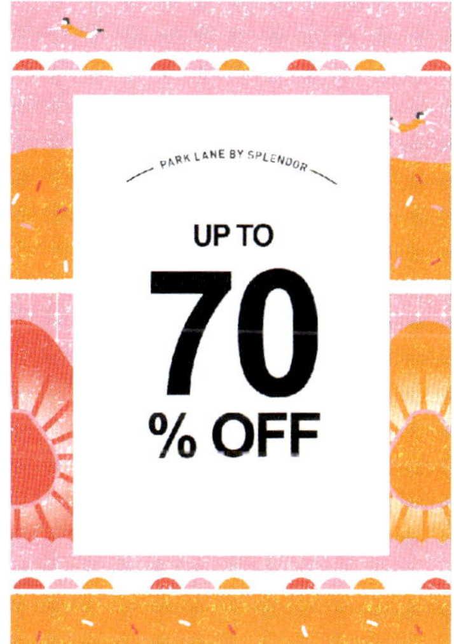

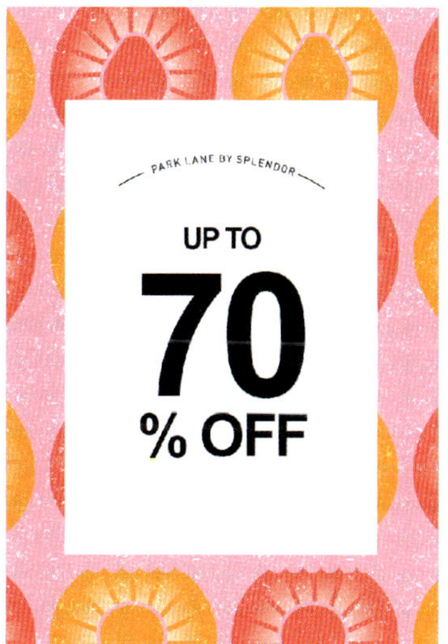

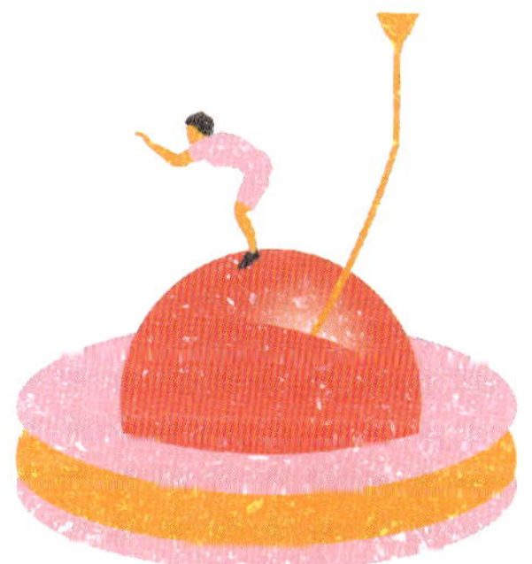

Happy Birthday!
甜心頭

This series of direct mail material is designed to celebrate the anniversary of Park Lane, during which time the mall would hold many sale events. The illustration is a cake , which layer by layer symbolizes the layers of discounts and surprises, and in which people are having fun from one layer to another. A sense of celebration is added by the colorful color.

Summer Fantasy Poster

Designer	**Client**	**photographer**
ZhongXing.H	**Park Lane by Splender**	**Senyong Liu**

Key Diagram

Font	Paper	Size
Helvetica (English) A-OTF Gothic (Chinese)	Coated paper	260×375mm

Sans serif font reduces the burden brought by the crowded information.

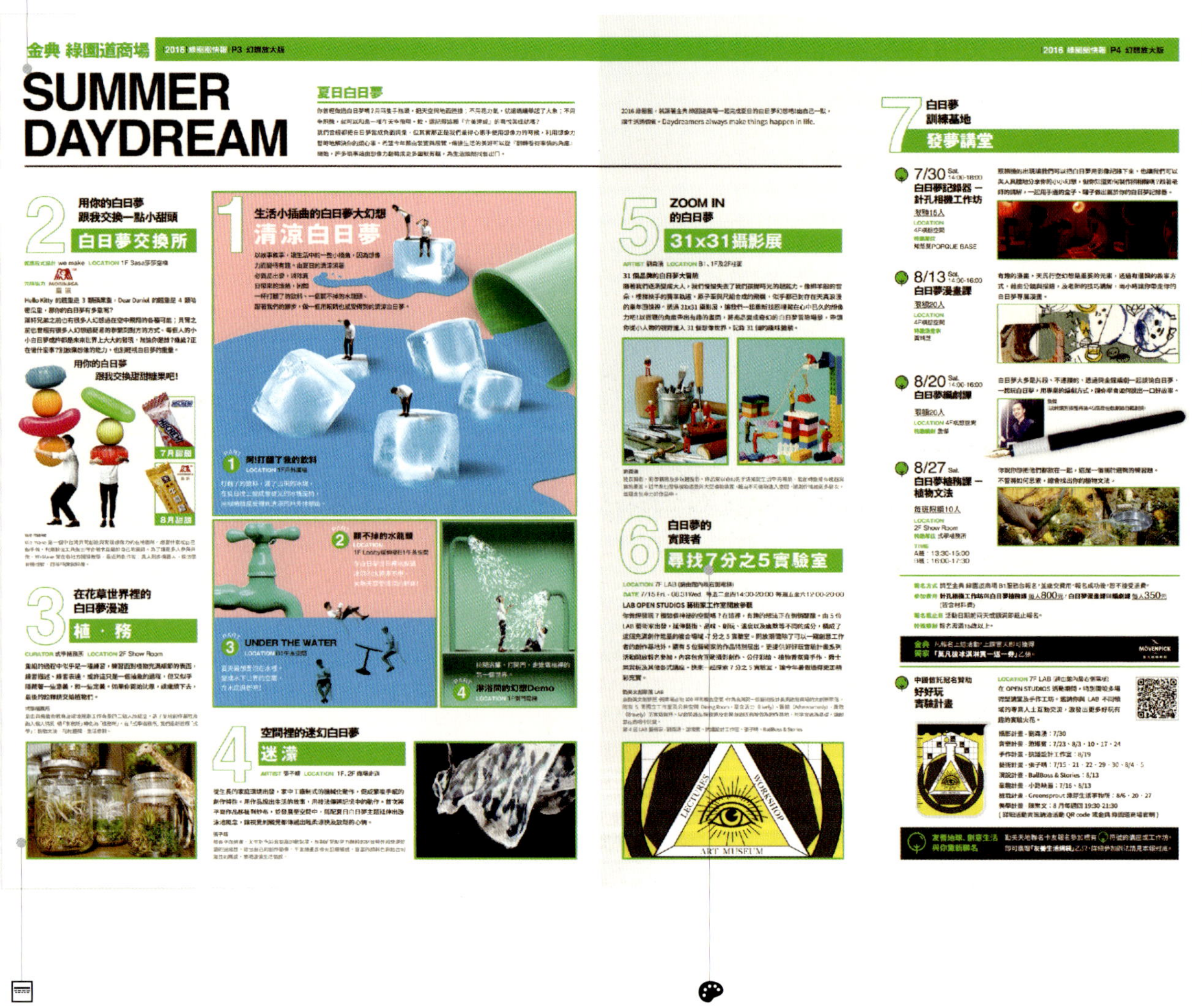

A number of contrasting elements are applied: font size, colors, and image size.

The design is based on cool green color; the vivid color echoes the themes.

Grid

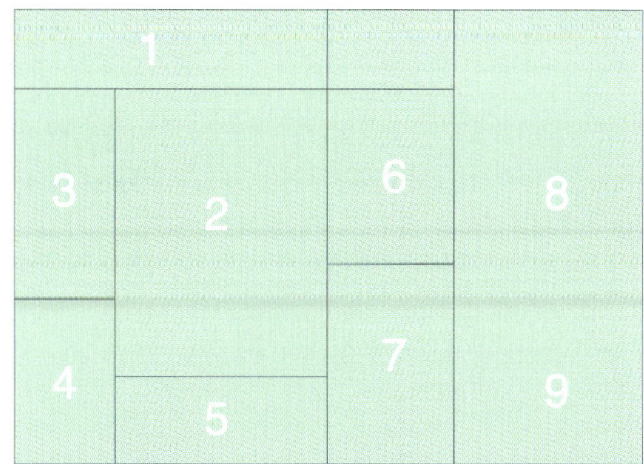

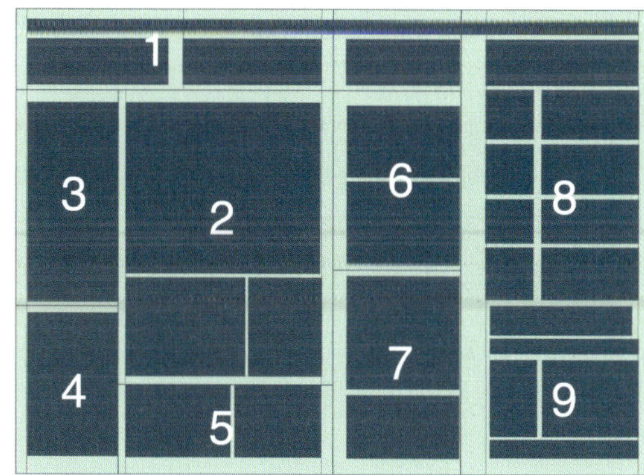

Visual Flow

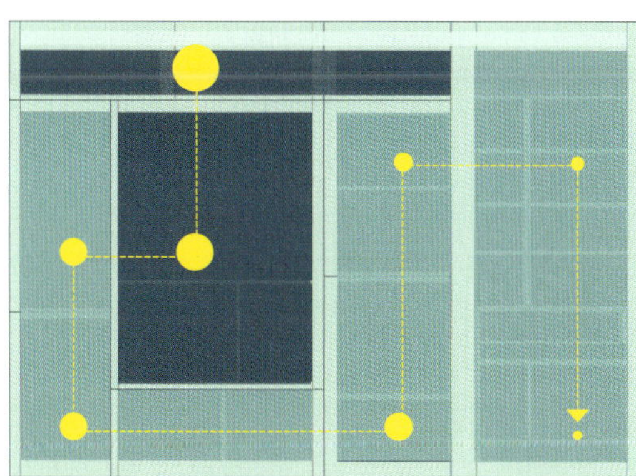

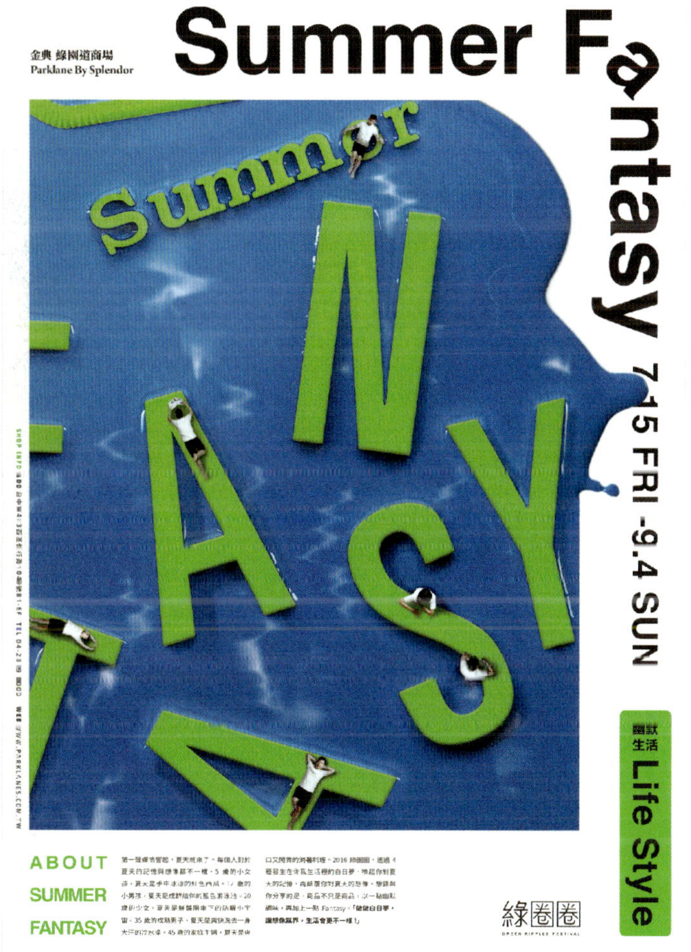

Summer Fantasy is a promotional project designed for Park Lane's summer art festival. The products are divided into four themes visually: foods, drink, beauty care, and accessories. Seeing the products in different angles lets us appreciate a summer full of imagination and energy.

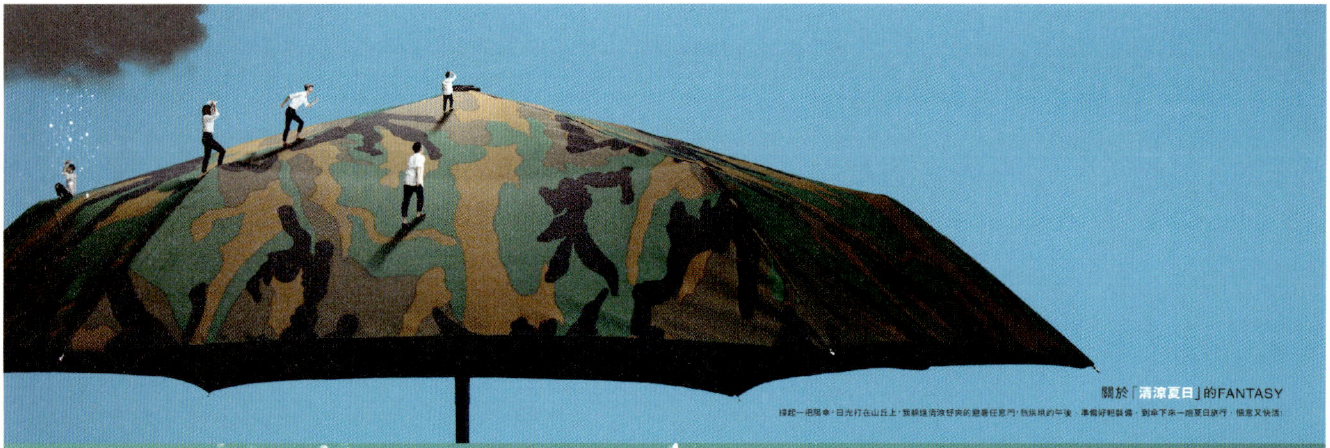

關於「清涼夏日」的FANTASY

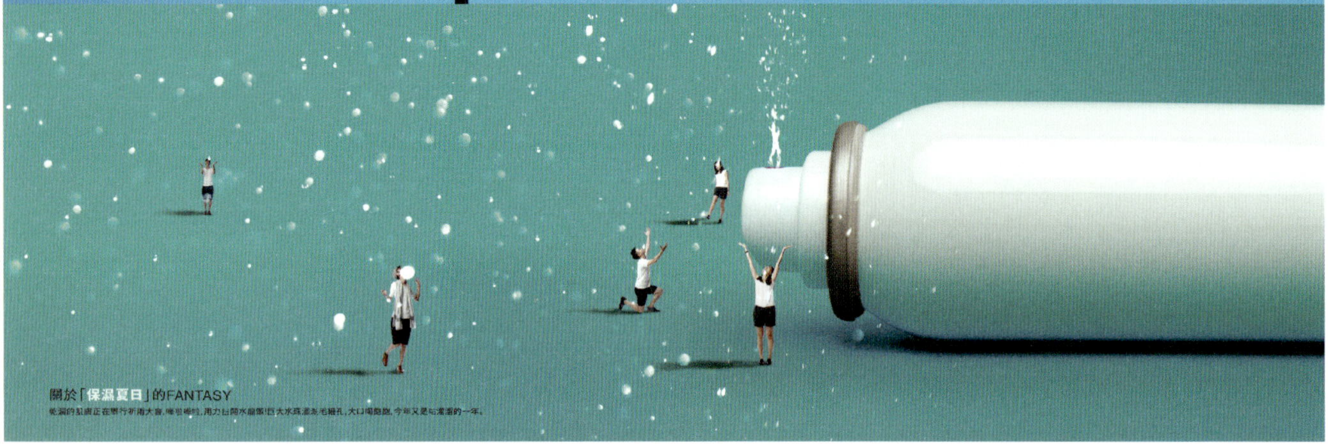

關於「保濕夏日」的FANTASY

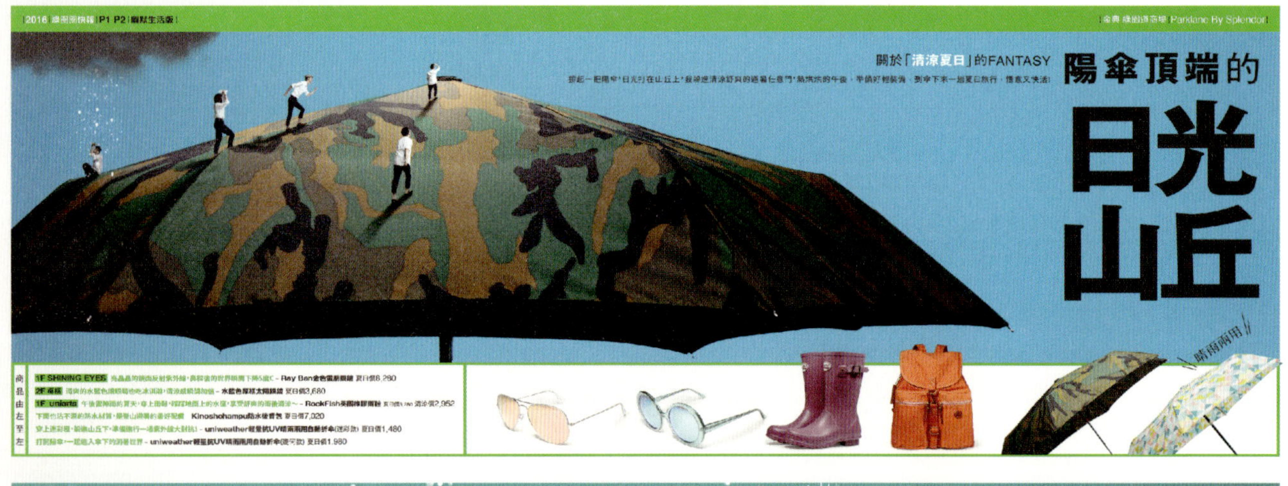

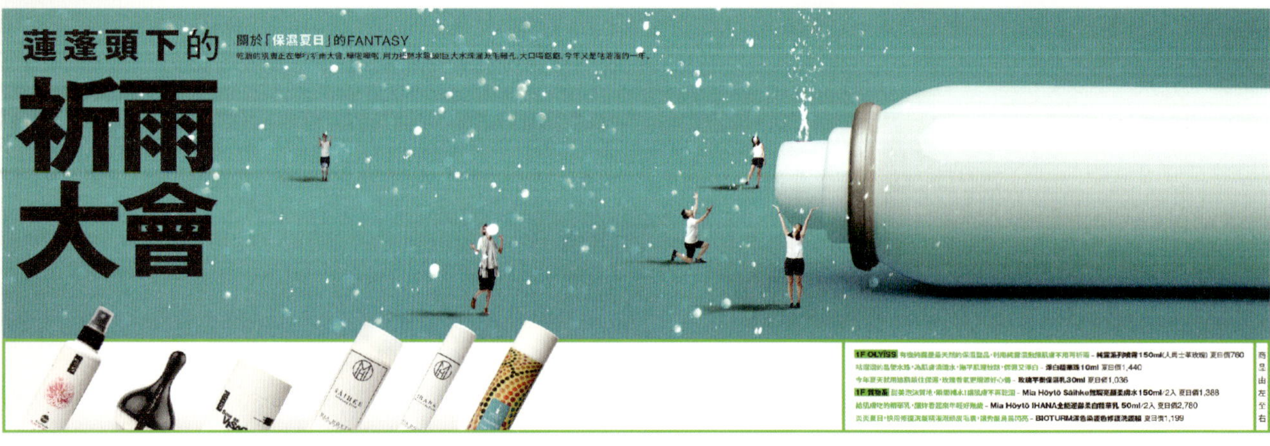

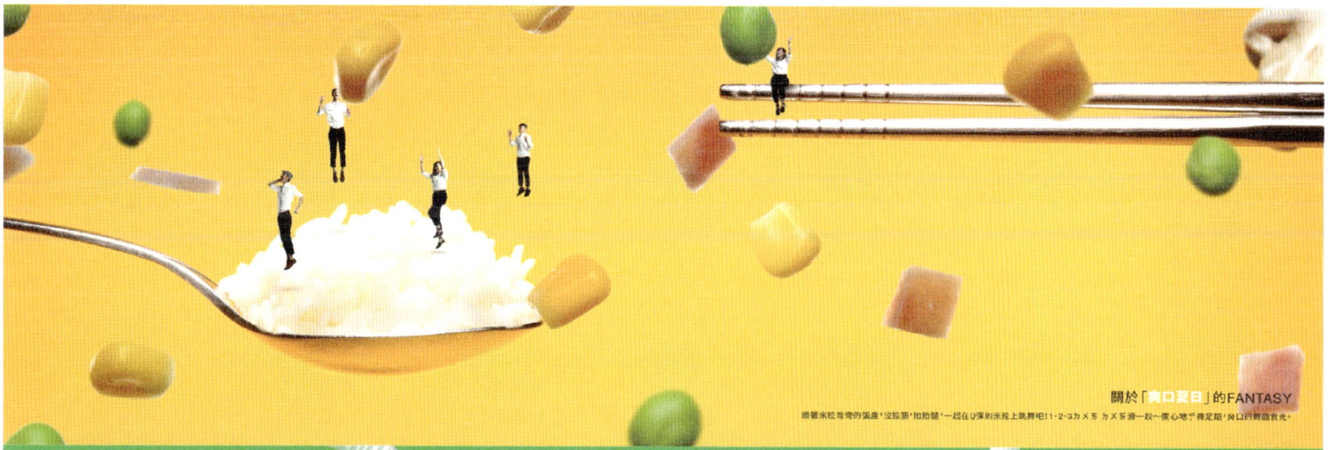

關於「爽口夏日」的FANTASY

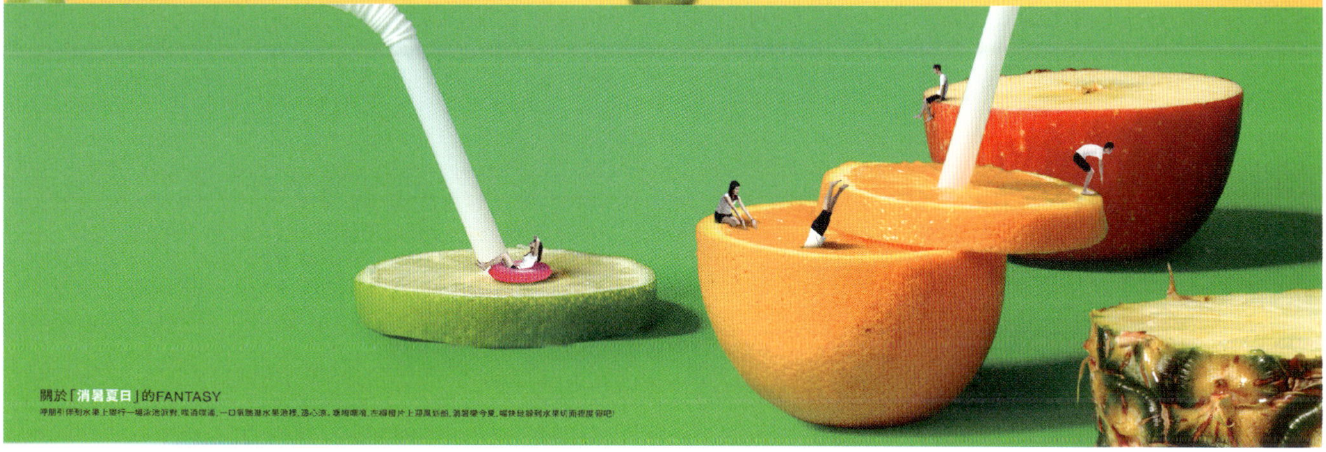

關於「消暑夏日」的FANTASY

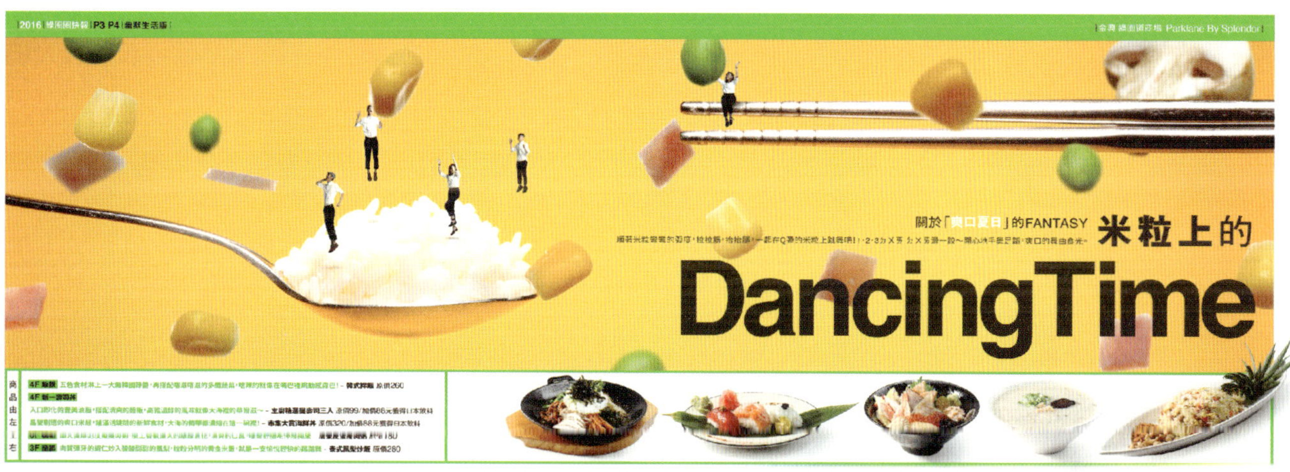

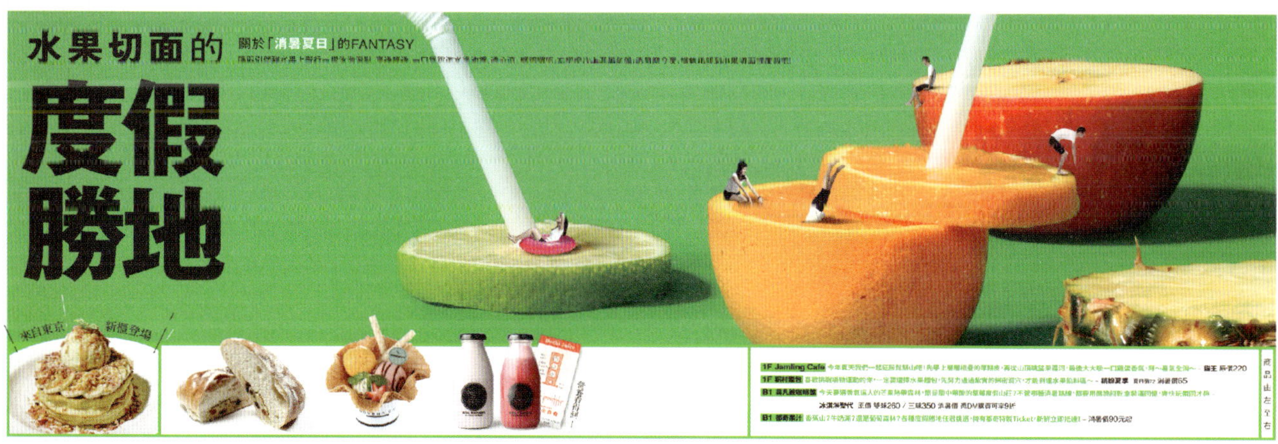

Atre Oimachi Golden Week & Mother's Day Poster

Designer

Takao Nakagawa

Client

Atre Oimachi

Key Diagram

Paper

Coated paper

Size

210×297mm (A4)

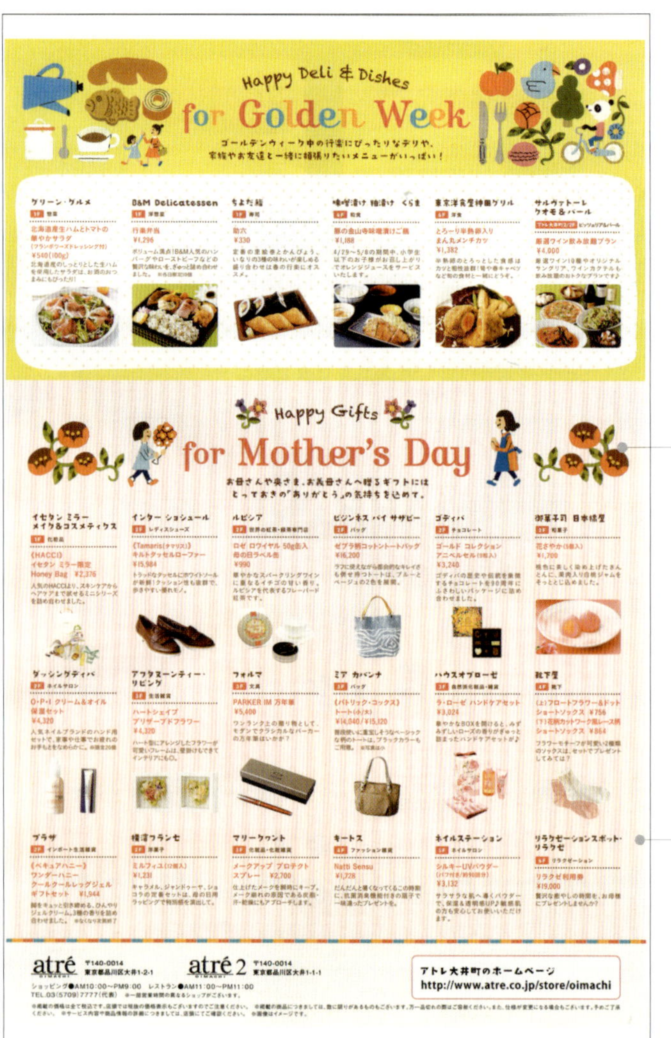

Golden Week corresponds to warm yellow, Mother's Day corresponds to warm red and the overall color is filled with a pleasant atmosphere. In addition, information such as the floor the product is located on and the promotional price is marked red, allows consumers to get the information they need more quickly.

The layout has less negative space so it can contain tons of information, which is in line with the needs of the mall. At the same time, combined with the design principle of proximity and repetition, the text is arranged with a certain rhythm and is well organized.

Grid

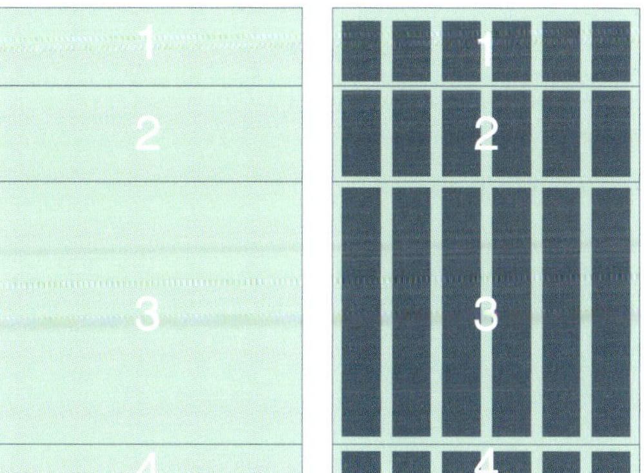

Visual Flow

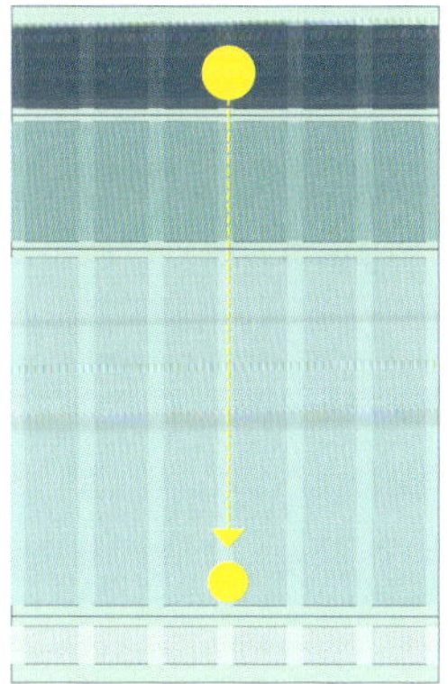

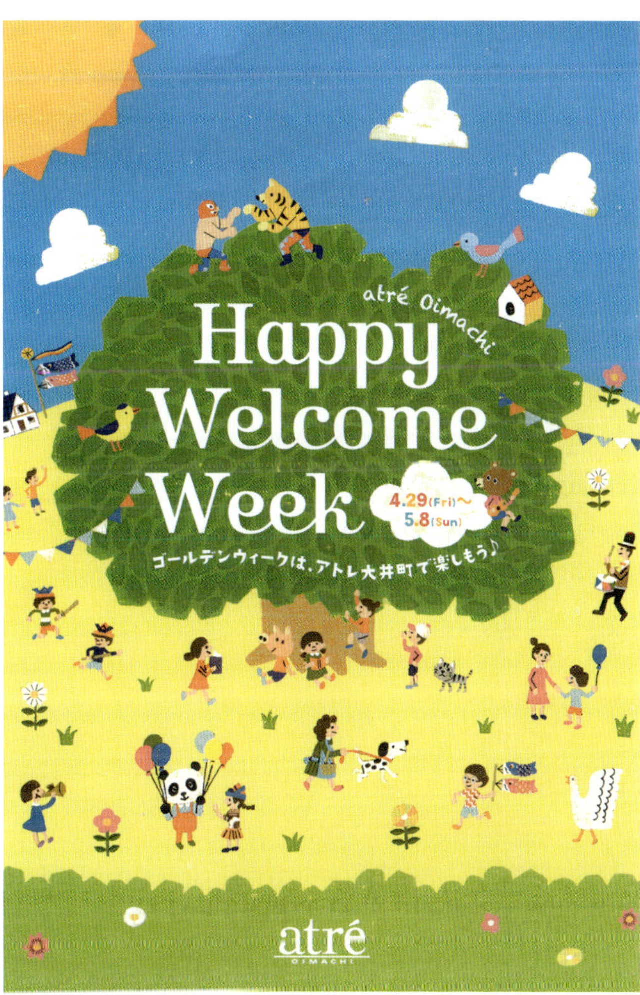

This is a promotional piece for the Golden Week and Mother's Day launched by the Atre Oimachi Shopping Mall. Atre Oimachi. Since there would be activities for children in the shopping mall during the period, the designer imagined an atmosphere that was lively and enjoyable and tried to present them in the design. A fun atmosphere is shown in the poster: Human beings and animals are enjoying being together.

Yiwan Living Space Posters

Designer

Peigen Junior

Client

Yiwan Living Space

Key Diagram

Font

Lexis
Hei-ED

Paper

High art silk

Size

483×329mm (A3+)

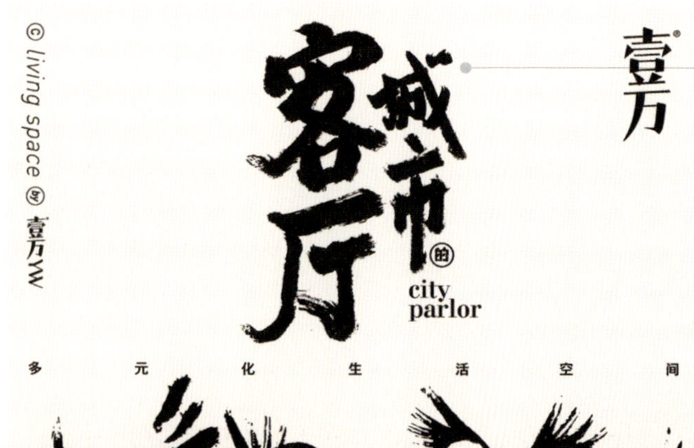

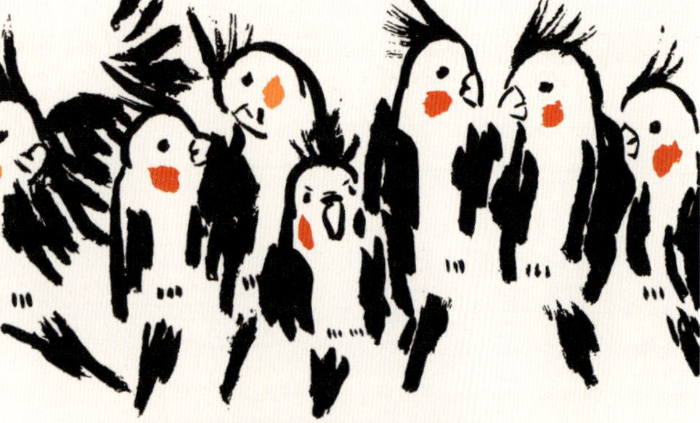

The font is square and upright and its strokes are thick and forceful. The font is used to make the important messages become more eye-catching. The sizes of font vary greatly so that the layout seems to have a sense of rhythm.

The grey background with black characters appears antique and elegant. Bright red and orange colors intersperse the layout to make it not so boring.

The design elements are aligned to the center in order to keep the balance of the layout and leave the proper white space at both sides. The illustration of parrots divides the poster into two equal parts to deliver the symmetry beauty.

Grid

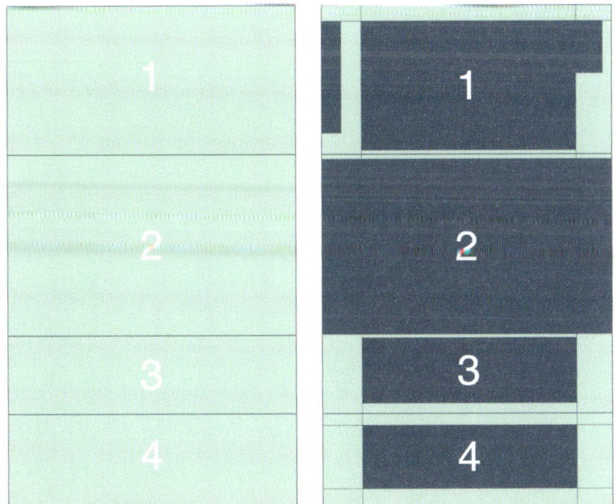

Visual Flow

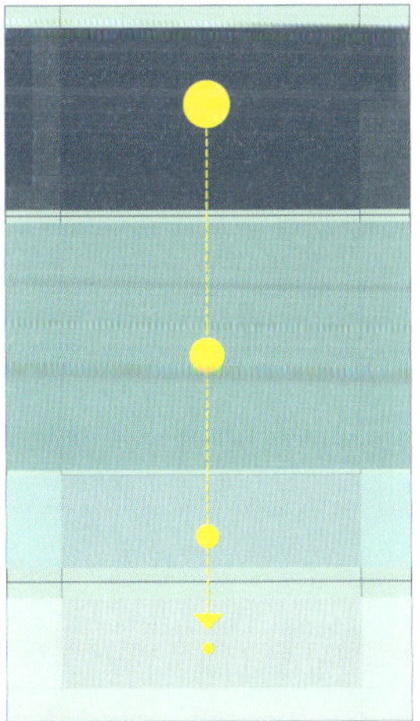

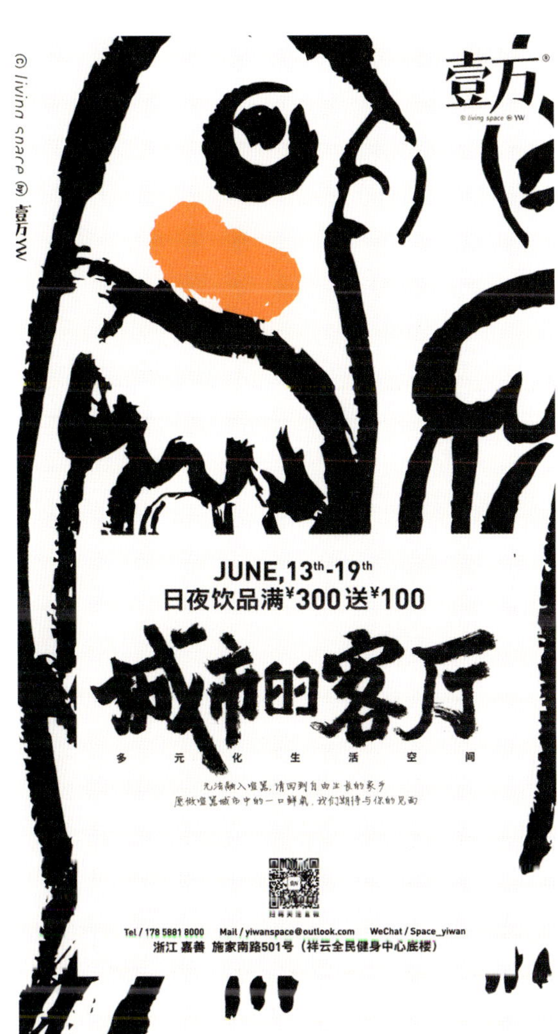

Yiwan Living Space originates from the idea of providing a peaceful place that makes people feel like they are at home. Although you may be far away from your parents and relatives, Yiwan can also give you warmth in the busy city. The designer combines his childhood memories with his understanding of home in the poster series. The parrot in the poster as the main element is to create a pleasant and relaxing atmosphere.

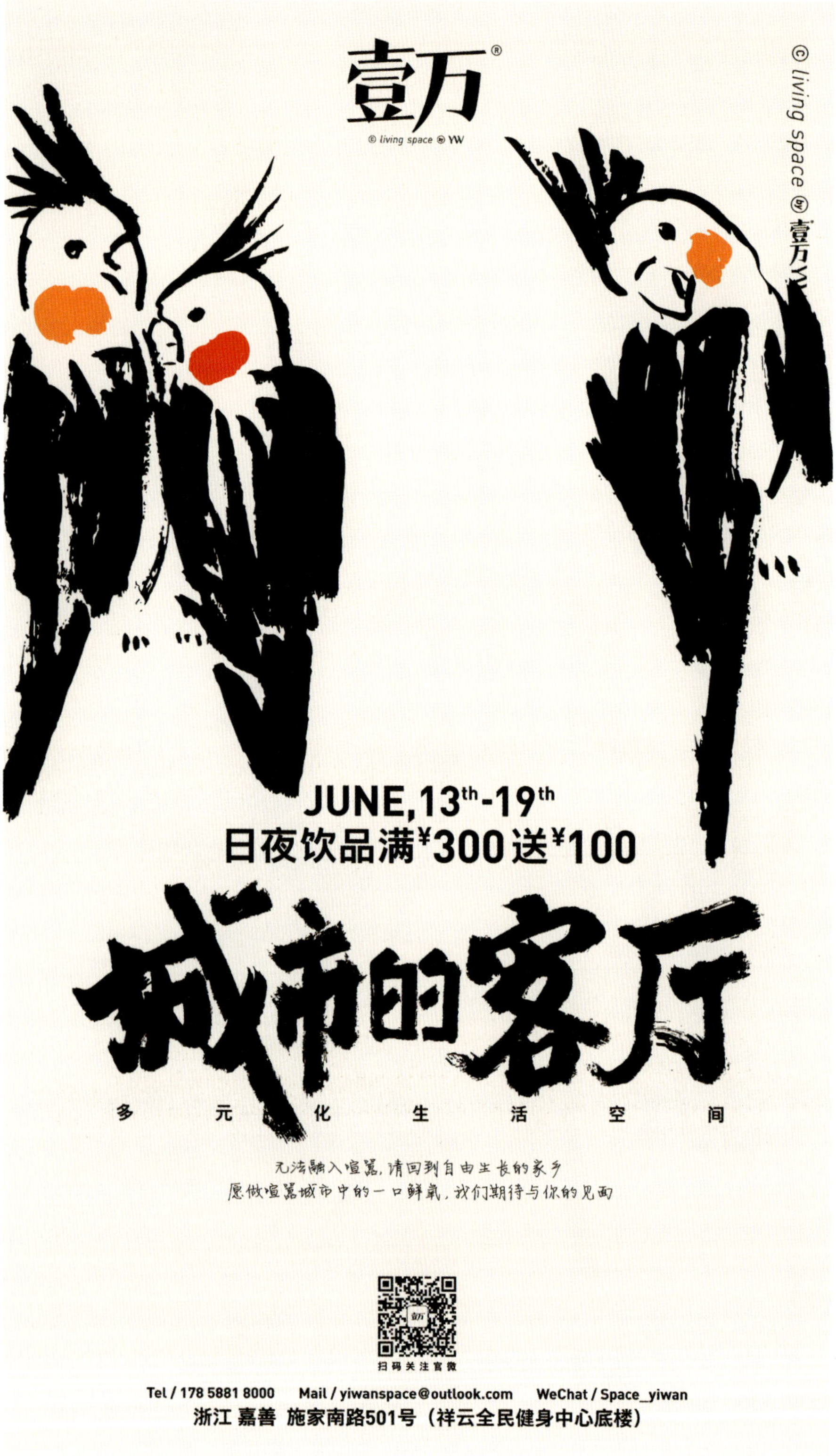

壹万®

® living space ® YW

© living space by 壹万YW

JUNE,13th-19th

日夜饮品满¥300送¥100

城市的客厅

多 元 化 生 活 空 间

无法融入喧嚣，请回到自由生长的家乡

愿做喧嚣城市中的一口鲜氧，我们期待与你的见面

扫码关注官微

Tel / 178 5881 8000 Mail / yiwanspace@outlook.com WeChat / Space_yiwan

浙江 嘉善 施家南路501号（祥云全民健身中心底楼）

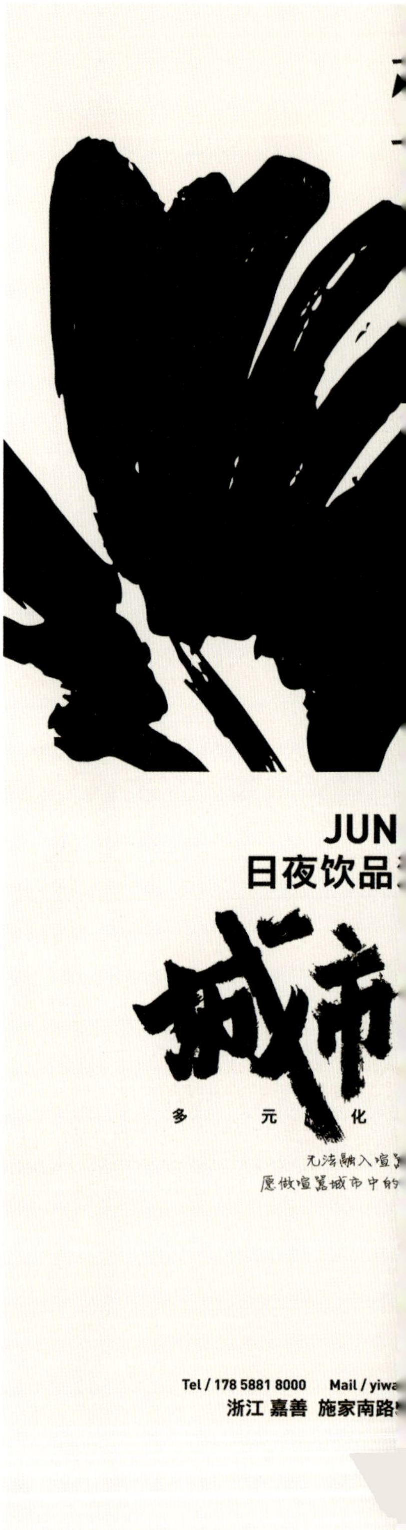

JUN

日夜饮品

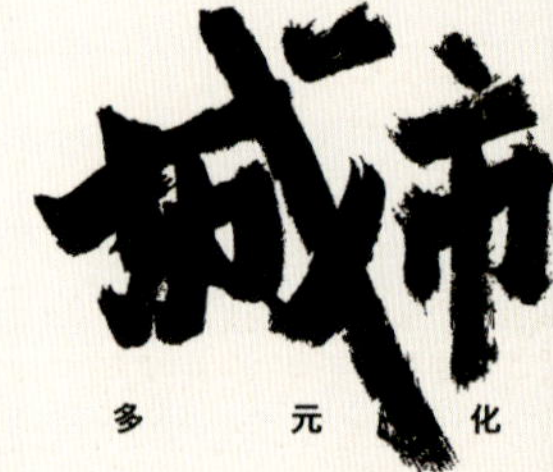

Tel / 178 5881 8000

浙江 嘉善

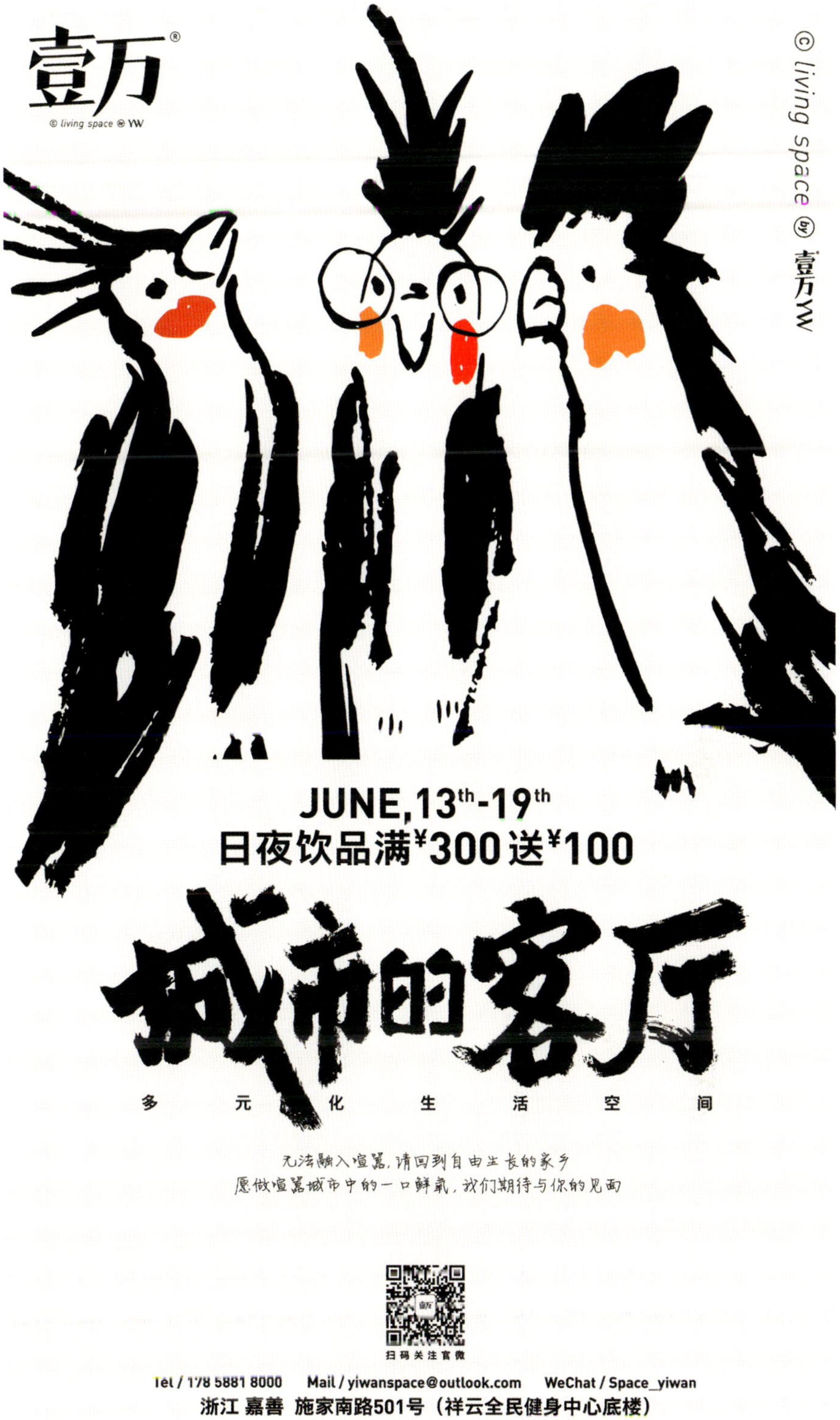

壹万®

© living space ® YW

© living space by 壹万YW

JUNE,13th-19th

日夜饮品满¥300送¥100

城市的客厅

多 元 化 生 活 空 间

无法融入喧嚣,请回到自由生长的家乡

愿做喧嚣城市中的一口鲜氧,我们期待与你的见面

扫码关注官微

Tel / 178 5881 8000 Mail / yiwanspace@outlook.com WeChat / Space_yiwan

浙江 嘉善 施家南路501号（祥云全民健身中心底楼）

Japanese Class Direct Mail

Designer

Singing Huang

Client

Master Educational Institute

Key Diagram

Paper

Coated paper

Size

210×297mm (A4)

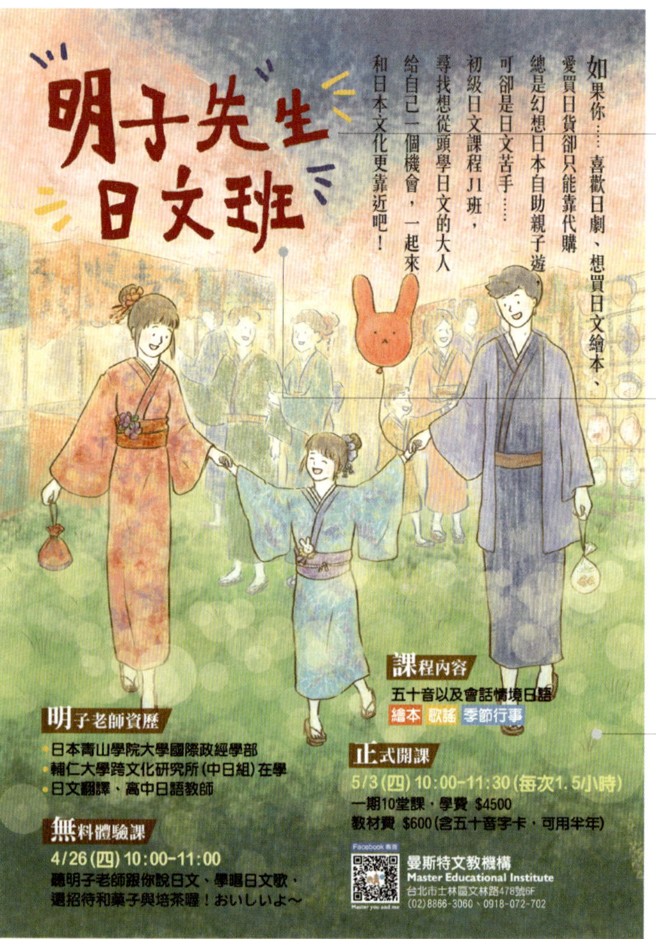

This design for Japanese language classes is based on the theme of a Japanese traditional festival.

Tт

The headline uses handwritten type, which differs from the main information part of the page, and is in harmony with the background of the illustration. The main information is applied with regular fonts to let consumers read the content clearly.

The titles are brown, which is consistent with the warm color of the illustration.

There is both vertical and horizontal text in the layout, so the whole page is divided into two areas. The information arrangement in the lower part is more important; gathering relevant information can help design the layout in a better way.

Grid

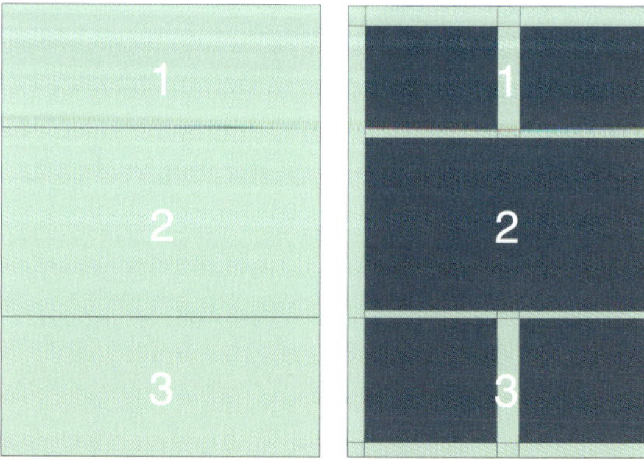

Visual Flow

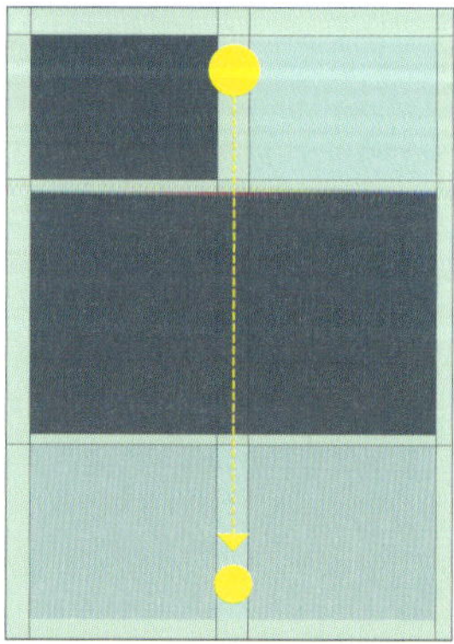

City Foodie

Designer
Connie Huang

Client
Eslite Dunnan Shop

Key Diagram

Font
Aquiline
Custom font

Paper
Coated paper

Size
210×297mm (A4)

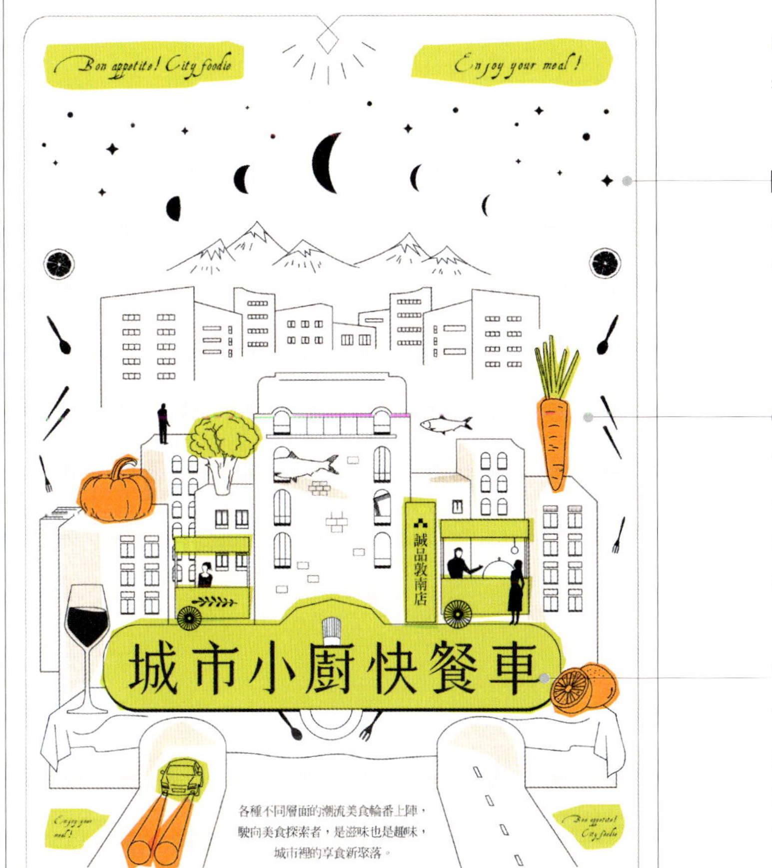

The project was inspired by a city at night, food, and books, and hence, the illustration is created with some surreal elements.

Symmetrical layout makes the whole design very balanced, stable, and full of harmonious beauty.

The use of color is quite surreal, too. By transferring the color black onto moons and stars and other small decorative elements, the whole visual is in white instead and seems to present a city in the daytime.

Tт

Two different fonts are used in the design. The handwriting is less readable, but can be fully integrated into the illustration and become one of the decorative elements. The Chinese serif font is highly recognizable and can accurately convey information to consumers.

Grid

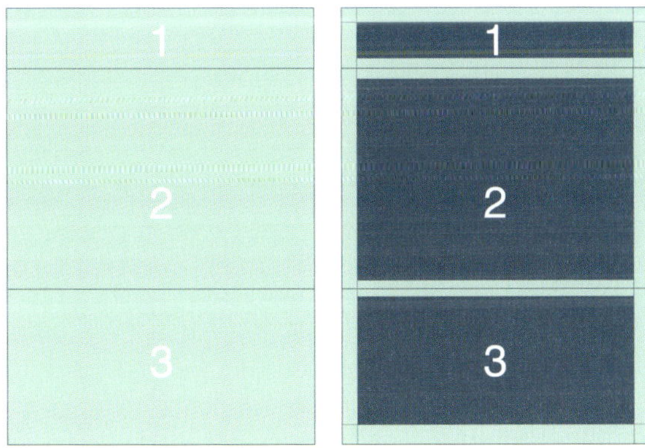

Visual Flow

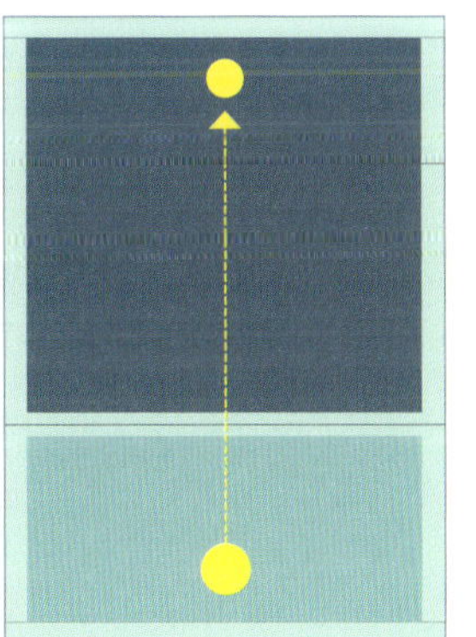

Table Mountain National Park Brochure

Designer

Benthe Derks

Client

South African Table Mountain National Park

Key Diagram

Font

Futuyre PT (Body copy)
Levele Black (Headings)

Paper

170g Premium coated (Neo Star Matt)

Size

200×200mm

Sans serif fonts work well with flat illustrations, both of them convey a minimalist and modern feel.

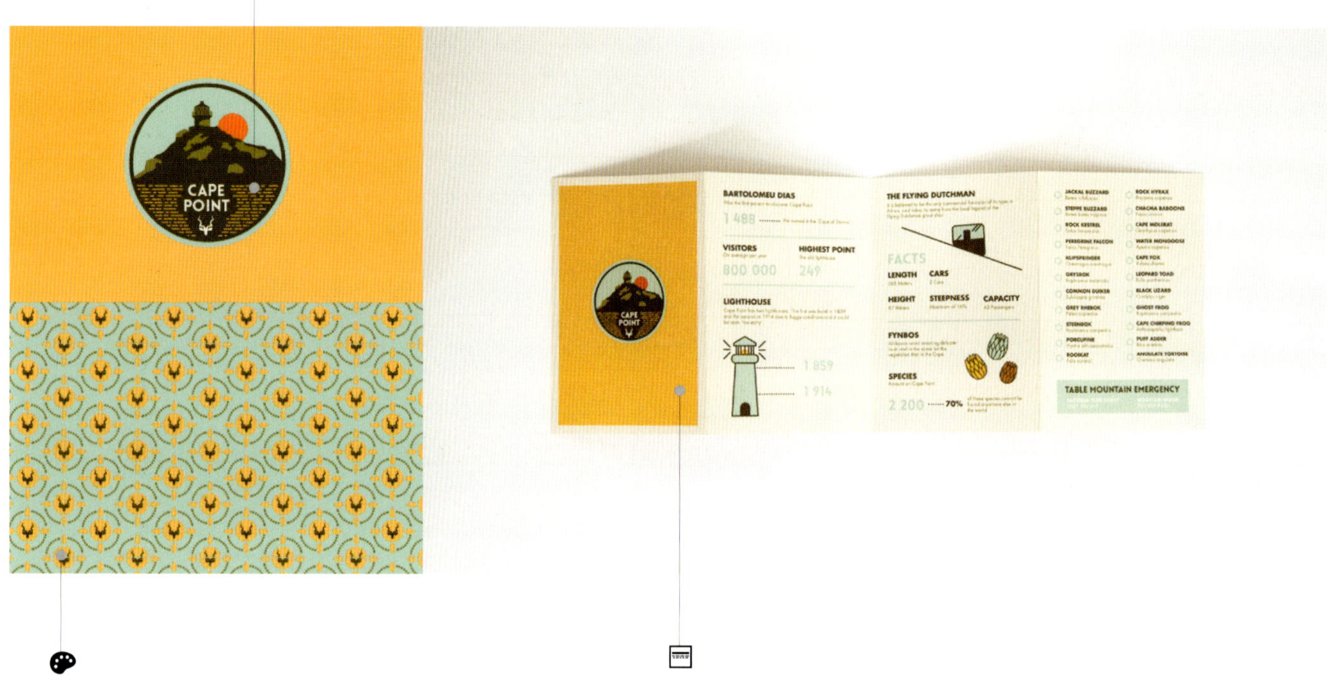

The main color is light green and ochre, which is reminiscent of nature. And the color contrast is strong.

The information in the five national parks is arranged neatly and rhythmically by the design principle of proximity. A lot of negative space leaves enough spacing between the graphic and the text, making the layout more breathable.

Grid

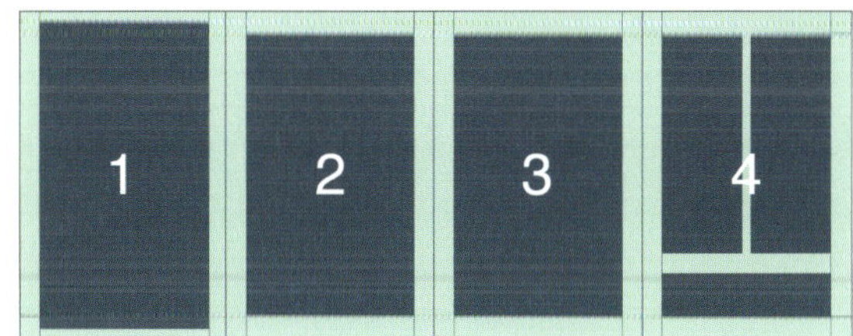

Visual Flow

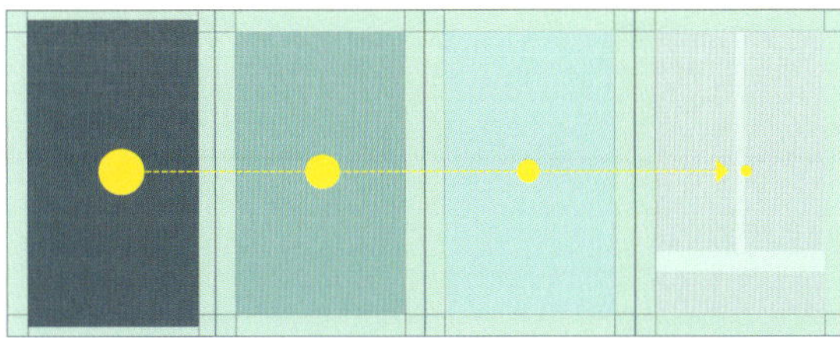

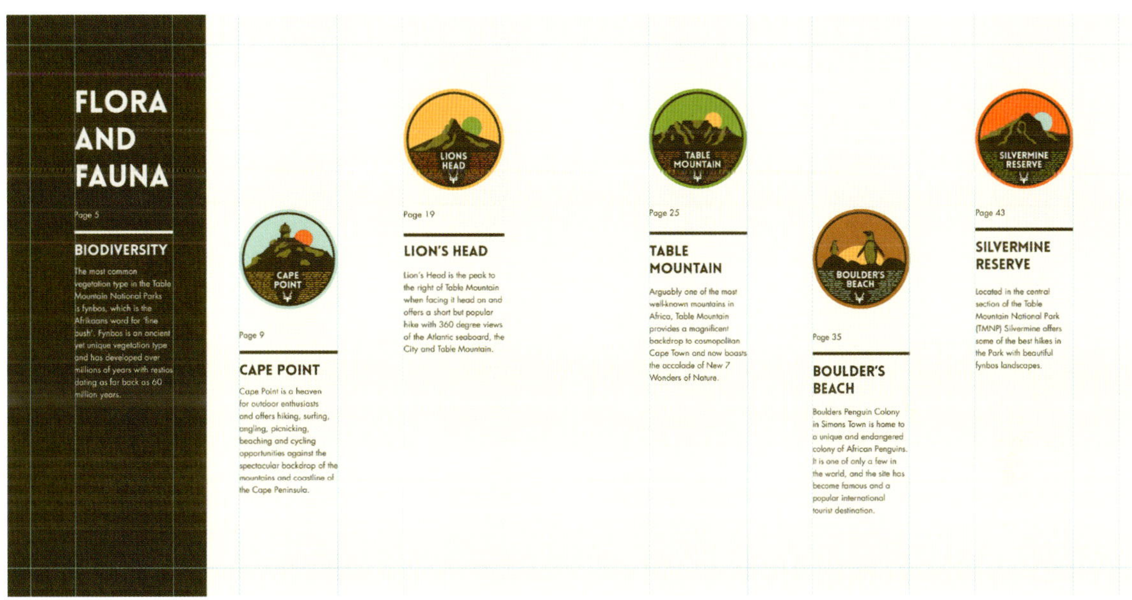

Table Mountain National Park consists of five parks as shown in the brochure. Each park has its own logo, color palette, and pattern. The main brochure is designed as a coffee table book with detailed information and beautiful photography of the parks. There is a pocket edition with facts and a map that can be taken on trips.

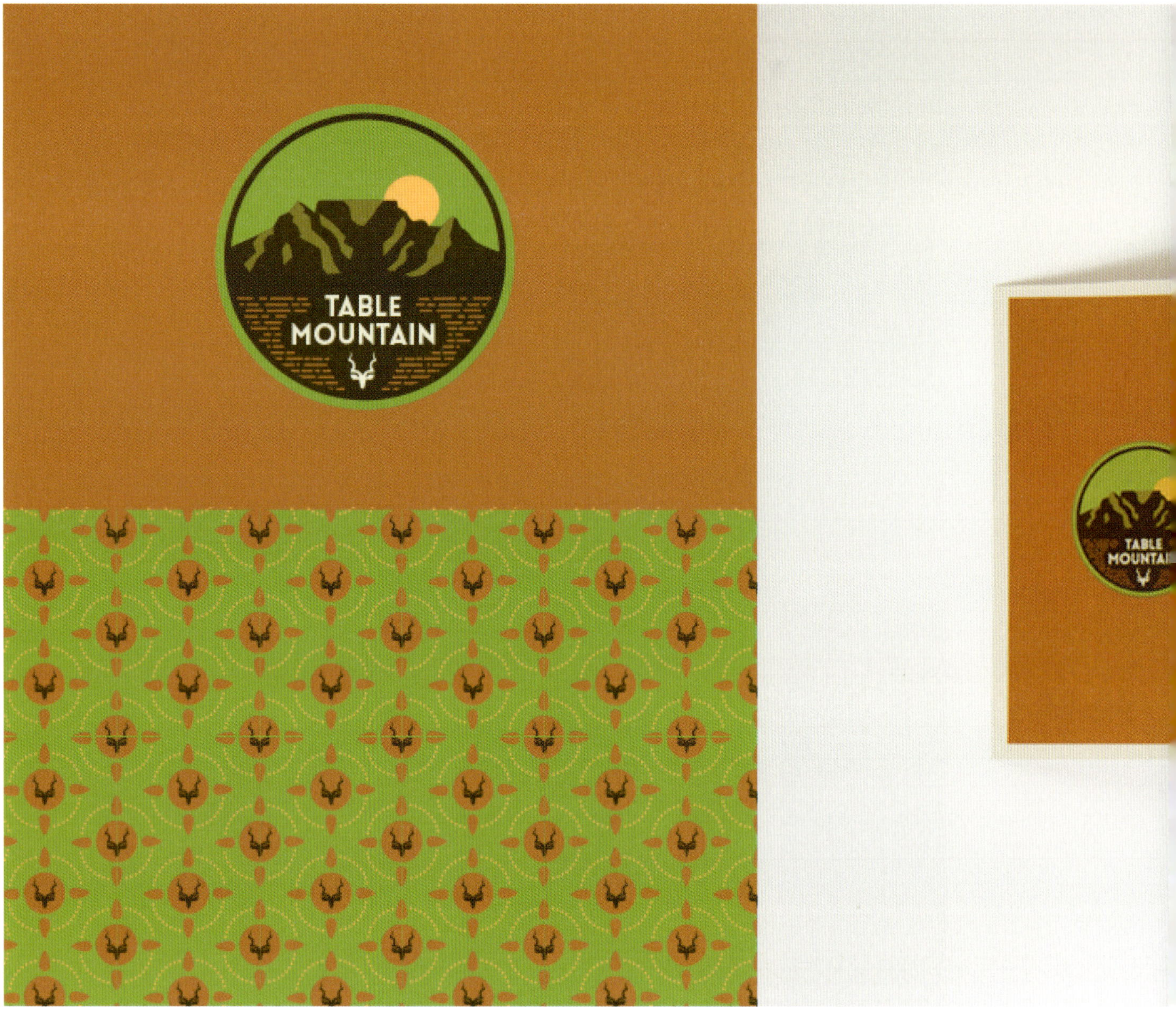

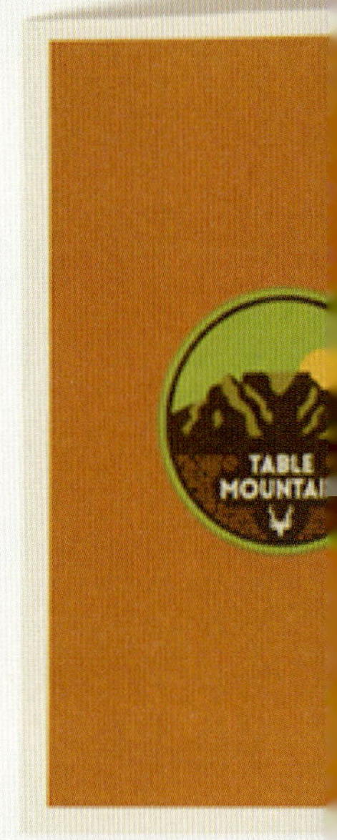

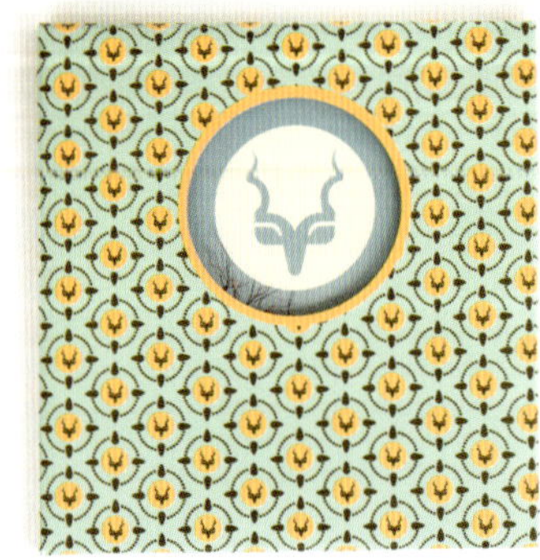

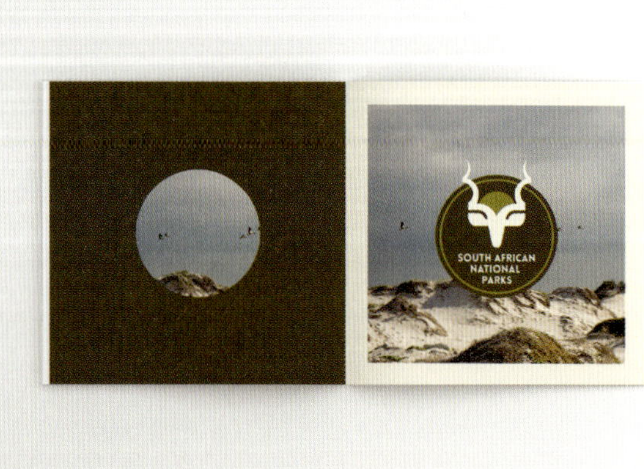
SOUTH AFRICAN
NATIONAL
PARKS

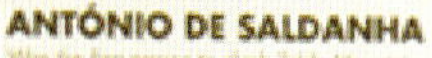
ANTÓNIO DE SALDANHA
1 503
EXISTENCE
GEOLOGY

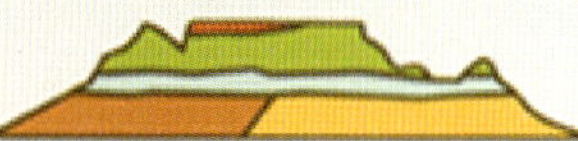
PAKHUIS FORMATION
PENINSULA FORMATION
GRAAFWATER FORMATION
CAPE GRANITE
MALMESBURY GROUP

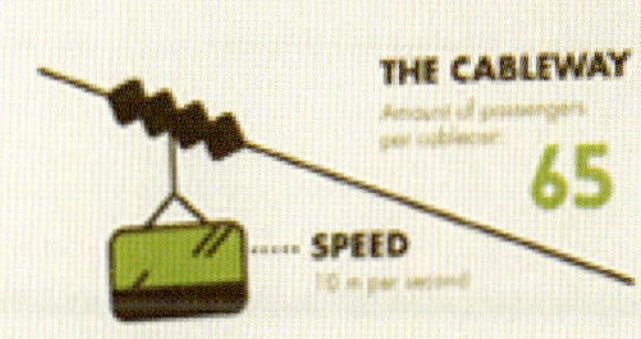
THE CABLEWAY
65
SPEED
1 929
VISITORS
800 000
HIGHEST POINT
1 086
FYNBOS
SPECIES
2 200
70%
JACKAL BUZZARD
STEPPE BUZZARD
ROCK KESTREL
PEREGRINE FALCON
KLIPSPRINGER
GRYSBOK
COMMON DUIKER
GREY RHEBOK
STEENBOK
PORCUPINE
ROOIKAT
ROCK HYRAX
CHACMA BABOONS
CAPE MOLERAT
WATER MONGOOSE
CAPE FOX
LEOPARD TOAD
BLACK LIZARD
GHOST FROG
CAPE CHIRPING FROG
PUFF ADDER
ANGULATE TORTOISE
TABLE MOUNTAIN EMERGENCY
NATIONAL PARK SAFETY
0861 106 417
MOUNTAIN RESCUE
021 937 0300

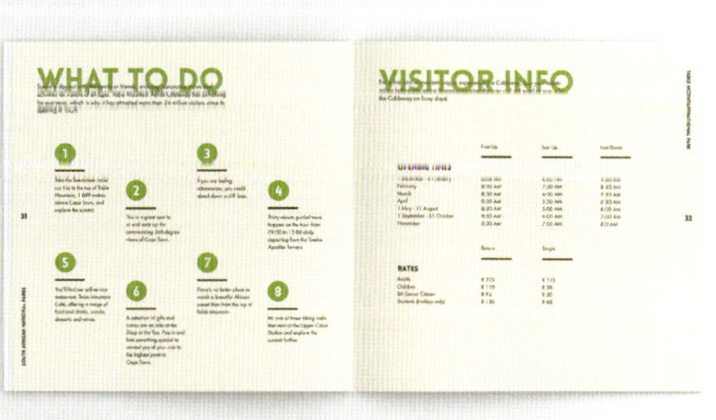
WHAT TO DO
VISITOR INFO

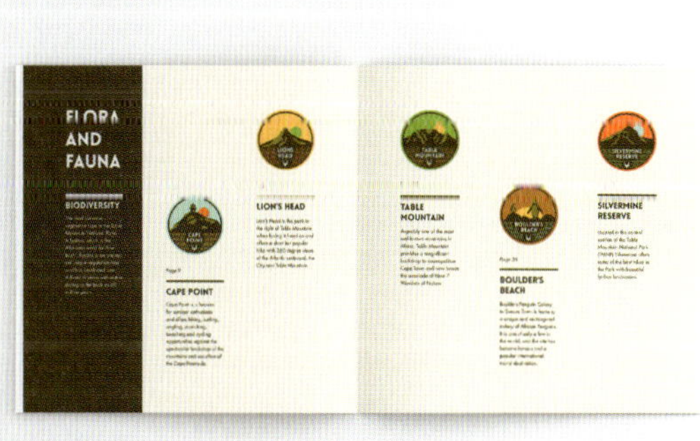
FLORA AND FAUNA

Pentameter Studio Branding

Designer

Thomas Birch

Client

Pentameter

Key Diagram

Font	Paper	Size
Apercu Fortescue	G.F. Smith Wild (business cards)	Various

Apercu is an amalgamation of classic realist typefaces.

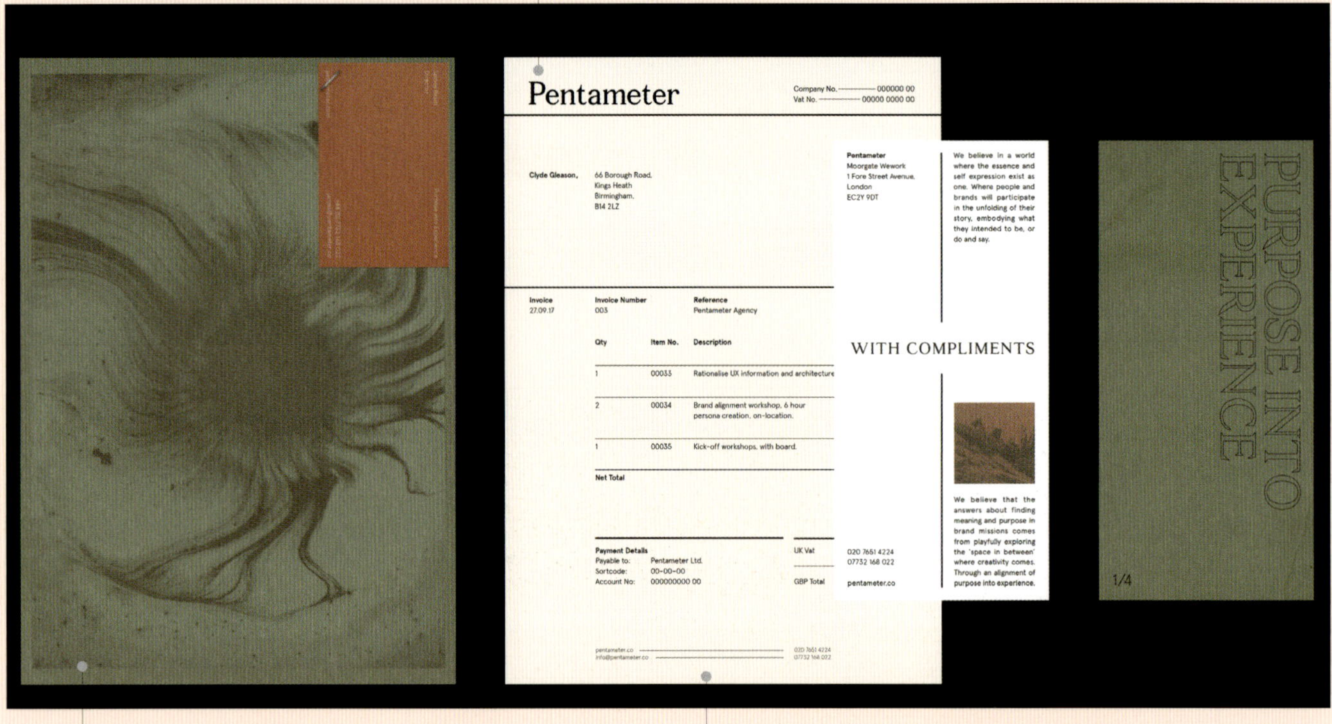

Modern brands should be adaptable when facing the newest trend, and its branding design has to evolve alongside the company organically. The comprehensive grid system is used to make this flexible layout, where different parts of content have their own tone of voice.

Pentameter aims for an elegant image that distances itself from the typical corporate tropes. The client's values of "mindfulness" and natural aesthetics are reflected in the muted color palette, foil-printed stationery, and tactile materials.

Grid

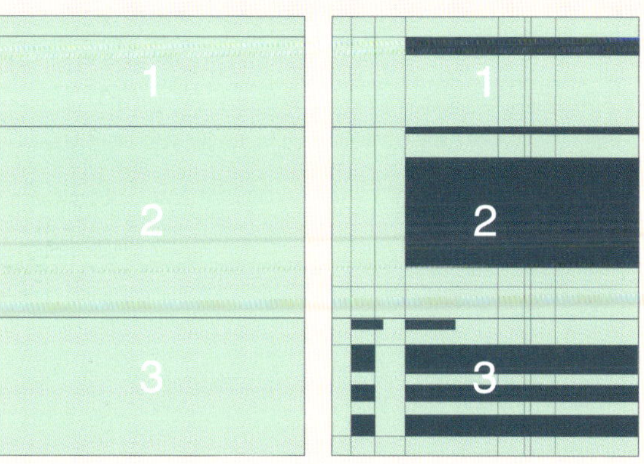

Visual Flow

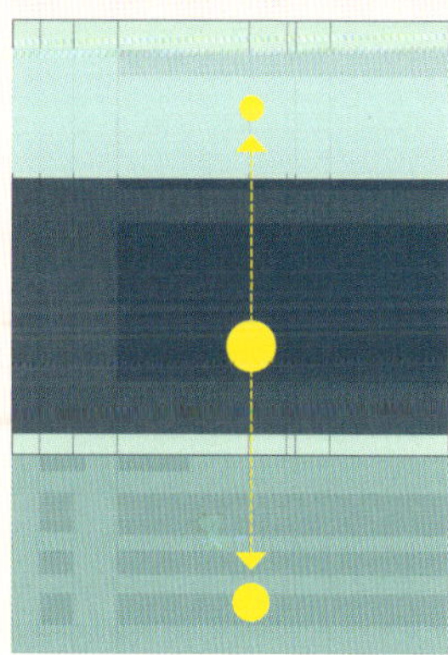

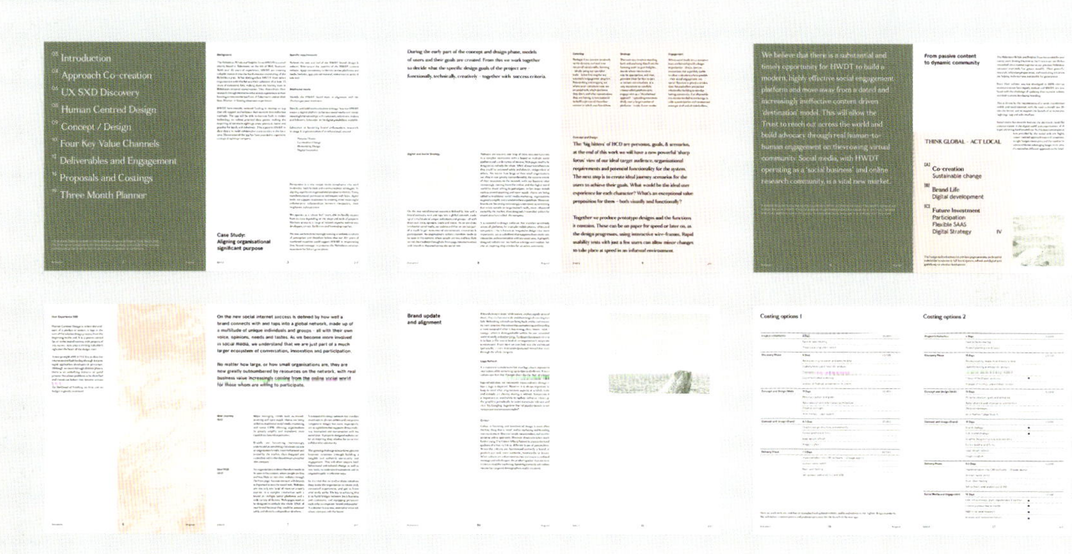

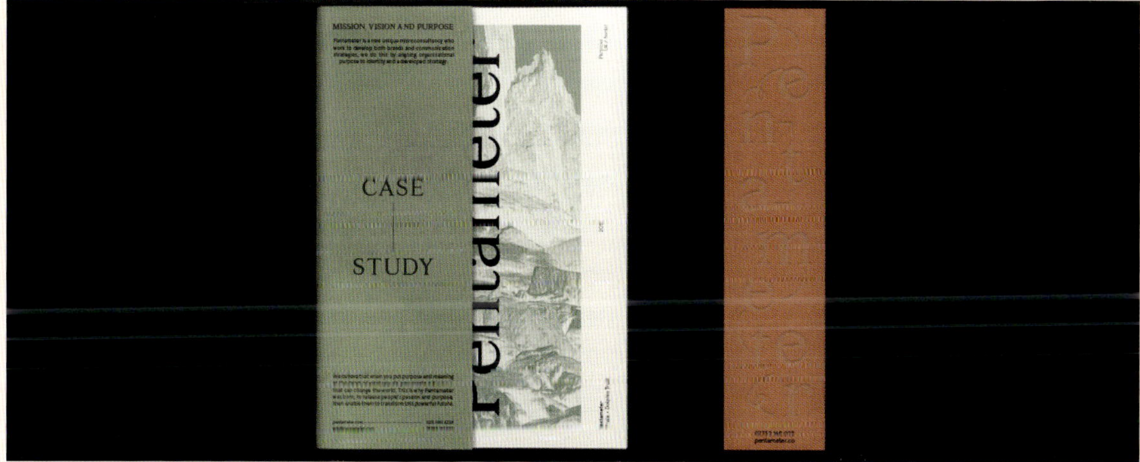

Pentameter provides consultancy in design, culture, and digital innovation to facilitate change within people and businesses. As a startup company, they needed a branding design to establish a identity and convey their values.

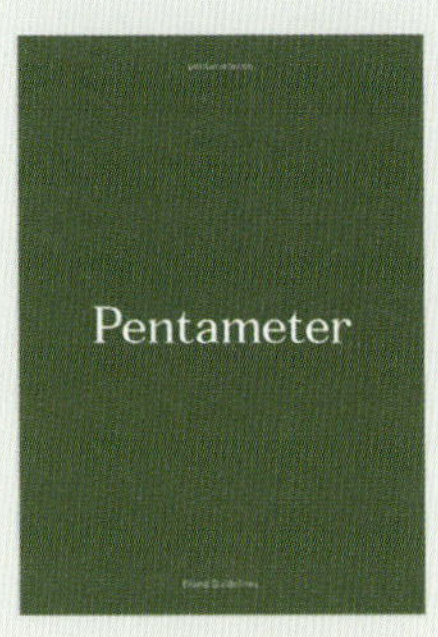
Pentameter

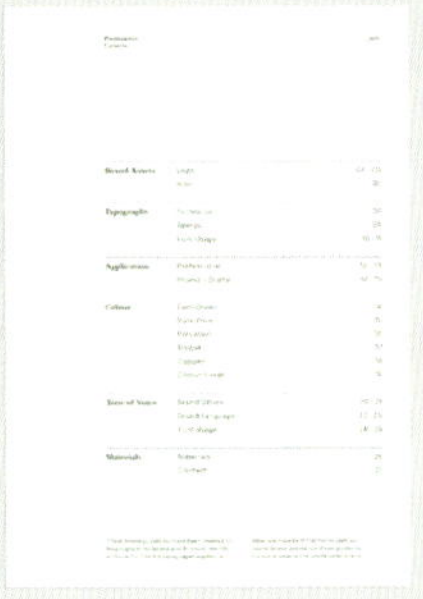

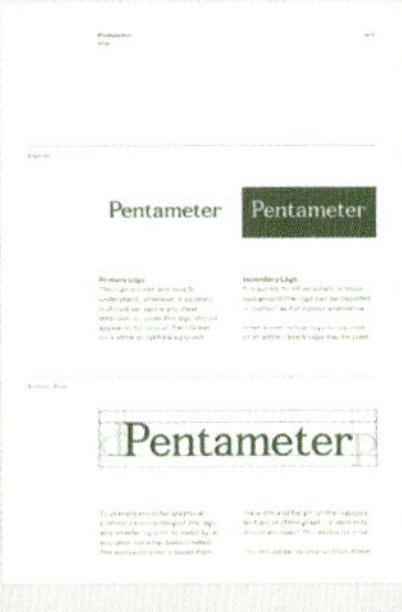
Pentameter
Pentameter
Pentameter

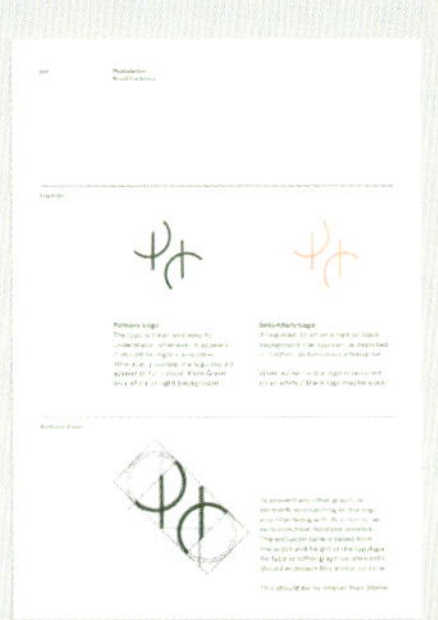

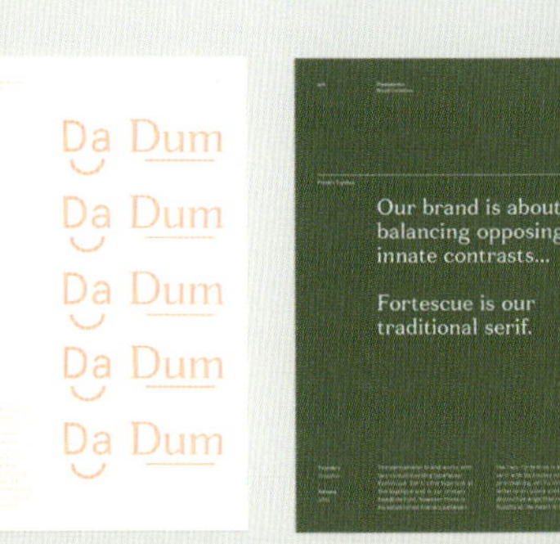
Da Dum
Da Dum
Da Dum
Da Dum
Da Dum
Our brand is about balancing opposing innate contrasts...
Fortescue is our traditional serif.

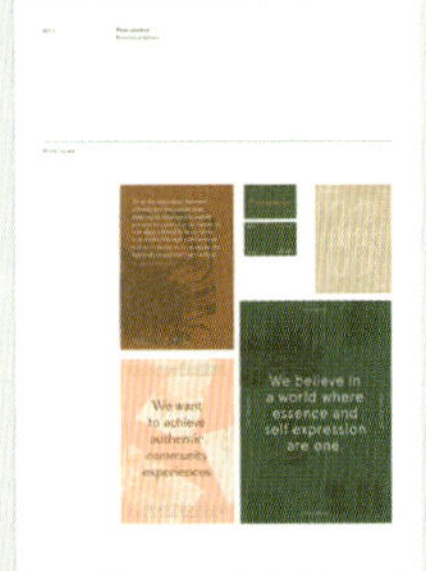

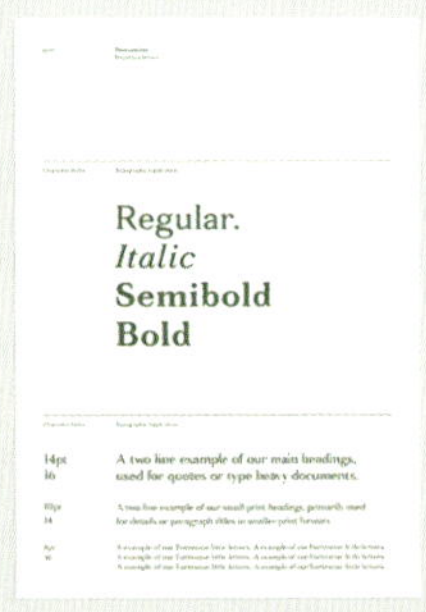
Regular.
Italic
Semibold
Bold
A two line example of our main headings, used for quotes or type heavy documents.

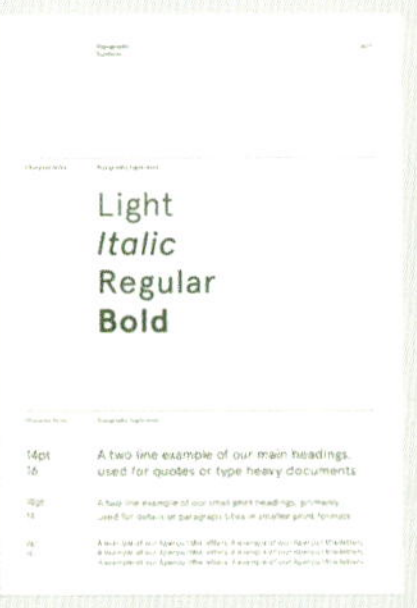
Light
Italic
Regular
Bold
A two line example of our main headings used for quotes or type heavy documents

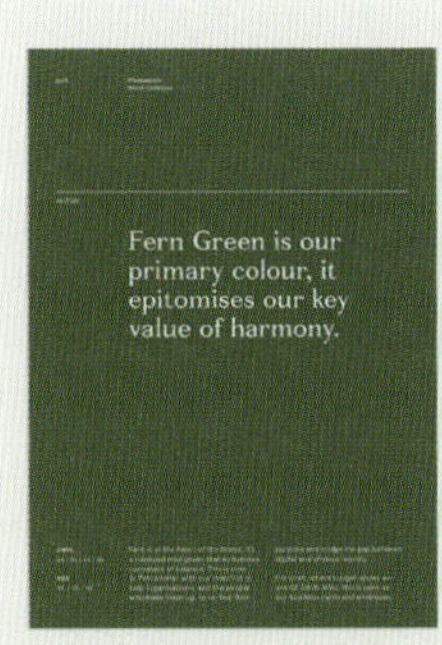
Fern Green is our primary colour, it epitomises our key value of harmony.

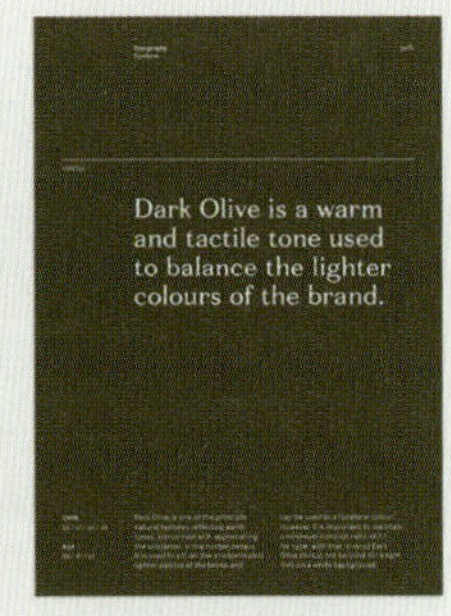
Dark Olive is a warm and tactile tone used to balance the lighter colours of the brand.

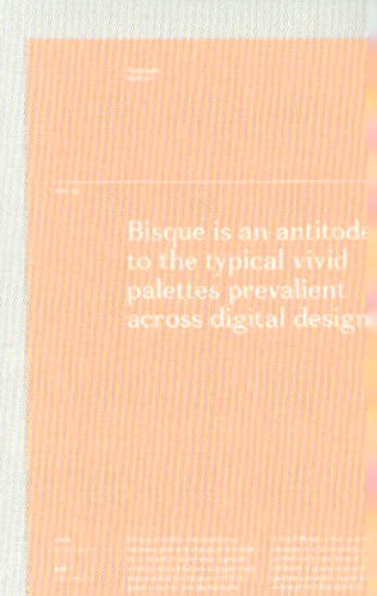

and exploring the space that exists between the two.

Aperçu is our supporting sans.

ria.

Listening

Perhaps if not counter intuitively to the dynamic and real time nature of social media, listening – ideally using our specialist tools – is the first step for any successful engagement program. Researching and mapping out where your customers most are on social web, which platforms they don't, and what conversations they are *having*, is now essential to build a picture of the online context in which your brand lives.

Strategy

The next step involves standing back and analysing data from the listening audit to gain insights, decide where intervention may be appropriate, and then generate ideas for how to join or initiate conversations. It is very important to carefully choose which platform(s) to engage with as a 'blunderbuss' approach – spreading resources thinly over a large number of platforms – rarely if ever works.

Engagement

When social media lets a customer have a relationship with a larger organisation – that is, have an interaction that is publicly visible to other customers where possible – then social engagement can occur. However in practice it takes time, focused effort and patient relationship building to develop lasting community. If at all possible it is recommended to encourage as wide a participation and involvement amongst staff and all stakeholders.

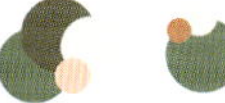

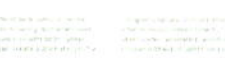

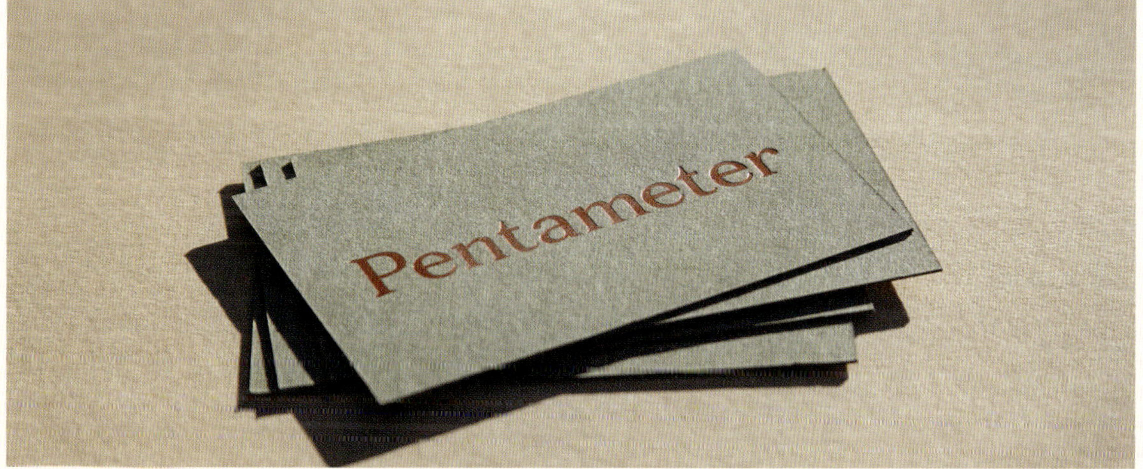

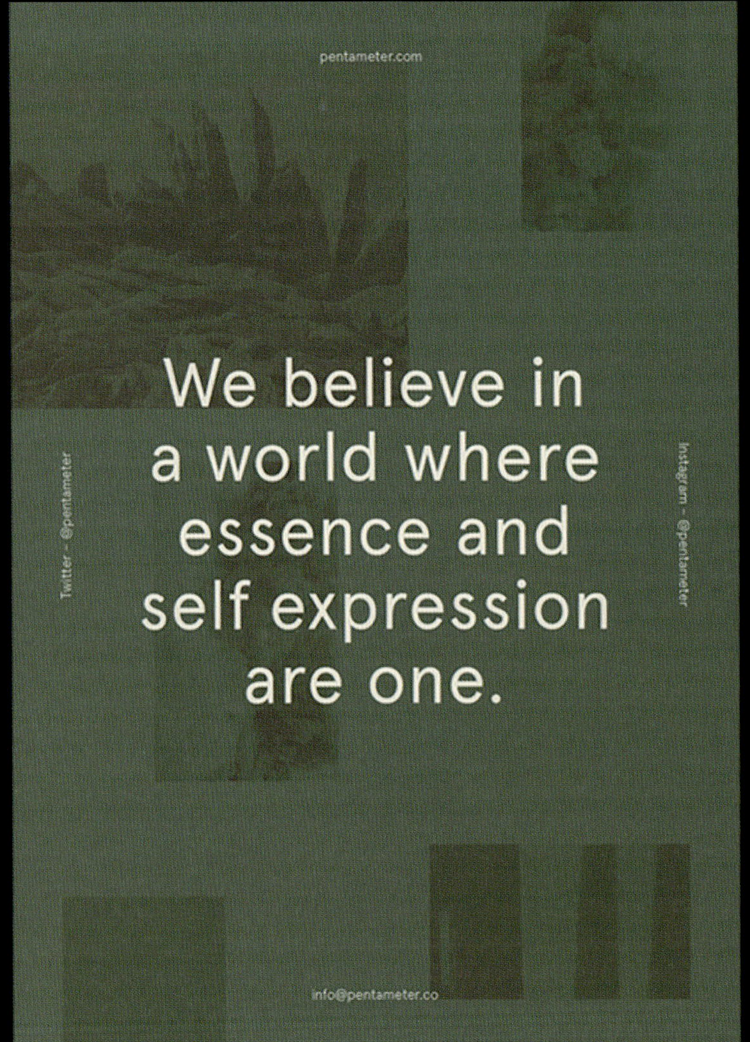
pentameter.com
We believe in
a world where
essence and
self expression
are one.
Twitter - @pentameter
Instagram - @pentameter
info@pentameter.co

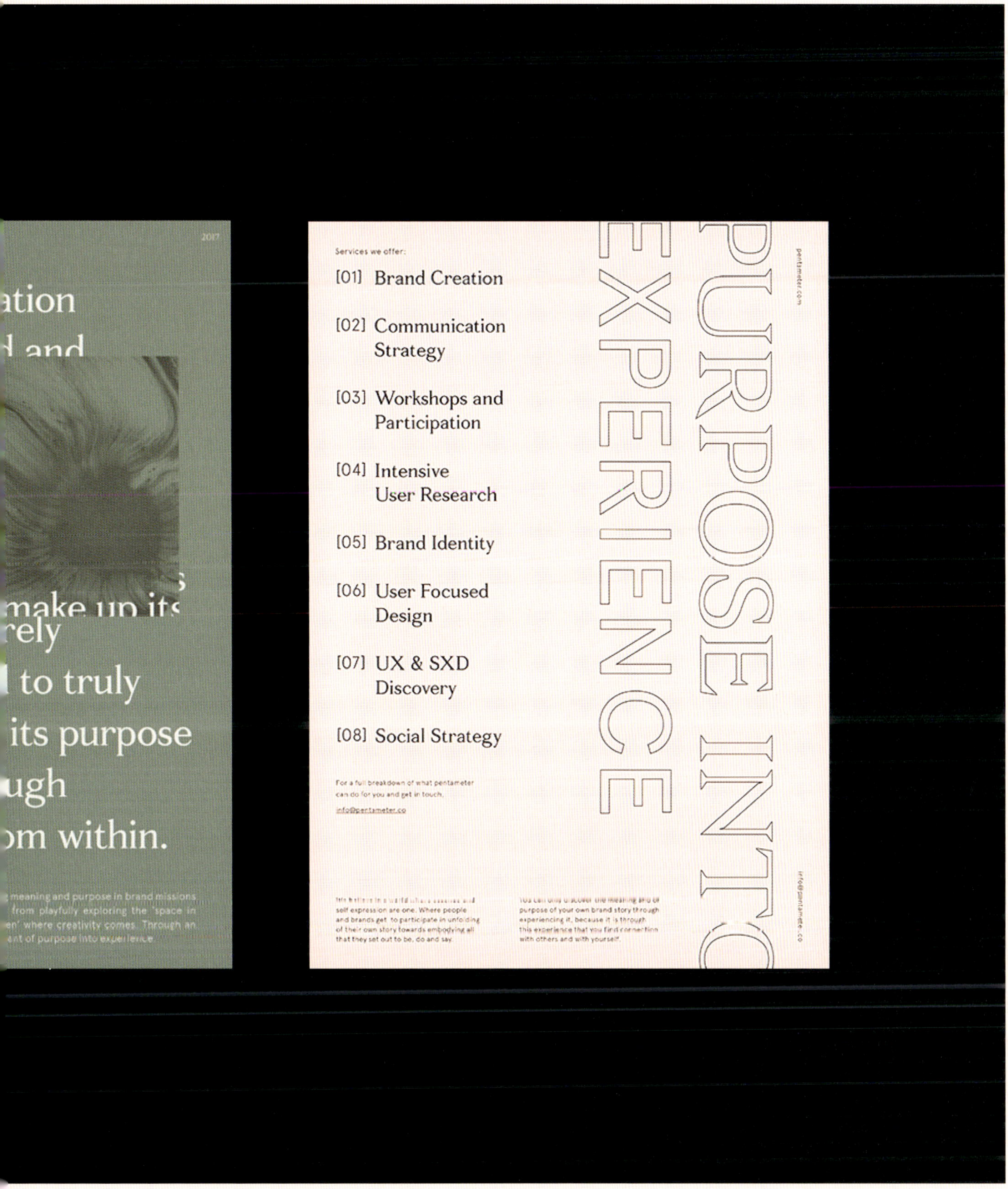

2017

ation
l and
make up its
rely
to truly
its purpose
ugh
om within.

meaning and purpose in brand missions
from playfully exploring the 'space in
en' where creativity comes. Through an
ent of purpose into experience

Services we offer:

[01] Brand Creation

[02] Communication Strategy

[03] Workshops and Participation

[04] Intensive User Research

[05] Brand Identity

[06] User Focused Design

[07] UX & SXD Discovery

[08] Social Strategy

For a full breakdown of what pentameter can do for you and get in touch.

info@pentameter.co

PURPOSE INTO EXPERIENCE

pentameter.com

self expression are one. Where people and brands get to participate in unfolding of their own story towards embodying all that they set out to be, do and say.

purpose of your own brand story through experiencing it, because it is through this experience that you find connection with others and with yourself.

info@pentameter.co

Shimada Corporation Brochure

Designer	**Client**
Masaomi Fujita	**Shimada Corporation**

Key Diagram

Font	Paper	Size
Alpin Gothic CG	Matt-coated paper	176×250mm (B5)

The condensed font Alpin Gothic CG is clear and the shape conveys a sense of the effective corporate working relationship of the company.

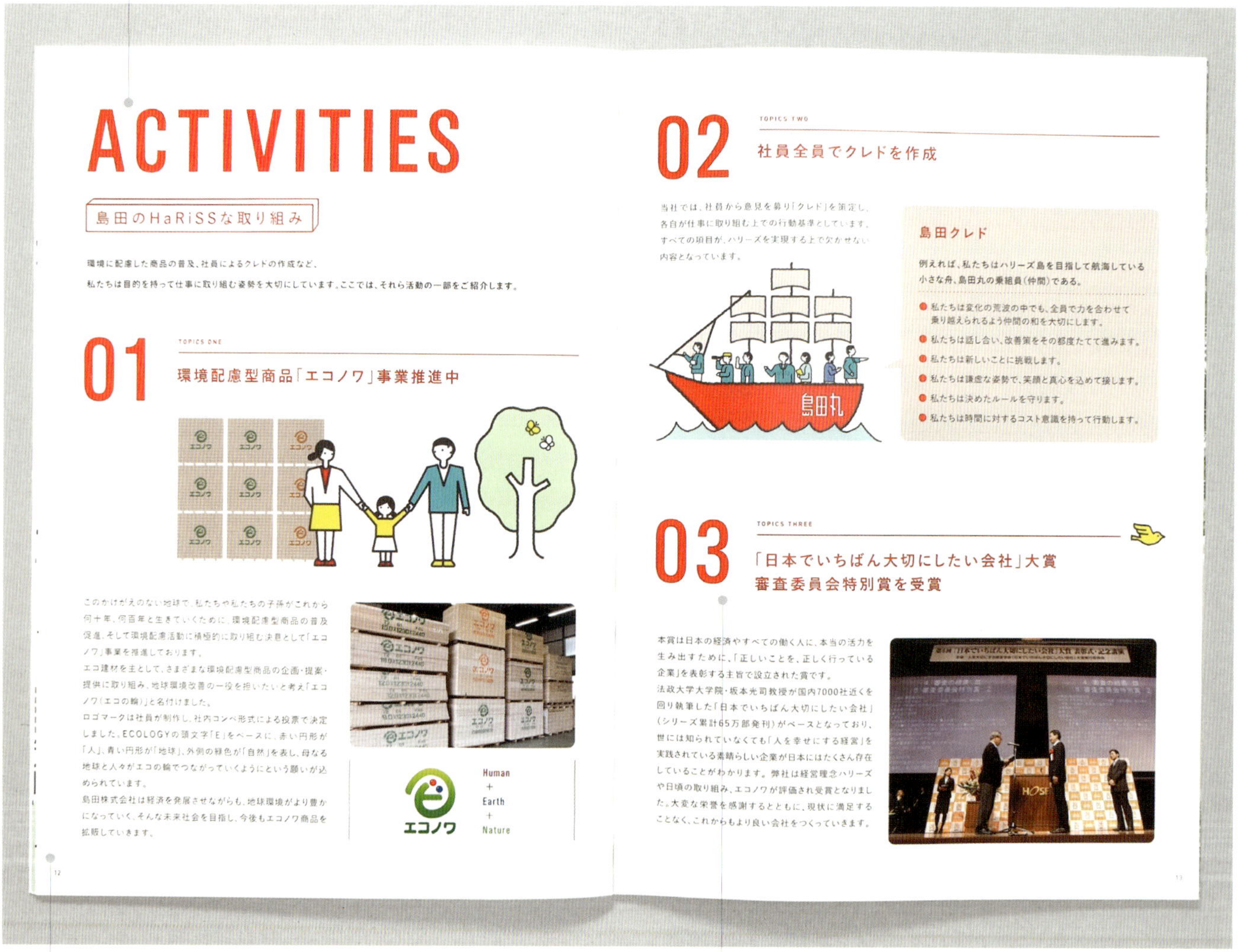

The layout uses content modules as a visual guide; readers will read the content in the order of the modules' arrangement. Reading from top to bottom and from left to right is quite a common practice.

The color red for all titles comes from the symbolic color of the company. The limited use of color allows more attention to the text.

Grid

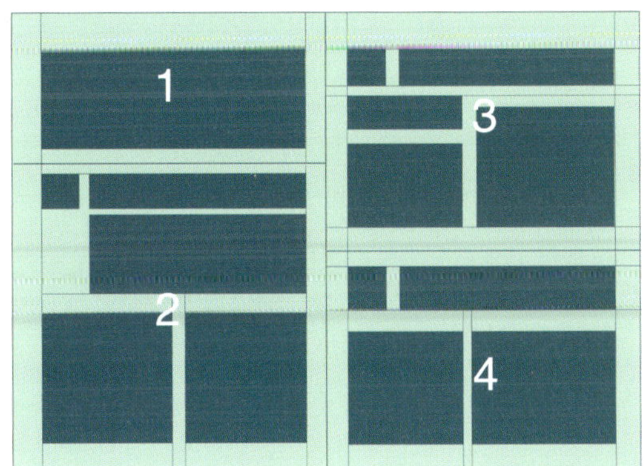

Visual Flow

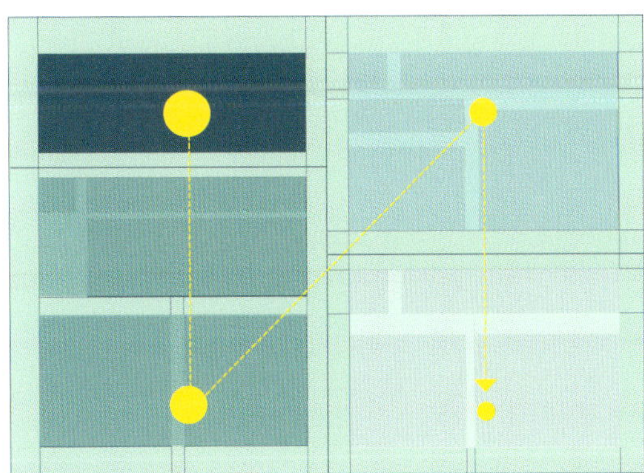

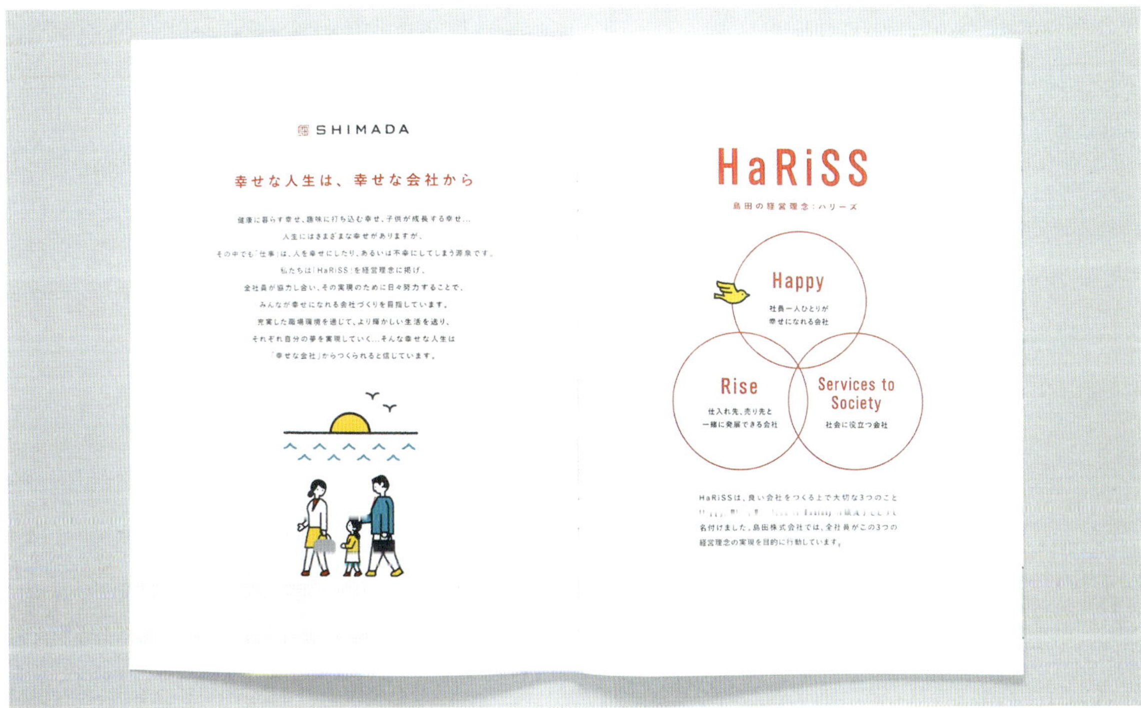

For the page structure of this brochure, the main focus was introducing the company's business philosophy "HaRiSS"—Happy, Rise, Services to Society. The text that explains the philosophy has been refined, so that they would properly reflect new messages from the renewed company. The original illustrations were used as the main graphics of the brochure to visualize how the employees interact with one another, and the kind of relationships they have built with their business partners, local people, and family members. The readers will get to know how Shimada's staff members are committed to work and how they value "interaction between people", as well as the fun atmosphere of the workplace.

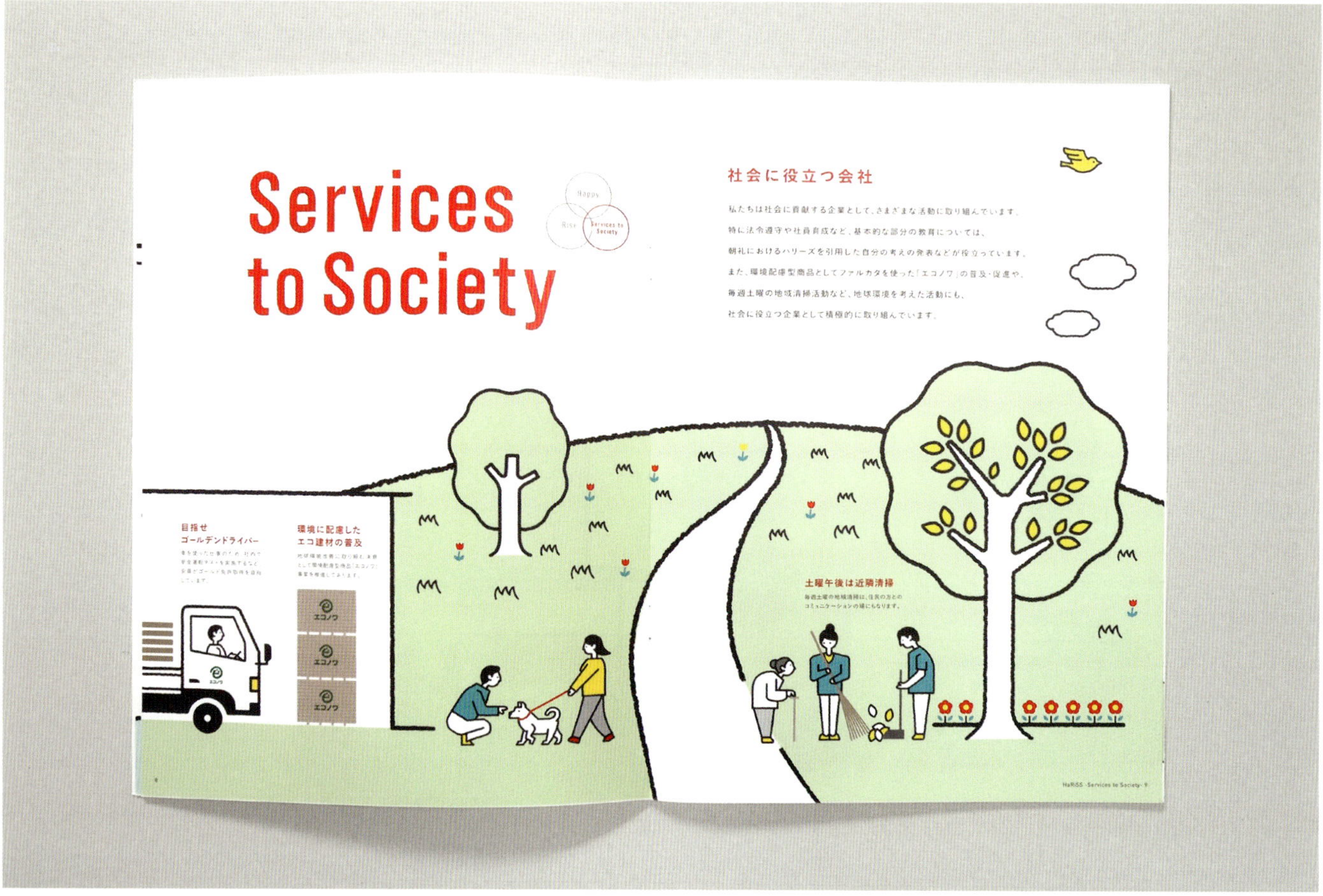

Services to Society

社会に役立つ会社

私たちは社会に貢献する企業として、さまざまな活動に取り組んでいます。
特に法令遵守や社員育成など、基本的な部分の教育については、
朝礼におけるハリーズを引用した自分の考えの発表などが役立っています。
また、環境配慮型商品としてファルカタを使った「エコノワ」の普及・促進や、
毎週土曜の地域清掃活動など、地球環境を考えた活動にも、
社会に役立つ企業として積極的に取り組んでいます。

目指せ ゴールデンドライバー

環境に配慮した エコ建材の普及

土曜午後は近隣清掃

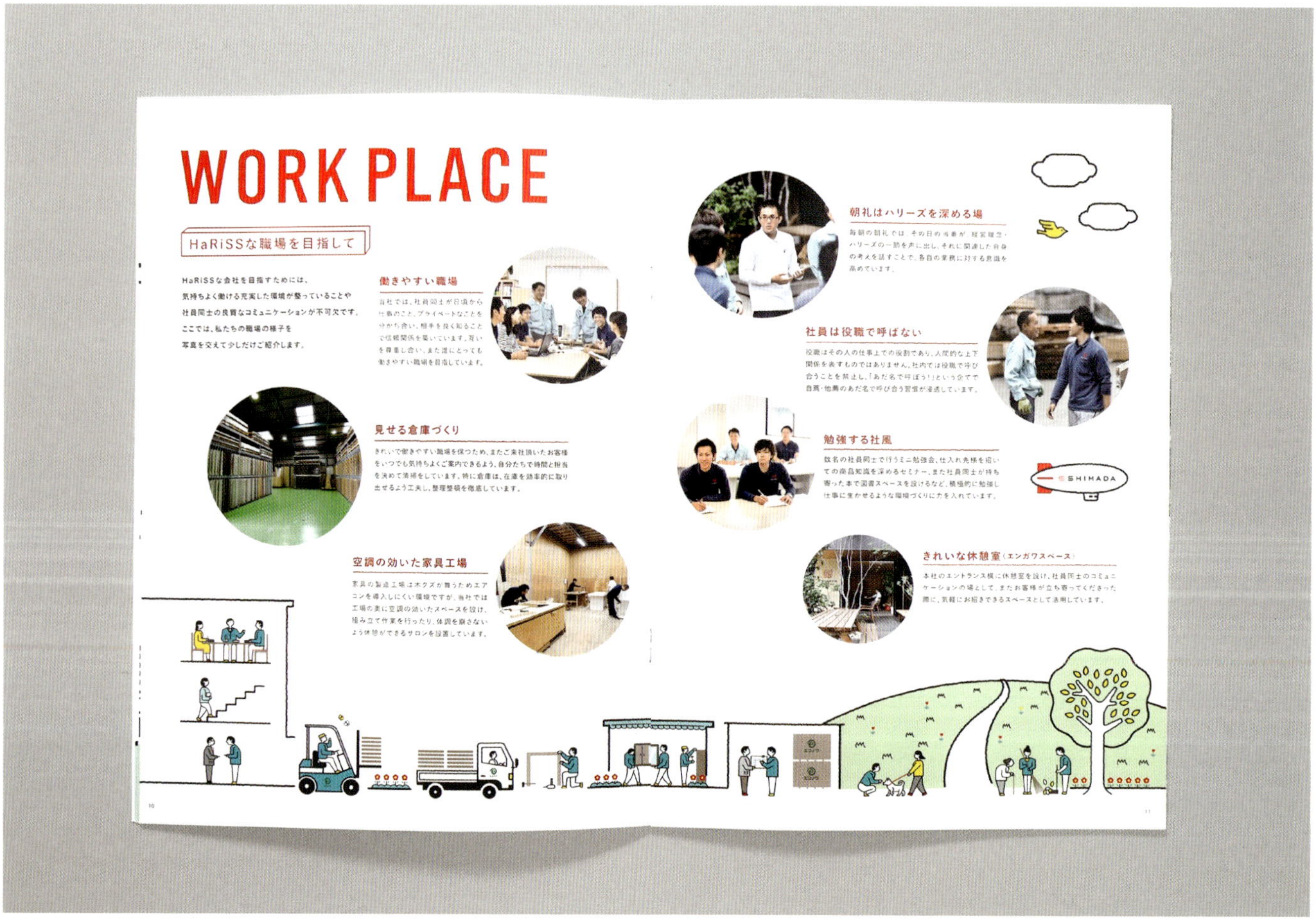

WORK PLACE

HaRiSSな職場を目指して

HaRiSSな会社を目指すためには、
気持ちよく働ける充実した環境が整っていることや
社員同士の良質なコミュニケーションが不可欠です。
ここでは、私たちの職場の様子を
写真を交えて少しだけご紹介します。

働きやすい職場

当社では、社員同士が日頃から仕事のこと、プライベートなことを分かち合い、相手を良く知ることで信頼関係を築いています。互いを尊重し合い、また誰にとっても働きやすい職場を目指しています。

見せる倉庫づくり

空調の効いた家具工場

朝礼はハリーズを深める場

社員は役職で呼ばない

勉強する社風

きれいな休憩室（エンガワスペース）

SHIMADA

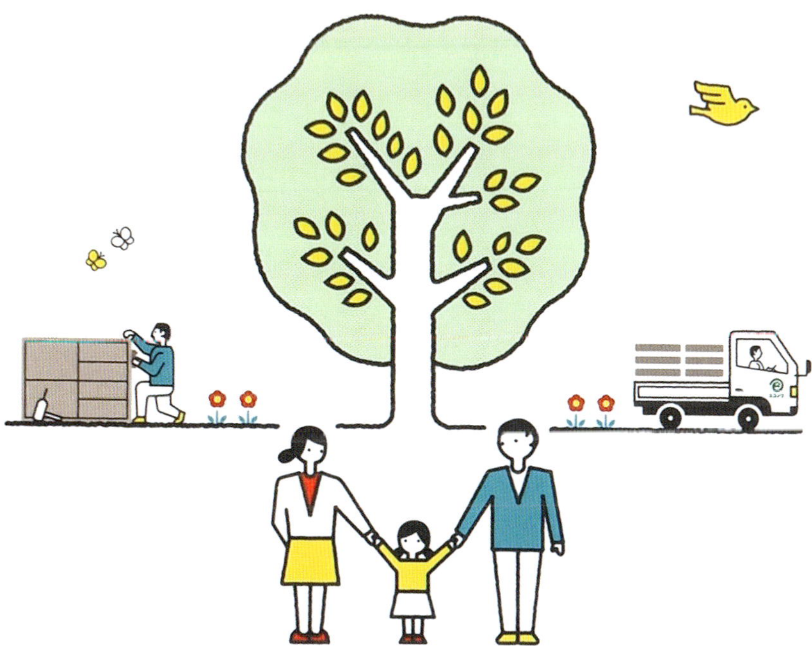

［ハリーズ］

HaRiSS

Happy / Rise / Services to Society

Apartment Farming 101 Infographic Brochure

Designer

Gloria Assé

Client

Apartment Farming 101

Key Diagram

Font

Various

Paper

Coated paper

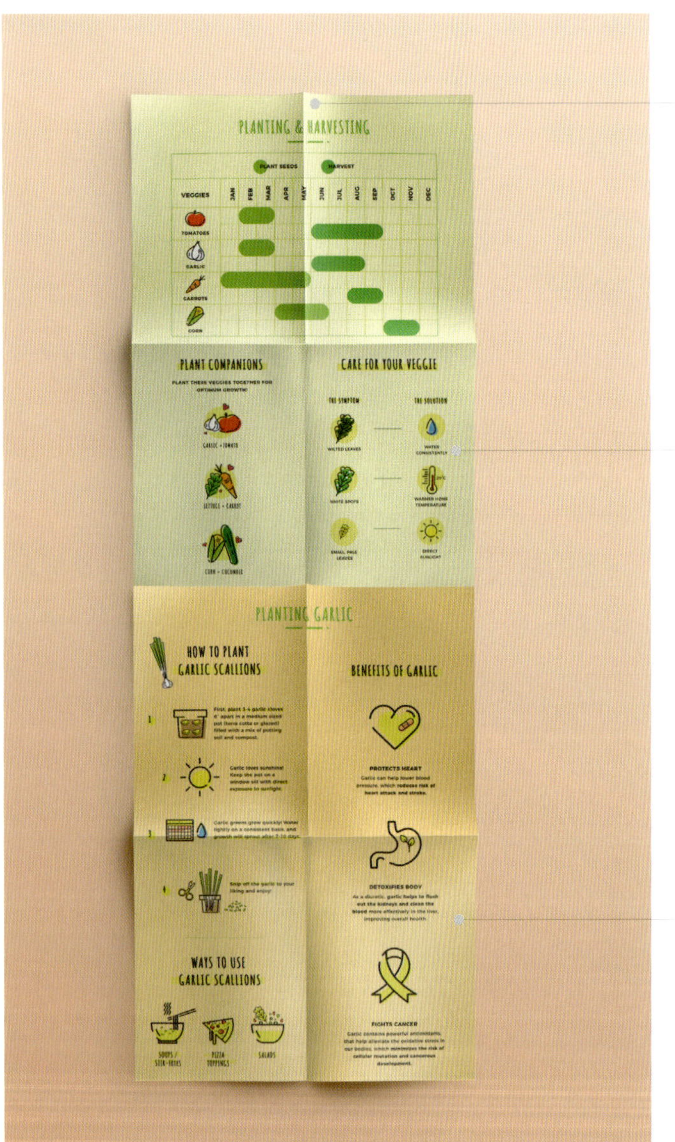

There are four kinds of font. The comparison between each of them classifies the text.

As the main colors of the brochure, green and brown symbolize the plant and soil which is echoed from the theme of the project.

An infographic seems the best way to present a comprehensive guide like this. The balanced proportion of text and images and the long and narrow columns make reading easier and smoother, allowing the newbie "farmers" to quickly begin their journey.

Grid

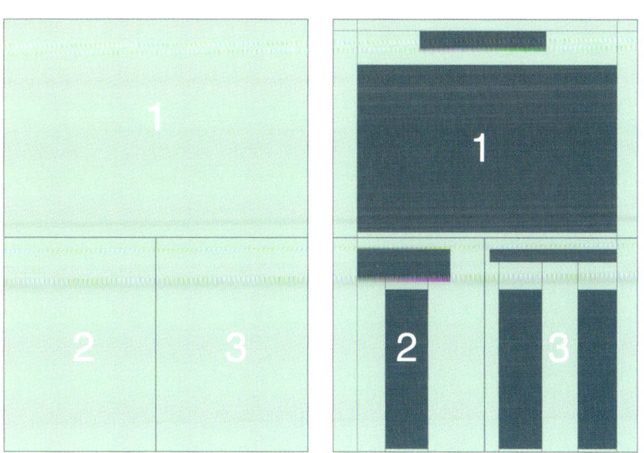

Visual Flow

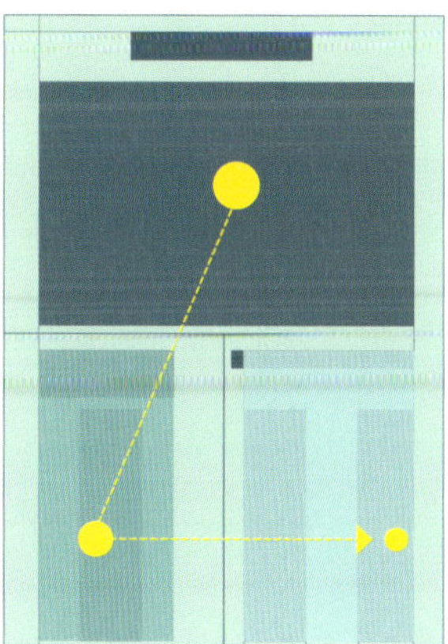

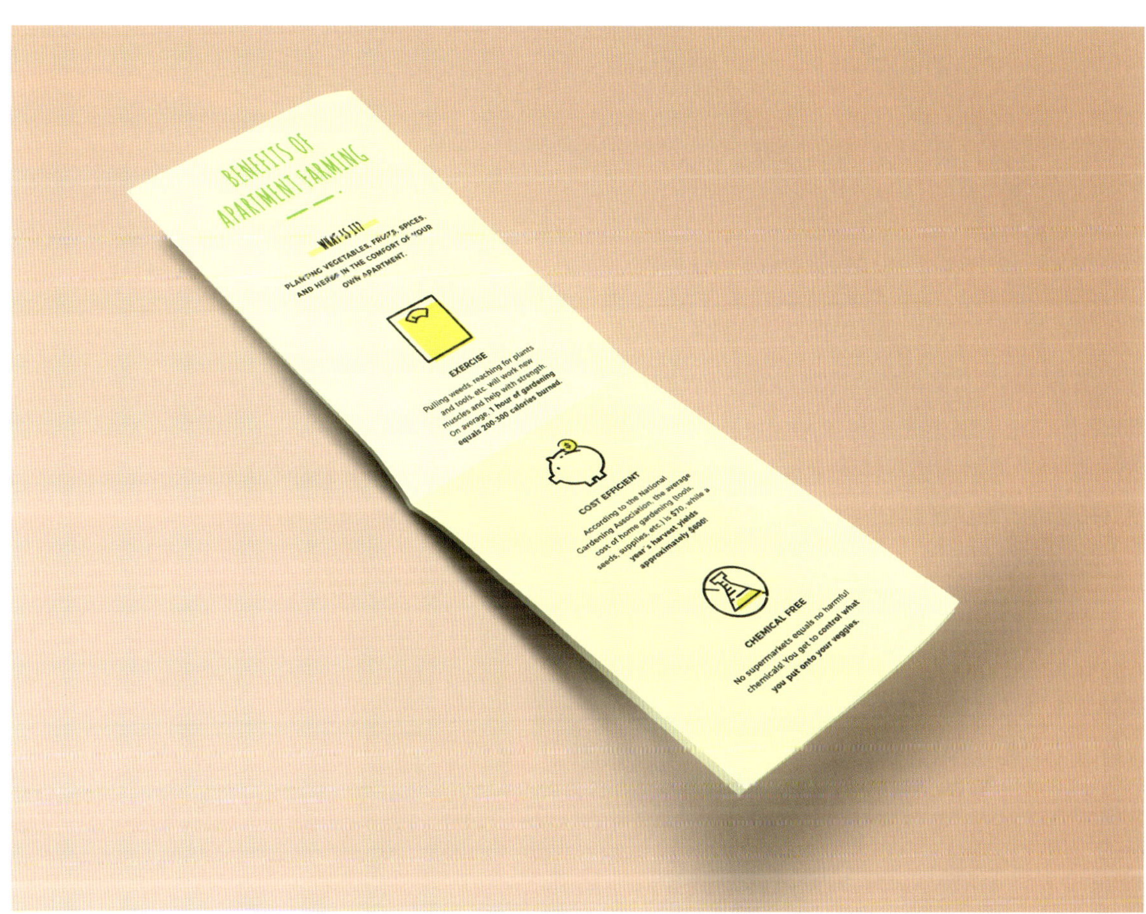

"Apartment Farming 101" is a brochure that informs its target audience, young adults in Toronto who live in apartments, how to begin planting vegetables in their homes.

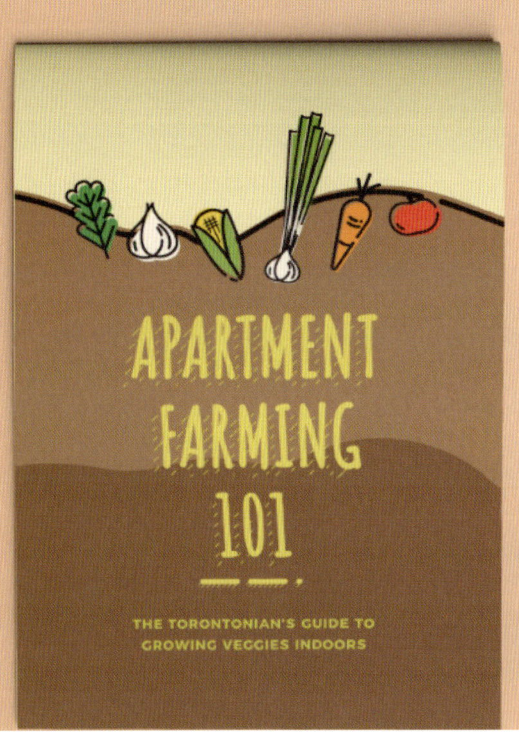

WAYS TO USE
GARLIC SCALLIONS

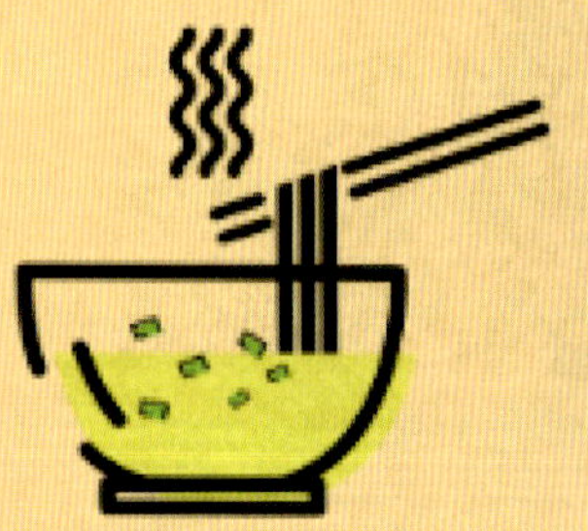

SOUPS /
STIR-FRIES

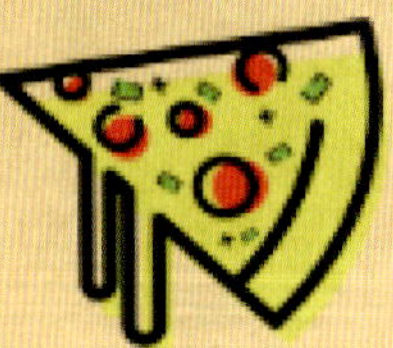

PIZZA
TOPPINGS

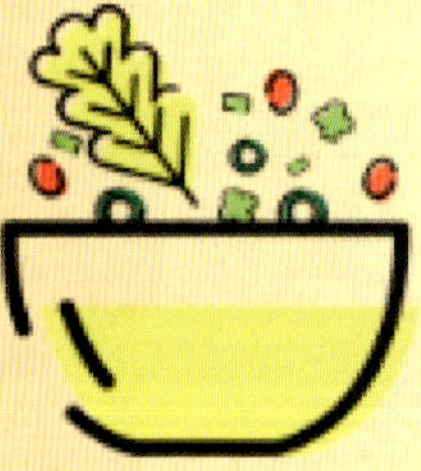

SALADS

PLANT PERSONALITY QUIZ

WHICH VEGGIE IS FOR YOU?

PLANTING VEGGIES CAN BE A GREAT EXPERIENCE IF YOU CHOOSE THE RIGHT ONES. FIND OUT WHICH VEGGIE IS THE ONE FOR YOU!

DO YOU SPEND MOST OF YOUR TIME AT HOME?

YES NO

ARE YOU PATIENT?

YES NO

DO YOU HAVE A LOT OF LIVING SPACE?

YES NO

IF YOU ANSWERED...

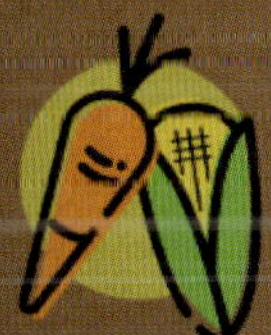

MOSTLY "YES"

CARROTS, CORN, CAULIFLOWER

Veggies like corn, carrots, and cauliflower require a lot of space, maintenance, and care!

MOSTLY "NO"

GARLIC, TOMATOES, GREENS

Veggies like garlic, tomatoes, and leafy greens are lower maintenance, take less time to plant, and take up less space.

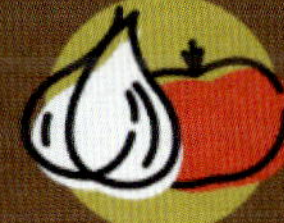

Training Campaign Flyer

Designer

Chao Tan

Client

Training Campaign

Key Diagram

Font	Paper	Size
Heiti	Ivory cardboard	70mm×220mm (Folded) 297mm×420mm (Unfolded)

The classic sans serif fonts have a minimalist and clean style which reflects the professionalism of the company.

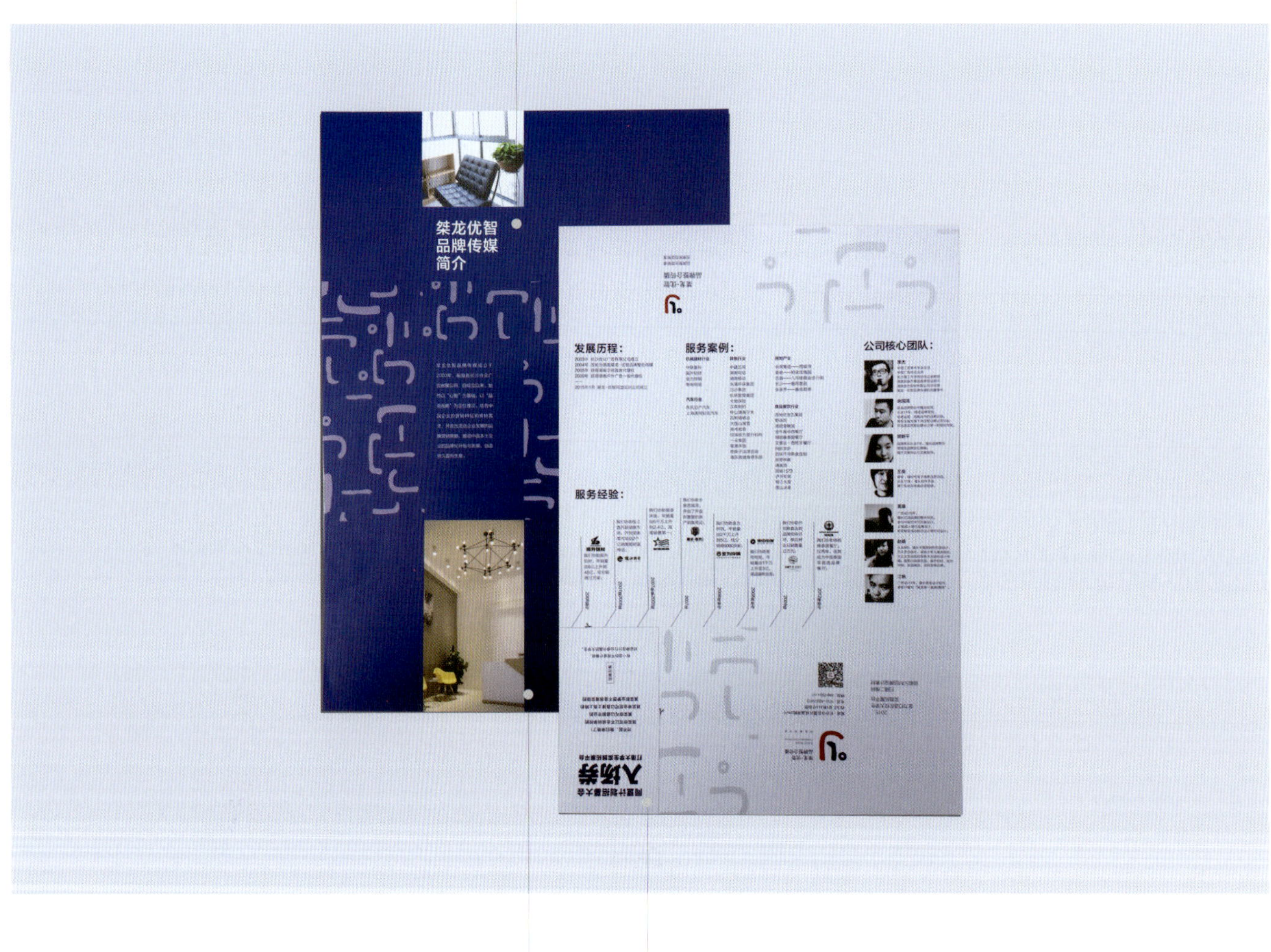

The negative space improves the visual effect of the layout, helping the students read the brochure in a quick way by highlighting the information.

The colors bluish purple and white communicate the calm and stable characteristics of the company.

Grid

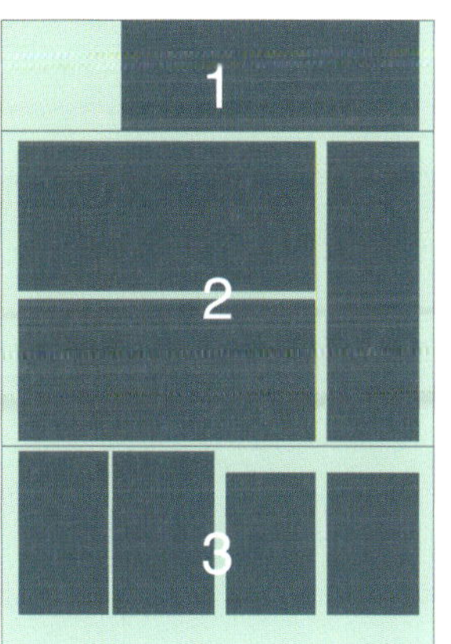

Visual Flow

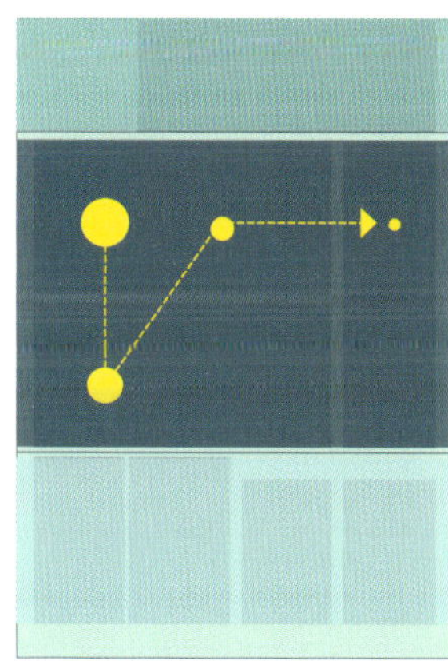

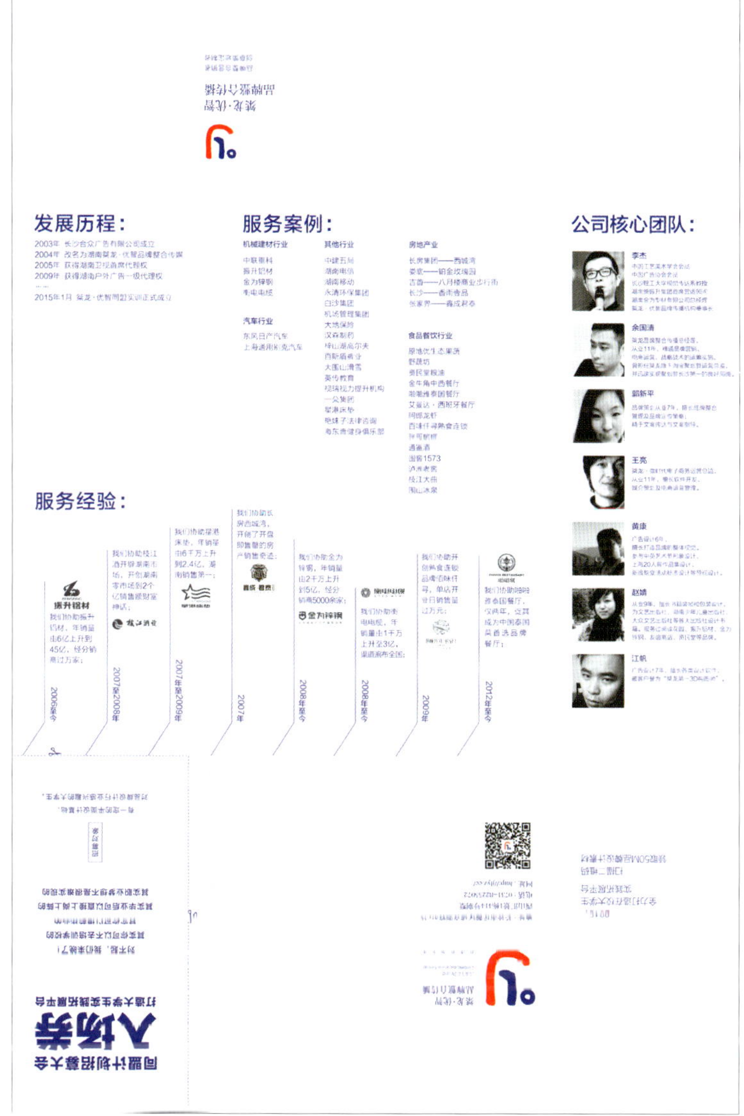

The Training Campaign is aimed at college students, so they need a flyer for enrollment. The content of the flyer includes information about the teachers from this design company who have rich experience in design and teaching; other relevant information is also included. A double-sided printed paper is folded into a small flyer. It saves cost and makes it easier to inspire reader's curiosity, and then drive people to read the information when they receive the flyer.

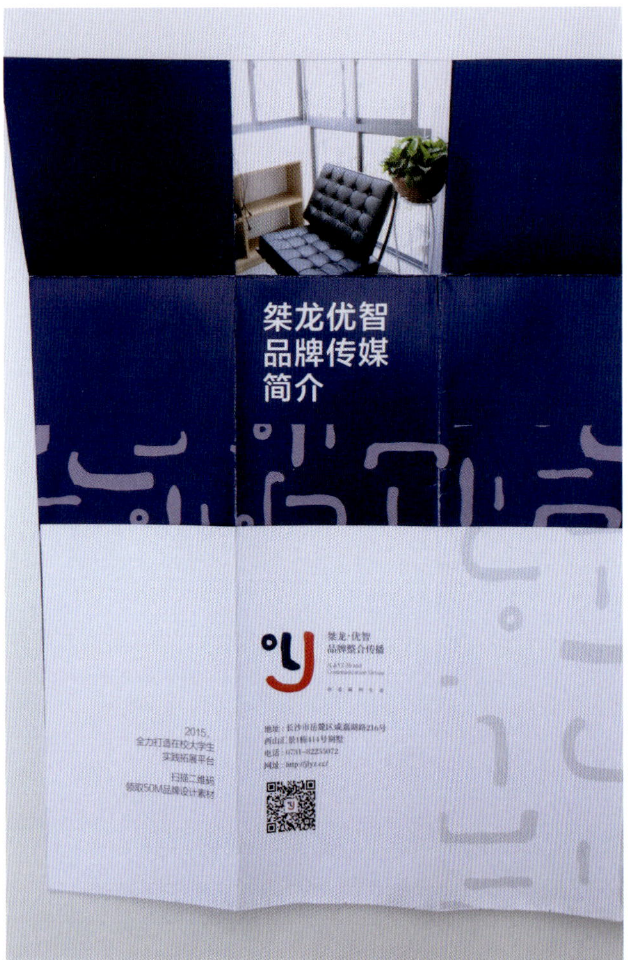
桀龙优智
品牌传媒
简介
桀龙·优智
品牌整合传播
2015,
全力打造在校大学生
实践拓展平台
扫描二维码
领取50M品牌设计素材

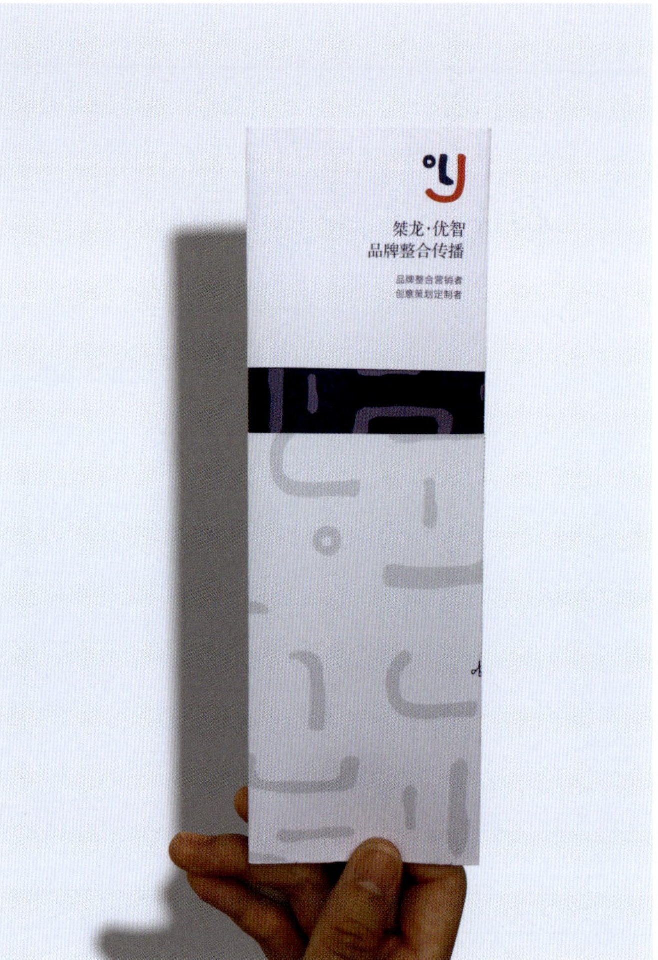
桀龙·优智
品牌整合传播
品牌整合营销者
创意策划定制者

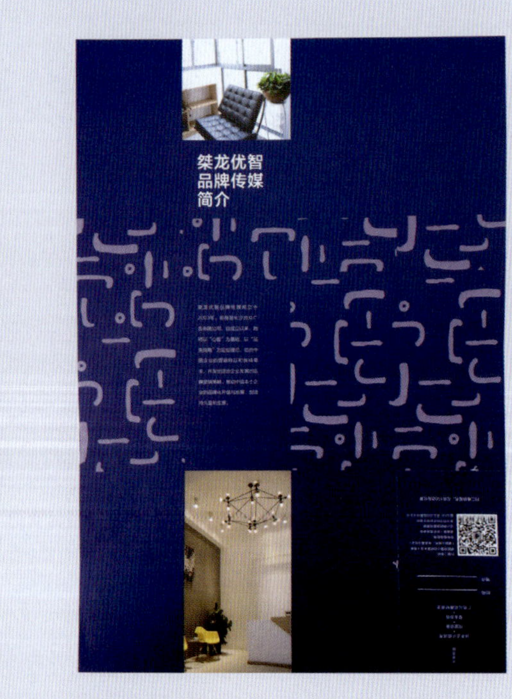
桀龙优智
品牌传媒
简介

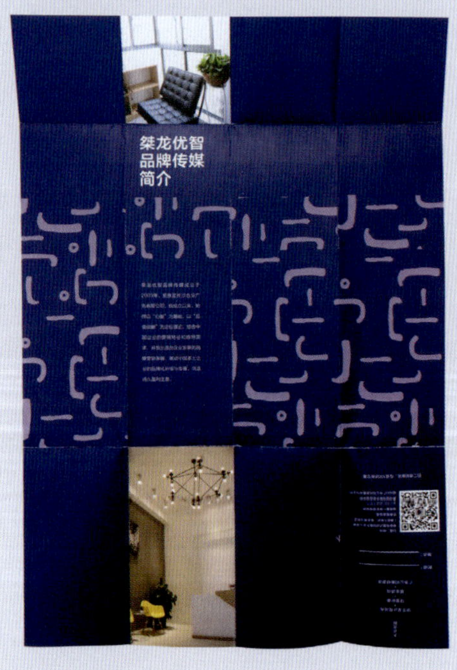
桀龙优智
品牌传媒
简介

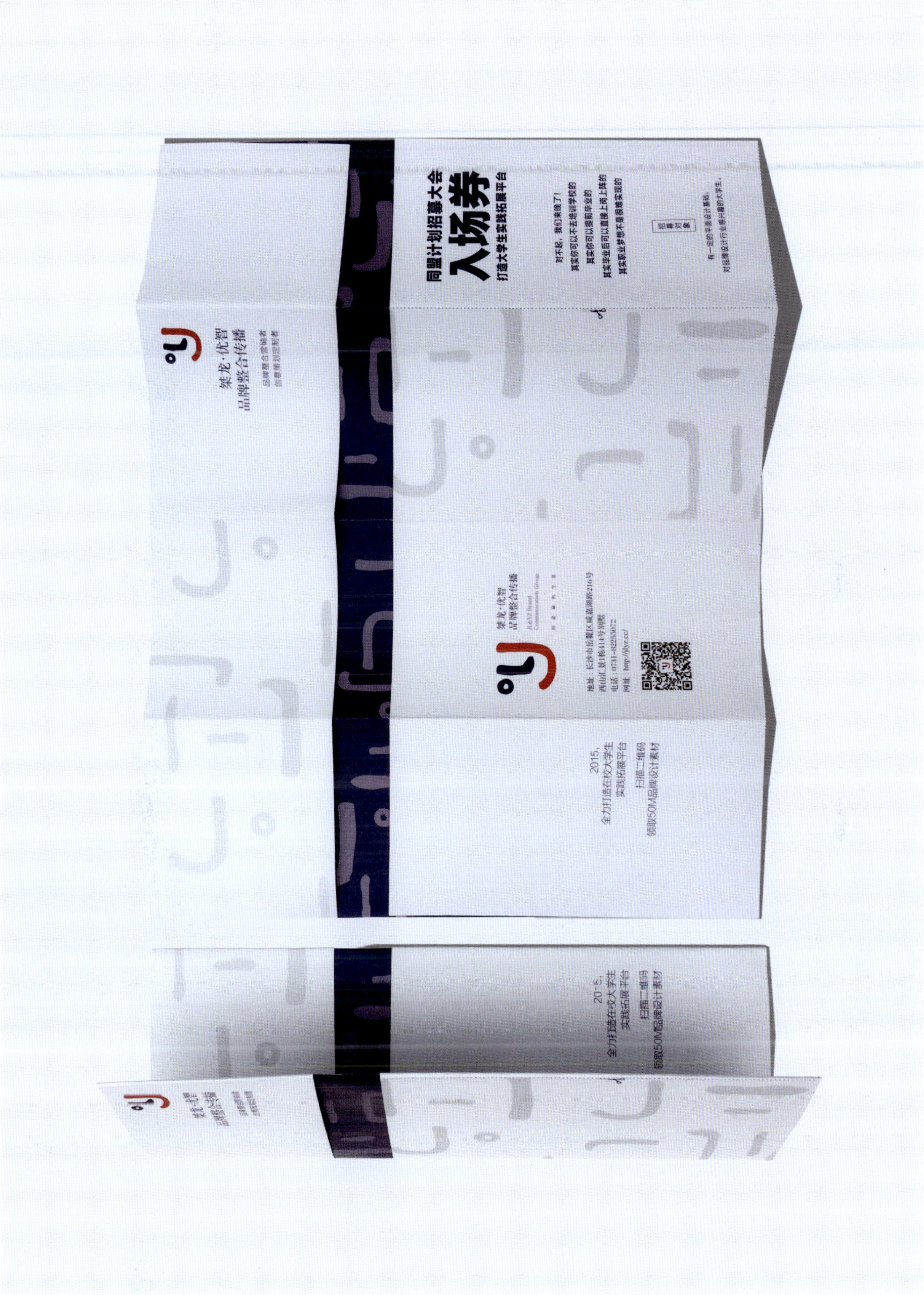

同盟计划招募大会
入场券
打造大学生实践拓展平台

对不起，我们来晚了！
其实你可以不去培训学校的
其实你可以提前毕业的
其实毕业后可以直接上岗上阵的
其实职业梦想不是很难实现的

招募对象
有一定的平面设计基础，
对品牌设计行业感兴趣的大学生。

品牌整合传播

2015，
全力打造在校大学生
实践拓展平台
扫描二维码
领取50M品牌设计素材

Walker Design Co. Promotional Mail

Designer

Bebold Creative

Client

Walker Design Co.

Key Diagram

Font

House Slant
Gotham
Bebas

Paper

150g Matt stock

Size

594×420mm (A2)

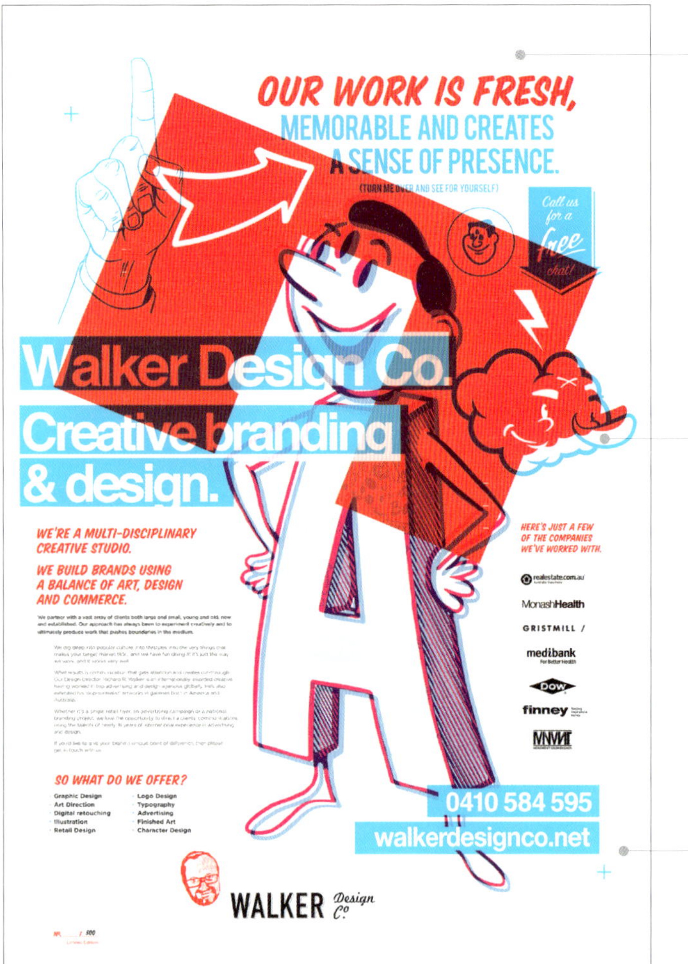

Three typefaces were used which enhanced the entire visual effect. The handwritten style of the House Slant in red is full of vitality; the Bebas in blue are condensed and neat; the white Gotham in blue background has tight letter-spacing with a classic quality.

The upper part of the layout is eye-catching because of the intense contrast of colors. It quickly leads viewers' attention to the headline and the main copy.

The layout is distinguished by different types of contrast: colors, font sizes, and even between the rigid color blocks and the lively cartoon character.

Grid

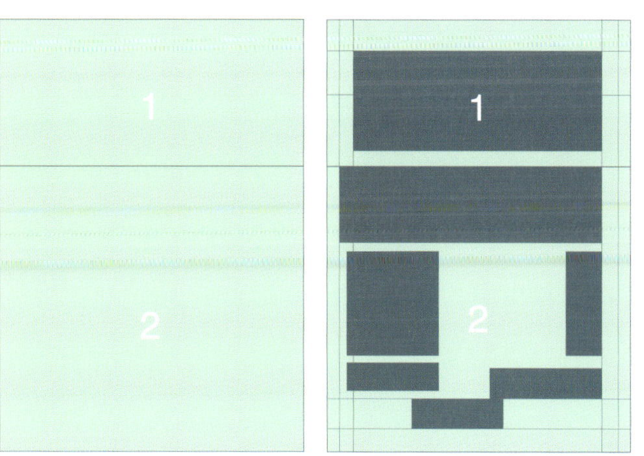

Visual Flow

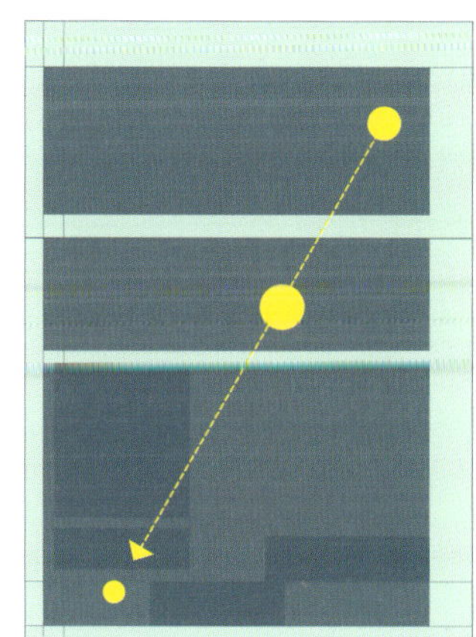

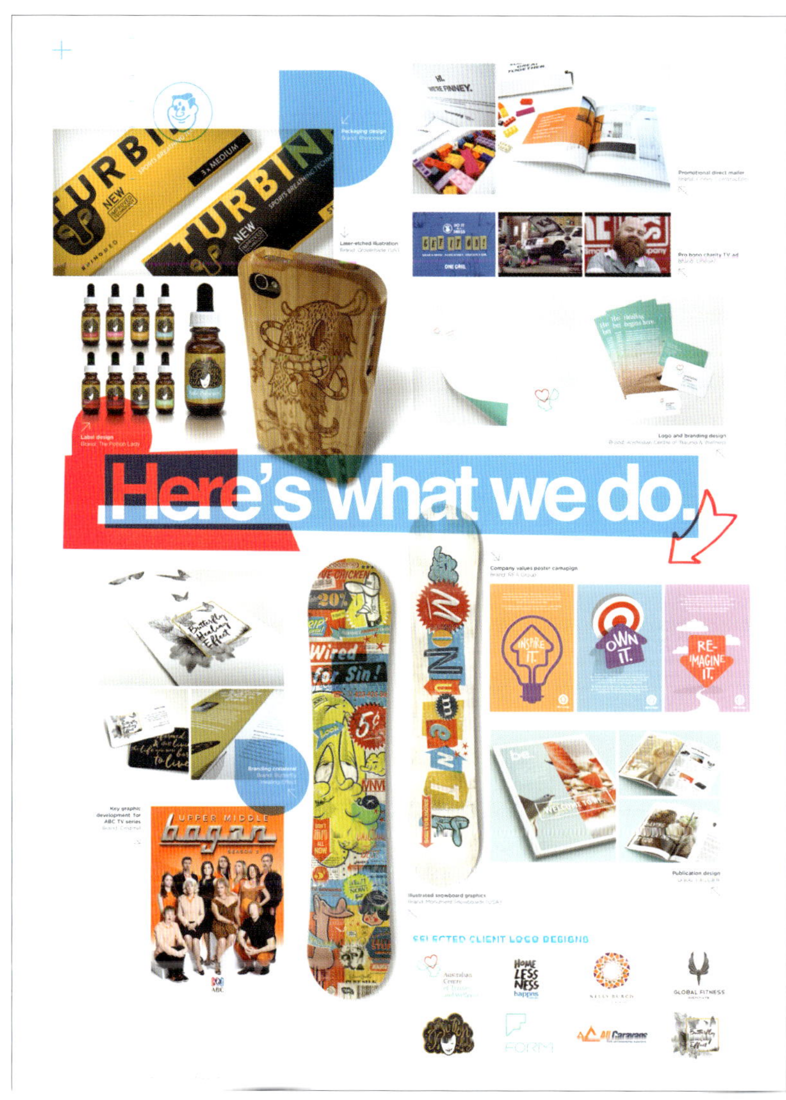

This is a design from the designers themselves, a promotional email sent out to potential clients. The design studio had been experimenting with different layouts to achieve the best result, with emphasis on how the layout would engage viewers and, more importantly, gain their trust.

Flux Brochure

Designer

TSUBAKI KL

Client

Matic Degree

Key Diagram

Font	Paper	Size
Avant Garde	Antalis cocoon (recycled paper)	148×210mm (A5)

Avant Garde is the one of the sans serifs which can deliver the beauty of geometry. It boasts personality and modernity.

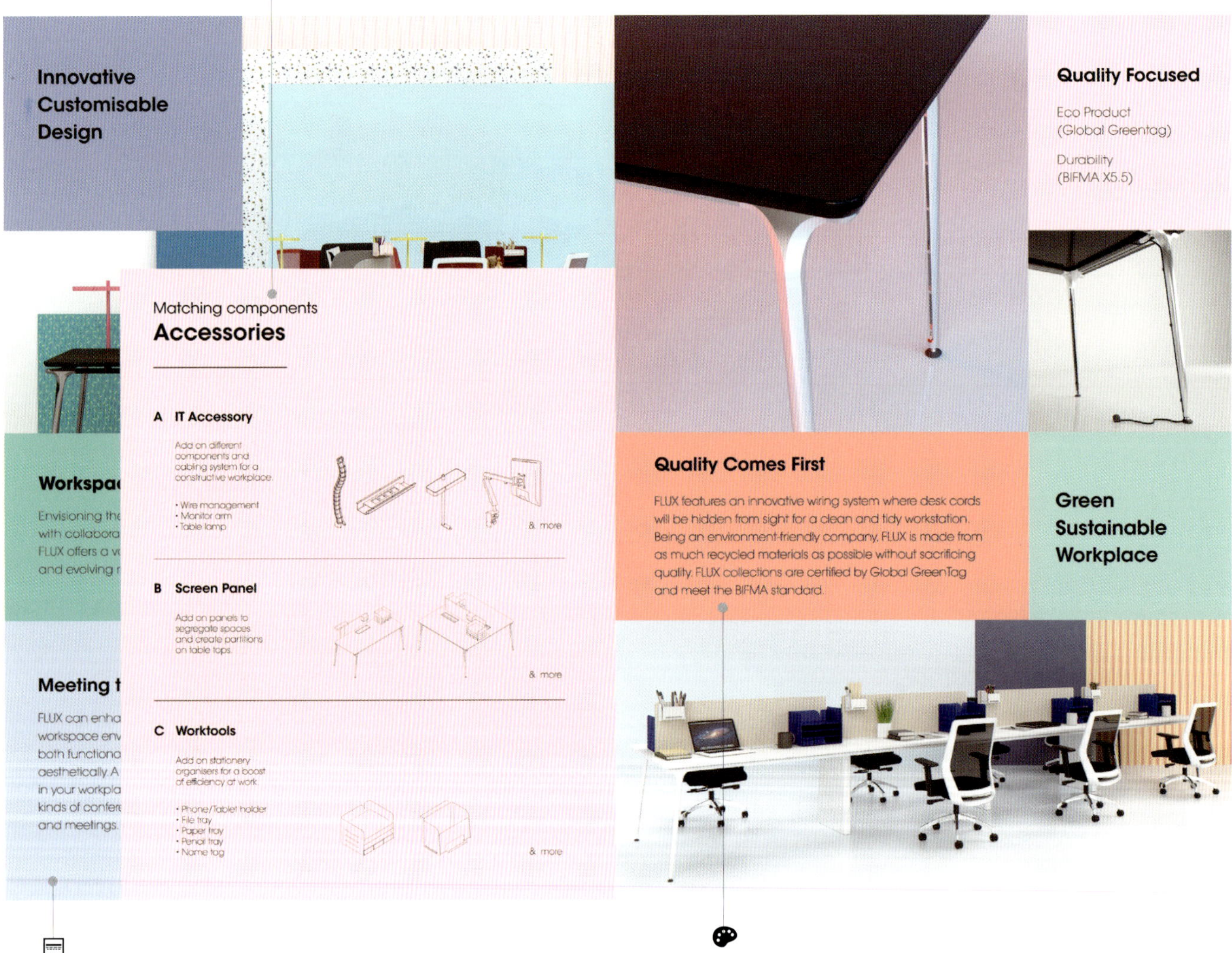

The module-based layouts are well-arranged in order yet dynamic. The larger proportion for images allows a pleasant and smooth reading experience.

The harmony of this differently colored visual is owed to the consistent low-saturation colors. Each color is assigned to a specifc content, making it easier to read. What's more, such a riot of colors gives off energy and fun.

Grid

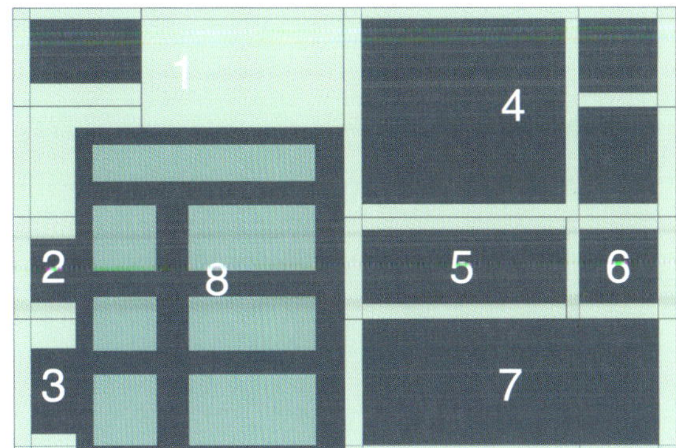

Visual Flow

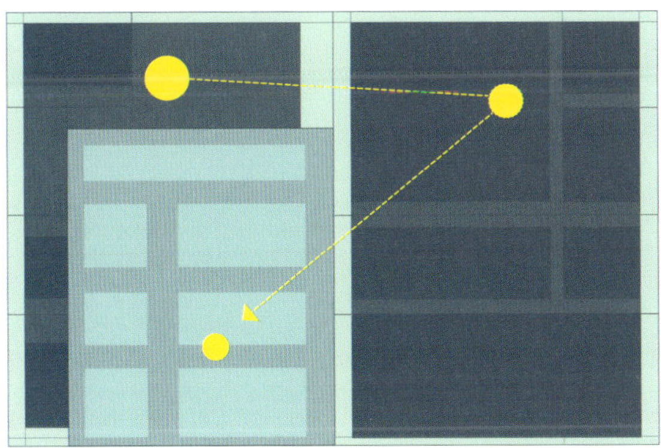

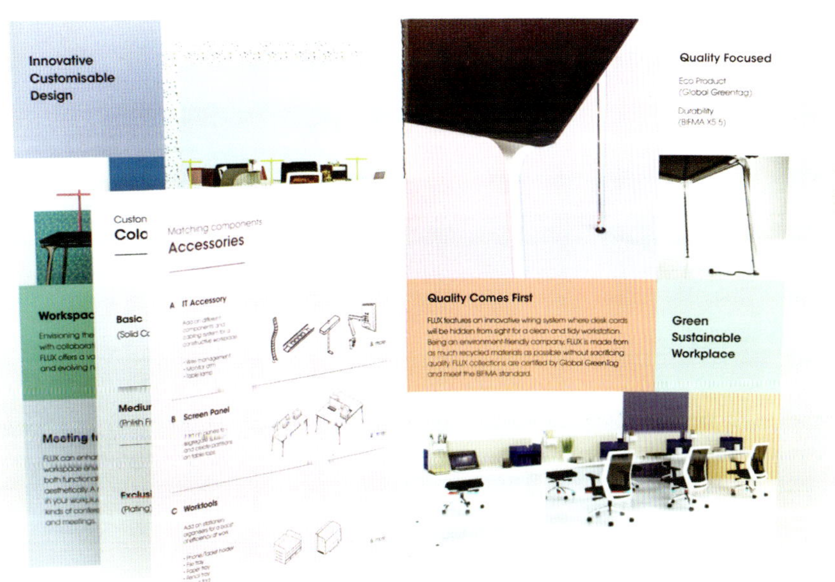

Flux is a newly-launched office furniture series which Matic Company designs. Flux furniture is devoted to creating an enjoyable and modern office environment for workers. It is not limited to the norm, but stands out with its bold and unique maximalist aesthetics.

To exhibit its personality, diversity,and applicability, the designer selects varying page sizes for the brochure. The overall design is distinct enough to grab readers' attention and allows them to have a novel reading experience.

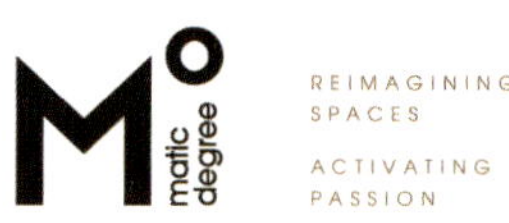

FLUX

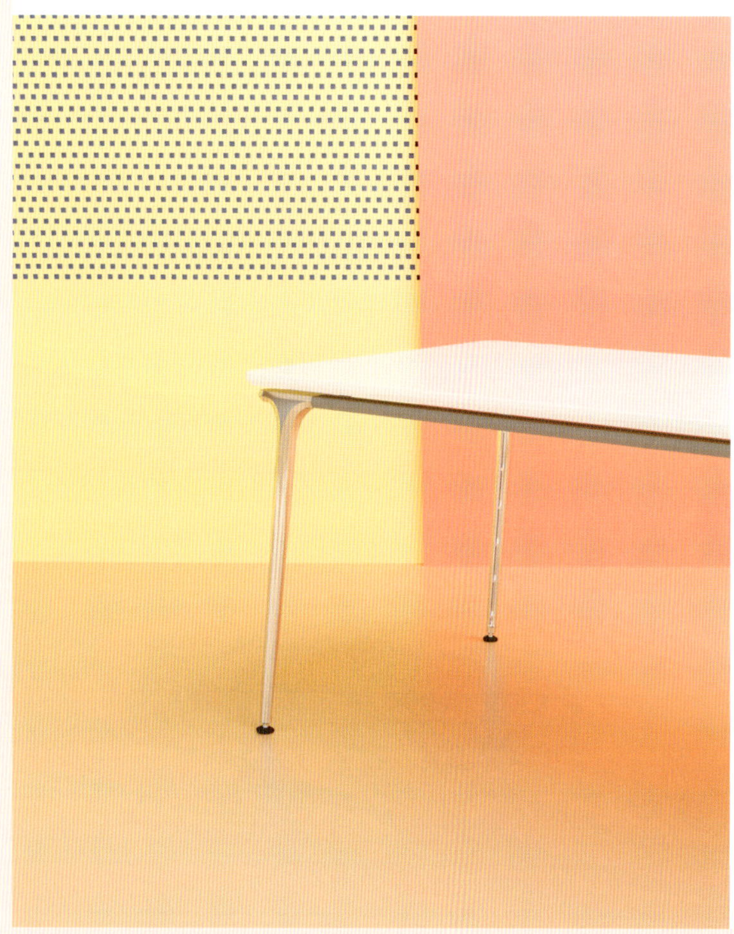

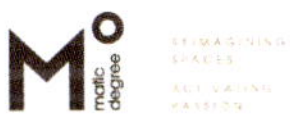

FLUX

User Experience Focus

FLUX redefines the workspace experience as a direct result of our purpose driven, user-centered design philosophy. FLUX blends form and function with its unique, space-efficient modular accessory mounting system. A growing catalogue of highly functional accessories can be easily attached to the FLUX table base creating an endless range of possible customised configurations from lighting and device holders to storage and privacy partitions.

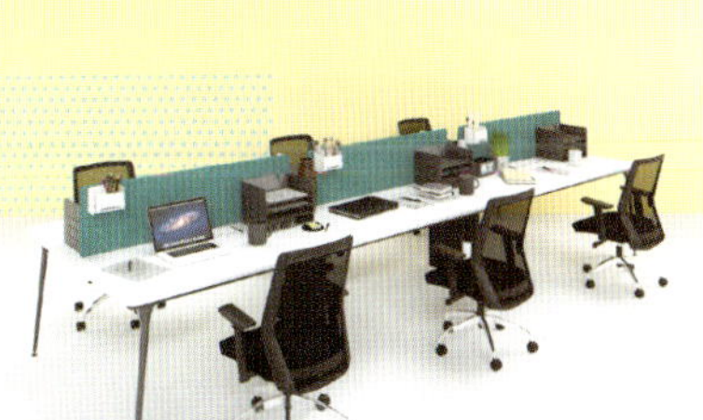

The MATIC Flux series is designed with a bold and unique maximalist aesthetic FLUX allows users to proclaim and express their unique personalities. The design features flexible personalisation and collaborative culture that encourages open workspace

Bold Lines, Soft Curves

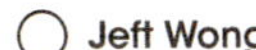

Jeff Wong
+6012 330 5038
jeffwong@maticdegree.com

Calvin Ong
+6017 613 7188
calvinong@maticdegree.com

Edwin Teoh
+6019 213 3330
edwinteoh@maticdegree.com

Connie Heu
+6012 2027119
connieheu@maticdegree.com

Matic Office System Sdn Bhd
(547300-D)

maticdegree.com

info@maticdegree.com

AOO Catalog

Designer

Martí Canillas

Client

AOO

Key Diagram

Font

Miller Display
Founders Grotesk

Paper

Munken Pure Rough 20

Size

110×190mm

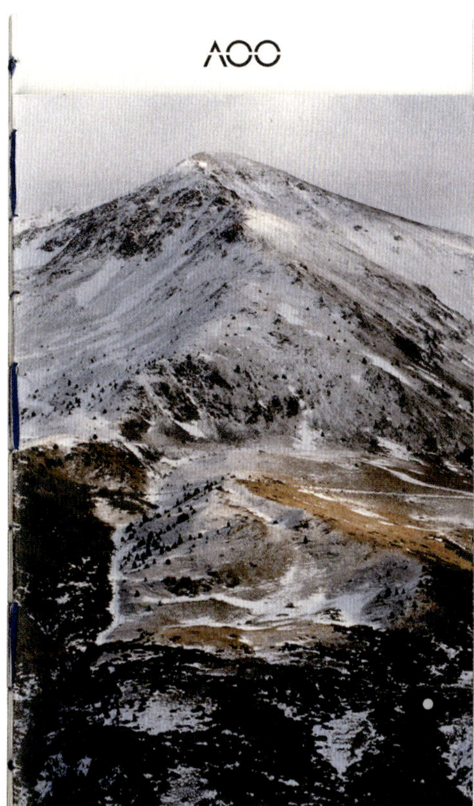

In order to give prominence to products, images have been priority for the layout. Text occupies only a small part. All the effort also allows reading quickly but clearly.

Grid

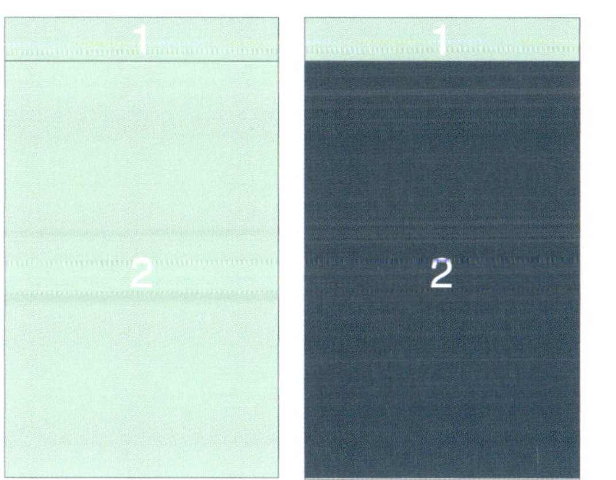

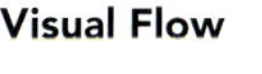

Visual Flow

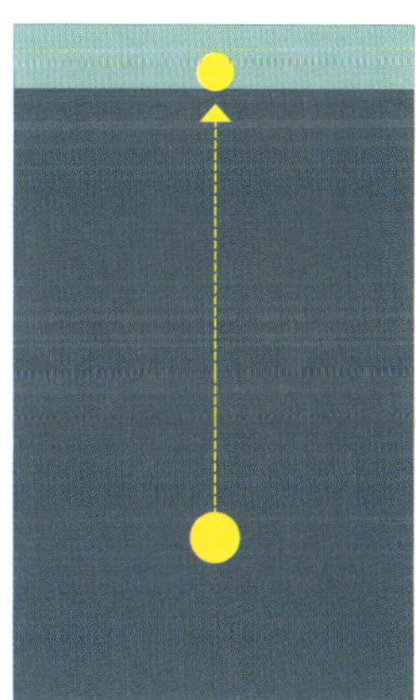

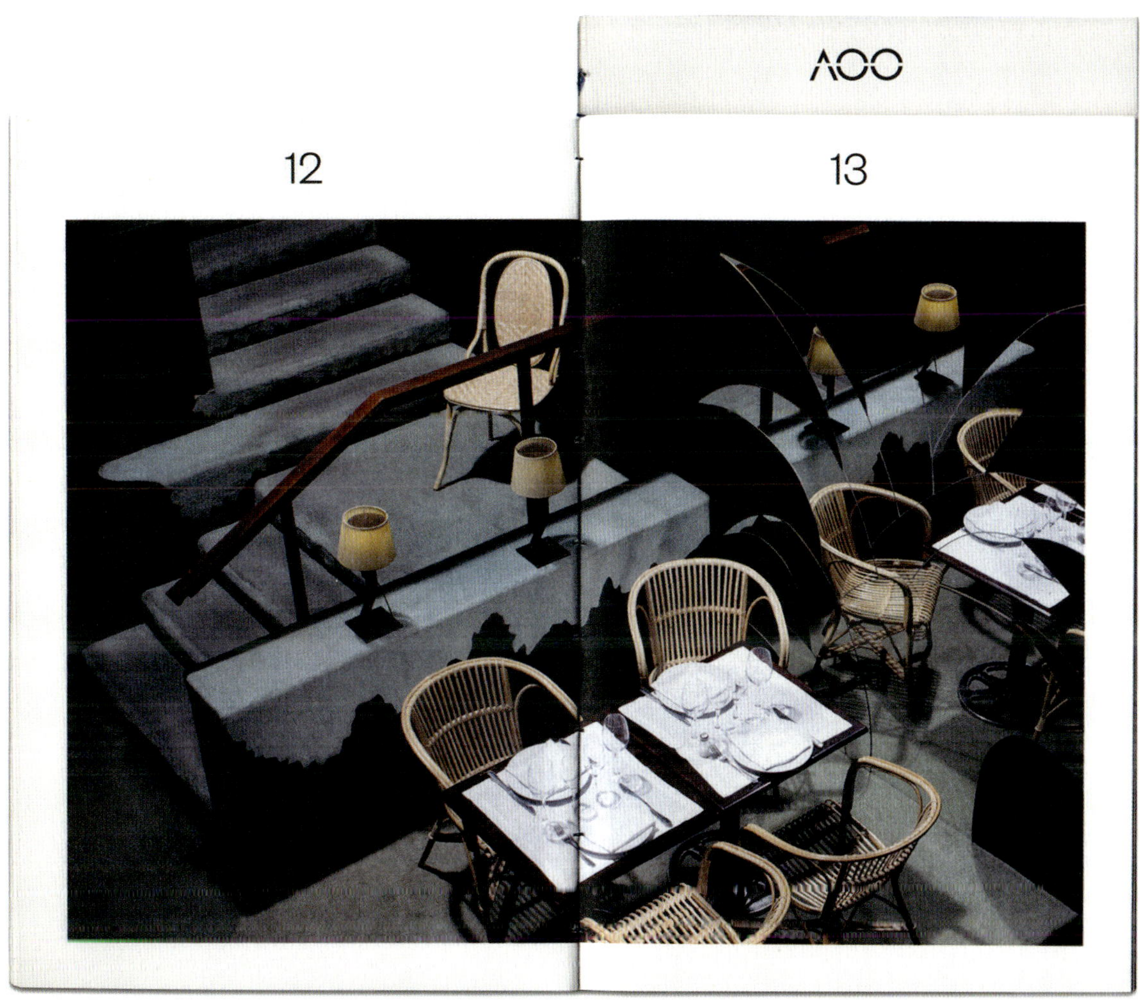

The piece for AOO was designed with the intention of being an unconventional multi-format catalog. Meant for interior designers and clients that would be using the pieces, the designers wanted it to stand out from other catalogs by printing in an uncommon format and by breaking it up into two sections. One where the pieces are shown in the context of how they could be used, and the other where the technical photos and dimensions of the furniture are shown.

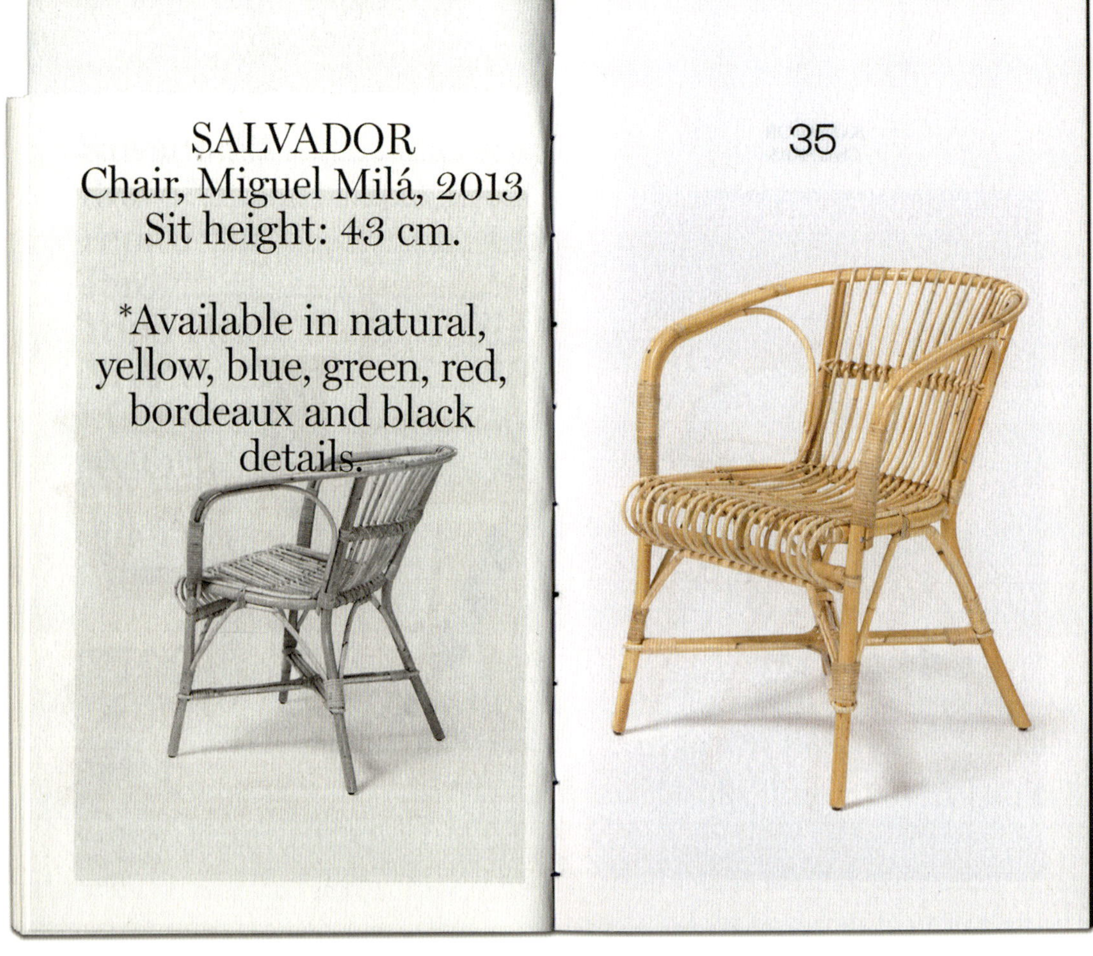
SALVADOR
Chair, Miguel Milá, 2013
Sit height: 43 cm.
*Available in natural, yellow, blue, green, red, bordeaux and black details.
35

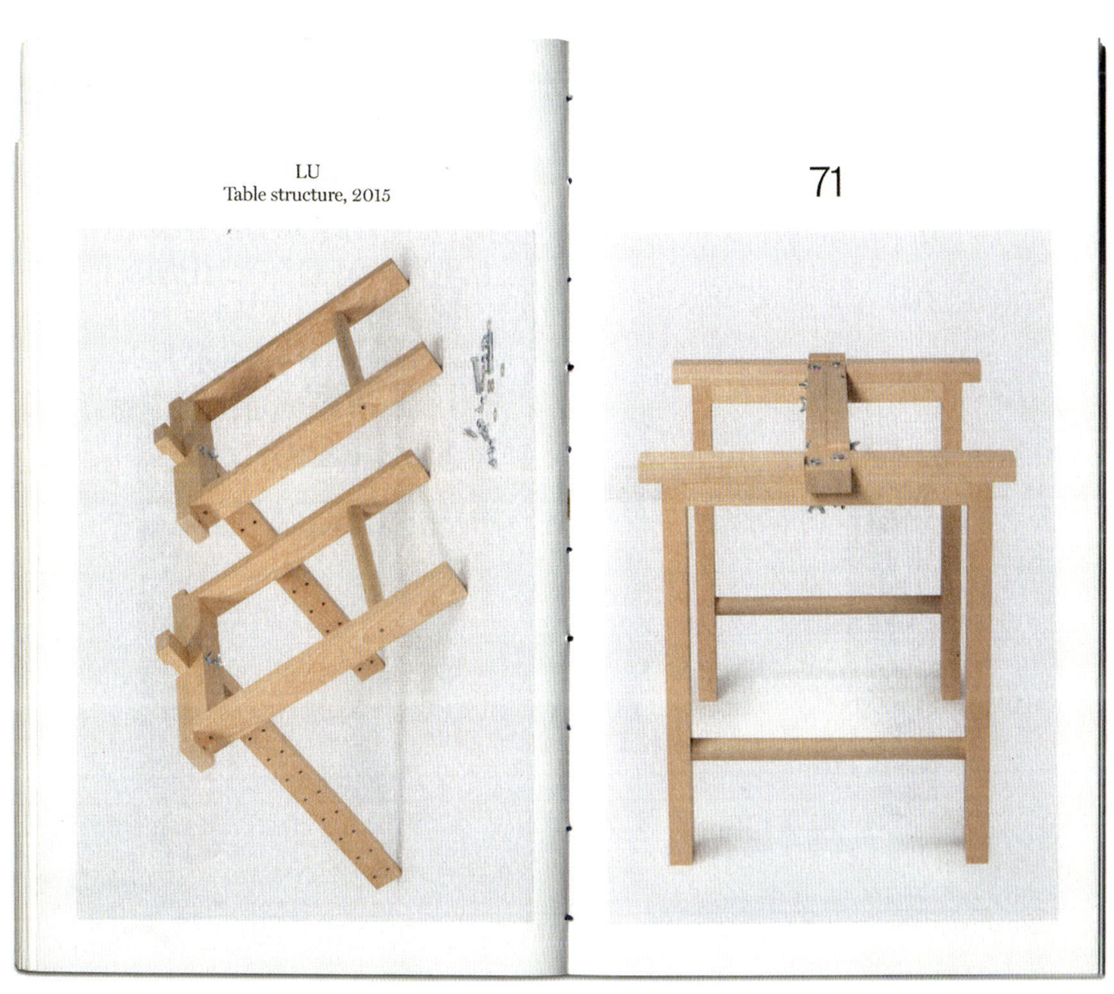
LU
Table structure, 2015
71

Murtle Booklet

Designer

Sourab Biswas

Client

Murtle

Key Diagram

Font	Paper	Size
Bison, Hk Grotesk	Coated paper	105×148mm

Bison and Hk Grotesk can generate a modern feeling.

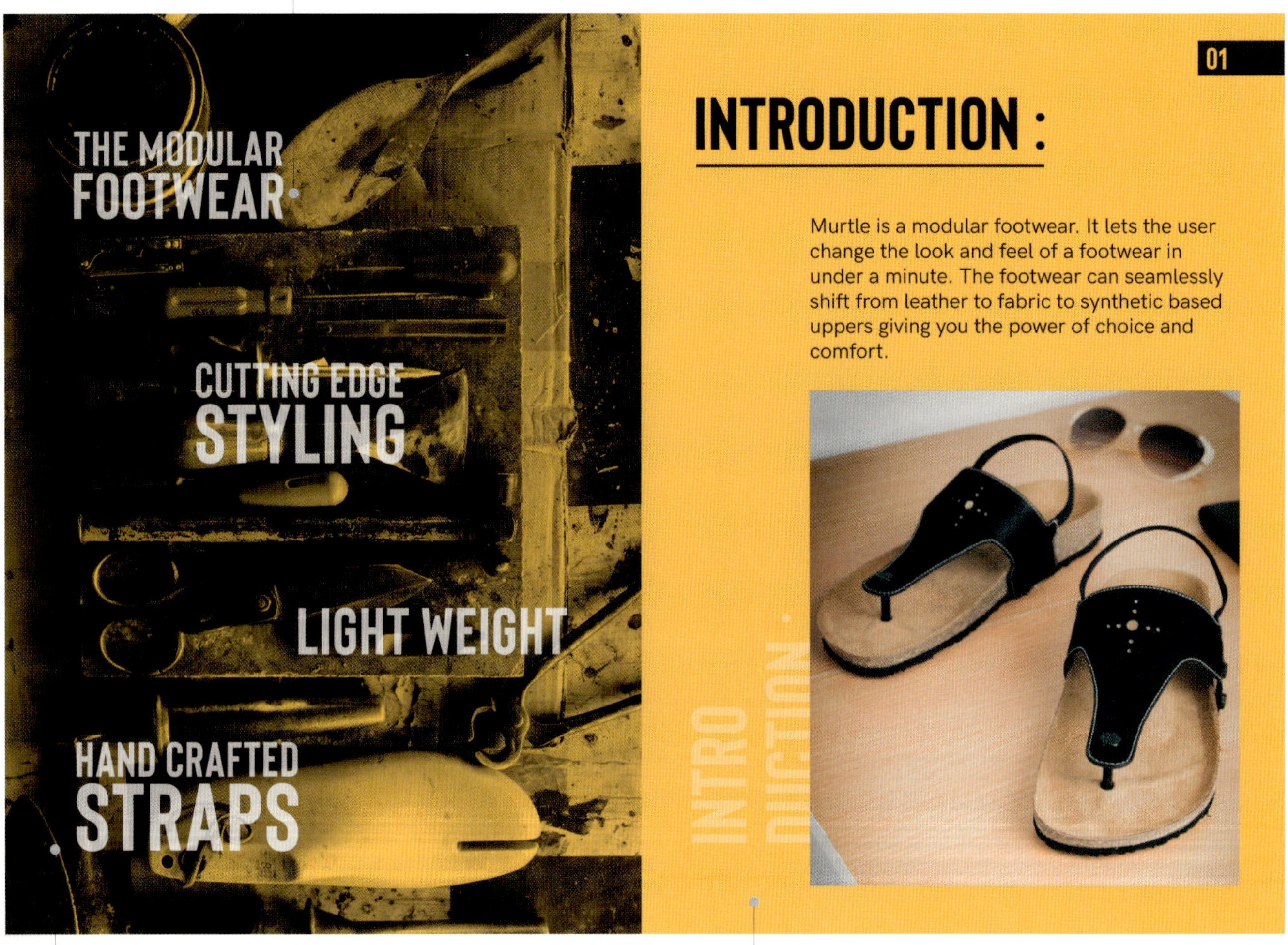

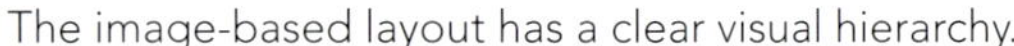

The image-based layout has a clear visual hierarchy.

Yellow is sharp and energetic which can draw the customers' attention at the first glance. It also reflects the design values of the brand.

Grid

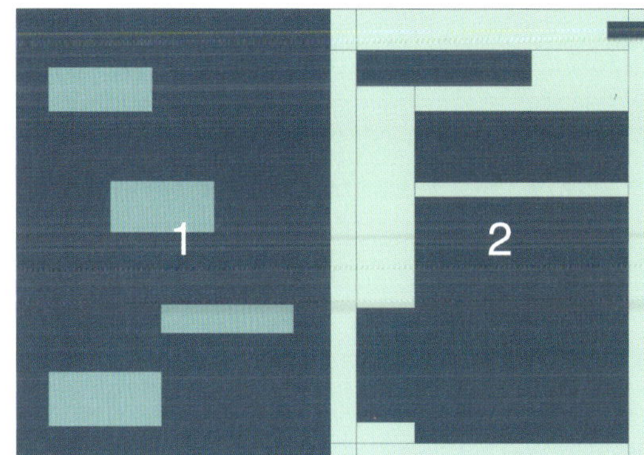

Visual Flow

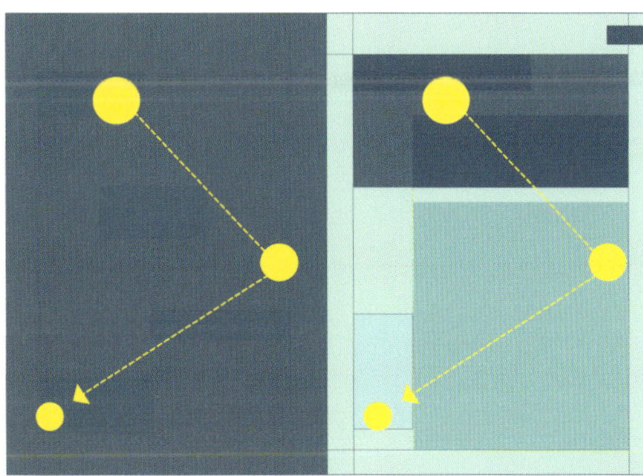

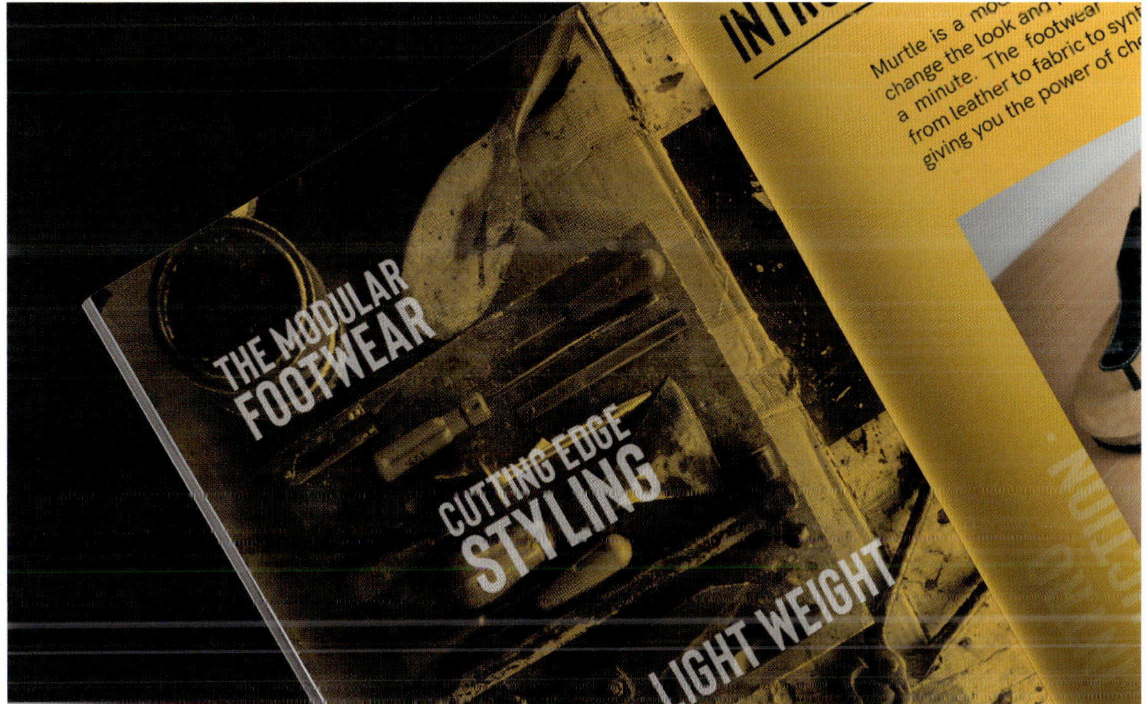

Murtle is a modular footwear. Its products have flexible modules that can allow the users to change the look and feel of the footwear within one minute. The booklet was created to promote this start-up company; it will be used on every purchase of their footwear.

04

KNOW WHO MADE YOUR MURTLE

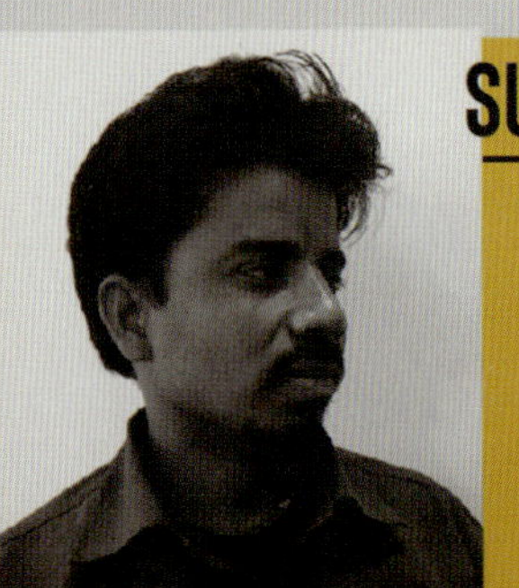

SUNIL

Aged about 34, is married for 12 years now and has three children who go to school. He is very sincere and dedi-cated to his work and do not mind stretching on holidays.

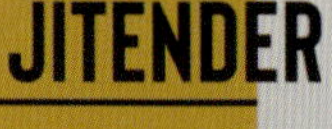

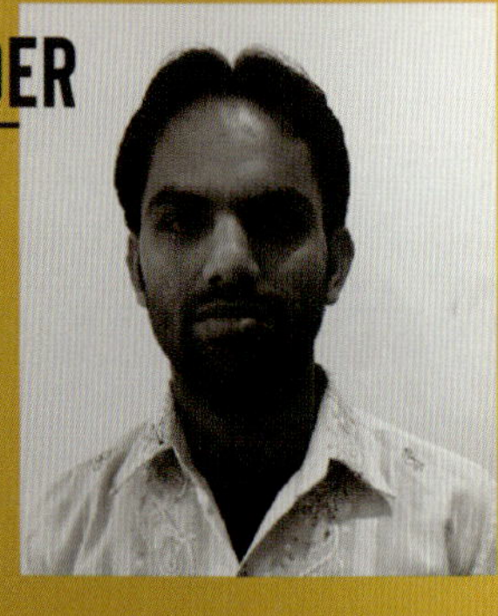

Aged about 28 is married for 6 years now and has one daughter who is just an year old. He is fast at executing any task, grasps the instruction in a jiffy and gets to work in blink of an eye.

HOW IS MURTLE IMPACTING ENVIRONME

The changeable strap as a concept is step towards sustainable fashion as materials can be used without worryi durability since all one has to do is ch strap on a Murtle to flaunt a new footw way whopping 70% wastage is avoided.

MURTLE'S IMPACT ON SOCIETY

All the Murtles are hand crafted from sc skilled artisans from Agra and assembl historical city of Hyderabad. Every stitch has a human element and you proud that its made just for you. We wage and ensure their children go to sc

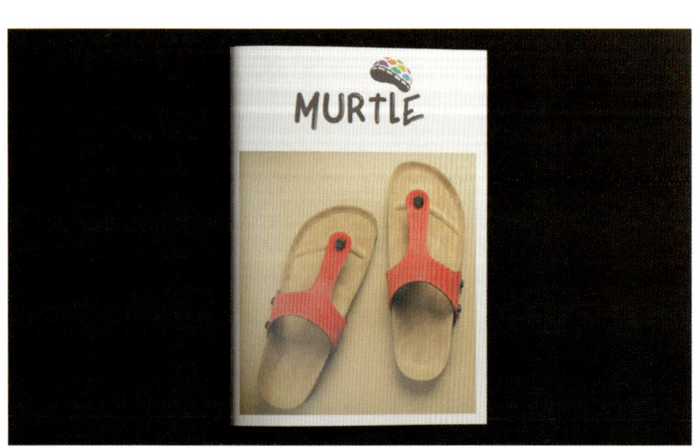

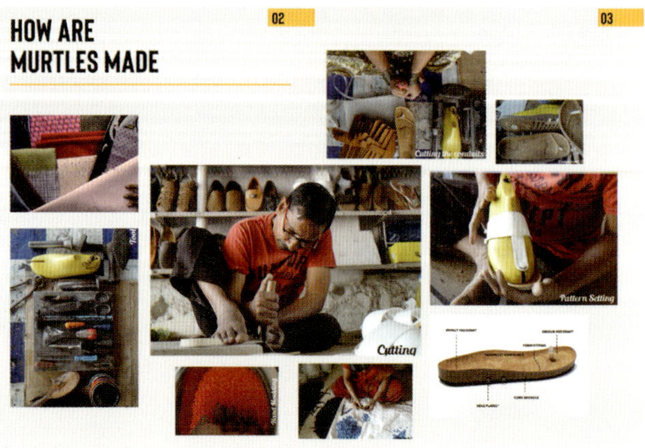

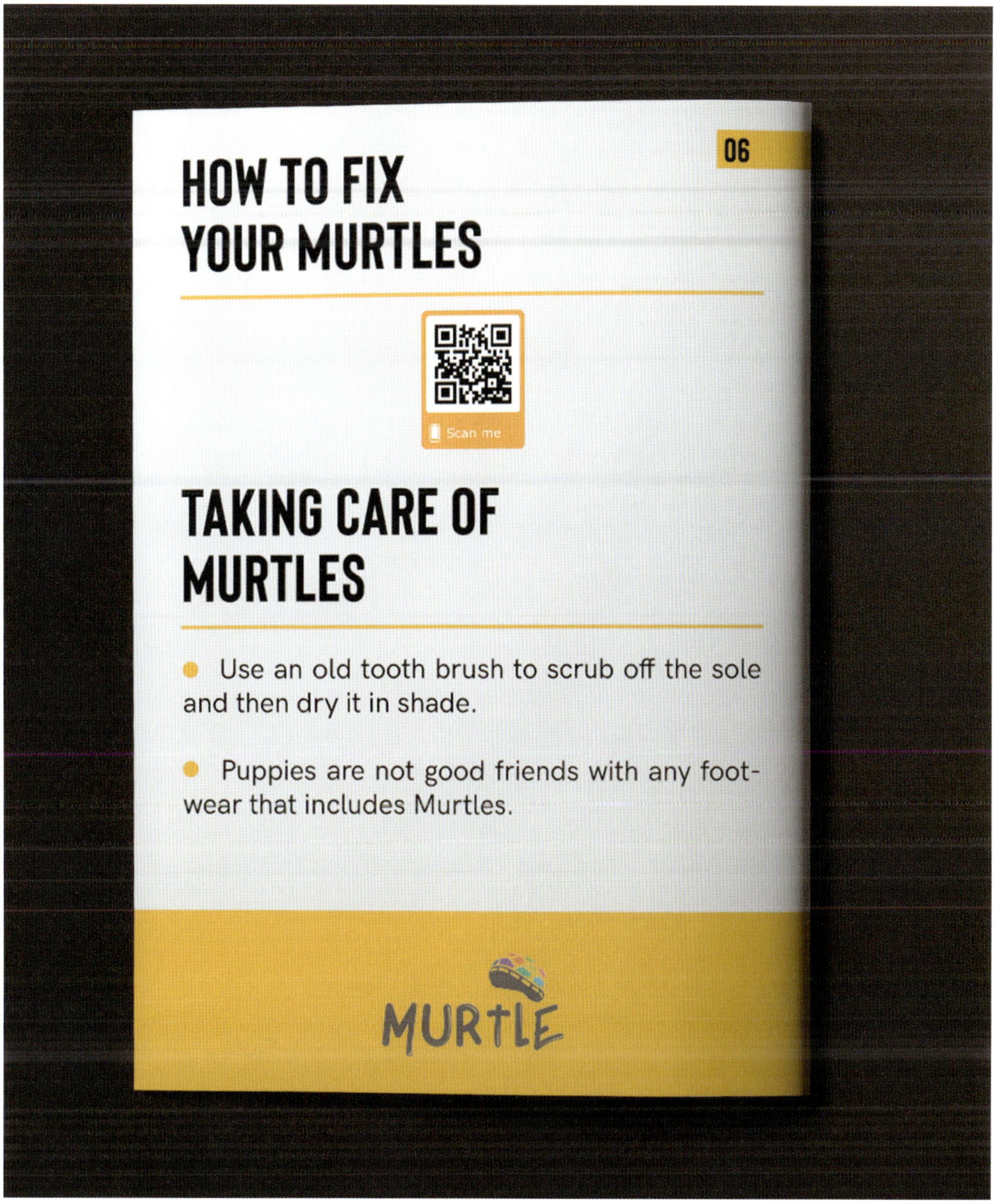

06

HOW TO FIX YOUR MURTLES

Scan me

TAKING CARE OF MURTLES

- Use an old tooth brush to scrub off the sole and then dry it in shade.
- Puppies are not good friends with any foot-wear that includes Murtles.

MURTLE

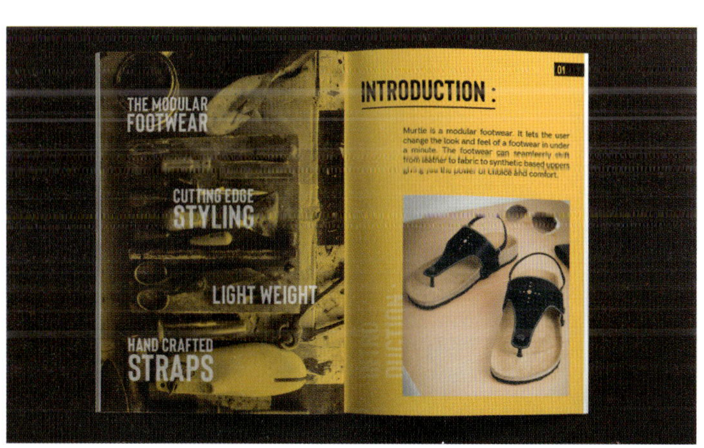

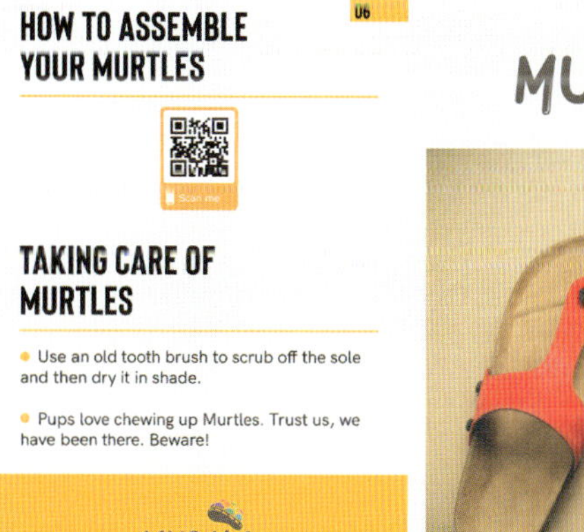

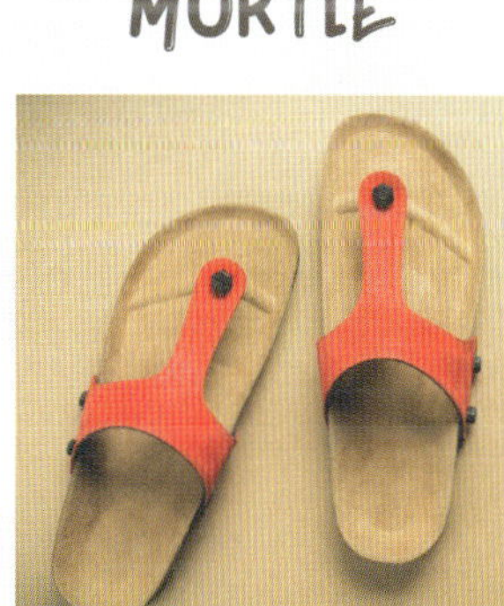

Make My Home Flyer

Designer

Nguyen Thanh Minh

Client

Make My Home Furniture

Key Diagram

Font	Paper	Size
Gotham (Bold / Light)	300g Couche paper	148×210mm (A5)

Using the bold and slim versions of the font to make text uniform, and adding shadows, is a way of highlighting the font area.

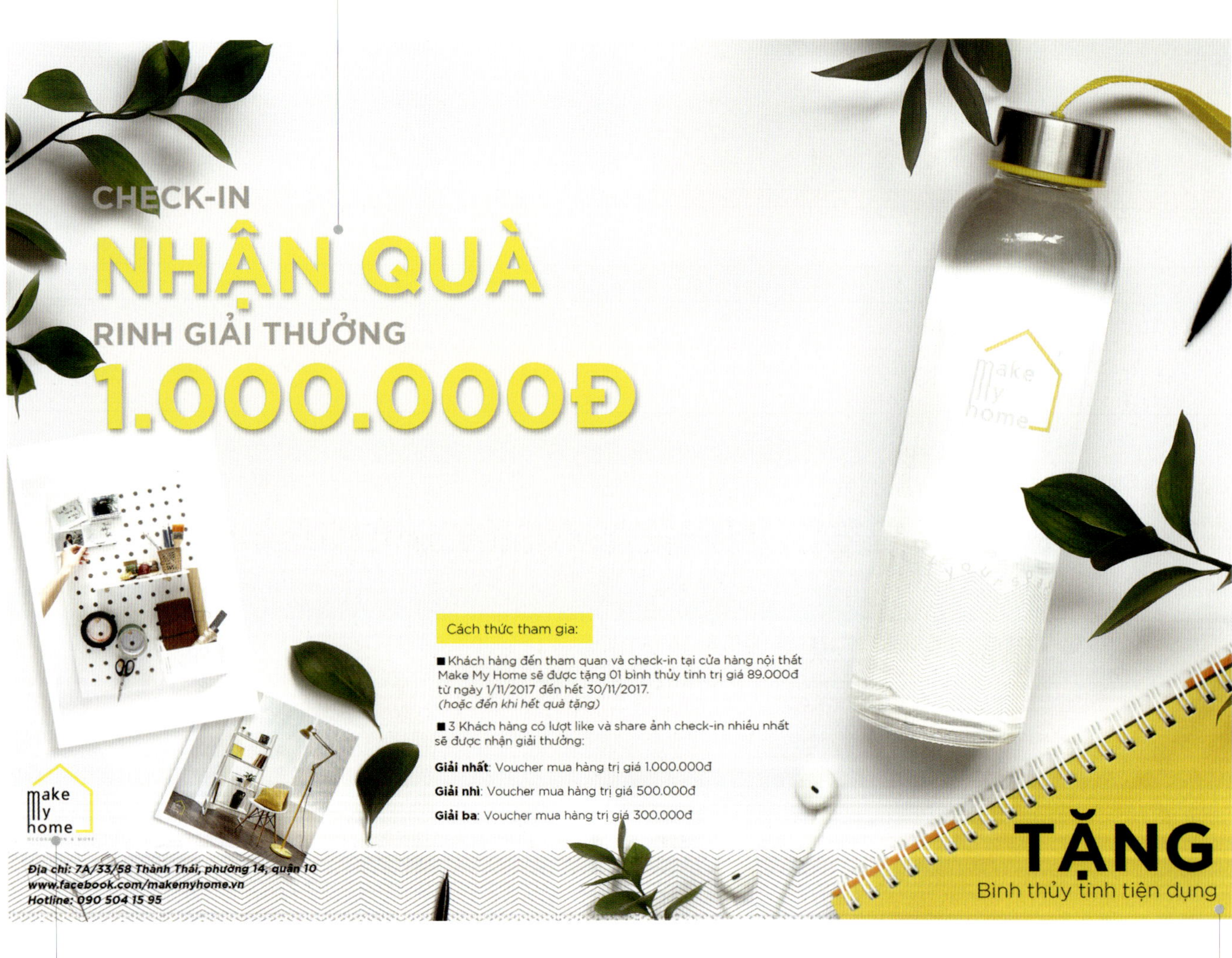

Large areas of negative space enhance the sense of breathing in the layout, the center of gravity is in the lower part of the page, stabling the minimalist visual.

Embellishing with the bright yellow and contrasting with the green leaves, echoes the young fashion characteristics of the furniture company.

Grid

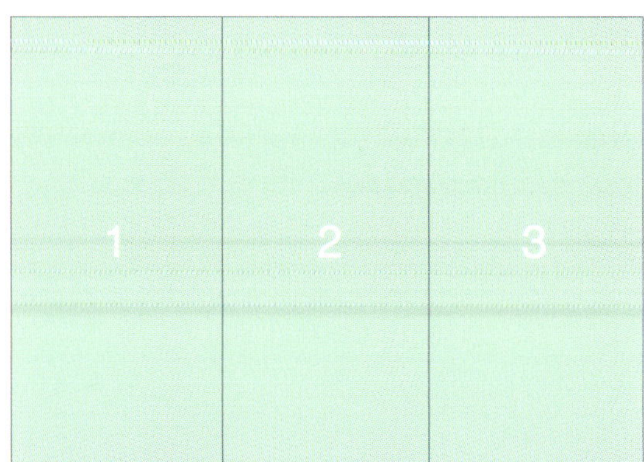

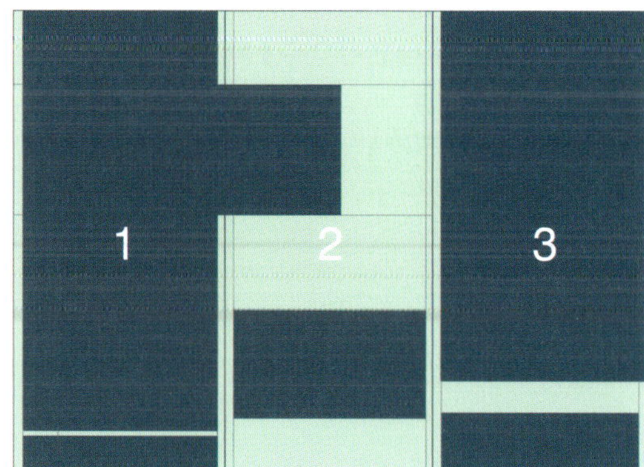

Visual Flow

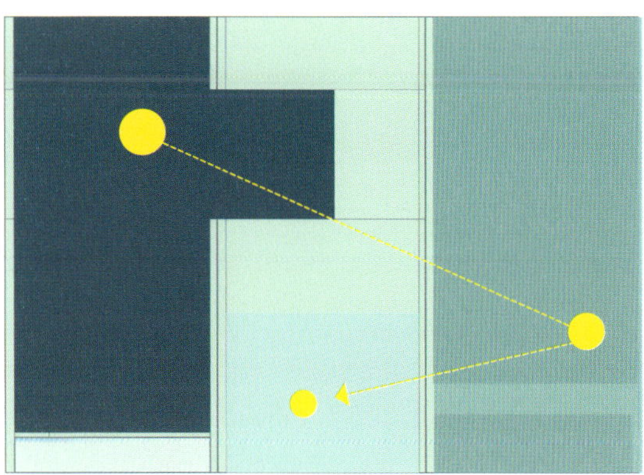

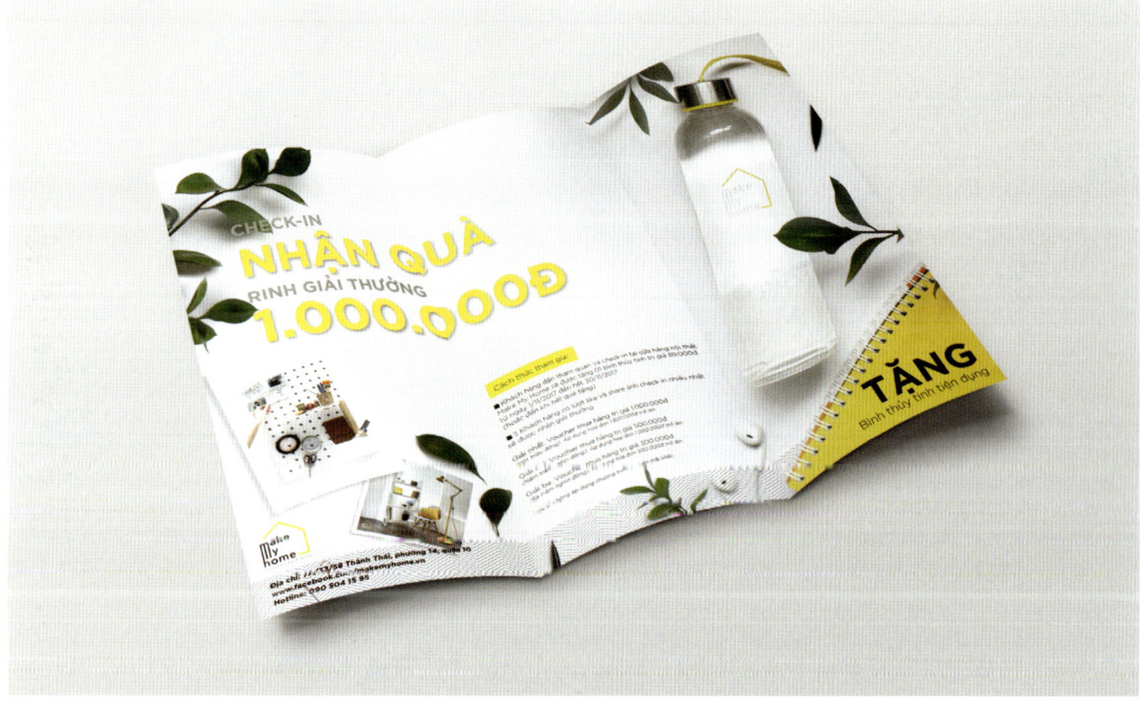

The flyers were used to promote the image of Make My Home Furniture Company, accompanied by a voucher to attract customers. The flyers use modern images, minimalist style, and bright and youthful color.

ACC Academy Leaflet

Designer

Hwayoung Lee

Client

ACC (Asia Culture Center)

Key Diagram

Font	Paper	Size
GT Walshim (English) SD Gothic Neo (Korean)	Semi-Gloss	150×210mm

The English and Korean text look like they belong to the same typeface, but in actuality they are different typefaces which share similar style.

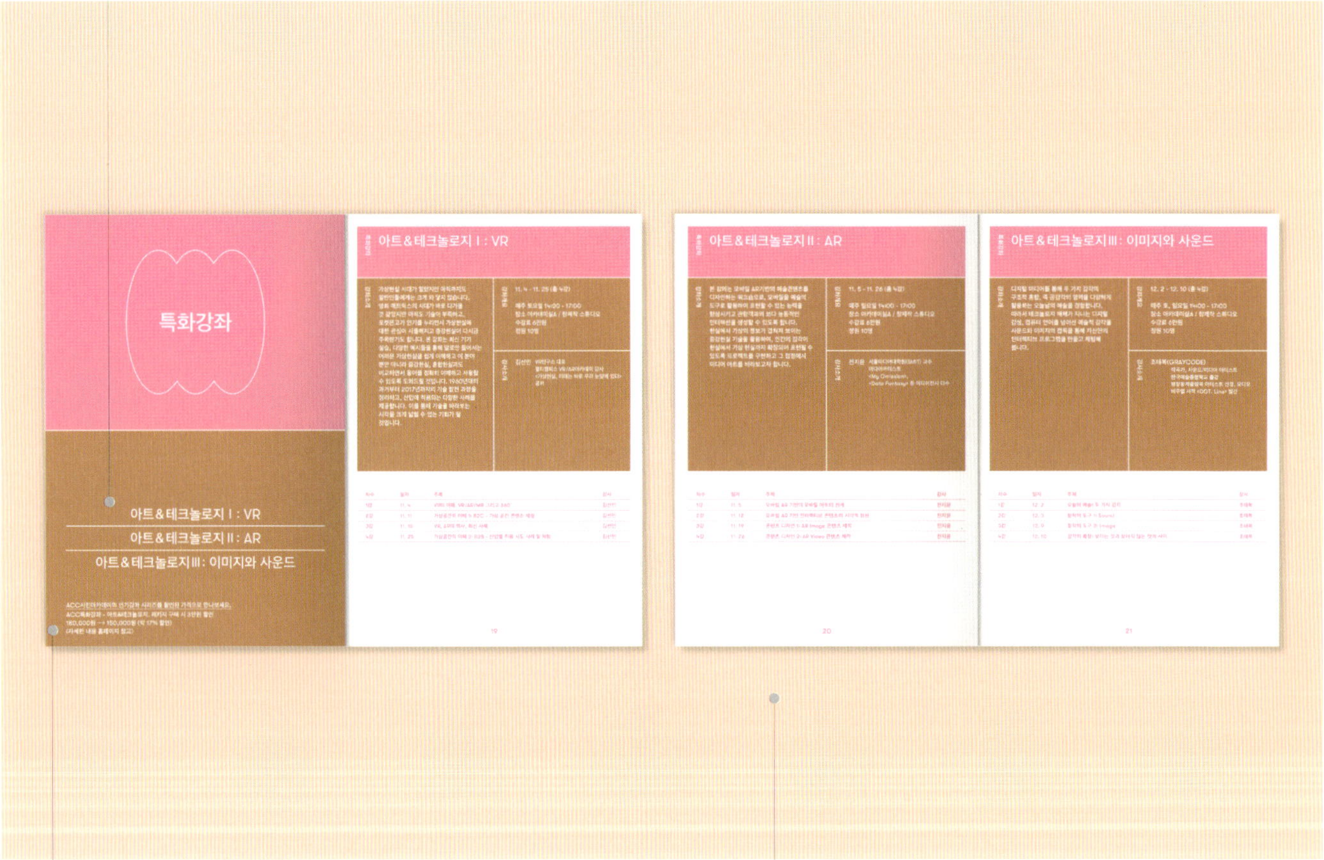

The use of tables makes content more well-arranged and easier to browse. A unified layout creates a regular reading pattern.

In spite of the variety of contents, the different colors presenting different types of information have made it more accessible. The color scheme of blue, gold, and pink is particularly eye-catching.

Grid

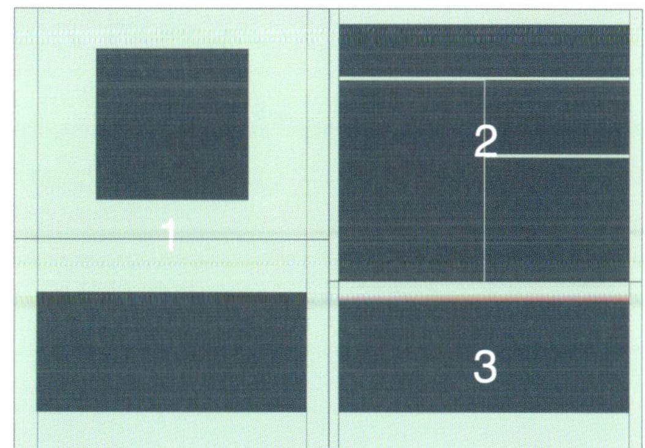

Visual Flow

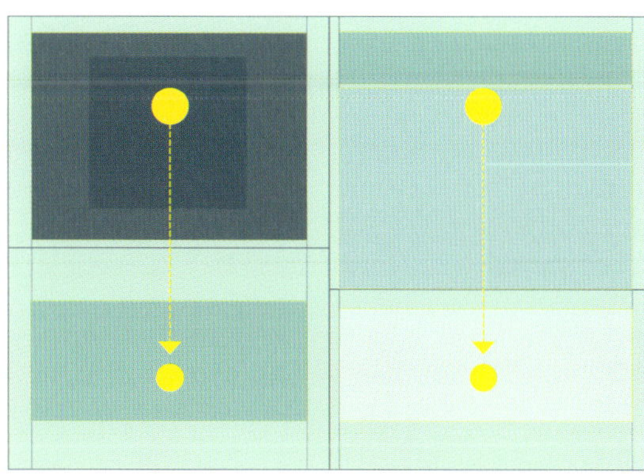

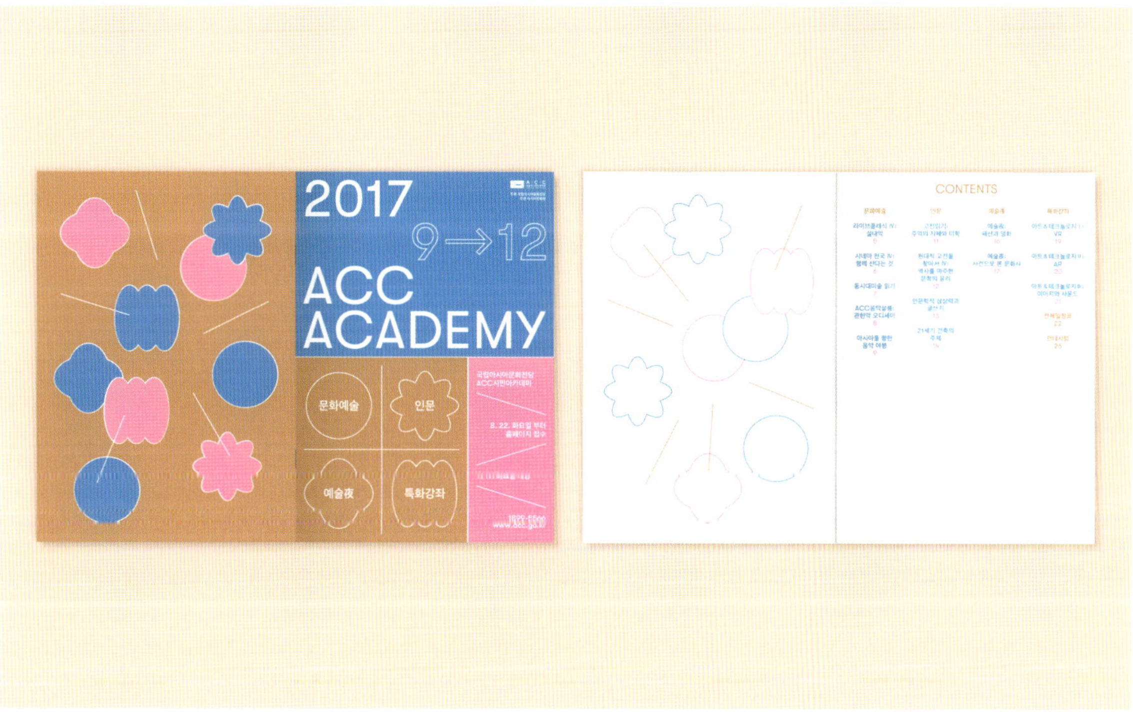

ACC Academy is an educational program for the citizens in Gwangju City at the art culture center in South Korea. The program consists of four categories: art, culture, humanities, and lecture. The graphic identity of the leaflet is based on the four categories, four graphic figures represent each of them.

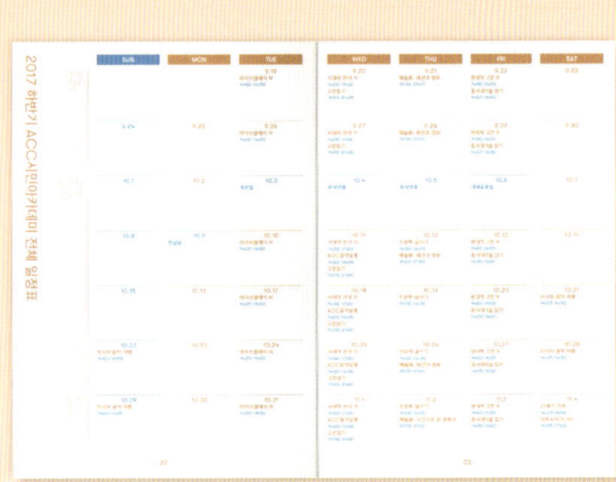

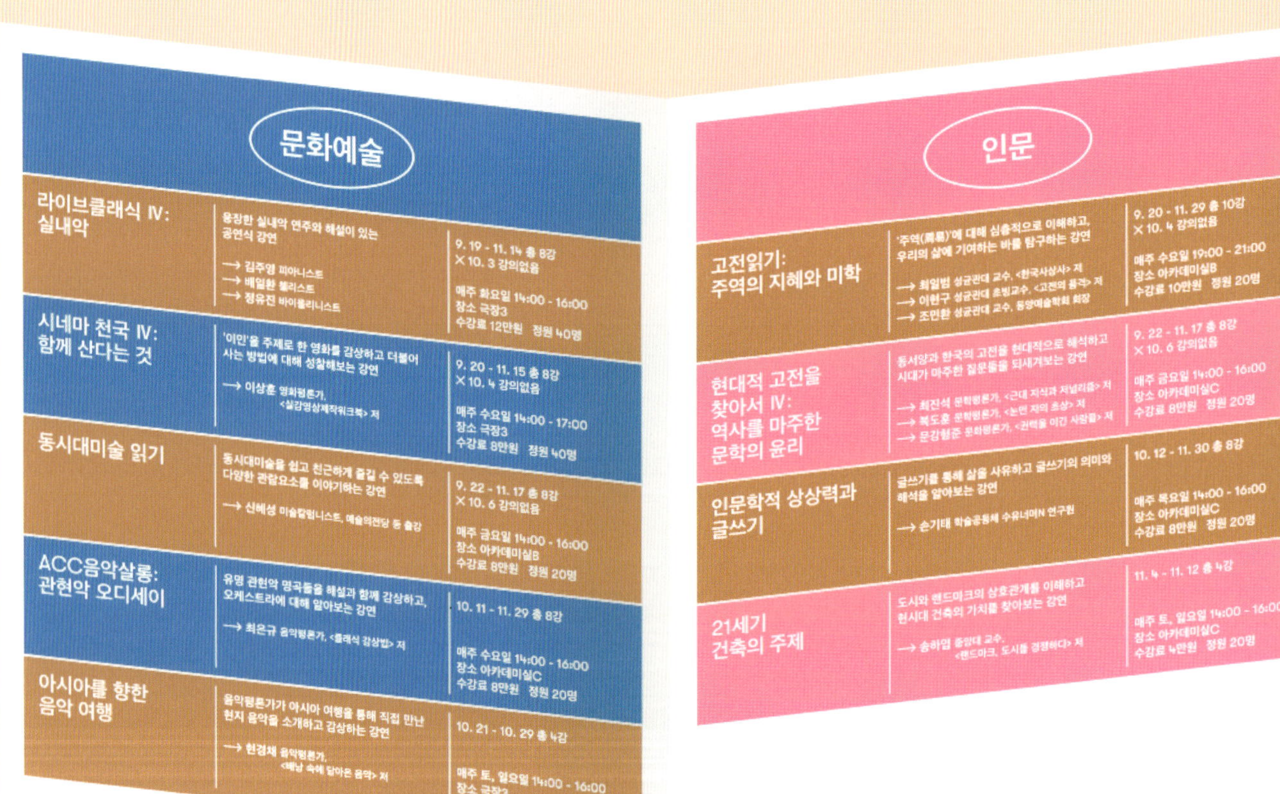
문화예술
라이브클래식 IV: 실내악
웅장한 실내악 연주와 해설이 있는 공연식 강연
→ 김주영 피아니스트
→ 배일환 첼리스트
→ 정유진 바이올리니스트
9. 19 - 11. 14 총 8강
× 10. 3 강의없음
매주 화요일 14:00 - 16:00
장소 극장3
수강료 12만원 정원 40명
시네마 천국 IV: 함께 산다는 것
'이민'을 주제로 한 영화를 감상하고 더불어 사는 방법에 대해 성찰해보는 강연
→ 이상훈 영화평론가, <실감영상제작워크북> 저
9. 20 - 11. 15 총 8강
× 10. 4 강의없음
매주 수요일 14:00 - 17:00
장소 극장3
수강료 8만원 정원 40명
동시대미술 읽기
동시대미술을 쉽고 친근하게 즐길 수 있도록 다양한 관람요소를 이야기하는 강연
→ 신혜성 미술칼럼니스트, 예술의전당 등 출강
9. 22 - 11. 17 총 8강
× 10. 6 강의없음
매주 금요일 14:00 - 16:00
장소 아카데미실B
수강료 8만원 정원 20명
ACC음악살롱: 관현악 오디세이
유명 관현악 명곡들을 해설과 함께 감상하고, 오케스트라에 대해 알아보는 강연
→ 최은규 음악평론가, <클래식 감상법> 저
10. 11 - 11. 29 총 8강
매주 수요일 14:00 - 16:00
장소 아카데미실C
수강료 8만원 정원 20명
아시아를 향한 음악 여행
음악평론가가 아시아 여행을 통해 직접 만난 현지 음악을 소개하고 감상하는 강연
→ 현경채 음악평론가, <해남 속에 담아온 음악> 저
10. 21 - 10. 29 총 4강
매주 토, 일요일 14:00 - 16:00
장소 극장3
수강료 4만원 정원 20명
인문
고전읽기: 주역의 지혜와 미학
'주역(周易)'에 대해 심층적으로 이해하고, 우리의 삶에 기여하는 바를 탐구하는 강연
→ 최일범 성균관대 교수, <한국사상사> 저
→ 이현구 성균관대 초빙교수, <고전의 품격> 저
→ 조민환 성균관대 교수, 동양예술학회 회장
9. 20 - 11. 29 총 10강
× 10. 4 강의없음
매주 수요일 19:00 - 21:00
장소 아카데미실B
수강료 10만원 정원 20명
현대적 고전을 찾아서 IV: 역사를 마주한 문학의 윤리
동서양과 한국의 고전을 현대적으로 해석하고 시대가 마주한 질문들을 되새겨보는 강연
→ 최진석 문학평론가, <근대 지식과 저널리즘> 저
→ 복도훈 문학평론가, <눈먼 자의 초상> 저
→ 문강형준 문화평론가, <권력을 이긴 사람들> 저
9. 22 - 11. 17 총 8강
× 10. 6 강의없음
매주 금요일 14:00 - 16:00
장소 아카데미실C
수강료 8만원 정원 20명
인문학적 상상력과 글쓰기
글쓰기를 통해 삶을 사유하고 글쓰기의 의미와 해석을 알아보는 강연
→ 손기태 학술공동체 수유너머N 연구원
10. 12 - 11. 30 총 8강
매주 목요일 14:00 - 16:00
장소 아카데미실C
수강료 8만원 정원 20명
21세기 건축의 주제
도시와 랜드마크의 상호관계를 이해하고 현시대 건축의 가치를 찾아보는 강연
→ 송하엽 중앙대 교수, <랜드마크, 도시를 경영하다> 저
11. 4 - 11. 12 총 4강
매주 토, 일요일 14:00 - 16:00
장소 아카데미실C
수강료 4만원 정원 20명
2017 ACC AC

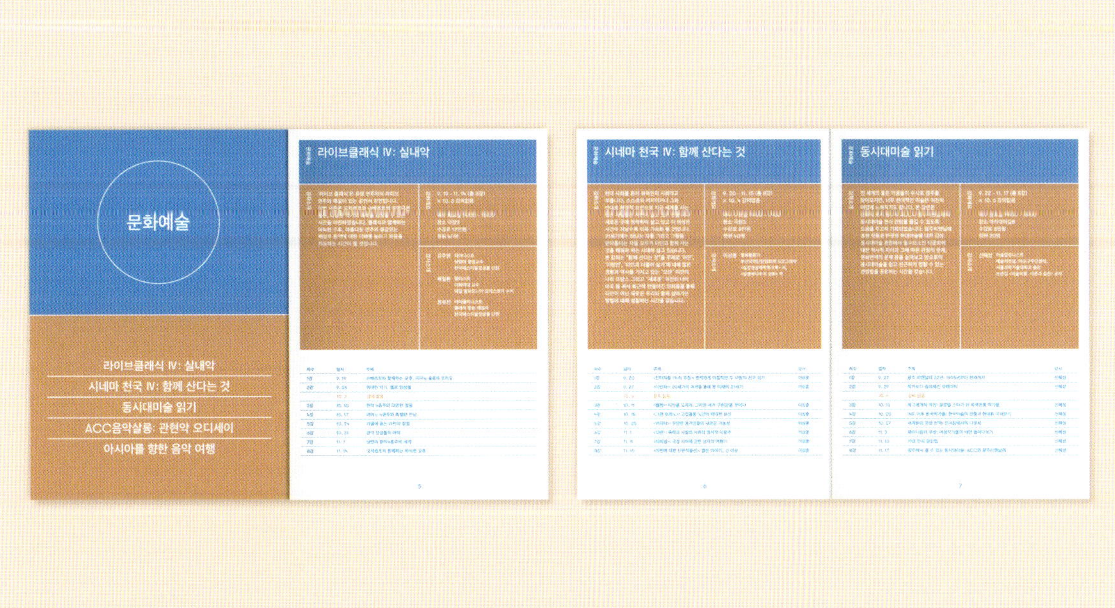
문화예술
라이브클래식 IV: 실내악
시네마 천국 IV: 함께 산다는 것
동시대미술 읽기
ACC음악살롱: 관현악 오디세이
아시아를 향한 음악 여행
라이브클래식 IV: 실내악
시네마 천국 IV: 함께 산다는 것
동시대미술 읽기

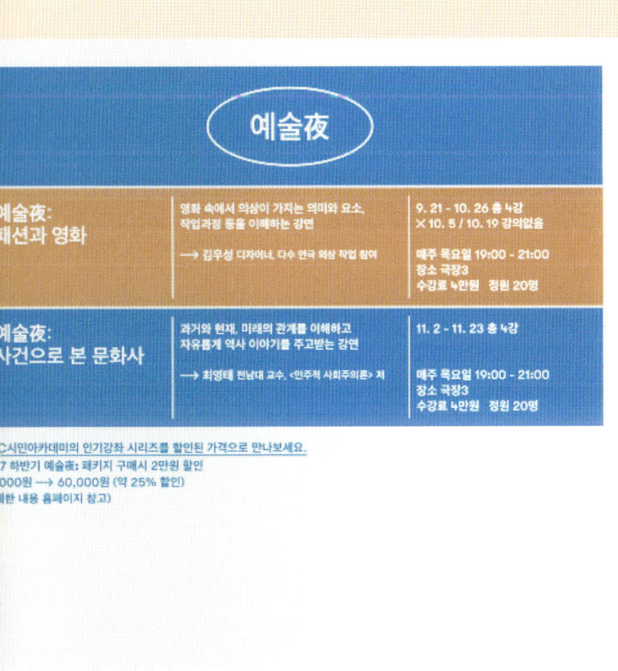
예술夜
예술夜:
패션과 영화
영화 속에서 의상이 가지는 의미와 요소,
작업과정 등을 이해하는 강연
→ 김우성 디자이너, 다수 연극 의상 작업 참여
9. 21 - 10. 26 총 4강
× 10. 5 / 10. 19 강의없음
매주 목요일 19:00 - 21:00
장소 극장3
수강료 4만원 정원 20명
예술夜:
사건으로 본 문화사
과거와 현재, 미래의 관계를 이해하고
자유롭게 역사 이야기를 주고받는 강연
→ 최영태 전남대 교수, <민주적 사회주의론> 저
11. 2 - 11. 23 총 4강
매주 목요일 19:00 - 21:00
장소 극장3
수강료 4만원 정원 20명
C시민아카데미의 인기강좌 시리즈를 할인된 가격으로 만나보세요.
7 하반기 예술夜: 패키지 구매시 2만원 할인
000원 → 60,000원 (약 25% 할인)
세한 내용 홈페이지 참고)

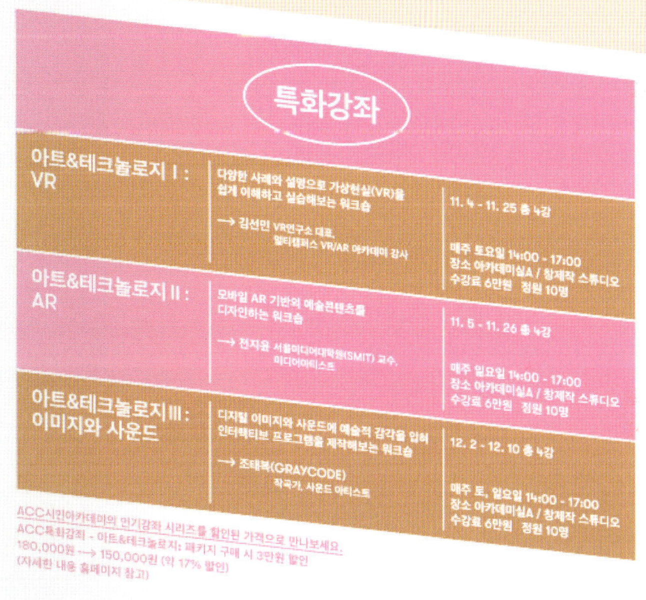
특화강좌
아트&테크놀로지 I :
VR
다양한 사례와 설명으로 가상현실(VR)을
쉽게 이해하고 실습해보는 워크숍
→ 김선민 VR연구소 대표,
멀티캠퍼스 VR/AR 아카데미 강사
11. 4 - 11. 25 총 4강
매주 토요일 14:00 - 17:00
장소 아카데미실A / 창제작 스튜디오
수강료 6만원 정원 10명
아트&테크놀로지 II :
AR
모바일 AR 기반의 예술콘텐츠를
디자인하는 워크숍
→ 천지윤 서울미디어대학원(SMIT) 교수,
미디어아티스트
11. 5 - 11. 26 총 4강
매주 일요일 14:00 - 17:00
장소 아카데미실A / 창제작 스튜디오
수강료 6만원 정원 10명
아트&테크놀로지 III :
이미지와 사운드
디지털 이미지와 사운드에 예술적 감각을 입혀
인터랙티브 프로그램을 제작해보는 워크숍
→ 조태복(GRAYCODE)
작곡가, 사운드 아티스트
12. 2 - 12. 10 총 4강
매주 토, 일요일 14:00 - 17:00
장소 아카데미실A / 창제작 스튜디오
수강료 6만원 정원 10명
ACC시민아카데미의 인기강좌 시리즈를 할인된 가격으로 만나보세요.
ACC특화강좌 - 아트&테크놀로지: 패키지 구매 시 3만원 할인
180,000원 → 150,000원 (약 17% 할인)
(자세한 내용 홈페이지 참고)
ADEMY 9→12

ESCAC Brochure

Designer

Walabi

Client

ESCAC (Cinema and Audiovisual School of Catalonia)

Key Diagram

Font

Merriweather
Source Sans Pro

Paper

Munken Kristai

Size

170×240mm

Two different typefaces maintain a balance modernity between and professionalism.

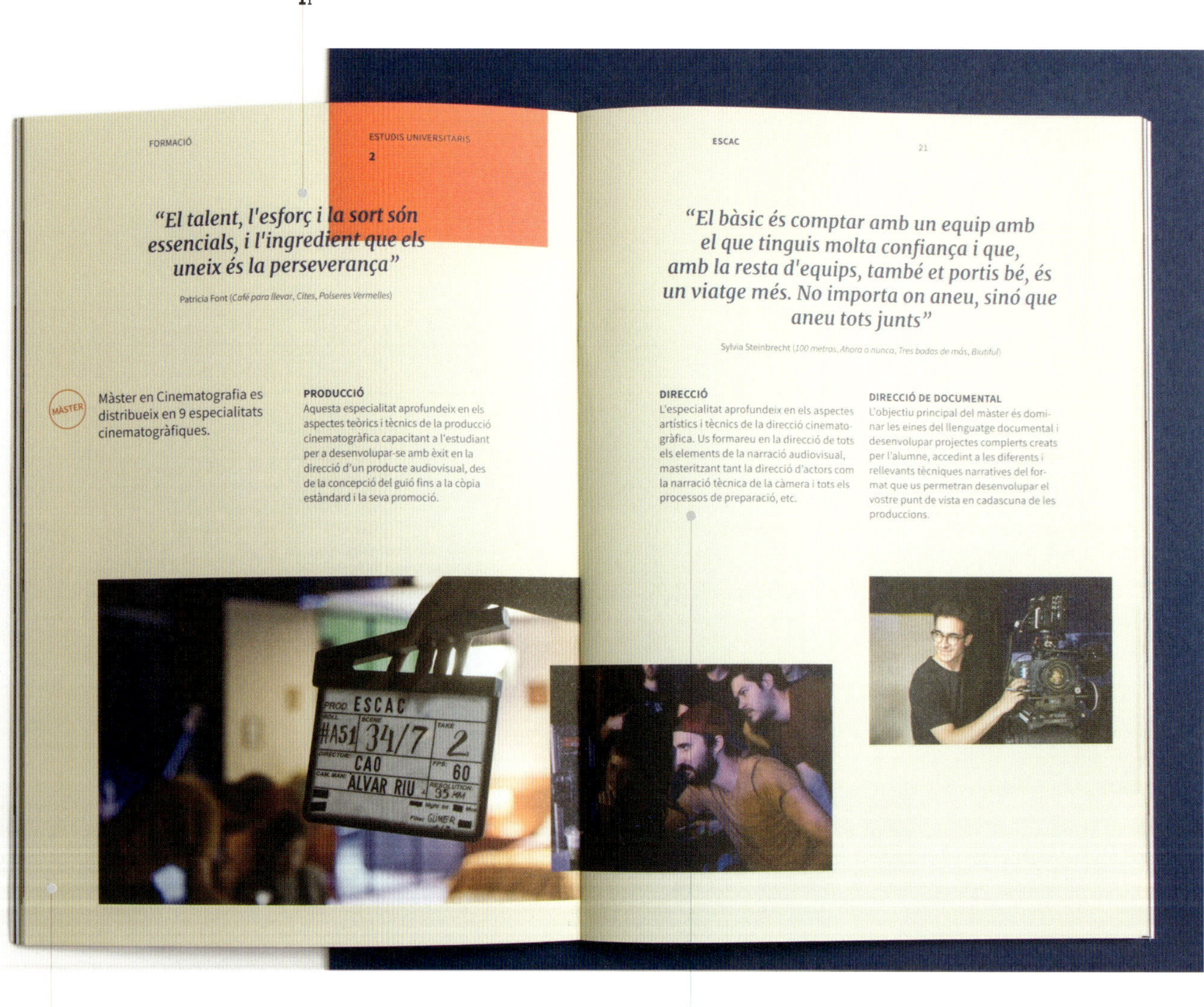

The grid system is flexible, without a fixed repeated layout. The contents are arranged into the various layout with specific demands.

A palette of fresh and relaxing colors is used to establish a close relationship with young people.

Grid

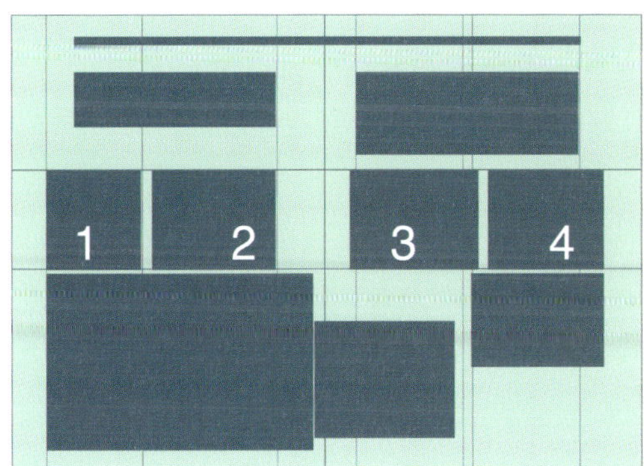

Visual Flow

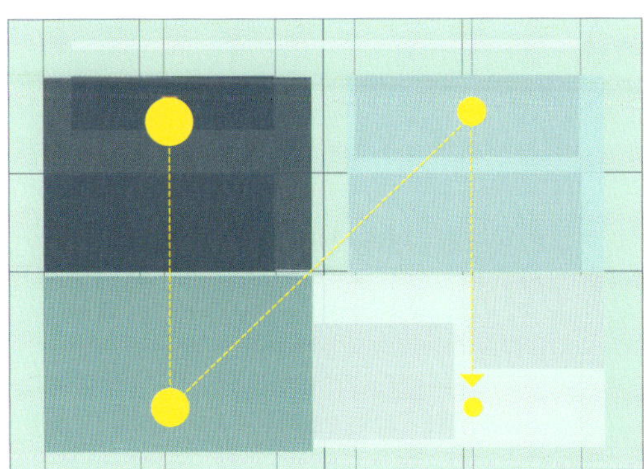

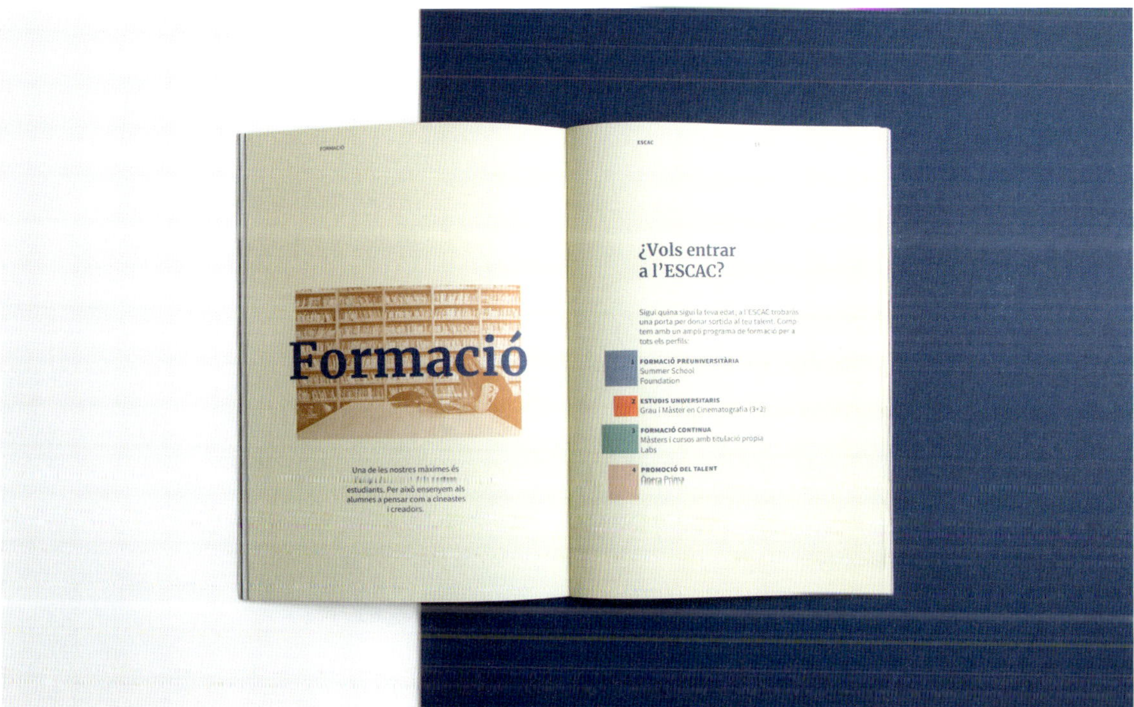

This brochure for the Cinema and Audiovisual School of Catalonia features serious and professional contents so a contemporary and dynamic design is needed to target the young audience.

ESCAC FILMS

ESCAC Films

La productora acadèmica de l'ESCAC té per objectiu assentar les bases i consolidar un tipus de producció que possibiliti la promoció i la incorporació dels joves talents formats a l'ESCAC a la indústria del cinema i de l'audiovisual.

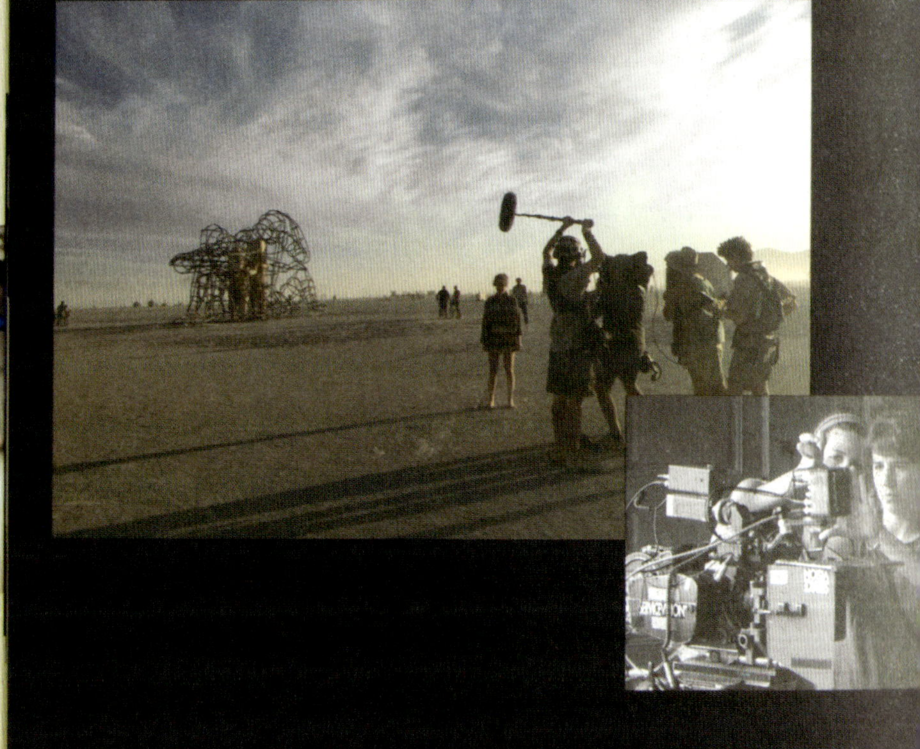

Des de la seva creació el 2012, la productora acadèmica ha obtingut nombrosos reconeixements nacionals i internacionals amb els projectes de graduació dels alumnes, tant ficcions com documentals:

- ***En la azotea*** de Damià Serra va estar seleccionat a la Berlinale després de guanyar el Primer Premi en la SEMINCI, i el premi al Millor Guió en els Premis Nova Autoria SGAE del Festival de Sitges. Nominat als Premis Goya i als Premis Gaudí 2017.
- ***Víctor XX*** d'Ian Garrido: Tercer Premi de Cinéfondation (Festival de Cannes), Diploma especial al Festival de Tampere, Premi al Millor curt nacional a Almeria en Curt i en els Premis ASECAN del cinema andalús i Millor Curtmetratge al Festival Internacional de cinema d'Elx.
- ***Lina*** de Nur Casadevall és premiat amb la Millor Direcció al Festival de Màlaga i obté el premi Silver Screen (Young Directors Awards) a Short Film EUROPE.
- ***Café para llevar*** de Patricia Font, Goya 2015 al Millor curt de ficció, té en el seu palmarès el Tercer Premi en Alcine, i el Primer Premi en Festival Zoom, en FASCURT, en CortoEspaña.
- ***Néboa*** de Claudia Costafreda: Millor Curtmetratge i Millor Guió al Festival Internacional de Cinema d'Osca.
- ***Ringo*** d'Adrià Pagès: Guanyador del Premi Sundance TV Shorts.
- ***Rocco*** de Gerard Nogueira: Bronze Tadpole en Camerimage Film Festival.
- ***Elegía*** d'Alba Tejero, Millor Direcció al Festival Internacional de Cinema de Palència.
- ***Bus Story*** de Jorge Yúdice: Primer Premi en Festival Cinespaña (Toulouse).
- ***Una hora, un paso*** de Bernat Gual i Aitor Iturriza amb mencions especials a South West Int FF de Londres i Videomaker Film Festival.
- ***Sasha*** de Felix Colomer, Menció especial en SEMINCI 2016 i nominat als Premis Gaudí 2018.
- ***Històries de l'Arrabassada*** de Ferran Romeu, Millor Documental de la Secció Premier Pas de Visions du Réel (Suïssa).
- ***Huellas de ausencia*** d'Anna Monràs, premi DOC-U al Docs Barcelona.

Osteo Poly Clinic Flyer

Designer
Vlad Ermolaev

Client
Osteo Poly Clinic

Key Diagram

Font	Paper	Size
New Paris Skyline	Olin regular	200×83mm 105×245mm

The letters O and C from this typeface are plump looking, having a shape very similar to the main visual element of a circle. Some part of the text has been inverted in a way to suggest the physical status the of the human body.

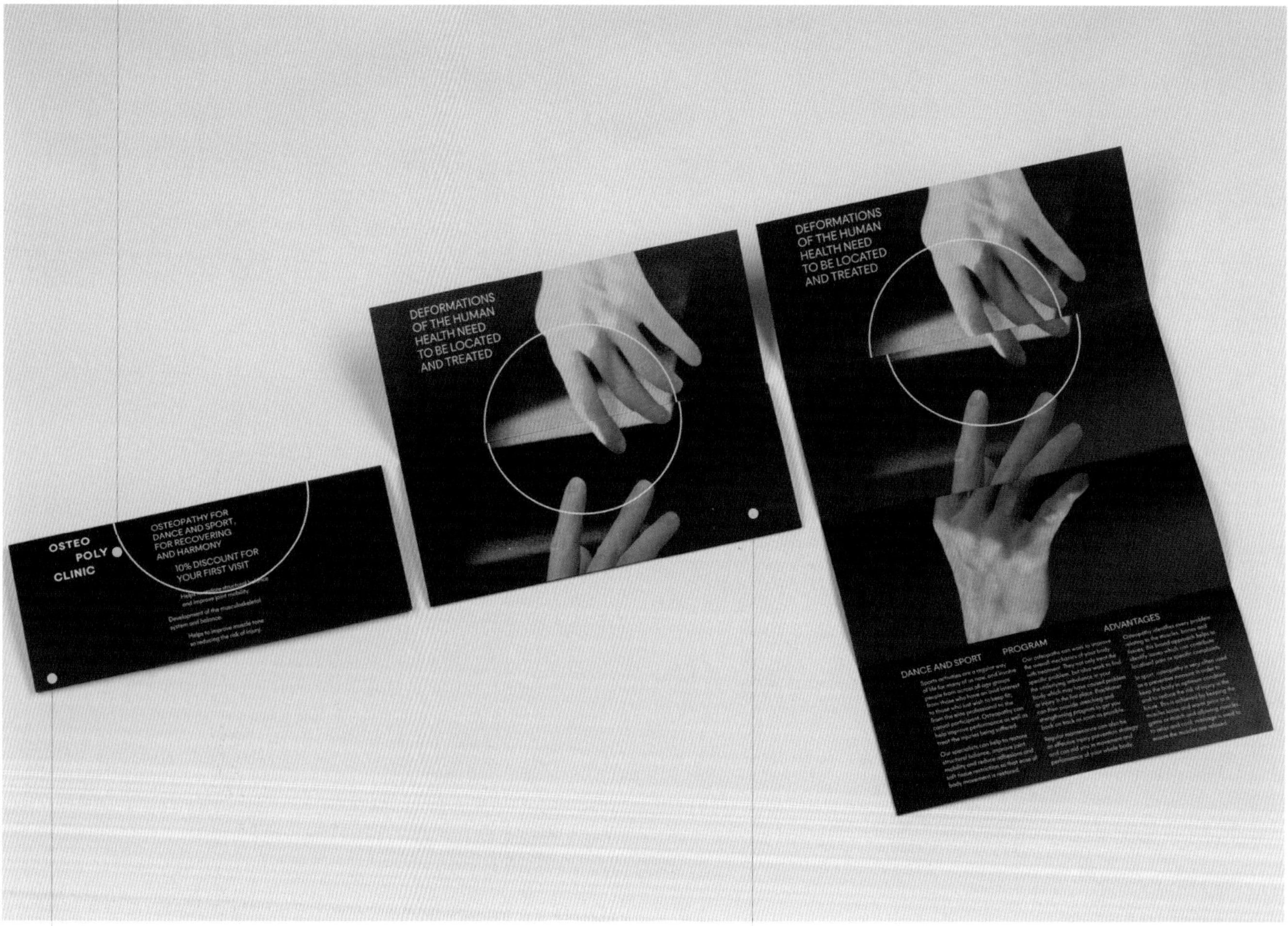

The large blank space leaves more room for contemplating, and allows more attention onto the circles and images.

The use of the monochrome black and white is to be visually calm and reliable. This is consistent with the professionalism of the clinic.

Grid

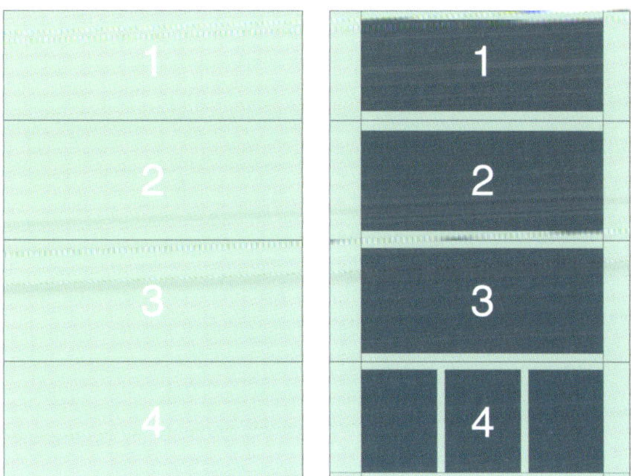

Visual Flow

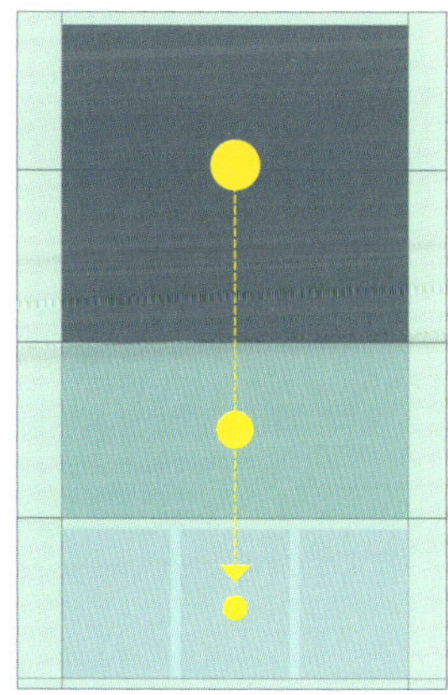

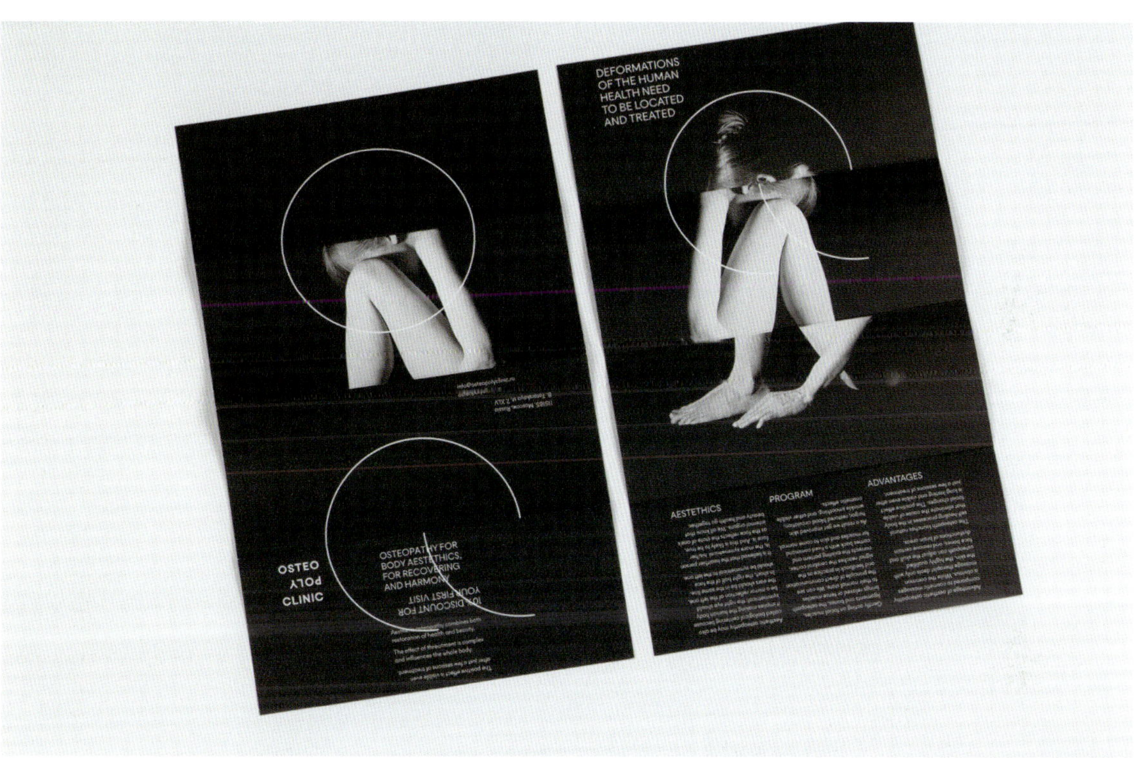

Osteo Poly Clinic is a health center that provides osteopathic medicine. The leaflet mainly promotes the core philosophy of the Osteo Poly Clinic and its programs. The circles in the leaflet represent the physical status of the human being. The broken circle implies some problems with health while the perfect circle means recovery from illness. The five circular shapes in the name of the company also implies the healing fingers of doctors.

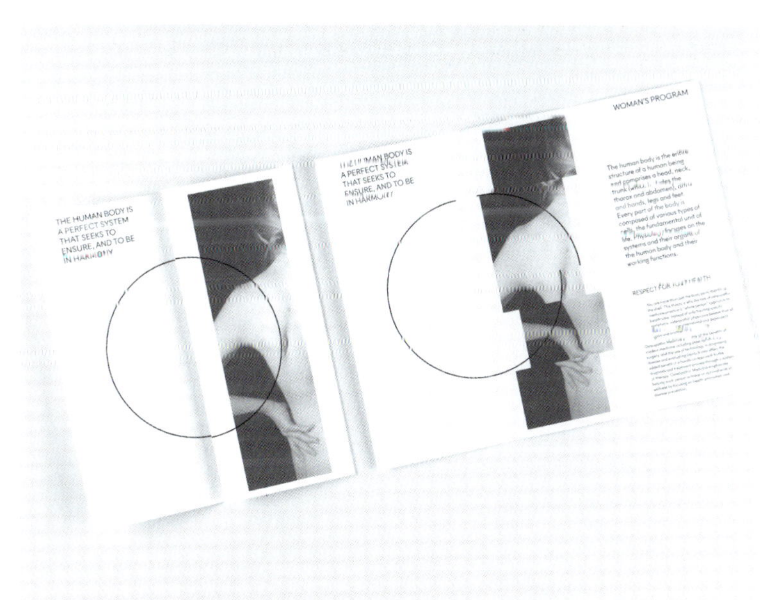

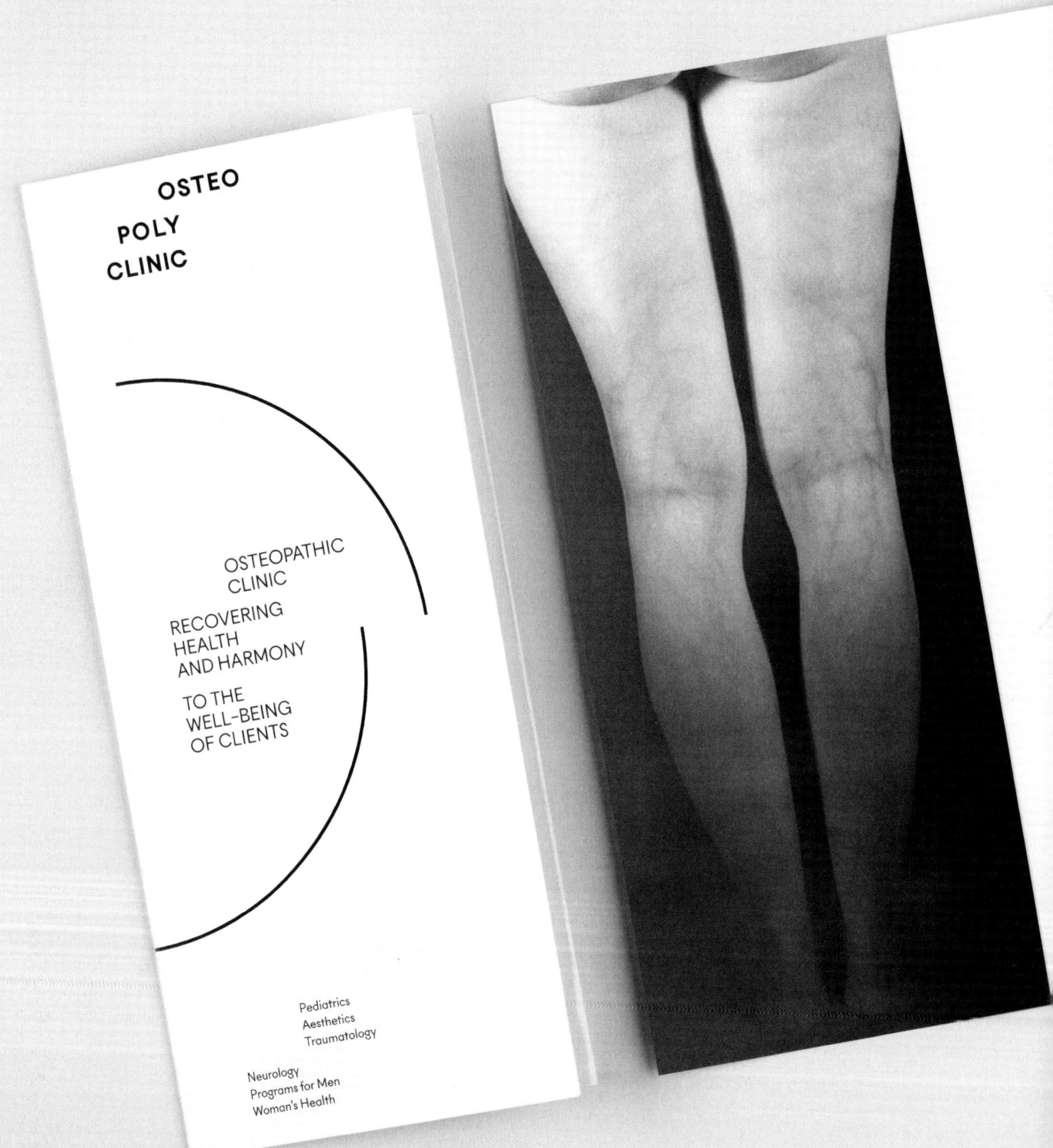
OSTEO
POLY
CLINIC
OSTEOPATHIC
CLINIC
RECOVERING
HEALTH
AND HARMONY
TO THE
WELL-BEING
OF CLIENTS
Pediatrics
Aesthetics
Traumatology
Neurology
Programs for Men
Woman's Health

THE HUMAN BODY IS A PERFECT SYSTEM THAT SEEKS TO ENSURE, AND TO BE HEALTHY. THE BODY IS THE ENTIRE STRUCTURE OF A HUMAN BEING

The human body is the entire structure of a human being and comprises a head, neck, trunk (which includes the thorax and abdomen), arms and hands, legs and feet. Every part of the body is composed of various types of cells, the fundamental unit of life. Physiology focuses on the systems and their organs of the human body and their working functions.

The human body consists of many interacting systems. Each system contributes to the maintenance of homeostasis, of itself, other systems, and the entire body.

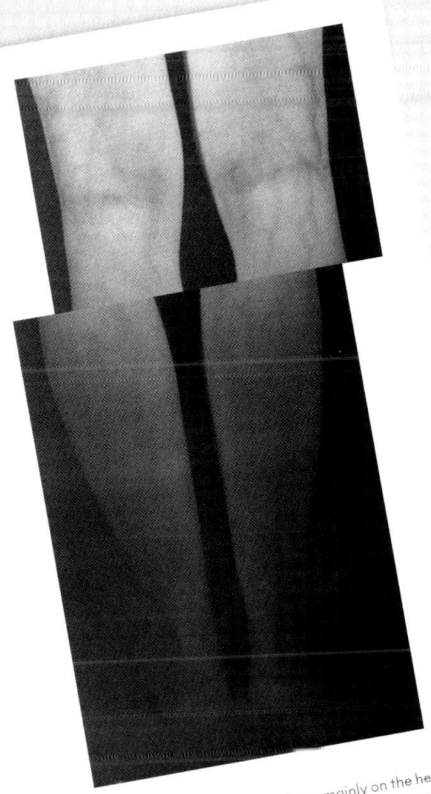

Clinical practitioners focus mainly on the health of individuals, while public health practitioners consider the overall health of communities and populations. Workplace wellness programs are increasingly adopted by companies for their value in improving the health and well-being of their employees, as are school health services in order to improve the health and well-being of children. This system can be split up into the muscular system and the skeletal system. The main function of the lymphatic system / Immune system is to extract, transport and metabolize lymph, the fluid found in between cells.

Many teens suffer from mental health issues in response to the pressures of society and social problems they encounter. Some of the key mental health issues seen in teens are: depression, eating disorders, and drug abuse. There are many ways to prevent these health issues.

CHILDREN'S HEALTH

The human body consists of many interacting systems. Each system contributes to the maintenance of homeostasis, of itself, other systems, and the entire body. A system consists of two or more organs, which are functional collections of tissue. Systems do not work in isolation.

Index

ACKNOWLEDGEMENTS

We would like to thank all the designers and contributors who have been involved in the production of this book; their contributions have been indispensable to its creation. We would also like to express our gratitude to all the producers for their invaluable opinions and assistance throughout this project. And to the many others whose names are not credited but have made helpful suggestions, we thank you for your continuous support.

FUTURE COLLABORATIONS:

If you wish to participate in SendPoints' future projects and publications, please send your website or portfolio to editor02@sendpoints.cn.